Contents

Contents

Abbreviations

The following abbreviations are used in the References:

ELH	*Journal of English Literary History*
JEGP	*Journal of English and Germanic Philology*
MLR	*Modern Language Review*
N & Q	*Notes and Queries*
PMLA	*Publications of the Modern Language Association of America*
RES	*Review of English Studies*
SEL	*Studies in English Literature, 1500–1900*
TLS	*Times Literary Supplement*

Introduction

THIS volume is a thorough revision of the one with the same title published in 1973. The layout of the volume has been modified to permit the inclusion of two chapters (instead of one) on the English history plays, and of one on New Approaches to Shakespeare. Nine of the chapters are entirely new; others have been rewritten by their original authors. The aim is to provide a selectively critical guide to the best in Shakespeare scholarship and criticism. Contributors have been free to organize their material in their own ways, though they have been asked to represent the main points of view on the works with which they are concerned. They have been encouraged to recommend the good rather than to castigate the bad. Though they do not offer histories of criticism, they recommend writings of earlier ages which still have something to offer. The most discussed works have chapters to themselves; the rest are grouped with others of their kind. Chapters on important background subjects—textual scholarship and theatre history—are included. The opening chapter offers guidance on writings of a still more general kind; its sections on Bibliographies and Periodicals should help readers to keep up with new writings as well as to find ones not mentioned elsewhere in this volume.

The References section to each chapter lists in alphabetical order the writings there recommended. Editions of books later than the first are cited when they are substantially revised. Many of the books are available in paperback reprints, listed in the catalogues *British Books in Print* (UK) and *Paperbound Books in Print* (US); and anthologies of criticism and scholarship often include chapters of books, and articles, listed here.

STANLEY WELLS

1 | The Study of Shakespeare

STANLEY WELLS

This volume aims to help readers to find their way among the immense amount of scholarly and critical writings about Shakespeare. It is not intended as a comprehensive bibliography: on the contrary, contributors have been asked to be selective and to provide critical guides to reading in their allotted areas. The bulk of the volume is made up of chapters on separate works or groups of works. Other chapters are devoted to studies of Shakespeare's text and of his plays in relation to the theatre both of his own time and of later ages; there is also a chapter offering guidance on recent developments in criticism. Though authors of chapters on the works touch on these topics where they are specially relevant, it seemed desirable also to offer sustained independent treatments of them, since each has its own necessary background. This opening chapter attempts to provide guidance to other, more general aspects of the study of Shakespeare: to reference books, background studies, and books concerned less with individual plays than with his overall achievement.

BIBLIOGRAPHIES

Four volumes attempt to provide comprehensive bibliographies up to 1958. The most engagingly idiosyncratic is William Jaggard's *Shakespeare Bibliography* of 1911. More reliable and systematic is Ebisch and Schücking's continuation published twenty years later, with a Supplement in 1936. Their work is continued in Gordon Ross Smith's *A Classified Shakespeare Bibliography, 1936–1958*, a massive compilation with a complicated classification system that needs to be mastered in order to make full use of the volume's rich contents. These are primarily research tools, supplemented and carried forward by sections in the *Annual Bibliography of English Language and Literature* and the special numbers of *Shakespeare Quarterly*. William Godshalk is General Editor of

the Garland Shakespeare Bibliographies (New York and London),
a series of volumes of variable quality primarily surveying
scholarship published since 1940, usually with one volume to a
play though, for instance, *Hamlet* has a volume for each decade
while the three Henry VI plays are treated together. A summary
of each item is provided.

More useful to undergraduates and general readers are deliberately selective bibliographies. David Bevington's *Shakespeare* (1978) in the Goldentree series offers an ample selection
helpfully arranged. Somewhat more idiosyncratic in its listings
is McManaway and Roberts's *Selective Bibliography of Shakespeare*
(1975). Larry S. Champion's *The Essential Shakespeare* (1986) is an
annotated bibliography of modern studies; David M. Bergeron's
and Geraldo U. de Sousa's *Shakespeare: A Study and Research
Guide* (1987) offers more discursive guidance. *The Cambridge
Companion to Shakespeare Studies* (1986), edited by Stanley Wells,
has chapters on critical and scholarly writings, and lists are
provided in *The New Cambridge Bibliography of English Literature*,
compiled by George Watson. Detailed critical studies of each
year's publications appear in *The Year's Work in English Studies*
and in *Shakespeare Survey* (Cambridge, from 1948), where they
are presented in three sections, one on the Life, Times, and Stage,
another on Critical Studies, and a third on Editions and Textual
Studies.

PERIODICALS

The oldest of the four main current periodicals devoted to Shakespeare is the annual *Shakespeare Jahrbuch*, which first appeared
in 1865. Since 1965 two versions have appeared, *Shakespeare
Jahrbuch* from East Germany and *Deutsche Shakespeare-Gesellschaft West Jahrbuch* from West Germany. Some of the articles
and reviews are in English. The English *Shakespeare Survey* has
appeared annually since 1948. The articles in each volume centre
on a main theme, and there are also critical surveys of scholarship, criticism, and performances. Some volumes include retrospective surveys of writings related to the volume's main topic.
The American *Shakespeare Quarterly* began in 1950. It includes
articles, shorter notes, reviews of books and performances, and
an annotated bibliography of the year's publications. The American *Shakespeare Studies*, first published in 1965, is an annual
collection of essays and book reviews.

THE LIFE

The most systematic overall scholarly study of Shakespeare's life and theatrical career is provided by E. K. Chambers in his monumental but ageing work of 1930, which includes studies of the facts and problems associated with each play, reprints and transcripts of all the records known at the time Chambers was writing, along with allusions to Shakespeare up to 1640 and other relevant material reliably if unalluringly presented. A useful abbreviation of Chambers's work, by Charles Williams, gives as much as the general reader is likely to require. Somewhat more limited in scope, though far more lively and attractive in presentation, is S. Schoenbaum's *William Shakespeare: A Documentary Life* (1975), in which a comprehensive collection of photographic facsimiles is accompanied by a detailed narrative commentary. The revised *William Shakespeare: A Compact Documentary Life* (1977, paperback 1978), also by Schoenbaum, includes the complete narrative and a selection of the documents; this is now to all intents and purposes the standard biography. The *Documentary Life* is supplemented by Schoenbaum's *Records and Images* (1981), which includes sections on Shakespeare's handwriting, Shakespeare forgeries, and portraits of Shakespeare. Shakespeare's links with the English Midlands are exhaustively studied in Mark Eccles's admirable *Shakespeare in Warwickshire* (1961). E. A. J. Honigmann's *Shakespeare: The 'Lost Years'* (1985) combines scholarship with speculation in an investigation of Shakespeare's early manhood.

There have been many attempts to tell the story of Shakespeare's life and to set it in a historical context. Among studies that can be recommended to the serious student are the closely argued section on the life in Peter Alexander's *Shakespeare* and Peter Quennell's more leisurely and discursive biography. There are attractive pictorial biographies by F. E. Halliday (1953) and Anthony Burgess (1970). Richard Dutton's *William Shakespeare: A Literary Life* (1989) offers a careful, balanced account of Shakespeare's literary career. A mass of information, especially on the Warwickshire background, is presented in E. I. Fripp's *Shakespeare: Man and Artist*, which is on as large a scale as Chambers's two volumes but presents its material in a narrative framework.

One of the best books on Shakespeare's life is actually a study of other people's attempts to recount it, S. Schoenbaum's

Shakespeare's Lives (1970), an authoritative and entertaining work that recounts the development of biographical studies of Shakespeare. Its excellent index makes it a valuable work of reference. Schoenbaum includes a study of attempts to prove that Shakespeare was someone else. Readers looking for an account of Shakespeare's life combined with a study of his achievement are probably still best served by Alexander's book, or by M. M. Reese's *Shakespeare: His World and His Work* (revised 1980).

GENERAL REFERENCE BOOKS

Several handbooks arranged in alphabetical order of entries provide information about a range of topics likely to be of interest to the student of Shakespeare and his times. F. E. Halliday's *A Shakespeare Companion 1564–1964* is reliable, economically written, and full up to the date of its completion. Campbell and Quinn's *Shakespeare Encyclopedia* (1966) is bulkier, more diffuse, and slightly less reliable, but includes more material relating to criticism of the plays. Stanley Wells's *Shakespeare: An Illustrated Dictionary* (revised 1985) is a more modest compilation with some emphasis on recent stage history. He has also edited *The Cambridge Companion to Shakespeare Studies* (1986), which has seventeen chapters on various aspects of Shakespearian interest including the background, the writings, and the textual, critical, and performance history. The three volumes of *William Shakespeare: His World, His Work, His Influence*, edited by John F. Andrews, include sixty essays on the historical and cultural context of Shakespeare's work, his career, and his influence from his own time to the present.

LANGUAGE

The standard one-volume concordance is Marvin Spevack's *The Harvard Concordance to Shakespeare* (1973), keyed to the Riverside text. Of more specialized interest is Spevack's *Complete and Systematic Concordance to the Works of Shakespeare* in 9 volumes (1968–80). Overall introductions to Shakespeare's language are provided in G. L. Brook's *The Language of Shakespeare* (1976) and N. F. Blake's *Shakespeare's Language: An Introduction* (1983). Assistance with the details of the language is often best obtained from well-annotated editions, but two basic books are Onions's *A Shakespeare Glossary* in its revised form and E. A. Abbott's *A Shakespearian Grammar*, still valuable after over a century. The specialist will need to use W. Franz's *Die Sprache Shakespeares in Vers und Prosa* (1939), a revised and enlarged edition of his *Shakespeare-Grammatik* (1898–1900), as well as Alexander Schmidt's *Shakespeare-Lexicon*, originally published in 1874–5. More specialized assistance on an aspect of Shakespeare's vocabulary neglected in some reference books is provided by Eric Partridge's *Shakespeare's Bawdy* (1947, 1968) and by E. A. M. Colman in *The Dramatic Use of Bawdy in Shakespeare* (1974). Helge Kökeritz's *Shakespeare's Pronunciation* (1953) was for long a standard study; its findings are supplemented and to some degree challenged in Fausto Cercignani's *Shakespeare's Works and Elizabethan Pronunciation* (1981), well indexed but still not easy to use. These studies are usefully supplemented by E. J. Dobson's *English Pronunciation 1500–1700* (1957). An invaluable guide to Shakespeare's use of proverbs and other wise saws and modern instances is R. W. Dent's *Shakespeare's Proverbial Language: An Index* (1981). Hilda M. Hulme's *Explorations in Shakespeare's Language* (1962) is a more selectively critical study. F. W. Ness's *The Use of Rhyme in Shakespeare's Plays* (1941) is the standard work on its subject, as is Brian Vickers's *The Artistry of Shakespeare's Prose* (1968).

EDITIONS

Guidance on editions of individual plays is provided in the following chapters. Readers who need a collected edition in one volume are variously served. In England the tradition has been to print collected editions with no annotation, though sometimes with introductory material and collective glossaries. In America the most popular collected editions are those prepared specifically for classroom use, with explanatory notes on the page. The Complete Oxford Shakespeare (1986; general editors Stanley Wells and Gary Taylor; available in various formats as well as an original-spelling edition) applies the results of the mid-twentieth century revolution in Shakespeare textual studies, offering for example two texts of *King Lear*, one based on the Quarto, the other on the Folio, and a Folio-based *Hamlet*. The newly modernized texts are arranged in a freshly considered chronological order. The edition includes a General Introduction and brief introductions to individual works; an annotated edition with fuller Introductions is in preparation. The thinking behind this edition is expounded in the editors' *William Shakespeare: A*

Textual Companion (1987), which also includes more general information about the canon and chronology of Shakespeare's works. The most generally approved, traditionally edited plain-text edition is that of Peter Alexander (1954), which can be had both in a single volume and in a four-volume set. C. J. Sisson's edition (1954) has the merit of including a complete, modernized text of *Sir Thomas More*. The American Riverside edition, edited by G. Blakemore Evans (1974), has thorough annotation, full critical Introductions, a good deal of ancillary material, and a text that incorporates numerous archaic spellings. David Bevington's annotated edition of the *Complete Works* (1980) is a thorough revision and re-presentation of Hardin Craig's, itself based on the Globe.

SHAKESPEARE'S REPUTATION AND INFLUENCE

Raw material for the study of Shakespeare's reputation during his lifetime and throughout the seventeenth century is provided in *The Shakspere Allusion-Book*, edited by John Munro, a valuable compilation which nevertheless has long stood in need of revision. E. A. J. Honigmann in *Shakespeare's Impact on His Contemporaries* (1982) re-examines the conventional view of Shakespeare as derived from contemporary allusions, seeks to establish that his earliest works date from the 1580s, and re-argues the case that *The Troublesome Reign* is an imitation rather than a source of *King John*. A partial study of Shakespeare's early reputation is G. E. Bentley's *Shakespeare and Jonson: Their Reputations in the Seventeenth Century Compared* (1945), which should be read along with David Frost's *The School of Shakespeare. The Influence of Shakespeare on English Drama 1600–1642* (1968). Frost essays a refutation of both Bentley's methods and his conclusions, the most striking of which is that Jonson's reputation stood higher than Shakespeare's during the period investigated.

The six volumes of Brian Vickers's *Shakespeare: The Critical Heritage* (1974–81) form a valuable anthology of criticism published up to 1801; the work also includes extracts from theatrical adaptations and from textual studies, and the editor provides helpful introductory material.

Perhaps the most important single event in the development of Shakespeare's posthumous reputation was the jubilee organized in 1769 by David Garrick. The best documentary account of this remarkable occasion is Johanne M. Stochholm's (1964); Martha

W. England's study (1964) represents a more serious attempt to assess its sociological significance. Its nineteenth-century counterpart is studied by Richard Foulkes in *The Shakespeare Tercentenary of 1864* (1984). D. Nichol Smith's scholarly and concise study (1928) of eighteenth-century interest in Shakespeare is still worth reading. There is no equivalent for the nineteenth century, but both F. E. Halliday (1957) and Louis Marder (1964) have written readable general accounts of Shakespeare's reputation. Oswald LeWinter's anthology *Shakespeare in Europe* (1963) reprints some of the most important Continental writings from Voltaire to Jean-Louis Barrault. Jonathan Bate's *Shakespeare and the English Romantic Imagination* (1986) is a scholarly critical study.

There is no adequate full account of the history of Shakespeare criticism, but Arthur M. Eastman (1968) gives a thoughtful survey of the work of the major critics and concise accounts are to be found in *The Cambridge Companion to Shakespeare Studies* (1986) edited by Stanley Wells. S. Viswanathan's *The Shakespeare Play as Poem: A Critical Tradition in Perspective* (1980) is concerned particularly with the influence of G. Wilson Knight. Shakespeare's impact on the visual arts, manifested especially through illustrations to editions, designs for the theatre, and paintings with Shakespearian subjects, is studied in W. Moelwyn Merchant's *Shakespeare and the Artist* (1959), a book which makes interesting critical use of its material.

SOURCES AND INFLUENCES

The principal studies of the sources of individual plays are referred to in the appropriate chapters. The more important narrative and dramatic sources and analogues are reprinted and discussed in Geoffrey Bullough's invaluable volumes (1957–75). Kenneth Muir's *The Sources of Shakespeare's Plays* (1977) offers concise critical accounts of the sources of each work. Some writings exercised a pervasive influence on Shakespeare; the influence of others was more local. Notes to the more fully annotated editions often provide the best source of information about the latter. Among more generally influential books, the Bible is the subject of Richmond Noble's scholarly but rather drily academic study, *Shakespeare's Biblical Knowledge and Use of the Book of Common Prayer* (1935); more restricted in its coverage, though also more informative, is Naseeb Shaheen's *Biblical References in Shakespeare's Tragedies* (1987).

There is no comprehensive study of the influence of Ovid. R. A. Brower's *Hero and Saint: Shakespeare and the Graeco-Roman Heroic Tradition* (1971) studies the tragedies in relation to classical influences, and in *Shakespeare's Rome* (1983) Robert S. Miola stresses the influence of Virgil in a critical study of Shakespeare's use of Roman themes in poems as well as plays. Leo Salingar's *Shakespeare and the Traditions of Comedy* (1974) offers a learned account of the classical, medieval, and Italian background to Shakespeare's comedies. Emrys Jones's *The Origins of Shakespeare* (1976) is concerned particularly with dramatic influences on Shakespeare's early plays. Carol Gesner's *Shakespeare and the Greek Romance* (1970) is principally relevant to the late plays. Robert Weimann studies the influence of popular traditions in his *Shakespeare and the Popular Tradition in the Theatre* (1978, first published in German in 1967). Medieval and later influences are considered in Ann Thompson's *Shakespeare's Chaucer: A Study in Literary Origins* (1978) and in Alan C. Dessen's *Shakespeare and the Late Moral Plays* (1986). In *Shakespeare and the Allegory of Evil* (1958) Bernard Spivack offers a study of the dramatic character type known as the vice with particular, but not exclusive, reference to *Othello*. The matter of the relationship between the young Shakespeare and his contemporaries is often bedevilled by problems of chronology, but G. K. Hunter has an acute section on the relationship between Lyly and Shakespeare in his book on Lyly (1962). F. P. Wilson's *Marlowe and the Early Shakespeare* (1953) is both learned and readable. E. A. Armstrong's subtle and fascinating *Shakespeare's Imagination* (1946) is concerned mostly with non-literary influences.

HISTORICAL, SOCIAL, AND PHILOSOPHICAL BACKGROUND

The two-volume work *Shakespeare's England*, edited by Lee and Onions (1916) in commemoration of the three-hundredth anniversary of Shakespeare's death, is still valuable. Made up of thirty sections by many different contributors, it is full of information about Elizabethan and Jacobean society and culture. It is supplemented and brought up to date in some respects by *Shakespeare in His Own Age*, a collection of essays edited by Allardyce Nicoll and originally published in commemoration of the four-hundredth anniversary of Shakespeare's birth as *Shakespeare Survey* 17, and by John F. Andrews's *William Shakespeare: His World, His Work, His Influence* (see 'General Reference Books' above). J. Dover Wilson's *Life in Shakespeare's England* (1911, 1968) is a documentary anthology, partial in scope but enduring in popularity. Shakespeare's relationship to his own time is also the theme of New Historicist studies mentioned in Chapter 19 of this book.

Probably the most accessible of books concerned with the intellectual environment of Shakespeare and his audience is E. M. W. Tillyard's *The Elizabethan World Picture* (1943). Though it has been criticized for presenting an excessively simplified and schematic picture, it remains a valuable introduction to an important topic. More detailed studies of the same subject are Hardin Craig's *The Enchanted Glass* (1936) and J. B. Bamborough's *The Little World of Man* (1952). Shakespeare's religious background is a matter of perennial controversy. Roland Mushat Frye's *Shakespeare and Christian Doctrine* (1963) may be found useful for its learning even by those who cannot accept its basically secular point of view.

Special aspects of Shakespeare's environment are studied in a number of individual works. K. M. Briggs has two books concerned with fairies, witchcraft, and magic. D. H. Madden's *The Diary of Master William Silence: A Study of Shakespeare and Elizabethan Sport* (1897, 1907) is an imaginatively conceived book which has the status of an independent work of art while also being founded on sound scholarship. It is acknowledged as a special influence on T. R. Henn's *The Living Image* (1972), which is particularly concerned with imagery derived from field sports. One of Henn's special topics is studied at greater length in Paul A. Jorgensen's *Shakespeare's Military World* (1956). Alan Brissenden has a lively and informative study of *Shakespeare and the Dance* (1981).

SHAKESPEARE AND MUSIC

Music is important in Shakespeare's plays, which in turn have influenced and inspired much music. A standard study is Edward W. Naylor's *Shakespeare and Music*, first published in 1896 and revised in 1931. John H. Long has surveyed the field in three books: *Shakespeare's Use of Music: A Study of the Music and Its Performance in the Original Production of Seven Comedies* (1955), *Shakespeare's Use of Music: The Final Comedies* (1961), and *Shakespeare's Use of Music: the Histories and Tragedies* (1971). The most detailed work on songs in Shakespeare is Peter J. Seng's *The Vocal Songs in the Plays of Shakespeare: A Critical History* (1967).

Each song is printed, with information in a New Variorum style about texts, music, and critical commentary. F. W. Sternfeld's *Music in Shakespearean Tragedy* (1963) is a thorough, scholarly, and original study extending beyond the limits suggested by its title; it includes transcriptions of early music. *Shakespeare in Music* (1964), edited by Phyllis Hartnoll, includes a useful essay by John Stevens on 'Shakespeare and the Music of the Elizabethan Stage' and also Winton Dean's invaluable 'Shakespeare and Opera', virtually a monograph in its own right. There are also chapters on 'Song and Part-Song Settings of Shakespeare's Lyrics, 1660–1960', and on 'Shakespeare in the Concert Hall'. The bibliographical aspects of the volume will be superseded by the *Shakespeare Music Catalogue*, edited by Bryan N. S. Gooch and David S. Thatcher (Oxford, forthcoming).

REFERENCES

BIBLIOGRAPHIES

Annual Bibliography of English Language and Literature (Modern Humanities Research Association, London, from 1920).

Bergeron, David M., and Geraldo U. de Sousa, *Shakespeare: A Study and Research Guide* (Lawrence, Kan., 1987).

Bevington, David, *Shakespeare* (Goldentree Bibliographies in Language and Literature, Arlington Heights, Ill., 1978).

Champion, Larry S., *The Essential Shakespeare* (Boston, Mass., 1986).

Ebisch, W., and L. L. Schücking, *A Shakespeare Bibliography* (Oxford, 1931); *Supplement for the Years 1930–35* (Oxford, 1937).

Jaggard, William, *Shakespeare Bibliography* (Stratford-upon-Avon, 1911).

McManaway, James G., and Jeanne Addison Roberts, *A Selective Bibliography of Shakespeare: Editions, Textual Studies, Commentary* (Washington, DC, 1975).

Smith, Gordon Ross, *A Classified Bibliography, 1936–1958* (University Park, Pa., 1963).

Watson, George (ed.), *The New Cambridge Bibliography of English Literature* (Cambridge, 1974).

Wells, Stanley (ed.), *The Cambridge Companion to Shakespeare Studies* (Cambridge, 1986).

PERIODICALS

Jahrbuch der Deutschen Shakespeare-Gesellschaft (1865–1964). (Two separate publications thereafter: *Jahrbuch 1965*, etc., published by the Deutsche Shakespeare-Gesellschaft West, Heidelberg, and *Shake-*

speare Jahrbuch 100/101 (1964–5), etc., published by the Shakespeare-
Gesellschaft East, Weimar.)
Shakespeare Quarterly (Washington, DC, from 1950).
Shakespeare Studies (Cincinnati, Ohio, from 1965; subsequently Nashville,
Tenn., and Columbia, SC).
Shakespeare Survey (Cambridge, from 1948).

THE LIFE

Alexander, Peter, *Shakespeare* (London, 1964).
Burgess, Anthony, *Shakespeare* (London, 1970).
Chambers, E. K., *William Shakespeare: A Study of Facts and Problems*, 2
vols. (Oxford, 1930; reprinted 1989); abridged by Charles Williams, *A
Short Life of Shakespeare with the Sources* (Oxford, 1933).
Dutton, Richard, *William Shakespeare: A Literary Life* (London, 1989).
Eccles, Mark, *Shakespeare in Warwickshire* (Madison, Wis., 1961).
Fripp, E. I., *Shakespeare, Man and Artist*, 2 vols. (London, 1938).
Halliday, F. E., *Shakespeare: A Pictorial Biography* (London, 1953).
Honigmann, E. A. J., *Shakespeare: The 'Lost Years'* (Manchester, 1985).
Quennell, Peter, *Shakespeare* (London, 1963; Penguin Shakespeare Lib-
rary, Harmondsworth, 1969).
Reese, M. M., *Shakespeare: His World and His Work* (London, 1953; rev.
1980).
Schoenbaum, S., *Shakespeare's Lives* (Oxford, 1970, rev. edn. 1991).
——*William Shakespeare: A Compact Documentary Life* (Oxford, 1977;
paperback 1978).
——*William Shakespeare: A Documentary Life* (Oxford, 1975).
——*William Shakespeare: Records and Images* (London, 1981).

GENERAL REFERENCE BOOKS

Andrews, John F. (ed.), *William Shakespeare: His World, His Work, His
Influence*, 3 vols. (New York, 1985).
Campbell, O. J., and E. G. Quinn (eds.), *The Reader's Encyclopedia of
Shakespeare* (also published as *A Shakespeare Encyclopedia*) (New
York, 1966).
Halliday, F. E., *A Shakespeare Companion 1550–1950* (London, 1952; 2nd
edn., *A Shakespeare Companion 1564–1964*, Harmondsworth, 1964).
Wells, Stanley, *Shakespeare: An Illustrated Dictionary* (London, 1978;
paperback Oxford, 1981; rev. 1985).
——(ed.) *The Cambridge Companion to Shakespeare Studies* (Cambridge,
1986).

LANGUAGE

Abbott, E. A., *A Shakespearian Grammar* (London, 1869).
Blake, N. F., *Shakespeare's Language: An Introduction* (London, 1983).

Brook, G. L., *The Language of Shakespeare* (London, 1976).

Cercignani, Fausto, *Shakespeare's Works and Elizabethan Pronunciation* (Oxford, 1981).

Colman, E. A. M., *The Dramatic Use of Bawdy in Shakespeare* (London, 1974).

Dent, R. W., *Shakespeare's Proverbial Language: An Index* (Berkeley, Calif., and London, 1981).

Dobson, E. J., *English Pronunciation 1500–1700*, 2 vols. (Oxford, 1957).

Franz, Wilhelm, *Die Sprache Shakespeares in Vers und Prosa* (Halle/Salle, 1939).

Hulme, Hilda M., *Explorations in Shakespeare's Language: Some Problems of Lexical Meaning in the Dramatic Text* (London, 1962).

Kökeritz, Helge, *Shakespeare's Pronunciation* (New Haven and London, 1953).

Ness, F. W., *The Use of Rhyme in Shakespeare's Plays* (New Haven and London, 1941).

Onions, C. T., rev. Robert D. Eagleson, *A Shakespeare Glossary* (Oxford, 1986).

Partridge, Eric, *Shakespeare's Bawdy* (London, 1947; 2nd edn., 1968).

Schmidt, Alexander, *Shakespeare-Lexicon*, 2 vols. (1874–5, rev. and enlarged by G. Sarrazin, Berlin, 1962).

Spevack, Marvin, *The Harvard Concordance to Shakespeare* (Cambridge, Mass., 1973).

—— *A Complete and Systematic Concordance to the Works of Shakespeare*, 9 vols. (Hildesheim, 1968–80).

Vickers, Brian, *The Artistry of Shakespeare's Prose* (London, 1968).

EDITIONS

Alexander, Peter (ed.), *William Shakespeare: The Complete Works* (London, 1951).

Bevington, David (ed.), *The Complete Works of Shakespeare* (Glenview, Ill., 1980).

Evans, G. Blakemore, *et al.* (eds.), *The Riverside Shakespeare* (Boston, Mass., 1974).

Sisson, C. J. (ed.), *William Shakespeare: The Complete Works* (London, 1954).

Wells, Stanley, and Gary Taylor (gen. eds.), *William Shakespeare: The Complete Works* (Oxford, 1986; compact edn., 1988).

Wells, Stanley, and Gary Taylor, with John Jowett and William Montgomery, *William Shakespeare: A Textual Companion* (Oxford, 1987).

SHAKESPEARE'S REPUTATION AND INFLUENCE

Bate, Jonathan, *Shakespeare and the English Romantic Imagination* (Oxford, 1986).

Bentley, G. E., *Shakespeare and Jonson: Their Reputations in the Seventeenth Century Compared*, 2 vols. (Chicago, Ill., 1945).

Eastman, Arthur M., *A Short History of Shakespearean Criticism* (New York, 1968).

England, Martha W., *Garrick's Jubilee* (Columbus, Ohio, 1964).

Foulkes, Richard, *The Shakespeare Tercentenary of 1864* (London, 1984).

Frost, David, *The School of Shakespeare. The Influence of Shakespeare on English Drama 1600–1642* (Cambridge, 1968).

Halliday, F. E., *The Cult of Shakespeare* (London, 1957).

Honigmann, E. A. J., *Shakespeare's Impact on His Contemporaries* (London, 1982).

LeWinter, Oswald (ed.), *Shakespeare in Europe* (Cleveland, Ohio, 1963; Penguin Shakespeare Library, Harmondsworth, 1970).

Marder, Louis, *His Exits and His Entrances* (London, 1964).

Merchant, W. Moelwyn, *Shakespeare and the Artist* (London, 1959).

Munro, John, rev. E. K. Chambers, *The Shakspere Allusion-Book*, 2 vols. (London, 1932).

Smith, D. Nichol, *Shakespeare in the Eighteenth Century* (Oxford, 1928).

Stochholm, Johanne M., *Garrick's Folly: The Stratford Jubilee of 1769 at Stratford and Drury Lane* (London, 1964).

Vickers, Brian (ed.), *Shakespeare: The Critical Heritage, 1623–1801*, 6 vols. (London, 1974–81).

Viswanathan, S., *The Shakespeare Play as Poem; a Critical Tradition in Perspective* (Cambridge, 1980).

SOURCES AND INFLUENCES

Armstrong, E. A., *Shakespeare's Imagination: A Study of the Psychology of Association and Inspiration* (London, 1946).

Brower, R. A., *Hero and Saint: Shakespeare and the Graeco-Roman Heroic Tradition* (Oxford, 1971).

Bullough, Geoffrey (ed.), *Narrative and Dramatic Sources of Shakespeare*, 8 vols. (London, 1957–75).

Dessen, Alan C., *Shakespeare and the Late Moral Plays* (Lincoln, Nebr., and London, 1986).

Gesner, Carol, *Shakespeare and the Greek Romance* (Lexington, Ky., 1970).

Hunter, G. K., *John Lyly: The Humanist as Courtier* (London, 1962).

Jones, Emrys, *The Origins of Shakespeare* (Oxford, 1976).

Miola, Robert S., *Shakespeare's Rome* (Cambridge, 1983).

Muir, Kenneth, *The Sources of Shakespeare's Plays* (London, 1977).

Noble, Richmond, *Shakespeare's Biblical Knowledge and Use of the Book of Common Prayer* (London, 1935).

Salingar, Leo, *Shakespeare and the Traditions of Comedy* (Cambridge, 1974).

Shaheen, Naseeb, *Biblical References in Shakespeare's Tragedies* (Newark, Del., 1987).

Spivack, Bernard, *Shakespeare and the Allegory of Evil* (New York and London, 1958).

Thompson, Ann, *Shakespeare's Chaucer: a Study in Literary Origins* (Liverpool, 1978).

Weimann, Robert, *Shakespeare and the Popular Tradition in the Theatre* (Baltimore, Md., and London, 1978).

Wilson, F. P., *Marlowe and the Early Shakespeare* (Oxford, 1953).

HISTORICAL, SOCIAL, AND PHILOSOPHICAL BACKGROUND

Bamborough, J. B., *The Little World of Man* (London, 1952).

Briggs, K. M., *The Anatomy of Puck: An Examination of Fairy Beliefs among Shakespeare's Contemporaries and Successors* (London, 1959).

—— *Pale Hecate's Team: An Examination of the Beliefs on Witchcraft and Magic among Shakespeare's Contemporaries and His Immediate Successors* (London, 1962).

Brissenden, Alan, *Shakespeare and the Dance* (London, 1981).

Craig, Hardin, *The Enchanted Glass: The Elizabethan Mind in Literature* (New York, 1936).

Frye, Roland Mushat, *Shakespeare and Christian Doctrine* (Princeton, NJ, 1963).

Henn, T. R., *The Living Image* (London, 1972).

Jorgensen, Paul A., *Shakespeare's Military World* (Berkeley, Calif., 1956).

Lee, Sidney, and C. T. Onions (eds.), *Shakespeare's England: An Account of the Life and Manners of His Age*, 2 vols. (Oxford, 1916).

Madden, D. H., *The Diary of Master William Silence: A Study of Shakespeare and Elizabethan Sport* (London, 1897; 2nd edn., 1907).

Nicoll, Allardyce (ed.), *Shakespeare in His Own Age* (*Shakespeare Survey* 17). (Cambridge, 1964; reprinted 1976).

Tillyard, E. M. W., *The Elizabethan World Picture* (London, 1943).

Wilson, John Dover, *Life in Shakespeare's England* (London, 1911; Penguin Shakespeare Library, Harmondsworth, 1968).

SHAKESPEARE AND MUSIC

Hartnoll, Phyllis (ed.), *Shakespeare in Music* (London, 1964).

Long, John H., *Shakespeare's Use of Music: A Study of the Music and Its Performance in the Original Production of Seven Comedies* (Gainesville, Fla., 1955).

—— *Shakespeare's Use of Music: The Final Comedies* (Gainesville, Fla., 1961).

—— *Shakespeare's Use of Music; The Histories and Tragedies* (Gainesville, Fla., 1971).

Naylor, Edward W., *Shakespeare and Music* (London, 1896; 2nd edn., 1931).

Noble, Richmond, *Shakespeare's Use of Song* (Oxford, 1923).

Seng, Peter J., *The Vocal Songs in the Plays of Shakespeare: A Critical History* (Cambridge, Mass., 1967).

Sternfeld, F. W., *Music in Shakespearean Tragedy* (London, 1963).

2 | Shakespeare's Text

NORMAN SANDERS

It is ironical that Shakespeare, the most highly esteemed writer of the modern world, should have been served quite so badly by the printing process as he was. And although one might wish to believe that things would have been different if he had, in the words of his first editors, 'himself . . . lived to have set forth and overseen his own writings', there is no real evidence that his death alone prevented our possessing an accurate, authoritative text of his plays. It would appear that in England plays were not considered as 'literature' at all until Ben Jonson produced his Folio of plays in 1616; and Shakespeare apparently made no effort to have his works published in good versions, although the existence of well-printed and perhaps personally supervised editions of his two narrative poems suggests that he knew how to go about the task had he so wished.

As it is, our knowledge of what Shakespeare wrote for the stage rests on a variety of publications, which were set up from manuscripts of many different kinds and origins, and of which the standards of accuracy and printing range from the appallingly bad to the relatively good. The study of Shakespeare's text during the past two hundred and fifty years is the record of people's attempts, first, to locate and correct the inaccuracies for which Elizabethan printing practices were responsible; second, to determine by examination of the early printed versions what kind of manuscripts lay behind them; and third, to arrive at a formula for editing that will record as near as we can get to what Shakespeare actually wrote, and that will incorporate the evidence on which this edited form is based.

THE EARLY EDITIONS

During Shakespeare's lifetime thirteen of his plays were published singly in reasonably accurate texts usually called 'good quartos': *Titus Andronicus* (1594), *Richard II* (1597), *Richard III* (1597), 1

Henry IV (1598), *Love's Labour's Lost* (1598), *Romeo and Juliet* (1599), *2 Henry IV* (1600), *The Merchant of Venice* (1600), *A Midsummer Night's Dream* (1600), *Much Ado About Nothing* (1600), *Hamlet* (1604–5), *King Lear* (1608), *Troilus and Cressida* (1609); and *Othello* was published in the same format, six years after his death, in 1622. In addition, the following plays were published in quarto form, and are usually called 'bad quartos' because they show various degrees of textual corruption when compared with other extant texts of the same plays: the play known in the Folio as *2 Henry VI* (1594), which bears the title *The First Part of the Contention betwixt the Two Famous Houses of York and Lancaster*; the play known in the Folio as *3 Henry VI* (1595 octavo), which is called *The True Tragedy of Richard Duke of York*; *Romeo and Juliet* (1597); *Henry V* (1600); *The Merry Wives of Windsor* (1602); *Hamlet* (1603); and *Pericles* (1609). Quartos of two other plays, which clearly have a connection with Shakespeare's plays on the same subjects, were also published in corrupt form: *The Troublesome Reign of King John* (1591) and *The Taming of A Shrew* (1594). Reprints of the various quartos in type facsimile appeared during the nineteenth century, the most prominent being the forty-eight-volume set edited by J. O. Halliwell-Phillipps (1862–71) and the forty-three-volume series prepared by F. J. Furnivall between 1880 and 1891. In 1939 W. W. Greg began 'Shakespeare's Quartos in Collotype Facsimile' for the Shakespeare Association and more recently there has appeared the single-volume *Shakespeare's Plays in Quarto* (1981) in which M. J. B. Allen and K. Muir offer fine-screen offset facsimiles of all the first 'good' quartos of plays, and some 'bad' ones.

All the plays that appeared first in some quarto form were included in the First Folio edition of the collected works, edited by two of Shakespeare's fellow actors, John Heminges and Henry Condell, and published in 1623. In this volume an additional sixteen plays were printed for the first time: *The Tempest, The Two Gentlemen of Verona, Measure for Measure, The Comedy of Errors, As You Like It, All's Well That Ends Well, Twelfth Night, The Winter's Tale, 1 Henry VI, Henry VIII, Coriolanus, Timon of Athens, Julius Caesar, Macbeth, Antony and Cleopatra,* and *Cymbeline.* Of the nineteenth- and early twentieth-century facsimiles of the Folio most frequently referred to in Shakespeare studies, Sidney Lee's of 1902 and 1910 is the most accurate reproduction of mainly a single copy; but this, as all others, has been superseded by Charlton Hinman's *Norton Facsimile* (1968), which is based upon the Folger Shakespeare Library's collection of eighty copies, being made up from the clearest and most correct pages available in the various copies.

The 1623 volume was reprinted as the 'Second Folio' of 1632, which formed the basis for the 'Third Folio' of 1663, of which the issue of 1664 contains *Pericles* and six plays sometimes attributed to Shakespeare: this was reprinted as the 'Fourth Folio' of 1685. The text of *Pericles* included in the Third Folio was reprinted from the 1609 quarto, facsimiles of which were published by Sidney Lee in 1905 and by W. W. Greg in 1940. Of the 'apocryphal' plays that are in the Third Folio only *Pericles* is generally accepted as being mainly by Shakespeare; although, among the fourteen other plays that have most frequently been claimed to be totally or in part by Shakespeare, *The Two Noble Kinsmen* appears to be emerging as the favourite for inclusion in the canon. It has been included in a number of twentieth-century complete editions such as the Nonesuch, Kittredge, Signet, New Penguin, River-side, and Oxford; and it will be in the Arden and New Variorum series. Thirteen printed plays that have been seen to contain evidence of Shakespeare's hand, together with the manuscript play, *Sir Thomas More*, were edited by C. F. Tucker Brooke in *The Shakespeare Apocrypha* (1908; 1918). These are discussed in Chapter 18 of this book. Facsimile editions of the non-dramatic works (*Venus and Adonis* (1593), *The Rape of Lucrece* (1594), *The Passionate Pilgrim* (1599), *The Phoenix and the Turtle* (1601), and the *Sonnets* (1609)) are listed in the References to Chapter 4.

THE EIGHTEENTH AND NINETEENTH CENTURIES

During the late seventeenth and early eighteenth centuries, when Shakespeare's works came to be considered 'classics', the texts of his plays began to receive a great deal of scholarly attention. Of the editions that appeared during the eighteenth century the most important textually are those of Nicholas Rowe (1709), Alexander Pope (1725), Lewis Theobald (1733), Thomas Hanmer (1743–4), William Warburton (1747), Samuel Johnson (1765), Edward Capell (1768), George Steevens (1778), and Edmond Malone (1790). All these editions (as well as many of those in the nineteenth century) have been reissued in the reprint series 'Major 18th and 19th Century Editions of the Works of Shake-speare'.

In almost every category of editorial change (correction of printing errors, emended readings, relineation, repunctuation, reassignment of speeches, correction and supplying of stage directions, act and scene divisions, the identification of locales, etc.) these editors supplied the vast bulk of the basic materials and possibilities, and contributed most to the texts as they are traditionally viewed.

While it is dangerous to make large generalizations about so varied a body of editorial work, it is probably true to say (1) that the work of these early editors was carried out in relative ignorance of the theatrical and printing conditions that prevailed in Shakespeare's day; (2) that the emendations they made were governed by the literary, grammatical, and linguistic standards of their time and by the stylistic and theatrical tastes of the individual editors; (3) that, while the 'good' and 'bad' quartos received a good deal of attention and use in the preparation of editions, scholarly opinion had not really crystallized into any settled view of their varying claims to authority. However, it should be noted that, for example, Dr Johnson perceived the dependence of the Second, Third, and Fourth Folios on the First and denied them any independent textual value; and Capell sorted out with some accuracy the various claims of the 'good' and 'bad' quartos. The ways in which some of the eighteenth-century editors, Capell in particular, anticipated some of the twentieth-century editorial methods can be sampled in the studies of S. K. Sen, R. B. McKerrow, and Alice Walker.

During the nineteenth century other editions appeared, many from the hands of distinguished scholars like J. Payne Collier (1842–4), Henry H. Hudson (1851–6), J. O. Halliwell-Phillipps (1853–65), and Alexander Dyce (1857), which added something of permanent value to the body of textual work already done. But the editorial methods employed and the principles governing emendation were not greatly different from those of their eighteenth-century predecessors. However, again there were some scholars who pursued studies on more scientifically analytical and less eclectic lines than their contemporaries. For example, Tycho Mommsen made a close scrutiny of the Folio and Quarto texts of *Romeo and Juliet* and *Hamlet*; W. Sidney Walker classified the errors found in Shakespeare's text; T. Kenny argued the case for memorially reconstructed texts; and P. A. Daniel made a useful analysis of the 'bad quarto' of *the Merry Wives of Windsor* and did still-useful work on the relationship between the Folio text of *Richard III* and the various quartos from which it may have been set up.

The culmination of nearly two centuries of textual study was the *Cambridge Shakespeare*, edited by W. G. Clark, J. Glover, and W. A. Wright, which appeared in its final revision 1891–3. This edition was not only the basis for the famous one-volume 'Globe Shakespeare' to which many works of reference like J. Bartlett's *Concordance* are keyed, but also led to the starting of the *New Variorum Shakespeare*, which is still in progress.

THE NEW BIBLIOGRAPHY

The new approach to Shakespeare's text which developed during the early part of the present century has been traced by F. P. Wilson in his model essay in the history of scholarship, *Shakespeare and the New Bibliography*, and by J. Dover Wilson in a series of articles in *Shakespeare Survey*.

The nature of this new approach to the problem was defined by R. B. McKerrow in his review of K. Deighton's *The Old Dramatists: Conjectural Readings* (1896), a book that is a glaring example of the kind of ingenious tinkering with textual possibilities that had become popular in the late nineteenth century:

Until some curious inquirer makes a thorough investigation into all the technical details of Elizabethan printing, and from this and a comparison of handwritings arrives at some definite statement of the relative probability of various misreadings and misprintings, emendation must remain in much the same state as medicine was before dissection was practised.

This was the course the 'New Bibliographers' followed. First, the ascertaining of what published materials were available for study, which led to the finding lists published by W. W. Greg in *The Library* at the turn of the century and ultimately to the *Short-Title Catalogue*, edited by A. W. Pollard and G. R. Redgrave, and Greg's *A Bibliography of English Printed Drama to the Restoration*. Second, the intricacies of the Elizabethan publishing trade were explored. Edward Arber had published his transcript of the Registers of the Stationers' Company from 1875 to 1877, and his work was supplemented by that of Greg, E. Boswell, and W. A. Jackson on the records of the Company's Court of Assistants. This material was studied with a view to establishing such things as the business relationships that were possible between printer, publisher, and bookseller; the methods by which plays could get into print; the interpretation of the book entries in the Company's registers; the nature of the licensing process by the civil and ecclesiastical authorities; the Company's procedure for establishing a printer's ownership of a copy; and the nature of 'piracy' (illegal printing of plays against the wishes of the author and/or the theatre companies, or in violation of the claims of another printer). Studies that clarified such matters appeared in various periodicals, particularly *The Library*, during the early years of this century, but many of the conclusions arrived at and the problems raised are discussed in such books as Greg's *Companion to Arber, Some Aspects and Problems of London Publishing between 1500 and 1650*, and *The Shakespeare First Folio*; A. W. Pollard's *Shakespeare Folios and Quartos* and *Shakespeare's Fight With the Pirates*; E. M. Albright's *Dramatic Publication in England*; J. Q. Adams's *Dramatic Records*; and Leo Kirschbaum's *Shakespeare and the Stationers*.

The most important area of research was the determining from the extant texts of the exact nature of the Elizabethan printing process. For forty years R. B. McKerrow's *An Introduction to Bibliography for Literary Students* (1928) was the classic textbook showing how the transmission of the literary texts of the English Renaissance were affected by the contemporary printing practices. Then in 1972 Philip Gaskell published *A New Introduction to Bibliography*, which incorporated the results of research done on printing technology since McKerrow's day and includes the first systematic description of the practices of the machine-press era. The analytical techniques developed from the kind of knowledge McKerrow and Gaskell cover were applied first to the quartos, and many early successes were scored. Among the most notable of these were W. W. Greg's, W. J. Neidig's, and A. W. Pollard's demonstration that a collection of nine quartos variously dated were actually printed by Thomas Pavier in 1619; Greg's study of the variants of *King Lear*; and Fredson Bowers's analysis of the system of proof correction used in the same play. Perhaps the best demonstration, between 1900 and 1950, of the application of such techniques on a large scale is E. E. Willoughby's *The Printing of the First Folio of Shakespeare* which, although many of its conclusions have been changed and vastly expanded by Charlton Hinman's later work, still offers a fine display of the methods and results of the New Bibliography.

All the bibliographers working at this time were aware that the object of their researches was to penetrate the printed surface of the plays so as to be able to postulate with some degree of accuracy the kind of manuscript the printer used. One aid to this end was the study of all the extant dramatic manuscripts. W. W. Greg made a beginning with the inclusion of several 'plots' (scene analyses prepared by the players for theatre use) and a player's part in his *Henslowe Papers*; and the Malone Society and other publishers put out accurate transcriptions of the extant plays in manuscript between 1910 and 1929, the most important of which was Greg's edition of *Sir Thomas More*. The study of Elizabethan handwriting, of which these editions were a product, also led to a series of facsimiles illustrating the literary hands of the period in *English Literary Autographs 1500–1650*, to discussions of dramatic manuscripts in E. K. Chambers's *The Elizabethan Stage* and *William Shakespeare*, to Greg's complete survey of the extant remains in his *Dramatic Documents from the Elizabethan Playhouses*, and to two notable studies of individual plays that well illustrate the conclusions arrived at by such research: Greg's analysis of two stage abridgements (Robert Greene's *Orlando Furioso* and George Peele's *Battle of Alcazar*), and R. C. Bald's work on Thomas Middleton's *A Game at Chess*.

It was work of this kind used in conjunction with the analysis of the printed texts that enabled scholars to identify the various classes of manuscript that could lie behind any printed version: 'foul papers'—the author's first or early draft; fair copy—the author's final version, which was submitted to the theatre company; the prompt book—the manuscript prepared for theatre production, which could be either a theatrical editing of the fair copy or a new version prepared by the company's bookkeeper; scribal copies of any of these; and memorially constructed copy —the hypothetical source of the 'bad quartos'. One particular manuscript study was to have far-reaching results so far as Shakespeare was concerned. This was the discovery of the writing characteristics of Ralph Crane, a scrivener who copied for Shakespeare's company, the King's Men, manuscripts designed for publication in the First Folio. His scribal habits are summarized by Greg in *The Shakespeare First Folio*; see also T. H. Howard-Hill's 'Spelling and the Bibliographer.'

With the knowledge gained from playhouse manuscripts, Elizabethan printing and publishing practices, and the probable day-to-day workings of a theatre company of the time (derived principally from the study of *Henslowe's Diary*), scholars proceeded to determine the nature of the printers' copy for the various printed versions of the plays. The best summary of the state of knowledge up to 1955 is to be found in W. W. Greg's *The Shakespeare First Folio*. The texts of *The Tempest, The Two Gentlemen of Verona, The Merry Wives of Windsor, Measure for Measure*, and *The Winter's Tale* seem to have been printed from manuscripts specially prepared for the First Folio by Ralph Crane. Theatre copy of some sort was thought to lie behind the Folio texts of *As You Like It, Twelfth Night, Richard III, Julius Caesar, Macbeth, Hamlet, Othello, King Lear*, and *Cymbeline*. Authorial manuscript was thought to have been used to some extent in the preparation of *The Comedy of Errors, Much Ado About Nothing, Love's Labour's Lost, A Midsummer Night's Dream, The Merchant of Venice, The Taming of the Shrew, All's Well That Ends Well, King John, Richard II, 1 Henry IV, 2 Henry IV, Henry V, 1 Henry VI, 2 Henry VI, 3 Henry VI, Henry VIII, Troilus and Cressida, Coriolanus, Titus Andronicus, Romeo and Juliet, Timon of Athens*, and *Antony and Cleopatra*. However in many cases the Folio texts appear to have been set up with varying degrees of conflation of a manuscript and a printed text where one existed. Many of the 'good quartos' seem to have been based on Shakespeare's own manuscript at one or two removes.

So far as the origins of the 'bad quartos' are concerned the problems are very much more complex. To account for their characteristic features a theory of 'memorial reconstruction' was developed. This posits that these texts are versions of what an actor or actors could recall from having played one or more roles (usually of a comparatively minor sort) in an authorized production of the play. W. W. Greg was the first to explore the implications of the theory in connection with the 'bad quarto' of *The Merry Wives of Windsor*, and other studies of individual plays followed. Among the most important of these are Peter Alexander's and Madeleine Doran's work on *The Contention* and *The True Tragedy*; H. R. Hoppe's on *Romeo and Juliet*; H. T. Price's on *Henry V*; J. Dover Wilson's and B. A. P. van Dam's on *Hamlet*; W. W. Greg's and Fredson Bowers's on *King Lear*; and two important analyses of the same play by G. I. Duthie, who examined and rejected the possibility that transcription by one of the two shorthand systems available to Elizabethans may have been responsible for many of the features exhibited by the 'bad quartos'. Two historical studies

which show how the textual problems of plays have been tackled
are Madeleine Doran's *The Text of 'King Lear'* and D. L. Patrick's
The Textual History of 'Richard III'.

One other important matter occupied the attention of the New
Bibliographers. This was how to use the results of their labours
to produce a definitive edition of the works. Much consideration
was given to such topics as the principles that should govern
textual emendation, by W. W. Greg and others; the selection of
the proper copy texts for modern editions, by Greg, R. B. Mc-
Kerrow, and Fredson Bowers; the degree to which faith may be
placed in the punctuation of Elizabethan printers, by R. M.
Alden, Hilary Jenkinson, Percy Simpson, and Peter Alexander;
how far the printer followed the orthography of the manuscript
and how far his own system, by J. Dover Wilson and A. W.
Pollard; the possibility that plays were revised by the author
over a number of years by Dover Wilson in his New Cambridge
editions of the plays.

THE AGE OF BOWERS

In general, textual work done since the 1950s has continued along
the lines of the New Bibliography; but new methods and refine-
ments of older ones have been used to test the findings of earlier
scholars. The best way of appreciating the kind of work done is to
read through the volumes of *Studies in Bibliography* between 1947
and the present, the issues of *The Library* for the same years, and
the annual review articles in *Shakespeare Survey* written by
James G. McManaway and his successors. Certain large achievements stand out. First, methods by which the texts may be made
to yield the secrets of the printing process have become greatly
sophisticated. The identification of the work of individual compositors is now possible by the tabulation and analysis of type,
the spellings preferred when there are no mechanical factors
inhibiting choice. The idea that compositors can be identified by
variations in spelling had first been suggested by Thomas Satchell
in 1929, but the method was much refined by Alice Walker and
Charlton Hinman. Perhaps the most convenient discussion of
the theory behind this analytical technique is to be found in T.
Howard-Hill's 'Spelling and the Bibliographer'. Second, analysis
of the process of sheets through the press, the distribution of the
manuscript between various compositors, the breaks in the
printing process, and the practice of leaving certain unvarying

parts of the type standing from page to page and forme to forme have enabled bibliographers to work out time schedules for the printing of individual works.

The outstanding example of the kind of results such techniques can produce is Charlton Hinman's *The Printing and Proofreading of the First Folio of Shakespeare*. Using a machine of his own invention, Hinman collated all eighty copies of the First Folio in the Folger Shakespeare Library. This enabled him to chart in great detail such things as the compositors' habits, the occurrences of 'distinctive types' (pieces of type characteristically-enough damaged to be individually identified and associated with a single printer's case), the kinds of errors made and the degree of fidelity with which different compositors followed their copy, the implications of the practice of 'casting off copy' (i.e. the system of dividing the manuscript to be set between two workmen for simultaneous setting, thus making it necessary to spread out or compress the printed text at the points of juncture), the system of proof correction, the use of cancelled leaves, corrected and uncorrected pages, the transfer of standing type from one part of the volume to another, and the employment of lines and rules to divide the text on the page. The conclusions based on such researches allowed Hinman to provide us with an account of how the First Folio came into being, which will probably be modified only in its details.

Other scholars re-investigated many of the other problems first tackled by the New Bibliographers. For example, the whole dramatic outputs of the printers who handled the Shakespeare texts have been analysed: G. Walton Williams scrutinized the play texts that came from the shop of Thomas Creede as preparation for an edition of *Romeo and Juliet*; and Craig Ferguson and Alan Craven closely studied the quartos printed by Valentine Simmes with sometimes very different conclusions. Certainly the fullest enquiry of this kind is Peter Blayney's *The Texts of 'King Lear' and Their Origins*, which exhaustively details the practices of Nicholas Okes's Jacobean printing-house. The relationship between quarto and Folio texts has been much theorized about; the deduction of the types of manuscript copy from the printed pages has become a very complex and much disputed matter; and there has been extensive discussion of how such evidence can be used and recorded in the preparation of modern editions.

After the death of W. W. Greg one name dominated the study of Shakespeare's text—that of Fredson Bowers. In almost every area of bibliography he assumed Greg's mantle. He codified the principles of descriptive bibliography in his *Principles of Bibliographical Description*; under his founding editorship *Studies in Bibliography* published a great deal of the most exciting and representative work done during the past thirty years; he has contributed fundamental research to the difficult problems posed by the text of such plays as *Hamlet, King Lear,* and *Richard III*; he has been ever ready to define the theory and objectives of the whole subject in books like *The Bibliographical Way, Textual and Literary Criticism,* and *On Editing Shakespeare and Other Elizabethan Dramatists*; and he has put his editorial principles into practice in his old-spelling editions of the works of Thomas Dekker and of Beaumont and Fletcher.

RECENT WORK AND TRENDS

In recent years much of the work done on Shakespeare's text has been an extension of that produced by the 'School of Bowers'. For example Hinman's conclusions about the compositors of the First Folio have been questioned and refined in such studies as T. H. Howard-Hill's *A Reassessment of Compositors B and E in the First Folio Tragedies*. There has been much work and as much disagreement on the relationships between the Folio, and the 'good' and 'bad' quartos; and immense ingenuity has been employed to deduce the nature of the manuscripts underlying the various printed versions of the plays in work such as that done by Eleanor Prosser on the scribe and the compositor of the Folio *2 Henry IV*, and that of Howard-Hill on the plays copied by the scrivener Ralph Crane.

However, in the late 1970s and 1980s there has also been a marked change, not so much in the nature and techniques of bibliographical analysis as in the questioning of the assumptions underlying the whole subject since Pollard, Greg, and McKerrow enunciated the principles of the New Bibliography at the beginning of this century. Between that time and now textual critics have generally assumed that the ultimate aim of all work in the field is to arrive at a definitive text of the plays in the canon—that is, the one as close as the accidents of time will allow to the final holograph as it left the author's hand. Further it has been believed that the surest way to discover such a text is the application of as nearly a scientific and objective method of analysis as was humanly possible.

Very few scholars today would subscribe any longer to this idea. There have emerged in recent writings attitudes (derived ultimately, one supposes, from the ideas of some contemporary physicists and psychologists) that question the reliance on measurement and quantification in the analysis of textual evidence. Thus Peter Davison warns us that the bibliographical method itself is not scientific, that the scholar's findings may be based upon exceptional rather than 'normal' practice, that human behaviour is not logical, that even so 'objective' a critic as Hinman can be led to conclusions by the subjectiveness of his selection of evidence.

The numbers, percentages, and charts that we have become so accustomed to in articles on compositor analysis apparently no longer carry the conviction they once did; and there is a widespread awareness of the limitations of bibliographical data. There were twenty years ago rare early warnings of such scepticism. E. A. J. Honigmann in *The Stability of Shakespeare's Text* observed bleakly that 'optimists are at their most dangerous precisely when they offer the world new "bibliographical facts" '; and D. F. McKenzie's history of the Cambridge University Press from 1696 to 1712, which is based on very full records including workmen's vouchers for composition, correction and presswork, contains indications that some of the assignments of compositorial stints and timetables of presswork should be viewed less confidently than they were wont to be.

Perhaps the work done on the 1598 quarto of *Love's Labour's Lost* since the late 1970s may serve to illustrate the new doubt. G. R. Price, John Kerrigan, Paul Werstine, M. Draudt, and Stanley Wells all applied well-tried analytical techniques to the problems of this text and came to divergent conclusions. Price identified four compositors at work, while Werstine finds only two, and Draudt seems to assume that a single worker set the type; and their conclusions become even more tentative when the discussion moves to the manuscript copy and the quarto's relationship to the version found in the Folio. Wells's pronouncement on so small a matter as the errors in the Latin quotations may represent the lack of anything like a consensus on the whole problem: 'It is impossible to determine with absolute confidence which errors should be attributed to the compositor, which to Shakespeare, and which to his characters'.

By far the clearest illustration of the change in assumptions that has occurred in textual studies is offered by *King Lear*. This play has always been the bibliographers' Everest; and Honigmann's mild speculation some years ago as to whether a finished form of the text of this or any other play ever existed has been developed in the detailed work of Peter Blayney, Michael Warren, S. Urkowitz, P. W. K. Stone, Stanley Wells, Gary Taylor, and others in *The Division of the Kingdoms* into a full-blown case for the hypothesis that we possess in the 1608 quarto and the First Folio texts of *King Lear* Shakespeare's original version and his own revision of the play; and it is editions of both of these that appear side by side in Wells's and Taylor's *Oxford Shakespeare*.

It is eminently appropriate that such an hypothesis should be translated into editorial practice in this most recent scholarly edition of the works. Many other editions have appeared in the last forty years or so, designed to serve a variety of readerships (such as Alexander's, Sisson's, Dover Wilson's Cambridge, the New Arden, the Riverside, the New Penguin, and the New Cambridge and Oxford multi-volume series now in progress); and all contain original textual work. But it is the massive achievement of the Oxford edition that has caused the greatest amount of controversy and is certainly the most innovative and daring in its editorial decisions to have appeared this century. The Oxford Press's provision for the reader is lavish: a one-volume modernized edition, a textual commentary of enormous scope, an old-spelling version, and the plays separately edited in single volumes. Almost all aspects of this edition demonstrate its originality. Problems have been faced with a mental freshness and scholarly honesty: in the treatment of the stage directions, in grappling with the difficulties of modernizing Elizabethan English, in the handling of the linkage of half-lines of verse, and in the digesting anew of the vast amount of previous scholarship on matters such as canon and chronology, Folio composition, and the summation of the current areas of agreement about the text of each play.

It will take many years for the scholarly world to absorb and evaluate the conclusions offered in these volumes and they will be the basis for much future work—in fact, they may well become the textual equivalent of A. C. Bradley's *Shakespearean*

Tragedy in criticism: they are where future labourers will start, what they will have to discuss first—whether they agree with them or not. When such headline-making novelties as the change of Falstaff's name to Oldcastle in *1 Henry IV* or the addition of 'Shall I die?' to the poetic canon or the unfamiliar titles *All is True* (for *Henry VIII*) and *The First Part of the Contention* (for *2 Henry VI*) have lost their novelty and have become safely buried, I believe it is the edition's whole-hearted embracing of the idea of the indeterminacy of Shakespeare's text that will take surest hold. The fluent, masterpiece-producing Bard may well have gone forever to be replaced by the constantly scribbling blotter of many a thousand lines.

REFERENCES

THE EARLY EDITIONS

Allen, M. J. B., and Kenneth Muir (eds.), *Shakespeare's Plays in Quarto* (Berkeley, Calif., 1981).

Brooke, C. F. Tucker (ed.), *The Shakespeare Apocrypha* (Oxford, 1908; corr. 1918).

Furnivall, F. J. *et al.* (eds.), *Plays and Poems in Quarto*, 43 vols. (Shakespeare Association Facsimiles, London, 1880–91).

Greg, W. W. (ed.), *Pericles. The Quarto of 1609* (Shakespeare Association, London, 1940).

—— and Charlton Hinman (ed.), *Shakespeare Quarto Facsimiles* (Shakespeare Association, London and Oxford, 1939–   ).

Halliwell-Phillipps, J. O. (ed.), *Collection of Lithographic Facsimiles of the Early Quarto Editions . . .* , 48 vols. (London, 1862–71).

Hinman, Charlton (ed.), *The Norton Facsimile. The First Folio of Shakespeare* (New York, 1968).

Lee, Sidney (ed.), *Shakespeare's Comedies, Histories, and Tragedies* (Oxford, 1902; London, 1910).

—— (ed.), *Shakespeare's Poems and 'Pericles'*, 5 vols. (Oxford, 1905).

THE EIGHTEENTH AND NINETEENTH CENTURIES

Clark, W. G., J. Glover, and W. A. Wright (eds.), *The Cambridge Shakespeare*, 9 vols. (Cambridge, 1863–6; 2nd edn., 1867; 3rd edn., 1891–3).

Daniel, P. A., Introductions to facsimiles of the First, Third, and Sixth Quartos of *Richard III* (London, 1886, 1888, 1889).

—— Introduction to facsimile of the First Quarto of *The Merry Wives of Windsor* (London, 1881).

Furness, H. H. *et al.* (eds.), *A New Variorum Edition of Shakespeare* (Philadelphia, Pa., 1871–   ).

Kenny, Thomas, *The Life and Genius of Shakespeare* (London, 1864).

McKerrow, R. B., *The Treatment of Shakespeare's Text by His Earliest Editors, 1709–1768*, British Academy Lecture 1933.

Mommsen, Tycho, 'Hamlet', *Neue Jahrbücher für Philologie und Paedagogik*, 72 (1885), 57, 107, 159.

—— *Shakespeares Romeo und Julie* (Oldenburg, 1859).

Sen, S. K., *Capell and Malone, and Modern Critical Bibliography* (Calcutta, 1960).

Walker, Alice, *Edward Capell and His Editions of Shakespeare*, British Academy Lecture 1962.

Walker, W. Sidney, *A Critical Examination of the Text of Shakespeare*, ed. W. N. Lettsom (London, 1860).

THE NEW BIBLIOGRAPHY

Adams, J. Q. (ed.), *Dramatic Records of Sir Henry Herbert* (New Haven, Conn., 1917).

Albright, Evelyn M., *Drama Publication in England 1580–1640* (New York, 1927).

Alden, R. M. 'The Punctuation of Shakespeare's Printers', *PMLA* 39 (1924), 557–80.

Alexander, Peter, *Shakespeare's 'Henry VI' and 'Richard III'* (Cambridge, 1929).

—— *Shakespeare's Punctuation*, British Academy Lecture 1945.

Bald, R. C. (ed.), *Thomas Middleton's 'A Game at Chess'* (Cambridge, 1929).

Bowers, Fredson, 'Current Theories of the Copy-Text', *Modern Philology*, 48 (1950), 12–20.

—— 'An Examination of the Method of Proof Correction in *Lear*', *The Library*, 2 (1947), 20–44.

Chambers, E. K., *The Elizabethan Stage*, 4 vols. (Oxford, 1923).

—— *William Shakespeare: A Study of Facts and Problems*, 2 vols. (Oxford, 1930; reprinted 1989); abridged by Charles Williams, *A Short Life of Shakespeare with the Sources* (Oxford, 1933).

Dam, B. A. P. van, *The Text of Shakespeare's 'Hamlet'* (London, 1924).

Doran, Madeleine, *Henry VI* (Iowa City, I., 1928).

—— *The Text of 'King Lear'* (Stanford, Calif., 1931).

Duthie, G. I., *Elizabethan Shorthand and the First Quarto of 'King Lear'* (Oxford, 1949).

—— *Shakespeare's 'King Lear', a Critical Edition* (Oxford, 1949).

Gaskell, Philip, *A New Introduction to Bibliography* (Oxford, 1972).

Greg, W. W., *A Bibliography of English Printed Drama to the Restoration*, 4 vols. (London, 1951–62).

—— *A Companion to Arber* (London, 1967).

—— *Dramatic Documents from the Elizabethan Playhouses*, 2 vols. (London, 1931).

—— *Henslowe Papers* (London, 1907).

—— 'On Certain False Dates in Shakespearian Quartos', *The Library*, 9 (1908), 113–31, 381–409.

—— *Principles of Emendation in Shakespeare*, British Academy Lecture 1928.

—— 'The Rationale of the Copy-Text', *Studies in Bibliography*, 3 (1950), 19–36.

—— *The Shakespeare First Folio* (Oxford, 1956).

—— *Some Aspects and Problems of London Publishing between 1500 and 1650* (Oxford, 1956).

—— *Two Elizabethan Stage Abridgements* (Malone Society Reprints, Oxford, 1923).

—— *Variants in the First Quarto of 'King Lear'* (London, 1940).

—— *et al.*, *English Literary Autographs 1500–1650* (London, 1925–32).

—— (ed.), *The Booke of Sir Thomas More* (Malone Society Reprints, Oxford, 1911).

—— (ed.) *Shakespeare's 'Merry Wives of Windsor', 1602* (Oxford, 1910).

—— and E. Boswell (eds.), *Records of the Court of the Stationers' Company 1576–1602* (London, 1930).

Henslowe, Philip, *Henslowe's Diary*, 2 vols., ed. W. W. Greg (London, 1904–8).

—— *Henslowe's Diary, with Supplementary Material, Introduction and Notes*, ed. R. A. Foakes and R. T. Rickert (Cambridge, 1961).

Hoppe, H. R., *The Bad Quarto of 'Romeo and Juliet', a Bibliographical and Textual Study* (Cornell, NY, 1948).

Jackson, W. A. (ed.), *Records of the Court of the Stationers' Company 1602–1640* (London, 1957).

Jenkinson, Hilary, 'Notes on the Study of English Punctuation of the Sixteenth Century', *RES* 2 (1926), 152–8.

Kirschbaum, Leo, *Shakespeare and the Stationers* (Columbus, Ohio, 1955).

McKerrow, R. B., *An Introduction to Bibliography for Literary Students* (Oxford, 1927).

—— *Prolegomena for the Oxford Shakespeare* (Oxford, 1939).

Neidig, W. J., 'The Shakespeare Quartos', *Modern Philology*, 8 (1910–11), 145–63.

Patrick, D. L., *The Textual History of 'Richard III'* (Stanford, Calif., 1936).

Pollard, A. W., 'Elizabethan Spelling as a Literary and Bibliographical Clue', *The Library*, 4 (1923), 1–8.

—— *Shakespeare's Fight with the Pirates* (Cambridge, 1920; 2nd edn. (1937).

—— *Shakespeare Folios and Quartos, 1594–1685* (London, 1909).

—— and G. R. Redgrave (eds.), *A Short-Title Catalogue of Books Printed in England, Scotland, and Ireland and of English Books Printed Abroad, 1475–1640* (London, 1926); (2nd edn. rev. Jackson, Ferguson, and Pantzer, vol. i, *A–H* (Oxford, 1986), vol. ii, *I–Z* (Oxford, 1976).

Price, H. T., *The Text of 'Henry V'* (Newcastle-under-Lyme, 1920).

Simpson, Percy, *Shakespearian Punctuation* (Oxford, 1911).

Willoughby, E. E., *The Printing of the First Folio of Shakespeare* (London, 1932).

Wilson, F. P., *Shakespeare and the New Bibliography*, rev. and ed. Helen Gardner (Oxford, 1970).

Wilson, John Dover, *The Manuscript of Shakespeare's 'Hamlet', and the Problems of Its Transmission*, 2 vols. (Cambridge, 1934).

—— 'The New Way with Shakespeare's Texts', *Shakespeare Survey* 7 (1954) 48–56; 8 (1955) 81–99; 9 (1956) 69–80; 11 (1958) 78–88.

THE AGE OF BOWERS

Blayney, Peter, *The Texts of 'King Lear' and Their Origins*, vol. i, *Nicholas Okes and the First Quarto* (Cambridge, 1982).

Bowers, Fredson, *The Bibliographical Way* (Lawrence, Kan., 1959).

—— *On Editing Shakespeare and Other Elizabethan Dramatists* (Philadelphia, Pa., 1955).

—— *Principles of Bibliographical Description* (Princeton, NJ, 1949).

—— *Textual and Literary Criticism* (Cambridge, 1959).

—— (ed.), *The Dramatic Works in the Beaumont and Fletcher Canon* (Cambridge, 1966–).

—— (ed.), *The Dramatic Works of Thomas Dekker*, 4 vols. (Cambridge, 1953–61).

—— and L. Beaurline (eds.), *Studies in Bibliography* (Charlottesville, Va., annually since 1947).

Craven, Alan E., 'The Reliability of Simmes's Compositor A', *Studies in Bibliography*, 32 (1979), 186–9.

—— 'Simmes' Compositor A and Five Shakespeare Quartos', *Studies in Bibliography*, 26 (1973), 37–60.

Ferguson, W. Craig, *Valentine Simmes* (Charlottesville, Va., 1968).

Hinman, Charlton, *The Printing and Proofreading of the First Folio of Shakespeare*, 2 vols. (Oxford, 1963).

Howard-Hill, T. H., 'Spelling and the Bibliographer', *The Library*, 18 (1963), 1–28.

Nicoll, Allardyce, Kenneth Muir (from 1966), and Stanley Wells (from 1981) (eds.), *Shakespeare Survey* (Cambridge, annually since 1948).

Smidt, Kristian (ed.), *The Tragedy of King Richard III* (Oslo and New York, 1969).

Walker, Alice, *Textual Problems in the First Folio* (Cambridge, 1953).

Walton, J. K., *Copy for the First Folio Text of 'Richard III'* (Auckland, NZ, 1955).

—— *The Quarto Copy for the First Folio of Shakespeare* (Dublin, 1971).

Williams, G. Walton (ed.), *Romeo and Juliet* (Durham, NC, 1964).

RECENT WORKS AND TRENDS

Alexander, Peter (ed.), *William Shakespeare: The Complete Works* (London, 1951).

Blayney, Peter, *The Texts of 'King Lear' and Their Origins*, vol. i, *Nicholas Okes and the First Quarto* (Cambridge, 1982).

Brockbank, Philip (gen. ed.), *The New Cambridge Shakespeare* (Cambridge, 1984–).

Davison, Peter, 'The Selection and Presentation of Bibliographic Evidence', *Analytical and Enumerative Bibliography*, 1 (1977), 101–36.

Draudt, M., 'Printer's Copy for the Quarto of *Love's Labour's Lost (1598)*, *The Library*, 6 (1981), 119–31.

—— 'The "Rosaline-Katherine Tangle" in *Love's Labour's Lost*', *The Library*, 6 (1982), 381–96.

Ellis-Fermor, Una, Harold F. Brooks, Harold Jenkins and Brian Morris (eds.), *The New Arden Shakespeare* (London, 1951–).

Evans, G. Blakemore (ed.), *The Riverside Shakespeare* (Boston, Mass., 1974).

Honigmann, E. A. J., 'Shakespeare's Revised Plays: *King Lear* and *Othello*', *The Library*, 6 (1982), 142–73.

—— *The Stability of Shakespeare's Text* (London, 1965).

Howard-Hill, T. H., *Ralph Crane and Some Shakespeare First Folio Comedies* (Charlottesville, Va., 1972).

—— *A Reassessment of Compositors B and E in the First Folio Tragedies* (Columbia, SC, 1977).

Jackson, MacD. P., 'Fluctuating Variation: Author, Annotator, or Actor', in *The Division of the Kingdoms: Shakespeare's Two Versions of 'King Lear'*, ed. Gary Taylor and Michael Warren (Oxford, 1983), 313–49.

Kerrigan, J., '*Love's Labour's Lost* and Shakespearean Revision', *Shakespeare Quarterly*, 33 (1982), 337–9.

—— 'Revision, Adaptation, and the Fool in *King Lear*' in *The Division of the Kingdoms: Shakespeare's Two Versions of 'King Lear'*, ed. Gary Taylor and Michael Warren (Oxford, 1983), 195–245.

—— 'Shakespeare at Work: the Katherine-Rosaline Tangle in *Love's Labour's Lost*', *RES* 33 (1982), 129–36.

—— (ed.), *Love's Labour's Lost* (New Penguin Shakespeare, Harmondsworth, 1982).

McKenzie, D. F., *The Cambridge University Press, 1696–1712*, 2 vols. (Cambridge, 1966).

Price, G. R., 'The Printing of *Love's Labour's Lost* (1598)', *Papers of the Bibliographical Society of America*, 72 (1978), 405–34.

Prosser, Eleanor, *Shakespeare's Anonymous Editors: Scribe and Compositor in the Folio Text of '2 Henry IV'* (Stanford, Calif., 1980).

Sisson, C. J., *New Readings in Shakespeare*, 2 vols. (Cambridge, 1956).

—— (ed.), *William Shakespeare: The Complete Works* (London, 1954).

Spencer, T. J. B., and Stanley Wells (gen. eds.), *The New Penguin Shakespeare* (Harmondsworth, 1967–).

Stone, P. W. K., *The Textual History of 'King Lear'* (New York, 1980).

Taylor, Gary, 'The Date and Authorship of the Folio Version', in *The Division of the Kingdoms: Shakespeare's Two Versions of 'King Lear'*, ed. Gary Taylor and Michael Warren (Oxford, 1983), 351–468.

—— 'Four New Readings in *King Lear*', *N. & Q.* NS 29 (1982), 121–3.

—— 'The War in *King Lear*', *Shakespeare Survey* 33 (1980), 27–34.

—— and Michael Warren (eds.), *The Division of the Kingdoms: Shakespeare's Two Versions of 'King Lear'* (Oxford, 1983).

Urkowitz, Steven, *Shakespeare's Revision of 'King Lear'* (Princeton, NJ, 1980).

Warren, Michael, 'Quarto and Folio *King Lear* and the Interpretation of Albany and Edgar', in *Shakespeare, Pattern of Excelling Nature*, ed. David M. Bevington and Jay L. Halio (Newark, Del., 1978), 95–107.

Wells, Stanley, 'The Copy for the Folio Text of *Love's Labour's Lost*', *RES* 33 (1982), 137–47.

—— 'Introduction: The Once and Future *King Lear*', in *The Division of the Kingdoms: Shakespeare's Two Versions of 'King Lear'*, ed. Gary Taylor and Michael Warren (Oxford, 1983), 1–22.

—— and Gary Taylor, with John Jowett and William Montgomery, *William Shakespeare: A Textual Companion* (Oxford, 1987).

—— and Gary Taylor (gen. eds.), *William Shakespeare: The Complete Works*. Modern Spelling Edition (Oxford, 1986); Original Spelling Edition (Oxford, 1987); multi-volume series in progress.

Werstine, Paul, 'The Editorial Usefulness of Printing House and Compositor Studies', in *Play-Texts in Old Spelling: Papers from the Glendon Conference*, ed. G. B. Shand and Raymond C. Shady (New York, 1984), 35–64.

—— 'Editorial Uses of Compositor Study', *Analytical and Enumerative Bibliography*, 2 (1978), 153–65.

—— 'Folio Editors, Folio Compositors, and the Folio Text of *King Lear*', in *The Division of the Kingdoms: Shakespeare's Two Versions of 'King Lear'*, ed. Gary Taylor and Michael Warren (Oxford, 1983), 247–312.

—— 'Variants in the First Quarto of *Love's Labour's Lost*', *Shakespeare Studies*, 12 (1979), 35–47; supplemented in *Papers of the Bibliographical Society of America*, 73 (1979), 493–4.

Wilson, J. Dover, A. T. Quiller-Couch, *et al.* (eds.), *The New Shakespeare* (Cambridge, 1921–66).

3 | Shakespeare in Performance

MICHAEL JAMIESON

Shakespeare was a popular playwright in his own day, and at most subsequent periods in our theatre his main works have been regularly staged. A critical approach to Shakespeare based on a study of the plays as works to be performed is illuminating in itself, and can also be an antidote to the kind of literary criticism which occasionally conveys insights and nuances which no actor or director could communicate to an audience. All students of Shakespeare should have a general notion of the stage conditions of Elizabethan times because this knowledge helps to explain the form the play takes on the printed page. It is desirable that readers of Shakespeare should also be playgoers or have experience of his works on film or television, since this gives them some understanding of how individual texts work in performance today. Familiarity with Shakespeare's fortunes on the stage between his day and our own is less important, but the stage history of a particular play or a group of plays sometimes sheds fresh light on the characters and their interplay, or reminds us that a scene that makes dull reading has been found significant or memorable in a past performance. Theatrical and critical views do not, or need not, conflict. The stage interpretation from the fifties onwards of Shakespeare's plays on English history, for example, showed that there had been a feedback from the critical and scholarly work of the forties; and Peter Brook's innovative productions of *King Lear* and *A Midsummer Night's Dream* in 1962 and 1970 drew in part on ideas given currency in the writing of Jan Kott. Any chronological list of interpreters of Shakespeare that includes such critics as Johnson, Hazlitt, Bradley, Bradbrook, and Weimann should cite also performers like Garrick, Siddons, Kean, Irving, Gielgud, and Ashcroft, directors like Phelps, Poel, Barker, and Brook, adaptors like Brecht, and film-makers like Olivier, Kozintsev, Kurosawa, and Welles.

SHAKESPEARE AND THE ELIZABETHAN STAGE

Biographers have been unable to establish the exact moment at which Shakespeare entered the theatre, but his arrival in London coincided with the first and greatest upsurge in our history of regular, commercial, metropolitan play production. In 1576, twelve years after Shakespeare's birth at Stratford, James Burbage erected at Shoreditch what seems to have been the second custom-built public playhouse in London, the Theatre, the timbers of which were used in 1599 as the basis for the Globe on Bankside. From early in his career Shakespeare was associated with Burbage's sons, Richard and Cuthbert, in speculative theatrical enterprises as an actor, as a company-sharer in the leading troupe of the age, and as a part-owner of the Globe and later of Blackfriars. Shakespeare's standing gave him more authority within his company than any mere playwright, and he must have written his plays with unique knowledge of the capabilities of his friend Richard Burbage and their fellow players and of the artistic effects possible at the Globe and at Blackfriars. S. Schoenbaum's large format *William Shakespeare: A Documentary Life* not only comments on but reproduces in facsimile the main documents and records.

Two massive works of scholarship and reference, E. K. Chambers's four-volume *The Elizabethan Stage* and its accompanying two-volume *William Shakespeare: A Study of Facts and Problems*, together with G. E. Bentley's seven-volume continuation *The Jacobean and Caroline Stage*, show that there is no lack of facts about playhouse buildings, about the organization, personnel, and repertories of the various companies, about players and playwrights, about the legislation and control of playing, and about performances at Court, in inn-yards, in halls and colleges, and in the public and private playhouses of London. The general reader will find most of what he wants to know about these facts, and the inferences that can legitimately be made from them, in A. M. Nagler's brief *Shakespeare's Stage* and in two helpful accounts by Andrew Gurr, *The Shakespearean Stage, 1574–1642* and *Playgoing in Shakespeare's London*. Gurr's first volume aimed at providing a redaction of Chambers and Bentley; but it lucidly summarizes the ascertainable facts and modern scholarly opinion on the main topics: the companies, the players, the playhouses, the staging, and the audiences. The sequel amplifies the conspectus with much lively social and historical detail. One appendix names and describes 162 people known to have attended play-houses between 1567 and 1642, whilst a second reprints 205 passages about playgoing (the later ones retrospective or nostalgic) written between 1563 and 1699. Among older scholars, F. P. Wilson distilled within a single lecture given in 1955 his views on the Elizabethan theatre, and George Fulmer Reynolds in *On Shakespeare's Stage* (four lectures, posthumously published in 1967, which deserve a wider readership) engagingly discussed the problems of Elizabethan staging, a subject on which he was the leading and the most judicious scholar for over fifty years.

In 1968 G. E. Bentley in *The Seventeenth Century Stage* reprinted four Renaissance accounts of the English stage as prologue to eleven scholarly articles on the theatrical context. Later he made available much of his own prodigious research into such matters as censorship and the contracts and earnings of playwrights and players in two briskly organized books, *The Profession of Dramatist in Shakespeare's Time, 1590–1640* and its sequel *The Profession of Player*. Three volumes that trace the evolution of the stage from its medieval origins are Glynne Wickham's *Early English Stages*; another discursive work of reference, this time by various hands, is *The Revels History of Drama in English*, the third and fourth volumes of which cover the years 1576–1660. Much important evidence is visual, and every known representation in this period of a playhouse, real or imagined, is printed in *Illustrations of the English Stage, 1580–1642* by R. A. Foakes, whose own comments are brief and pointed. Wickham observed that in this field of study there is 90 per cent speculation to 10 per cent fact. While scholarly restraint is welcome, writers who undertake to explore the implications of the facts about public and private playhouses, acting style, or staging must all at times indulge in speculation.

THE PUBLIC PLAYHOUSE

Unlike most of his contemporaries, Shakespeare never wrote for the boy companies, and most of his plays were first acted by his fellow players at public playhouses, notably the Globe between 1599 and 1609. In some ways we know less about the wooden playhouses of Renaissance England than we do about the ancient stone-built theatres of Greece or Rome, which survive in the Mediterranean today, although excavations in the Spring of 1989 excitingly revealed the foundations of the Rose at Southwark.

The public playhouses were not necessarily all alike and the documentary evidence about them is scanty. A copy exists of a sketch a Dutch tourist made of the Swan around 1596, and there are builders' contracts for the Fortune (1599) and the Hope (1613). Various panoramic views of London show the exteriors of buildings on Bankside. Little of this relates directly to the playhouse we are most interested in, the Globe. Many scholars have attempted to reconstruct that particular 'wooden O', but A. M. Nagler believed that the evidence permits no more than the description of a generic type of Shakespearian stage. Where evidence is scanty, the kind of reconstruction individual scholars propose is governed (*a*) by their theories of the origins and evolution of the public playhouse, and (*b*) by their ideas about how the plays were staged. Deductions often have to be made not just from the stage directions but from the dialogue and implied action, which allow wide areas of interpretation. John Cranford Adams in *The Globe Playhouse: Its Design and Equipment* produced confident designs for Shakespeare's playhouse, and his work, with that of his colleague Irwin Smith, long formed the basis for several theatres built on American campuses for performances along Elizabethan lines. Yet Adams's design no longer commands assent. He believed (*a*) that the public playhouse evolved from earlier improvised playing-places in inn-yards— so that his galleried Globe recalls in its architectural detail Elizabethan domestic buildings, not to say 'Tudor Tea-shoppes' —and (*b*) that the Elizabethans staged plays with close attention to where each scene was set and that well-differentiated areas were used for particular kinds of locality. Adams's reconstruction gave great prominence to two areas, the *inner* and *upper* stages— the first term never used in Elizabethan texts and the second hardly ever. In *The Globe Restored*, first published in 1953, C. Walter Hodges suggested that the public playhouse evolved from strolling players setting up their trestle-stages with tiring-houses behind, inside the galleried bear- and bull-baiting houses which already existed on Bankside (a theory that one phrase in the Fortune contract seems to support). Hodges presented the visual evidence from contemporary English and Continental sources in a handsome book, and, being himself a brilliant draughtsman, he was also able to convey the spirit of his reconstruction in a series of drawings and sketches. Influenced by George R. Kernodle's *From Art to Theatre*, Hodges adopted for the tiring-house façade a baroque style, recalling not Tudor domestic architecture but the elaborately carved Renaissance screens that adorn the halls of English palaces, country houses, colleges, and inns of court (themselves often playing-places). That the play-house façade was not 'the bare machine for playing imagined by twentieth-century scholars' was argued by Kernodle in the 1959 issue of *Shakespeare Survey*—a volume which was principally concerned with past and present views of the Elizabethan theatre. Kernodle saw the playhouse as 'a complex symbol, combined out of several age-old medieval symbols'.

The publication in 1940 of G. F. Reynolds's influential *The Staging of Elizabethan Plays at the Red Bull Theater, 1605–25* led to rigorous and discriminating re-examination of the stage directions and dialogue of the plays in the various repertories. Scholars now agree that disproportionate emphasis was put on inner and upper stages, and suggest that in most plays most of the action took place on the great rectangular stage and that Elizabethan requirements for acting space at the rear and 'above' or 'aloft' were less frequent than J. C. Adams had claimed. Alfred Harbage found in 1955 that of eighty-six plays (seventeen by Shakespeare) staged in public playhouses between 1576 and 1608, forty-eight required no use of a gallery, thirty-nine no use of an enclosed space at the rear, and twenty-five no use of either. Subsequently the more detailed researches by Richard Hosley, in a series of searching articles addressed to the specialist (the gist of which is contained in his chapter in the third volume of *The Revels History*) and by T. J. King, in an authoritative book, have endorsed Harbage's findings that (*a*) when characters appear 'aloft' it is usually only for a brief scene in which one character overlooks others below, so that the gallery above the stage could normally be used by paying spectators as 'the Lords' Room', or after 1609 (when the customs of the private playhouses like Blackfriars extended to the Globe) by the musicians, or by both; and (*b*) that in those plays which require a curtained 'discovery-place' for tableau scenes the effect may have been contrived by curtaining the doors or by using a booth or 'tent'.

Two books on the Globe aroused controversy at the time of their first appearance, as their authors had intended. Leslie Hotson's *Shakespeare's Wooden O* postulated that the audience sat all round the players, that the tiring-house was below and not behind the stage, and that the actors made their entrances from 'houses'. Hotson's argument was based on his own view of the way plays were presented at Court. His hypothetical Globe, with its appalling sight-lines, has not been accepted by scholars or by theatre people. Frances A. Yates in *Theatre of the World*—which fascinatingly explores that territory where magic, science, and the Renaissance knowledge of Antiquity overlap—put forward a new theory of the evolution of the playhouse, claiming that James Burbage in building the Theatre and later the Globe made use of Vitruvius' theories about ancient architecture as propagated in England by John Dee. She also maintained that an illustration, engraved in Germany for Robert Fludd's *Ars Memoriae* (1623), depicts the Globe (others have since suggested it shows Blackfriars or was imagined). Few scholars have been convinced by the major argument, but Dame Frances's insight into the Globe as a moral emblem reinforces Kernodle's comments about the symbolism of that 'wide and universal theatre'.

Since 1970 much academic research, community effort, and show-biz publicity have been directed towards building a full-size reproduction of a Globe playhouse on Bankside and elsewhere. A paper by Walter Hodges examining the validity of such a project won endorsement at the first World Shakespeare Conference in Vancouver in 1971; and two years later in *Shakespeare's Second Globe, the Missing Monument* Hodges argued that the topographical drawings and engraved panorama or *Long View* of Bankside by Wenceslaus Hollar provide an adequate basis for reconstructing the second Globe (which in 1613, within Shakespeare's life-time, replaced the original, which had been destroyed by fire). Hodges also co-edited with S. Schoenbaum *The Third Globe*, the proceedings of a symposium of scholars and architects held at Wayne State University to explore the practicalities of undertaking a reconstruction of the Globe in down-town Detroit. John Orrell, a scholar who participated in that symposium, published in 1983 *The Quest for Shakespeare's Globe*, a highly technical enquiry into 'the size, shape, and orientation of the main frame of the second Globe' (but with implications for the first Globe). Orrell, like Hodges, accepted the credibility of Hollar's meticulous perspective sketch for the *Long View*; he took account of the exact spot at which Hollar had set up his topographical glass or drawing-frame and this enabled him to make calculations and measurements. He came to favour 'a larger, less intimate house than was once thought likely, truly capable of

holding the three thousand spectators of contemporary report'—
also of a theatre 'apparently aligned to the midsummer sunrise'.
And although he granted that old Burbage and his illiterate
builder Peter Street could not have had Inigo Jones's scholarly
familiarity with Vitruvius, he yet suggested that the Globe may
have echoed the Vitruvian idea of the *homo ad quadratum*. Thus
he gave qualified support to Dame Frances Yates. Subsequently
in the revealingly titled *The Human Stage, English Theatre Design,
1567–1640*, a work that ranges far beyond the Globe, Orrell
argued that the theatres of the time of Shakespeare and Jonson
embodied what art historians call 'the architectural principles of
the age of humanism'. He followed Sydney Anglo, the scholar of
Tudor pageantry and spectacle, in seeing parallels between the
festive pavilions of courtly chivalry as revived in 1520 by Henry
VIII—structures that had cosmological symbolism—and the later
public amphitheatres at Shoreditch. He even hazarded that, if
the Globe resembled the ideal theatre of Antiquity as envisaged
by Sebastiano Serlio in his *Book of Architecture* (1545; translated
into English only in 1611), this was because Peter Street had
access via English surveyors' handbooks to the theoretical, even
mystical principles of Italian humanism. The 'goodly frame'
which Orrell commends to us is a far cry from that playhouse
derived from John Cranford Adams, which was confidently
recreated in Olivier's film of *Henry V* in 1944.

That 'argufying' over the interpretation of dry facts about the
Globe matters even to as close, quirky, and brilliant a reader of
Shakespeare as Sir William Empson is demonstrated by the
posthumous publication in 1986 of his long piece 'The Globe
Theatre' in *Essays on Shakespeare*. That scholarship is essential in
any attempt at full-scale reconstruction is indicated by the fact
that Sam Wanamaker, exuberant impresario of the Globe project
at Bankside, has amongst his advisers both Professor Gurr and
Professor Orrell, joint authors of *Rebuilding Shakespeare's Globe*.

THE PRIVATE PLAYHOUSES

In 1575, the year before Burbage built the Theatre, Sebastian
Westcott opened an indoor playhouse for Paul's Boys, and in
1576 Richard Farrant moved the boys from the Chapel Royal at
Windsor into a similar theatre at Blackfriars. These were the so-
called 'private' playhouses, where companies of well-trained
boys, under their choir-master, acted Lilliputian entertainments,

usually satirical or pastoral. Shakespeare alluded in *Hamlet* to their success. In 1596 the Burbages purchased and reconstructed Blackfriars, but did not succeed in opening it as an adult play-house until about 1610. From then until 1642 the King's Men played by candle-light at the second Blackfriars in the winter and in the bigger, open-air Globe (rebuilt after the fire of 1613) in the summer. W. A. Armstrong's pamphlet, *The Elizabethan Private Theatres*, summarized the main facts and problems. H. N. Hille-brand's superbly researched *The Child Actors: A Chapter in Eliza-bethan Stage History* evokes in detail the milieu of the 'little eyases'. The history and physical dimensions of the first and second Blackfriars are dealt with in Irwin Smith's bulky book, while Richard Hosley proposed a reconstruction of the second Blackfrairs in a short article, later incorporated in the third volume of *The Revels History*. G. E. Bentley, in an important paper, 'Shakespeare and the Blackfriars Theatre', speculated that the acquisition of the smaller theatre had implications for Shake-speare and suggested that in *Pericles*, *Cymbeline*, *The Winter's Tale*, and *The Tempest* Shakespeare was making increasingly successful experiments in a new form of entertainment, influenced by Beaumont and Fletcher, and specifically designed both for the new stage conditions at Blackfriars and for a more courtly, aristocratic audience. The fullest and most up-to-date discussion of the buildings, repertory, and audience is in Keith Sturgess's *Jacobean Private Theatre* (1987); one chapter evokes *The Tempest* as it might have been performed at Bankside. Orrell's architectural study *The Theatres of Inigo Jones and John Webb*, though primarily about Court and academic playing-places, is relevant to the whole privileged milieu, as is a brief book to be mentioned later, Stephen Orgel's *The Illusion of Power*.

THE AUDIENCE

The size and social composition of the audiences at the public and private playhouses have stimulated research and aroused controversy. An early attempt at this kind of theatrical sociology was Louis B. Wright's chapter in *Middle Class Culture in Elizabethan England*, and W. A. Armstrong scrutinized evidence about private theatre audiences in the years 1575–1642 in an article. The first comprehensive coverage was Alfred Harbage's *Shakespeare's Audience*, which claimed that the Globe could hold about 2,400 people from all ranks of society, whereas a private theatre would seat a more select audience of perhaps 700. Harbage explored the implications for practising playwrights of the two kinds of audience in his subsequent book *Shakespeare and the Rival Traditions* where he maintained that a split developed between the 'Theatre of the Nation' and the 'Theatre of the Coterie' with a gradual loss of vitality in private theatre plays. Harbage's democratic assumptions of the American forties were challenged in the first year of Reagan's presidency by Ann Jennalie Cook in *The Privileged Playgoers of Shakespeare's London, 1576–1642* (1981). Drawing on authoritative recent historical scholarship (economic, sociological, demographic) she produced a model of society in Shakespeare's London that is different from Harbage's; and she asserted that those at the bottom of the Elizabethan-Jacobean social scale could seldom have had either the time or the money to be regular playgoers in the afternoons. Only the privileged, who exercised patronage and power, would have had the leisure to frequent both private and public playhouses. These conclusions have been questioned by Gurr in *Playgoing in Shakespeare's London*. They were even more sharply disputed by Martin Butler in an appendix to *Theatre and Crisis, 1632–1642*; he held out for a modified version of the Harbage thesis. The composition of the audience is central to some recent political criticism of Shakespeare. There is no evidence that the King's Men distinguished between Globe plays and Blackfriars ones; and many writers still feel that Shakespeare's perennial appeal stems from the fact that he addressed a wide audience.

THE STAGING

Much of the documentary evidence about Elizabethan staging (or what we would nowadays call production) occurs in property-lists, which survive among the papers of Philip Henslowe, the chief rival to James Burbage, and further inferences can be made from the plays themselves, particularly their stage directions. R. A. Foakes and R. T. Rickert have edited Henslowe's 'diary' to which Neil Carson has provided a functional abstract, *A Companion to Henslowe's Diary*. The Elizabethans seem to have combined realism of presentation with extreme stylization, even in the same play. Henslowe's list shows that large free-standing properties existed, and possibly painted back-cloths—for example 'rock', 'cage', 'tomb', 'Hell Mouth', 'the City of Rome'. Stage directions are often ambiguous, but expressions like '*A bed thrust forth, on it Frank in a slumber'* seem to indicate that large properties were carried on to the stage. Since the publication in 1933 of J. Isaacs's pamphlet *Production and Stage Management at the Black-friars Theatre* it has been assumed that techniques were more elaborate at Blackfriars than at the Globe, and that performances were similar in their visual and musical splendours to the Court masque. T. J. King in his exhaustive *Shakespearean Staging, 1599–1642* concluded that the staging requirements of public and private theatre plays show no significant differences, and he divided plays into four categories according to their basic require-ments. His analysis of 276 plays establishes that eighty-seven require only a floor space in front of an unlocalized facade with two entrances through which properties can be brought on or thrust out; forty-five plays need in addition an acting place above the stage; 102 require a covered space where actors can hide, or where properties, or actors, or both, can be discovered; and forty-five plays require a trap-door, thus necessitating a platform stage. King's book is a research aid, to be consulted rather than read. In it a student can find quickly *all* known contemporary performances of particular Elizabethan plays, and it is the first book to summarize the bibliographers' findings on each play. Where playhouse manuscripts or prompt-books exist, or where the printed text is demonstrably based on playhouse copy, the stage directions reflect production methods. King shows that most plays could have been staged simply in a hall or in a playhouse. Henslowe's inventories also include details about the wardrobe. Using this and other evidence, Hal H. Smith in an informative article, 'Some Principles of Elizabethan Stage Costume', demonstrated that Elizabethan costumes were often elaborate and that more use was made of historical costume, especially in plays about classical antiquity such as *Troilus and Cressida*, than earlier scholars have suggested. The standard work is M. C. Linthicum's *Costume in the drama of Shakespeare and His Contemporaries* (1936).

Music was a feature of private theatre entertainment and, from 1609, of public playhouse performances also. Hosley thinks that the gallery above the stage at the public theatres housed both spectators and musicians, as well as, on occasions, actors 'aloft'. Music in Shakespeare's tragedies has been studied by F. W. Sternfeld, and John H. Long has devoted two volumes to Shake-speare's use of music in the great comedies and in the last plays.

Also informative is Alan Brissenden's *Shakespeare and the Dance*. A technical account of Shakespeare's use of sound-effects has been given by Frances Shirley.

THE PLAYERS AND THE PLAYING

Muriel Bradbrook's *The Rise of the Common Player* is, with Bentley's *The Profession of Player*, the most illuminating commentary on the Elizabethan actors and on the high place their leaders won for themselves in society in their metamorphosis from strollers to servants of the king. Bentley emphasized that most players died poor. The clowns Richard Tarlton and Will Kempe early achieved national celebrity, to be succeeded in popular esteem by the tragedians Edward Alleyn (Henslowe's leading player), and his rival, Richard Burbage. The biographical facts about the players (more revealing about their litigation than their prowess on the boards) are in the reference books by Chambers and Bentley, in Edwin Nungezer's still useful *Dictionary of Actors*, and in Bentley's *The Profession of Player*. It was to the company rather than to the owners of the playhouse that the players owed allegiance, though control of both often overlapped. No company in English stage history has survived as long as the Lord Chamberlain's/King's Men nor has any other group created a comparable repertory of plays. T. W. Baldwin in *The Organisation and Personnel of the Shakespearean Company* set forth all that can be recovered about the running of this troupe, even attempting the impossible by attributing each part in Shakespeare to a particular player. An article by William A. Ringler, Jr., 'The Number of Actors in Shakespeare's Early Plays', raised questions about company organization and ultimately about the quality of the acting, for Ringler proved that, with doubling, as few as sixteen players could act all the parts in the eighteen plays Shakespeare wrote before his company moved to the Globe in 1599. Stephen Booth in his 'Speculations on Doubling in Shakespeare's Plays', contributed to *Shakespeare: The Theatrical Dimension*, was not necessarily reflecting Elizabethan stage-practice in postulating that the same person might play Cordelia and the Fool in *Lear*.

Acting is ephemeral, and Elizabethan stage-playing eluded detailed description by contemporaries, so that its spirit and technique cannot be recaptured now. William Worthen in *The Idea of the Actor*, only a third of which focuses on Elizabethan playing, challenges many assumptions by exploring what it meant morally and artistically to be an actor in three different cultural periods. Some scholars argue that Elizabethan acting must have been extremely formal and rhetorical, others that it was realistic and convincing. Such terms are always relative and often ambiguous. The puzzle might be solved if we could only know what sort of gesture Burbage made when as Hamlet he said to the players, 'Nor do not saw the air *too much* with your hand *thus . . .*', and how consistent Burbage's own playing was with Hamlet's advice. Alan Downer's 'Prolegomenon to a Study of Elizabethan Acting' is a serious introduction to the problems of discussing the acting of the past, while Lise-Lone Marker's later essay 'Nature and Decorum in the Theory of Elizabethan Acting' re-examines the documents and statements about stage-playing in the light of Renaissance thinkers' theories about Imitation and Nature. Bertram Joseph, between editions of his book *Elizabethan Acting* in 1951 and 1964, modified his view that acting was formal, and that its techniques were analogous to those of rhetoric and oratory as taught in grammar schools. Joseph's comparison of theatrical gesture with the system of manual motions evolved for the deaf and dumb by John Bulwer in 1644 provoked discussion. Alfred Harbage had argued for formal acting in *PMLA* in 1939, a view he later modified. Marvin Rosenberg, answering the question 'Elizabethan Actors: Men or Marionettes?', put the case for Shakespeare's actors projecting human personalities. Andrew Gurr's ideas on actors are contained in articles upon which he drew in *The Shakespearean Stage*. He believed that Alleyn 'strutted and bellowed' but that Burbage did not, and he discerned an ascending order of achievement in the Elizabethan words *playing* (the work of common strollers), *acting* (originally used only for the decorous 'action' of the orator), and *personation* (the art of individual characterization). The Elizabethans did not have a sophisticated language for analysing stage-playing. No doubt there were good and bad actors then as in other ages; and the robust playing to the holiday apprentices at the Red Bull was probably less admired by the judicious than the personated passion of Burbage as Lear or Macbeth. The fact that great moments in Elizabethan drama often show men in almost pathological states of rage or grief has led some scholars to seek clues about the acting of such scenes in Elizabethan writings on melancholy or madness. R. A. Foakes's excellent article 'The Player's Passion' explored the connections between Elizabethan psychology and acting, suggesting that Burton's description of a jealous man might indicate how Othello was originally played. Foakes pointed out that the order the Elizabethan theorists imposed on experience might suggest stylized acting at times. Certainly stage directions like *'Isabella falls in love'* in a minor play of the period reflect stock reactions; and there seem to have been conventional ways of portraying malcontents, of presenting ghosts and visions, and of conveying invisibility. The fact in the adult companies that youths played the women's parts might confirm that all playing was formalized. Michael Jamieson, after reviewing the evidence about the boy actors and their training in 'Shakespeare's Celibate Stage', concluded that some boys must have acted uncommonly well to have held the stage in roles like Rosalind or Cleopatra. Conventions are unquestioningly accepted in their own day, but feminist critics have come to see more than Pirandellian resonances in the cross-dressing of boy players who were enacting women who themselves resort to cross-dressing. The realistic representation of fights, torture, mutilation, grief, rage, and hysteria may well have co-existed within a single play with conventionalized presentation and stylized acting (especially in dumb-shows, the subject of an entire book by Dieter Mehl). John Russell Brown's view that acting was changing in Shakespeare's age, that formalism was 'fast dying out', and that a new naturalism was 'a kindling spirit' in Shakespeare's theatre, is convincing. The development of Shakespeare's blank verse seems to reflect an evolution in acting also.

SOME PERFORMANCE-ORIENTATED STUDIES

What is the usefulness and significance of studying Shakespeare in the context of Elizabethan stage-practice? This approach has always enabled writers to explore and explicate Shakespeare's dramaturgy and assess his professional skills. J. L. Styan in *Shakespeare's Stagecraft* did precisely that; and Ann Pasternak Slater described her *Shakespeare the Director* as an exercise in the 'stage-orientated study of Shakespeare's imagery'. Bernard Beckerman's *Shakespeare at the Globe, 1599–1609* is an earlier and very illuminating account of Shakespeare's stagecraft in the fifteen Globe plays. Three volumes in the Theatre Production Studies are complementary rather than overlapping. In the first, *Elizabethan Popular Theatre, Plays in Performance*, Michael

Hattaway located several texts, including *Titus Andronicus*, in their immediate theatrical context, often elucidating those scenic moments when visual elements combine significantly with dialogue—moments which, following Brecht, he termed 'gests'. In the second, *Shakespeare's Theatre*, Peter Thomson dealt mainly, as had Beckerman, with the Globe repertory, concentrating on *Twelfth Night*, *Hamlet*, and *Macbeth*, but also pondering the implications of the move to Blackfriars. In the third, *Jacobean Private Theatre*, mentioned earlier, Keith Sturgess took up the question of indoor staging. In 1967 Styan wrote of 'aspects of Shakespeare's code of signals'. *Semiotics* had become a key-word by 1984, when David Bevington—whose first book *From 'Mankind' to Marlowe* (1962) remains the best account of what Shakespeare's generation inherited from the tradition of the Morality Play—published his study of the complex way in which nonverbal elements operate, *Action is Eloquence: Shakespeare's Language of Gesture*. Sidney Homan's collection of twelve articles *Shakespeare's 'More Than Words Can Witness': Essays on Visual and Nonverbal Enactment in the Plays* also deals with these matters as does a book by one of his contributors, Alan C. Dessen's *Elizabethan Drama and the Viewer's Eye*. Marion Lomax, too, in her well-illustrated *Stage Images and Traditions: Shakespeare to Ford* strove to recover meaningful aspects of plays which are now closed to us—partly by investigating mythological, classical, religious, literary, and theatrical iconography, but also by reporting on the visual inventions and solutions of recent directors in main-line and experimental theatres.

Behind much of the new, wide-ranging social and political analysis of Shakespearian texts looms Robert Weimann, the learned East German Marxist whose most influential book *Shakespeare und die Tradition des Volktheaters: Sociologie. Dramaturgie. Gestaltung* appeared in 1967. The work itself, like its title, may have lost some resonance in its American adaptation as *Shakespeare and the Popular Tradition in the Theater: Studies in the Social Dimension of Dramatic Form and Function*. Weimann firmly placed Shakespeare within the culture and society of his time, stressing the rich native and vernacular heritage but never ignoring the tradition of classical humanism. He also emphasized such theatrical notions as the stage-positioning of characters in the public playhouse. Indeed his hypothesis of an upstage *locus* or specific setting for 'high' characters, and an unlocalized *platea* downstage near the groundlings for the Vice or Clown gained wide currency. But surely if Lance, Gobbo, and later Falstaff had this confiding access to the pit, so too had Hamlet and Macbeth in soliloquy? Five works which bring the urgency of the new historicist or materialist criticism to bear upon Elizabethan drama, with varying degrees of concentration on Shakespeare, must be cited here. Stephen Orgel's brilliant short study *The Illusion of Power: Political Theater in the Renaissance* (1975) suggestively contrasted a court drama, which expressed the age's assumption about monarchy, with a public theatre which can be seen—within limits—'as a democratizing institution'. Walter Cohen's much longer *Drama of a Nation, Public Theater in Renaissance England and Spain* (1985) addressed the big question of why these countries, so divided in religion and culture, yet produced theatres uniquely similar. His detailed analysis led him to conclude that both theatres (and thus Calderòn, Lope de Vega, and Shakespeare) fused classical with popular—and at times radical—elements. Michael D. Bristol's *Carnival and Theater: Plebeian Culture and the Structure of Authority in Renaissance England* (1985), whose title indicates a debt to the ideas of Mikhail Bakhtin, predictably examined theatre as a social institution, festive and political as well as literary. David Wiles's *Shakespeare's Clown, Actor and Text in the Elizabethan Playhouse* (1987), which is much more closely concerned with Shakespeare, was also influenced by Bakhtin; his double hypothesis that Falstaff (a) is structurally the clown's part and (b) was originally played by Will Kemp can be seen as a strategy to reclaim for Sir John plebeian, radical status. The up-to-date bibliography on Fools and Clowns is useful. Finally, Stephen Mullaney's *The Place of the Stage: License, Play, and Power in Renaissance England* (1988) set up intriguing links between the topographical marginality of playhouses built near lazar-houses and brothels, the ambivalent social status of players, and the considerable ideological range and licence of *Henry IV*, *Macbeth*, and *Measure for Measure*. Orrell in a prologue to *The Human Stage* imagined himself and his readers hovering over Elizabethan London and finding 'almost everything in the scene below . . . the work of man'. Mullaney's first chapter is a different evocation of the same city-scape. Walter Cohen concluded that what makes the drama 'an attractive subject for a radical, active-orientated criticism' is the social heterogeneity and the popular elements.

Scholars and critics alike continue to write revealingly of
Shakespeare in the context of his own theatre, and their work has
relevance not just to readers, but also to theatre people. The
playhouse that Sir Tyrone Guthrie built at Stratford, Ontario,
and the new Swan Theatre at Stratford-upon-Avon are in their
different ways splendid attempts at recapturing in contemporary
terms the Shakespearian actor-audience relationship. Now Sam
Wanamaker plans to build the Globe at Bankside with an indoor
playhouse, the Cockpit, nearby. A remark of Walter Hodges
deserves pondering: 'The ancient tradition which nourished the
Elizabethan playhouses died when the last of them was pulled
down; since when it may almost be said that no play of Shakespeare's has been acted, except in adaptation.'

SHAKESPEARE IN PERFORMANCE, 1660 TO THE PRESENT

If the evidence about Elizabethan, Jacobean, and Caroline performances of Shakespeare has tantalizing lacunae, the sheer bulk
of information about presentations of the plays between the
Restoration and our own day is overwhelming. The facts are
contained in old-fashioned volumes of theatrical history, in
magisterial works of reference like *The London Stage*, in eye-
witness accounts of great performances, in modern scholarly
discussions of the stage history of separate plays or groups of
plays, in the biographies of players like Edmund Kean or William
Charles Macready or of a scholar-crank like William Poel, in
books on the leading theatrical companies, and in prompt books,
playbills, press cuttings, and ephemera preserved in the theatrical
collections of Britain, the United States, and Europe.

The history of Shakespearian staging is itself inextricably
linked with political and social change, with modification in
literary taste, and with innovations in playhouse design, acting
technique, and stage practice. The student of Shakespeare who
asks himself 'What did Dryden really do to *Antony and Cleopatra*
in *All for Love?*', or 'Why was Hazlitt so thrilled by Mrs Siddons
and Edmund Kean in their Shakespearian roles?', or 'Was Bernard
Shaw fair in his incessant attacks in the *Saturday Review* on Sir
Henry Irving as an actor-producer of Shakespeare?', or 'Why did
Brecht adapt *Coriolanus?*', gets involved in matters which take
him beyond stage history (itself merely a branch of antiquarian-
ism) to general questions about the culture of a period and
specific questions about the theatrical and critical interpretation

of Shakespeare. These questions, in turn, may stimulate a student's own reading of the plays, since the way characters and scenes have been presented in the theatre often sheds light on their significance, and suggests possibilities of interpretation which might not occur in the study—a topic explored by John Russell Brown in 'Theatre Research and the Criticism of Shakespeare and His Contemporaries'. His own book, *Shakespeare's Plays in Performance*, grounded on knowledge of the plays' fortunes on the stage in the past and in our own day, sought to find in the text the 'stage reality that lies there waiting to be awakened'.

There have been, broadly speaking, four movements in the history of Shakespeare in performance—the first dominated by the adapters, the second by the great players of the eighteenth- and nineteenth-century stage, the third by that international figure of the twentieth-century theatre, the director, and the fourth by the technological revolution of film, television, and video. Two and a half centuries of Shakespearian staging were surveyed by George C. D. Odell in *Shakespeare—from Betterton to Irving*, an old-fashioned, plodding theatrical chronicle, which has been amplified and corrected but never replaced by later scholarship. Arthur Colby Sprague, *doyen* of modern stage historians, gave a selective history of this same subject in *Shakespearean Players and Performances*, each chapter of which recreated a significant stage interpretation—Betterton's Hamlet, Garrick's King Lear, Booth's Iago, etc. Sprague's earlier book, *Shakespeare and the Actors*, recovered from semi-oblivion those illustrative touches of stage business which accumulated in successive performances, an aspect of theatrical custom which fascinated traditionalists like Sir John Gielgud and Sir Donald Wolfit. Writing for the playgoer, Norman Marshall gave a readable account of changes in Shakespearian staging in three chapters of *The Producer and the Play* which stress the final emergence of the director as the artist responsible for the overall interpretation in the theatre of a Shakespeare script. Robert Speaight's wide-ranging survey *Shakespeare on the Stage*, profusely illustrated, is no mere coffee-table book; it describes not just British but American and European performances and productions over the centuries. Gāmini Salgādo's *Eyewitnesses of Shakespeare: First-hand Accounts of Performances, 1590–1890* is an anthology of brief comments and extracts from reviews. Charles H. Shattuck's *Shakespeare on the American Stage, from the Hallams to Edwin*

Booth, commissioned for the Bicentennial Year, covers the eventful years from 1752 to 1876. Most of the above scholars concerned themselves with what performers did. Carol Jones Carlisle in *Shakespeare from the Greenroom: Actors' Criticism of Four Tragedies* took a fresh approach by piecing together what British and American actors and actresses from Betterton onwards (including the donnish Speaight) have said or written on Shakespeare, usually about the characters. Joseph G. Price's *The Triple Bond*, essays gathered in honour of Sprague, contains work by distinguished stage historians.

Other contributors to the present volume discuss the usefulness to readers and critics of the stage histories of individual plays or of groups of plays. Most editions of single plays now include a good deal of such material. For the New (Cambridge) Shakespeare of Dover Wilson and Quiller-Couch quite full stage histories of each play were compiled in the form of annals first by Harold Child and later by C. B. Young. Today this information is usually integrated into the critical introduction. The general editors of the Oxford Shakespeare and of the New Cambridge Shakespeare expect the individual editors to discuss performances, frequently with illustrations of past productions. Each Cambridge volume includes conjectural reconstructions, sketched by Walter Hodges, of two key incidents in the Elizabethan playhouse. In the seventies John Russell Brown presented for the American Harbrace Theater Edition five plays with production photographs and a stage-based running commentary. From the late eighties the Bristol Classical Press has included *King Lear*, *Othello*, and *Richard III* in its *Plays in Performance* editions, with text on one page and a moment-by-moment commentary, necessarily selective, on what past players and directors have done with lines and actions. Two paperback series, Michael Scott's 'Text and Performance' and J. R. Mulryne's 'Shakespeare in Performance', invite contributors to re-create selected past performances in short studies of single plays.

Some researchers go into stage history in minute detail. Sprague's *Shakespeare's Histories: Plays for the Stage* chronicles the rediscovery and revaluation of these plays in the theatre, particularly at the Birmingham Rep and at Stratford in the postwar years. Examples of books that deal with the stage fortunes of a single text are: Dennis Bartholomeusz's *Macbeth and the Players*, Margaret Lamb's *'Antony and Cleopatra' on the English Stage*,

Joseph G. Price's *The Unfortunate Comedy* which is about *All's Well That Ends Well*, and John Ripley's *'Julius Caesar' on Stage in England and America, 1599–1973*. Marvin Rosenberg's trilogy of stage-related character expositions comprises *The Masks of Othello*, *The Masks of King Lear* and *The Masks of Macbeth*. *Hamlet* has understandably obsessed stage historians. Messrs Mander and Mitchenson compiled a picture-book illustrating past perform-ances and productions. Works have been devoted to individual actors in the play—Charles H. Shattuck's on Edwin Booth and Rosamond Gilder's on John Gielgud, while two actors who supported Richard Burton on Broadway published their separate recollections of that production. There are also academic mono-graphs on William Poel's three productions of *Hamlet*, including the quarto and *Fratricide Punished*, and on the famous version which Gordon Craig designed and directed at Stanislavski's invitation for the Moscow Arts Theatre. J. C. Trewin's *Five & Eighty Hamlets* is the record of a compulsive playgoer. An in-valuable research tool is Shattuck's *The Shakespeare Promptbooks*, a catalogue of the surviving theatre copies, which indicate the ways in which various actors and directors have handled, or mishandled, Shakespeare's texts.

Superb research by a team of American scholars in the eleven volumes of *The London Stage, 1660–1800* and by J. P. Wearing, a heroic Englishman, in his nine-volume *The London Stage, 1890–1929* enable a student to find out what was happening day by day in London theatres during those two periods. And another American co-operative enterprise, *A Biographical Dictionary of Actors, Actresses, etc. in London, 1660–1800*, yields much factual information. Scenes from Shakespeare had been performed clandestinely during the Commonwealth, as Leslie Hotson showed in *The Commonwealth and Restoration Stage*, but between 1660 and 1700 Shakespeare came second to Beaumont and Fletcher among the old dramatists, and his plays were either adapted as spectacular operas, as readers of Pepys will remember, or were regularized to comply with neoclassic taste. This movement was described, and the main adaptations summarized, by Hazelton Spencer in *Shakespeare Improved*, to which Christopher Spencer provided a convenient adjunct by editing *Five Restoration Adaptations of Shakespeare*. Nahum Tate's *King Lear* (1681) with its excision of the Fool, its romance between Cordelia and Edgar, and its restoration of King Lear to the throne, formed the basis of all acting texts, Shakespeare's play not being completely restored until Macready's revival in 1834. Colley Cibber's alteration of *Richard III* (1700) long remained the actor-manager's Saturday night stand-by, some of its melodramatic lines being retained in Laurence Olivier's film of 1956.

Betterton's acting created a vogue for some of Shakespeare's plays around 1700, but it was not until the 1730s that Shakespeare achieved pre-eminence among older dramatists and that a number of his plays became part of the staple fare of playgoers who judged the excellence of players by their powers in Shakespearian roles. In the period 1747–76, when David Garrick made Drury Lane the premier theatre in Europe, both for acting and stage presentation, about 20 per cent of his repertory was Shakespearian, albeit in adaptation. The annals of London performances are contained in C. B. Hogan's *Shakespeare in the Theatre, 1701–1800*, which is in some ways superseded by *The London Stage* (on which Hogan collaborated), where Shakespearian performances are listed in the illuminating context of general theatrical activities. In the prefaces the five editors, including Hogan, discussed the Shakespearian element in the London repertories, and one of them, A. H. Scouten, analysed the significance of Shakespeare's growing stage fame in an article 'The Increase in Popularity of Shakespeare's Plays in the Eighteenth Century: A *Caveat* for Interpreters of Stage History'.

Eye-witness accounts of Burbage, Betterton, and even Garrick can be disappointing to students of Shakespeare. The age that saw Mrs Siddons in maturity and Edmund Kean at the height of his romantic powers was also the time of the great dramatic critics and theatrical reporters. To read Hazlitt or Leigh Hunt on Mrs Siddons as Lady Macbeth or Constance and on Kean as Shylock or Richard III is to be reminded that the prime interpreter was the individual player and that critical attention focused on Shakespeare's character portrayal. The nineteenth-century actor-producers, particularly Charles Kean and Henry Irving, lavished upon the plays a wealth of period costumes and scenery, archaeologically accurate, and such cumbersome staging necessitated ruthless cutting of the text. We should not, however, see the Victorians entirely from Shaw's point of view. Richard Foulkes's collection of essays on Shakespeare in the Victorian Theatre is entertaining and enlightening, whilst Alan Hughes in *Henry Irving, Shakespearean*—though recording that some 1,507 or 46 per cent of the lines were cut from *Lear*—defends the actor as an interpreter of Shakespeare. In the 1890s, when G.B.S. was attacking Irving for such extravagance, the scholarly, eccentric William Poel mounted a series of unfashionable, experimental presentations of Shakespearian and Elizabethan plays in which he tried to recapture the original conventions. Poel's theories (discussed in Robert Speaight's biography) were championed by Shaw in the *Saturday Review* and influenced Harley Granville Barker, whose own productions of Shakespeare in the West End from 1912 to 1914 proved seminal in their respect for their text, the pace of the verse-speaking, and the brilliant modern sets and costumes. Barker (the subject of several studies, the best of which is by Dennis Kennedy) became frustrated at the absence of a subsidized National Theatre in England and turned to writing the series *Prefaces to Shakespeare* (1927–47). His elucidation of some fourteen of the plays showed the insight of a director, and led to greater understanding by academics of Shakespeare as a man of the theatre as well as influencing a new generation of producers at such specialized theatres as the Old Vic in London and the Shakespeare Memorial Theatre at Stratford. Changes in Shakespearian production in the years between the wars are dealt with in such books as *Old Vic Saga* by Harcourt Williams, himself a director there, and *The Stratford Festival* by T. C. Kemp and J. C. Trewin, but by far the best account is *The Shakespeare Revolution: Criticism and Performance in the Twentieth Century* by J. L. Styan whose heroes include Poel, Barker, Jackson, Guthrie, and Brook. Trewin's indefatigable playgoing is chronicled in the later sections of *Shakespeare on the English Stage, 1900–1964* and in *Going to Shakespeare*. In collaboration with Sprague he examined changing attitudes to such things as cutting the text, stage business, character portrayal, and stage design in *Shakespeare's Plays Today: Some Customs and Conventions of the Stage*. Sprague's pamphlet *The Doubling of Parts in Shakespeare's Plays* is succinct; and, like W. J. Lawrence in 1918, he dismissed as theatrically implausible the doubling of Cordelia and the Fool. Idiosyncratic and lively impressions of Shakespearian acting and production, mainly in the years between the wars, are gathered in two collections of theatre reviews—*Brief Chronicles* by James Agate and *The Shakespearean Scene* by Herbert Farjeon. From his undergraduate days Kenneth Tynan brilliantly evoked the heroic performances of Gielgud, Olivier, Valk, and Wolfit in reviews published in 1950 as *He That Played the King*. His later more socially committed collections record the impact of Brecht and Brook on Shakespeare production.

J. L. Styan in *The Shakespeare Revolution* took the story as far as Brook's *Dream* at the Royal Shakespeare Company in 1970. But from the fifties onwards the flow of books, articles, reminiscences, interviews, and notices becomes impossible to record. Richard David's *Shakespeare in the Theatre* serves as a continuation of Styan for it, too, deals with stage interpretation and scholarly consensus, mainly by examining in detail twenty-two productions of the seventies—all, except for a National Theatre *Hamlet*, at the RSC. Stanley Wells in his brief *Royal Shakespeare* (1976) analysed and evaluated four RSC productions, two by Peter Hall and two by John Barton. This company's approach to Shakespeare has continued to attract scholarly documentation as well as critical and journalistic interest. In addition to two new histories called *The Royal Shakespeare Company*, one by David Addenbrooke subtitled *The Peter Hall Years*, the second by Sally Beauman *A History of Ten Decades*, there are full-length books devoted to individual directors, and even to single productions. Thus a student interested in Peter Brook's long commitment to Shakespeare would find on his book-list the following: J. C. Trewin's biography; Brook's own *The Empty Stage* and *The Shifting Point: Forty years of Theatrical Exploration, 1946–87*; Richard Proudfoot's essay 'Peter Brook and Shakespeare'; David Selbourne's *The Making of 'A Midsummer Night's Dream': An Eye-Witness Account of Peter Brook's Production from First Rehearsal to First Night*; and what is possibly the first such paperback to be devoted to a director, David Williams's *Peter Brook: A Theatrical Casebook*, which reprints Charles Marowitz's 'A *Lear* Log', his review of the *Dream*, and Kenneth Tynan's ecstatic notice linking the *Lear* of 1962 with Beckett. A student enquiring into John Barton's more traditionalist approach to Shakespeare would have a list almost as lengthy: Michael Greenwald's *Directions by Indirections: John Barton of the Royal Shakespeare Company*; the text of the trilogy *The Wars of the Roses* as adapted and partly re-written by Barton for the RSC in 1963 and subsequently televised by the BBC; Barton's own *Playing Shakespeare*; and chapters from David and Wells. RSC actors and actresses have discussed the way they approach the creation of Shakespeare's characters in two volumes of essays *Players of Shakespeare* and in a feminist collection

Clamorous Voices: Shakespeare's Women Today for which the interviewer Carol Rutter talked with younger RSC actresses like Fiona Shaw and Juliet Stevenson. Antony Sher's best-selling *Year of the King, An Actor's Diary and Sketchbook* records his obsessive preoccupation with Richard Crookback from the first rumours that he might play that star part at the RSC in 1984. Not all articles on the work of the RSC have been approving. Alan Sinfield in his polemical 'Royal Shakespeare: Theatre and the Making of Ideology', contributed to *Political Shakespeare* (ed. Jonathan Dollimore and Alan Sinfield), discerned 'a great deal of genuine radical purpose' but also 'a strain of opportunism'. The new school of cultural materialists has sometimes found the RSC, like the BBC, guilty of using Shakespeare as 'a hegemonic instrument'. *The Shakespeare Myth*, edited by Graham Holderness in 1988 for the Cultural Politics series, subjects some of the theatre people interviewed to fierce rebuttal. In her *Modern Shakespearean Offshoots* Ruby Cohn explored that interesting phenomenon, the creation of independent works derived from Shakespeare by, amongst others, Bond, Brecht, Ionesco, Stoppard and—in his collages—Marowitz, whose own essays *Prospero's Staff* and collection *The Marowitz Shakespeare* are relevant. Sinfield commended Bond for reconstituting in his *Lear* aspects of Shakespeare's text so that they became the vehicle of radical values.

Actors and directors, however, continue to explore and present Shakespeare. Ralph Berry in *On Directing Shakespeare: Interviews with Contemporary Directors* by putting questions to a Pole, an Italian, and a North American as well as to Jonathan Miller and Trevor Nunn reminded us that Shakespeare is not the exclusive property of the RSC or even of the English-speaking theatre. It is not always easy to find information except in back-files of newspapers on such innovative productions as Ariane Mnouchkine's *Richard II* or the Ninagawa Company of Tokyo's *Macbeth* and *The Tempest*, but a good place to start is the *Bloomsbury Theatre Guide* (ed. Griffiths and Woddis 1988), which is also informative about groups like Cheek by Jowl and Red Shift. Several books emanating from Cambridge University Press, often in the 'Directors in Perspective' series, bring out the significant ways in which foreign directors like Roger Planchon or Peter Stein have responded to Shakespeare; and Margot Heinemann in 'How Brecht Read Shakespeare', her acute contribution to *Political Shakespeare*, observed in a footnote that in Germany going to Shakespeare need not be 'an irredeemably elitist experience; for he is far more accessible to ordinary audiences in translation . . . than in the archaism and compression of the original English'. Questions about 'accessibility' and 'relevance' in modern productions have been aired by that most articulate of the enemies of 'Mandarin bardolatry' Jonathan Miller, frequently in interviews but also in his book about what he calls 'the afterlife of masterpieces', *Subsequent Performances*. Students who wish to keep abreast of developments in the staging of Shakespeare should consult the British annual *Shakespeare Survey*, which has since its inception in 1948 carried review articles by scholars like Richard David, Gareth Lloyd Evans, John Russell Brown, and Stanley Wells, and also the American *Shakespeare Quarterly*, which devotes space in its Autumn number to reviews of plays at both Stratfords (War-wickshire and Ontario) and at such Elizabethan playhouses as those at San Diego and Ashland.

SHAKESPEARE ON FILM, TELEVISION, AND VIDEO

Whether Shakespearian playgoing is elitist or not, most people have little access to theatres and Shakespeare has long provided material for film-makers, so that a vast, international audience now encounters Shakespeare in the cinema, on television, or on video. Roger Manvell's *Shakespeare on Film* (1971) was a pioneering survey, while Charles W. Eckert's casebook *Focus on Shakespearean Films* (1972) was an early assemblage of interviews, reminis-cences, and film reviews. Jack J. Jorgens's *Shakespeare on Film* (1977) stressed not the *problems* of rendering Shakespeare on film but the *possibilities* and he used frame blow-ups rather than publicity stills for his illustrations. A later work, which is critically aware and also scholarly, is Anthony Davies's *Filming Shake-speare: The Adaptations of Laurence Olivier, Orson Welles, Peter Brook, and Akira Kurosawa* (1988); it has both a select filmography and a model bibliography. *Shakespeare Survey 39* appeared about the same time and was largely devoted to film and television; and it is perhaps revealing that the Cambridge *Companion to Shake-speare Studies*, which has gone through several transformations since the thirties, in its latest form included a chapter on film and television. The growth of Media Studies and the advent of Film Theory have led to much more publication in this field, both sociological and aesthetic. Holderness in his own essay in *Political Shakespeare* and with his fellow-authors in *The Shakespeare Myth* addressed questions of 'radical potentiality and institutional closure' in the filming and televising of Shakespeare as well as Shakespeare's place in popular culture. J. C. Bulman and H. R. Coursen brought together much of the relevant material as editors of *Shakespeare on Television* (1988). There is now a *Shakespeare on Film Newsletter*. Some of the most 'Shakespearian' of the Shakespeare films have not been in English; it is as if translating *Hamlet* and *Lear* into Russian or transposing *Macbeth* and *Lear* into Japanese as *Throne of Blood* and *Ran* is cinematically liberating. The experience of Shakespeare's plays in the theatre, on film, on television, in video, or even on radio keeps readers and students in touch with a living Shakespeare.

REFERENCES

SHAKESPEARE AND THE ELIZABETHAN STAGE

Adams, John Cranford, *The Globe Playhouse: Its Design and Equipment* (Cambridge, Mass., 1942: 2nd edn., London, 1961).

Armstrong, William A., 'The Audience of the Elizabethan Private Theatres', *RES* NS 10 (1959), 234–49; reprinted in *The Seventeenth Century Stage*, ed. G. E. Bentley (Chicago, Ill., 1968).

—— *The Elizabethan Private Theatres: Facts and Problems* (London, 1958).

Baldwin, Thomas Whitfield, *The Organisation and Personnel of the Shakespearean Company* (Princeton, NJ, 1927; reprinted New York, 1961).

Beckerman, Bernard, *Shakespeare at the Globe, 1599–1609* (New York, 1962).

Bentley, G. E., *The Jacobean and Caroline Stage*, 7 vols. (Oxford, 1941–68).

—— *The Profession of Dramatist in Shakespeare's Time, 1590–1640* (Princeton, NJ, 1971).

—— *The Profession of Player in Shakespeare's Time, 1590–1640* (Princeton, NJ, 1984).

—— (ed.). *The Seventeenth Century Stage: A Collection of Critical Essays* (Chicago, Ill., 1968).

—— 'Shakespeare and the Blackfriars Theatre', *Shakespeare Survey 1* (Cambridge, 1948), 38–50; reprinted in his *Shakespeare and His Theatre* (Lincoln, Nebr., 1964).

Bevington, David, *Action is Eloquence: Shakespeare's Language of Gesture* (Cambridge, Mass., 1984).

—— *From 'Mankind' to Marlowe* (Cambridge, Mass., 1962).

Booth, Stephen, 'Speculations on Doubling in Shakespeare's Plays', in *Shakespeare, the Theatrical Dimension*, ed. Philip McGuire and David Samuelson (New York, 1979), 103–31; reprinted in his *'King Lear'*, *'Macbeth', Indefinition, and Tragedy* (New Haven, Conn., 1983).

Bradbrook, Muriel C., *The Rise of the Common Player: A Study of Actor and Society in Shakespeare's England* (London, 1962).

Brissenden, Alan, *Shakespeare and the Dance* (London, 1981).

Bristol, Michael D., *Carnival and Theatre: Plebeian Culture and the Structure of Authority in Renaissance England* (London, 1985).

Butler, Martin, *Theatre and Crisis, 1632–1642* (Cambridge, 1984).

Carson, Neil, *A Companion to Henslowe's Diary* (Cambridge, 1988).

Chambers, E. K., *The Elizabethan Stage*, 4 vols. (Oxford, 1923).

—— *William Shakespeare: A Study of Facts and Problems*, 2 vols. (Oxford, 1930; reprinted, 1989); abridged by Charles Williams, *A Short Life of Shakespeare with the Sources* (Oxford, 1933); index to both works by Beatrice White (Oxford, 1934).

Cohen, Walter, *Drama of a Nation, Public Theater in Renaissance England and Spain* (Ithaca, NY, 1985).

Cook, Ann Jennalie, *The Privileged Playgoer in Shakespeare's London, 1576–1642* (Princeton, NJ, 1981).

Dessen, Alan C., *Elizabethan Drama and the Viewer's Eye* (Chapel Hill, NC, 1977).

—— *Elizabethan Stage Conventions and Modern Interpreters* (Cambridge, 1984).

Downer, Alan S., 'Prolegomenon to a Study of Elizabethan Acting', *Maske und Kothurn*, 10 (1965), 625–36.

Empson, William, 'The Globe Theatre', in his *Essays on Shakespeare*, ed. David Pirie (Cambridge, 1986), 158–222.

Foakes, R. A., *Illustrations of the English Stage, 1580–1640* (London, 1985).

—— 'The Player's Passion: Some Notes on Elizabethan Psychology and Acting', *Essays and Studies*, NS 7 (1954), 62–77.

Greg, W. W. (ed.), *Dramatic Documents from the Elizabethan Playhouse*, 2 vols. (Oxford, 1931).

Gurr, Andrew, 'Elizabethan Action', *Studies in Philology*, 63 (1966), 144–56.

—— *Playgoing in Shakespeare's London* (Cambridge, 1987).

—— *The Shakespearean Stage, 1574–1642* (Cambridge, 1970).

—— 'Who Strutted and Bellowed?', *Shakespeare Survey* 16 (1963), 95–102.

—— with John Orrell, *Rebuilding Shakespeare's Globe* (London, 1989).

Harbage, Alfred, 'Elizabethan Acting', *PMLA* 54 (1939), 685–708; reprinted in his *Theatre for Shakespeare* (Toronto, 1955).

—— *Shakespeare and the Rival Traditions* (New York, 1952).

—— *Shakespeare's Audience* (New York, 1941).

—— *Theatre for Shakespeare* (Toronto, 1955).

Hattaway, Michael, *Elizabethan Popular Theatre, Plays in Performance* (London, 1982).

Henslowe, Philip, *Henslowe's Diary, with Supplementary Material, Intro-*

duction and Notes, ed. R. A. Foakes and R. T. Rickert (Cambridge, 1961).

Hillebrand, Harold Newcomb, *The Child Actors: A Chapter in Elizabethan Stage History* (University of Illinois Studies in Language and Literature, Urbana, Ill., 1926).

Hodges, C. Walter, *The Globe Restored: A Study of the Elizabethan Theatre* (London, 1953; 2nd edn., London 1968).

—— *Shakespeare's Second Globe, the Missing Monument* (London, 1973).

—— and S. Schoenbaum (eds.), *The Third Globe, Symposium for the Reconstruction of the Globe Playhouse* (Detroit, Mich., 1979).

Homan, Sidney (ed.), *Shakespeare's 'More Than Words Can Witness': Essays on Visual and Nonverbal Enactment in the Plays* (Lewisburg, Pa., 1980).

Hosley, Richard, 'The Discovery-Space in Shakespeare's Globe', *Shakespeare Survey* 12 (Cambridge, 1959), 35–46; reprinted in *The Seventeenth Century Stage*, ed. G. E. Bentley (Chicago, Ill., 1968).

—— 'The Gallery over the Stage in the Public Playhouse of Shakespeare's Time', *Shakespeare Quarterly*, 8 (1957), 15–31.

—— 'The Origins of the Shakespearian Playhouse', *Shakespeare Quarterly*, 15 (1964), 29–39.

—— 'A Reconstruction of the Second Blackfriars', in *The Elizabethan Theatre*, 1, ed. David Galloway (Toronto, 1969), 74–88.

—— 'The Second Blackfriars Playhouse (1596)', *The Revels History of Drama in English*, vol. iii, ed. Clifford Leech and T. W. Craik (London, 1975), 197–226.

—— 'Shakespeare's Use of a Gallery over the Stage', *Shakespeare Survey* 10 (Cambridge, 1957), 77–89.

—— 'The Staging of Desdemona's Bed', *Shakespeare Quarterly*, 14 (1963), 57–65.

—— 'The Use of the Upper Stage in *Romeo and Juliet*', *Shakespeare Quarterly*, 5 (1954), 371–9.

—— 'Was There a Music-Room in Shakespeare's Globe?', *Shakespeare Survey* 13 (Cambridge, 1960), 113–23.

Hotson, Leslie, *Shakespeare's Wooden O* (London, 1959).

Isaacs, J., *Production and Stage Management at the Blackfriars Theatre* (London, 1933).

Jamieson, Michael, 'Shakespeare's Celibate Stage', in *Papers Mainly Shakespearian*, ed. G. I. Duthie (Edinburgh and London, 1964), 21–39; reprinted in *The Seventeenth Century Stage*, ed. G. E. Bentley (Chicago, Ill., 1968).

Joseph, Bertram, *Elizabethan Acting* (London, 1951; 2nd edn., 1964).

Kernodle, George R., *From Art to Theatre: Form and Convention in the Renaissance* (Chicago, Ill., 1944).

—— 'The Open Stage: Elizabethan or Existentialist?, *Shakespeare Survey* 12 (1959), 1–7.

King, T. J., *Shakespearean Staging, 1599–1642* (Cambridge, Mass., 1971).

Leech, Clifford, and T. W. Craik (gen. eds.), *The Revels History of Drama in English*, vol. iii, *1576–1613* and vol. iv, *1613–1660* (London, 1975 and 1981).

Linthicum, M. C., *Costume in the Drama of Shakespeare and His Contemporaries* (Oxford, 1936).

Lomax, Marion, *Stage Images and Traditions: Shakespeare to Ford* (Cambridge, 1987).

Long, John H., *Shakespeare's Use of Music: The Comedies* and *The Last Plays*, 2 vols. (Gainesville, Fla., 1955 and 1961).

Marker, Lise-Lone, 'Nature and Decorum in the Theory of Elizabethan Acting', in *The Elizabethan Theatre II*, ed. David Galloway (Toronto, 1970), 87–107.

Mehl, Dieter, *The Elizabethan Dumb Show: The History of a Dramatic Convention* (London, 1965).

Mullaney, Stephen, *The Place of the Stage: License, Play, and Power in Renaissance England* (Chicago, Ill., 1988).

Nagler, A. M., *Shakespeare's Stage* (New Haven, Conn., 1958).

Nungezer, Edwin, *A Dictionary of Actors and of Other Personages Associated with the Public Presentation of Plays in England before 1642* (New Haven, Conn., 1929).

Orgel, Stephen, *The Illusion of Power: Political Theater in the Renaissance* (Berkeley, Calif., 1975).

Orrell, John, *The Human Stage, English Theatre Design, 1567–1640* (Cambridge, 1988).

—— *The Quest for Shakespeare's Globe* (Cambridge, 1983).

—— *The Theatres of Inigo Jones and John Webb* (Cambridge, 1985).

Reynolds, George Fulmer, *On Shakespeare's Stage*, ed. R. K. Knaub (Boulder, Colo., 1967).

—— *The Staging of Elizabethan Plays at the Red Bull Theater, 1605–25* (New York, 1940).

Ringler, William A., Jr., 'The Number of Actors in Shakespeare's Early Plays', in *The Seventeenth Century Stage*, ed. G. E. Bentley (Chicago, Ill., 1968), 110–34.

Rosenberg, Marvin, 'Elizabethan Actors: Men or Marionettes', *PMLA* 69 (1954), 915–27; reprinted in *The Seventeenth Century Stage*, ed. G. E. Bentley (Chicago, Ill., 1968).

Schoenbaum, S., *William Shakespeare: A Documentary Life* (Oxford, 1975).

Shirley, Frances Ann, *Shakespeare's Use of Off-Stage Sounds* (Lincoln, Nebr., 1963).

Slater, Ann Pasternak, *Shakespeare the Director* (Brighton, 1982).

Smith, Hal H., 'Some Principles of Elizabethan Stage Costume', *Journal of the Warburg and Courtauld Institutes*, 25 (1962), 240–57.

Smith, Irwin, *Shakespeare's Blackfriars Playhouse: Its History and Its Design* (New York, 1964).

—— *Shakespeare's Globe Playhouse: A Modern Reconstruction* (New York, 1956).

Sternfeld, F. W., *Music in Shakespearean Tragedy* (London, 1963).

Sturgess, Keith, *Jacobean Private Theatre* (London, 1987).

Styan, J. L., *Shakespeare's Stagecraft* (Cambridge, 1967).

Thomson, Peter, *Shakespeare's Theatre* (London, 1983).

Weimann, Robert, *Shakespeare and the Popular Tradition in the Theater: Studies in the Social Dimension of Dramatic Form and Function*, ed. Robert Schwartz (Baltimore, Md., 1978).

Wickham, Glynne, *Early English Stages, 1300–1600*, 3 vols. (1959–81).

Wiles, David, *Shakespeare's Clown, Actor and Text in the Elizabethan Playhouse* (Cambridge, 1987).

Wilson, F. P., 'The Elizabethan Stage', *Neophilologus*, 39 (1955), 40–58; reprinted in his *Shakespearian and Other Studies*, ed. Helen Gardner (Oxford, 1969).

Worthen, William B., *The Idea of the Actor: Drama and the Ethics of Performance* (Princeton, NJ, 1984).

Wright, Louis B., *Middle Class Culture in Elizabethan England* (San Marino, Calif., 1935; 2nd edn., London, 1964).

Yates, Frances A., *Theatre of the World* (London, 1969).

SHAKESPEARE IN PERFORMANCE, 1660 TO THE PRESENT

Addenbrooke, David, *The Royal Shakespeare Company, The Peter Hall Years* (London, 1974).

Agate, James, *Brief Chronicles: A Survey of Plays by Shakespeare and the Elizabethans in Actual Performance, 1923–42* (London, 1943).

Avery, Emmett L., Charles Beecher Hogan, *et al.* (eds.), *The London Stage: A Calendar of Plays, Entertainments and Afterpieces, 1660–1800*, 11 vols. (Carbondale, Ill., 1960–5).

Bartholomeusz, Dennis, *Macbeth and the Players* (Cambridge, 1969).

Barton, John, *Playing Shakespeare* (London, 1984).

Beauman, Sally, *The Royal Shakespeare Company. A History of Ten Decades* (Oxford, 1982).

Berry, Ralph (ed.), *On Directing Shakespeare, Interviews with Contemporary Directors* (London, 1977).

Brockbank, Philip (ed.), *Players of Shakespeare: Essays in Shakespearean Performance by Twelve Players with the Royal Shakespeare Company* (Cambridge, 1985).

Brook, Peter, *The Empty Stage* (London, 1968).

—— *The Shifting Point: Forty Years of Theatrical Exploration, 1946–87* (London, 1988).

Brown, John Russell, *Shakespeare's Plays in Performance*, with 'Theatre

Research and the Criticism of Shakespeare and His Contemporaries' as appendix (London, 1966; Penguin Shakespeare Library, Harmondsworth, 1969).

Bulman, J. C., and H. R. Coursen (eds.), *Shakespeare on Television* (Hanover, NJ, 1988).

Burnim, Kalman A., Philip H. Highfill, and Edward A. Langhans (eds.), *A Biographical Dictionary of Actors, Actresses, Musicians, Dancers, Managers, & Other Stage Personnel in London, 1660–1800*, in progress (Carbondale, Ill., 1973–).

Campbell, Oscar James, and Edward G. Quinn (eds.), *A Shakespeare Encyclopaedia* (London, 1966).

Carlisle, Carol Jones, *Shakespeare from the Greenroom: Actors' Criticism of Four Major Tragedies* (Chapel Hill, NC, 1969).

Cohn, Ruby, *Modern Shakespearean Offshoots* (Princeton, NJ, 1985).

Daost, Yvette, *Roger Planchon: Director and Playwright* (Cambridge, 1981).

David, Richard, *Shakespeare in the Theatre* (Cambridge, 1978).

Davies, Anthony, *Filming Shakespeare: The Adaptations of Laurence Olivier, Orson Welles, Peter Brook and Akira Kurosawa* (Cambridge, 1988).

Dollimore, Jonathan, and Alan Sinfield (eds.), *Political Shakespeare: New Essays in Cultural Materialism* (Manchester and Ithaca, NY, 1985).

Eckert, Charles W. (ed.), *Focus on Shakespearean Films* (Englewood Cliffs, NJ, 1972).

Farjeon, Herbert, *The Shakespearean Scene: Dramatic Criticisms, 1913–44* (London, 1949).

Foulkes, Richard (ed.), *Shakespeare and the Victorian Stage* (Cambridge, 1986).

Gilder, Rosamond, *John Gielgud's Hamlet: A Record of Performance*, with 'The Hamlet Tradition' by John Gielgud (London, 1937).

Greenwald, Michael L., *Directions by Indirections: John Barton of the Royal Shakespeare Company* (Newark, NJ, 1985).

Griffiths, Trevor R., and Carole Woddis (eds.), *Bloomsbury Theatre Guide* (London, 1988).

Hogan, Charles Beecher, *Shakespeare in the Theatre: A Record of Performances in London, 1701–1800*, 2 vols. (Oxford, 1952–7).

Holderness, Graham (ed.), *The Shakespeare Myth* (Manchester, 1988).

Hotson, Leslie, *The Commonwealth and Restoration Stage* (Cambridge, Mass., 1928).

Houtchens, Lawrence, and Carolyn Houtchens (eds.), *Leigh Hunt's Dramatic Criticism, 1808–1831* (New York, 1949).

Howe, P. P. (ed.), *The Complete Works of William Hazlitt*, vol. xviii, *Art and Dramatic Criticism* (London, 1933).

Hughes, Alan, *Henry Irving, Shakespearean* (Cambridge, 1981).

Jackson, Russell, and R. L. Smallwood (eds.), *Players of Shakespeare 2,*

Further Essays in Shakespearean Performance by Players with the Royal Shakespeare Company (Cambridge, 1988).

Jorgens, Jack J., *Shakespeare on Film* (Bloomington, Ind., 1977).

Kemp, T. C., and J. C. Trewin, *The Stratford Festival* (Birmingham, 1953).

Kennedy, Dennis, *Granville Barker and the Dream of Theatre* (Cambridge, 1985).

Lamb, Margaret, *'Antony and Cleopatra' on the English Stage* (Cranbury, NJ, 1980).

Lundstrum, Rinda F., *William Poel's Hamlets: The Director as Critic* (Ann Arbor, Mich., 1984).

Mander, Raymond, and Joe Mitchenson, *Hamlet through the Ages. A Pictorial Record from 1709* (London, 1952).

Manvell, Roger, *Shakespeare on Film* (London, 1971).

Marowitz, Charles, *Prospero's Staff: Acting and Directing in the Contemporary Theatre* (Bloomington, Ind., 1986).

—— *The Marowitz Shakespeare, Adaptations and Collages* (London, 1978).

Marshall, Norman, *The Producer and the Play* (London, 1957).

Miller, Jonathan, *Subsequent Performances* (London, 1986).

Odell, George C. D., *Shakespeare—from Betterton to Irving*, 2 vols. (London, 1920; reprinted New York, 1963).

Patterson, Michael, *Peter Stein, Germany's Leading Theatre Director* (Cambridge, 1981).

Price, Joseph G., *The Unfortunate Comedy: A Study of 'All's Well That Ends Well' and Its Critics* (Liverpool, 1968).

—— (ed.), *The Triple Bond, Plays Mainly Shakespearean in Performance* (University Park, Pa., 1975).

Proudfoot, Richard, 'Peter Brook and Shakespeare', in *Themes in Drama 2*, ed. James Redmond (Cambridge, 1980), 157–89.

Ripley, John, *'Julius Caesar' on Stage in England and America, 1599–1973* (Cambridge, 1980).

Rosenberg, Marvin, *The Masks of King Lear* (Berkeley, Calif., 1971).

—— *The Masks of Macbeth* (Berkeley, Calif., 1978).

—— *The Masks of Othello: The Search for the Identity of Othello, Iago and Desdemona by Three Centuries of Actors and Critics* (Berkeley, Calif., 1961).

Rutter, Carol (ed.), *Clamorous Voices: Shakespeare's Women Today* (London, 1988).

Salgādo, Gāmini, *Eyewitnesses of Shakespeare: Firsthand Accounts of Performances 1590–1890* (London, 1975).

Scouten, Arthur H., 'The Increase in Popularity of Shakespeare's Plays in the Eighteenth Century: A *Caveat* for Interpreters of Stage History', *Shakespeare Quarterly*, 7 (1956), 189–202.

Selbourne, David, *The Making of 'A Midsummer Night's Dream', An Eye-Witness Account of Peter Brook's Production from First Rehearsal to First Night* (London, 1982).

Senelick, Laurence, *Gordon Craig's Moscow 'Hamlet'* (Westport, Conn., 1982).

Shattuck, Charles H., *The Hamlet of Edwin Booth* (Urbana, Ill., 1969).

—— *Shakespeare on the American Stage*, vol. ii, *From Booth & Barrett to Sothern and Marlowe* (Washington, DC, 1987).

—— *Shakespeare on the American Stage. From the Hallams to Edwin Booth* (Washington, DC, 1976).

—— *The Shakespeare Promptbooks: A Descriptive Catalogue* (Urbana, Ill., 1965).

Shaw, G. Bernard, *Our Theatres in the Nineties*, 3 vols. (London, 1932); ed. Edwin Wilson, *Shaw on Shakespeare* (New York, 1961; Penguin Shakespeare Library, Harmondsworth, 1969).

Sher, Antony, *Year of the King, an Actor's Diary and Sketchbook* (London, 1985).

Speaight, Robert, *Shakespeare on the Stage, an Illustrated History of Shakespearian Performance* (London, 1973).

—— *William Poel and the Elizabethan Revival* (London, 1954).

Spencer, Christopher (ed.), *Five Restoration Adaptations of Shakespeare* (Urbana, Ill., 1965).

Spencer, Hazelton, *Shakespeare Improved* (Cambridge, Mass., 1927).

Sprague, Arthur Colby, *The Doubling of Parts in Shakespeare's Plays* (London, 1966).

—— *Shakespeare and the Actors: The Stage Business in His Plays, 1660–1905* (Cambridge, Mass., 1944; reprinted New York, 1963).

—— *Shakespeare's Histories: Plays for the Stage* (London, 1964).

—— *Shakespearian Players and Performances* (London, 1954).

—— *The Stage Business in Shakespeare's Plays: A Postscript* (London, 1953).

—— and J. C. Trewin, *Shakespeare's Plays Today: Some Customs and Conventions of the Stage* (London, 1970).

Styan, J. L., *The Shakespeare Revolution: Criticism and Performance in the 20th Century* (Cambridge, 1977).

Trewin, J. C., *Five & Eighty Hamlets* (London, 1989).

—— *Going to Shakespeare* (London, 1978).

—— *Peter Brook, A Biography* (London, 1971).

—— *Shakespeare on the English Stage, 1900–1964* (London, 1964).

Tynan, Kenneth, *Curtains* (London, 1961).

—— *He That Plays the King* (London, 1950).

—— *Tynan Right and Left* (London, 1967).

Wearing, J. P. (ed.), *The London Stage, A Calendar of Plays and Players, 1890–1929*, 9 vols. (Metuchen, NJ, 1976–84).

Wells, Stanley, *Royal Shakespeare: Four Major Productions at Stratford-upon-Avon* (Manchester, 1977).

Williams, David (ed.), *Peter Brook: A Theatrical Casebook* (London, 1988).

Williams, Harcourt, *Old Vic Saga* (London, 1949).

4 | The Non-dramatic Poems

KATHERINE
DUNCAN-JONES

Facsimiles of the earliest printed texts of the *Sonnets* and other non-dramatic poems are assembled in the Yale Elizabethan Club quatercentenary volume. Sources and analogues are explored expansively in T. W. Baldwin's book on their *Literary Genetics* (1950), and more concisely by Geoffrey Bullough (narrative poems only, however) in his *Narrative and Dramatic Sources*. Among the few book-length studies of Shakespeare's non-dramatic poems (other than the *Sonnets*) are Muriel Bradbrook's *Shakespeare and Elizabethan Poetry* and G. Wilson Knight's *The Mutual Flame*.

The narrative poems

TEXTS

Venus and Adonis (1593) and *Lucrece* (1594), both dedicated to the Earl of Southampton, were initially printed by Shakespeare's Stratford contemporary, Richard Field, though Field quickly sold his rights in them—perhaps for a good price—to other publishers. Though outstandingly successful in Shakespeare's lifetime, being frequently alluded to and frequently reprinted, the narrative poems have, compared with the *Sonnets*, been edited relatively rarely in modern times. Their position at the end of the volume in many one-volume editions of Shakespeare tends to make them seem like supplementary works that can acceptably be overlooked. Hyder Rollins's New Variorum edition (1938) is a mine of information, but scarcely a 'reading text'. F. T. Prince's New Arden (1960) is bulked out with the addition of *The Passionate Pilgrim* and 'The Phoenix and the Turtle'; J. C. Maxwell's New Cambridge

(1966) contains in addition *A Lover's Complaint.* In terms of secondary information, Prince's volume is useful on sources and critical history, Maxwell's for textual and linguistic comment. It is curious that though *Lucrece* (see below) has come in for more adverse comment, probably, than any other indubitably authentic work of Shakespeare, it has achieved at least one separate modern edition by a scholar who takes it seriously, J. W. Lever, in his 1971 New Penguin edition. *Venus and Adonis*, Shakespeare's earliest published work, and the poem most critics have preferred, has yet to appear as an independent text in comparably accessible form.

CRITICISM AND COMMENTARY

Perhaps alone among Shakespeare's works, the narrative poems have not been greatly admired by those who have undertaken to edit them. Modern editors have not been quite so blunt as Edmond Malone, who in the *Supplement* to his great Shakespeare edition in 1780 complained of 'the wearisome circumlocution with which the tale of each of them is told', comparing the process of reading them to a journey in which the reader 'is led through many an intricate path, and after travelling for some hours finds his inn yet at a distance.' Both Prince and Maxwell, taking their cue from Coleridge, find much to admire in the pace, the sensuousness, the intense perception of natural detail so distinctive to *Venus and Adonis*. As Prince puts it, Shakespeare

creates the poem in a kind of double consciousness, in two concurrent lives, made possible by intense activity of mind and feeling.

However, though Prince makes a sensitive and appreciative attempt to categorize the mythological eroticism of *Venus and Adonis* as comic, he does not seem to expect to take his audience with him in this appreciation, prefacing his remarks with the prediction that 'few English or American readers nowadays will respond to such happily wanton fancies as *Venus and Adonis*.' Maxwell accepts the notion of the poem as a comedy, but modifies it, stressing rather 'the role of the central myth in the poem', together with its natural detail, which he finds reminiscent of Burns.

Neither editor makes high claims for *Lucrece*. Prince finds it 'obvious that the poem, as a whole, is a failure', with 'glaringly obvious' 'defects of rhetoric'. Worse than this, he finds the central story in itself uninteresting, and thinks Shakespeare handles it in an off-putting way. While acknowledging that Lucrece develops into a tragic heroine after her violation, he thinks that 'we are never wholly convinced that she deserves the part', and that the excesses of rhetoric undermine it—'she is forced to express herself in a way which dissipates the real pathos of the situation'. Maxwell, again, refines what is fundamentally the same view. Though he finds moral complexity in Shakespeare's presentation of Tarquin, he has little time for Lucrece's rhetoric. He sees *Lucrece*, 'unsatisfactory, uneven, and inchoate', as interesting mainly as the seedbed from which later and greater works, such as *Macbeth*, grew. Lever, too, sees *Lucrece* as artistically faulty, and like Price and Maxwell thinks the lady protests too much.

It is in books and articles that the critical life of the poems has been most vigorously sustained, despite Douglas Bush's discouraging verdict that 'Shakespeare, at the age of twenty-nine and thirty, chose to write not merely one unsatisfactory classical poem, but two'. Discussion of *Venus and Adonis* has most often been concerned with the question of its tone, and consequent generic status. Rufus Putney was one of the earliest critics to see the poem as comic—even burlesque or farcical—suggesting, in a strongly argued article in 1953, that Shakespeare 'deliberately and deftly avoided the pathos the legend contained'. Later writers have felt that Putney overstates the case, but they have not eliminated comic and ironic elements altogether, subordinating them instead as some among many components of a complexly ordered mythological artefact. William Keach's important book on *Elizabethan Erotic Narratives* (1977) places Shakespeare's poem in the context of Ovidian poetry in general, and Elizabethan epyllia in particular, showing that 'Shakespeare intensifies every aspect of Ovid's episode, but . . . in a manner which remains deeply Ovidian'. Keach does justice to the complexity of the poem, tackling those elements in it—including the humour—which are disconcerting or ambivalent. His implicit linkage of Shakespeare's poem with the iconography of Venus and Adonis in Renaissance painting, suggested in the illustrations to his book, is taken further by Clark Hulse, and has become a regular feature of discussions of both poems, which are perhaps the closest Shakespeare ever came to poetic 'speaking pictures' as defined in Sidney's *Defence of Poesy*. In a short but meaty article

in 1983 Gordon Williams develops an analogy between Shakespeare and Titian, originally suggested by Panofsky, in their
handling of the Venus and Adonis story. Unlike Panofsky, he
attributes the analogy to 'a shared cultural climate', rather than
direct influence.

Possibly some such 'shared climate' explains the fact that
Shakespeare's choice of subject in his second, 'graver', poem
corresponds with Sidney's account of the 'right poet', who is like
the 'more excellent' kind of painter:

who having no law but wit, bestow that in colours upon you which is
fittest for the eye to see: as the constant but lamenting look of Lucretia,
when she punished in herself another's fault, wherein he painteth not
Lucretia, whom he never saw, but painteth the outward beauty of such a
virtue.

Sidney's *Defence* was not published until 1595, but it was written
in 1580 or so, and may conceivably have been known to the
young Shakespeare in manuscript. *Lucrece* has generated a good
deal of critical debate, much of it concerned with the question of
whether—as suggested in the passage from Sidney—his Lucrece is
to be seen as unequivocally admirable, or whether, as proposed
by D. C. Allen and others, Shakespeare shows awareness of the
debate about her moral status initiated by St Augustine. According
to Augustine, ably summarized by Allen, 'Lucrece should have
defended herself to the death, or, having been forced, lived free
of blame with a guiltless conscience'. In his wide-ranging book
The Rapes of Lucretia (1982) Ian Donaldson also assumes that
Shakespeare was aware of the post-Augustinian controversy,
and that his presentation of Lucrece either is, or should be, to
some extent ironic. However, Richard Levin (1981) shows that
the 'ironic' reading is not supported by a single contemporary
allusion, and furnishes a chilling countercheck to many elaborately
subtextual readings of Renaissance literature. Probably the
iconographic approach is more promising, and has not yet been
exhausted. As an extended and fully articulated exploration of a
female consciousness *Lucrece* seems also ripe for feminist criticism.
Nancy J. Vickers combines these two approaches in her analysis
of the importance of 'heraldry' in the poem. Developments of
such approaches may eventually bring the narrative poems, so
often hitherto perceived as marginal, somewhere nearer to the
centre of the canon of Shakespeare's work. Their correct chronological placing in the Oxford Shakespeare assists this integration.

Sonnets and *A Lover's Complaint*

TEXTS

These texts appeared together in the volume entitled *SHAKE-SPEARES SONNETS* published by Thomas Thorpe in 1609. An ever recurring tendency by editors to believe that they can achieve a more coherent arrangement than that of 1609 began with the second edition, John Benson's radically rearranged text (1639/40), in which the sonnets were given fancy titles, run together to form longer lyrics, mingled with *A Lover's Complaint* and *Passionate Pilgrim* pieces, and re-written to make it appear that the persona's beloved friend was female. Unsatisfactory though this version may seem, Benson's text has its place in literary history, for it was in this form that Shakespeare's *Sonnets* were read and admired by poets of the period, such as Sir John Suckling, and it formed the basis of the earliest eighteenth-century editions. Malone's edition (1780) restored the 1609 text, emended with scrupulous moderation, but it also initiated a long divorce between the *Sonnets* and their 1609 companion, *A Lover's Complaint*, by intercalating the largely inauthentic *Passionate Pilgrim*. Dover Wilson's Cambridge text is closely based on that of Malone, as were most of the nineteenth-century editions, a rare exception being George Wyndham's ultra-conservative text (1898), based closely on 1609. Hyder Rollins's magnificently inclusive two-volume New Variorum edition (1944) is an indispensable reference work, giving a detailed history of earlier editions of the *Sonnets* and theories about them. However, he too excludes *A Lover's Complaint*, perhaps persuaded by the opinions of many previous editors that it was not by Shakespeare. More surprisingly, Stephen Booth, who offers a facsimile text of the 1609 quarto alongside his own modernized version, also stops short at the succeeding *Complaint*, though its catchword 'A' appears on the final page reproduced. His edition is the most extreme example of an annotated text of the *Sonnets* in which readers are told, in immense detail, what to think about them. Though his 'analytic commentary' has some value as a basis for seminar discussion, it is not so unassumingly helpful as the annotated text by Ingram and Redpath, which is lucidly set out, with notes on verso, sonnets on recto, and offers comments on language and meaning which the editors are sometimes content to leave open-ended. Their modernization of punctuation is less satisfactory, however, as the frequent use of strong points such as dashes and exclamation marks destroys some ambiguities and suggests a rather declamatory style of reading. C. K. Pooler's (old) Arden edition is unusual for its period, in retaining the integrity of the 1609 text, though he claims only that *A Lover's Complaint* 'contains lines that might have been written by Shakespeare'. His notes give useful cross-references to the rest of Shakespeare's work and to other Elizabethan writers. But the reunion of *Sonnets* and *A Lover's Complaint* has been most confidently accomplished by John Kerrigan in his New Penguin edition (1986), which is a copiously annotated text, recalling Booth in its tone of authoritative assertion both about the value (or lack of it) of previous work, and about how individual lines and passages should be read. However, Kerrigan is generous with information, often providing original or unusual illustrative material, and in the absence of a revised Arden his edition is clearly the one with most to offer to new readers of the *Sonnets*. Students should, however, be warned that not all emendations of the 1609 text have been recorded, e.g. Capell's emendation of 'cross' for 'loss' in 34. 12; nor is the text treated quite so conservatively as is claimed, cf. 'travel' for 'travaile' in line 2 of the same sonnet, also unnoted. For detailed collations, readers should refer to the *Textual Companion* to the Oxford Shakespeare.

For readers who prefer a more compact text of the *Sonnets*, Martin Seymour-Smith's (1963) is one of the best. William Burto's Signet (1964) has an introductory essay by W. H. Auden. G. B. Harrison's old Penguin (1938) represents the 1609 text, including *A Lover's Complaint*, fairly closely. There are also many 'plain' texts of the *Sonnets*, including one with an introduction by Stanley Wells (1985).

CRITICISM AND COMMENTARY

Critical analysis of the *Sonnets* began with the publisher John Benson, mentioned above, who pleaded rather defensively for a lucidity which was at least partly the product of his own re-arrangement: 'you shall find them serene, clear and elegantly plain . . . no intricate or cloudy stuff to puzzle intellect, but perfect eloquence'. Few subsequent commentators have felt the *Sonnets* to be at all clear or plain. Debate has surrounded four main issues: (i) the nature and status of the text; (ii) the connotations of

Thorpe's description of a 'Mr. W.H.' as 'onlie begetter' of the sonnets; (iii) the date of composition and the extent to which this is reflected in the order of the sonnets; (iv) the connexions of particular parts of the sequence with real-life figures, corresponding to 'Mr. W.H.' (who may or may not also be the young friend to whom Sonnets 1–126 appear to be addressed), the 'rival poet' apparently alluded to in 76–86, and the 'dark lady' celebrated in 127–52. Underlying these enquiries is the more radical question of the relationship of the *Sonnets* to Shakespeare's own experience —whether, as Wordsworth said, 'with this key / Shakespeare unlocked his heart'. Finally, (v), some of the best writers on the *Sonnets* have discussed them in literary terms with minimal reference to these knotty problems.

(i) Perhaps because of the subject matter of the *Sonnets*, in which the majority of the poems are addressed to a male friend rather than to a female mistress, a belief that the text was pirated, stolen, or even published out of malice by Shakespeare's enemies, bent on disgracing him, was common among nineteenth- and early twentieth-century scholars. A concomitant of this belief was general uncertainty about the authenticity both of the sonnets and their arrangement. Sidney Lee perhaps went furthest and with most authority (as an eminent bibliographer) in undermining the status of Thorpe's text, partly provoked by George Wyndham's thoroughgoing defence of it. However, Lee's attack on Thorpe's supposedly dishonest career and low standards of printing did not command complete support. Percy Simpson, among others, defended the sensitivity with which the *Sonnets* are punctuated, and E. K. Chambers and G. B. Harrison are among those who have considered, *pace* Lee, that Shakespeare himself may have authorized publication. My own examination of the rest of Thorpe's publications has suggested that Shakespeare is quite likely to have sold the text directly to Thorpe, who had recently done good work for Jonson and Marston, among others; and a comparison of the 1609 quarto with other sonnet volumes points to its being an artistic unit not unfamiliar in the period, made up of sonnets, 'anacreontic poems' (153–4), and 'complaint'. John Kerrigan's edition is based on the presumption that the 1609 text presents an artistic whole. Close stylistic analysis by MacD. P. Jackson (who has also analysed the printing of the 1609 quarto) has supported the likelihood that *A Lover's Complaint* is authentic Shakespeare, of circa 1600.

(ii) Thomas Thorpe's capitalized dedication of the 'INSUING. SONNETS.' to a 'Mr. W.H.', their 'ONLIE. BEGETTER', has given rise to more speculation than can be chronicled here. Some have thought that 'begetter' might mean 'procurer', but Ingram and Redpath, among others, suggest that the word will not easily carry that meaning. Some, building on the idea that it was he who procured the text, have thought Mr. W.H. the dedicator, rather than the dedicatee; this reading, too, seems very strained. Rollins gives a full account of theories about the dedication up to 1944, and Kenneth Muir and John Kerrigan record some later developments. One of the few certainties about the dedication is that its format, in capitals and with a stop after each word, was intended to resemble a Latin lapidary inscription. The dedication of another Thorpe publication, Jonson's *Volpone* (1607), is visually similar, but without the stops.

(iii) Opinions about the date of composition of individual sonnets and of *A Lover's Complaint* have varied within a range of some twenty-five years, 1583–1608. Leslie Hotson's attempt to assign some sonnets to the 1580s has not commanded much support, but should not be disregarded; the same is true of the thoroughgoing work of Claes Schaar, who also gives very early dates to some sonnets. Sonnet 107, with its plethora of what appear to be topical references, such as 'The mortall Moone hath her eclipse indur'de' (death of Elizabeth?) has provoked an enormous amount of commentary, conveniently summarized by Kerrigan. Some of the most far-reaching attempts to date all the sonnets in the sequence have approximated to creative writing rather than scholarship, a notable example being John Padel's version, in which, having rearranged the sonnets in his preferred, supposedly chronological, order, he actually gives them the catchpenny title *New Poems by Shakespeare* (1981). A more scholarly, but in the end almost equally unconvincing, rearrangement was undertaken by Brents Stirling in 1968. Painstaking stylistic analysis along the lines of studies undertaken by MacD. P. Jackson and others may prove ultimately to be the most rewarding method for dating the components of the 1609 volume. But given the number of variables, such as the possibility of repeated revision, and indeterminate gaps in time between composition and ordering, it seems unlikely that it will ever be possible to date all the poems with confidence, or even to determine their relative order. The genesis of an analogous poetic sequence from a later period, Tennyson's *In Memoriam*, can be traced in some detail because of the survival of authorial manuscripts recording stages of composition during a period of seventeen years. In the case of Shakespeare's *Sonnets*, for which such manuscript evidence does not survive, we shall probably always have to rest content with much uncertainty.

(iv) The two strongest contenders for the rôle of 'Mr. W.H.' are William Herbert, Third Earl of Pembroke, who was to be one of the dedicatees of the First Folio in 1623, where he was described as having favoured Shakespeare in his lifetime; and Henry Wriothesley, Earl of Southampton, to whom Shakespeare dedicated the narrative poems. Chambers and Dover Wilson are among Pembroke's most weighty supporters, but many other scholars have favoured Southampton, despite the need to reverse his initials. Pembroke's patronage is studied in detail by Michael Brennan, and among book-length studies of Southampton and Shakespeare are those by G. P. V. Akrigg and A. L. Rowse. The last named has made a well-documented case for a third 'W.H.', Sir William Harvey, who became Southampton's stepfather in 1598. Other candidates include William Hart (Shakespeare had both a brother-in-law and a nephew of this name), William Hughes (an imaginary young actor), William Hatcliffe (a student of Gray's Inn discovered by Leslie Hotson), William Hathaway, and 'William Himself'.

The 'rival poet' has been variously linked with Marlowe, Chapman, Drayton, Gervase Markham and others. More scraps of evidence seem to point to Chapman than to any of the others; for instance, the six-foot lines of his great translation of Homer might be aptly described as 'the proud full sail of his great verse' (86. 1). However, the question can by no means be described as settled.

Still less, despite claims by A. L. Rowse to have solved all the problems of the *Sonnets*, is the identity of the Dark Lady held by most scholars to be resolved. She is identified by Rowse with a member of a family of Italian musicians, Emilia Lanier, née Bassano. While it is difficult to prove decisively that the 'woman coloured ill' referred to in the *Sonnets* was *not* based on Emilia Lanier, several other candidates, such as Mary Fitton and Lucy Negro, are also hard to eliminate completely. Emilia Lanier has the attraction of being better documented than most non-aristo-cratic women of Shakespeare's period, for she visited the astrologer and diarist Simon Forman, and was a published poetess. However, the probabilities may be in favour of the real-life original—if any, for praise of black beauty was extremely fashionable in the late sixteenth century—belonging to that vast majority of Elizabethan women who have left little trace in surviving records. Among such is Shakespeare's wife. In the previous *Bibliographical Guide* J. M. Nosworthy predicted that 'it may yet emerge that Anne Hathaway appears in Thorpe's collection more frequently than has been hitherto supposed'. This prophecy was fulfilled in Barbara Everett's long review-article of John Kerrigan's edition (1986), in which she made ingenious play with a theory that Anne Hathaway was in some rarefied yet compelling sense the master-mistress of the poet's passion. Her article provoked a lively correspondence, which rapidly left both the *Sonnets* and Kerrigan's edition far behind. This centrifugal tendency has beset many discussions of the biographical background.

(v) The critics who have written best on the *Sonnets* have for the most part made little or no reference to all these problems. C. S. Lewis's few pages on them in *English Literature in the Sixteenth Century* are characteristically powerful, both in generalization—'In certain senses of the word "love", Shakespeare is not so much our best as our only love poet'—and in specimen analyses of style. Others whose accounts have much to offer, and are in different ways fresh or original, include Rosalie Colie, J. B. Leishman, Molly Mahood, Giorgio Melchiori, and Hallett Smith. Alastair Fowler's structural analysis (1970) is among other things remarkable for its inclusion of *A Lover's Complaint* as an integral part of the overall structure.

The *Complaint* itself is best analysed, in literary terms, by Kerrigan.

Other poems

TEXTS

In addition to facsimiles and editions already mentioned, the Oxford Shakespeare's section of 'Various poems' is unusually inclusive, with some unfamiliar poems ascribed to Shakespeare in manuscript texts.

CRITICISM AND COMMENTARY

Shakespeare's contribution to a curious collection of poems associated with Sir John Salusbury, compiled by Robert Chester in 1601, was his most famous short lyric 'The Phoenix and the Turtle'. This was largely overlooked until the twentieth century, when it has received much attention of various kinds. Its inclusion in Helen Gardner's anthology of *Metaphysical Poets* (1957) marks the perception of it by mid-twentieth-century critics such as Empson; it has also been extravagantly admired by Wilson Knight. The lyric's social and literary context has been investigated by, among others, Carleton Brown and John Buxton. Attempts to read it as contemporary allegory, for instance as an account of Elizabeth's relationship with Essex, have often paid too little heed to the occasional character of the volume. Work on it is usefully summarized by R. A. Underwood.

While 'The Phoenix and the Turtle' has been examined with great sophistication, discussion of other short poems has been relatively primitive, and largely confined to questions of authenticity. The proportion of Jaggard's piratical *Passionate Pilgrim* (1599) that can be accepted as Shakespeare's is uncertain, apart from its texts of Sonnets 138 and 144; the other poems have accordingly received relatively little attention.

REFERENCES

GENERAL

Baldwin, T. W., *On the Literary Genetics of Shakespere's Poems and Sonnets* (Urbana, Ill., 1950).

Bradbrook, Muriel C., *Shakespeare and Elizabethan Poetry* (London, 1951).

Bullough, Geoffrey, *Narrative and Dramatic Sources of Shakespeare* (London, 1966), i. 161–99.

Knight, G. Wilson, *The Mutual Flame* (London, 1955).

Martz, L., J. M. Osborn, and E. M. Waith (eds.), *Shakespeare's Poems: A Facsimile of the Earliest Editions* (Elizabethan Club Series 3; New Haven, Conn. and London, 1964).

Narrative Poems

TEXTS

Lever, J. W. (ed.), *The Rape of Lucrece* (New Penguin, Harmondsworth, 1971).

Malone, Edmond, *Supplement to the Edition of Shakespeare's Plays Published in 1778*, 2 vols. (London, 1780); *Poems* in i. 397–760.

Maxwell, J. C. (ed.), *The Poems* (Cambridge, 1966).

Prince, F. T. (ed.), *The Poems* (The Arden Shakespeare, London; Cambridge, Mass., 1960).

Rollins, Hyder E. (ed.), *The Poems* (New Variorum Shakespeare, Philadelphia, 1938).

CRITICISM AND COMMENTARY

Allen, D. C., 'Some Observations on *The Rape of Lucrece*', *Shakespeare Survey* 15 (1962), 89–98.

Bush, Douglas, *Mythology and the Renaissance Tradition in English Poetry* (Minneapolis, Minn., 1932), 139–55.

Coleridge, S. T., *Biographia Literaria*, chap. 15, in *Works*, ed. James Engell and W. Jackson Bate (Princeton, NJ, 1983), vii. 19–28.

Donaldson, Ian, *The Rapes of Lucretia: A Myth and Its Transformations* (Oxford, 1982).

Hulse, Clark, *Metamorphic Verse: The Elizabethan Minor Epic* (Princeton, NJ, 1981).

Keach, William, *Elizabethan Erotic Narrative: Irony and Pathos in the Ovidian Poetry of Shakespeare, Marlowe and Their Contemporaries* (London, 1977).

Levin, Richard, 'The Ironic Reading of *The Rape of Lucrece* and the Problem of External Evidence', *Shakespeare Survey* 34 (1981), 85–92.

Panofsky, Erwin, *Problems in Titian, Mostly Iconographic* (New York, 1969), 140.

Putney, Rufus, 'Venus *Agonistes*', *University of Colorado Studies: Series in Language and Literature*, 4 (1953), 52–66.

Sidney, Sir Philip, *Miscellaneous Prose*, ed. K. Duncan-Jones and J. van Dorsten (Oxford, 1973), 80–1.

Vickers, Nancy J., 'The Blazon of Sweet Beauty's Best: Shakespeare's *Lucrece*', in *Shakespeare and the Question of Theory*, ed. P. Parker and G. Hartman (London, 1985), 95–115.

Williams, Gordon, 'The Coming of Age of Shakespeare's Adonis', *MLR* 78 (1983), 769–76.

Sonnets and A Lover's Complaint

TEXTS

Benson, John (publisher), *Poems Written by Wil. Shakespeare. Gent.* (London, 1640); also available in facsimile, ed. H. M. Klein (Hildesheim, 1979).

Booth, Stephen, *Shakespeare's Sonnets: Edited with Analytic Commentary* (New Haven, Conn., and London, 1977).

Burto, William H. (ed.), *Sonnets* (New York, 1964).

Harrison, G. B. (ed.), *The Sonnets and A Lover's Complaint*, (London, 1938).

Ingram, W. G., and T. Redpath (eds.), *Shakespeare's Sonnets* (London, 1964).

Kerrigan, John (ed.), *The Sonnets and A Lover's Complaint* (New Penguin, London and New York, 1986).

Lee, Sidney (ed.), *Sonnets of Shakespeare* (London, 1905).

Malone, Edmond, *Supplement to the Edition of Shakespeare's Plays Published in 1778* (London, 1780), i. 581–706, 739–60.

Pooler, C. K. (ed.), *Sonnets* (The Arden Shakespeare, London, 1918).

Rollins, Hyder E. (ed.), *The Sonnets* (New Variorum Shakespeare, Philadelphia, Pa., and London, 1944), 2 vols.

Seymour-Smith, Martin (ed.), *The Sonnets* (1963).

Wells, Stanley (ed.), *Shakespeare's Sonnets and A Lover's Complaint* (Oxford, 1985).

Wilson, John Dover (ed.), *The Sonnets* (New Shakespeare, Cambridge, 1966; rev. edn., 1967).

Wyndham, George (ed.), *The Poems of Shakespeare* (London, 1898).

CRITICISM AND COMMENTARY

Akrigg, G. P. V., *Shakespeare and the Earl of Southampton* (London, 1968).

Brennan, Michael G., *Literary Patronage in the English Renaissance: The Pembroke Family* (London and New York, 1988).

Chambers, E. K., *William Shakespeare: A Study of Facts and Problems* (Oxford, 1930; reprinted 1989); abridged by Charles Williams, *A Short Life of Shakespeare with the Sources* (Oxford, 1933), i. 555–76.

Colie, Rosalie, *Shakespeare's Living Art* (Princeton, NJ, 1974), 68–134.

Duncan-Jones, Katherine, 'Was the 1609 *SHAKE-SPEARES SONNETS* Really Unauthorized?', *RES* 34 (1983), 151–71.

Everett, Barbara, 'Mrs Shakespeare', *London Review of Books*, vol. viii, no. 22 (1986), 7–10.

Fowler, Alastair, *Triumphal Forms: Structural Patterns in Elizabethan Poetry* (Cambridge, 1970).

Hotson, Leslie, *Shakespeare's Sonnets Dated, and Other Essays* (London, 1949).

Jackson, MacD. P., 'Punctuation and the Compositors of Shakespeare's Sonnets, 1609', *The Library*, 5th ser. 30 (1975), 1–24.

—— 'Shakespeare's *A Lover's Complaint*: Its Date and Authenticity', *University of Auckland Bulletin*, 17; English Series, 13 (Auckland, 1965).

Leishman, J. B., *Themes and Variations in Shakespeare's Sonnets* (London, 1961).

Lewis, C. S., *English Literature in the Sixteenth Century* (Oxford, 1954), 498–509.

Mahood, Molly M., *Shakespeare's Wordplay* (London, 1957), 89–110.

Melchiori, Giorgio, *Shakespeare's Dramatic Meditations: An Experiment in Criticism* (Oxford, 1976).

Muir, Kenneth, *Shakespeare's Sonnets* (London, 1979).

Nosworthy, J. M., 'The Sonnets and Other Poems', in *Shakespeare: Select Bibliographical Guides*, ed. Stanley Wells (Oxford, 1973), 44–53.

Padel, John, *New Poems by Shakespeare: Order and Meaning Restored to the Sonnets* (London, 1981).

Rowse, A. L., *Shakespeare's Sonnets: The Problems Solved* (London, 1973).

—— *Shakespeare's Southampton* (London, 1965).

—— *Simon Forman: Sex and Society in Shakespeare's Age* (London, 1974).

Schaar, Claes, *Elizabethan Sonnet Themes and the Dating of Shakespeare's Sonnets* (Lund Studies in English, 32; Lund, 1962).

Simpson, Percy, *Shakespearian Punctuation* (Oxford, 1911).

Smith, Hallett, *The Tension of the Lyre: Poetry in Shakespeare's Sonnets* (San Marino, Calif., 1981).

Stirling, Brents, *The Shakespeare Sonnet Order* (Berkeley, Calif., 1968).

Other poems

Brown, Carleton (ed.), *Poems by Sir John Salusbury and Robert Chester* (Early English Text Society Extra Series, 113, 1914).

Buxton, John, 'Two Dead Birds: A Note on *The Phoenix and Turtle*', in *English Renaissance Studies: Presented to Dame Helen Gardner in Honour of Her Seventieth Birthday*, ed. J. Carey (Oxford, 1980), 44–55.

Empson, William, 'The Phoenix and the Turtle', *Essays in Criticism*, 16 (1966), 147–53.

Gardner, Helen (ed.), *The Metaphysical Poets* (London, 1957).

Underwood, R. A., *Shakespeare's 'The Phoenix and the Turtle': A Survey of Scholarship* (Salzburg, 1974).

5 | The Early Comedies

D. J. PALMER

TEXTS

Among several good modern-spelling editions of the plays in separate volumes, the new Arden Shakespeare provides the fullest critical apparatus on the text, date, sources, interpretation, and stage history.

The standard of inexpensive paperback editions of Shakespeare has improved considerably, and those mentioned here have all attracted the services of distinguished scholars. Choice between them must be determined by what is offered in addition to a reliable text. Each volume in the New Penguin Shakespeare contains a substantial and lucid introductory analysis of the play, with a summary of relevant works for further reading; the most valuable feature of this edition, however, is the ample commentary which, together with the textual apparatus, is printed at the back of the volume. The Signet Classic Shakespeare is less adequately annotated, but each volume in this series reprints three or four important critical essays and source material where appropriate, while the editorial introductions are sound and sometimes brilliant (particularly Harry Levin's introduction to *The Comedy of Errors*). The Pelican Shakespeare also contains some excellent editorial essays, notably by Paul A. Jorgensen on *The Comedy of Errors*, Richard Hosley on *The Taming of the Shrew*, and Alfred Harbage on *Love's Labour's Lost*; the commentaries, however, are too brief to be of much help for detailed study. More extensive introductions to the text, its sources, and the meaning of the play are provided by editions of individual plays in The Oxford Shakespeare and the New Cambridge Shakespeare, but both series are as yet incomplete. The New Cambridge edition places particular emphasis upon stage history.

CRITICAL STUDIES AND COMMENTARY

Two factors have traditionally circumscribed the critical reputation
of Shakespeare's early comedies: they are early, and they are
comedies. Overshadowed by the later masterpieces, they have
been patronized or defended as the uncertain prentice work of
immaturity, until we have become more accustomed to make
allowances for their supposed limitations than to recognize their
subtlety, superb craftsmanship, and depth of vision. Moreover,
they have suffered from what H. B. Charlton described, in the
book with which the modern study of Shakespearian comedy
begins, as 'the enormous lee-way into which the consideration
of comedy has fallen in comparison with the progress which has
been made in exploring the grounds of criticism in tragedy'.
Developments in the criticism of the early comedies during the
past twenty years have therefore been particularly concerned
with overcoming this double barrier to a proper estimate of their
value, by improving our knowledge of Shakespeare's cultural
heritage, and by challenging what R. A. Foakes, in his introduction
to *The Comedy of Errors*, refers to as 'a long tradition of regarding
comedy in general as inferior to "serious" plays, and Shakespeare's comedies in particular, as entertainments, plays of escape
into a careless world'. Researches into Shakespeare's early life
and schooling, together with the evidence produced by textual
scholars for accepting the intregrity of the early plays as Shakespeare's own work, have exploded those hoary myths of the ill-
educated dramatist who began his career by refurbishing other
men's plays. Critics now have a more substantial foundation for
regarding the early Shakespeare, in the words of A. C. Hamilton,
'as a sophisticated literary craftsman', and consequently are
more predisposed to give the early plays their due as accomplished
achievements without need of apology. But the special problem
of interpreting the comedies is posed for the critic by
Foakes: 'let him, however, probe beneath the vocabulary commonly used to describe the comedies, gay, warm, enchanting,
romantic, lively, and so forth, and he is at once liable to invite the
scorn of the many who believe interpretation to be unnecessary,
and provoke the hostility of those for whom the experience
afforded by the comedies is a sort of inviolate glow, sacred and
not to be profaned.' Through the insights and approaches summarized here, the reader may discover that by taking Shake-

speare's early comedies seriously he improves both his enjoyment and his understanding of them.

Despite the progress of modern scholarship, in one fundamentally important respect our ignorance remains. There is not sufficient evidence to allow us to say exactly when the early comedies were written, or in what order. Most scholars would accept that the five plays were probably composed between 1590 and 1595, and that *The Comedy of Errors, The Taming of the Shrew, The Two Gentlemen of Verona,* and *Love's Labour's Lost* preceded *A Midsummer Night's Dream.* This is the order now commonly accepted, but it is at best conventional and open to occasional dispute.

Where the objective criteria are more than usually inconclusive, critics considering the early comedies as a group have been free to arrange their own sequence according to their differing conceptions of the relationships between the five plays. This has sometimes proved a dangerous liberty to critics theorizing about Shakespeare's development, as for instance in Charlton's assumption that after *Love's Labour's Lost* and *The Two Gentlemen of Verona* Shakespeare underwent a 'recoil from romanticism' and produced *The Comedy of Errors* and *The Taming of the Shrew.* On the other hand Virgil Whitaker finds support for the conventional sequence listed above in 'a decreasing dependence upon the classics and a growing familiarity with contemporary literature' (though one wonders whether the Ovidian spirit of *A Midsummer Night's Dream* bears this out: we still await a proper study of Shakespeare's use of Ovid). Peter G. Phialas also accepts the conventional sequence of *The Comedy of Errors, The Taming of the Shrew,* and *The Two Gentlemen of Verona* on the grounds of the relative emphasis upon wooing and romantic love' between the three plays. B. O. Bonazza's highly schematic analysis of four kinds of plot-structure in the same sequence of plays, 'to follow the steps in his progress from tentative experimentation to full competence', is particularly vulnerable to the two principal objections to which all such reconstructions are open, namely the circular reasoning which assumes what it sets out to prove by approaching the plays in a certain order, and the supposition that Shakespeare's artistic growth necessarily followed the orderly progression of the critic's logic. Bonazza's argument is also considerably weakened by his omission of *The Taming of the Shrew.* Whatever grouping of these early comedies is adopted, it is more useful as a framework for comparison and mutual illumination than as a reliable indication of Shakespeare's development. There is general agreement, however, with Charlton's estimate of *A Midsummer Night's Dream* as 'Shakespeare's first masterpiece' and the crowning achievement of the early comedies.

The study of Shakespeare's work as a whole must, of course, take account of both the continuity and the development of his art, and most critics of the early comedies have observed in them the emergence of what were to become major characteristics of their successors. But beginning with Charlton, whose book is an 'attempt to trace in Shakespeare's comedies the growth of his "comic idea"', there has been a persistent tendency in dealing with the evolution of Shakespearian comedy to relegate the first group of plays to the status of preliminary and only partially successful drafts for the incontestably superior plays that were to follow them, as though Shakespeare at the start of his career was trying imperfectly to do the same kind of thing he later did so well. Terms such as 'immature' and 'experimental', so frequently applied to the early comedies, have tended to obscure and undervalue their intrinsic qualities.

Of late, however, there are signs that criticism is turning from this retrospective view of the early plays, in favour of an approach through their antecedents in both learned and popular forms. Thanks to T. W. Baldwin's indefatigable researches, we are now aware that the Elizabethan school curriculum enabled Shakespeare to begin his career already well versed in the principles of dramatic composition, although we may not go all the way with Baldwin's conviction that Shakespeare practised the regular five-act structure as expounded by the Renaissance commentators on Terentian comedy. Apart from his academic models, Shakespeare's debts to contemporary dramatists in his early comedies include none greater than that to the sophisticated court dramatist John Lyly, and the relationship between them has been explored in detail by G. K. Hunter, and more briefly outlined by Marco Mincoff. Geoffrey Bullough's indispensable edition of the principal sources allows us to judge for ourselves the remarkable adroitness with which from the beginning of his career Shakespeare was adapting materials to his own purposes. The image of the early Shakespeare which emerges from these studies bears little resemblance to that of a novice working with crude or elementary skills. Sophistication and complexity are already the notable features of the early comedies, and A. C. Hamilton summarizes what we can recognize if we are not prejudiced by our admiration for the later achievements of Shakespearian comedy, namely that 'the subtlety and comprehensiveness of Shakespeare's dramatic genius are present from the beginning of his life as a writer.'

Charlton's antithesis between 'classical' and 'romantic' comedy, which is the basis of his approach to the plays, was the first real attempt to define the kind of comedy we call Shakespearian, to understand its conventions, and to describe its characteristics. Following Charlton, E. C. Pettet has provided a fuller introduction to the romance tradition underlying the comedies, and Nevill Coghill has traced their non-classical character to medieval Christian ideas of comedy. But the most original modern approaches to Shakespearian comedy are those of Northrop Frye and C. L. Barber. Both are concerned with a conception of comic form more highly developed than a rudimentary interest in plot and character. Frye regards the conventions of comedy as structural patterns related to an archetypal ritual celebration of the victory of summer over winter, life over death. He finds that Shakespeare's 'dramatic instinct' led him to shape his material into these conventional patterns, which organize human experience comprehensively and inclusively. Frye therefore tends to treat the plays as artefacts divorced from reality, contained within the structural patterns that give form and meaning to the dramatic actions. Barber's interpretation is related to Frye's in deriving comic structure from patterns of ritual celebration, but his approach is more specifically historical in its 'exploration of the way the social form of Elizabethan holidays contributed to the dramatic form of festive comedy'. He finds in the traditional pastimes and merry-making customs of Shakespeare's England a natural kinship to the 'saturnalian pattern' of the comedies, with their 'basic movement through release to clarification'. Alongside the academic and courtly models, therefore, the influence and meaning of many traditional kinds of games, pageants and revelry must be included in our awareness of the elements that compose Shakespearian comedy. Edward Berry, on the other hand, relates the theories of modern anthropology concerning the rites of passage from adolescence to maturity to Elizabethan social practice and the progression of a Shakespeare comedy.

Modern criticism generally endorses Bertrand Evans's observation that in Shakespeare's early comedies 'technique itself
occupies a proportionately large place in the total work'. If this is
a genuine sign of the beginner, it also displays what H. F. Brooks
points out as 'the command he shows, from the very outset of his
career as a playwright, of the elements of dramatic construction'.
For some critics, dexterity in plotting is a relatively humble
mechanical skill; Charlton, for instance, saw Shakespeare in his
'classical' comedies as submitting himself to a discipline 'which,
however uncongenial to the spirit, was a salutary apprenticeship
to the mechanics of play-building'. One suspects that the spirit
to which it is 'uncongenial' in this case is the critic's and not
Shakespeare's; conceived as the prosaic carpentry of fitting a
number of scenes together, structural technique is somewhat
beneath the attention of the critic who wishes to dwell upon the
higher beauties of poetic vision. Hence Charlton's evident distaste for the 'classical' kind of comedy represented in his view by
The Comedy of Errors and *The Taming of the Shrew*, in which clever
intrigue associates ingenious plotting with a low moral tone. But
of course Shakespeare's virtuosity in the art of plotting is not
confined to the so-called classical plays; it is evident throughout
his early comedies, and is nowhere more apparent than in *A
Midsummer Night's Dream*. Moreover, it is far more than a matter
of 'technical expertness in plotting', in the sense that Charlton
uses that phrase. 'The supreme power manifest in Shakespeare's
art of dramatic construction is the combinative power,' writes
H. F. Brooks, referring to his skill in selecting 'great significant
patterns' and in relating them analogously to each other. The
study of Shakespeare's structural techniques in the early comedies
is therefore not merely a matter of observing the ingenious
complication and resolution of an intricate plot, but involves an
understanding of the ways in which conventional motifs are
employed, and of the relationship between different elements in
the total design. Shakespeare's indebtedness to the conventions
of Latin and Italianate comedy is amply illustrated in Leo Salingar's
authoritative account of this literary tradition.

THE PLAYS

Emphasis upon the importance of structural design is particularly
evident in modern interpretations of those two comedies which
Charlton considered as Shakespeare's 'recoil from romanticism',

The Comedy of Errors and *The Taming of the Shrew*. In the former, which may well have been Shakespeare's first comedy, and which is certainly his most classical in the sense that the main plot is derived from Plautus, Charlton noted that by doubling the set of twins in the source 'the plot becomes a sort of mathematical exhibition of the maximum number of erroneous combinations of four people in pairs'. Technical ingenuity of this kind was for Charlton of a very low order of artistic merit, and he regarded the play as a farce, in which 'the general temper of the life depicted' is 'crude, coarse, and brutal'. In treating the 'romantic' story of Aegeon and the love interest centred upon Luciana as 'alien' and 'incongruous' elements, Charlton was oblivious to the vital aspect of Shakespeare's structural method which concerns his skill in weaving disparate elements into a new whole. As Phialas notes, *The Comedy of Errors* 'shows his general predilection for combining multiple actions into mutually qualifying relationships'. Moreover, Madeleine Doran has made the point that 'it may have seemed to Renaissance dramatists that their romantic plots were less unclassical than we think of them', and therefore that 'Shakespeare, in having the parents as well as the children "lost" and discovered is only elaborating a familiar pattern'. This elaboration of the original Plautine plot, particularly when it is considered in connection with the play's extensive references to St. Paul's dealings with the Ephesians (explored by T. W. Baldwin), gives to the play a more substantial kind of interest than the term 'farce' suggests, and thus provides an instructive example of the relationship between structural design and meaning. 'His play deepens from farce', writes Geoffrey Bullough, 'touching on the relations of husbands and wives, parents and children, in a moralizing way', and, while this last phrase seems to go too far in the opposite direction, we can surely endorse Foakes's view, expressed in the Introduction to his edition, that 'it does more than merely provoke laughter, or release us temporarily from inhibitions and custom into a world free as a child's affording delight and freshening us up. It also invites compassion, a measure of sympathy, and a deeper response to the disruption of social and family relationships which the action brings about'.

Charlton was too busy with what he called the 'rollickingly anti-romantic' spirit of *The Taming of the Shrew* to notice the subtlety of a dramatic structure to which G. R. Hibbard pays tribute in his Introduction: 'It is no exaggeration to say that the first audience to witness a performance of the play . . . were seeing the most elaborately and skilfully designed comedy that had yet appeared on the English stage'. And apart from the other arguments concerning the relationship between Shakespeare's play and the anonymous *The Taming of a Shrew* (which many, but by no means all, scholars now regard as a corrupted version of Shakespeare's play), Richard Hosley makes a powerful point about the structural adroitness it displays: 'It is doubtful whether by 1594 any English dramatist other than Shakespeare was sufficiently skilled in plot-construction to write such a carefully and subtly integrated triple-action play.' At least, as C. C. Seronsy writes, 'agreement among Shakespearian editors and critics is well-nigh universal that in *The Taming of the Shrew* the three plot strands of shrew-taming, loving intrigue or "supposes", and induction are interwoven with great skill and that Shakespeare, as presumable author, has brought them into a unity far superior to that achieved by the anonymous contemporary play *The Taming of a Shrew*'. Here again it is Shakespeare's ability to bring different kinds of conventional material into significant relationship with each other which critics regard as the essence of his technique in this comedy. The induction was a familiar Elizabethan device for creating two levels of dramatic reality, but by making the trick played upon Christopher Sly turn upon what T. N. Greenfield terms 'an experiment in human nature' in which Sly 'is a part of a comic juxtaposition of two contrasting worlds . . . the unimaginative subject in a test of the power of the imagination', Shakespeare was creating an image of the relationship between the spectator and the play. 'Shakespeare's particular emphasis brings his Induction into an organic relationship with the main play', says Greenfield; 'the contrast between the literal world of Sly and the world of dramatic poetry is emphatic and meaningful'. Such a self-conscious reflection upon his own art anticipates Shakespeare's use in *A Midsummer Night's Dream* of that other Elizabethan convention of double illusion, the play-within-the-play, and indeed Sly has more than a little in common with Bottom. Seronsy, however, points out that the induction is even more closely related to the double plot of the main play in terms of the transformations of character that take place in each, a perception conveniently summarized by Hosley, who notes that 'taken together, the three actions constitute a complex of compared and contrasted poses and "supposes" '. The source of the plot of Bianca's wooing is the earlier Elizabethan comedy *Supposes*, Gascoigne's translation of a play by Ariosto, and Seronsy shows us how the idea of 'supposes' is the link between Sly's metamorphosis into a lord, the disguises and mistaken identities of the Bianca plot, and the method by which Petruchio supposes or assumes 'qualities in Katherina that no one else, possibly even the shrew herself, ever suspects', until she discovers them in herself. Thus, in Hibbard's words, 'whether at the elementary and obvious level of a transformation of the outward appearance, such as Lucentio and Tranio undergo, or at the deeper one of a psychological change like Katherina's, this idea runs all through the play'. *The Taming of the Shrew* has inevitably attracted the interest of feminist critics, such as Coppélia Kahn, who sees the play as a satire on man's urge to dominate women. More shrewdly, Ann Thompson examines the ironies and ambiguities by which directors and performers undercut or contradict the surface meaning of the text.

As with *The Comedy of Errors*, therefore, an analysis of the play's structural method has important implications for its interpretation. There is clearly more to it than Charlton suggests by treating it simply as a knockabout farce. 'Naturally,' wrote Charlton, 'a tale of taming makes both the tamer and the tamed more like dwellers in a menagerie than in the polite world.' But as we have seen, the shrew plot cannot be isolated from the total design, which directs our interest to a series of external and internal transformations. The coarseness and brutality of the traditional shrew-taming has been humanized, as Petruchio relies, not on physical force, but on a subtler psychological approach to convince Kate that she is not what she seems. The play is no less funny seen in this way, but it is considerably more interesting.

Of the five early comedies, *The Two Gentlemen of Verona* is the one unanimously declared a failure. Opinions differ only on the reasons for the disaster, and these have not been developed much further since Charlton's diagnosis that 'Shakespeare's first attempt to make romantic comedy had only succeeded so far that it had unexpectedly and inadvertently made romance comic'. Charlton's account of the disaster makes hilarious reading at Shakespeare's expense; there is just the possibility, however, as Clifford Leech and A. C. Hamilton believe, that the dissolution of romance into comedy was neither unexpected nor inadvertent, but that Shakespeare was in control and quite deliberately ridiculing the extravagances of the romantic code of behaviour upon which his plot is based. J. F. Danby, on the other hand, represents the school of interpretation which believes that a better understanding of the conventions will solve some at least of the difficulties in the play.

Certainly a great deal of the overt mockery comes from the two clowns, whose function reflects one of the more successful aspects of the play's dramatic structure. H. F. Brooks observes that 'Shakespeare, in the parts he has given to Speed and Launce, is developing his play by means of comic parallels that illustrate and extend his themes', and his essay is a perceptive analysis of the way in which the clowns (and the dog) are used to burlesque the situations of the main plot. We may not therefore agree with Charlton that 'both Launce and Speed come into the play for no reason whatever but to be unmistakably dolts', yet he does suggest an unfortunate consequence of this comic parallelism upon the romantic hero Valentine: 'one begins to feel that it will be extremely difficult to make a hero of a man who is proved to be duller of wit than the patent idiots of the piece'. Stanley Wells finds that the basic failure of the play 'arises from the fact that Shakespeare is still a tyro in dramatic craftsmanship', and more specifically that 'the organic deficiencies of the play are the result of Shakespeare's failure to devise a plot which will enable characters conceived within the conventions of romantic love to behave in a manner compatible with these conventions'. The structural method of juxtaposing different elements, which we have seen as a characteristic of the early comedies, here seems to have created the difficulties that these critics find with the play; for the composition of the play not only concerns the parallels between masters and servants, but also turns upon the conventional antithesis of the rival claims of love and friendship, and upon the 'balancing of character against character and situation against situation' described by Norman Sanders in his edition. As Bullough points out, the influence of Lyly is apparent 'in the dramatic use of the courtly and amorous code', and in the symmetries of character relationship. But G. K. Hunter observes that 'this Lylian kind of structure will, however, only work when the characters are as simple as Lyly's', and that Proteus is conceived too psychologically for the balance of conflicting ideals to be preserved in the notorious final scene. This assumes, of course, that we are not meant to laugh at that point. Inga-Stina Ewbank directs our attention to the rhetorical artifice of the play, and finds in it 'an awareness that conventionalized language, like conventionalized behaviour, may be false', but also a failure in the last scene to make the language adequate to the depth of feeling. 'Cool, reticent and somewhat rueful' is how Alexander Leggatt summarizes the play's effect in his elegant and un-dogmatic account of love in the comedies.

When Charlton referred to 'the insouciant romantic formless-ness' of *Love's Labour's Lost*, he meant that 'it is deficient in plot and characterization. There is little story in it. Its situations do not present successive incidents in an ordered plot'. In fact none of the early comedies shows more clearly the principles of Shakespeare's structural technique, for, as M. C. Bradbrook says, 'the contrast of different characters in terms of their different idiom, played off or chiming in together, constitutes the "form" of the comedy'. And C. L. Barber points out that 'what is striking about *Love's Labour's Lost* is how *little* Shakespeare used exciting action, story, or conflict, how far he went in the direction of making the piece a set exhibition of pastimes and games . . . story interest is not the point: Shakespeare is presenting a series of wooing games, not a story'.

In the absence of a story in the play, several attempts have been made in the past to remedy the deficiency by discovering a story behind the play, in the form of covert allusions to court rivalries. Much ingenuity has been devoted to identifying the historical 'originals' of the *dramatis personae*, none more confidently than by Frances Yates, who declared more than fifty years ago that 'everyone is agreed that *Love's Labour's Lost* is the most topical of all Shakespeare's plays, that it bristles with allusions to con-temporary events and living persons. . . . I think one may say that this theory is now more or less generally accepted. The studious young men in the play can be interpreted as representing either the Raleigh group, immersed in their studies, or the Essex–Southampton group who laugh at schemes of that kind'. A theory that permits two such quite contrary interpretations arouses suspicions about the validity of either, but for a refutation of the textual and historical basis of the theory, Strathmann's article should be consulted. As Hamilton observes, 'the characters most suspected of historical originals are the most conventional literary types'. Alfred Harbage, in his edition, roundly dismisses such theories: 'none of them carries conviction except to those under the hypnosis induced by the shimmering nature of the evidence. A few suggestive phrases in the play there certainly are, but neither the characters nor the episodes resemble in the least the persons and events they are supposed to shadow forth'.

The elaborate design of the play, as most modern critics describe it, rests upon the contrapuntal relationships of the various groups of characters—courtiers, academics, and rustics—and the sophistication and artifice of the design corresponds to the stylistic self-consciousness of the language; in Barber's words, 'the effect is that each social level and type is making sport with words in an appropriate way, just as the lord's infatuation with the ladies is paralleled by Costard's and then Armado's attentions to Jaquenetta'. Such a skilfully patterned structure might almost be enjoyed for its own sake, as Harley Granville-Barker suggests: 'We must think of it all in terms of music, of contrasts in tone and tune, rhythm and the breaking of rhythm. . . . All plays exist, plots and character schemes beside, as schemes of sound, as shifting pictures, in decoration of thought and phrase, and the less their dependence on plot or conflict of character the more must they depend on such means to beauty and charm. . . . We are, indeed, never very far from the formalities of song and dance.' And following Granville-Barker, Bobbyann Roesen (Anne Barton) finds that 'the quality of the whole is very much that of a musical composition, an inexorable movement forward, the appearance and reappearance in the fabric of the play of certain important themes, forcing the harmony into a series of coherent resolutions consistent with each other and with the drama as a whole'. But those 'certain important themes' concern the very idea of artifice for its own sake, divorced from reality: 'it is the most artificial of all Shakespeare's comedies', wrote Bradbrook, 'and comes nearer than any other to containing a manifesto against artifice'. The influence of Lyly upon the courtly mode of the comedy and its elaborate symmetries is patent, although G. K. Hunter notes an essential difference in *Love's Labour's Lost*, which is 'concerned, as Lyly's never are, with "placing" or judging wit and cultivation in terms which are outside these values themselves'. And in this critical awareness of the limits of artifice, itself an added dimension to the drama of self-conscious sophistication, Cyrus Hoy finds 'the basic pattern of Shakespearian comedy: a pattern which consists in a movement from the artificial to the natural, always with the objective of finding oneself'. Such artifice in *Love's Labour's Lost* is related by Rosalie L. Colie to the conventions of the love sonnet, 'so that we accept the less programmatic, however artificial and stylized it may be, as the truer to some unexplained "reality".' In his edition of the play, John Kerrigan also highlights its concern with the artifice of playmaking. 'Not about French politics, and still less about "the school of night"', he writes, '*Love's Labour's Lost* investigates drama, and, in doing so, it inquires into the character of that sociable, sophisticated, and essentially dramatic animal, man.'

By common consent, *A Midsummer Night's Dream* is not only the most perfectly constructed of the early comedies, it is also the last of them and seems to occupy a special position in Shakespeare's development, as his first major triumph. Even Charlton was disposed to spare a few words of praise for its structural beauty, although not without the characteristically slighting reference to 'technical expertness in plotting'; 'the unity of the comic idea, not the joinery of episodes, is what makes the greatness of *A Midsummer Night's Dream*'. As we have seen, in more recent appraisals of the preceding comedies, this is a distinction without a difference as far as Shakespeare's methods of composition are concerned. David P. Young's comprehensive study of the play describes its construction in words that might well be applied to the aim, if not always the achievement, of Shakespeare's methods from the beginning of his career: 'the particular quality of his achievement in this case seems to have stemmed from his ability to bring a great variety of comic materials into a complete harmony, a synthesis or fusion by which he was able to make them his own'. 'Three contrasted worlds', writes Bradbrook,'—the lovers', the rustics', and the fairies'—have each their own idiom and their own codes, but in the woods of Athens . . . divided worlds meet and intermingle . . . *A Midsummer Night's Dream* combines in the most paradoxical way the natural and to Elizabethan eyes pastoral and humble beauty of the woodland and its fairies with the highly sophisticated pattern of the lovers' quarrel and the straight burlesque provided by the loves of Pyramus and Thisbe'. Even single elements of the play reflect Shakespeare's synthesizing and transforming power: the fairies, for instance, derive from a fusion of Ovidian mythology and English folklore. The background to Shakespeare's mutation of the dangerous fairies of rustic superstition into mischievous but benevolent 'spirits of another sort' has been studied by M. N. Latham and more recently by K. M. Briggs. 'They do illustrate the rich traditional meanings available in the materials Shakespeare was handling', as Barber says.

Of one of the play's most celebrated confrontations between contrasting worlds, described by Barber as 'the climax of the polyphonic interplay', David P. Young writes, 'as Bottom meets Titania, analogies begin to surround them: the popular stage joins hands with the world of court entertainment; folklore is introduced to myth; grossness chats with refinement; bestiality dwells with spirituality'. The play therefore proclaims through the analogies of its structure, as well as through the title and the incidents of its plot, the transforming power of the imagination, which most critics regard as its central preoccupation. 'The poet's confident assertion of the transforming power of the poetic imagination, in a play that is a testimony of that power,' says A. C. Hamilton, 'balances the dramatist's confidence in his craft that allows him the mockery of the poetic imagination in the Pyramus and Thisbe interlude.' Barber expands the point: 'the consciousness of the creative or poetic act itself, which pervades the main action, explains the subject matter of the burlesque accompaniment provided by the clowns . . . the clowns provide a broad burlesque of the mimetic impulse to become something by acting it, the impulse which in the main action is fulfilled by imagination and understood by humor'. And R. W. Dent emphasizes the importance of the last act of the play, with Theseus's speech as the prelude to the play-within-the-play: 'the heart of the comedy, its most pervasive unifying element, is the partially contrasting role of imagination in love and in art'. John Russell Brown also notes the structural analogy between the lovers' experiences and our own perception of the play, mirrored in burlesque fashion by the Pyramus and Thisbe interlude: 'Shakespeare was deeply concerned with the ways in which actors and audience accept the "truth" of dramatic illusion, and, as a poet, he saw in these relationships an image of man's recognition of imagined truths.'

Critics have therefore found in the highly-wrought dramatic structure Shakespeare's own reflections on his art; David Young, for instance, asks, 'may not this play, since it contains an inner play and discussions of drama, poetry, and the imagination, represent a very conscious effort on the part of the dramatist to advance the scope and level of his art and thus be a vital source for our understanding of Shakespeare's own ideas about the character and purpose of his art?' R. W. Dent calls it 'Shakespeare's closest approximation to a "Defense of Dramatic Poesy" in general'. So considered, A. C. Hamilton says, 'the play suggests Shakespeare's awareness of the rounding out of the first stage of his works'.

The emphasis of modern criticism upon the structural skill displayed by the early comedies has not been a limited interest in the mere technicalities of Shakespeare's art, but a recognition of his ability to combine conventional meanings. There are no better illustrations of this than the two comedies which, following Charlton, E. C. Pettet found to be 'the polar opposite of Shakespeare's romantic comedies'. Yet far from being antithetical to Shakespeare's characteristic preoccupations in comedy, *The Comedy of Errors* and *The Taming of the Shrew* have both been shown to exemplify in more than rudimentary form the abiding interests of Shakespearian comedy. The motif of mistaken identity which is the cause of so much hilarious confusion in *The Comedy of Errors* is one of the simplest of all comic devices, but Shakespeare exploits it to penetrate the more fundamental and disturbing questions of personal identity itself. The strange coincidence of identical twins presents the problem of identity most acutely, for, as Harry Levin observes, 'duplication, in particular, seems an affront to human dignity (one is almost tempted to call it a loss of face)—to be always mistaken for, to be indistinguishable from, somebody else'. Moreover, while the resultant errors in the play provide laughter for us, their victims speak of madness and hallucination, as Harold Brooks points out: 'mistakes of identity all but destroy relationship, and loss of relationship calls true identity in question; the chief persons suspect themselves or are suspected of insanity, or of being possessed, surrounded, or assailed by supernatural powers— madness or demoniac possession would be the eclipse of the true self, and sorcery might overwhelm it'. 'Real horror attaches to the notion of the *complete* identity of two human beings', says G. R. Elliott; 'all normal persons (and especially Shakespeare) set so much store by human individuality that they shrink from the thought of its being submerged. . . . And *The Comedy of Errors* has a note of real weirdness just when its mirth is keenest.' 'Yet,'

Brooks adds, 'the hazard of metamorphosis and of the loss of present identity is also the way to fresh or restored relationship.'

Shakespeare did not introduce identical twins again until *Twelfth Night*, but his comedies employ the device of mistaken identity, and the pattern of loss and recovery, which together form the action of *The Comedy of Errors*. The fact that Cyrus Hoy is writing with particular reference to *Love's Labour's Lost* when he describes the typical movement of Shakespearian comedy as having 'the objective of finding oneself' serves to corroborate the significance of *The Comedy of Errors*.

This profounder conception of identity has also been noticed in *The Taming of the Shrew* in terms of the unifying motif of 'supposes' analysed by Seronsy. Writing on Katherina's transformation of character, Bullough remarks that 'a mistake in identity is after all less deeply comic than one in assessing a person's nature. *The Taming of the Shrew* shows that Shakespeare was already moving from the outer world of appearances and situation to the inner world of character and ethical implication'. The theme of identity is here treated in relation to another characteristic preoccupation of Shakespearian comedy, which Hibbard describes as 'the notion of metamorphosis'. The transformation of Katherina, as Seronsy notes, is 'an interior one', revealing, in Hibbard's words, that 'Shakespeare is already very much interested, in this play, in the working of the imagination, which he was to explore further in *A Midsummer Night's Dream*'. Moreover, as Greenfield has shown, in its use of the induction *The Taming of the Shrew* makes a typically Shakespearian association between the metamorphic power of the imagination and the art of theatrical illusion.

In the light of these recent interpretations, therefore, the radical distinctions drawn by Charlton between Shakespeare's 'classical' and 'romantic' comedies are seen to be misleading and inadequate. Levin's conclusion, that 'even within the venal and angular precincts of Latinate comedy, he can make us aware of unpathed waters, undreamed shores, and things in heaven and earth that philosophy has not fathomed', represents the emphasis of modern criticism upon Shakespeare's ability to transform convention, and upon the remarkable continuity of the comedies. The other comedies of the early group apply the same preoccupations with true and false identity, metamorphosis, and illusion to the conventions of courtly behaviour, especially in love. Norman Sanders notes the interesting use of disguise in *The Two Gentlemen of Verona*, for instance, 'which makes Julia physically what Proteus is both nominally and morally: that is, a shape-changer, a metamorphosis'. Cyrus Hoy's summary of Shakespeare's comic 'objective', in the context of *Love's Labour's Lost*, 'to find oneself is to escape from artificiality into the natural, to leave off deceiving oneself by setting about to know oneself', is as relevant to *The Taming of the Shrew* as it is to *The Two Gentlemen of Verona*, which, as Phialas says, deals with 'the opposition between the conventions or poetics of love and the realistic or matter-of-fact concept of it'. Moreover, this 'escape from the artificial into the natural' as a process of psychological reorientation is often accompanied by a corresponding physical movement, from the court world to the pastoral. Northrop Frye sees this pattern adumbrated in *The Two Gentlemen of Verona*, where 'the action of the comedy begins in a world represented as a normal world, moves into the green world, goes into a metamorphosis there in which the comic resolution is achieved, and returns to the normal world', and in the forest where the characters assemble for the notorious dénouement of this play he finds 'the embryonic form of the fairy world of *A Midsummer Night's Dream*'. A similar preoccupation in *Love's Labour's Lost* is described by Bobbyann Roesen in terms of the movement from the world of enclosed artifice to the wider perspectives of reality. 'Through *Love's Labour's Lost*', she writes, 'the play has been a symbol of illusion, of delightful unreality, the masque of Muscovites, or the pageant of the Nine Worthies, and now it becomes apparent that there was a further level of illusion above that of the plays within the play. The world of that illusion has enchanted us; it has been possessed of a haunting beauty, the clear loveliness of the landscapes in the closing song. But Shakespeare insists that it cannot take the place of reality itself, and should not be made to'.

Not unexpectedly, these interrelated themes of identity, metamorphosis, and the role of imagination have been most extensively studied in *A Midsummer Night's Dream*, for of the early comedies it is the play that treats them most fully, and that develops furthest what J. L. Calderwood calls 'Shakespeare's continuing exploration of the nature, function, and value of art'. 'He does seem unusually and consistently aware', Calderwood writes, 'of how the illusions foisted upon and generated by characters within the play are related to the master illusion which is the play, and which is similarly foisted upon and generated by the audience.' The episode which has attracted much attention in this respect is Theseus's speech and Hippolyta's reply at the beginning of the last act, after the lovers' 'dream' and before the interlude of Pyramus and Thisbe, for Theseus specifically associates the lover's imagination with that of the poet, not to mention the lunatic. It is a focal point for two divergent approaches to the play, as Calderwood points out: 'criticism of *A Midsummer Night's Dream* has on the whole followed the contrasting leads of Theseus and Hippolyta in their responses to the lovers' story of the night.'

Critics in the camp of Theseus share his allegiance to the values of reason as opposed to those of imagination; moreover they tend to assume that Theseus is the spokesman of Shakespeare's point of view. Thus Charlton: 'Sanity, cool reason, common sense, is the pledge of Theseus against the undue ravages of fancy and of sentiment in human nature. . . . With Theseus, the philosophy of comedy is finding its voice, and his "cool reason" is its prevailing spirit.' Here certainly is Charlton's 'recoil from romanticism'. Marco Mincoff also regards Theseus as 'a choric figure expounding objective values', values which he says are reflected in 'the mature, rational, unswerving love of Theseus and Hippolyta', that serves 'as a frame to the whole play and a standard by which love is to be measured'. In a learned but sometimes overburdened interpretation of the play's courtly symbolism, Paul A. Olson manages to side with Theseus's rationalism without slighting the value of poetic imagination, by suggesting that 'Theseus makes some implicit distinctions between the poet and his mad colleagues. It is only lovers and madmen who are said to exhibit fantasies which descend beyond the comprehension of reason. Implicitly, poets, however much they are possessed by a *furor poeticus*, may deal in imaginings apprehensible in more rational terms'. One wishes that Shakespeare (or Theseus) had not left such an important point merely 'implicit'.

'If we take our stand shoulder to shoulder with Theseus,' writes Barber, 'the play can be an agency for distinguishing what is merely "apprehensible" from what is "comprehended".' But, as he goes on to remind us, Theseus 'does not quite have the last word . . . his position is only one stage in a dialectic'. 'Hippolyta supplies the necessary corrective', writes Stanley Wells; 'she can conceive what the lovers have been through and her use of the word "transfigured" helps to suggest that the woodland scenes represent for them a genuine shaping experience.' R. W. Dent and David Young recognize that this 'dialectic' is a reflection of certain ambivalences within the Elizabethan conception of the imagination (their discussion of the relevant background should be supplemented by reference to Rossky's article). Dent suggests that 'being good Elizabethans, we may well remember that not all dreams are the product of divided, passion-stimulated, never-sleeping imagination. Some dreams are divine revelations of truth, however difficult to expound.' Young's point is that 'anyone who wished to undertake a defense of the imagination might easily have done so, drawing upon the inherent contradiction in contemporary theories between the feeling that imagination was deceitful and destructive, and the creative powers commonly granted it as part of the epistemological hierarchy'.

As for Theseus, Dent indicates the irony undermining his position: 'Himself a creation from "antique fable" unconsciously involved in "fairy toys", Theseus believes in neither. . . . A noble governor, quite willing to accept poetry for a wedding-night pastime and to acknowledge it as the well-intended offering of his faithful subjects, he at no time implies any respect for it. Shakespeare's entire play implies a contrary view, despite the humility of its epilogue.' J. L. Calderwood similarly believes that 'the modesty of Shakespeare's epilogue is transformed by humorous irony into something of this order: "If it makes you feel more 'reasonable', adopt Theseus's view and regard the play as an idle dream—at best a way of passing the time; but, like the lovers who also converted drama into dream, whether you realize it or not, you have experienced something here of enduring value and with a reality of its own".'

'A major kind of knowledge which *A Midsummer Night's Dream* makes available to its audience', says Calderwood, 'is the inner forms and impulses of the human mind itself—the tricks and shaping fantasies of strong imagination and the forces that direct it, but the range and limits of cool reason as well. The mind that comes to focus upon the play, and especially upon the drama of the forest, comes to focus upon itself. . . . The theatrical experience made possible by the play thus mirrors the fictional experience presented *in* the play.' It is above all in the significant ordering of this experience that we find the quality and value of the poetic imagination; in the words of David Young, 'the coherence and constancy are in the poet's art, and they spring from his consistent use of the metamorphic principle as a device not only for reflecting experience but for controlling it and expressing its unity.'

REFERENCES

TEXTS

Foakes, R. A. (ed.), *The Comedy of Errors* (Arden Shakespeare, London, 1962).

Jorgensen, Paul A. (ed.), *The Comedy of Errors* (Pelican Shakespeare, Baltimore, Md., 1964).

Levin, Harry (ed.), *The Comedy of Errors* (Signet Shakespeare, New York, 1965).

Wells, Stanley (ed.), *The Comedy of Errors* (New Penguin Shakespeare, Harmondsworth, 1972).

Heilman, Robert (ed.), *The Taming of the Shrew* (Signet Shakespeare, New York, 1966).

Hibbard, G. R. (ed.), *The Taming of the Shrew* (New Penguin Shakespeare, Harmondsworth, 1968).

Hosley, Richard (ed.), *The Taming of the Shrew* (Pelican Shakespeare, Baltimore, Md., 1964).

Morris, Brian (ed.), *The Taming of the Shrew* (Arden Shakespeare, London, 1981).

Oliver, H. J. (ed.), *The Taming of the Shrew* (Oxford Shakespeare, Oxford, 1982).

Thompson, Ann (ed.), *The Taming of the Shrew* (New Cambridge Shakespeare, Cambridge, 1984).

Evans, Bertrand (ed.), *The Two Gentlemen of Verona* (Signet Shakespeare, London, 1964).

Jackson, Berners A. W. (ed.), *The Two Gentlemen of Verona* (Pelican Shakespeare, Baltimore, Md., 1964).

Leech, Clifford (ed.), *The Two Gentlemen of Verona* (Arden Shakespeare, London, 1969).

Sanders, Norman (ed.), *The Two Gentlemen of Verona* (New Penguin Shakespeare, Harmondsworth, 1968).

Arthos, John (ed.), *Love's Labour's Lost* (Signet Shakespeare, New York, 1965).

David, Richard (ed.), *Love's Labour's Lost* (Arden Shakespeare, London, 1951).

Harbage, Alfred (ed.), *Love's Labour's Lost* (Pelican Shakespeare, Baltimore, Md., 1963).

Hibbard, G. R. (ed.), *Love's Labour's Lost* (Oxford Shakespeare, 1989).

Kerrigan, John (ed.), *Love's Labour's Lost* (New Penguin Shakespeare, Harmondsworth, 1982).

Brooks, Harold F. (ed.), *A Midsummer Night's Dream* (Arden Shakespeare, London, 1979).

Clemen, Wolfgang (ed.), *A Midsummer Night's Dream* (Signet Shakespeare, London, 1963).

Doran, Madeleine (ed.), *A Midsummer Night's Dream* (Pelican Shakespeare, Baltimore, Md., 1959).

Wells, Stanley (ed.), *A Midsummer Night's Dream* (New Penguin Shakespeare, Harmondsworth, 1967).

CRITICAL STUDIES AND COMMENTARY

Baldwin, T. W., *Shakespeare's Five-Act Structure* (Urbana, Ill., 1947).

Barber, C. L., *Shakespeare's Festive Comedy* (Princeton, NJ, 1959).

Berry, Edward, *Shakespeare's Comic Rites* (Cambridge, 1984).

Bonazza, B. O., *Shakespeare's Early Comedies* (The Hague, 1966).

Brooks, H. F., 'Themes and Structure in *The Comedy of Errors*', in *Early Shakespeare* (Stratford-upon-Avon Studies 3, ed. J. R. Brown and B. Harris, London, 1961), 54–71.

Bullough, Geoffrey (ed.), *Narrative and Dramatic Sources of Shakespeare*, vol. i (London, 1957).

Charlton, H. B., *Shakespearian Comedy* (London, 1939).

Coghill, Nevill, 'The Basis of Shakespearian Comedy', *Essays and Studies* (1950); reprinted in *Shakespeare Criticism 1935–1960*, ed. Anne Ridler (World's Classics, London, 1963), 201–27.

Evans, Bertrand, *Shakespeare's Comedies* (Oxford, 1960).

Frye, Northrop, 'The Argument of Comedy', *English Institute Essays 1948* (New York, 1949); reprinted in *Shakespeare: Modern Essays in Criticism*, ed. Leonard F. Dean (New York, 1957; 2nd edn., 1967), 79–89.

Hamilton, A. C., *The Early Shakespeare* (San Marino, Calif., 1967).

Hunter, G. K., *John Lyly: The Humanist as Courtier* (London, 1962).

Leggatt, Alexander, *Shakespeare's Comedy of Love* (London, 1974).

Mincoff, Marco, 'Shakespeare and Lyly', *Shakespeare Survey 14* (1961), 15–24.

Pettet, E. C., *Shakespeare and the Romance Tradition* (London, 1949).

Phialas, Peter G., *Shakespeare's Romantic Comedies* (Chapel Hill, NC, 1966).

Salingar, Leo, *Shakespeare and the Traditions of Comedy* (Cambridge, 1974).

Whitaker, Virgil K., *Shakespeare's Use of Learning* (San Marino, Calif., 1953).

THE PLAYS

Baldwin, T. W., *Shakspere's Five-Act Structure* (Urbana, Ill., 1947).

Bradbrook, Muriel C., *Shakespeare and Elizabethan Poetry* (London, 1951).

Briggs, K. M., *The Anatomy of Puck* (London, 1959).

Brooks, Harold F., 'Two Clowns in a Comedy (to say nothing of the Dog): Speed, Launce (and Crab) in *The Two Gentlemen of Verona*', *Essays and Studies* (1963), 91–100.

Brown, John Russell, *Shakespeare and His Comedies* (London, 1957; 2nd edn., 1962).

Bullough, Geoffrey (ed.), *Narrative and Dramatic Sources of Shakespeare*, vol. i (London, 1957).

Calderwood, J. L., '*A Midsummer Night's Dream*: The Illusion of Drama', *Modern Language Quarterly*, 26 (1965), 506–22.

Charlton, H. B., *Shakespearian Comedy* (London, 1938).

Colie, Rosalie L., *Shakespeare's Living Art* (Princeton, NJ, 1974).

Danby, J. F., 'Shakespeare Criticism and *The Two Gentlemen of Verona*', *Critical Quarterly*, 2 (1960), 309–21.

Dent, R. W., 'Imagination in *A Midsummer Night's Dream*', *Shakespeare Quarterly*, 15 (1964), 115–29.

Doran, Madeleine, *Endeavours of Art* (Madison, Wis., 1954).

Elliott, G. R., 'Weirdness in *The Comedy of Errors*', *University of Toronto Quarterly*, 60 (1939); reprinted in *Shakespeare's Comedies: An Anthology of Modern Criticism*, ed. Laurence Lerner (Penguin Shakespeare Library, Harmondsworth, 1968), 19–31.

Ewbank, Inga-Stina, ' "Were man but constant, he were perfect": Constancy and Consistency in *The Two Gentlemen of Verona*', in *Shakespearian Comedy* (Stratford-upon-Avon Studies 14, ed. M. Bradbury and D. J. Palmer, London, 1972), 31–57.

Granville-Barker, Harley, *Prefaces to Shakespeare*, First Series (London, 1927).

Greenfield, T. N., 'The Transformation of Christopher Sly', *Philological Quarterly*, 33 (1954), 34–42.

Hamilton, A. C., *The Early Shakespeare* (San Marino, Calif., 1967).

Hoy, Cyrus, '*Love's Labour's Lost* and the Nature of Comedy', *Shakespeare Quarterly*, 13 (1962), 31–40.

Kahn, Coppélia, *Man's Estate: Masculine Identity in Shakespeare* (Berkeley and Los Angeles, Calif., 1981).

Latham, M. W., *The Elizabethan Fairies* (New York, 1930).

Olson, Paul, A., '*A Midsummer Night's Dream* and the Meaning of Court Marriage', *ELH* 24 (1957), 95–119.

Phialas, Peter G., *Shakespeare's Romantic Comedies* (Chapel Hill, NC, 1966).

Roesen, Bobbyann, *'Love's Labour's Lost'*, *Shakespeare Quarterly*, 4 (1953), 411–26.

Rossky, W., 'Imagination in the English Renaissance: Psychology and Poetic', *Studies in the Renaissance*, 5 (1958), 49–78.

Seronsy, C. C., ' "Supposes" as a Unifying Theme in the *Taming of the Shrew'*, *Shakespeare Quarterly* 14 (1963), 15–30.

Strathmann, E. A., 'The Textual Evidence for "The School of Night" ', *Modern Language Notes*, 56 (1941), 176–86.

Wells, Stanley, 'The Failure of *The Two Gentlemen of Verona'*, *Shakespeare Jahrbuch*, 94 (1963), 161–73.

Yates, Frances A., *A Study of 'Love's Labour's Lost'* (Cambridge, 1936).

Young, David P., *Something of Great Constancy* (New Haven, Conn., 1966).

6 | The Middle Comedies

R. L. SMALLWOOD

Editions

When the late Gāmini Salgādo began his elegant discussion of criticism of the middle comedies for the first edition of this book, he could report only the partial availability of the five plays we are here concerned with in the new Arden and New Penguin editions. Not only are both these series now complete in their coverage of the comedies (as of almost everything else), but a revised version of the new Ardens is already in preparation and two new series, the New Cambridge and the Oxford, are already well advanced, though by chance only the New Cambridge has so far published editions of any of the middle comedies. The general scope of each of these series is described earlier in this volume (see Chapter 1); I offer here some brief remarks on the distinctive qualities of the texts relevant to this chapter.

John Russell Brown's new Arden edition of *The Merchant of Venice*, though in some ways a little dated, still offers a lively introduction with a sharp sense of the play in performance and an alertness to the idea of 'wealth' (monetary and spiritual) that later critics have developed further. W. Moelwyn Merchant's New Penguin edition, sound and readable as usual in this series, has interesting comment on the trial scene and makes a determined effort to keep Portia at the play's centre. Molly Mahood's New Cambridge edition provides good material on the play in its contemporary context, on attitudes to Venice and to Jews and usury, and also deals well with the play's afterlife in the ebbs and flows of response to its principal characters in the theatre.

Arthur Humphreys's new Arden *Much Ado about Nothing* is among the latest volumes in the series. Its long introduction offers helpful comment on the text (in particular the rather special characteristics of the quarto), on the sources, and on the style and form of the play, and presents an optimistic interpretation of 'the world of Messina', its mood and its relationships. The New Penguin, edited by R. A. Foakes, is brisk and sensible in its introduction and pithy (sometimes a little too pithy) in its notes. F. H. Mares's New Cambridge edition is generous in its introductory account of the play's theatre history, at least in Britain, and helpfully insinuates into its critical commentary a sense of changing responses to the play in past and present criticism.

H. J. Oliver's new Arden text of *The Merry Wives of Windsor* carefully argues the case for the now more or less generally accepted belief that the play was written in 1597 when the patron of Shakespeare's company, Lord Hunsdon, received his Garter Knighthood. In the New Penguin edition G. R. Hibbard fights a rearguard action for the older view that the play belongs just after the turn of the century, with the specific Garter references of Act V a survival from an entertainment provided by Shakespeare for an earlier occasion. Both editors write well on the play's social world.

The new Arden *As You Like It*, edited by Agnes Latham, is helpful on matters of text, dating, and sources (a particularly useful section here); the more directly critical portion of its introduction concentrates on analysis of the principal characters. H. J. Oliver's New Penguin considers the play in relation to its source in Lodge's *Rosalynde* and has helpful commentary, too, on its relation to the pastoral convention more generally, and to the convention of stage disguise.

The new Arden *Twelfth Night* of J. M. Lothian was posthumously completed by T. W. Craik, its introduction being very full on sources and analogues and offering a scene-by-scene analysis of the play on the ground that 'the reading of plays backwards is a kind of blasphemy against drama'. M. M. Mahood's New Penguin edition is particularly observant of the play's language. Its crisp and sensitive introduction is good too on mood and atmosphere. The New Cambridge edition by Elizabeth Story Donno concentrates on character analysis in its introduction; its stage history is well illustrated, with a distinct bias towards Stratford-upon-Avon in its later stages.

Among the many other single-play-per-volume editions, readers of this Guide will probably find the Signet series most useful for its generous extracts from the published criticism of several centuries. Less accessible pieces made available in the

Signet middle comedy editions include E. E. Stoll on Shylock, Lewis Carroll, Bernard Shaw, and W. H. Auden on *Much Ado about Nothing*, Max Beerbohm on *As You Like It*, and Charles Lamb on Malvolio.

Scholarly Studies

Two of the plays in this group have so far been the subject of volumes in the impressively thorough Garland series of annotated bibliographies. Jay Halio and Barbara C. Millard cover *As You Like It* and Thomas Wheeler *The Merchant of Venice*. The readiest way to recent textual scholarship on the comedies is via the *Textual Companion* to the Oxford Shakespeare by Stanley Wells and Gary Taylor. Though primarily concerned with their own textual and editorial decisions, the volume discusses and provides access to much recent textual work on these plays.

Another impressive achievement of Shakespeare scholarship in recent decades is Geoffrey Bullough's *Narrative and Dramatic Sources of Shakespeare* in eight monumental volumes which reprint all the direct sources and offer extracts from analogues, with a judicious discussion of Shakespeare's indebtedness to, and departures from, the texts that influenced him. *The Merchant of Venice* is dealt with in Volume I, the other four middle comedies in Volume II. Kenneth Muir's *The Sources of Shakespeare's Plays* provides briefer accounts of the adaptation of source material in these plays. More detailed studies of the sources and background of comedies in this group are C. T. Prouty's of *Much Ado about Nothing*, Marco Mincoff's of *As You Like It*, Robert C. Melzi's of *Twelfth Night*, and William Green's of *The Merry Wives of Windsor* (the last concerned not so much with sources—the play is virtually sourceless—as with the play's occasion). Although its principal thesis—that *Twelfth Night* was written and rehearsed in a matter of days for a special performance before Don Virginio Orsino, Duke of Bracciano, on Twelfth Night 1601, and that several of its characters reflect identifiable members of the Court—has by no means won general assent, Leslie Hotson's *The First Night of 'Twelfth Night'* also deserves mention here, for it provides much information on the background to the play's themes, setting, characters, and language.

The more general background to the comedies is the subject of Leo Salingar's *Shakespeare and the Traditions of Comedy*, which provides a full discussion of the classical and Italian models from which Shakespearian comedy derives. Nevill Coghill's 'The Basis of Shakespearian Comedy' locates the origins of Shakespearian comic form in the medieval biblical drama of man's redemption. E. C. Pettet's *Shakespeare and the Romance Tradition* remains useful for its discussion of a different, but equally important area of influence. Stanley Wells's essay 'Shakespeare and Romance' places *Twelfth Night* (among other plays outside the scope of this chapter) in this broader context. Here, however, as with Thomas McFarland's *Shakespeare's Pastoral Comedy* or David Young's *The Heart's Forest*, which examine some of Shakespeare's comedies in relation to the more general pastoral tradition of Renaissance literature, the more strictly 'scholarly' category is merging into the critical.

CRITICISM AND COMMENTARY

General

The proliferation of critical writing on comedy in general, on Shakespearian comedy, and on Shakespeare's comedies has in recent years been so enormous that any account of it within the present limits has necessarily to be rather brutal in its selectivity.

Students of Shakespearian comedy who wish to see it against the background of comedy considered more generally will find the collection *Comedy* edited by Wylie Sypher a useful starting point. It includes the classic pieces of Henri Bergson on 'Laughter' and George Meredith on 'Comedy' and a long essay by the editor on 'The Meanings of Comedy'. A broader selection of essays and extracts is in Robert W. Corrigan's *Comedy: Meaning and Form*. This includes a range of twentieth-century treatments of comedy both specific and theoretical (including Suzanne Langer's important comments from *Feeling and Form*) as well as some valuable earlier writing. Robert B. Heilman's *The Ways of the World: Comedy and Society* is a more discursive examination of a range of approaches to comic drama from Aristophanes to the present, with a good deal of attention to Shakespeare. Much briefer, and inevitably therefore more partial, but stimulating and readable, is Moelwyn Merchant's *Comedy* in the Critical Idiom series. Among studies that narrow their sights to the Shakespearian period, though not exclusively to Shakespeare, are Muriel Bradbrook's *The Growth and Structure of Elizabethan Comedy*, David Farley-Hills's *The Comic in Renaissance Comedy*, and John Weld's *Meaning in Comedy: Studies in Elizabethan Romantic Comedy*. Each of them treats a selection of Shakespeare's comedies against the background of the growth and development of Elizabethan comedy. Professor Bradbrook still provides the fullest sense of the historical context, in terms both of theatrical conditions and dramatic developments. Farley-Hills's opening essay offers some interesting broad perspectives on Elizabethan and Jacobean comedies (and on comedy more generally); the bulk of the book consists of essays on specific plays, mostly not Shakespearian. Weld is concerned essentially to provide an introduction to Elizabethan romantic comedy both in general terms and through a selection of specific texts. His stopping point is 1597 so that, apart from a concluding chapter on *The Merchant of Venice*, his work is useful mainly as background to the plays under review here.

In turning to criticism of Shakespearian comedy more specifically, one recalls Gāmini Salgādo's assertion, in the first edition of this Guide, that Northrop Frye's *A Natural Perspective* was the 'best book' ever written on Shakespearian comedy. With the benefit of another fifteen years' perspective, it is such terms as 'most influential' or 'seminal' that one would now tend to substitute for that brave value judgement. Certainly no one who wishes to understand modern thinking about Shakespearian comedy can afford to neglect Frye's book, or the essay 'The Argument of Comedy' of 1948 that heralded it and in many ways now seems to mark the beginning of serious criticism of the comedies. (Readers of this chapter who wish to sample the earlier critical tradition might most usefully do so through H. B. Charlton's *Shakespearian Comedy*, the counterpart for the comedies of Bradley's book on the tragedies and, like its great predecessor, approaching its subject mainly through character analysis. The same is true of another classic from this earlier period, John Palmer's *Shakespeare's Comic Characters*.) In a study that engages with all Shakespeare's comedies and romances, and with their origins in Greek New Comedy and the Roman dramatists Shakespeare would have studied at school, Frye defines many of the concepts now taken for granted in comedy criticism: the juxtaposition of a 'green' world and a normal world, the idea of identity lost and rediscovered, the relationship of comic patterns of separation and reunion, or of death and resurrection, to the seasonal cycle which brings spring after winter, the expulsion from the harmonious community that comedy celebrates of the egocentric, malevolent, anti-social individual. After Frye, theme and form replace character and style as the principal concerns of comedy criticism.

If Frye's work, with its broad brush strokes and bold general-izations, is perhaps receding a little into critical history, C. L. Barber's *Shakespeare's Festive Comedy* remains, thirty years after its first appearance, entirely current. Based on some of the same general assumptions about comedy as Frye's work, it sharpens their focus and adds an anthropological dimension by relating them to the tradition of social festival (May games, lords of misrule, mummings, and other seasonal and ritual celebrations) and examines several Shakespearian comedies against this back-ground, seeing in it, and in the plays, a recurrent pattern which moves, as he puts it, 'through release to clarification'. Although Barber's work starts from archetypal models, his comment on the plays themselves never becomes diffused or generalized. His work has recently been taken further (into a wider range of plays and a fuller examination of the background of social festivity) in the work of the French scholar François Laroque, whose *Shake-speare et la Fête* of 1988 is about to be published in English as *Shakespeare's Festive World*.

Approaching the comedies from the same general direction of social background is Edward I. Berry's sharply written and illuminating study *Shakespeare's Comic Rites*, which relates the comedies to Elizabethan social customs of initiation, courtship, and marriage, seeing the plays as recording the 'rites of passage' through the rituals of wooing of characters who pass in them from adolescence to adulthood and to that 'myth of romantic marriage that Shakespeare, more than any other writer, has perpetuated'. Refining and re-exploring ideas ultimately deriving from Frye is a long essay by Sherman Hawkins, 'The Two Worlds of Shakespearean Comedy'. Hawkins identifies a closed world and a green world (actual or latent) in all these plays, with comedy shaped by the movement of characters between the two. The closed world is 'a metaphor for the human heart. The force which knocks at its closed door is love.' The essay has, perhaps, a tendency to create too much unity among the divergencies of Shakespearian comedy, but its juxtapositions are apt and fre-quently illuminating.

The archetypal approach through mythology and anthropology moves into specifically Christian religious terms in the work of

Robert Grams Hunter and R. Chris Hassel. Hunter's *Shakespeare and the Comedy of Forgiveness* relates several of the comedies to the patterns of fifteenth- and early sixteenth-century moralities, with their erring Everyman figures, sinful, deserving condemnation, but finally penitent, forgiven, and saved. His concerns are mostly with the later comedies and romances, but there is an interesting chapter on the Claudio of *Much Ado About Nothing*. R. Chris Hassel's *Faith and Folly in Shakespeare's Romantic Comedies* examines the middle comedies in their contemporary Christian humanist context, bringing to bear on the plays the Pauline and Erasmian paradoxes of the reversals of wisdom and folly in a study that offers an instructive new dimension to the criticism of these plays.

Among the many recent general books on the middle comedies Alexander Leggatt's *Shakespeare's Comedy of Love* is perhaps the most consistently illuminating and helpful. It offers a chapter on each of the plays and though the starting point for each was 'some instance of tension between different kinds of style or dramatic idiom', the book makes no attempt to homogenize the comedies into a unity but instead celebrates the diversity of their exploration of the common theme of romantic love. Also focusing on love—'love's wealth', 'love's truth', 'love's order', and on the variety of Shakespeare's explorations of comic form—is John Russell Brown's rather older study *Shakespeare and His Comedies*, still worth looking at for the perceptive detail of its analyses of relationships in the plays and its occasional excursion into the theatrical implications of those analyses. Kenneth Muir's *Shakespeare's Comic Sequence* provides a chapter on each of the plays that is, as one would expect from this critic, a model of good sense and wisdom, unfussily presented and genuinely helpful. More quirky and challenging is Ralph Berry's *Shakespeare's Comedies: Explorations in Form*, which provides a far from optimistic reading of many of the comedies and thus a useful antidote (or irritant at least) to some current interpretations. Richard Levin's *Love and Society in Shakespearian Comedy* has similar aims. This is a crisply written and self-consciously unsentimental book, looking at the social relationships of the plays with an eye alert to tensions and imperfections, offering overall a strongly revisionist stance against the romantic-festive approach to the comedies. Bertrand Evans's *Shakespeare's Comedies* considers the plays exclusively from the point of view of Shakespeare's exploitation of discrepant levels of awareness among characters, with the audience always at the top of the tree of knowledge. The approach becomes mechanical at times, but the determined application of the formula creates many useful insights—among this group of plays perhaps especially for *Much Ado about Nothing* and *The Merry Wives of Windsor*.

If Barber's notion of comedy, that it takes its persons (and its audience) 'through release to clarification' is right, then one of its constant concerns is its capacity to effect change. Two studies connected with this metamorphosing aspect of the plays are Ruth Nevo's *Comic Transformations in Shakespeare* and William Carroll's *The Metamorphoses of Shakespearean Comedy*. Ruth Nevo's book is fundamentally about comic form and about Shakespeare's adaptation of his inheritance from Greek and Roman dramatists, above all his development of the process of 'turmoil' through which the fiction passes to transform initial incompleteness into the final fulfilment of the comedy ending. Carroll's book more directly treats a selection of the comedies as 'specimens of transformation', linking metamorphosis with love and its fulfilment and with the energies of comedy itself in an illuminating and fruitful argument.

A particular, indeed a defining, aspect of comedy is its happy ending. Stanley Wells's useful preliminary survey of 'Happy Endings in Shakespeare' has been taken further by a number of critics. R. S. White's *'Let Wonder Seem Familiar': Endings in Shakespeare's Romantic Vision* examines the conclusions to the comedies against the background of endings in Elizabethan prose romance and earlier Elizabethan comedy, and also as part of Shakespeare's 'continuing engagement with the problems of time'. This is a sensitive and valuable study, though in covering all the comedies and romances in a single short volume its treatment of individual plays is inevitably brief. Zvi Jagendorf looks at Shakespeare's comedy endings in relation to two other major seventeenth-century dramatists. His *The Happy End of Comedy: Jonson, Molière, and Shakespeare* is a stimulating short book, offering an introduction on the formal structure of comedy and a wide range of examples from many periods and media before its chapters on Jonson and Molière, and thus coming to Shakespeare with an illuminatingly various context already well established.

The concern with comic structure involved in the study of endings makes Philip Edwards's *Shakespeare and the Confines of*

Art relevant at this point. Edwards sees Shakespeare 'engaged in a continuous battle . . . against his own scepticism about the value of his art as a model of human behaviour'. Every play, seen in this light, becomes an experiment with its own form and the thesis produces some excellent commentary on the comedies and the whole idea of the 'happy ending', though only two of the middle comedies (*As You Like It* and *Twelfth Night*) are treated at any length. The same two endings are the subject of a splendid essay by Anne Barton. Her '*As You Like It* and *Twelfth Night*: Shakespeare's Sense of an Ending' argues (convincingly) that in all of Shakespeare's comedies up to *Twelfth Night* 'a retrospective view from the final scene is encouraged and alters our understanding of the play as a whole'. The 'tremor' of Jaques's departure from the ending of *As You Like It* is seen as drawing attention to, rather than undermining, the poise of the rest of the comic conclusion; in *Twelfth Night*, on the other hand, the juxtaposition of the romantic plot and the play's harsher elements shows Shakespeare beginning to 'unbuild his own comic form at the point of greatest vulnerability: the ending'. Though concentrating on the two plays of its title, this important essay has much to teach us about Shakespearian comedy more generally.

A useful essay that examines a number of characters from a range of comedies is R. A. Foakes's 'The Owl and the Cuckoo: Voices of Maturity in Shakespeare's Comedies'. It is the tone of compassion, tolerance, often moral authority or social responsibility that 'reminds us of the world of time outside the play' that interests Foakes here and he locates it in a surprisingly varied group: Jaques, Theseus, Beatrice and Benedick, Feste. It is useful to be asked to think about these people together.

The clown roles of the middle comedies have been the subject of some illuminating, if sometimes speculative, critical attention since Enid Welsford's pioneering study *The Fool: His Social and Literary History*. William Willeford covers some of the same ground as Welsford in *The Fool and His Sceptre*, a wide-ranging survey that moves from the court jester and his predecessors to the comedians of the silent film and to realms of psychological speculation beyond that, but finds time en route to say some interesting things about Shakespeare's fools. More exclusively Shakespearian are Robert Goldsmith's *Wise Fools in Shakespeare*, with a useful chapter on each of the major roles, and Gareth Lloyd Evans's 'Shakespeare's Fools: The Shadow and the

Substance of Drama', sometimes contentious, but with an alert awareness of performance, Elizabethan and modern.

Much of Shakespearian comedy is in prose. The best general discussion of the subject is in Brian Vickers's *The Artistry of Shakespeare's Prose*, though the book is perhaps a little uneven on this group of plays, with the Falstaff scenes of *The Merry Wives of Windsor* eliciting the most penetrating commentary.

Chapter 19 of this book offers guidance on new critical approaches to Shakespeare. The middle comedies have so far engaged the new critics less urgently than other genres. Elliott Krieger's *A Marxist Study of Shakespeare's Comedies* insists, usefully, no doubt, but in the end unproductively when it is repeated in different forms so often, that the elegant world of Shakespearian comedy is built upon, and enshrines, the rigidities of an immoveable class structure. Among new historicist studies, Malcolm Evans's 'Deconstructing Shakespeare's Comedies' provides a starting point, with its overview of recent critical trends in response to the comedies and its suggestions for possible new areas of critical enquiry. Keir Elam's *Shakespeare's Universe of Discourse: Language Games in the Comedies* applies advanced techniques of discourse analysis and semiotics to the verbal intricacies of the 'language games' of the comedies. It is fair to say, however, that those interested in linking modern linguistics to Shakespeare criticism will find this book more useful than will the average general reader.

Feminist criticism of the comedies has of late been particularly lively. A good introduction to such approaches would be Catherine Belsey's 'Disrupting Sexual Difference: Meaning and Gender in the Comedies', which examines the conceptions of marriage, the family, and sexual difference in a series of comedies against the background of contemporary social assumptions. *The Woman's Part: Feminist Criticism of Shakespeare*, a large collection of essays that attempted to be representative when published in 1980, contains only one essay wholly on this group of plays, that by Janice Hays on *Much Ado about Nothing*, though several of the other middle comedies receive mention in essays on broader themes. This collection proved the herald to a series of books presenting feminist approaches to Shakespeare, many of them devoting attention to the comedies. In *Shakespeare's Division of Experience* Marilyn French looks at the comic heroines as examples of the 'inlaw feminist principle' by which women are presented as superhumanly virtuous (the alternative being the 'outlaw' (sub-human) woman of the tragedies). This 'chaste constant' heroine, offering the possibility of harmonious sexual relationships, removes the destructive potential of sexuality which Shakespeare explores in other plays and which intrudes fitfully even here. In her book *Comic Women, Tragic Men* Linda Bamber devotes a chapter to the comedies within the framework of her conception of all the plays as explorations of the tensions and challenges between the 'masculine self' and the 'feminine other'. The comedies are seen, on the whole, as presenting that relationship at its most fruitful and untroubled, mainly through the avoidance of choice on the part of the female characters. There is a chapter on the middle comedies as a group and a separate chapter devoted to giving and taking in *The Merchant of Venice* in Marianne Novy's *Love's Argument: Gender Relations in Shakespeare*. She perceives a constant tension, in Shakespeare's exploration of gender relations, between patriarchy and mutuality, the latter presented at its most optimistic in such a play as *As You Like It*. For Marilyn L. Williamson, on the other hand, Shakespeare's comedies 'may seem protofeminist' but they are in fact 'patriarchal to the core'. Her aim to 'introduce a historical perspective on feminist criticism of Shakespeare's plays' produces an invigorating discussion of power relationships in the comedies, though her remarks on the problem comedies and the late romances are perhaps more substantial and far-reaching than her chapter on the middle comedies. This whole field is one in which new work is constantly appearing and is certainly one of the liveliest areas of critical debate on this group of plays.

I turn now to criticism of individual plays within this group; because of limitations of space I make virtually no further reference to the general studies already mentioned, even when they have separate chapters on individual plays.

The Merchant of Venice

The Merchant of Venice has for long been a battleground of critical debate, its very status as 'comedy' frequently under attack and its Christian community sometimes seen in recent commentary as being as responsible as Shylock for the racial hatred explored in the play. Some of the theoretical bases for that debate, and the historical and economic context of the play that informs it, are examined in a challenging essay by Walter Cohen '*The Merchant of Venice* and the Possibilities of Historical Criticism'. Laurence Danson's full-length study *The Harmonies of 'The Merchant of Venice'*, the most substantial discussion of the play to date, explores in its introduction the history of 'ironic' and 'idealistic' responses to the play and argues, sensitively and in detail in the following chapters, in favour of the latter, seeing the play as moving, through the transformation of a series of impediments and conflicts, to the complex harmonies of the final scene. This is as full, and as carefully argued, a description of the play as romantic comedy as one could hope for. The ironic reading, on the other hand, is perhaps best encapsulated in another monograph, that of A. D. Moody. For Moody even the ending is ironic, the Venetian Christians generally a shallow and insubstantial group personified in the inanities of Gratiano, and Portia as trivial in her pleasure-seeking as the rest. Shylock, in this interpretation, becomes the scapegoat for the Christians' shortcomings, cast out before the fools' paradise of the conclusion in moonshine. In the same mood, though with different emphases, is Graham Midgley's essay '*The Merchant of Venice*: A Reconsideration'. For him the only dramatically effective figures of the play are Shylock and Antonio, both lonely outcasts: 'As Shylock is to Venetian society, so is Antonio to the world of love and marriage'. Antonio's lonely, defeated exit in Act V thus parallels that of the broken Shylock in Act IV. Sigurd Burckhardt ('*The Merchant of Venice*: The Gentle Bond') sees the play as presenting two worlds —love/hate, Belmont/Venice, the ring/the bond—in opposition. Only by confronting the harsh world of Shylock, by bringing Belmont to Venice, by conforming to the harshness of the bond even more than Shylock, can Portia transform it and reassert that other bond of love. Burckhardt's secondary thesis, that the process is akin to Shakespeare himself facing the harshnesses and anfractuosities of his source story in order to discover the liberating truths beyond them, is perhaps a little less persuasive, but this is an important essay, taking account of both the main critical responses to the play and attempting a reconciliation. Several of Burckhardt's points are explored further and modified by Robert Hapgood. His essay 'Portia and the Merchant of Venice' is especially useful for its concentration on Portia as teacher. Also concerned with the idea of bonds is Jan Lawson Hinely whose essay sees *The Merchant of Venice*, more than any other of Shakespeare's comedies, as concentrating on 'those who lose as well as those who win'. Its discussion of Antonio is particularly interesting. The sexual politics of the opposition between Portia and Antonio for possession of Bassanio are the focus of Keith Geary's trenchant essay. In the achievement of her uncompromising victory he sees Portia as crushing both Shylock and Antonio, leaving them emotionally destitute. The 'unlessoned girl' turns out to be 'the most adept businessman of them all'.

Among this group of publications specifically on *The Merchant of Venice*, two may finally be singled out for providing (what a number of the general items mentioned in the first section of Criticism and Commentary above also provide) a sense of the play within the context of Shakespeare's work as a whole: J. W. Lever explores the oppositions of the play, seeing them as ultimately reducible to the confrontation between Portia (personifying the values of love and community) and Shylock (the opposite of those values), a confrontation resolved here by a comic device, and an issue that Shakespeare will return to more seriously in the tragedies. R. F. Hill's essay '*The Merchant of Venice* and the Pattern of Romantic Comedy' examines several aspects of the play against the paradigm of Shakespeare's other romantic comedy plots; the variations (and the coincidences) which Hill identifies are instructive and offer an interpretation of the play that sees it looking forward to *Measure for Measure* in its exploration of love in the larger context of charity and justice.

The Merry Wives of Windsor

Criticism of *The Merry Wives of Windsor* has persistently been diverted into two fundamentally unrewarding side-channels: comparison of the Falstaff of this play with his namesake in the two parts of *Henry IV*; and obsession with the occasion of the play rather than with its achievement as comedy. Work on the latter issue has been mentioned in the first section of this chapter; the present review is concerned with studies of the play for its own sake, though Hazlitt's essay, in his *Characters of Shakespear's Plays*, doubles very nicely as a representative grumble about the alleged decline of Falstaff and a cheerful celebration of the play's comic form. That form is unique, of course, in Shakespeare's comic output in being wholly English in geographical location and largely bourgeois in social setting. Alexander Leggatt includes it, therefore, not in his book on Shakespeare's 'Comedy of Love' but in his *Citizen Comedy in the Age of Shakespeare*, where it appears alongside the city comedies of Jonson, Middleton, and Dekker. Its status as bourgeois comedy is also explored by G. K. Hunter in an essay that compares it illuminatingly with Dekker's *The Shoemaker's Holiday*. Anne Barton's 'Falstaff and the Comic Community' considers the play in relation to Shakespearian comedy generally and to Shakespeare's dramatic inheritance in the comic genre. The essay is particularly successful in its discussion of Windsor as social organism and in its response to the outsiders (Falstaff and Fenton) whose presence triggers the play's action. Muriel Bradbrook's chapter on *The Merry Wives of Windsor* is strong in praise of its professional craftsmanship, though its conclusion that this is 'the very best second best Shakespeare' may sound more patronizing than complimentary. Her study nevertheless has valuable things to say about the play's theatrical vigour and effectiveness. An illuminating examination of the play's self-conscious theatricality is offered in William Carroll's essay ' "A Received Belief": Imagination in *The Merry Wives of Windsor*'; his remarks are particularly useful on the 'play within the play' in the final scene in Windsor Forest. The background to that scene is investigated by John M. Steadman in his 'Falstaff and Actaeon'. The extra interpretative dimension that this study provides has been further extended by Jeanne Addison Roberts in the fullest discussion of the play to date. Her book *Shakespeare's English Comedy: 'The Merry Wives of Windsor' in Context* offers excellent appraisal of current scholarly thinking on the text, date, and background of the play, a balanced review of critical attitudes since the eighteenth century, and a vigorous and sensitive assessment of the play's achievement, both in itself and in relation to Shakespearian comedy more generally.

Much Ado about Nothing

Criticism of *Much Ado about Nothing* has tended, on the whole, to emphasize the double plot of the play either by celebrating the success of the presentation of Beatrice and Benedick or by worrying about the awkwardnesses and angularities of the story of Hero and Claudio. In his chapter on the latter in his *Shakespeare and the Comedy of Forgiveness* Robert Grams Hunter attempts a defence of Claudio as a prototype of later Shakespearian erring husbands and lovers—Angelo, Posthumus, Leontes—finally achieving, through the benevolence and grace of comedy, forgiveness and love. The argument is salutary, though perhaps

more relevant to the literary form of the play than to the impact
its characters make in performance. John Wain, in his essay 'The
Shakespearian Lie-detector', offers no easy resolutions to this
division in the play. For him the story of Hero and Claudio, and
the verse in which it is presented, both fail; Shakespeare, conscious
of this, puts even more energy into the other plot (Beatrice,
Benedick, Dogberry) to create a play that is at once lop-sided and
brilliant. That brilliance is the theme of Graham Storey's 'The
Success of *Much Ado about Nothing*' which concentrates on the
play's proposition that 'man is a giddy thing' and his consequent
capacity for self-deception, with the opportunities for comedy
that this affords, most magnificently realized in Dogberry. It is
on this element of self-deception that J. Dennis Huston concentrates in his chapter on *Much Ado about Nothing* in his *Shakespeare's Comedies of Play*. Concerned mainly with the earlier
comedies, the book concludes with an excellent discussion of
this play's exploration of comic form, fuller than that of its
predecessors, its romance characters rescued from an apparently
irresistible tendency to cast themselves in a tragedy by the
professional skills of a Dogberry 'unaccountably tied to the
powers of goodness'. A. P. Rossiter's essay also celebrates Dogberry's marauding forays on language in its crisp, witty, and
elegant exploration of the play's concern with deception. The
essay would be an excellent starting point for anyone embarking
on the criticism of *Much Ado about Nothing*. A fuller exploration of
Dogberry's contribution to the play, linguistic and structural, is
provided by John A. Allen's purposeful (and perhaps slightly
over-earnest) essay on the role and its place among the many
examples of the 'infatuation of the ego with itself' to be found in
Much Ado about Nothing. Allen's reading is an optimistic one,
presenting the play's perception of human behaviour as in the
end profoundly tolerant, as Dogberry's presiding genius makes
clear. Pursuit of the play's darker moods through concentration
on the alleged problems of Claudio, has, on the other hand, led
some critics (and even some directors) to denigrate the whole
ethos of the society of Messina. This is the theme of Michael
Taylor's essay '*Much Ado about Nothing*: The Individual in Society',
which astutely probes the relationships between individual
characters and their social world, from the excessive isolationism
of Don John at one extreme to the excessive conformity of
Claudio at the other, with Beatrice and Benedick securing, though

not without difficulties and frictions, a satisfactory balance between the two. The idea of social disharmony is pushed further
by Walter N. King whose 'Much Ado about *Something*' sees the
play in large measure as a critique of a corrupt society, rescued
from its own capacity for moral blindness only by Dogberry,
struggling in vain to find an appropriate role for the wit its
principal characters so often misuse. For Barbara Everett, too,
the male world of Messina leaves much to be desired, though it is
ultimately rescued by the humane values represented in the
play's female characters, above all Beatrice; the idea of saving
grace through the female roles is pursued through this play, and
through many of the other comedies, in a sensitive and illuminating essay.

A much less optimistic reading of the play's sexual politics is
offered in essays by Carol Cook and Harry Berger. For Carol
Cook the masculine world, symbolized in the recurrent horn and
cuckold jokes, survives unchanged and (from within, at least)
unquestioned as the play ends: 'Hero remains dead in her
resurrection, as she is re-appropriated to the mode of perception
that killed her'. Harry Berger, in a witty and allusive essay, also
discerns rapaciousness and self-regard in what he calls the
Messina Men's Club, a community unaltered in its assumptions
as the play concludes—'in the nick of time', in his view.

One turns from the austerities of such writing, offering trenchant and, in their way, accurate descriptions, yet somehow inimical
to the spirit of celebration and community which the play is
capable of evoking in an audience, to the only critical monograph
on *Much Ado about Nothing* to have appeared so far. J. R. Mulryne's
short book confronts those elements that others have found
difficult and unattractive and, in a wide-ranging and open-
minded assessment of them in relation to the play as a whole
(characters, representative scenes, and language, all treated with
a lively responsiveness to theatricality), finds them not so dominant or so assertive that they cannot be absorbed within the
overall comic mood. That mood is nevertheless sharpened by its
anticipation of the contrasting treatment of 'mistaking' in love in
Othello and *The Winter's Tale*. Even this determined attempt at
integration of the play's disparities, however, finally admits that
although *Much Ado about Nothing* is a comedy, it is not a very
'happy' one. There remains a sense, for many critics, of incompatibility between the pain of the Hero/Claudio story and the

laughter of the Beatrice/Benedick relationship; it is, one suspects, an incompatibility discerned in criticism that in performance has helped to sustain the play's theatrical vitality.

As You Like It

The bustle of Messinan high society in *Much Ado about Nothing* is replaced in Shakespeare's next comedy by the pastoral landscape of Arden. The nature of that world is investigated in Mary Lascelles's 'Shakespeare's Pastoral Comedy', which looks at the general tradition from which Lodge's *Rosalynde* (the main source of the play) grew, and thence at Shakespeare's theatrical treatment of it, with its Robin Hood allusions and its insistence that all pastoral landscapes are countries of the mind from which characters must return to a real world of duty. Also concerned with the nature of Arden, and in particular the eccentricities of its time consciousness, is Jay Halio's ' "No clock in the forest": Time in *As You Like It*', a sensitive and persuasive examination of Rosalind's proposition that 'time travels in divers paces with divers persons', with the forest providing 'that repository of natural life devoid of artificial time barriers' to which the play's characters flee from the 'new régime' of Duke Frederick. Some of Halio's ideas are more fully explored (at times a little solemnly) in a later essay by Rawdon Wilson 'The Way to Arden: Attitudes toward Time in *As You Like It*'. Wilson's argument is that the movement from court to Arden is not a sudden jump but a gradual transition, 'the way of a mind's journey, a mental voyage of discovery' to 'a recognition of self', a 'new experience of the value of feeling' from which the characters return to a court which will never be the same again.

The sense of *As You Like It* moving between worlds, or between attitudes to the world, is reflected in other juxtapositions in the play, several of them explored in recent criticism. Two essays deserve mention: John Shaw's 'Fortune and Nature in *As You Like It*' and David Palmer's 'Art and Nature in *As You Like It*'. Shaw shows the two qualities he isolates pervading the play's plot and characters and controlling its conclusion. For Palmer 'Arden is a meeting place of Art and Nature' and the play's concern is always the relationship between them, a relationship that is ultimately reconciled as Nature is discovered through Art.

That technique of reconciliation through juxtaposition is a feature explored on a wider front in one of the most influential (and best) studies of *As You Like It*, that by Harold Jenkins. His analysis of the play's juxtapositions—court/country, idealism/ cynicism, real shepherd/pastoral-convention shepherd, and so on—shows the play as a series of conversations fascinating for their presentation of contrasting attitudes—to each other in their interlocutors, and to each other's views of life. An equally influential and important essay, close in date to Jenkins's, is Helen Gardner's. She too is concerned with the play's mixing of moods made possible through the perfunctory treatment of plot in order to reach 'a space to work things out', a space in which you may find melancholy as a weasel sucks eggs, or sermons in stones, just as you like it.

That sense of equipoise and balance between the celebratory and the melancholy described by Jenkins and Dame Helen is precisely caught in Anne Barton's essay on the play's conclusion mentioned above. Other writers on *As You Like It*, however, find the balance of the play tilting towards its less optimistic elements, particularly in their concentration on Jaques. For Michael Taylor in his essay 'The Penalty of Adam' Duke Senior's description of the forest as instructive is deliberately absurd; he compiles an impressive list of the hardships and dangers of life in Arden and draws attention to the anxiety of those exiled there to escape at the first possible opportunity. In 'Et in Arcadia Ego' Harry Morris looks at the presence of death in the play, in Touchstone's insistence on the process by which we 'rot and rot', in Jaques's description of the oblivion at the end of the 'ages of man', and in the reference, in this pastoral play, to the 'dead shepherd'. This is a stimulating essay, making interesting comparisons with treatments of this theme in the visual arts of the period. A. D. Nuttall's rather surprising coupling of Jaques with Caliban as 'Two Unassimilable Men' results in a provocative discussion of the conflict between Jaques and the Duke seen respectively as realist and fantasist and producing a tension as fierce as that between Prospero and Caliban. From that Nuttall develops a remarkable sense of the destructive, uneducable, anti-comic elements that sharpen the focus of Shakespearian comedy. D. J. Palmer's discussion of Jaques in his '*As You Like It* and the Idea of Play' sees him as the only character in this constant exploration of the nature of play who has himself no capacity for it, for in turning all the world into a stage he has turned himself into a perpetual observer—a role that, paradoxically, he sustains at the end while the rest abandon theirs. This is an entertaining and instructive essay.

With the only monograph so far published on *As You Like It* one returns to the attempt to see the play whole. Michael Jamieson's short book follows the play through in a scene-by-scene analysis which, although occasionally giving a sense of the dutiful, is a sane, balanced, and helpful commentary, keeping a deft eye on the play's theatricality and constantly sensitive to its language and to the poise of its movement between romance and sobriety, comedy and irony, adventure and common sense.

Twelfth Night

'Elusive' is a word that seems to arise rather often in critical accounts of *Twelfth Night*. It is, no doubt, the play's mingling of romantic comedy in its main plot (of Viola and Orsino) with the harsher story of the revenge on Malvolio of the subplot that is largely responsible for this mood. Perhaps the most acute critical analysis of the mixture, and its effect on the play's conclusion, is in Anne Barton's essay on 'Shakespeare's Sense of an Ending' referred to above. Several other critics have approached the play by way of the intense contrasts of its ending. In her essay 'Cupid's Whirligig and the Comic Providence of *Twelfth Night*' Joan Hartwig presents a clear and revealing analysis of the relationship between the two plots of the play and their final separation in the vengeful exit of Malvolio—the only character in *Twelfth Night* who refuses to submit himself to a design higher than his own will. William C. Carroll ('The Ending of *Twelfth Night* and the Tradition of Metamorphosis') also writes well on the final scene and on Malvolio's inability (or unwillingness) to participate in that process of transformation to which the audience itself is required to submit. Ralph Berry too is concerned with the audience's response to the final baiting of Malvolio, an example of what he calls 'theatre as bloodsport', which finally induces a sense of shame. While on the subject of the play's ending this may also be the place to mention A. C. Bradley's brief essay on 'Feste the Jester'—Bradleian character criticism no doubt, and scarcely escaping sentimentality, but still with something to communicate about the poignant and wistful mood of that final song.

The contention of many of these critics who approach *Twelfth Night* by way of its ending is that it shows us, in Anne Barton's phrase, Shakespeare beginning to 'unbuild his own comic form at its point of greatest vulnerability: the ending'. The play, the last of this group of so-called middle comedies, tends in this view to be regarded as a milestone in Shakespeare's development as a comic dramatist. This is very much Clifford Leech's theme in his short book *'Twelfth Night' and Shakespearian Comedy*. Leech examines the play's discordant elements, its sometimes disturbing mixture of romance and revenge, and sees the dramatist about to move on from what he calls its 'vulnerable delight' to a broader vision of human behaviour in the dark comedies that followed. That idea of the fragility of *Twelfth Night* is also the theme of Harold Jenkins's sensitive and graceful essay, an account of the play without the slightly elegiac tone of Leech's study, for Jenkins is concerned to celebrate its humane generosity and to offer an unusually positive appraisal of Orsino (as, of course, of Viola), though he has good things to say on the sub-plot by the way. So too does L. G. Salingar's study of the design of the play, with its deft comparisons with the sources and its concern to suggest the overall coherence and comic balance of the piece. Like Jenkins, D. J. Palmer in his densely argued essay 'Art and Nature in *Twelfth Night*' spends more time than most on Orsino, seeing him as one of the many self-deceivers in the play, at the beginning subject to a fiction, to art, but brought, through Viola's love, to a realization of her nature, and his own, a process of metamorphosis paralleled, much more harshly, in Malvolio's movement through the play. The capacity of so many of the play's characters for self-deception is the central concern of an earlier, but still valuable essay, 'The Masks of *Twelfth Night*' by Joseph H. Summers, which sees the movement towards resolution as a process of unmasking and of growing self-awareness. That movement, seen in terms of a passing through revels and indulgence to final epiphany (not unconnected with the play's title) is analyzed with sharp response to the play's language, and also to its music, in John Hollander's essay '*Twelfth Night* and the Morality of Indulgence'.

The language of *Twelfth Night*, the complex relationships between it and reality, the whole realm of illusion and role-play, the ability of language to regulate, and even create, what the characters perceive of themselves and of their world, is the subject of a subtle and intricate essay by Terence Eagleton. Michael Taylor sets *Twelfth Night* beside its alternative title

'What You Will' in an engaging discussion of the relationship between freedom from ambition and responsibility (in the spirit of Twelfth Night carnival) and pursuit of individual resolution, the search for 'what you will'. His division of the play's characters according to these criteria is revealing. Also concerned to remind us of the play's full title is Barbara Everett's 'Or What You Will', a constantly illuminating examination of the tone and mood of the play, of its 'lightness . . . as far as possible from triviality', of its apparent inconsequentiality and lack of urgency, its musicality, its complexity, and (to end where we began) its elusiveness. This is an excellent essay, acutely responsive to the verbal precision and subtlety of the play and communicating that response sharply and tellingly to its readers. One does not ask for more in Shakespeare criticism.

THE PLAYS IN PERFORMANCE

'The simple thing to do with a Shakespeare play', wrote Bernard Shaw, 'is to perform it; the alternative is to let it alone'—and much trouble would have been saved, one cannot help reflecting, in sorting through the writings of critics if the world had taken notice of him. That some insist on indulging themselves in criticism, however, does not prevent others from essaying the far from simple activity of performance. The middle comedies have long been, and continue to be, among the most frequently revived of Shakespeare's plays and there is much interesting writing on their effect in performance. General works on Shakespeare in performance are covered elsewhere in this Guide (see Chapter 3); I mention here a selection of significant publications on performances of the middle comedies.

Anthony Dawson's *Watching Shakespeare* offers chapters on *The Merchant of Venice, As You Like It,* and *Twelfth Night* which succinctly examine, with many well chosen examples, some of the choices that must be made in producing these plays. John Russell Brown's *Shakespeare's Plays in Performance* contains valuable essays on Shylock and on *Twelfth Night* in the theatre. The same author's *Shakespeare's Dramatic Styles* explores 'the theatrical life implicit in the printed words', particularly in relation to *As You Like It* and *Twelfth Night*. Toby Lelyveld's *Shylock on the Stage* provides a general survey of the changing theatrical fortunes of the role and the extremes of comic mockery and tragic pathos between which it has swung. Ralph Berry deals adroitly with recent trends in productions of *Twelfth Night* in one of the chapters of his *Changing Styles in Shakespeare*. Philip McGuire, in *Speechless Dialect: Shakespeare's Open Silences*, examines Antonio's and Sir Andrew's exits in the final scene of *Twelfth Night* with reference to their handling by a number of recent directors. Two of the plays in this group have so far been the subject of volumes in the 'Text and Performance' series: Lois Potter writes on *Twelfth Night* and Bill Overton on *The Merchant of Venice*. Both suffer from what seems to me the fundamental shortcoming of this series: the division, at their middle pages, between 'text' and 'performance', enshrining, in miniature, the 'never the twain shall meet' attitude that they are meant to combat. Both volumes nevertheless offer some excellent discussions of contrasted productions of their plays. For those interested in looking at some of the roles of comedy heroines in earlier theatrical manifestations a useful starting point would be Russell Jackson's essay 'Perfect Types of Womanhood: Rosalind, Beatrice, and Viola in Victorian Criticism and Performance'. From the same period Helena Faucit (Lady Martin) writes on her own performances of Beatrice and Rosalind in *On Some of Shakespeare's Female Characters*.

Turning to particular modern productions and performances of the middle comedies several pieces recommend themselves. There is an excellent essay on John Barton's 1976 Stratford *Much Ado about Nothing* in Richard David's *Shakespeare and the Theatre*. Stanley Wells deals in depth with the 1969 *Twelfth Night* at Stratford (also by John Barton) in his *Royal Shakespeare*. The Viola of that production, Dame Judi Dench, explores her relationship with Orsino (Richard Pasco) in a chapter of John Barton's *Playing Shakespeare*. The same volume contains a discussion between two recent Stratford Shylocks, Patrick Stewart and David Suchet. The Malvolio from John Barton's *Twelfth Night*, Donald Sinden, writes entertainingly, and informatively, on his performance in *Players of Shakespeare 1*, edited by Philip Brockbank. This collection also contains Sinead Cusack's account of her Stratford Portia of 1981, Patrick Stewart's essay on his Shylock of three years earlier, and John Bowe's on Orlando (1980). In *Players of Shakespeare 2*, edited by Russell Jackson and Robert Smallwood, there are further accounts of the preparation and performance of middle comedy roles from the players' point of view: Ian McDiarmid writes on a controversial Shylock (1984), Zoë Wanamaker on her Viola of 1983, Juliet Stevenson and Fiona

Shaw on Rosalind and Celia (1985), and Alan Rickman on Jaques (also 1985). Other volumes relevant to the middle comedies are forthcoming in this series and in the series 'Shakespeare in Performance' and 'Text and Performance'. It is through their theatricality that these comedies have survived over the centuries; fittingly, therefore, this account of recent writing on them ends by recording the fact that it is to their performance that the sharpest critical attention seems currently to be directed.

REFERENCES

EDITIONS

Gilman, Albert (ed.), *As You Like It* (Signet Classic Shakespeare, New York, 1963).

Latham, Agnes (ed.), *As You Like It* (Arden Shakespeare, London, 1975).

Oliver, H. J. (ed.), *As You Like It* (New Penguin Shakespeare, Harmondsworth, 1968).

Brown, John Russell (ed.), *The Merchant of Venice* (Arden Shakespeare, London, 1955).

Mahood, Molly M. (ed.), *The Merchant of Venice* (New Cambridge Shakespeare, Cambridge, 1987).

Merchant, W. Moelwyn (ed.), *The Merchant of Venice* (New Penguin Shakespeare, Harmondsworth, 1967).

Myrick, Kenneth (ed.), *The Merchant of Venice* (Signet Classic Shakespeare, New York, 1965).

Hibbard, G. R. (ed.), *The Merry Wives of Windsor* (New Penguin Shakespeare, Harmondsworth, 1973).

Oliver, H. J. (ed.), *The Merry Wives of Windsor* (Arden Shakespeare, London, 1971).

Foakes, R. A. (ed.), *Much Ado about Nothing* (New Penguin Shakespeare, Harmondsworth, 1968).

Humphreys, Arthur R. (ed.), *Much Ado about Nothing* (Arden Shakespeare, London, 1981).

Mares, F. H. (ed.), *Much Ado about Nothing* (New Cambridge Shakespeare, Cambridge, 1988).

Stevenson, David L. (ed.), *Much Ado about Nothing* (Signet Classic Shakespeare, New York, 1964).

Baker, Herschel (ed.), *Twelfth Night* (Signet Classic Shakespeare, New York, 1965).

Donno, Elizabeth Story (ed.), *Twelfth Night* (New Cambridge Shakespeare, Cambridge, 1985).

Lothian, J. M. (ed.), rev. T. W. Craik, *Twelfth Night* (Arden Shakespeare, London, 1975).

Mahood, Molly M. (ed.), *Twelfth Night* (New Penguin Shakespeare, Harmondsworth, 1968).

CRITICISM AND COMMENTARY

Allen, John A., 'Dogberry', *Shakespeare Quarterly*, 24 (1973), 35–53.

Bamber, Linda, *Comic Women, Tragic Men: A Study of Gender and Genre in Shakespeare* (Stanford, Calif., 1982).

Barber, C. L. *Shakespeare's Festive Comedy: A Study of Dramatic Form and Its Relation to Social Custom* (Princeton, NJ, 1959).

Barton, Anne, '*As You Like It* and *Twelfth Night*: Shakespeare's Sense of an Ending', in *Shakespearian Comedy*, ed. Malcolm Bradbury and David Palmer (Stratford-upon-Avon Studies, 14; London, 1972), 160–80.

—— 'Falstaff and the Comic Community', *Shakespeare's 'Rough Magic': Renaissance Essays in Honor of C. L. Barber*, ed. Peter Erickson and Coppélia Kahn (Newark, Del., 1985), 131–48.

Barton, John, *Playing Shakespeare* (London, 1984).

Belsey, Catherine, 'Disrupting Sexual Difference: Meaning and Gender in the Comedies', in *Alternative Shakespeares*, ed. John Drakakis (London, 1985), 166–90.

Berger, Harry L., 'Against the Sink-a-Pace: Sexual and Family Politics in *Much Ado about Nothing*', *Shakespeare Quarterly*, 33 (1982), 302–13.

Berry, Edward I., *Shakespeare's Comic Rites* (Cambridge, 1984).

Berry, Ralph, *Changing Styles in Shakespeare* (London, 1981).

—— *Shakespeare's Comedies: Explorations in Form* (Princeton, NJ, 1972).

—— '*Twelfth Night*: The Experience of the Audience', *Shakespeare Survey* 34 (1981), 111–19.

Bradbrook, Muriel C., *The Growth and Structure of Elizabethan Comedy* (London, 1955).

—— 'Royal Command: *The Merry Wives of Windsor*', in her *Shakespeare the Craftsman* (London, 1969), 75–96.

Bradley, A. C., 'Feste the Jester', in *A Book of Homage to Shakespeare*, ed. Israel Gollancz (London, 1916), 164–9; reprinted in A. C. Bradley, *A Miscellany* (London, 1929), 207–17.

Brockbank, Philip (ed.), *Players of Shakespeare 1* (Cambridge, 1985).

Brown, John Russell, *Shakespeare and His Comedies* (London, 1957; 2nd edn., 1962).

—— *Shakespeare's Dramatic Styles* (London, 1970).

—— *Shakespeare's Plays in Performance* (London, 1966; Penguin Shakespeare Library, Harmondsworth, 1969).

Bullough, Geoffrey (ed.), *Narrative and Dramatic Sources of Shakespeare*, 8 vols. (London, 1957–75).

Burckhardt, Sigurd '*The Merchant of Venice*: The Gentle Bond', *ELH*, 29 (1962), 239–62.

Carroll, William C., 'The Ending of *Twelfth Night* and the Tradition of Metamorphosis', in *Shakespearian Comedy*, ed. Maurice Charney (New York, 1980), 49–61.

—— *The Metamorphoses of Shakespearean Comedy* (Princeton, NJ, 1985).

—— ' "A Received Belief": Imagination in *The Merry Wives of Windsor*', *Studies in Philology*, 74 (1977), 186–215.

Charlton, H. B., *Shakespearian Comedy* (London, 1938).

Coghill, Nevill, 'The Basis of Shakespearian Comedy', *Essays and Studies*, NS 3 (1950), 1–28.

Cohen, Walter, '*The Merchant of Venice* and the Possibilities of Historical Criticism', *ELH* 49 (1982), 765–89.

Cook, Carol, ' "The Sign and Semblance of Her Honour": Reading Gender Difference in *Much Ado About Nothing*', *PMLA*, 101 (1986), 186–202.

Corrigan, Robert W., *Comedy: Meaning and Form* (Scranton, Pa., 1965).

Danson, Lawrence, *The Harmonies of 'The Merchant of Venice'* (New Haven, Conn., and London, 1978).

David, Richard, *Shakespeare in the Theatre* (Cambridge, 1978).

Dawson, Anthony, *Watching Shakespeare: A Playgoers' Guide* (London, 1988).

Eagleton, Terence, 'Language and Reality in *Twelfth Night*', *Critical Quarterly*, 9 (1968), 217–28.

Edwards, Philip, *Shakespeare and the Confines of Art* (London, 1968).

Elam, Keir, *Shakespeare's Universe of Discourse: Language Games in the Comedies* (London, 1984).

Evans, Bertrand, *Shakespeare's Comedies* (Oxford, 1960).

Evans, Gareth Lloyd, 'Shakespeare's Fools: The Shadow and the Substance of Drama', in *Shakespearian Comedy*, ed. Malcolm Bradbury and David Palmer (Stratford-upon-Avon Studies, 14; London, 1972), 142–59.

Evans, Malcolm, 'Deconstructing Shakespeare's Comedies', in *Alternative Shakespeares*, ed. John Drakakis (London, 1985), 67–94.

Everett, Barbara, '*Much Ado about Nothing*', *Critical Quarterly*, 3 (1961), 319–35.

—— 'Or What You Will', *Essays in Criticism*, 35 (1985), 294–314.

Farley-Hills, David, *The Comic in Renaissance Comedy* (Totowa, NJ, 1981).

Faucit, Helena (Lady Martin), *On Some of Shakespeare's Female Characters* (London, 1891).

Foakes, R. A., 'The Owl and the Cuckoo: Voices of Maturity in Shakespeare's Comedies', in *Shakespearian Comedy*, ed. Malcolm Bradbury and David Palmer (Stratford-upon-Avon Studies, 14; London, 1972), 121–41.

French, Marilyn, *Shakespeare's Division of Experience* (London, 1982).

Frye, Northrop, 'The Argument of Comedy', in *English Institute Essays 1948*, ed. D. A. Robertson (New York, 1949), 58–73.

——*A Natural Perspective: The Development of Shakespearian Comedy and Romance* (New York, 1965).

Gardner, Helen, '*As You Like It*', in *More Talking of Shakespeare*, ed. John Garrett (London, 1959), 17–32.

Geary, Keith, 'The Nature of Portia's Victory: Turning to Men in *The Merchant of Venice*', *Shakespeare Survey 37* (1984), 55–68.

Goldsmith, Robert Hillis, *Wise Fools in Shakespeare* (East Lansing, Mich., 1955; Liverpool, 1958).

Green, William, *Shakespeare's 'Merry Wives of Windsor'* (Princeton, NJ, 1972).

Halio, Jay L., '"No Clock in the Forest": Time in *As You Like It*', *SEL*, 2 (1962), 197–207.

——and Barbara C. Millard (eds.), '*As You Like It*': *An Annotated Bibliography, 1940–1980* (Garland Shakespeare Bibliographies; New York, 1985).

Hapgood, Robert, 'Portia and the Merchant of Venice', *Modern Language Quarterly*, 28 (1967), 19–32.

Hartwig, Joan, 'Feste's "Whirligig" and the Comic Providence of *Twelfth Night*', *ELH*, 40 (1973), 501–13.

Hassel, R. Chris, *Faith and Folly in Shakespeare's Romantic Comedies* (Athens, Ga., 1980).

Hawkins, Sherman, 'The Two Worlds of Shakespearean Comedy', *Shakespeare Studies*, 3 (1967), 62–80.

Hazlitt, William, '*The Merry Wives of Windsor*', in *Characters of Shakespear's Plays* (1817; Everyman's Library, London, 1906, etc.), 250–2.

Heilman, Robert B., *The Ways of the World: Comedy and Society* (Seattle, Wash., 1978).

Hill, R. F. '*The Merchant of Venice* and the Pattern of Romantic Comedy', *Shakespeare Survey 28* (1975), 75–87.

Hinely, Jan Lawson, 'Bond Priorities in *The Merchant of Venice*', *SEL*, 20 (1980), 217–39.

Hollander, John, '*Twelfth Night* and the Morality of Indulgence', *Sewanee Review*, 67 (1959), 220–38.

Hotson, Leslie, *The First Night of 'Twelfth Night'* (London, 1954).

Hunter, George K., 'Bourgeois Comedy: Shakespeare and Dekker', in *Shakespeare and His Contemporaries: Essays in Comparison*, ed. E. A. J. Honigmann (Revels Plays Companion Library, Manchester, 1986), 1–15.

Hunter, Robert Grams, '*Much Ado about Nothing*', in his *Shakespeare and the Comedy of Forgiveness* (New York, 1965), 85–105.

Huston, J. Dennis, 'The Evidence of Things Not Seen: Making Believe and the Self-Defensive Play of *Much Ado about Nothing*', in his *Shakespeare's Comedies of Play* (London, 1981), 122–50.

Jackson, Russell, 'Perfect Types of Womanhood: Rosalind, Beatrice, and Viola in Victorian Criticism and Performance', *Shakespeare Survey 32* (1979), 15–26.

—— and Robert Smallwood (eds.), *Players of Shakespeare 2* (Cambridge, 1988).

Jagendorf, Zvi, *The Happy End of Comedy: Jonson, Molière, and Shakespeare* (Newark, Del., 1984).

Jamieson, Michael, *Shakespeare: 'As You Like It'* (Arnold's Studies in English Literature, 25; London, 1965).

Jenkins, Harold, '*As You Like It*', *Shakespeare Survey 8* (1955), 40–51.

—— '*Shakespeare's Twelfth Night*', *Rice Institute Pamphlet*, 45 (1959), 19–42.

King, Walter N., 'Much Ado about *Something*', *Shakespeare Quarterly*, 15 (1964), 143–55.

Krieger, Elliott R., *A Marxist Study of Shakespeare's Comedies* (London, 1979).

Laroque, François, *Shakespeare et la fête* (Paris, 1988).

—— *Shakespeare's Festive World* (Cambridge, 1991).

Lascelles, Mary, 'Shakespeare's Pastoral Comedy', in *More Talking of Shakespeare*, ed. John Garrett (London, 1959), 70–86.

Leech, Clifford, '*Twelfth Night' and Shakespearian Comedy* (Toronto, 1965).

Leggatt, Alexander, *Citizen Comedy in the Age of Shakespeare* (Toronto, 1973).

—— *Shakespeare's Comedy of Love* (London, 1974).

Lelyveld, Toby, *Shylock on the Stage* (London, 1961).

Lenz, Carolyn Ruth Swift, Gayle Greene, and Carol Thomas Neely (eds.), *The Woman's Part: Feminist Criticism of Shakespeare* (Urbana, Ill., 1980).

Lever, J. W., 'Shylock, Portia, and the Values of Shakespearian Comedy', *Shakespeare Quarterly*, 3 (1952), 383–8.

Levin, Richard A., *Love and Society in Shakespearian Comedy: A Study of Dramatic Form and Content* (Newark, Del., 1985).

McFarland, Thomas, *Shakespeare's Pastoral Comedy* (Chapel Hill, NC, 1972).

McGuire, Philip, *Speechless Dialect: Shakespeare's Open Silences* (Berkeley and Los Angeles, Calif., 1985).

Melzi, Robert C., 'From Lelia to Viola', *Renaissance Drama*, 9 (1966), 67–81.

Merchant, W. Moelwyn, *Comedy* (Critical Idiom Series; London, 1972).

Midgley, Graham, '*The Merchant of Venice*: A Reconsideration', *Essays in Criticism*, 10 (1960), 119–33.

Mincoff, Marco, 'What Shakespeare Did to *Rosalynde*', *Shakespeare Jahrbuch*, 96 (1960), 78–89.

Moody, A. D., *Shakespeare: 'The Merchant of Venice'* (Arnold's Studies in English Literature, 21; London, 1964).

Morris, Harry, '*As You Like It*: Et in Arcadia Ego', *Shakespeare Quarterly*, 26 (1975), 269–75.

Muir, Kenneth, *Shakespeare's Comic Sequence* (Liverpool, 1979).

—— *The Sources of Shakespeare's Plays* (London, 1977).

Mulryne, J. R., *Shakespeare: 'Much Ado About Nothing'* (Arnold's Studies in English Literature, 16; London, 1965).

Nevo, Ruth, *Comic Transformations in Shakespeare* (London, 1980).

Novy, Marianne, *Love's Argument: Gender Relations in Shakespeare* (Chapel Hill, NC, 1984).

Nuttall, A. D., 'Two Unassimilable Men', in *Shakespearian Comedy*, ed. Malcolm Bradbury and David Palmer (Stratford-upon-Avon Studies, 14; London, 1972), 210–40.

Overton, Bill, '*The Merchant of Venice*' (Text and Performance Series; London, 1987).

Palmer, D. J., 'Art and Nature in *As You Like It*', *Philological Quarterly*, 49 (1970), 30–40.

—— 'Art and Nature in *Twelfth Night*', *Critical Quarterly*, 9 (1967), 201–12.

—— '*As You Like It* and the Idea of Play', *Critical Quarterly*, 13 (1971), 234–45.

Palmer, John, *Comic Characters of Shakespeare* (London, 1946).

Pettet, E. C., *Shakespeare and the Romance Tradition* (London, 1949).

Potter, Lois, '*Twelfth Night*' (Text and Performance Series; London, 1983).

Prouty, C. T., *The Sources of 'Much Ado about Nothing'* (New Haven, Conn., 1950).

Roberts, Jeanne Addison, *Shakespeare's English Comedy: 'The Merry Wives of Windsor' in Context* (Lincoln, Nebr., 1979).

Rossiter, A. P., '*Much Ado about Nothing*', in his *Angel with Horns: Fifteen Lectures on Shakespeare*, ed. Graham Storey (London, 1961), 65–81.

Salingar, L. G., 'The Design of *Twelfth Night*', *Shakespeare Quarterly*, 9 (1958), 117–39.

—— *Shakespeare and the Traditions of Comedy* (Cambridge, 1974).

Shaw, John, 'Fortune and Nature in *As You Like It*', *Shakespeare Quarterly*, 6 (1955), 45–50.

Steadman, John M., 'Falstaff as Actaeon: A Dramatic Emblem', *Shakespeare Quarterly*, 14 (1963), 231–44.

Storey, Graham, 'The Success of *Much Ado about Nothing*', in *More Talking of Shakespeare*, ed. John Garrett (London, 1959), 128–43.

Summers, Joseph H., 'The Masks of *Twelfth Night*', *University of Kansas City Review*, 22 (1955), 25–32.

Sypher, Wylie (ed.), *Comedy* (Garden City, NY, 1956).

Taylor, Michael, 'As You Like It: The Penalty of Adam', *Critical Quarterly*, 15 (1973), 76–80.

—— 'Much Ado about Nothing: The Individual in Society', *Essays in Criticism*, 23 (1973), 146–53.

—— 'Twelfth Night and What You Will', *Critical Quarterly*, 16 (1974), 71–80.

Vickers, Brian, *The Artistry of Shakespeare's Prose* (London, 1968).

Wain, John, 'The Shakespearian Lie-Detector: Thoughts on *Much Ado about Nothing*', *Critical Quarterly*, 9 (1967), 27–42.

Weld, John, *Meaning in Comedy: Studies in Elizabethan Romantic Comedy* (Albany, NY, 1975).

Wells, Stanley, 'Happy Endings in Shakespeare', *Shakespeare Jahrbuch*, 102 (1966), 103–23.

—— *Royal Shakespeare: Four Major Productions at Stratford-upon-Avon* (Manchester, 1977).

—— 'Shakespeare and Romance', in *Later Shakespeare*, ed. John Russell Brown and Bernard Harris (Stratford-upon-Avon Studies, 8; London, 1966), 48–79.

—— and Gary Taylor, with John Jowett and William Montgomery, *William Shakespeare: A Textual Companion* (Oxford, 1987).

Welsford, Enid, *The Fool: His Social and Literary History* (London, 1935).

Wheeler, Thomas, (ed.), 'The Merchant of Venice': An Annotated Bibliography (Garland Shakespeare Bibliographies; New York, 1985).

White, R. S., 'Let Wonder Seem Familiar': Endings in Shakespeare's Romantic Vision (Princeton, NJ, and London, 1985).

Willeford, William, *The Fool and His Sceptre: A Study in Clowns and Jesters and Their Audience* (London, 1969).

Williamson, Marilyn L., *The Patriarchy of Shakespeare's Comedies* (Detroit, Mich., 1986).

Wilson, Rawdon, 'The Way to Arden: Attitudes towards Time in *As You Like It*', *Shakespeare Quarterly*, 26 (1975), 16–24.

Young, David P., *The Heart's Forest: A Study of Shakespeare's Pastoral Plays* (New Haven, Conn., 1972).

7 | The Problem Plays

Troilus and
Cressida,
All's Well that
Ends Well,
and Measure for
Measure

JOHN WILDERS

GENERAL STUDIES

Of all Shakespeare's plays, these three have caused the greatest
critical disagreement. They have sometimes perplexed the critics
—Dowden omitted all consideration of *Troilus and Cressida* from
the first edition of his *Shakspere: His Mind and Art* because, as he
confessed, he did not know what to make of it—and they have
been interpreted in widely different, conflicting ways. Indeed
some critics have concluded that conflicting, incompatible responses are precisely what they were designed to produce.
Rossiter remarks that 'all the firm points of view . . . are felt to be
fallible. . . . Hence the "problem"-quality, and the ease with
which any critic who takes a firm line is cancelled out by
another', and Bradshaw, surveying the divergent interpretations
of *Troilus and Cressida*, concludes that it was 'designed to frame
and generate such disagreements'.

Most scholars believe that they were written when Shakespeare
was in his late thirties. *Troilus and Cressida* was probably written
in 1602 (a year after *Hamlet*, which some critics see as also a
problem play), *All's Well that Ends Well* in 1603, and *Measure for
Measure* in 1604, the same year as *Othello*. One of their features is
that they apparently do not fit into any of the conventional
dramatic forms. As Thomas says, they 'defy absorption into the
traditional categories of romantic comedies, histories, tragedies
and romances, but share striking affinities in terms of themes,

atmosphere, tone and style'. Since all three were also written during a fairly short space of time they have often been thought to constitute a distinct and separate group. Frye is alone in believing that *All's Well that Ends Well* and *Measure for Measure* are 'simply romantic comedies.'

Dowden believed that these plays were the product of a period in Shakespeare's life in which he underwent some kind of personal crisis which induced him to 'take a deep, passionate and tragical view of life' which 'spoilt him, at that time, for a writer of comedy' (Preface to the third edition). Dover Wilson also discerned in them 'the note of disillusionment and cynicism', an outlook which is 'cheerless and often unwholesome', and, although this biographical approach is now largely discredited, some critics still see the unresolved conflicts depicted in the plays as an expression of the tensions in the dramatist's own mind. 'Shakespeare' says French, 'placed increasing significance on chaste constancy. Parallel with this (although probably caused by actual events, and not simply his literary development), he suffered increasingly from disgust and sexual guilt. These attitudes and feelings reached their climax in the period in which he wrote the problem plays.'

The idea that the plays were the work of a troubled mind was forcefully attacked by Sisson in *The Mythical Sorrows of Shakespeare* and the tendency has been to concentrate on the nature of the plays themselves and not on the mind that created them. In 1896, Boas categorized them in terms of subject matter and effect. 'All these dramas', he affirmed, 'introduce us into highly artificial societies whose civilization is ripe unto rottenness. . . . At the close our feeling is neither simple joy nor pain; we are excited, fascinated, perplexed, for the issues raised preclude a completely satisfactory outcome'. It was Boas who first applied to them the term 'problem plays'.

In the first full-length study of them, published in 1931, Lawrence also rejected the biographical approach, asserting that there was no evidence that they were written to express Shakespeare's personal feelings or convictions. The essential characteristics he perceived were not unlike those recognized by Boas. 'The theme is handled', he explained, 'so as to arouse not merely interest or excitement, or pity or amusement, but to probe the complicated interrelations of character and action, in a situation admitting of different ethical interpretations.' Ethical ambiguity was also one of the elements which, in an influential essay, Rossiter identified. 'These plays', he argued, 'throw opposed or contrary views into the mind: only to leave the resulting equations without any settled or soothing solutions.' Thomas, in an extensive study of all three plays, comes to a similar conclusion: 'They expose fundamental problems . . . within a framework which makes the audience acutely aware of the problems without providing amelioration through the provision of adequate answers or a dramatic mode which facilitates a satisfactory release of emotions.' It is heartening to see that during the ninety years between Boas's remarks and Thomas's detailed analysis, there has been a steady progress in our understanding of the problem plays and an increasing agreement about their characteristics. At the same time, however, we have come to realize that the troubling, unresolved conflicts and the ambiguities present in these plays are typical not simply of this particular group but of Shakespeare's work generally. Schanzer demonstrated that *Julius Caesar* and *Antony and Cleopatra* are as ethically unstable as any of the problem plays and that *Timon of Athens* and *King Lear* could well be added to the group. The habit of associating the three plays, Schanzer believed, had caused harm 'by fencing plays off from their kindred, exaggerating the supposed similarities between those within the pale and their supposed differences from those outside it', and should therefore be abandoned. Although his advice has not been followed and a number of studies of the group have been published since he issued this warning in 1963, nevertheless there has been a growing awareness that in a great many of Shakespeare's works he creates essentially unresolvable conflicts of which he invites us to hold simultaneous and conflicting views which are not finally reconciled. Perhaps the most valuable result of a century of enquiry into these works has been to make us realize the 'problematical' nature of Shakespeare's art generally.

Troilus and Cressida

TEXTS

Of the recent editions, the most useful are the Oxford, edited by Kenneth Muir, the Arden, edited by Kenneth Palmer, and the New Penguin, edited by R. A. Foakes. All three have illuminating introductions and informative commentaries. The first two are designed primarily for university students and professional Shakespearians, and Foakes's New Penguin, although designed for less advanced students, is nevertheless of great value to all readers. The texts of all three are based partly on the Quarto. The text in the Oxford edition of *The Complete Works* is based on the Folio, which the editors believe includes the dramatist's own revisions.

CRITICAL STUDIES AND COMMENTARY

Although the title-page of the First Quarto edition of *Troilus and Cressida* (1609) declares that it was acted at the Globe theatre, the Epistle that prefaced the second issue (also 1609) implies that it had never been performed at all and was perhaps never designed for the public stage. Alexander argues that it was composed for performance at one of the Inns of Court. It has been one of Shakespeare's least popular plays in the theatre and, although a wholesale adaptation by Dryden with the same title held the stage from 1679 to 1734, Shakespeare's original was not performed in England until 1907, when a 'costume recital' was acted by amateurs; the 'main result' according to *The Times*, 'was the conviction that it was impossible to arrange for the stage'. Since then, however, there have been a number of successful productions, including Tyrone Guthrie's at the Old Vic in modern dress (1956), and the productions in classical costume by the Royal Shakespeare Company under the direction of Peter Hall and John Barton in collaboration (1960) and by John Barton alone (1968). Terry Hands's production for the same company in 1981 emphasized the satirical element and was said to have been interpreted 'from the perspective of Thersites'.

From the time it was first published there has been uncertainty about its dramatic genre. In the First Quarto it was called a history, in the Epistle added to the second issue of the Quarto it was called a comedy, and in the First Folio it was inserted between the tragedies and the histories. It has also been called a 'comical satire' and a 'heroic farce'. Coleridge found it the hardest of Shakespeare's plays to characterize and Frye regarded it as 'an experimental play in a special category'. Its failure to conform to any of the conventional genres has been explained as a manifestation of the lack of any consistent principles expressed by the play itself. According to Edwards, Shakespeare created a form 'which forbids the more obvious compensations of order, meaning and hope which inevitably seem implicit in the structure and plot of more conventional plays' and Fly connects the 'radical instability' of its form with the 'devastating and form-denying vision informing it'.

It is a highly argumentative, intellectual play, 'more peculiarly analytic in language and dramatic meaning than any other work of Shakespeare' (Knight). Two of the longest scenes consist of actual philosophical debates, one in the Greek camp about the nature of social order, the other among the Trojan leaders about the nature of value, and some critics have suggested that these arguments are conducted on the basis of two contrasting sets of ideals. 'On one side', says Ornstein, 'is a decaying world of chivalry, courtly and romantic . . . on the other side is a purely masculine, realistic world of soldiery and empire, pragmatic in its values, uncritical of its goals, concerned only with the attainment of power.' What many critics have emphasized, however, is that the ideals extolled by Ulysses among the Greeks and by both Troilus and Hector among the Trojans are abandoned in practice by the very characters who have propounded them. 'The Trojans, debating even now whether the war is worth fighting, can achieve nothing decisive with their chivalric code of war with honour. The Greeks, crippled by disaffection and insubordination, can achieve nothing even with the resources of rhetoric and contrivance which lie in Ulysses' (Edwards). The rhetoric of Ulysses and the other Greek generals is, according to Long, satirically presented and deliberately inflated so as to appear ridiculous. He describes their debate as 'a council of the inept and disaffected, stuffed to the chops with grievances they cannot digest, yet still trying to talk big, still clutching hopelessly after the magniloquent phrase and the magnificent gesture or sentiment.' Ulysses' grandiose exposition of the principles governing the universe, moreover, is the prelude to nothing more than a ruse designed to lure Achilles back into action, a proposal 'that two major warriors should be treated like simple-minded children' (Palmer). Nor is Ulysses' trick any more effective than his philosophizing. It makes the boorish Ajax even more conceited and leaves Achilles unmoved. Achilles is certainly roused to action at the end of the play but not as a result of Ulysses' persuasions. His one desire is to avenge the death of Patroclus.

Many critics have pointed out that Hector is, in his way, just as inconsistent as Ulysses. At first he proposes that the Trojans should accept Nestor's invitation to end the war and return Helen on the perfectly sensible grounds that she is 'not worth what she does cost the keeping'. Troilus, however, declares that reason is itself inimical to the ideals of chivalry, and he pleads on the grounds of 'manhood and honour' that they should continue to fight for Helen. The two brothers are engaged in a clash of principles, as Hector realizes, but although he pours scorn on Troilus' arguments as impulsive and naïve, he finally sides with him and agrees that the war should go on. The wisdom of his change of heart is, moreover, further challenged when Helen's entrance in the third act reveals that 'the face that launched a thousand ships belongs to a woman of extreme silliness and affectation' (Muir). Hence 'the principal characters defy the sound political theories which they expound with so much eloquence' (Campbell) and their supposedly high-principled orations, subsequently ignored, seem in retrospect to have been little more than 'rant and cant' (Thomson). Ulysses and Hector, moreover, are not the only characters to undergo a radical change of heart and action. Troilus experiences a profound change of attitude towards Cressida, and Achilles, who at first regards the war with a contemptuous detachment, later becomes fiercely engaged in it. Such contradictory behaviour may make us feel that the characters are inconsistent but, according to Adamson, such a reaction would be beside the point. The play, she suggests, 'raises questions about such volatilities and vacillations, and about how these are linked with the desire for satisfaction, stability, concord, unity; and also it seems to raise even more basic questions about what constitutes the distinct individuality of a particular self'. Thomas also regards 'the abundance of references to the identity and nature of the characters' as a distinctive feature of the play.

There has been disagreement about the soundness of Troilus' political principles. Knight believes that the Trojans generally 'stand for human beauty and worth' and that their cause is admirable 'if only because they believe in it'. Rossiter, on the other hand, regards Troilus' arguments as 'quite specious and self-deluding'; they are 'nonsense and meant to be taken as nonsense'. Similar disagreement has arisen about Troilus' feelings as a lover and the nature of his feelings for Cressida. Whereas Knight describes them as essentially 'pure, noble . . . hallowed by constancy', a 'mystic apprehension of romantic love', Campbell sees them merely as the appetites of 'an expert in sensuality', a 'sexual gourmet' towards whom we should be 'continuously critical and derisive'. Both critics assume extreme positions and neither does justice to the complex, contradictory character Shakespeare actually created. Our response to the climactic moment in which Troilus discovers Cressida's infidelity is determined by our view of him in the earlier scenes. For some readers he grows in tragic stature in an experience which is 'brutally and pitilessly effective' (Morris); for others he displays a hysterical disregard of realism which shows no 'tragic potentiality' (Campbell). His final return to battle has similarly been considered as a chivalrous enterprise undertaken for 'the fine values of humanity, fighting against the demon powers of cynicism' (Knight) and as a descent into mere brutality: 'At the very outset of the play . . . he could dismiss the warmongers as "Fools on both sides". Now he is one of them, lover turned savage warrior, a thing of courage to whom mercy is "a vice" ' (Dollimore).

Whatever their disagreements about individual characters, most critics agree that the love story and the political action run in parallel, each portraying the collapse of the ideals which inspired it. As Yoder says, 'Hector's death carries us to the same conclusion as the disillusionment of Troilus: namely, that the ugly realities of this world are at cross-purposes with the codes of courtly love and honour that seem to govern it.' But although there is general agreement that this is the way in which the play is constructed, there are widely different views about how this evidence should be interpreted. It can be interpreted as an expression of absolute moral nihilism, a demonstration on Shakespeare's part that all ideals are merely consoling illusions. 'It has been advanced', says French, 'that *Troilus* is about men's failure to live up to their ideals. But the presentation of those ideals is so satirical that it is evident that the play is really concerned with the delusive nature of the ideals themselves.' Foakes puts forward a totally opposite view. 'Whatever the limitations of the Greek and Trojan warriors', he declares, 'they are capable of grand aspirations and noble ideals. . . . The play is not disillusioned, even nihilistic, as some critics argue; it is, however, notably realistic in the sense that it portrays men and women in society trying in their muddled way to cope with public demands that clash with private desires, and always with the pressure of time upon them.' Adamson also sees the play as not totally pessimistic and cynical, but rests her case less on Shakespeare's words than on an audience's instinctive reaction to them. 'The play does compel our assent to the lethal logic of Hector's assassination of Patroclus, or the Myrmidons' of Hector', but it 'simultaneously compels our feelings to *dissent* from such things. These lives are fragile, they do not last; but that does not mean that we acquiesce in their extinction'.

Our response to the play as a whole is further complicated by the presence in it of two satirical commentators, the buffoonish Pandarus whose sexual pragmatism consistently undermines Troilus' 'impassioned rhapsodising' (Rossiter), and Thersites the cynic who dismisses the entire action of the play as nothing but 'wars and lechery'. In fact the critics reveal their view of *Troilus and Cressida* by the way in which they regard Thersites. Some see him as an authoritative spokesman, a reliable guide to what is actually happening. Thomas thinks that he is not just a 'degenerate railer' because he is 'so accurate in his pronounce-ments'. Adamson also sees a good measure of truth in his scabrous invective, but believes that this is no reason for taking it as the whole truth. 'With Thersites, as with all the others, the play gives considerable salience to his views while also casting a quizzical, inquisitive light on them.' Bradshaw puts forward a similar view. We should, he believes, not accept Thersites' nihilistic outlook because he is precisely 'the kind of person to whom such a conclusion would appeal'; 'to be the play's most scurrilous unpacker of human motives is his pride and pleasure, but because the play also unpacks that pride and pleasure, it suggests that such reductivism could satisfy only those who are physically and emotionally warped—are, in human terms, func-tionally incomplete.' Thersites is, however, only the most un-sympathetic character in a play populated entirely by people with whom we cannot wholly identify ourselves. All of them are egocentric, or treacherous, or unfaithful, or prurient, or at best unstable. If we are to find some kind of norm by which to judge them it is we, as French argues, who must supply and assert it. Unfortunately, however, the critics have so far failed to agree on what such a norm might be.

All's Well that Ends Well

TEXTS

The new Arden edition, edited by G. K. Hunter, the New Cambridge, edited by Russell Fraser, and the New Penguin, edited by Barbara Everett, are the best available texts and all three have perceptive, informative introductions. The explanatory notes in the New Penguin are simpler and less detailed than those in the other two.

CRITICAL STUDIES AND COMMENTARY

Although *All's Well that Ends Well* was probably written in 1602, it did not appear in print until 1623 when it was included in the First Folio edition of Shakespeare's plays, and there is no record of a production before 1741. Its theatrical history has been written by Joseph G. Price who concludes that it has been 'produced infrequently and the productions have received scant critical attention'. He also believes that no 'really satisfying production of *All's Well* has yet been accomplished in a major theatre'. His survey, however, did not extend far enough to include the two excellent productions by the Royal Shakespeare company, the first directed by John Barton in 1967 with Ian Richardson as Bertram, the second, set in the late nineteenth century, directed in 1981 by Trevor Nunn in which Dame Peggy Ashcroft played the Countess. It was also very successfully directed for BBC Television by Elijah Moshinsky in 1980.

The themes of *All's Well that Ends Well* have been fully elucidated by Hunter in his edition. These are the contrast between youth and age, the 'moral frailty' of the young, especially Bertram and Parolles, and the moral stability of the old as represented by Bertram's late father, the King, the Countess, and Lafew. This contrast is connected with another idea, subtly examined by Donaldson, that the death of the older generation offers liberation to the young: 'the beginning of *All's Well* is thus concerned with an apparent ending which turns out to be indeed a beginning'. Another contrast discussed by Hunter, and which Bradbrook sees as the play's central concern, is between the inherited rank of Bertram and the innate virtue of the humbly born Helena, two different kinds of 'honour' on which the King delivers a formal *ex cathedra* speech (II. iii. 117–44). Closely related to this distinction, as Knight points out, is the question of female 'honour', or virginity, and the honourable state of matrimony consummated by the loss of virginity, a paradox which Helena and Parolles talk about towards the end of the first scene: 'the final use of her virginity is the purchase of honour not only for herself but also, as a ransom, for her husband' (Hunter). Honour of a different kind—the credit awarded to a distinguished soldier—is also what Bertram hopes to win by going to the war. Hence, as French says, 'Shakespeare pits an exemplar of the legitimate masculine principle, Bertram, who is capable of juggling morals to suit his own purposes . . . against an exemplar of chaste constancy, Helena, who is powerless and morally absolute'. These contrasts are accompanied by the idea that human beings are never wholly good or bad but made, as the First Lord declares, 'of a mingled yarn, good and ill together'. This idea, discussed by Rossiter and Fraser, lies behind the ambiguous impression created by the characters and the conflicting judgements passed upon them by the critics.

Bertram was roundly condemned by Samuel Johnson who denounced him as 'a man noble without generosity, and young without truth; who marries *Helen* as a coward, and leaves her as a profligate; when she is dead by his unkindness, sneaks home to a second marriage, is accused by a woman he has wronged, defends himself by falsehood, and is dismissed to happiness'. Coleridge, on the other hand, found himself 'unable to agree with the solemn abuse which the critics have poured upon Bertram. . . . He was a young nobleman in feudal times, just bursting into manhood, with all the feelings of pride and birth and appetite for pleasure and liberty natural to a character so circumstanced. Of course he had never regarded Helena otherwise than as a dependant in the family . . . [He] had surely good reason to look upon the King's forcing him to marry as a very tyrannical act'. These two conflicting opinions, the one denouncing Bertram as 'weak, cowardly, mean-spirited, false and ill-natured' (Rossiter), the other emphasizing his energy, youth, and need for freedom (French), recur throughout the play's critical history. Although, as everyone agrees, Shakespeare made his behaviour towards Helena callous and unfeeling, he also made his conduct understandable by emphasizing his immaturity. Bertram is a 'young cub', an 'unseasoned courtier', an example of 'unbaked and doughy youth' who seeks honour in battle but is trapped into marriage. What Everett calls his 'well-bred loutishness' is 'fitted to his age and understanding'. Moreover it is not simply Helena's superiority of character that puts him in an unfavourable light. In adapting his source, as Smallwood explains, Shakespeare also makes the older characters speak disparagingly of him and compare him, to his disadvantage, with Helena.

Her character has also aroused critical disagreement. The plot requires that she should behave with a determination and deviousness which some readers have found distasteful, especially Masefield who complains that she 'practises a borrowed art, not for art's sake nor for charity, but woman-fashion, for a selfish end'. Even her admirers admit that in her infatuation with Bertram she is blind to his faults. 'She does not seek to know what he is as a man', says Foakes, 'but is content with what she imagines him to be; and she never troubles to discover whether Bertram cares for her. In her own way she is as self-centered as Bertram and Parolles.' Yet comparison between Shakespeare's play and its source, as Smallwood demonstrates, shows that the dramatist tried to portray her in a favourable light and to protect her from 'those charges of predatoriness, of husband-hunting', to which some critics have objected. At the other extreme, Knight believes that she can do no wrong. She not only has the sincerity, intelligence, and humility which Bertram lacks, but is the agent of a sacrificial and redeeming love which makes her 'a semi-divine person, or some new type of saint'. Each one of these conflicting views, however, arises from some aspect of Helena which is actually in the play. She is, moreover, not simply complex (and wholly credible) in herself, but creates different impressions on the other characters. We admire or dislike her depending on whether we look at her through the eyes of the Countess and the King or from the standpoint of the man who is compelled to marry her. The conflicting opinions held by the critics are actually present in the play itself.

There has been closer agreement about the character of Parolles. He is, as his name indicates, a man of 'words' rather than deeds (Bradbrook), whose words are 'not only boastful, but of the newest cut. . . . The latest slang, the latest fashionable clothes are Parolles' stock-in-trade' (Hunter). His function is to serve as a foil to Bertram. The hero's immaturity is revealed by his initial respect for Parolles; his final exposure is paralleled by the earlier unmasking of Parolles (Rossiter); and his growth in experience is marked by his rejection of Parolles. Bertram's attraction to Parolles, as Smallwood puts it, is 'no more than the symptom of what is wrong with Bertram—his shallowness, his unthinking careless-ness, and lack of thought for others'. Yet, as Leech points out, Parolles also grows in maturity at the end and 'acquires an awareness of his own nature that Bertram never reaches'. He is not therefore merely despicable, though comparisons of him with Falstaff once made by Johnson and others now seem ex-aggerated and irrelevant.

Lavache, whose frank statements on sex and hell spring un-expectedly from so minor a character, serves a function in the total organization of the play. He and Parolles, says Foakes, 'seem to represent something in the bedrock of human beings; something of what they are is present in all; as, for example, the lust of the flesh that drives Lavache to think of marriage also urges Bertram to the bed of Diana later on, and perhaps has analogies with the lust of the eye which drives Helena to seek Bertram'. The fact that such sexual impulses motivate so many of the characters may, argues Fraser, encourage us to be more tolerant towards Bertram.

The critical disagreements which the characters of Bertram and Helena have provoked arise from the many-faceted quality of their personalities and the problematical nature of the situations in which Shakespeare placed them. The most worrying situation of all, however, is the one in which Bertram finds himself as the play comes to its conclusion. Here, as Smallwood describes it, 'we have an elaborate stage spectacle which allows Bertram to expose his cowardice, lust, dishonesty, and fear to all those characters whom he most wishes to impress', and in this degraded condition he is asked, indeed compelled, to accept once more the wife he has deserted. He does so in a single rhymed couplet, the brevity and conditional nature of which raise serious doubts about the genuineness of his words and the extent to which he has repented. 'Helena never saves Bertram,' declares Edwards, 'He is irredeemable: Shakespeare could not save him'; and Fraser agrees: 'Bertram, who never changes, never repents'. The King's closing words, 'All yet seems well', however, may suggest that the hero could still redeem himself and be genuinely united with the heroine at some time in the future. This possibility is made stronger if we recognize, as Donaldson does, that in this play 'endings often fail to come when we most expect them':

'*All's Well that Ends Well* speaks constantly of an end which is not finally realized within its dramatic framework, but pushed forward into an undramatized future'. What this ending may ultimately consist of we can never know, for it lies outside the scope of this complex and elusive play.

Measure for Measure

TEXTS

There are editions designed to serve the needs of a wide range of different readers. On the one hand there is the New Variorum, edited by Mark Eccles, which has an exhaustive textual and critical apparatus and contains the texts of Shakespeare's sources and copious extracts from critical studies of the play. At the other extreme there is the New Penguin, edited by J. M. Nosworthy, designed for the general reader, and between the two there is the Arden, edited by J. W. Lever, which has a selective apparatus and an informative, well-balanced introduction.

CRITICAL STUDIES AND COMMENTARY

A play called 'Mesur for Mesur' by 'Shaxberd' is recorded as having been performed before James I at Whitehall on 26 December 1604, but allusions in the text, examined by Eccles and Lever, suggest that it had been written and probably performed during the preceding summer. Although a radically adapted version by Sir William Davenant, *The Law against Lovers*, was produced in 1662 and another adaptation by Charles Gildon, *Measure for Measure, or Beauty the Best Advocate*, was put on in 1700, Shakespeare's original text was not performed again until 1720. It has not been very popular in the theatre but there have been successful productions in the twentieth century of which the most memorable was directed at Stratford-on-Avon by Peter Brook with Sir John Gielgud as Angelo, Barbard Jefford as Isabella, and Harry Andrews as the Duke. Like the other two problem plays, this 'great undefinable poem or unclassifiable play', as Swinburne called it, has been interpreted in widely differing ways. Schanzer is probably right to claim that 'no other play by Shakespeare . . . has aroused such violent, eccentric and mutually opposed responses.' Its central characters have been variously extolled and reviled and the play has been seen, at one extreme, as an expression of Shakespeare's disgust with humanity and, at the other, as a Christian parable of the atonement. Whereas for Coleridge it was 'the most painful—say rather the only painful' work that Shakespeare wrote, it has also been called 'a more Christian piece of thinking' than that of 'nine out of ten professional Renaissance theologians' (E. M. Pope).

The character who has aroused the strongest disagreement has been Isabella. Her refusal to sacrifice her chastity to save her brother's life has been judged as evidence either of saintliness or of rigid inhumanity. As early as 1753 Charlotte Lennox went so far as to denounce her as 'a mere vixen in her virtue' with 'the Manners of an affected Prude', an attack which provoked the Victorian critic Anna Jameson to praise her 'moral grandeur', 'saintly grace', and 'vestal dignity': 'She is like a stately and graceful cedar, towering on some alpine cliff, unbowed and unscathed amid the storm.' The divergency of opinion, and something of the passion, of both ladies has reappeared in the work of subsequent commentators. Whereas Sisson believes that Isabella represents 'something in womanhood' which Shakespeare 'reveres with all his heart' and R. W. Chambers compares her single-minded virtue to that of a Christian martyr, Ellis-Fermor regards her as 'hard as an icicle': 'Weak as [Claudio] is, his self-indulgence cannot stand comparison with hers, with the pitiless, unimaginative, self-absorbed virtue which sustains her.' An accurate interpretation lies between—or, rather, encompasses —both extremes. Leavis is right to suggest that although, in her confrontations with Angelo, she 'must command a measure of sympathy in us', nevertheless we should not 'regard her with pure uncritical sympathy as representing an attitude endorsed by Shakespeare himself'. Gless, in a full-length study of the play, associates her with the tradition of Protestant anti-monastic satire which criticized members of the religious orders for being more anxious to abide by 'the letter of their man-made laws' than 'the spiritual meaning of the scriptures': 'the essence of her nature lies in her allegiance to a system of man-made laws that are fundamentally at odds with other, transcendent laws to which the play's language persistently alludes.' Her final plea for Angelo's life, though legalistically expressed, reveals how profoundly her suffering has changed her and that she has acquired a capacity for mercy which was lacking in her treatment of her brother.

Angelo's attempt to impose the death penalty for fornication did not appear as improbable in Shakespeare's time as it no doubt does to modern audiences. McGinn, R. G. Hunter, and Thomas all point out that it was a policy seriously recommended by the more strict and extreme Puritan divines and that less than half a century after the play was written incest and adultery became felonies punishable by death, and fornication carried a sentence of three months' imprisonment. Claudio's plight is therefore 'not merely a requirement of the plot but a situation which could become a social reality' (Thomas). Angelo himself may well have been a recognizably Puritan type, the kind who 'seek for a name of righteousness because they be very stout and sore against other men's faults' (Erasmus, quoted by Gless). Hence, as Hawkins suggests, the most severe punishment he receives 'may be his total and irrevocable loss (comparable to a loss of chastity for Isabella) of personal integrity and self-respect'. No one realizes better than Angelo himself how far he has failed to live up to the moral standards he has tried to impose on others.

There is general agreement about the dramatic functions of the Duke which, indeed, are clear and simple enough: he sets the conflict in motion by handing over the responsibility of government to Angelo, takes charge of the situation when its consequences threaten to become dangerous, and sits in judgement over his subjects when they have recognized their own inadequacies. There has, however, been violent disagreement about the Duke's character, motivation, and the way in which he administers justice at the conclusion. Knight was the first critic to notice that his relationship to the other characters was comparable to that of God towards his creatures. His character, Knight believes, is 'that of the prophet of an enlightened ethic. . . . His sense of human responsibility is delightful throughout; he is like a kindly father, and all the rest are his children.' Gless also sees him as acting in a way analogous to God: 'we are compelled to view him as a human link, with human limitations, in a great chain, delegating to Angelo gifts that heaven first delegated to him.' 'He is,' says Miles, 'the benign but objective ruler who acts out the play's request for tolerance and compromise'. Lever, on the other hand, regards him as less than godlike: 'he is not infallible, omniscient or omnipotent, but has to resort to the shifts and stratagems of an earthly ruler'. Other critics have emphasized his fallibility: 'he plays upon the consciences of the other characters', says Hawkins, 'sets up and then removes the rod of the law; arbitrarily orders people into, and out of, death-row; and finally issues pardons for all offences.' His most severe critic is Long, who complains that the Duke 'feels himself licensed to lie, manipulate and bamboozle, responsive only to the neat execution of his own designs.' If Shakespeare really did intend him to seem as unprincipled as this, then he could not also have designed him as a portrait of James I, the ruling monarch. Yet several scholars, including Bradbrook and Schanzer, have shown that the Duke and the King were temperamentally similar. Like Duke Vincentio, James I preferred 'the life removed', disliked to 'haunt assemblies', and had a fondness for governing by subterfuge. Moreover the tempering of justice with mercy which the Duke displays in the final scene corresponds both with the King's principles, set out in his own treatise on 'the properties of government', the *Basilicon Doron* (or 'Royal Gift'), published shortly before the play was written, and with his actual, often capricious practice. Bennett, in an extensive study of the play, has no doubt that the Duke was a character 'whose acts and whose theories of government would be interesting to the new age and its new King because they were so carefully like the ones which the King had identified as his own'. It is hard to think of a Shakespearian character who has elicited such conflicting interpretations; to adjudicate between them would tax the ingenuity even of the Duke himself.

The most heated critical arguments have been about Shakespeare's management, through the Duke, of the play's conclusion. Practically none of the characters gets what he asks for. Angelo, shamed by the public exposure of his guilt, begs for death but is given life and marriage to the woman he has formerly rejected. Isabella, whose devotion to her religious vocation has sustained her throughout the assaults of Angelo, is offered marriage to the Duke, and Lucio, at first condemned to death for slander, is suddenly condemned to what he regards as a fate worse than death and is forced to marry the whore who has borne his child. These multiple marriages are clearly not of the joyful, fulfilling kind that occur in the last acts of Shakespeare's earlier comedies. (Marriage in this play, says French, is seen as a punishment.) Only Claudio is reunited with the woman he has loved all along, but he has endured the prolonged terror of a death sentence, which the Duke could at any point have annulled. To these judicial decisions the critics have responsed in a variety of ways. Some, like Leavis and Weil, have found them thoroughly satisfactory, 'a consummately right and satisfying fulfilment of the essential design'. 'The last scene,' says Owen, 'is . . . a confirmation . . . of the rest of the play.' Others, including Gless, have praised the Duke's verdict on political and judicial grounds: he manages to 'work a popular reprieve for the mildly guilty Juliet and Claudio, catch out an amusing but potentially dangerous slanderer, and expose to corrosive public shame a deeply corrupt chief magistrate'. As for Isabella's prospective marriage, it 'confirms her departure from bondage . . . and her entry into a world governed by fruitful, married love'. Those critics who are less concerned with the psychology of the characters than with the symbolism of the play's whole design believe that the ending depicts the fulfilment of its Christian teaching: 'Justice, charity, and wisdom are all present' according to Battenhouse 'centered in the Duke and richly exhibited in the plotted peace and merciful comedy which he effects.' Yet the people who find the conclusion wholly satisfactory overlook the fact that it creates almost as many difficulties as it resolves. As Hawkins puts it, 'the very marriage that structurally clinches the comic resolution . . . may bring to mind problems left unresolved on the psychological, emotional, level of action' and this is reflected in the number of characters (Angelo, Isabella, Julietta, Claudio, and Barnadine) who remain silent in response to the Duke's judgements. The reason may be that it is not the Duke but the playwright who is unable to deal satisfactorily with the dilemmas he has created (Knights, Mincoff, and Edwards), or that the problems are inherently insoluble. *Measure for Measure*, like the other problem plays, 'confronts the audience, as well as its characters, with conflicts that are no more amenable to a final solution in art, or, for that matter, to critical resolution, than they are amenable to a final solution in real life' (Hawkins). The arguments which the play has aroused for the last two centuries—and which still continue—may well have been precisely the effect Shakespeare hoped for.

REFERENCES

GENERAL STUDIES

Boas, F. S., *Shakspere and His Predecessors* (London, 1896).

Bradshaw, Graham, *Shakespeare's Scepticism* (Brighton, 1987).

Coleridge, S. T., *Coleridge's Shakespeare Criticism*, ed. T. M. Raysor, 2 vols. (London, 1930; Everyman's Library, London, 1962); *Coleridge on Shakespeare*, ed. Terence Hawkes (Penguin Shakespeare Library, Harmondsworth, 1969).

Dowden, Edward, *Shakspere: His Mind and Art* (London 1875).

Edwards, Philip, *Shakespeare and the Confines of Art* (London, 1968).

Foakes, R. A., *Shakespeare: The Dark Comedies to the Last Plays: From Satire to Celebration* (London, 1971).

French, Marilyn, *Shakespeare's Division of Experience* (New York, 1981).

Frye, Northrop, *The Myth of Deliverance: Reflections on Shakespeare's Problem Comedies* (Toronto and Buffalo, NY, 1983; Brighton, 1983).

Lawrence, W. W., *Shakespeare's Problem Comedies* (New York, 1931; Penguin Shakespeare Library, Harmondsworth, 1969).

Long, Michael, *The Unnatural Scene: A Study in Shakespearean Tragedy* (London, 1976).

Rossiter, A. P., *Angel with Horns* (London, 1961).

Schanzer, Ernest, *The Problem Plays of Shakespeare* (London, 1963).

Sisson, C. J., *The Mythical Sorrows of Shakespeare*, British Academy Lecture, 1934).

Thomas, Vivian, *The Moral Universe of Shakespeare's Problem Plays* (London, 1987).

Wilson, John Dover, *The Essential Shakespeare* (London, 1932).

Troilus and Cressida

TEXTS

Foakes, R. A. (ed.), *Troilus and Cressida* (New Penguin Shakespeare, Harmondsworth, 1987).

Muir, Kenneth (ed.), *Troilus and Cressida* (Oxford Shakespeare, Oxford, 1982).

Palmer, Kenneth (ed.), *Troilus and Cressida* (Arden Shakespeare, London, 1982).

CRITICAL STUDIES AND COMMENTARY

Adamson, Janet, *Troilus and Cressida* (Harvester Critical Introductions to Shakespeare, Brighton, 1987).

Alexander, Peter, 'Troilus and Cressida, 1609', *The Library*, 9 (1928), 267–86.

Campbell, O. J., *Shakespeare's Satire* (New York, 1943).

Dollimore, Jonathan, *Radical Tragedy: Religion, Ideology and Power in the Drama of Shakespeare and His Contemporaries* (Brighton, 1984; 2nd edn., 1989).

Fly, Richard D., ' "Suited in Like Conditions as our Argument": Imitative Form in Shakespeare's *Troilus and Cressida*', *SEL* 15 (1975), 273–92.

Foakes, R. A., '*Troilus and Cressida* Reconsidered', *University of Toronto Quarterly*, 32 (1962–3), 142–54.

Knight, G. Wilson, *The Wheel of Fire: Interpretations of Shakespearian Tragedy* (London, 1930; rev. edn., 1949).

Morris, Brian, 'The Tragic Structure of *Troilus and Cressida*', *Shakespeare Quarterly*, 10 (1959), 481–91.

Muir, Kenneth, '*Troilus and Cressida*', *Shakespeare Survey 8* (1955), 28–39.

Ornstein, Robert, *The Moral Vision of Jacobean Tragedy* (Madison, Wis., 1960).

Thomson, Patricia, 'Rant and Cant in *Troilus and Cressida*', *Essays and Studies*, 22 (1969), 33–56.

Yoder, R. A., ' "Sons and Daughters of the Game": An Essay on Shakespeare's *Troilus and Cressida*', *Shakespeare Survey 25* (1972), 11–25.

All's Well that Ends Well

TEXTS

Everett, Barbara (ed.), *All's Well that Ends Well* (New Penguin Shakespeare, Harmondsworth, 1970).

Fraser, Russell (ed.), *All's Well that Ends Well* (New Cambridge Shakespeare, Cambridge, 1985).

Hunter, G. K. (ed.), *All's Well that Ends Well* (Arden Shakespeare, London, 1959).

CRITICAL STUDIES AND COMMENTARY

Bradbrook, Muriel C., *Shakespeare and Elizabethan Poetry* (London, 1951).

Donaldson, Ian, '*All's Well that Ends Well*: Shakespeare's Play of Endings', *Essays in Criticism*, 27 (1977), 34–54.

Johnson, Samuel, *Samuel Johnson on Shakespeare*, ed. W. K. Wimsatt (New York, 1960); reprinted as *Dr. Johnson on Shakespeare* (Harmondsworth, 1969).

Knight, G. Wilson, *The Sovereign Flower* (London, 1958).

Masefield, John, *William Shakespeare* (London, 1911).

Price, Joseph G., *The Unfortunate Comedy* (Toronto and Liverpool, 1968).

Smallwood, R. L., 'The Design of *All's Well that Ends Well*', *Shakespeare Survey 25* (1972), 45–61; reprinted in *Aspects of Shakespeare's Problem Plays*, ed. Kenneth Muir and Stanley Wells (Cambridge, 1982). 26–42.

Measure for Measure

TEXTS

Eccles, Mark (ed.), *Measure for Measure* (New Variorum Edition, New York, 1980).

Lever, J. W. (ed.), *Measure for Measure* (Arden Shakespeare, London, 1965).

Nosworthy, J. M. (ed.), *Measure for Measure* (New Penguin Shakespeare, Harmondsworth, 1969).

CRITICAL STUDIES AND COMMENTARY

Battenhouse, R. W., '*Measure for Measure* and Christian Doctrine of the Atonement', *PMLA* 61 (1946), 1029–59.

Bennett, Josephine Waters, '*Measure for Measure' as Royal Entertainment* (New York, 1966).

Bradbrook, Muriel C., *Shakespeare and Elizabethan Poetry* (London, 1951).

Chambers, R. W., *Man's Unconquerable Mind* (London, 1939).

Ellis-Fermor, U. M., *The Jacobean Drama: An Interpretation* (London, 1936).

Gless, Darryl J., *Measure for Measure: The Law and the Convent* (Princeton, NJ, 1979).

Hawkins, Harriett, *Measure for Measure* (Harvester New Critical Introductions to Shakespeare, Brighton, 1987).

Hunter, Robert Grams, *Shakespeare and the Comedy of Forgiveness* (New York, 1965).

Jameson, Anna, *Characteristics of Women*, 2 vols. (London, 1832).

Knight, G. Wilson, *The Wheel of Fire: Interpretations of Shakespearian Tragedy* (London, 1930; rev. edn., 1949).

Knights, L. C., 'The Ambiguity of *Measure for Measure*', *Scrutiny*, 10 (1942), 222–33.

Leavis, F. R., '*Measure for Measure*', in *The Common Pursuit* (London, 1952).

Lennox, Charlotte, *Shakespear Illustrated*, 3 vols. (London, 1753).

McGinn, D. J., 'The Precise Angelo', in *J. Q. Adams Memorial Studies*, ed. J. G. McManaway *et al.* (Washington DC, 1948), 129–39.

Miles, Rosalind, *The Problem of 'Measure for Measure'* (London, 1976).

Mincoff, Marco, '*Measure for Measure*: A Question of Approach', *Shakespeare Studies*, 2 (Cincinnati, Ohio, 1966), 141–52.

Ornstein, Robert, *The Moral Vision of Jacobean Tragedy* (Madison, Wis., 1960).

Owen, Lucy, 'Mode and Character in *Measure for Measure*', *Shakespeare Quarterly*, 25 (1974), 17–32.

Pope, E. M., 'The Renaissance Background of *Measure for Measure,*
Shakespeare Survey 2 (1949), 66–82.

Swinburne, A. C., *A Study of Shakespeare* (London, 1880).

Weil, Herbert, 'Form and Contexts in *Measure for Measure*', *Critical*
Quarterly, 12 (1970), 55–72.

8 | The Late Comedies

MICHAEL TAYLOR

TEXTS

There are no competing early texts for any of the late comedies. *Cymbeline*, *The Winter's Tale*, and *The Tempest* appear only in the 1623 First Folio; *Pericles* makes a scruffy debut in a 'debased' quarto of 1609 (reproduced as a photographic facsimile with an Introduction by W. W. Greg in 1940) but, for some reason, does not appear in a Folio until the Third in 1664. The three Folio plays present no major textual problems; *The Tempest* is, indeed, in its advertising position as the first play in the Folio, a model of its kind. And while the 1609 text of *Pericles* is clearly not a model one, it is nonetheless the only substantive, authoritative early edition from which all the others derive. The absence of *Pericles* from the First Folio and the fact that the others appear in it out of sequence indicate that the compilers did not apparently envisage these plays as a group. *The Tempest* is the first play in the Folio, heading the section of comedies; *The Winter's Tale* is the last in this section and was almost left out altogether (the fate of *Pericles*), and *Cymbeline* comes at the end of the tragedies and is the final play in the Folio. Such indifference to family resemblance on the part of Heminges and Condell puts into perspective the subsequent critical concern with the romances as the interweaving instruments of a quartet.

Of modern single editions of these plays the Arden series has set the highest standards. Particularly to be recommended for the perspicuity of their Introductions in this series are Frank Kermode's edition of *The Tempest* ('extraordinary for the density, range, and intelligence of its documentation' as Harry Berger remarks) and J. M. Nosworthy's edition of *Cymbeline*. In some ways, another series, the New Penguin, has proven to be more readable than the Arden, without sacrificing scholarly standards (its notes, for instance, do not clutter up the actual text of the play). Particularly to be recommended in this series, again for the strength of their Introductions, are Philip Edwards's edition of *Pericles*, Anne Righter's of *The Tempest*, and Ernest Schanzer's of *The Winter's Tale*. Three Signet editions can be warmly recommended: Ernest Schanzer's *Pericles*, Robert Langbaum's *The Tempest*, and Frank Kermode's *The Winter's Tale*. Still interesting for the modern reader (partly because of an engaging quirkiness in the treatment of the plays) are the editions of the New (Cambridge) Shakespeare, especially J. C. Maxwell's discerning *Pericles*. In a class of its own is the first of the romances to be published in the Oxford Shakespeare series, Stephen Orgel's fine edition of *The Tempest*.

CRITICISM AND COMMENTARY

'Tales, Tempests and such like Drolleries': What Is Romance and Why Did Shakespeare Write It?

A great deal of hard thought and imaginative speculation has been expended by critics of the romances in the pursuit of a persuasive definition of Shakespearian romance and the reasons for the playwright's turning to it at the end of his career. The term's resistance to easy categorization is not surprising considering how intractable romance, a hybrid conglomerate if ever there was one, has always been to its anatomizers and definers. One can therefore sympathize with the despairing critic who wants to back out of the problem altogether by maintaining that Shakespeare's romances are uncategorizable, something or other peculiarly and uniquely Shakespearian; as A. D. Nuttall puts it, 'There is a sense in which the last plays of Shakespeare are *sui generis*, so that any word would do (the blanker the better)' (1966). The eloquence of this notion of blankness is reinforced by the reminder from Stanley Wells that the word romance was never used by Shakespeare, nor by the Elizabethans to describe any play, nor was the adjective recorded until 1659. The critic who offers us the most celebrated, and celebrative, attempt to see the romances as anything but *sui generis* is, of course, Northrop Frye, whose book, *A Natural Perspective: The Development of Shakespearean Comedy and Romance*, revels in the reliance of these last plays on the operatic conventions of romance whose popularity rests squarely on what Frye calls its 'mythic descent'. The kind of reality celebrated in the romances is one 'symbolized by nature's power of renewal; it is the world we want; it is the world we hope our gods would want for us if they were worth worshipping'; the romances offer us 'an imaginative model of desire' in which death is an unnatural force. And it is a world and a mode towards which, so Frye assures us, Shakespeare has been pulled throughout his career; there is a 'logical evolution toward romance in Shakespeare's work'.

Many, perhaps most, critics who have dealt seriously with Frye have taken issue to some extent with his anatomy of Shakespearian romance, while acknowledging its coherence and power. There are large and significant differences, Diana Childress reminds us, between Frye's formulation of romance—a category for him that transcends generic boundaries—and our experience of Shakespeare's romances themselves: above all, our experience of the estranging grotesque in them, she argues, might well make Shakespeare's romances not really romances at all. Perceptions of the estranging grotesque, or weaker versions of it at least, dominate the criticism of commentators who see Shakespearian romance as generically unstable (although it is not altogether clear to me why the grotesque should be considered, in some essential way, inimical to romance). *The Tempest's* 'confinements, contortions, problems', according to Richard Hillman, militate against its being thought of as a romance and, while acknowledging that Shakespeare's romances are clearly in the traditions of classical romance and the chivalric romance of the late Middle Ages, Howard Felperin, in a major book on the late comedies, *Shakespearean Romance*, stresses the largely unoperatic way Shakespeare in them combines the reality and pleasure principles, with the former invariably having the last word. He notices, for instance, that Shakespeare's romances, 'like Milton's, are on one level a stern reprimand of romance (while remaining romance) and test to the breaking point not only the characters they contain but the mode they employ', though he would doubtless agree with Frye that they are more Sidneian than Baconian and, like R. G. Hunter, he sees them finally as examples of a 'comedy of atonement'.

A comedy of atonement: variations on this formula are commonplace. For D. G. James (1937) the notion of atonement survives in the romances even though they exist for him primarily as poetic meditations on issues and themes that have 'no interest in humanity'. The atonement or, in his terminology, 'renewal', consists of the recovery of lost royalty despite the acknowledged tragedy of human life and the terrific presence of evil. G. Wilson

Knight supplies us with a more exuberant, perhaps more way-ward, version of this position, in which the plays are triumphant 'myths of immortality', shunning, so he would have us believe, the 'side-issues of Elizabethan and Jacobean manners, politics, patronage, audiences, revolutions and explorations' for the sake of 'poetic quality and human interest', though it is hard for us to imagine just what Knight leaves human for Shakespeare to be poetic about. A number of critics see in explicitly Christian terms what J. P. Brockbank more decorously describes as 'some solace of immortality' (1971). S. L. Bethell, for instance, argues that the romances' interest in bygone times is an attempt 'to recreate a vanished blessedness', with *The Winter's Tale*, in particular, an 'adequate literary expression of Christian humanism'; and Bonamy Dobrée sees throughout the romances a 'diffusion of Christian Charity, an all-understanding love'. For Louis Martz, A. D. Nuttall (1972), and others the humanism is more Greek than Christian, especially for *The Winter's Tale* and *The Tempest*. Roy Battenhouse, however, allies himself with Bethell, noting that their approach meets with the disapproval of 'critics un-accustomed to typological interpretation'. This sort of thing is pursued on the secular plane by D. A. Traversi who thinks of the last plays as symbolic poems: 'the plot has become simply an extension, an extra vehicle of the poetry'. His position, and others like it, is put in its place by Philip Edwards, most notably, who talks of 'the pallidness of all interpretations of the last plays which insist that they are symbolic utterances' (1958). The more moderate, less 'typological' notion of a morally coherent universe in Shakespeare's romances is pursued by D. L. Peterson. An earlier version of this view is E. M. W. Tillyard's belief that the romances are the final phase of the tragic pattern—'his *Eumenides* to the already completed *Agamemnon*'.

Expressions of such certainty now seem rather old-fashioned. 'What kind of emotional responses were the Romances designed to arouse?' asks Philip Edwards (1958) with perhaps a touch of asperity. For Ruth Nevo the question is still not easily answered as the romances constitute a 'taxonomic scandal'. It is necessary according to her thesis to restore to them their essential uncanni-ness by invoking 'the findings and methods of present-day post-psychoanalytic semiotics' in order 'to discover an informing or generating fantasy, or ensemble of fantasies, in each play'. The chief method or technique of promoting fantasy turns out to be—for all the plays, not just the romances—a process whereby the major characters are nearly all 'split figures, doubles or proxies for each other'. Although her book makes stimulating reading, her heavy reliance on this one stratagem on Shakespeare's part (if indeed it is one) strains credulity; there are too many rhetorical leaps of faith of the kind indicated by her question about Cleon: 'Is Cleon, proxy father for Pericles, also his masochistic self-image?' I doubt whether Nevo would take no for an answer to this question. Nonetheless, some evidence for some kind of taxonomic scandal can be seen in the critical obsession with genre itself. *The Tempest*, for instance, as Gary Schmidgall points out, has been read as romance, morality play, initiation ritual, refinement of the *commedia dell'arte*, topical response to New World voyages, masque, comedy, tragedy, hymeneal celebration, fairy tale, myth, and autobiographical palinode. Schmidgall himself offers the epic as his contribution to the classification debate, a notion peculiarly (perhaps paradoxically) congenial to *The Tempest* with its Virgilian echoes (see Orgel's Oxford edition of the play). If critics *do* see the plays mainly as romances the word seems almost to have become a mere appendage to its more significant qualifier—tragi-comic, pure (Uphaus on *Pericles*), problem (Uphaus on *Cymbeline*), historical (Brockbank on *Cymbeline* (1958), with interesting variations on the idea of what constitutes its historicity by Harris, Moffet, and Emrys Jones), ethical, and so on.

Almost as much effort as went into the investigation of the nature of Shakespearian romance has also gone into explaining why Shakespeare turned to writing it when he did. Although variations, usually of a milder kind, on Lytton Strachey's notorious charges of indifference and boredom still occasionally surface, by and large the more persuasive interpretations insist on the supremacy of theatrical and professional concerns to explain Shakespeare's fascination with the revival of romance. Frank Kermode (1963) puts the case for this approach convincingly:

the most profitable explanation is that which postulates a revival of theatrical interest in romance, and seeks the reason for it not so much in the older drama as in the great heroic romances of the period, Sidney's *Arcadia* and Spenser's *Faerie Queene*.

Kermode is working here in a fairly popular field of enquiry. G. E. Bentley's paper, for example, written in 1948, is a more than useful introduction to the theatrical context of the romances, especially in its emphasis on the importance of the purchase of the private playhouse, Blackfriars, by Shakespeare's company in 1608 (cf. Muir 1974)). A. C. Kirsch talks of the last plays in the context of the 'operatic' conventions exploited by Marston, Fletcher, and Jonson. Dennis Bartholomeusz's history of *The Winter's Tale* in the theatre provides us with a focused view of the importance of theatrical convention in our understanding of the play as a romance. E. C. Pettet's book emphasizing the power of the romance tradition for Shakespeare's cast of mind is still well worth reading, as is Carol Gesner's on Shakespeare and the Greek romance. Perhaps the most stimulating direction that this kind of approach has recently taken—more stimulating, for instance, than the traditional one advocated by A. H. Thorndike and his student F. H. Ristine of the influence of Beaumont and Fletcher—has been in the work of critics, like Schmidgall, Frye (1978), Proudfoot, and Jacquot, who insist on the huge importance of the court masque in the early seventeenth century as an influence on the drama of the time, especially on Shakespeare's late comedies. Schmidgall describes the masque as 'the period's most intriguing, astonishing, and innovative art form', particularly important from a political point of view, while Frye sees Shakespeare's romances as 'a kind of democratized version of the same form, a people's masque'.

'You speak a language that I understand not': Language and Structure in the Late Comedies.

'The possibilities of language dominate the main issues we have to face in the last plays' writes Jonathan Smith in an important article on *The Winter's Tale*, and he goes on to demonstrate how vital it is for us to know the social status of words in Shakespeare's time in order to understand, for instance, the extent and intensity of a character's social, political, or familial alienation. (Information about the social status of words is something that the Oxford editions of the plays give in fair measure.) Characteristic of speakers in the last plays (notably Leontes in *The Winter's Tale*), so Anne Barton argues in a pair of important articles, is an unawareness of the primary meaning of words, part of a widening disjunction between language and speaker, accentuating (cf. Hallett Smith) the way language is used to emphasize the occasion rather than to characterize the speaker. She talks of 'linguistic mis-meetings' (1971) where 'Words define the gap between individuals; they do not bridge it'. Mis-meetings, misunderstandings, gaps, all signal the use of a language that no one really understands: 'the Romances are written in a form of otherspeaking' remarks Philip Edwards provocatively (1958). And in a book on *The Winter's Tale* which 'stands . . . as an invitation . . . for continued payment of loving attention to this still much-tooneglected masterpiece', Charles Frey surrenders himself to the play's 'vastness and opacity'. Little wonder, then, given language's dramatized inadequacy, that the gaps between the words should loom larger sometimes than the words themselves; in *The Tempest*, 'the absent, the unspoken . . . is the most powerful and problematic presence' writes Stephen Orgel (1986). (Cf. W. T. Jewkes who talks of 'the power of paralanguage' in *The Tempest*, though we should note that the unspoken has traditionally been seen in beneficent visionary terms, as, in Tinkler's tautology, the 'still movelessness of the ideal vision'.) The gaps between the words are the linguistic equivalent of the gap between the words' maker and the life he describes, leading J. M. Nosworthy, for one, to claim that 'the Jacobean Shakespeare is a more anonymous and more enigmatic person than the Elizabethan one'.

The verse itself is often tortuously compressed and Metaphysical in conceit: a 'verse of an hysterical virtuosity' as Frank Kermode describes its workings in *Cymbeline* (1963), a necessary virtuosity perhaps for a play, in Taylor's words, 'blown stylistically between the opposing winds of fairy-tale and case-history'. And there is pain too here in the marriage of harsh form with harsh content, first noticed particularly by F. C. Tinkler: '[*Cymbeline*'s verse] has a hard corrugated texture . . . from the persistent recreation of feelings of a particular kind of physical pain'. Stephen Orgel writes of *The Winter's Tale*: 'even the syntax is tragic' (1986), and Russ McDonald almost concurs: 'even the syntax is tragi-comic'. When Leontes sees the truth of things he begs for 'verbal excoriation', as C. T. Neely puts it. In all the romances, Barbara Mowat tells us, there are 'violent conjunctions of representational and presentational style'. It is hardly surprising, then, that an equation is often made between, say, *Cymbeline*'s difficult, tumid language and its 'embroiled, darkly skeptical world view', as Maurice Hunt chooses to describe it, while the language itself of *The Tempest* sometimes has to bear the burden of its speakers' imperialism: Stephen Greenblatt, for example, argues trenchantly that the play insists on our noticing the extent to which the 'New World is a vast, rich field for the plantation of the English language'. Much too is made of the deliberate stylistic awkwardness of some of the romances. According to Rosalie Colie, in a fine book on Shakespeare, *The Winter's Tale* is 'a truncated torso of a play', one 'conspicuously ill-made'. (There are other voices. Fitzroy Pyle's rather pedestrian book on *The Winter's Tale*, for instance, makes an impassioned defence of the play's essential shapeliness).

Much is also made of the fact that the awkwardness of these plays is frequently conveyed by a deliberate cultivation of the archaic, the primitive, the *faux-naïf*. Here is how J. P. Brockbank (1971) puts it:

For it happened at the beginning of the seventeenth century, and would happen again at the end of the eighteenth, that a society with a highly complex and civilized literary culture looked back to old tales and to the Middle Ages in search of rich simplicities, expressible in innocent speech and show.

Pericles is a particular target of this approach. Philip Edwards's New Penguin edition boldly talks of the 'great deal of subtlety and care [that] went into giving the impression of a work of artless simplicity, even naivety'. He writes: 'An atavism of technique casts over the whole the sentimental glow of times past so important for the nostalgic Elizabethans'. Howard Felperin tells us that we have to 'unlearn our sophisticated notions of dramatic story-telling' (1967). A brilliant examination of *Pericles* along these lines can be found in Andrew Welsh's article. I suppose it is only fair to point out that sometimes these and other defenders of the perspicuity of primitive technique seem to have gone over to the other side of idolatry in their determination to give Shakespeare the benefit of the doubt over every ill-tuned string.

'Thou madest thy daughters thy mother': The Family in Shakespeare's Late Comedies

It has often been observed that much of Shakespeare's drama is about families, and his romances make explicit the paradox, as Meredith Skura reminds us in an essay on *Cymbeline*, of the immense importance of the family to the play's characters and at the same time the necessity for them to bring about its destruction in one way or another: 'both parents and children have to find

the right balance between holding on and letting go'. Putting it
in this blandly sociological way does not do justice to the fervency
of Shakespeare's presentation in the romances of rejection, per-
secution, and conciliation within the family, nor to the extraordinary radiating significance of the workings-out of this process.
David Bergeron in *Shakespeare's Romances and the Royal Family*
catches something of the magic at work here in his enlightening
contrast between Shakespeare's treatment of the family and the
early seventeenth century satiric dramatists', of whom Shakespeare is only an occasional member. Satire demystifies and
demythologizes the family, argues Bergeron; Shakespeare politi-
cizes and mythicizes it. Bergeron is much less impressive when
he is writing directly on the main topic of his book, the alleged
intimate connections between the presentation of the family in
Shakespeare's plays and the actual historical circumstances of
the English royal family. In this he resembles all the other royal
watchers he castigates—principally Frances Yates and Glynne
Wickham—though we would probably all agree with the former
when she writes: 'the atmosphere of Elizabethan revival around
the younger royal generation is the atmosphere to which Shakespeare's Last Plays belong'.

Criticism that attempts to go beyond atmosphere without
falling into the mire of biographical and excessively topical
speculation could do worse than begin with Charles Frey's
observation that in the romances 'problems of sons as tragic
victims of their fathers' feuds are largely eliminated'. He goes on
to say that 'only daughters are looked to for continuation of the
central family', but adds the important warning that they are
'exalted more as potential wives and father-comforters than as
persons in their own right' (1980). He concludes his essay with
an even more dire warning: '[the romances] may be more patriarchal and patrilineal in perspective than Shakespearean interpreters have yet cared or dared to recognize', indulging, in fact,
what David Sundelson calls a 'paternal narcissism'.

Some critics have at least dared to recognize an ill-disguised
sexual disgust in the romances, reminiscent of the problem
comedies. Coppélia Kahn writes: '*Pericles*, *The Winter's Tale* and
The Tempest all mirror anxiety about—even disgust at—desire,
female sexuality, and procreation'. According to Patricia Gourlay,
the mysogynistic male order of *The Winter's Tale* is destroyed by
'subversive woman, truth-teller and . . . artist', or the 'maternal

super-ego' in Murray Schwartz's (1975) psychoanalytic terminology. Stephen Orgel talks of the 'psychoanalytic shape' (1986) of
The Tempest in which an absent mother and wife are replaced by
'surrogates and a ghostly family' and a 'violently libidinized
adolescent Ferdinand'. Violently libidinized! It is perhaps in this
context that we should ponder the ambiguous case of Lysimachus
and Marina in *Pericles*: 'much of the heart is taken out of the play'
writes Edwards (1976) if we do not imagine that Marina has
succeeded in smiling Lysimachus' depravity out of act.

As one might expect, given the obvious fact that the late
comedies all end in tranquillity, more optimistic views about the
workings of human sexuality and the role of women in the
romances can be found in the work of a number of critics. D. W.
Harding's article 'Shakespeare's Final View of Women' describes
how in the tragedies, especially in *Macbeth*, *Antony and Cleopatra*,
and *Coriolanus*, men are dominated and destroyed by women. In
the romances, except for Dionyza and Cymbeline's Queen, the
women are supremely beneficent, especially the younger ones
who do not yet have 'the more severe and formidable possibilities
of the mature woman'. Harding makes discreet use of the possibilities of royal flattery and the possible significance of the
death of Shakespeare's son, Hamnet, as motivating factors in the
construction of these plays and he makes much of the fact that
Cymbeline and Prospero *free* their daughters. Cyrus Hoy writes
in a similar vein when he insists that in the romances Shakespeare attempts to liberate his imagination from the 'shrill
mistress-wife-mother figures' of his earlier plays. In an earlier,
extremely influential, article, C. L. Barber (1969) sees these beneficent women as indispensable catalysts in the regenerative
transformations of the older generation: 'where regular comedy
deals with freeing sexuality from the ties of the family, these late
romances deal with freeing family ties from the threat of sexual
degradation', with the young women, in Ernest Schanzer's words,
standing as 'emblems of the state of innocence which their elders
have lost' (1969).

*'Your actions are my dreams': Psychology and Politics and the Late
Comedies*

As we have seen in the previous section, most modern critics
have been influenced in some measure (sometimes without
knowing it) by the 'psychoanalytic shape' that these plays etch

on the cortex. What this approach, the psychologizing one, has in common with the political is an unusual emphasis on an awareness (some readers might think an overawareness) of the extent to which Shakespeare's plays are, in Stephen Orgel's words, 'collaborative fantasies' (1986), with us, the readers, as implicated analysts:

That is why every generation, and perhaps every reading, produces a different analysis of its Shakespearean texts.

The resulting waywardness and cocksureness, in more ways than one, of the psychological approach are well conveyed by Murray Schwartz's confident pronouncement on Cloten's remark in *Cymbeline* about British noses: 'Britain's a world by itself, and we will nothing pay for wearing our own noses' (III. i. 13–14). He writes: 'The nose obviously here assumes a phallic significance, displaced upward, and Cloten imagines it as detachable'. In Shakespeare's emphasis here on Cloten's largely out-of-character, temporary, transfiguring patriotism, Cloten's remark is, in terms of his 'psychology', simply and desirably unanalysable. Norman Holland's self-critical diffidence in his role as psychoanalyst of the text in his article on Caliban (1968) seems to me no more than appropriate in the circumstances.

Politicizers of the text also frequently acknowledge the degree of creative collaboration involved in their readings, though they would probably shy away from the word 'fantasies'. A remarkably confident and influential statement of their credo can be found in Tony Bennett's article in a collection of essays, *Re-Reading English*, designed for the undergraduate:

The position which a text occupies . . . at the originating moment of production is . . . no necessary indicator of the position which it may subsequently come to occupy in different historical and political contexts . . . [it is] not a question of what texts mean but of what they might be *made to mean* politically.

What they might be made to mean politically can and does cut across the ideological spectrum, from large (and conservative) claims like Schmidgall's that the last plays reveal an 'astonishing recovery of political optimism' on the part of a writer who, unlike Marston, refuses to 'sequester himself in misanthropy', to views that see them as Schmidgall sees *King Lear, Timon of Athens*, and *Coriolanus*: as 'the bleak obverse of *The Book of the Courtier*'.

Schmidgall's book is almost entirely devoted to *The Tempest*, a play whose profligate, vulnerable openness to all manner of interpretation requires a section to itself.

'Spirits to control, art to enchant': *The Tempest*.

Articles and books on *The Tempest* outnumber all the works on the rest of the late comedies put together. The play's interpretative malleability, especially its invitation to allegorists of all stripes, has set subtle and not so subtle minds a-racing. 'This is a multiple, complex allegory' Brockbank claims (1966), and its multiplicity cannot be better demonstrated than in Michael Srigley's contention that the play 'is virtually a Rosicrucian document'. Anne Righter (Barton) notes more generally and more acutely: '*The Tempest* is an extraordinarily obliging work of art. It will lend itself to almost any interpretation, any set of meanings imposed on it: it will even make them shine' (1968). Sometimes complexity falls victim to the lure of a simple topicality as when Prospero is seen, in Patrick Grant's article, as James I or John Dee. Sometimes it falls victim to an elaborate religious mysticism as in the case of Colin Still's work (1936). (E. E. Stoll's *PMLA* article remains an excellent antidote to Still's and others' religiosity.) Occasionally topicality and other interests combine as in the case of Lorie Leininger's feminist argument that sees the marriage between Miranda and Ferdinand in terms of the real one between Elizabeth and Frederick in 1613, and, in a good-humoured attempt to rewrite the play, advocates a compensatory subversive alliance between Miranda and Caliban.

A great deal of imaginative speculation has concerned itself with those supremely enigmatic creations, Ariel and Caliban, especially Caliban, 'the core of the play' as Frank Kermode (1962) describes him. Harry Levin notes that Caliban has become

a mouthpiece for cosmic speculation in Browning's *Caliban upon Setebos, or, Natural Theology in the Island*, for revolutionary ideology in Renan's *Caliban: Drame Philosophique*, and for a Jamesian commentary on the play itself in *The Sea and the Mirror* by W. H. Auden.

Sometimes complexity (and everything else) falls victim to the furthest reaches of the interpreter's imagination as in D. G. James's desperate belief in his nonetheless stimulating book *The Dream of Prospero* that *The Tempest* is a dream of Prospero's who has in fact never left Milan. An attempt to put all this speculation into some kind of theoretical perspective can be found in A. D. Nuttall's *Two Concepts of Allegory*, but the book's declared objective to 'show that allegorical poetry is more curiously and intimately related to life than was allowed by C. S. Lewis's petrifying formula' now seems to be arguing against a thesis that perhaps never should have been taken terribly seriously, and its conclusion that the island and most elements of the play are 'pre-allegorical' is not very helpful (cf. P. Yachnin's notions of 'autobiographical allegory' and 'pseudo-allegory'). Nuttall's later essay on the play, where he describes its ending as 'sick with ambiguity' (1972) is, word for word, much more stimulating.

Schmidgall describes *The Tempest* as a 'political *summum bonum*' and compares it interestingly to Book VI of *The Faerie Queene*: in both the drama consists in large part of the 'conquest of civic monsters by idealized courtiers'; in both great stress is laid on the importance of obedience. Unlike the tragedies, wisdom and power are reconciled but, according to Paul Cantor, only through unbelievably good fortune: 'the case is only an ideal, a dream'. Most political and other commentary on *The Tempest* is more in Cantor's vein than Schmidgall's; Howard Felperin (1980), for instance, believes that the play 'has broken irreparably with its mythic source and entered the realm of ironic secularity'. The question most asked about the play, whether or not in terms of its ironic secularity (though nowadays usually in precisely these terms), is: who or what is Shakespeare/Prospero? The parameters of the debate were established in 1969 in a seminal article on *The Tempest* by Harry Berger Jr. who, taking issue with what he describes as the sentimentalist's reading of the play, gives us a world-weary, embattled, and cynical Prospero. Richard Abrams, very much an ironic secularist, thinks of Prospero in terms of the 'villain-playwright analogy'. The meaning of Prospero's magic, the meaning of his abjuration of it, and the meaning of his apparent change of heart in his pursuit of revenge, are stimuli for obsessive conjecture. The complexity of Prospero as mage is investigated by Barbara Mowat in an illuminating article whereby Prospero should be seen both as a serious magician and a carnival illusionist (1981). After an impressively learned disquisition on the provenance of Prospero's magic, D. G. James comes to the remarkable conclusion that it is a 'far cry' from the 'last frenzies of Faustus to Prospero's serene abjuration of magic and all its ways' (cf. Sisson's article). Once a popular word with

commentators on *The Tempest*, 'serene' has become *the* word to
be shunned. Margreta de Grazia formulates Prospero's change of
heart a little too starkly perhaps, but her formulation focuses on
the nub of the issue: 'as the result of virtually nothing, a momentous change occurs in *The Tempest*'.

In recent years the most fashionable direction for allegorical
and symbolic interpretation to take has been the political, especially the politics of colonialism. At one time (and still to some
extent) this approach could remain married to the credo of
'serenity' whereby Prospero's colonizing triumph could be seen,
in Leo Marx's seminal essay, as affirming 'an intellectual and
humanistic ideal of high civilization'. Nowadays, Prospero is
much more likely to be seen, according to Thomas Cartelli, as a
kind of Kurtzian figure dispossessing Caliban of his rightful
inheritance. Howard Felperin in fact directly compares *The
Tempest* with *Heart of Darkness*, that 'ultimate modernist
ironization of the romance form it adopts' (1978). An even more
provocative version of this debunking approach can be found in
Paul Brown's article where the island of *The Tempest* is seen in
terms of the Ireland of the early seventeenth century, though the
argument is clearly fuelled by Ireland's situation in the twentieth.
Brown stresses the paradoxical mutuality of Prospero and Caliban
whereby, for instance, Caliban's swooning raptures over the
island's sweet airs represent (scandalously) 'a utopian moment
where powerlessness expresses *a desire for powerlessness*'. Stephen
Greenblatt agrees with Brown: Shakespeare 'places Caliban at
the outer limits of difference only to insist upon a mysterious
measure of resemblance', and he asks us to see this mysterious
attraction, as does Brown, in a larger context of colonialism,
noting the 'disturbing allure' that the concept of the Wild Man
has traditionally held for the Western imagination. Stephen
Orgel argues that in their new encounter with American natives,
Britons saw their own past, while Europeans thought of themselves as versions of American Indians: 'it was claimed that if
Indian babies were kept out of the sun, they would grow up
white' (1985).

POSTSCRIPT: CRITICAL SURVEYS

One way of keeping track of the changing critical fortunes of
these plays is to consult a number of critical surveys. Philip
Edwards supplied one in 1958 which covered the years from 1900

to 1957. The first decade of the century, he notes, was dominated by the biographical approach, which then gave way to the theatrical, particularly the importance of the move to the Blackfriars. Later, the two dominant influences moved away from the theatre and out of the author's life, concentrating instead on the literary properties of the late comedies: the nature of dramatic romance (a perennially fascinating conundrum as we have seen) and the play's mythic, symbolic, and allegorical significances.

In 'Shakespeare's Romances since 1958: A Retrospect' F. D. Hoeniger in 1976 traced two important lines of development. One involves a busy expansion of the investigation of theatrical considerations in our understanding of the romances, especially the one that lays such stress on the influence of the masque (Hoeniger asks us to think of *The Tempest*, for instance, in terms of Mozart's *The Magic Flute*). The other line of enquiry emphasizes a return to a more sophisticated examination of Shakespeare's sources, with his earlier plays in particular providing useful insights into the last ones: here, Hoeniger singles out the work of R. A. Foakes and David Young. A category all to himself in this period, as far as Hoeniger is concerned, is Northrop Frye. Another is what Hoeniger calls 'unsolemn approaches'. Norman Sanders in 1978 also provided us with 'An Overview of Critical Approaches to the Romances', which is especially useful in tracing the importance of the visionary response to the late comedies, primarily the Christian and the anthropological.

REFERENCES

TEXTS

Maxwell, J. C. (ed.), *Cymbeline* (New Shakespeare, Cambridge, 1960).
Nosworthy, J. M. (ed.), *Cymbeline* (Arden Shakespeare, London, 1955).

Edwards, Philip (ed.), *Pericles* (New Penguin Shakespeare, Harmondsworth, 1976).
Greg, W. W. (ed.), *Pericles 1609* (Shakespeare Quarto Facsimiles, 5; London, 1940).

Hoeniger, F. D. (ed.), *Pericles* (Arden Shakespeare, London, 1963).
Maxwell, J. C. (ed.), *Pericles* (New Shakespeare, Cambridge, 1956).
Schanzer, Ernest (ed.), *Pericles* (Signet Classic Shakespeare, New York, 1965).

Kermode, Frank (ed.), *The Tempest* (Arden Shakespeare, London, 1954).
Langbaum, Robert (ed.), *The Tempest* (Signet Classic Shakespeare, New York, 1964).
Orgel, Stephen (ed.), *The Tempest* (Oxford Shakespeare, Oxford, 1987).
Quiller-Couch, A. T., and J. D. Wilson (eds.), *The Tempest* (New Shakespeare, Cambridge, 1921).
Righter, Anne (Barton) (ed.), *The Tempest* (New Penguin Shakespeare, Harmondsworth, 1968).

Kermode, Frank (ed.), *The Winter's Tale* (Signet Classic Shakespeare, New York, 1963).
Pafford, J. H. P. (ed.), *The Winter's Tale* (Arden Shakespeare, London, 1963).
Schanzer, Ernest (ed.), *The Winter's Tale* (New Penguin Shakespeare, Harmondsworth, 1969).

CRITICISM AND COMMENTARY

Abrams, Richard, 'The Tempest and the Concept of the Machiavellian Playwright', *English Literary Renaissance*, 8 (1978), 43–66.
Barber, C. L., ' "Thou that beget'st him that did thee beget": Transformation in *Pericles* and *The Winter's Tale*', *Shakespeare Survey* 22 (1969), 59–67.
Bartholomeusz, Dennis, *'The Winter's Tale' in Performance in England and America 1611–1976* (Cambridge, 1982).
Barton, Anne, 'Leontes and the Spider: Language and Speaker in Shakespeare's Last Plays', in *Shakespeare's Styles: Essays in Honour of Kenneth Muir*, ed. Philip Edwards *et al.* (Cambridge, 1980), 131–50.
—— 'Shakespeare and the Limits of Language', *Shakespeare Survey* 24 (1971), 19–30.
Battenhouse, Roy, 'Theme and Structure in *The Winter's Tale*', *Shakespeare Survey* 33 (1980), 123–38.
Bennett, Tony, 'Text and History', *Re-reading English*, ed. Peter Widdowson (London, 1982), 223–36.
Bentley, G. E., 'Shakespeare and the Blackfriars Theatre', *Shakespeare Survey* 1 (1948), 40–9.
Berger, Harry, Jr., 'Miraculous Harp: A Reading of Shakespeare's *Tempest*', *Shakespeare Studies* 5 (1969), 253–83.
Bergeron, David M., *Shakespeare's Romances and the Royal Family* (Lawrence, Kan., 1985).
Bethell, S. L., *The Winter's Tale: A Study* (London, 1947).
Brockbank, J. P., 'History and Histrionics in *Cymbeline*', *Shakespeare Survey* 11 (1958), 42–9.
—— 'Pericles and the Dream of Immortality', *Shakespeare Survey* 24 (1971), 105–16.

——— 'The Tempest: Conventions of Art and Empire', in *Later Shakespeare*, ed. J. R. Brown and Bernard Harris (London, 1966), 183–201.

Brown, Paul, ' "This thing of darkness I acknowledge mine": *The Tempest* and the Discourse of Colonialism', in *Political Shakespeare: New Essays in Cultural Materialism*, ed. Jonathan Dollimore and Alan Sinfield (Manchester, 1985), 48–71.

Cantor, Paul, 'Prospero's Republic: The Politics of Shakespeare's *The Tempest*', in *Shakespeare as Political Thinker*, ed. John Alvis and T. G. West (Durham, NC, 1981), 239–55.

Cartelli, Thomas, 'Prospero in Africa: *The Tempest* as Colonialist Text and Pretext', in *Shakespeare Reproduced: The Text in History and Ideology*, ed. Jean Howard and Marion O'Connor (New York, 1987), 99–115.

Childress, Diana T., 'Are Shakespeare's Late Plays Really Romances?', in *Shakespeare's Late Plays*, ed. Richard Tobias and P. G. Zolbrod (Athens, Ohio, 1974), 44–55.

Colie, Rosalie, *Shakespeare's Living Art* (Princeton, NJ, 1974).

Dobrée, Bonamy, 'The Last Plays', in *The Living Shakespeare*, ed. Robert Gittings (London, 1960), 140–54.

Edwards, Philip, 'Shakespeare's Romances: 1900–1957', *Shakespeare Survey 11* (1958), 1–18.

Felperin, Howard, 'Romance and Romanticism: Some Reflections on *The Tempest* and *Heart of Darkness*, or When Is Romance No Longer Romance?', *Critical Inquiry*, 6 (1980) 691–706; reprinted in *Shakespeare's Romances Reconsidered*, ed. C. M. Kay and H. E. Jacobs (Lincoln, Nebr., 1978), 60–76.

——— *Shakespearean Romance* (Princeton, NJ, 1972).

——— 'Shakespeare's Miracle Play', *Shakespeare Quarterly*, 18 (1967), 363–74.

Foakes, R. A., *Shakespeare: The Dark Comedies to the Last Plays: From Satire to Celebration* (London, 1971).

Frey, Charles, *Shakespeare's Vast Romance: A Study of 'The Winter's Tale'* (New York, 1980).

Frye, Northrop, *A Natural Perspective: The Development of Shakespearean Comedy and Romance* (New York, 1955).

——— 'Romance as Masque', in *Shakespeare's Romances Reconsidered*, ed. C. M. Kay and H. E. Jacobs (Lincoln, Nebr., 1978), 11–39.

Gesner, Carol, *Shakespeare and the Greek Romance: A Study of Origins* (Lexington, Ky., 1970).

Gourlay, Patricia S., ' "O my most sacred lady": Female Metaphor in *The Winter's Tale*', *English Literary Renaissance*, 5 (1975), 375–95.

Grant, Patrick, 'The Magic of Charity: A Background to Prospero', *RES* NS 27 (1976), 1–16.

Grazia, Margreta de, '*The Tempest*: Gratuitous Movement or Action without Kibes and Pinches', *Shakespeare Studies*, 14 (1981), 249–65.

Greenblatt, Stephen, 'Learning to Curse', in *First Images of America*, ed. Fredi Chiapelli (Berkeley, Calif., 1976), 561–80.

Harding, D. W., 'Shakespeare's Final View of Woman', *TLS* (30 November 1979), 59+.

Harris, Bernard, ' "What's past is prologue": *Cymbeline*, and *Henry VIII* ', in *Later Shakespeare*, ed. John Russell Brown and Bernard Harris, (London, 1966), 203–33.

Hillman, Richard, '*The Tempest* as Romance and Anti-Romance', *University of Toronto Quarterly*, 55 (1985–6), 141–60.

Hoeniger, F. D., 'Shakespeare's Romances since 1958: A Retrospect', *Shakespeare Survey 29*, (1976), 1–10.

Holland, Norman N., 'Caliban's Dream', *Psychoanalytic Quarterly*, 37 (1968), 114–25.

Hoy, Cyrus, 'Fathers and Daughters in Shakespeare's Romances', in *Shakespeare's Romances Reconsidered*, ed. C. M. Kay and H. E. Jacobs (Lincoln, Nebr., 1978), 77–90.

Hunt, Maurice, 'Shakespeare's Empirical Romance: *Cymbeline* and Modern Knowledge', *Texas Studies in Language and Literature*, 22 (1980), 322–42.

Hunter, R. G., *Shakespeare and the Comedy of Forgiveness* (New York, 1965).

Jacquot, Jean, 'The Last Plays and the Masque', in *Shakespeare 1971: Proceedings of the World Shakespeare Congress, Vancouver, August 1971*, ed. Clifford Leech and J. M. R. Margeson (Toronto, 1972), 156–73.

James, D. G., *The Dream of Prospero* (Oxford, 1967).

—— 'The Failure of the Ballad-Makers', in *Scepticism and Poetry: An Essay on the Poetic Imagination* (London, 1937), 205–41.

Jewkes, W. T., ' "Excellent dumb discourse": The Limits of Language in *The Tempest*', in *Essays on Shakespeare*, ed. Gordon Ross Smith (Philadelphia Pa., 1964), 196–210.

Jones, Emrys, 'Stuart *Cymbeline*', *Essays in Criticism*, 11 (1961), 84–99.

Kahn, Coppélia, 'The Providential Tempest and the Shakespearean Family', in *Representing Shakespeare: New Psychoanalytic Essays*, ed. M. M. Schwartz and Coppélia Kahn (Baltimore, Md., 1980), 217–43.

Kermode, Frank, *Shakespeare and the Final Plays* (Writers and Their Work Series, 155; London, 1963).

Kirsch, A. C., '*Cymbeline* and Coterie Dramaturgy', *ELH* 34 (1967), 285–306.

Knight, G. Wilson, *The Crown of Life: Essays in Interpretation of Shakespeare's Final Plays* (London, 1947).

Leininger, Lorie, 'The Miranda Trap: Sexism and Racism in Shakespeare's *The Tempest*', in *The Woman's Part: Feminist Criticism of Shakespeare*, ed. Carolyn Lenz *et al.* (Chicago, Ill., 1980), 285–94.

Levin, Harry, 'Two Magian Comedies, *The Tempest* and *The Alchemist*', *Shakespeare Survey 22* (1969), 47–58.

Martz, Louis, L., 'Shakespeare's Humanist Enterprise: *The Winter's Tale*', in *English Renaissance Studies: Presented to Dame Helen Gardner in Honour of Her Seventieth Birthday*, ed. John Carey (Oxford, 1980), 114–31.

Marx, Leo, 'Shakespeare's American Fable', *Massachusetts Review*, 2 (1960–1), 40–71.

McDonald, Russ, 'Poetry and Plot in *The Winter's Tale*', *Shakespeare Quarterly*, 36 (1985), 215–29.

Moffet, Robin, '*Cymbeline* and the Nativity', *Shakespeare Quarterly*, 13 (1962), 207–18.

Mowat, Barbara A., *The Dramaturgy of Shakespeare's Romances* (Athens, Ga., 1976).

—— 'Prospero, Agrippa, and Hocus Pocus', *English Literary Renaissance*, 11 (1981), 281–303.

Muir, Kenneth, 'Theophanies in the Last Plays', in *Shakespeare's Late Plays*, ed. Richard Tobias and P. G. Zolbrod (Athens, Ohio, 1974), 32–43.

Nevo, Ruth, *Shakespeare's Other Language* (London, 1987).

Neely, C. T., '*The Winter's Tale*: The Triumph of Speech', *SEL* 15 (1975), 321–38.

Nuttall, A. D., *Two Concepts of Allegory: A Study of Shakespeare's 'The Tempest' and the Logic of Allegorical Expression* (London, 1967).

—— 'Two Unassimilable Men', in *Shakespearian Comedy*, ed. Malcolm Bradbury and David Palmer (Stratford-upon-Avon Studies, 14; London, 1972), 210–40.

—— *William Shakespeare: The Winter's Tale* (Studies in English Literature, 26; London, 1966).

Orgel, Stephen, 'Prospero's Wife', in *Rewriting the Renaissance: The Discourses of Sexual Difference in Early Modern Europe*, ed. Margaret W. Ferguson *et al.* (Chicago, Ill., 1986), 50–64.

—— 'Shakespeare and the Cannibals', in *Cannibals, Witches, and Divorce: Estranging the Renaissance*, ed. Marjorie Garber (Selected Papers from the English Institute, 1985, NS 11; London, 1987), 40–66.

Peterson, D. L., *Time, Tide and Tempest: A Study of Shakespeare's Romances* (San Marino, Calif., 1973).

Pettet, E. C., *Shakespeare and the Romance Tradition* (London, 1949).

Proudfoot, Richard, 'Shakespeare and the New Dramatists of the King's Men, 1606–1613', in *Later Shakespeare*, ed. John Russell Brown and Bernard Harris (Stratford-upon-Avon Studies, 8; London, 1966), 235–61.

Pyle, Fitzroy, '*The Winter's Tale*': *A Commentary on the Structure* (London, 1968).

Ristine, F. H., *English Tragicomedy: Its Origin and History* (New York, 1910).

Sanders, Norman, 'An Overview of Critical Approaches to the Romances', in *Shakespeare's Romances Reconsidered,* ed. C. M. Kay and H. E. Jacobs (Lincoln, Nebr., 1978), 1–10.

Schmidgall, Gary, *Shakespeare and the Courtly Aesthetic* (Berkeley, Calif., 1981).

Schwartz, Murray M., 'Between Fantasy and Imagination: A Psychological Exploration of *Cymbeline*', in *Psychoanalysis and Literary Process,* ed. F. C. Crews (London, 1970), 219–83.

——'*The Winter's Tale*: Loss and Transformation', *American Imago,* 32 (1975), 145–99.

Sisson, C. J., 'The Magic of Prospero', *Shakespeare Survey* 11 (1958), 70–7.

Skura, Meredith, 'Interpreting Posthumus's Dream from Above and Below: Families, Psychoanalysts, and Literary Critics', in *Representing Shakespeare,* ed. M. M. Schwartz and Coppélia Kahn (Baltimore, Md., 1980), 203–16.

Smith, Hallett, *Shakespeare's Romances: A Study of Some Ways of the Imagination* (San Marino, Calif., 1972).

Smith, Jonathan, 'The Language of Leontes', *Shakespeare Quarterly,* 19 (1968), 317–27.

Srigley, Michael, *Images of Regeneration: A Study of Shakespeare's 'The Tempest' and Its Cultural Background* (Studia Anglistica Upsaliensa, 58; Uppsala, 1985).

Still, Colin, *Shakespeare's Mystery Play: A Study of 'The Tempest'* (London, 1921); enlarged as *The Timeless Theme* (London, 1936).

Stoll, E. E., '*The Tempest*', *PMLA* 47 (1932), 699–726.

Sundelson, David, 'So Rare a Wonder'd Father: Prospero's *Tempest*', in *Representing Shakespeare,* ed. M. M. Schwartz and Coppélia Kahn (Baltimore, Md., 1980), 33–53.

Taylor, Michael, 'The Pastoral Reckoning in *Cymbeline*', *Shakespeare Survey* 36 (1983), 97–106.

Thorndike, A. H., *The Influence of Beaumont and Fletcher upon Shakespeare* (Worcester, Mass., 1901).

Tillyard, E. M. W., *Shakespeare's Last Plays* (London, 1938).

Tinkler, F. C., '*Cymbeline*', *Scrutiny,* 7 (1938–9), 5–20.

Traversi, Derek A., *Shakespeare: The Last Phase* (London, 1954).

Uphaus, R. W., *Beyond Tragedy: Structure and Experiment in Shakespeare's Romances* (Lexington, Ky., 1981).

Wells, Stanley, 'Shakespeare and Romance', in *Later Shakespeare,* ed. John Russell Brown and Bernard Harris (Stratford-upon-Avon Studies, 8; London, 1966), 49–79.

Welsh, Andrew, 'Heritage in *Pericles*', in *Shakespeare's Late Plays,* ed. Richard Tobias and P. G. Zolbrod (Athens, Ohio, 1974), 89–113.

Wickham, Glynne, 'Riddle and Emblem: A Study in the Dramatic Structure of *Cymbeline*', in *English Renaissance Studies: Presented to*

Dame Helen Gardner in Honour of Her Seventieth Birthday, ed. John Carey (Oxford, 1980), 94–113.

—— 'Shakespeare's Investiture Play: The Occasion and Subject of *The Winter's Tale*', *TLS* (18 December 1969), 1456.

Yachnin, P., ' "If by Your Art": Shakespeare's Presence in *The Tempest*', *English Studies in Canada*, 14 (1988), 119–34.

Yates, Frances A., *Shakespeare's Last Plays: A New Approach* (London, 1975).

Young, David, *The Heart's Forest: A Study of Shakespeare's Pastoral Plays* (New Haven, Conn., 1972).

9 | Titus Andronicus and Romeo and Juliet

R. S. WHITE

Titus Andronicus and *Romeo and Juliet* are Shakespeare's two earliest tragedies (though dating is difficult the first is normally placed 1589–90 and the second 1594–6), and they have sometimes been considered together for this reason, notably by Nicholas Brooke and G. K. Hunter. Hunter writes:

As one might expect with a playwright finding his way into his craft, similar structural skeletons serve for both plays, though the flesh hung on top of them is very different.

A. C. Hamilton places the two in the context of Shakespeare's youthful works, and James L. Calderwood deals with them in a book which argues for Shakespeare's developing 'metadramatic' self-reflexiveness (that is, an explicit use of the stage as metaphor in his plays). However, comparison and even arguments for 'development' are strained and only marginally revealing, since the plays are so different. *Titus Andronicus* is a development from a ferocious genre which centres on revenge, while *Romeo and Juliet* draws upon romance of love. Taken together, they teach a salutary lesson that Shakespeare did not just work in a single form called 'tragedy', but instead that he experimented with and brought to maturity several quite different and even antithetical traditions of tragedy. This fact can be appreciated most clearly if we compare each play with its source, an exercise which shows us both how derivative Shakespeare was, and how inspired he was in adaptation. The sources, and some helpful preliminary commentary, are to be found in Geoffrey Bullough's monumental volumes.

The commentary on each play will be considered separately here, and the fact that *Romeo and Juliet* is given more space reflects not only the ratio of criticism available but also the fact that the latter is a great favourite for study in schools and universities while the former is not often set for study. In both cases, a good place to start critical reading is Dieter Mehl's book, which gives brief, trustworthy introductions to both plays.

TEXTS

Which text you will want to work with depends on the way in which you wish to deal with the plays. The complete works of Shakespeare which matter are first the old-fashioned, unannotated but serviceable one edited by Peter Alexander, second the more ambitious 'Riverside' edition by G. Blakemore Evans, which has introductions to each play and notes, and third the new Oxford edition, by Stanley Wells and Gary Taylor, which makes some bold textual decisions. As for single-text editions, the main choice lies between the new Arden (*Titus Andronicus* is edited by J. C. Maxwell, *Romeo and Juliet* by Brian Gibbons), which contains scholarly introductions and copious notes of which by no means all are relevant to most readers; the New Penguin (of these two plays only *Romeo and Juliet* edited by T. J. B. Spencer is so far available), which has a very clear text and helpful critical introduction and notes; the New Cambridge (*Romeo and Juliet*, again, is the only one of these two plays available, edited by G. Blakemore Evans), whose introduction is valuable for its emphasis on staging possibilities, and which contains full textual apparatus and useful notes; (the series should not be confused with the earlier Cambridge editions, which were edited in rather cavalier fashion by John Dover Wilson); and the Oxford *Titus Andronicus* edited by Eugene M. Waith. I should recommend the Oxford *Titus Andronicus* and the New Cambridge *Romeo and Juliet*.

Titus Andronicus

Although there is testimony from Ben Jonson that *Titus Andronicus* was one of the most popular plays on the Elizabethan stage, it has not had much critical acclaim since then. Right up to the 1940s the play met with howls of disapproval, and critics have been willing either to give it away in embarrassment as not written by Shakespeare, or admit it into the canon only as an aberrant, 'barbarous' work. The more generous have conceded that, as Shakespeare's first tragedy (perhaps his first play), we can forgive an experimental and deeply flawed work. There is a clear line of disapproval stretching from Edward Ravenscroft who in 1686 absolved Shakespeare of any part in the writing of 'the most incorrect and indigested piece in all his Works, It seems rather a heap of Rubbish than a Structure'. The line leads beyond T. S. Eliot who called it 'one of the stupidest and most uninspired plays ever written, a play in which it is incredible that Shakespeare had any hand at all'. No wonder anybody who wishes to make a positive statement about the play starts off very much on the defensive. One relative sympathizer is J. C. Maxwell who edited the play, and he makes the corrective and valid point that it is a promising forecast of Shakespeare's unquestionably great tragedies, one planned in its own right 'on the grand scale, achieving a result that, however little it may appeal to us, is beyond the powers of any other dramatist writing at the time'. Hereward T. Price, whose specific intention is to attribute the play to Shakespeare rather than Peele, makes the point that the first scene is thoroughly 'Shakespearian' in both its structure and its underlying debate about justice. In the only book-length study, Maurice Charney makes many illuminating comparisons with *King Lear*, and praises *Titus Andronicus* in its own right. There is much in this book to repay careful reading.

Serious criticism of *Titus Andronicus* dates from 1940, when Fredson Bowers placed it in a tradition of revenge plays, comparing it (as Jonson did) with the great sensation of the Elizabethan stage, Kyd's *The Spanish Tragedy*, and later *Hamlet*. Bowers argues that, given the conventions of the genre of revenge tragedy, the atrocities are largely justified as they drive the essentially virtuous protagonist towards his own decision to take revenge. He also draws attention to the striking quality shown in the characterization of the black villain, Aaron, comparing him to Marlowe's Barabas (in *The Jew of Malta*) as one who takes 'delight in villainy for its own sake'. Bowers concedes, however, that Aaron is not fully integrated into the design. Whatever else we feel about the play, it must be admitted that Aaron in conception is the first fully 'Shakespearian' character. Eldred Jones examines the significance of his blackness, while Bernard Spivack sees him as one of the 'Family of Iago', a figure emerging from late medieval dramatic tradition. As well as

concentrating on Aaron, Spivack presents an interpretation of
the play as a whole, arguing that it has 'a large political theme,
the unity of Rome'. Other critics, notably Ribner and Hamilton,
have followed Bowers in interpreting the play as a serious development from Senecan revenge tragedy.

It comes as something of a surprise when, in 1944, we find
E. M. W. Tillyard describing *Titus Andronicus* as 'an abounding
play': 'There are beautiful lyrical passages, fresh descriptions of
nature, while Aaron is a magnificent comic villain.' However, his
analysis is based on aspects of the play which can hardly be
called central to its design, and can even be seen as exceptions
rather than any rule. Tillyard, anxious to advance a largely
conservative and now discredited orthodoxy of 'The Elizabethan
World Picture' based on order and strong control, follows through
the political questions of 'title and succession'. These certainly
are important and even fundamental at the beginning and end,
but the play's treatment cannot really sustain Tillyard's insistence
on order and monarchy, for it is the very act of relinquishing
elected power in favour of hereditary rule that implicates Titus in
the mayhem that follows. The political theme is interesting in
itself, but not in the way that Tillyard infers. When reading
Tillyard, we must remember that he was writing towards the end
of the Second World War (and in the decade afterwards), when
he cannot have been alone in yearning for a social stability which
he equates with strong monarchical rule, after the atrocities of
war. In other words, we may not agree with his views but we can
understand why he held them.

Another critic who takes the play seriously is M. C. Bradbrook
who, in 1951, saw it as 'more like a pageant than a play'. She
argues that its genre is at first the Complaint, leading up to 'a
kind of ballet of lamentation' in Act III. Only after this, she
argues, does it become a revenge play. This certainly seems more
perceptive about the structure than simpler explanations. Although she is dismissively patronizing of 'the groundlings' who,
she says, would not have understood much except the sensational
episodes, Bradbrook captures tones quite subtly, as when she
juxtaposes the earlier 'heraldic' presentation against Titus' later
wit and irony. She notices the presence of Ovidian material,
which Eugene Waith was to see as crucial to the play's 'organising
principle'. First, Waith says, Shakespeare learned from Ovid the
technique of 'portraying the extraordinary pitch of emotion to

which a person may be raised by the most violent outrage'. He
extends this perception by examining imagery of metamorphosis,
which indicates again Shakespeare's intention to portray transformations of powerful emotion, rather than to construct a neat,
Senecan plot. D. J. Palmer follows Waith's lead, reading the play
as Shakespeare's bold attempt to enact through ritual a paradoxical
expression of the unutterable in such powerful passages as this:

> MARCUS. But yet let reason govern thy lament.
> TITUS. If there were reason for these miseries,
>   Then into limits could I bind my woes.
>   When heaven doth weep, doth not the earth o'erflow?
>   If the winds rage, doth not the sea wax mad,
>   Threat'ning the welkin with his big-swol'n face?
>   And wilt thou have a reason for this coil?
>   I am the sea; hark how her sighs do blow.
>
>   (III. i. 219–26)

The critical attention given the play in the 1940s and 1950s no
doubt contributed to a star-studded production by Peter Brook
(1955), in which Laurence Olivier graphically proved the power
of such speeches. The production was very much influenced by
theories about 'Theatre of Cruelty' current at the time, and to
which Charney returns.

Before moving on to more recent critical approaches, we should
consider a reading which has surfaced from time to time, and
which still has some adherents. H. B. Charlton in 1948 roundly
declared that 'Titus Andronicus is melodrama'. He sees 'a night-
mare of horrors' and sensations, presented with little structural
or ethical coherence. Charlton himself takes a high moral tone
about this:

... melodrama, lacking an inner world, can have none of the philosophic
significance which is the peculiar function of tragedy; it can throw no
light on the great mysteries of human fate.

Others, beginning from the assumption that the play is melodrama, are not so contemptuous of the genre. John Dover Wilson,
believing Titus to be Shakespeare's reworking of a play by
George Peele, reads the play as a parody: 'Once catch the trick of
it, you can see [Shakespeare] laughing through most of the
scenes he rehandled'. He finds the description of the dismembered
Lavinia almost hilarious. Dover Wilson may have been drawing
on Mark Van Doren who, in 1939, had treated Titus Andronicus as

a parody of the genre of 'Tragedy of Blood', and also on T. S. Eliot who seems to have been the first to suggest the play is 'farce'. More generally, the approach had its heyday in performances during the 1960s, when Jacobean tragedy was often viewed as 'savage farce'. This approach conveniently forgets that *Titus* belonged to a fashion more than a decade earlier than the appearance of plays like *The Revenger's Tragedy*.

Since it is a superficially tempting interpretation, allowing us to feel superior in our detachment, some words should be said about this approach. Certainly *Titus* can be played as a parody, and even when played seriously it can raise laughs which are sometimes dramatically justified and sometimes arise out of a modern squeamish embarrassment at so many physical atrocities. Also, as Douglas H. Parker shows (while not supporting the reading of the play as one of 'black humour'), *Titus Andronicus* does draw on certain traditional comic conventions. Most of Shakespeare's tragedies share this trait, and it is one of his trademarks. But an overall approach to the play which turns it into a systematic debunking of tragic effects does not stand up to close scrutiny. At least on *reading* the play one can feel that Shakespeare is relentlessly serious to the point of grimness. (This may in itself constitute a problem to audiences attuned to expect 'comic relief'.) There is surely some confusion in critics who can find the rape and dismemberment of Lavinia risible while proclaiming the blinding of Gloucester in *King Lear* to be harrowing. It rather looks as if the earlier scene were a premonition of the later, and should be interpreted as having a similar function and effect. We can admit two things. After he has undertaken the mission of revenge, Titus begins to find grim relish in the task. His 'Ha, ha, ha!' at III. i. 264, which so shocks Martius, marks a turning point. Second, Aaron has an amoral vitality that expresses itself in sarcasm. (He too can be seen as a prototype of Edmund in *King Lear* and also the Bastard in *King John*.) These two insights, however, have serious rather than comic consequences. Aaron's extreme abdication from moral values, as in

> But I have done a thousand dreadful things
> As willingly as one would kill a fly,
> And nothing grieves me heartily indeed
> But that I cannot do ten thousand more
>
> (v. i. 141–4)

serves not to add humour but to highlight the hypocrisy of characters like Saturninus and Tamora, who claim righteous justifications of revenge for their deadly deeds. At least Aaron is not deceiving himself. Similarly, Titus' later recklessness contrasts with his earlier inability to 'dissemble' (I. i. 438 and III. i. 219 ff.) and his scruples about killing a fly (III. ii. 52 ff.—the very image used later by Aaron) until he recalls what part Aaron has played in the destruction of his family. He has been morally cauterized —reduced to the same callousness—as the world around him. Rome is a 'wilderness of tigers' (III. i. 54), a phrase used in the title of an essay by Alan Sommers on the play's structure and symbolic meaning. Each preys ruthlessly upon its own species and even family in futile and desperate attempts at survival. The metaphor may be unfair to tigers. Titus, after being initially a noble and selfless character, is now no better and no worse than the rest in his sadism, and this is as a result of what has been done to him and his family. In a balanced discussion, Reuben A. Brower (1971) comments on IV. iii:

At this point in the play we may say, 'Exit Titus, tragic hero', for the 'frantic wretch' of later scenes acts for the most part with little humanity or heroism.

C. L. Barber examines the family, both as metaphor and reality, seeing *Titus Andronicus* as an 'Abortive Domestic Tragedy'. Barber's chapter is one of the most interesting contributions, but it reveals its full power when read in the context of his book, which is an examination of the family in Shakespeare from a Freudian point of view.

Given the overwhelming evidence for the Elizabethan attitude that drama was educative (most eloquently expressed in Sir Philip Sidney's *Defence of Poetry*), contemporary audiences could have been expected to realize the causes of Titus' moral degeneration and to have noted the disastrous consequences of counter-revenge rather than regarding the tonal change as being one towards ghoulish farce. An interest in ethics, and more specifically in justice, marks some interpretations, such as G. K. Hunter's. R. S. White argues that the fate of Lavinia is an implicit condemnation of the society in which she lives where 'justice' is a matter of self-destructive, male revenge even when carried out by a woman such as Tamora. Lavinia's role is a 'blueprint' for those of other feminine victims such as Lucrece, Ophelia,

Desdemona, and Cordelia, as well as children in plays like *King John*, *Richard III*, and *Macbeth*. Catharine R. Stimpson, comparing the play with *The Rape of Lucrece*, writes

> Few of Shakespeare's dramas about traumatic injustice are as clear, or as severe, as those about the raped woman who must be punished because she endured an aggression she never sought and against which she fought.

By and large, critics feel more qualified to comment on matters of aesthetics rather than ethics. Albert H. Tricomi traces through *Titus Andronicus* the gory train of mutilation, arguing a case about the design of the play: 'Only in the literalization of its metaphors, it appears, does the tragedy seem to be at ease with itself.' Wolfgang Clemen also has interesting insights into the use of imagery, and Richard Marienstras links imagery and theme in considering the significances of the forest, hunting, and sacrifice.

Romeo and Juliet

The critical history of *Romeo and Juliet* began inauspiciously with an entry by Samuel Pepys in his Diary, dated 1 March 1662:

> . . . and thence to the Opera, and there saw "Romeo and Julett", the first time it was ever acted. But it is the play of itself the worst that ever I heard in my life, and the worst acted that ever I saw these people do.

'The first time it was ever acted' is at first sight puzzling in the light of the title page of the First Quarto, which indicates appreciative audiences in Shakespeare's day:

> An excellent conceited Tragedie of Romeo and Juliet. As it hath been often (with great applause) plaid publiquely, by the right Honourable the L. of Hunsdon his Seruants.

Pepys meant that it was the first performance since the closing of the theatres in 1642. We cannot explain away his contempt by dwelling on the inferior quality of the acting: he is quite explicit about 'the play of itself'. But when considering the comments of any critic it is important to remember that such people are, like the rest of us, the products of their time and class. Pepys was a hardheaded man who rose to be Secretary to the Admiralty, and although he was a great theatregoer he may not have approved of the indiscipline and financial recklessness involved in the passion of these young lovers.

The eighteenth and nineteenth centuries were kinder because, especially in the Romantic period, they were more respectful of strong emotions. It is arguable that critics of these ages provided more original, sympathetic insight into this play than those of the twentieth century. Nicholas Rowe in 1709 anticipated the two main lines of modern criticism by pinpointing two general areas of interest: the punishment of the families for their unreasonable feud, and the passion of the love story itself. Shakespeare, he says, 'has shown something wonderfully Tender and Passionate in the Love-part, and very Pitiful in the Distress'. Dryden in 1672 raised the fertile problem of the role of Mercutio, while Samuel Johnson in 1765 suggested that the Nurse was 'one of the characters in which the author delighted', a judgement that has become the frame of reference for modern critics when dealing with this character. His description of her as 'at once loquacious and secret, obsequious and insolent, trusty and dishonest' is, in its inclusiveness, still among the best commentaries on this character. The Romantic critics of the early nineteenth century took their cue from the great German commentator, August Wilhelm Schlegel (1811), in focusing on the lyricism and passion of the lovers expressed through their poetry. Both Hazlitt and Coleridge quote (the latter, notoriously, without acknowledgement) Schlegel's impression which, significantly, turns the play into a 'poem':

Whatever is most intoxicating in the odour of a southern spring, languishing in the song of the nightingale, or voluptuous in the first opening of the rose, is to be found in this poem. (Hazlitt's quotation)

It is significant that Hazlitt calls it a 'poem' rather than a play, a symptom of a common Romantic tendency. He and Coleridge played down Schlegel's equally important perception that the play 'at the same time is a melancholy elegy in its interest and imparted frailty; it is at once the apotheosis and the obsequies of love'. Our own century has found more to pursue in the darker second comment than in the idealizing of the first. Hazlitt's essay is particularly fine, and it comes from a great theatre man as well as critic. He incidentally builds into his essay on the play an argument that Shakespeare has captured an entire philosophy of life, one that lives in the innocent anticipation of youth rather than the critical disappointment of experienced hindsight. Like Pepys, Hazlitt is a man of his age, and he is partly using the play to criticize Wordsworth's philosophy of backward-looking nostalgia. A host of Victorian critics followed in Hazlitt's footsteps in praising the romantic aspect of the play and the ardency of Juliet.

Twentieth-century criticism, with its generally quizzical and ambivalent temper, has been less rhapsodic. Guided by the juxtaposing of violence and sentiment, many critics want to resist what they see as a naïvely sentimental response, and they have sometimes located their doubts in the play's execution. They may be taking their lead from A. C. Bradley who remarked that *Romeo and Juliet* is 'a pure tragedy, but it is an early work, and in some respects an immature one'. The distinction between 'a pure tragedy' and 'an immature one' is curious and may reveal an element of moral fastidiousness in Bradley, a great Victorian critic but, we suspect, one temperamentally unable to yield up his sympathies wholeheartedly to the pleasures of young lovers. (It may not be simply the youthfulness of the lovers that he is out of sympathy with, since he also significantly excludes *Antony and Cleopatra* from his list of the four great tragedies.)

Many modern critics disagree even with Bradley's cryptic phrase 'a pure tragedy'. Since the 1950s there has been a tendency to emphasize the 'mixed' quality of Shakespeare's drama and also ambivalent points of view expressed in each play. F. M. Dickey argues that *Romeo and Juliet* 'conforms surprisingly to the pattern of encouraging laughter at the folly of love' which we find in the comedies. James L. Calderwood also finds links with the comedies, and argues that the appropriate comparison is not with other tragedies but with *Love's Labour's Lost*, a romantic comedy which ends unexpectedly with separation of lovers rather than marriage. He argues that the real subject of both plays is language, the relationship of words to truth. Susan Snyder dwells on the 'comic matrix' of the play. Early in the play, she argues, the movement is essentially comic, containing many conventions from comedy. With Mercutio's death, however, the family feud becomes a matter of deeply felt hatred, and this tone, with the increasing helplessness of the lovers, turns the play-world into one of tragedy. *Romeo and Juliet* is then seen as a tragedy based upon comic formulas. One of the implications, as we shall see other critics arguing, is that 'For this once in Shakespearian tragedy, it is not what you are that counts, but the world you live in'. (As I have suggested, much the same might be said of critics.) One way of reconciling the comic elements with the tragic ending is suggested by R. S. White who argues that, at least in dealing with love, tragedy and comedy have a common generic source in romance. Love at first sight, separations, lucky and unlucky accidents, defiance of parents, high emotions, and improbable motifs such as sleeping potions occur again and again in ancient Greek and in Elizabethan romance, just as similar things (without the potions) happen in modern romances and soap-operas. The outcome, either happy or tragic, seems sometimes arbitrary. It is significant, for example, that *Othello*, another tragedy with a romance source, is analyzed by Snyder in a similar way to *Romeo and Juliet*.

Three books that look at Shakespeare's treatment of love itself in tragedy indicate other lines of approach, and again, given the range of views expressed, we may often feel that critics are revealing their own cultural assumptions rather than necessarily finding a 'truth' about the play. H. A. Mason, while acknowledging a 'sacred' quality (the word is borrowed from T. S. Eliot) in the powerful effect of the 'balcony' scene, the 'supreme moment in the play', tends nevertheless to accept Bradley's overall opinion, and in doing so he follows the judgemental and comparative critical method of Eliot and the 'Cambridge school' of critics. Mason criticizes the play for not unifying love and death 'in significant wholes' and uses it to analyse later plays 'in which Shakespeare appears to have been trying to accomplish what he failed to do in *Romeo and Juliet*'. It is quite common for academic critics to complain of a play's failure when audiences give it their resounding blessing. Mason provides a detailed comparison between the play and its source, a prose work by Arthur Brooke translated from French, itself translated from Italian concluding that where Shakespeare emphasizes Fate, Brooke shows Fortune at work. This rather metaphysical distinction has fuelled many an essay. Bertrand Evans (in a book which includes a chapter on *Titus Andronicus*), beginning with the notion of 'unawareness' (the characters do not know what we know because they have not heard the Prologue), argues that *Romeo and Juliet* is 'a tragedy of Fate'. 'Fate is the controlling practiser, and the entire action of the play represents her at work in the details of her housekeeping'. F. M. Dickey considers Elizabethan Platonic attitudes to love, a subject dealt with also by John Vyvyan. Dickey diplomatically builds into his approach a fusing of two apparently incompatible lines that the play is a tragedy of providence and also one of character, since fate is seen to be working through characters to punish the feuding families. Derick R. C. Marsh avoids trying to 'arrive at some neatly formulated abstraction which will represent Shakespeare's attitude to love', preferring to treat the play individually. He sees the love as 'doomed' because it is of a particular kind—'first love, that intense sexual attraction that by its very nature cannot long remain as it is'. Marjorie Garber refines this view by tracing a rapid maturation in the lovers from adolescence to maturity, as they are forced to come to terms with the painful realities of life. Given the plurality of versions of love amongst critics, it seems that love itself is as much a series of cultural constructions as critical interpretations of the play.

Others have seen the love as 'doomed' in a different sense. Molly M. Mahood, whose book is primarily about Shakespeare's varying forms of punning on words but also reaches deep into the plays she deals with, sees *Romeo and Juliet* as a 'dramatic experience' rather than as an arid philosophical debate about fate, character, or love (a preference shared by John Lawlor). Mahood finds the play a tragedy of love of a particular kind, but not the same kind as Marsh's. She sees it as *liebestod*, tragic passion which seeks its own destruction, such as that of Wagner's Tristan and Isolde, as defined by Denis de Rougemont (1939). Mahood writes:

When we explore the language of *Romeo and Juliet* we find that both its wordplay and its imagery abound in those concepts of love as a war, a religion, a malady, which de Rougemont has suggested as the essence of *amour-passion*.

The formulation allows her to describe a 'tragic equilibrium' between love and death, as the former is seen as something which inevitably includes the latter as part of its most intense manifestation. This approach has been questioned and denied by other critics, but at least it has the quality of preserving the idealistic fullness of experience played out by the lovers, the quality that places Romeo and Juliet amongst such celebrated myth figures of love as Tristan and Isolde and Heloise and Abelard. Julie Kristeva has produced a variation upon the nexus of love-death by connecting love-hate involved in 'transgression love, outlaw love', which exists because it violates social norms.

Quoting Juliet's 'My only love sprung from my only hate' (i. v. 139) and other similar lines, Kristeva argues that it is *because* there is the backdrop of family hatred that the love can exist so intensely between the young people, and that an element of potential hatred exists even within the relationship.

Norman Rabkin, in his stimulating book *Shakespeare and the Common Understanding*, finds not 'equilibrium' but irreconcilable paradoxes contained in a vision of 'complementarity'. Starting from the constant use of oxymoron in the play ('living, all is death's' iv. v. 40), he moves towards the overall view that the play is founded on a set of tragic paradoxes which the lovers while alive can neither resolve nor survive. They must live and die in 'the cursed mingling of two unreconcilable lives', although the further paradox also applies that, in dying, they lose all and yet achieve 'all there is to be gained' from love. Philip Edwards sees the fusion of 'contrary evaluations' in the play, a concept similar to Rabkin's.

In terms of what love means to the individual protagonists, the most interesting perceptions have come from critics who concentrate on Juliet's feelings. After all, as Coleridge pointed out, Romeo is not so innocent at the outset, and indeed he may be suspect in the rapidity with which he switches his attentions from Rosaline to Juliet. Irene Dash writes from a Juliet-centred perspective, analysing with particular acuteness the adolescent woman's ambivalent relationship with her mother and the equally important female, the Nurse. Diane Elizabeth Dreher takes the complementary but different line that Juliet is importantly involved in a relationship with her father based on his desire to dominate and hers to defy. Michael Goldman, in his suggestive book on the 'unsounded self' in Shakespeare, says our final image is 'not of the lovers as a couple, but of each as a separate individual grappling with internal energies that both threaten and express the self . . .'.

Other, conflicting views have been arrived at by concentrating on one of the three important characters other than the lovers, namely Friar Lawrence, Mercutio, and the Nurse. M. C. Bradbrook, dwelling as carefully as Mahood on imagery that links love and death, draws the opposite conclusion. Aligning herself with the Friar, she finds the love dangerous in its swiftness and she fears that 'quick bright things come to confusion' (*A Midsummer Night's Dream*, i. i. 149). The lovers are 'too impulsive to live

safely in the electric atmosphere that surrounds them'. Clifford
Leech implicitly supports the Friar in regarding the lovers as too
careless of their lives, but he is really arguing a different case
that, because it is so easy to take this line, the play is not fully
tragic. He is rather prescriptive in his notion of tragedy, saying
that it must become 'an ultimate confrontation with evil' to
qualify fully for the genre. The lovers, according to this argument,
are not evil but simply reckless. Bradbrook uses the Friar's moderation to criticize the lovers for their irrationality, while Leech uses
it to condemn the play as it stands for its very lack of the truly
irrational mystery of evil. Commitment to a single character's
perspective can (as we find over and over again in Shakespeare)
lead to opposite interpretations of the play as a whole.

Mercutio's status, problematic enough in its own right, was
confused still further by a legend perpetuated by Dryden (1672)
that Shakespeare had drawn the character so strongly 'that he
was forc'd to kill him in the third Act to prevent being kill'd by
him'—in other words, that the presence of Mercutio's vitality
risks overbalancing the play and distracting us from the lovers.
(Dryden himself, it should be said, does not agree with this
opinion, thinking Mercutio to be 'exceeding harmless'). Samuel
Johnson (1765) sagely points out that once Mercutio has fulfilled
his dramatic role in the construction of the play, there is no more
room for his 'wit, gaiety and courage'. Bernard Shaw (1895), ever
iconoclastic, regrets what he sees as the degeneration of Mercutio
from 'a wit and fantasist of the most delicate order' to a 'detest-
able and intolerable cad . . .'. Nicholas Brooke supplies a careful
analysis of the actual scene in which Mercutio is killed, presumably the one where Shaw thinks he is a cad. His other great
scene is where he speaks with strangely embittered intensity of
Queen Mab, a kind of anti-goddess of love, a note which in its
potential cynicism jars with the romantic elements and contributes
to an underlying, uneasy humour in the play. It is certainly a
scene in which adolescent passion is placed against an altogether
bleaker and more cynical version of love. Mercutio's death is not
only a pivotal moment for the plot, giving Romeo the impetus to
kill Tybalt, but also the occasion for his expressing outrage
against the family feud which is causing so much violence: 'A
plague o'both your houses' (III. i. 101, Arden edition).

The Nurse, who, along with Mercutio is Shakespeare's inspired
addition to his sources, is hardly cynical, but her attitude to love

is as different from that of the lovers as is Mercutio's. In fact, love hardly exists in her vision. She can understand sexual union as a bawdy, physical affair, and although initially she aids the Friar in allowing Romeo and Juliet to marry, she rapidly retrenches when the going gets tough and condones an arranged marriage between Juliet and Paris. Barbara Everett writes with memorable insight about the Nurse's comically verbose speeches in I. iii. Stanley Wells examines the associative logic, broken syntax, false connections, and circumstantial and bawdy details in the same speeches, discovering 'a kind of innocence' behind the words. An important function of the Nurse's monologues is, Wells argues, to lay great stress on Juliet's youthfulness.

It is important, after examining certain issues and characters in a play, to try to see it as a whole and to regard all elements as equally contributive to the total design and effect. An approach (with its own variations) emphasizing the total, dramatic context as much as the individual characters, is one that regards all the characters who die as in some respect the victims of the society in which they live. Mark Van Doren anticipated this approach when he saw the lovers as 'being alone in a world which does not understand them'. G. R. Hibbard says 'Romeo and Juliet move in a world which is either hostile to or, at the best, uncomprehending of and unsympathetic to their ideals and aspirations'. Philip Edwards, seeing the play as a 'mingled drama', finds the world of love sacrificed in a paradox to the enveloping world of hate: 'Hate breeds love, hate destroys love . . .'. And again, 'This love exists in—indeed, is born from—a world of malice and pettiness'. Coppélia Kahn, a feminist critic, specifies the 'malice' as masculine in origin. She sees the real tragic force in the play not as something mystical like 'fate' but 'in a realistic social sense', the feud between the families which is *patriarchal* in nature. The lovers cannot successfully negotiate their rites of passage towards adulthood because of the worldly, repressive obstacles put in their way by the violence of a predominantly male ethos. At least a part of this argument is textually justified when, at the end, the Prince directly accuses the heads of the respective families of causing the deaths:

> Where be these enemies? Capulet, Montague?
> See what a scourge is laid upon your hate,
> That heaven finds means to kill your joys with love!
>
> (v. iii. 291–3)

Capulet admits over the corpses that they are 'Poor sacrifices of our enmity!' (v. iii. 310). It is arguable that Juliet's fate in particular expresses an adolescent wish that death will, in the code of martyrdom, heal family wounds, eradicate conflict, and produce harmony from a conflict for which she has, by tragic circumstances, been made to feel responsible. Another important feminist study of Shakespeare's works is Juliet Dusinberre's *Shakespeare and the Nature of Women*, although there are only a few pages on *Romeo and Juliet*. Dusinberre emphasizes the 'reciprocal idolatry' between the young lovers that replaces the male idolatry of the courtly love tradition with its 'preconceptions about the nature of women'. Dusinberre's thesis that Protestant ideology initiated debate about orthodoxies also has significance for the ways in which the play presents enforced, loveless marriage as unjust to a young woman.

For anybody interested in the stage adaptations and receptions of *Romeo and Juliet*, Jill L. Levenson's short book offers the most comprehensive account. She presents information about performances from those on the Elizabethan stage, through Garrick's revisions and Charlotte Cushman's acting of the part of Romeo (with her sister as Juliet), down to Zeffirelli's film and his less celebrated stage version. Harley Granville-Barker was a great director and critic, and his comments on many of Shakespeare's plays are worth considering.

REFERENCES

Titus Andronicus

TEXTS

Alexander, Peter (ed.), *William Shakespeare: The Complete Works* (Glasgow and London, 1951).

Evans, G. Blakemore (textual ed.), *The Riverside Shakespeare*, Boston, 1974.

Maxwell, J. C. (ed.), *Titus Andronicus* (Arden Shakespeare, London, 3rd edn., 1961).

Waith, Eugene M. (ed.), *Titus Andronicus* (Oxford Shakespeare, Oxford and New York, 1984).

Wells, Stanley, and Gary Taylor (eds.), *William Shakespeare: The Complete Works* (Oxford, 1986).

Wilson, John Dover (ed.), *Titus Andronicus* (New Shakespeare, Cambridge, 1948).

CRITICISM AND COMMENTARY

Barber, C. L., and Richard P. Wheeler, *The Whole Journey: Shakespeare's Power of Development* (Berkeley and Los Angeles, Calif., and London, 1986).

Bowers, Fredson, 'The School of Kyd', *Elizabethan Revenge Tragedy 1587–1642* (Princeton, NJ, 1940).

Bradbrook, M. C., 'Moral Heraldry: *Titus Andronicus, Rape of Lucrece, Romeo and Juliet*', in *Shakespeare and Elizabethan Poetry: A Study of His Earlier Work in Relation to the Poetry of the Time* (London, 1951).

Brower, Reuben A., *Hero and Saint: Shakespeare and the Graeco-Roman Tradition* (Oxford, 1971).

Bullough, Geoffrey (ed.), *Narrative and Dramatic Sources of Shakespeare*, 8 vols. (London, 1957–75), vol. vi.

Calderwood, James L., '*Titus Andronicus*: Word, Act, Authority', in *Shakespearean Metadrama: The Argument of the Play in 'Titus Andronicus', 'Love's Labour's Lost', 'Romeo and Juliet', 'A Midsummer Night's Dream' and 'Richard II'* (Minneapolis, Minn., 1971), 23–51.

Charlton, H. B., 'Apprentice Pieces: *Titus Andronicus, Richard III* and *Richard II*', in his *Shakespearian Tragedy* (Cambridge, 1948).

Charney, Maurice, *Titus Andronicus* (Harvester New Critical Introductions to Shakespeare, Hemel Hempstead, 1990).

Clemen, Wolfgang, *The Development of Shakespeare's Imagery* (London and New York, 1951).

Eliot, T. S., *Selected Essays: 1917–1932* (London, 1932).

Hamilton, A. C., 'The Early Tragedy: *Titus Andronicus*', in *The Early Shakespeare* (San Marino, Calif., 1967), 63–89.

Hunter, G. K., *Dramatic Identities and Cultural Tradition* (Liverpool, 1978) (reprints the essays 'Seneca and the Elizabethans: A Case Study in "Influence"', 'Seneca and English Tragedy', and 'Shakespeare's Earliest Tragedies', containing material also on *Romeo and Juliet*).

Jones, Eldred, *Othello's Countrymen: The African in English Renaissance Drama* (London, 1965).

Marienstras, Richard, 'The Forest, Hunting and Sacrifice in *Titus Andronicus*', in his *New Perspectives on the Shakespearean World*, trans. Janet Lloyd (Cambridge, 1985).

Mehl, Dieter, *Shakespeare's Tragedies: An Introduction* (English translation, Cambridge, 1986).

Palmer, D. J., 'The Unspeakable in Pursuit of the Uneatable: Language and Action in *Titus Andronicus*', *Critical Quarterly*, 14 (1972), 320–39.

Parker, Douglas H., 'Shakespeare's Use of Comic Conventions in *Titus Andronicus*', *University of Toronto Quarterly*, 56 (1987), 486–97.

Price, Hereward T., *Construction in Shakespeare* (Ann Arbor, Mich., 1951).

Ravenscroft, Edward, *Titus Andronicus,* or *The Rape of Lavinia* (London, 1687).

Ribner, Irving, 'Senecan Beginnings: *Titus Andronicus, Richard III, Romeo and Juliet*', in his *Shakespearian Tragedy* (London, 1960), 14–35.

Sommers, Alan, ' "Wilderness of tigers": Structure and Symbolism in *Titus Andronicus*', *Essays in Criticism*, 10 (1960), 275–89.

Spivack, Bernard, 'The Hybrid Image in Shakespeare', in his *Shakespeare and the Allegory of Evil: The History of a Metaphor in Relation to His Major Villains* (New York and London, 1958).

Stimpson, Catharine R., 'Shakespeare and the Soil of Rape', in *The Woman's Part: Feminist Criticism of Shakespeare*, ed. Carolyn Ruth Swift Lenz, Gayle Green, and Carol Thomas Neely (Urbana, Ill., 1980), 56–64.

Tillyard, E. M. W., 'The Early Shakespeare', in his *Shakespeare's History Plays* (London, 1944).

Tricomi, Albert H., 'The Aesthetics of Mutilation in *Titus Andronicus*', *Shakespeare Survey* 27 (1974), 11–20.

Van Doren, Mark, '*Titus Andronicus*', in his *Shakespeare* (New York, 1939), 38–43.

Waith, Eugene, 'The Metamorphosis of Violence in *Titus Andronicus*', *Shakespeare Survey* 10 (1957), 39–49.

White, R. S., 'Lavinia', in his *Innocent Victims: Poetic Injustice in Shakespearean Tragedy* (2nd edn., London, 1986), 26–35.

Willbern, David, 'Rape and Revenge in *Titus Andronicus*', *English Literary Renaissance*, 8 (1978), 159–82.

Romeo and Juliet

TEXTS

Evans, G. Blakemore (ed.), *Romeo and Juliet* (New Cambridge Shakespeare, Cambridge, 1984).

Gibbons, Brian (ed.), *Romeo and Juliet* (Arden Shakespeare, London, 1980).

Spencer, T. J. B. (ed.), *Romeo and Juliet* (New Penguin Shakespeare, Harmondsworth, 1967).

CRITICISM AND COMMENTARY

Bradbrook, Muriel C., *Shakespeare and Elizabethan Poetry* (London, 1951).

Bradley, A. C., *Shakespearean Tragedy* (London, 1904).

Brooke, Nicholas, *Shakespeare's Early Tragedies* (London, 1968).

Bullough, Geoffrey (ed.), *Narrative and Dramatic Sources of Shakespeare*, 8 vols. (1957–75), vol. i.

Calderwood, James L., *Shakespearean Metadrama: The Argument of the Play in 'Titus Andronicus', 'Love's Labour's Lost', 'Romeo and Juliet', 'A*

Midsummer Night's Dream', and *'Richard II'* (Minneapolis, Minn., 1971).

Coleridge, Samuel Taylor, *Shakespearean Criticism*, ed. T. M. Raysor (London, 1930), vol. 2.

Dash, Irene G., *Wooing, Wedding, and Power: Women in Shakespeare's Plays* (New York, 1981).

de Rougemont, Denis, *Passion and Society*, transl. Montgomery Belgion (revised edn., London, 1956).

Dickey, Franklin M., *Not Wisely but Too Well: Shakespeare's Love Tragedies* (San Marino, Calif., 1957).

Dreher, Diane Elizabeth, *Domination and Defiance: Fathers and Daughters in Shakespeare* (Lexington, Ky., 1986).

Dryden, John, *Defence of the Epilogue*, in *Essays of John Dryden*, ed. W. P. Ker (Oxford, 1901).

Dusinberre, Juliet, *Shakespeare and the Nature of Women* (London, 1975).

Edwards, Philip, *Shakespeare and the Confines of Art* (London, 1968).

Evans, Bertrand, *Shakespeare's Tragic Practice* (Oxford, 1979).

Everett, Barbara, *'Romeo and Juliet*: The Nurse's Story', *Critical Quarterly*, 14 (1972), 129–39, reprinted in *Shakespeare's Wide and Universal Stage*, ed. C. B. Cox and D. J. Palmer (Manchester, 1984), 134–45.

Garber, Marjorie, *Coming of Age in Shakespeare* (London, 1981).

Goldman, Michael, *Shakespeare and the Energies of Drama* (Princeton, NJ, 1972).

Granville-Barker, Harley, *Prefaces to Shakespeare* (London, 1930), vol. 2.

Hazlitt, William, *Characters of Shakespear's Plays* (London, 1817).

Hibbard, G. R., 'New Pathetique Tragedie', in his *The Making of Shakespeare's Dramatic Poetry* (Toronto, 1981).

Johnson, Dr Samuel, *The Yale Edition of the Works of Samuel Johnson: Johnson on Shakespeare*, ed. Arthur Sherbo (Yale, 1968).

Kahn, Coppélia, 'Coming of Age in Verona', *Modern Language Studies*, 8 (1977–8), 5–22; reprinted in *The Woman's Part: Feminist Criticism of Shakespeare*, ed. C. R. S. Lenz, G. Greene, and C. T. Neely (Urbana, Ill., 1980), and in her *Man's Estate: Masculine Identity in Shakespeare* (Berkeley and Los Angeles, Calif., 1981).

Kristeva, Julia, 'Romeo and Juliet: Love-Hatred in the Couple', in *Tales of Love*, transl. Leon S. Roudiez (New York, 1987), 209–28.

Lawlor, John, *'Romeo and Juliet'*, in *Early Shakespeare*, ed. B. Harris and J. R. Brown (Stratford-upon-Avon Studies, 3; London, 1961), 123–44.

Leech, Clifford, 'The Moral Tragedy of *Romeo and Juliet'*, in *English Renaissance Drama: Essays in Honor of Madeleine Doran and Mark Eccles*, ed. Standish Henning *et al.* (Carbondale and Edwardsville, Ill., 1976).

Levenson, L., *'Romeo and Juliet': Shakespeare in Performance* (Manchester, 1987).

Mahood, Molly M., *Shakespeare's Wordplay* (London, 1957).

Marsh, Derick R. C., *Passion Lends Them Power: A Study of Shakespeare's Love Tragedies* (Sydney, 1976).

Mason, H. A., *Shakespeare's Tragedies of Love* (London, 1970).

Pepys, Samuel, *The Diary of Samuel Pepys*, ed. R. Latham and W. Matthews (London, 1970), iii. 39.

Rabkin, Norman, *Shakespeare and the Common Understanding* (New York, 1967).

Rowe, Nicholas, *The Works of Mr William Shakespear* (London, 1709), vol. i.

Schlegel, August Wilhelm, *A Course of Lectures on Dramatic Art and Literature*, ed. Rev. A. J. W. Morrison, trans. John Black (London, 1846).

Shaw, G. Bernard, *Shaw on Shakespeare*, ed. Edwin Wilson (Harmondsworth, 1961).

Snyder, Susan, *The Comic Matrix of Shakespeare's Tragedies* (Princeton, NJ, 1979).

Van Doren, Mark, *Shakespeare* (New York, 1939).

Vyvyan, John, *Shakespeare and the Rose of Love: A Study of the Early Plays in Relation to the Medieval Philosophy of Love* (London, 1960).

Wells, Stanley, 'Juliet's Nurse: The Uses of Inconsequentiality', in *Shakespeare's Styles: Essays in Honour of Kenneth Muir*, ed. Philip Edwards *et al.* (Cambridge, 1980), 51–66.

White, R. S., *'Let Wonder Seem Familiar': Endings in Shakespeare's Romance Vision* (Princeton, NJ and London, 1985).

10 | Hamlet

DAVID DANIELL

Hamlet is a complex achievement of high Renaissance art in Europe, and in Aristotle's sense the first great tragedy for two thousand years. It has always been seen as deserving a special place. In some particular senses, however, it belongs to today's world: 'To be or not to be' is the most famous quotation in the world's dominant language: and everyone who knows the play recognizes in the Prince a too-familiar figure. William Hazlitt noted that Hamlet lived five hundred years before we were born, but all his thoughts 'we seem to know as well as we do our own. . . . Their reality is in the reader's mind. It is we who are Hamlet. This play has a poetic truth, which is above that of history.' The current of debate and disagreement, about an already dense and internally disjunctive drama, is unusually strong, making a flood which still rises. *Hamlet* has always been the most discussed work of literature in the world. It was said in 1900 that the criticism of the play was greater in bulk than the indigenous literature of several European states. Modern listings, like the annual *MLA Bibliography*, give some 1,200 books and articles solely on *Hamlet* published since 1960, about 700 of them since 1975. What follows is an attempt to map a very large territory indeed.

EDITIONS

Among the many modern editions of the play, three are especially noteworthy. Philip Edwards's for the New Cambridge Shakespeare in 1985 showed a greater dependence on the 1623 Folio text than had been fashionable since the work done by Dover Wilson for the earlier Cambridge edition in the 1930s, an endeavour which pressed the importance of the second Quarto text. G. R. Hibbard's edition for the Oxford Shakespeare in 1987 is still more dependent on the Folio. Both have lively critical introductions and good annotation. Pride of place has to be given to Harold Jenkins's magisterial new Arden of 1982, with a much fuller and more comprehensive introduction, and annotation

supported by 150 pages of additional notes; his text is based on
the second Quarto. All three of the above give detailed accounts
of the textual problems the play presents. The New Penguin
edition by T. J. B. Spencer (1980), and the New Clarendon by
George Rylands (1947), are sound, of interest, and fit the pocket.

CRITICAL REVIEWS AND COLLECTIONS

Furness's New Variorum edition (1879) gives extensive extracts
from 1710. C. C. H. Williamson (1950) illustrates some of the
diversity up to the mid-1940s. Morris Weitz (1965) discusses the
major critical issues up to the mid-1960s. The collection edited by
Kenneth Muir and Stanley Wells in 1979 gathers pieces from the
annual *Shakespeare Survey*. There are collections of essays in the
Stratford-upon-Avon Studies volume (no. 5, 1966) edited by J. R.
Brown and Bernard Harris; of extracts made by John Jump for the
Macmillan *Casebook* series (1968); and by David Bevington for
Prentice Hall's *Twentieth Century Interpretations* series, also in
1968. More comprehensive, though occasionally naïve in incidental commentary, is the assembly of long extracts of material
from 1698 to 1977, edited by Laurie Lanzen Harris and Mark W.
Scott for Gale (1984) with an annotated bibliography of additional
material. Michael Hattaway's 1987 volume in the *Critics Debate*
series directs attention to late twentieth-century critical theorizing.

CRITICISM AND COMMENTARY

Dryden in 1668 condemned the Player's Speech for smelling 'a
little too strongly of the buskin': over a hundred years later
Samuel Johnson admired the poise and decorum of Dryden's
criticism. It is easy for us to feel that Augustan critics continued
to miss the point rather grandly. Seventeenth-century references
show interest but critical puzzlement. As in the eighteenth
century, it was common to say that Shakespeare's undoubted
'genius' in creating such an eloquent and elevated avenger went
with some barbarity of judgement. So Jeremy Collier in 1698
deplored Ophelia's immodesty and thought that Shakespeare
should have contrived her madness better. 'Since he was resolv'd
to drown the lady like a Kitten he should have set her swimming
a little sooner.' Shakespeare's first named editor, Nicholas Rowe,
in 1709, recognized the stature of *Hamlet* as a tragedy, comparable
with Sophocles. Samuel Johnson's brief comments in 1765 (see
also James Lill, 1979) responded to the largeness of the play:

though Shakespeare was tender to Ophelia, he implied, Hamlet was offensive to her. His speech in the prayer scene was 'too horrible to be read or to be uttered'. Indeed Hamlet shows a central failure, which is Shakespeare's, the standard eighteenth-century charge of 'the irregularity of his genius' as Coleridge expressed it for them.

One reaction to Shakespeare's apparent failure, always open as an alternative, was wholesale butchery. Though Garrick restored many previous cuts, and understood, obviously, the combination of delicacy and melancholy in the prince, in his 1772 production he still cut most of Act Five, altering the play beyond recognition. Another response was Voltaire's in 1752, and condemnation of the play as 'a vulgar and barbarous drama, which would not be tolerated by the vilest populace of France, or Italy. Hamlet becomes crazy in the second act, and his mistress becomes crazy in the third . . .' Such surgery, and such condemnation, continue, of course. The story of the first two hundred years of *Hamlet* criticism, not yet fully told, can be followed partly in Brian Vickers's volumes in the *Critical Heritage* series, partly in Williamson, partly in Harris and Scott, and more comprehensively in the New Variorum. Voltaire's national chauvinism is set in context by J. D. Golder (1971).

Voltaire was attacked in 1767 by Lessing. For the eighteenth-century critic in general, this play especially had presented two problems, seen as Hamlet's apparent procrastination, and the need to find reasons for it. That a necessity for coming to fresh terms with *Hamlet* became a North European philosophical affair is shown by the importance of German criticism throughout the nineteenth century. A quite new Hamlet became visible (foreseen, separately, by two Scots, William Richardson and Henry Mackenzie). In 1795, Goethe's sensitive Hamlet had 'a beautiful, pure, noble and most moral nature', in effect a private being crushed by the stern public demands made on him. The prince was an oak tree planted in a precious vase: as the tree grew, the vase shattered—a fate common to mankind. Schlegel in 1808 first developed the play as *Gedankentrauerspiel*, a 'tragedy of thought': Hamlet was doubter and sceptic, questioning the value of action, moving from religious confidence to doubt. 'The criminals are at last punished, but, as it were, by an accidental blow'. Ulrici in 1839 took Schlegel further, allowing the doubt to penetrate the morality of revenge, checking Hamlet in his course: the prince was punished for over-reaching, and trying to be in himself a kind of Providence (for all the above, see the New Variorum). Such Romantic criticism of *Hamlet* was strongest in Coleridge and Hazlitt. What Coleridge thought about the play is not in fact easily open to view, though it seems to square with his general defence of Shakespeare's excellences unified by organic form. Coleridge's critical responses to *Hamlet* seem wide—on opening scenes, for example, and the quality of the poetry. But in its context the celebrated *Table Talk* remark, 'I have a smack of Hamlet myself, if I may say so', adumbrates something surely a little distasteful, something of that familiar figure who is so given to private thought as to be detached from the real world and constitutionally averse to action: someone far too sensitive to be asked to do the washing-up. Hazlitt's short essay in the collection called *Characters of Shakespear's Plays* puts such privatization into a different context, more concerned with the genius of Shakespeare's Hamlet than the apparently wilful impotence of Coleridge's, itself a descendant of Goethe's lovely Hamlet 'without the strength of nerve which forms a hero'. Hazlitt outlines kinds of mental woe in the play, including that in which 'powers of action have been eaten up by thought' as one among many. He presents the play as 'the most remarkable for the ingenuity, originality, and unstudied development of character. Shakespeare had more magnanimity than any other poet, and he has shown more of it in this play than in any other'. He sees Hamlet's refusal in the prayer scene as 'a refinement in malice, which is in truth only one excuse for his own want of resolution. . . . He is the prince of philosophical speculators. . .' His dilatoriness is because it is 'more to his taste to indulge his imagination in reflecting upon the enormity of the crime and refining on his schemes of vengeance, than to put them to immediate practice'. Hazlitt calls 'to think, not to act' his ruling passion, an identification which, like his account of the indulgence of imagination, gives the sense of liberty rather than impotence: Hamlet's character, he says, 'is made up of undulating lines: it has the yielding flexibility of "a wave o' th' sea" '.

In their different ways, nineteenth-century European writers on Hamlet, from Kierkegaard, Gervinus, Turgenieff, Nietzsche, Brandes and above all Freud, extended the implication of such privatization, occupying themselves in finding reasons for Hamlet's delay which tended to be existential, and all focusing on the

inner state of the prince. The most important British and Continental commentators tended to work privately themselves, at
study desk or analyst's couch rather than in the living theatre.
There were, of course, many others a touch less rarified who
wrote well: Williamson fills 250 pages with nineteenth-century
comments, mostly British, and the New Variorum has a similar
number up to 1877 (and see Harris and Scott). A sense of the
common world's fascination with the prince is overwhelming.
(Williamson's polemic Postscript refers in passing to a few
pleasingly dotty interpretations from that century, including
E. P. Vining's in 1881 [also noted by Bradley], where Hamlet in
the course of the play becomes a woman in love with Horatio and
jealous of Ophelia. It is not for us to feel smug, however, when
1984 can produce J. A. Bryant Jr.'s nonsense of a Hamlet as Christ,
with a holy Ghost, and much else.)

The one-and-a-half lectures on *Hamlet* in A. C. Bradley's
Shakespearean Tragedy of 1904 are a monument marking the end
of the century of criticism when Hamlet's character had been
central. Bradley's later detractors have not allowed him the full-
blooded tragic prince, 'a heroic, terrible figure' that he presents.
After listing examples of Hamlet's fearless vigour Bradley adds
'imagine Coleridge doing any of these things!'. It was asserted,
quite wrongly, that he had no liking for the theatre (see Cooke,
1972). Having pointed out, surely correctly, that 'if we had no
knowledge of his character, the story would hardly be intelligible',
in half a lecture he surveys previous theories about reasons
for delay; he also analyses Ophelia, Gertrude, and Claudius:
but the heart of his main lecture is his attribution of Hamlet's
delay to something he finds unique in Shakespeare, Hamlet's
disgust

at his uncle's drunkenness, his loathing of his mother's sensuality, his
astonishment and horror at her shallowness, his contempt for everything
pretentious or false, his indifference to everything merely external . . .
And then within a month—'O God! a beast would have mourned
longer'—she married again, and married Hamlet's uncle, a man utterly
contemptible and loathsome in his eyes; married him in what to Hamlet
was incestuous wedlock . . . an eruption of coarse sensuality, 'rank and
gross', speeding post-haste to its horrible delight.

This is cause enough for melancholy: but it is before he has
met the Ghost. Then, at that

hour of uttermost weakness . . . there comes on him, bursting the bounds of the natural world with a shock of astonishment and terror, the revelation of his mother's adultery and his father's murder, and with this, the demand on him, in the name of everything dearest and most sacred, to arise and act. . . . The rest of the story exhibits his vain attempts to fulfil this duty [of revenge], his unconscious self-excuses and unavailing self-reproaches, and the tragic results of his delay.

The understanding that a clue to the play has to lie in Hamlet's character did not die with Bradley: far from it; Levin L. Schücking's title for a book in 1922 partly concerned with *Hamlet* is *Character Problems in Shakespeare's Plays*. Bradley's lectures are a landmark because his judgements were so often telling, and because after him critics and commentators developed a host of profitable speculations about the play, of which much-extended character-analysis was only one part. After Bradley, such critics were, increasingly, professional academics, often with an undeclared stake in finding something new. The late nineteenth-century obsession with the prince's real or assumed madness led Oscar Wilde to contemplate writing an essay entitled 'Are the Commentators on *Hamlet* Really Mad, or Only Pretending to be?' But now, in the late twentieth century, the *Hamlet* sky is higher, and the horizons wider, than ever Wilde could have imagined. Moreover, however prolific the offerings of 'Eng. Lit.' in this century have been, criticism of stature has come from workers outside academia—a particularly European characteristic. For example, we follow Bradley further into Hamlet's melancholia and find Freud in 1900, and above all the essay by his disciple Ernest Jones (in various states from 1910, usually taken in the 1949 form) attributing Hamlet's paralysis to an Oedipus complex. In human terms, this is not foolish: the pathology of a link between what may be hidden deep in the psyche and an enervation of action is accepted (and see Lucas, 1951). As Dover Wilson pointed out, however, 'there is no Hamlet': that is, he is fiction. This has not prevented more recent analysts from pursuing the matter (Norman Holland in his 1964 book remarked that 'psychoanalysts seem to take to Hamlet like kittens to a ball of yarn'). Anna Nardo (1983) identified the 'double binds' in the play; Avi Erlich (1978) successfully challenged Freud and Jones. John P. Muller (1981) may lead us into that thorny brake where the more advanced ideas of Freudian psychoanalysis meet the more advanced theories of literature, with Lacan's essay on Desire in relation to *Hamlet*.

(Bradley himself noted that Hamlet's melancholy 'from the psycho-logical point of view . . . is the centre of the tragedy'. He added, however, 'but the psychological point of view is not equivalent to the tragic'). In 1920 a fashion for 'disintegrating' all Shakespeare was reaching its height under the double influence of the idea of a crude old play, worked on by 'a series of men', and psychoanalytic suggestions of intractable hidden forces. T. S. Eliot in 1920 reached his celebrated, unhappy judgements, that 'so far from being Shakespeare's masterpiece, the play is most certainly an artistic failure' and that, because Hamlet cannot objectify his feelings, 'his emotion is in *excess* of the facts as they appear'. (Less eccentrically, Eliot, in *On Poetry and Poets* thirty years later, was illuminating on the poetic strategy of the play's opening lines). Philip Edwards, in the introduction to his New Cambridge edition (1985), brought forward the originality both of Mallarmé (1886—important too for Joyce in *Ulysses*) and John Masefield (1911), the latter 'more interesting and valuable than Eliot's better-known pages'.

Distaste for Hamlet, as in Salvador de Madariaga's stress on his 'cruelty, egocentricity and aristocratic disdain' (1948), or in L. C. Knights finding him immature (1960), was not uncommon: or new, of course. Other developments independently set the compass swinging. Doubts about the nature of the Ghost became dominant. Though it is possible (see Hawkes, 1985) to mock Dover Wilson's entry into the arena, his three *Hamlet* volumes have been very properly influential. His *What Happens in Hamlet* (1935) suggested that Elizabethan attitudes to the play were recoverable, and essential; in particular, a new—reflecting Elizabethan—scepticism about the Ghost, 'the linch-pin of *Hamlet*'. Whether Hamlet's mission was divinely or demonically inspired is the subject of an essay by Philip Edwards on 'Tragic Balance' (1983): the fullest treatment of that debate to 1967, however, is in Eleanor Prosser's *Hamlet and Revenge* (1967; and see H. A. Mason, 1968). Since that time, Barbara Everett's 1977 essay and Arthur McGee's 1987 book have taken further the understanding of Ghost as demon. McGee occasionally overstates his case, but his study is incidentally to be cherished as the result of a life-time's work on *Hamlet* produced at the kitchen table— the European tradition of the non-academic enthusiast is still alive.

McGee, like the others, is a participant in the parallel, and noisy, argument about the religion of the court at Elsinore, or of Hamlet, or of his father (or, for that matter, of Shakespeare, or of *his* father). Bradley felt that the tragedies were not religious, and that no scheme of moral values could be deduced, but that *Hamlet*, exceptionally, had 'a more decided, though always imaginative, intimation of a supreme power concerned in human evil and good . . .'. Peter Alexander (1955) discussed the prince in relation to the doctrine of *hamartia* in Aristotle, and after: Roger Cox (1960) understood that to be Pauline, not pagan. Some, like H. D. F. Kitto (1956), saw *Hamlet* as a religious drama in the way that classical Greek dramas were. Others, like Patrick Cruttwell (1963), identified confusion between the Christian ethic and that of revenge. Sister Miriam Joseph (1962) found Hamlet on a path leading to damnation. 'Moral readings' have been common: unbiased religious explorations less so. Particularly illuminating is Alan Sinfield, who in 'Hamlet's Special Providence' found Shakespeare 'exploiting the contradictions in Stoicism and the embarrassments in Calvinism', and going much further, incidentally, than the remarks of T. S. Eliot in 'Shakespeare and the Stoicism of Seneca', in *Selected Essays* (1932, and see Gordon Braden, 1985). Sinfield concludes that Hamlet presents a not uncommon dissatisfaction with orthodox Protestant theology in an unusually coherent form. 'In *Hamlet*, Christian statements supersede pagan ones in a theologically precise form, but the action remains ambiguous'.

To the Cambridge of the late 1920s, Shakespeare's plays were primarily dramatic poems. G. Wilson Knight's brilliant, wrongheaded essay in *The Wheel of Fire* (1930) offered an interpretation of *Hamlet* which attempted to reconstruct the poet's vision, to find the basic, controlling thematic pattern, its spiritual core. This emerged as disease and death. His assertion of a healthy positive court and a sick Hamlet was widely attacked (see Holloway, 1961); but a study of the imagery by Caroline Spurgeon (1935), for example, also found a dominant disease-motif, a sick Hamlet spreading a kind of contagion. For all the veneer of newness such work was a late-Romantic flowering, a seeking of the soul of Shakespeare, and still much concerned with character, as reading L. C. Knights makes plain. Knights, like Wilson Knight, was open to the charge of subjective generalization (see Everett, 1960). Caroline Spurgeon's assembly of figures of speech was to give clues to hidden mysteries. Wolfgang Clemen (1951) was more rigorous, and brought out other issues in his demonstration of the development of Shakespeare's artistry. He illuminated Hamlet's concern with the everyday world—'Hamlet is no abstract thinker and dreamer'. In contemplating the design, later critics linked stage-pictures, as well as a far greater range of verbal images; related, for example, to war and violence (Maynard Mack, 1952; Maurice Charney, 1969; and Nigel Alexander, 1971, the last finding poison, play, and duel as dominant). Later criticism still more comprehensively understood that Elizabethan rhetorical training made both Shakespeare and Hamlet more verbally self-conscious ('words, words, words') than we readily grasp, and made it likely that many kinds of artifice must be in play at the point where illusion is created, strategies in which audiences of the time would have taken a keen pleasure. Jane Donawerth's chapter on *Hamlet* in her *Shakespeare and the Sixteenth-Century Study of Language* (1984) showed Shakespeare using ideas about language, with Renaissance copiousness and decorum, to an effect in this play which is rich and complex. Particularly influential in this field have been Molly Mahood's pages on Hamlet's punning in *Shakespeare's Wordplay* (1957); Inga-Stina Ewbank's 1977 essay, ' "Hamlet" and the Power of Words'; and George T. Wright's important exploration of one rhetorical device, curiously significant to the play, 'Hendiadys and Hamlet' (1981). Brian Vickers's *The Artistry of Shakespeare's Prose* (1968) showed the technique of prose as used for Hamlet's dissimulation and wit. Coming freshly to light is the play's new vocabulary in its 4,700 distinct words according to Spevack. Alfred Hart in 1943 found that in *Hamlet* Shakespeare used over 600 words for the first time; and in 1979 Paula Guntermann calculated that there are 144 coinages in the play (more than *OED* records).

Criticism as generalization, the expositing of grand and cloudy themes, still flourishes. It should not properly survive such rhetorical understanding, though no doubt it will. As Clemen pointed out as long ago as 1951, of 'And thus the native hue of resolution / Is sicklied o'er with the pale cast of thought', 'The customary interpretation of this passage, "reflection hinders action", does it an injustice. For Hamlet does not say "reflection hinders action", he simply utters this image . . .' The best criticism works from the text: Martin Dodsworth's interesting *Hamlet Closely Observed* (1985), for example, is such an analysis, repaying many readings.

The writing of *Hamlet* was a turning-point for Shakespeare, not only in matters of technique like vocabulary or use of certain tropes. Attempts such as E. E. Stoll's in 1919 to solve the traditional character problems by cutting through to the original stage-conventions were in fact bypassed as new facts came to light. Elizabethan ideas of revenge, and the curious customs of the revenge tragedy (first fully expounded by Fredson Bowers in 1940) were variously examined, to reveal how *Hamlet* differed from any convention. Eleanor Prosser (1967), as noted above, looked again at the evidence and found Hamlet living in a harsher and more. challenging ethical world than either the revenge tragedy systems, or universal critical stereotypes, had recognized (see also Harold Skulsky, 1970, and Mark Rose, 1971). William Empson's long essay in 1953, 'Hamlet When New', showed Shakespeare putting his modern, enigmatic prince into an old-fashioned play, and confiding in the audience his bewilderment at his predicament, saying 'You think this an awkward old play, and so it is, *but I'm in it*, and what can I do?' Shakespeare, Empson wrote, through the relation of Hamlet with his fellow players, made a calculated collapse of dramatic illusion even to the point of making the First Player the leader of a travelling company from the Globe, i.e. Burbage—who was, anyway, playing Hamlet—and then made that very collapse an illustration of the central theme. Here was visible an exhilarating artistic freedom from which Shakespeare never retreated.

The core of the late twentieth-century experience of *Hamlet* has been doubt, which affects every part, including how the audience is to react. There has been visible a growing sense of a baffling trick of doubleness and multiplicity in the play, from a linguistic *tic* of Hamlet's ('Oh God! Oh God!', 'Thrift, thrift', 'Except my life, except my life, except my life') to Claudius's egregious 'our sometime sister, now our queen': a multiplication which gives repetition instead of exploration, so that there are in all four sons impelled to avenge fathers (Hamlet, Fortinbras, Laertes, Pyrrhus), instead of, some would argue, adequate development of under-standing of that burden. Hamlet is paradoxically double, being scourge and minister at the same time. How can he be so? Fredson Bowers (1955) found him waiting for heaven to define his role. To Reuben Brower (1971), Hamlet was 'the most extreme example of Chapman's finely-meditating Homeric hero. . . . To be at once Achilles and the moral hero of the Virgilian and Christian tradition is beyond action and almost beyond expression. . . . His last word—and Shakespeare's—is "silence" '. Even those critics of an older generation who more firmly traced the ancient ritual qualities they found surviving in the play, as did Francis Fergusson (1949), were left only with analogies, and 'an essential mystery'. C. S. Lewis, in his 1942 lecture, pleaded for room for a less sophisticated critical response, more open to always-familiar childlike responses where doubts can remain. Harry Levin in 1959 found pervasive ironies, which allow us to face, but not solve, the contradictions produced by the play's questions and doubts. Frank Kermode's brief but very telling introduction to the play in *The Riverside Shakespeare* (1974) sets such matters in the fuller context of *Hamlet* studies.

Stephen Booth's 'On the value of Hamlet' (1969) is a clear statement of the frustration of any desire for certainty and coherence, focused on the audience's experience. Booth begins with the suggestion that the history of criticism makes us think we 'behold the frustrated and inarticulate Shakespeare furiously wagging his tail in an effort to tell us something': but what that turns out to be is 'a succession of actions upon the understanding of an audience'. The first scene, which Booth analyses at length and finely, 'is insistently incoherent and just as insistently coherent. The second presents 'still another kind of double understanding in double frames of reference'. . . . 'In *Hamlet* the problems the audience thinks about and the intellectual action of thinking about them are very similar. *Hamlet* is the tragedy of an audience that cannot make up its mind'. Booth develops 'the point where an audience's contrary responses come to consciousness'. Uniquely in this play 'the audience never has insight or knowledge superior to Hamlet's'. And so on, at vivacious length through points in the play 'that obviously make sense and . . . just as obviously cannot be made sense of'. It is fortunate that the most important exposition of doubt in *Hamlet* is also the most readable. On the same section of the track, and in its way progressing just as elegantly, is James L. Calderwood's *To Be And Not To Be* (1983). Calderwood begins by pointing out that in one sense Horatio's story, which closes the play, is 'merely a bad quarto of Shakespeare's play, a pirated edition based on memorial reconstruction by an actor who, though he knows much, cannot possibly know all . . .' He examines presence and absence, negation, erasure, juncture, the synchronic and the diachronic. He finds the audience drawn into a world of denials and contradictions, deconstructing and then reconstructing into paradox. This is a stimulating book-length study; as the title indicates, he shows that the play, satisfyingly, ultimately accepts and contains all the doubts.

Understanding of certain more secondary matters continually advances. To begin with likely sources and influences: Geoffrey Bullough, in the first two hundred pages of the *Major Tragedies* (vol. vii, 1973) in his *Narrative and Dramatic Sources of Shakespeare* introduced and printed the essential documents, and some unexpected analogues. Saxo Grammaticus was more fully presented by William H. Hansen in *Saxo Grammaticus and the Life of Hamlet*, a rewarding book which refreshes parts of Shakespeare's play that other critics do not reach.

The nature of the genre of *Hamlet* has been discussed widely: David Pirie's 'Hamlet without the Prince' (1972) explored some of the humour, and the chapter on *Hamlet* in Susan Snyder's *The Comic Matrix of Shakespeare's Tragedies* (1979) made a call for a closer relation to comedy than is customary. Louise George Clubb's 'The Arts of Genre: *Torrismondo* and *Hamlet*' (1980) is challenging, and J. P. Brockbank's 'Hamlet the Bonesetter' (1977) is a particularly interesting study of the play as tragedy and sacrificial ritual (and see N. Alexander (1967)). The title of H. D. F. Kitto's 'A Classical Scholar Looks at Shakespeare' (1959) tells its own story, as does that of D. W. Robertson's polemic lecture, 'A Medievalist Looks at *Hamlet*' (1980). Gilbert Murray's 'Hamlet and Orestes' of 1927 remains valuable. Moreover, if a 'source' is what was in Shakespeare's mind when he wrote, then we must not neglect the previous works of Shakespeare; among much else, Maynard Mack Jr. (1973) stressed the foreshadowing of Claudius in Bolingbroke.

A body of writing aims to set the play in its Elizabethan context: a problematic procedure, because that Uncertainty Principle by which the investigator influences the conditions being studied certainly applies. Since Stoll and Schücking, much has been written. Helen Gardner's 'The Historical Approach' (1959) is a classic statement of mainstream problems. Roland M. Frye's

The Renaissance Hamlet: Issues and Responses in 1600 (1984) attempted to analyse 'the complex and sophisticated concerns of
Elizabethan minds'; it is particularly useful on 'The Prince amid
the Tombs', and has a full bibliography. Lilian Winstanley in
1921 saw in the play a political allegory concerning Essex and
James VI. R. A. Foakes (1956) is illuminating on the conflicting
elements of formality and corruption in the Danish court. The
contemporary world is the subject of Martin Holmes in 1964, of
Keith Brown in 1969, on geography and cosmology, and of Ralph
Berry in 1984, where the six nations mentioned in the play make
'a rough mosaic of Shakespeare's mind'. Among analyses of the
more philosophical contents of Hamlet's mind are Robert Ellrodt's
subtle exploration of the suggestiveness of Montaigne (1975): the
standard, though brief, account by D. G. James in 1951, where the
play is put in a context including Bacon's *Advancement of Learning*,
and *King Lear*; and, expounding Shakespeare in an age of scepticism, S. Chaudhuri (1981).

The larger matter of the styles of Elizabethan acting available
to Burbage, and to Shakespeare, is well discussed by Peter
Holland (1984), and supported by interesting pages on *Hamlet* in
William B. Worthen's *The Idea of the Actor* (1984). Charles R.
Forker on theatrical symbolism is illuminating (1963). The practical theatricality of the play is the subject of Harley Granville-
Barker's fine and rewarding *Preface* (1930), and the large documentation of the stage history can be approached through John
A. Mills (1985). Peter Davison's *Hamlet: Text and Performance*
(1983) contains performance material from 1603, and crackles
with the sense of people involved and doing things. The standard
accounts of filmed Shakespeare (Roger Manvell, 1971; Jack L.
Jorgens, 1977) give weight to the work of Grigori Kozintsev. On
the modern stage, Tom Stoppard's *Rosencrantz and Guildenstern
Are Dead* (1967) makes metaphysical play with the play (discussed
in relation to Beckett by Robert Wilcher, 1979).

More such 'offshoots' are discussed by Ruby Cohn (1976); I
draw attention here to Richard Ellmann's *The Consciousness of
Joyce* (1977), supplementing William M. Schutte (1957), as a way
into the fertile fields of Joyce on *Hamlet*, not only in *Ulysses*; and
to Martin Scofield's exceptionally interesting *The Ghosts of Hamlet:
The Play and Modern Writers* (1980).

Granville-Barker expressed in 1930 his sense of three distinct
movements in the structure of the play. The construction has

been a particular modern concern. Fredson Bowers's two essays of 1964 are of special interest. O. B. Hardison (1960) found a pattern of three characters, one at the centre contrasted with two others. W. T. Jewkes (1984) wrote on perspective and structural explorations, D. J. Palmer on the dramatic use of eavesdropping, and G. R. Hibbard on the artistic leap Shakespeare made to the Henry IV plays and *Hamlet*. Joan Rees's *Shakespeare and the Story* (1978) is good on the excitements visible in the narrative shaping in *Hamlet*.

Jonathan Dollimore (1987) may illustrate the discovery of ideological implications in Shakespeare and his critics (and see Hattaway (1987)). Feminist readings include Linda Bamber's chapter in her *Comic Women, Tragic Men* (1982), where the changes that take place in Gertrude and Ophelia are brought out: and a rather more anti-male analysis of Gertrude in Rebecca Smith's 1980 essay.

I conclude with two puzzles which will, I suggest, always intrigue. 'Did the King See the Dumb-Show?' (and if so, why didn't he react?) is one of those hoary *Hamlet* questions which still yields insights. W. W. Robson's lecture of 1975 (and A. V. C. Schmidt's short answer in 1976), and M. R. Woodhead in 1979 must serve as a way in. Then, the often-declared universality of this play must be a tribute to its generosity: it patiently seems to survive mishandlings: Partridge chattering through Garrick's performance in Fielding's *Tom Jones* (Book X, Chapter X; and see Hassall, 1977); Mr Wopsle's difficulties in chapter 31 of Dickens's *Great Expectations* ('Whenever that undecided Prince had to ask a question or state a doubt, the public helped him out with it . . .'); even Jan Kott's perverse political distortions ('This production, deprived of the great soliloquies and of narrative quality . . .') mercifully not typical of all East European work. Tolstoy's famous dyspeptic dismissal is untypical of Russian reactions: that great nation has now had a special relation with this play for two centuries. There is something Russian called 'Hamletism', demonstrated, for example, in two very different books, Eleanor Rowe's *Hamlet: A Window on Russia* (1976) and Lawrence Senelick's *Gordon Craig's Moscow 'Hamlet'* (1982). There is the familiar Germanic identification with, if not ownership of, Hamlet (see Walter Mushg's 'Deutschland ist Hamlet', 1965). And so on. Surely this play suggests its universal truths wherever mankind finds it? Perhaps, perhaps. The curious reader is warmly directed to Laura Bohannan's 1956 account of taking to an African bush tribe the story of *Hamlet*.

REFERENCES

TEXTS

Edwards, Philip (ed.), *Hamlet, Prince of Denmark* (New Cambridge Shakespeare, Cambridge, 1985).

Hibbard, G. R. (ed.), *Hamlet* (Oxford Shakespeare, Oxford, 1987).

Jenkins, Harold (ed.), *Hamlet* (Arden Shakespeare, London, 1982).

Rylands, George (ed.), *Hamlet* (New Clarendon Shakespeare, Oxford, 1947).

Spencer, T. J. B. (ed.), *Hamlet* (New Penguin Shakespeare, Harmondsworth, 1980).

Wilson, J. Dover (ed.), *Hamlet* (New Shakespeare, Cambridge, 1934).

—— *The Manuscript of Shakespeare's 'Hamlet' and the Problems of Its Transmission*, 2 vols. (Cambridge, 1934).

CRITICAL REVIEWS AND COLLECTIONS

Bevington, David (ed.), *Twentieth Century Interpretations of 'Hamlet'* (Englewood Cliffs, NJ, 1968).

Brown, John Russell, and Bernard Harris (eds.), *Hamlet* (Stratford-Upon-Avon Studies, 5; London, 1963).

Furness, H. H. (ed.), *Hamlet*, 2 vols. (New Variorum Edition, London, 1879).

Harris, Laurie Lanzen, and Mark W. Scott (eds.), *Shakespearean Criticism*, (Detroit, Mich., 1984), vol. i.

Hattaway, Michael, *Hamlet* (The Critics Debate, London, 1987).

Jump, John (ed.), *Shakespeare, 'Hamlet': A Casebook* (London, 1968).

Muir, Kenneth, and Stanley Wells (eds.), *Aspects of 'Hamlet'* (Cambridge, 1979).

Williamson, Claude C. H. (ed.), *Readings on the Character of Hamlet* (London, 1950).

Weitz, Morris, *Hamlet and the Philosophy of Literary Criticism* (London, 1965).

CRITICISM AND COMMENTARY

Alexander, Nigel, 'Critical Disagreement about Oedipus and Hamlet', *Shakespeare Survey 20* (1967), 33–40; reprinted in *Aspects of 'Hamlet'*, ed. Kenneth Muir and Stanley Wells (Cambridge, 1979), 102–9.

—— *Poison, Play and Duel* (London, 1971).

Alexander, Peter, *Hamlet: Father and Son* (London, 1955).

Bamber, Linda, *Comic Women, Tragic Men: A Study of Gender and Genre in Shakespeare* (Stanford, Calif., 1982).

Berry, Ralph, *Shakespearean Structures* (London, 1984).

Bohannan, Laura, ' "Miching Mallecho: That Means Mischief" ', in *From the Third Programme: A Ten-Years' Anthology*, ed. C. J. Morris (London, 1956), 174–89; reprinted as 'Shakespeare in the Bush' in *Natural History*, 75 (1966), 28–33, and in *Every Man His Way: Readings in Cultural Anthropology*, ed. Alan Dundes (Englewood Cliffs, NJ, 1968).

Booth, Stephen, 'On the Value of *Hamlet*', in *Reinterpretations of Elizabethan Drama*, ed. Norman Rabkin (New York, 1969), 137–76.

Bowers, Fredson, 'Dramatic Structure and Criticism: Plot in *Hamlet*', *Shakespeare Quarterly*, 15 (1964), 207–18; reprinted in *Shakespeare 400: Essays by American Scholars on the Anniversary of the Poet's Birth*, ed. James G. McManaway (New York, 1964), 207–18.

—— *Elizabethan Revenge Tragedy, 1587–1642* (Princeton, NJ, 1940).

—— 'Hamlet as Minister and Scourge', *PMLA* 70 (1955), 740–9.

—— 'The Moment of Final Suspense in Hamlet: "We Defy Augury" ', in *Shakespeare 1564–1964: A Collection of Modern Essays by Various Hands*, ed. Edward A. Bloom (Providence, RI, 1964), 50–5.

Braden, Gordon, *Renaissance Tragedy and the Senecan Tradition: Anger's Privilege* (New Haven, Conn., 1985).

Bradley, A. C., *Shakespearean Tragedy* (London, 1904).

Brockbank, J. P., 'Hamlet the Bonesetter', *Shakespeare Survey 30* (Cambridge, 1977), 103–15.

Brower, Reuben, *Hero and Saint: Shakespeare and the Graeco-Roman Heroic Tradition* (New York, 1971).

Brown, Keith, 'Hamlet's Place on the Map', *Shakespeare Studies*, 4 (1969 for 1968), 160–82.

Bryant, J. A. Jr., 'Hamlet as Christian Malgré Lui', *Sewanee Review*, 92 (1984), 239–55.

Bullough, Geoffrey, *Narrative and Dramatic Sources of Shakespeare*,. vol. vii, *Major Tragedies* (London, 1973).

Calderwood, James L., *To Be and Not To Be: Negation and Metadrama in 'Hamlet'* (New York, 1983).

Charney, Maurice, *Style in 'Hamlet'* (Princeton, NJ, 1969).

Chaudhuri, Sukanta, *Infirm Glory* (Oxford, 1981).

Clemen, Wolfgang H., *The Development of Shakespeare's Imagery* (London, 1951; 2nd edn., with new preface, 1977).

Clubb, Louise George, 'The Arts of Genre: *Torrismondo* and *Hamlet*', *ELH* 47 (1980), 6657–69.

Cohn, Ruby, *Modern Shakespeare Offshoots* (Princeton, NJ, 1976).

Coleridge, S. T., *The Collected Works of Samuel Taylor Coleridge*. vol. v; *Lectures 1808–1819 On Literature*, ed. R. A. Foakes (Princeton, NJ and London, 1987).

Cooke, Katherine, *A. C. Bradley and His Influence in Twentieth-Century Shakespeare Criticism* (Oxford, 1972).

Cox, Roger L., 'Hamlet's *Hamartia*: Aristotle or St Paul?' *Yale Review*, 55 (1960), 347–64; reprinted in his *Between Earth and Heaven: Shakespeare, Dostoevsky, and the Meaning of Christian Tragedy* (New York, 1969).

Cruttwell, Patrick, 'The Morality of Hamlet—"Sweet Prince" or "Arrant Knave"?' in *Hamlet*, ed. J. R. Brown and B. Harris (Stratford-upon-Avon Studies, 5; London, 1963), 110–28.

Davison, Peter, *Hamlet: Text and Performance* (London, 1983).

Dodsworth, Martin, *Hamlet Closely Observed* (London, 1985).

Dollimore, Jonathan, *Radical Tragedy: Religion, Ideology and Power in the Drama of Shakespeare and His Contemporaries* (Brighton, 1984; 2nd edn., 1989).

Donawerth, Jane, *Shakespeare and the Sixteenth-Century Study of Language* (Urbana, Ill., 1984).

Edwards, Philip, 'Shakespeare and Kyd', in *Shakespeare, Man of the Theatre: Proceedings of the Second Congress of the International Shakespeare Association*, ed. Kenneth Muir, Jay Halio, and D. J. Palmer (Neward, Del., 1984), 148–54.

—— 'Tragic Balance in *Hamlet*', *Shakespeare Survey* 36 (1983), 43–54.

Eliot, T. S., 'Hamlet', in his *Selected Essays, 1917–1932*: (London, 1932, pp. 141–146).

—— 'Poetry and Drama', in his *On Poetry and Poets* (London, 1951).

—— 'Shakespeare and the Stoicism of Seneca', in his *Selected Essays, 1917–1932* (London, 1932), 126–40.

Ellmann, Richard, *The Consciousness of Joyce* (London, 1977).

Ellrodt, Robert, 'Self-Consciousness in Montaigne and Shakespeare', *Shakespeare Survey* 28 (1975), 37–50.

Empson, William, 'Hamlet When New', *Sewanee Review*, 61 (1953), 15–42, 185–205.

Erlich, Avi, *Hamlet's Absent Father* (Princeton, NJ, 1978).

Everett, Barbara, ' "Hamlet": A Time to Die', *Shakespeare Survey* 30 (1977), 117–23.

—— 'The Figure in Professor Knight's Carpet', *Critical Quarterly*, 2, (1960), 171–6.

Ewbank, Inga-Stina, ' "Hamlet" and the Power of Words', *Shakespeare Survey* 30 (1977), 85–92.

Fergusson, Francis, 'Hamlet, Prince of Denmark: The Analogy of Action', in his *The Idea of a Theater: A Study of Ten Plays* (Princeton, NJ, 1949, repr. 1968), 98–142.

Foakes, R. A., '*Hamlet* and the Court of Elsinore', *Shakespeare Survey* 9 (1956), 35–43.

Forker, Charles R., 'Shakespeare's Theatrical Symbolism and Its Function in *Hamlet*', *Shakespeare Quarterly*, 14 (1963), 215–29; reprinted in *Essays in Shakespearean Criticism*, ed. James L. Calderwood and Harold E. Toliver (Englewood Cliffs, NJ, 1970).

Frye, Roland Mushat, *The Renaissance Hamlet: Issues and Responses in 1600* (Princeton, NJ, 1984).

Gardner, Helen, 'The Historical Approach', in her *The Business of Criticism* (Oxford, 1959); reprinted in *Shakespeare. The Tragedies: A Collection of Critical Essays* (Englewood Cliffs, NJ, 1964).

Golder, J. D., '*Hamlet* in France 200 Years Ago', *Shakespeare Survey* 24 (1971), 79–86.

Granville-Barker, Harley, *Prefaces to Shakespeare,* vol. i, *Hamlet* (London, 1930).

Guntermann, Paula, 'Die Erstbelege im Wortschatz von Shakespeares *Hamlet*', *Shakespeare Jahrbuch (West)* (1978/1979), 58–72.

Hansen, William F., *Saxo Grammaticus and the Life of Hamlet: A Translation, History and Commentary* (Lincoln, Nebr., 1983).

Hardison, O. B., 'The Dramatic Triad in *Hamlet*', *Studies in Philology*, 57 (1960), 144–64.

Hart, Alfred, 'Vocabularies of Shakespeare's Plays' and 'The Growth of Shakespeare's Vocabulary', *RES* 19 (1943), 128–40 and 242–54.

Hassall, A. J., 'Fielding and *Tom Jones*', N & Q 222 (1977), 247–9.

Hawkes, Terence, 'Telmah', in his *That Shakespeherian Rag* (London, 1986), 92–119.

Hazlitt, William, *Characters of Shakespear's Plays* (1817; often reprinted).

Hibbard, G. R., '"Henry IV" and "Hamlet"', *Shakespeare Survey* 30 (1977), 1–12.

Holland, Norman N., *Psychoanalysis and Shakespeare* (New York, 1964).

Holland, Peter, '*Hamlet* and the Art of Acting', in *Drama and the Actor* (*Themes in Drama*, 6; Cambridge, 1984).

Holloway, John, *The Story of the Night: Studies in Shakespeare's Major Tragedies* (London, 1961).

Holmes, Martin, *The Guns of Elsinore* (London, 1964).

James, D. G., *The Dream of Learning: An Essay on 'The Advancement of Learning', 'Hamlet' and 'King Lear'* (Oxford, 1951).

Jewkes, W. T., '"To Tell My Story": The Function of Framed Narrative and Drama in *Hamlet*', in *Shakespearean Tragedy*, ed. Malcolm Bradbury and David Palmer (Stratford-upon-Avon Studies, 20; London, 1984), 31–46.

Jones, Ernest, *Hamlet and Oedipus* (London, 1949).

Jorgens, Jack L., *Shakespeare on Film* (Bloomington, Ind., 1977).

Joseph, Bertram L., *Conscience and the King: A Study of 'Hamlet'* (London, 1953).

—— '*The Spanish Tragedy* and *Hamlet*: Two Exercises in English Seneca', in *Classical Drama and Its Influence: Essays Presented to H. D. F. Kitto*, ed. M. J. Anderson (London, 1965), 121–34.

Joseph, Sister Miriam, '"Hamlet", a Christian Tragedy', *Studies in Philology*, 59 (1962), 119–40.

Kermode, Frank, Introduction to *Hamlet* in *The Riverside Shakespeare* (Boston, Mass., 1974), 1135–40.

Kitto, H. D. F., '*Hamlet*', in his *Form and Meaning in Drama: A Study of Six Greek Plays and of 'Hamlet'* (London, 1964), 246–337.

——'A Classical Scholar Looks at Shakespeare', in *More Talking of Shakespeare*, ed. John Garrett (London, 1959), 33–54.

Knight, G. Wilson, 'The Embassy of Death: An Essay on *Hamlet*', in his *The Wheel of Fire: Interpretations of Shakespearian Tragedy* (rev. edn., London, 1949), 17–46.

Knights, L. C., '*Hamlet' and Other Shakespearean Essays* (Cambridge, 1979).

——*An Approach to 'Hamlet'* (London, 1960).

Levin, Harry, *The Question of 'Hamlet'* (New York, 1959).

Lewis, C. S., 'Hamlet: The Prince or the Poem?', British Academy lecture 1942; reprinted in his *They Asked for a Paper* (London, 1962), 51–71, and in *Shakespeare's Tragedies: An Anthology of Modern Criticism*, ed. Laurence Lerner (Penguin Shakespeare Library, Harmondsworth, 1968), 65–77.

Lill, James, 'Samuel Johnson on *Hamlet*', *South Atlantic Quarterly*, 78 (1979), 333–41.

Lucas, F. L., *Literature and Psychology* (London, 1951).

McGee, Arthur, *The Elizabethan Hamlet* (New Haven, Conn., and London, 1987).

Mack, Maynard, 'The World of *Hamlet*', *Yale Review*, 41 (1952), 502–23; reprinted in *Modern Essays in Criticism*, ed. Leonard F. Dean (rev. edn., New York, 1967), 242–62; *Shakespeare. The Tragedies: A Collection of Critical Essays*, ed. Alfred Harbage (Englewood Cliffs, NJ, 1964), 44–60; and *Twentieth Century Interpretations of 'Hamlet'*, ed. David Bevington (Englewood Cliffs, NJ, 1968).

Mack, Maynard, Jr., *Killing the King: Three Studies in Shakespeare's Tragic Structure* (New Haven, Conn., and London, 1973).

Madariaga, Salvador, de, *On Hamlet* (London, 1948).

Mahood, Molly M., *Shakespeare's Wordplay* (London, 1957).

Manvell, Roger, *Shakespeare and the Film* (London, 1971).

Masefield, John, *William Shakespeare* (London, 1911; rev. 1954).

Mason, H. A., 'The Ghost in *Hamlet*', *Cambridge Quarterly*, 3 (1968), 127–52.

Mills, John A., '*Hamlet' on Stage: The Great Tradition* (Westport, Conn., 1985).

Muller, John P., 'Psychosis and Mourning in Lacan's *Hamlet*', *New Literary History*, 12 (1981), 147–65.

Murray, Gilbert, 'Hamlet and Orestes', in his *The Classical Tradition in Poetry* (Cambridge, Mass., 1927), 205–40.

Muschg, Walter, 'Deutschland ist Hamlet', *Shakespeare Jahrbuch West* (1965), 32–58.

Nardo, Anna K., 'Hamlet, "A Man to Double Business Bound" ', *Shakespeare Quarterly*, 34 (1983), 181–99.

Palmer, D. J., 'Stage Spectators in *Hamlet*', *Essays and Studies*, 47 (1966), 423–30.

Pirie, David, '*Hamlet* without the Prince', *Critical Quarterly*, 14 (1972), 293–314.

Prosser, Eleanor, *Hamlet and Revenge* (Stanford, Calif., 1967).

Rees, Joan, *Shakespeare and the Story* (London, 1978).

Robertson, D. W., Jr., 'A Medievalist Looks at *Hamlet*', in his *Essays in Medieval Culture* (Princeton, NJ, 1980), 312–31.

Robson, W. W., 'Did the King see the Dumb Show?', *Cambridge Quarterly*, 6 (1975), 303–26.

Rose, Mark, '*Hamlet* and the Shape of Revenge', *English Literary History*, 1 (1971), 132–43.

Rowe, Eleanor, *Hamlet: A Window on Russia* (New York, 1976).

Schmidt, A. V. C., untitled review, *N & Q* 221 (1976), 172–3.

Schücking, Levin L., *Character Problems in Shakespeare's Plays* (London, 1922).

Schutte, William M., *Joyce and Shakespeare: A Study on the Making of 'Ulysses'* (New Haven, Conn., 1957; Hamden, Conn., 1971).

Scofield, Martin, *The Ghosts of 'Hamlet': The Play and Modern Writers*, (Cambridge, 1980).

Senelick, Lawrence, *Gordon Craig's Moscow 'Hamlet': A Reconstruction*, (Westport, Conn., 1982).

Sinfield, Alan, 'Hamlet's Special Providence', *Shakespeare Survey* 33 (1980), 89–97.

Skulsky, Harold, 'Revenge, Honor, and Conscience in *Hamlet*', *PMLA* 85 (1970) 78–87; reprinted in revised form in his *Spirits Finely Touched: The Testing of Value and Integrity in Four Shakespearean Plays* (Athens, Ga., 1976), 51–86.

Smith, Rebecca, 'A Heart Cleft in Twain: The Dilemma of Shakespeare's Gertrude', in *The Woman's Part: Feminist Criticism of Shakespeare*, ed. Carolyn Ruth Swift Lenz, Gayle Greene, and Carol Thomas Neely (Urbana, Ill., 1980), 194–210.

Snyder, Susan, *The Comic Matrix of Shakespeare's Tragedies* (Princeton, NJ, 1979).

Spurgeon, Caroline F. E., *Shakespeare's Imagery and What It Tells Us* (Cambridge, 1935).

Stoll, Elmer Edgar, '*Hamlet': An Historical and Comparative Study* (Minneapolis, Minn., 1919).

Stoppard, Tom, *Rosencrantz and Guildenstern Are Dead* (London, 1967).

Tolstoy, Leo, 'Shakespeare and the Drama', reprinted in *Recollections and Essays*, trans. Aylmer Maude (World's Classics, Oxford, 1937), 307–83.

Vickers, Brian, *The Artistry of Shakespeare's Prose* (London, 1968).

—— *Shakespeare: The Critical Heritage*, 6 vols. (London, 1974–81).

Wilcher, Robert, 'The Museum of Tragedy', *Journal of Beckett Studies*, 4, (1979), 43–54.

Wilson, John Dover, *What Happens in 'Hamlet'* (Cambridge, 1935).

Winstanley, Lilian, *'Hamlet' and the Scottish Succession* (Cambridge, 1921).

Woodhead, M. R., 'Deep Plots and Indiscretions in "The Murder of Gonzago"', *Shakespeare Survey* 32 (1979), 151–61.

Worthen, William B., *The Idea of the Actor: Drama and the Ethics of Performance* (Princeton, NJ, 1984).

Wright, George T., 'Hendiadys and *Hamlet*', *PMLA* 96 (1981), 168–93.

11 | Othello

ROBERT HAPGOOD

Othello is among the half dozen plays that have been most central to major trends in Shakespearian scholarship and criticism during recent years. Textual scholars, stage-historians, performance critics, feminists, language analysts, new (and old) historicists, psychoanalytical critics—all of these and others have found an affinity between *Othello* and their various approaches. None of the recent efforts has achieved the classic standing of A. C. Bradley's chapters on the play in *Shakespearean Tragedy* (1904) or of G. Wilson Knight's 'The *Othello* Music' in *The Wheel of Fire* (1930). They remain the two best appreciations of the play and good places to start when studying it. Still, taken together, the newer work has significantly increased our understanding of *Othello* and promises further achievements along similar lines. It will be emphasized in this survey.

TEXTS AND TEXTUAL STUDIES

Textual experts today are more inclined than ever before to grant independent authority to the First Quarto and Folio editions, surmising that the latter reflects Shakespeare's revision of the former. In *The Stability of Shakespeare's Text*, Honigmann provides further support for Greg's view that the numerous variants between the Quarto and Folio texts include Shakespeare's first and second thoughts. He thus invites us to look over the play-wright's shoulder in the very process of writing and rewriting, substituting and transposing words and phrases as he goes. Looking at the end of such a process, Coghill examines the passages that the Folio includes but the Quarto does not. He pictures Shakespeare putting some finishing touches to his work after he has seen it performed, strengthening its exposition, playing up Brabanzio's obsession with Othello's 'foul charms', emphasizing the effect of kneeling, enlarging Emilia's part. In a subsequent article, Honigmann adds that the Folio-only passages reinforce 'the play's central concern with normal and abnormal sexuality' (p. 162).

It is rewarding to compare for one's self the hundreds of small differences between the First Quarto and Folio texts, using Schröer's parallel version or the facsimiles of each prepared by Hinman. Modern editions are eclectic, drawing on both texts to varying degrees while also noting alternative readings. In his conflation of the Quarto and Folio, Sanders frankly acknowledges that his edition—like all others—represents a 'third version' of his own devising, one which is 'to some extent similar to a stage production (which is always an interpretation) or a critical essay about it' (p. 207). The New Penguin (Muir) gives notably full glosses. In their editions Brown and Hankey place the text in a theatrical context. The Oxford Complete Shakespeare (Wells) is the edition cited in this chapter; employing a style of punctuation that is agreeably less exclamatory than usual, it gives special authority to the Folio, as the text closest to Shakespeare's final script for performance. The current text closest to the Quarto is Ridley's new Arden edition; its introduction has been found insensitive in matters of race and gender (Orkin, Newman).

CRITICISM AND COMMENTARY

The affinity between *Othello* and recent critical approaches is something new in the interpretative history of the play. Although never generally acclaimed—like *Hamlet* or *King Lear*—as *the* Shakespearian drama, *Othello* has always been ranked among his finest works. Yet hitherto it has won its place by sheer might not right—as its critics have seen the right. This is true even of Bradley and Knight. Bradley's chapters on the play stand out because he gives a fair-minded survey of the options for interpretation before developing his own choices. His over-emphasis on Iago's active malignity has acquired a new timeliness; it can provide a corrective to the current tendency to underrate Iago's influence. Knight immerses himself in the play's language, showing how the Miltonic 'music' of Othello—'highly-coloured, rich in sound and phrase, stately' yet at times 'sentimental' and 'exaggerated'—is turned to discord by the ugly, cynical intellectuality of Iago. Yet, as Gardner brings out, the play does not fit the predilections of either critic. Its disturbing finale, with Iago surviving, does not satisfy Bradley's need to feel 'reconciled' to the tragic way of the world. And for Knight, the play is primarily a 'story of intrigue' rather than the 'visionary statement' that he most values.

Like its hero, *Othello* has something alien about it. Shaw feels it to be more operatic and Bayley (1960) more novelistic than the Shakespearian norm. In a later book (1981) Bayley links *Othello* with *Hamlet* and *Macbeth* as 'tragedies of consciousness' but distinguishes it from them because in *Othello* the audience is entrapped within the split consciousness of Othello and Iago rather than liberated as in the other two. More than most of Shakespeare's tragedies, *Othello* draws on comic traditions (Snyder, de Mendonça, McDonald). It takes traditional love-conventions so seriously as to literalize them (Colie). Especially, it has resisted consideration as a form of dramatized moral philosophy. When Thomas Rymer finds the play 'very instructive' (presenting 'a warning to all good Wives, that they look well to their Linnen' and a 'lesson to Husbands, that before their Jealousie be Tragical, the proofs may be Mathematical'), his ironic mockery expresses a frustration that many subsequent moralists have shared.

Recent critical approaches, on the other hand, have been much more in tune with the play, thanks to a productive overlap between current concerns and *Othello*'s distinctive features. A heightened sensitivity to racial stereotyping has prompted studies of Othello's blackness by Hunter, Eldred Jones, Colie, Barthelemy, Newman; Orkin provides a guide to additional commentary (some of which sees Shakespeare as a racist), a compilation of the relevant evidence, and a thoughtful ventilation of the issues. As a study of sexual passions gone wild, *Othello* has fascinated critics of a psychoanalytical persuasion, both oedipal and pre-oedipal (Stewart, Holland, Kirsch, Wheeler). The play is the most domestic of Shakespeare's tragedies, and current sensitivity to gender stereotyping has prompted extensive analysis of its treatment of the relations between men and women. *Othello* figures promin-ently in almost all the books concerning gender in Shakespeare (French, Dash, Kahn, Erickson, Neely, Novy, Bamber); of them, Novy's chapter may be especially recommended for the balance in its sympathies and its assimilation of other work. The likelihood discussed above that *Othello* exists in more than one authoritative text has appealed to the post-modern taste for indeterminacy. Such productive overlaps with the play may be seen in other current approaches to be discussed below. For one, performance critics and stage-historians have done more justice than hitherto to *Othello*'s perennial theatrical power. And the play's focus on

Robert Hapgood

verbal deception has provided sound basis for its special appeal
to the post-modern self-consciousness about language and its
hazards. The cultural materialists are the exception; thus far they
have had little to say about the play.

The deconstructionist challenge to the dominance (or even
presence) of the author might seem especially appropriate to
Shakespeare, who is famous for his openness to interpretation.
Certainly it is a mistake to suppose that there is one right reading
of *Othello*. Yet to recognize that there can be more than one valid
reading does not preclude the possibility of wrong ones or that
certain readings may come closer to Shakespeare's apparent
intentions than others.

In *Othello* as elsewhere, Shakespeare's hand is most evident in
his dramatic actions. Bradley analyses what is unusual about the
action of *Othello*: 'In the first half of the play the main conflict is
merely incubating; then it bursts into life, and goes storming,
without intermission or change of direction, to its close' (p. 42).
Others also have remarked upon its distinctive rhythms. Fergusson
observes how the opening scene 'moves in the agile, sudden
rhythms of Iago's spirit', thus contrasting with the subsequent
Venetian scenes in which Othello sets the stately pace. Granville-
Barker calls attention to the speeding of events and drastic
compression of time at Cyprus until Lodovico's arrival; thereafter, he locates 'little or no time-compression' and in the final
scene 'None at all'. Even so the finale stands out from those of
other tragedies by Shakespeare. Nevo regards the hero's tragic
error (the murder of Desdemona) as almost unique in being
delayed to the very catastrophe. Foreman finds that no tragic
ending in Shakespeare is faster or more concentrated than that in
Othello.

Points of resemblance to other Shakespearian plots have been
analyzed by Emrys Jones, who sees in *Othello* yet another two-
part structure of the sort he finds in many of the plays, the first
part showing 'the preparation of Othello's jealousy' and the
second part 'Othello acting as a jealous man'. In an illuminating
essay Mack brings out additional features that the 'inward structure' of *Othello* shares with other tragedies by Shakespeare,
including 'mirror situations' (as when Bianca embodies 'the
prostitute figure that Desdemona has become in Othello's mind');
journeys that manifest inner change; and patterns in which 'the

hero tends to become his own antithesis', experiences madness, then recovers his original self.

After the plot, the next most reliable indicators of Shakespeare's intentions are to be found in the large patterns of language that run through the whole play (word and line readings, in contrast, are among the features most subject to interpretation). Rewarding studies have been made of such recurring images as those of animals, the sea, poisoning (Spurgeon, Knight, Clemen, Heilman) and such words as 'honest' and 'think' (Empson; Jorgensen, 1962, 1964); the play's unique lexicon (Martin Elliott), syntax (Doran), idiom (Bulman), oaths (Shirley), rhetorical patterns (Melchiori, Parker, Altman) and semantics (Danson) have all been analysed. These features add up to a universe of discourse that does much to define what Bradley called the distinctive 'atmosphere' of the play.

Large distinguishing patterns have also been seen in the speech of individual characters (Morozov). Calderwood examines Othello's proclivity for narrative and monologue. Mack contrasts the heroic overstatement of Othello with Iago's rationalism, Desdemona's high-minded innocence with Emilia's earthy realism. Hawkes (1973) underlines the Renaissance expectation of truthfulness in manly speech while Gohlke reveals the association of 'femininity with lies'.

Of characters there is always much dispute. Within broad outlines Shakespeare indicates leading traits and patterns of change but leaves wide latitudes in matters of emphasis. Hence very basic interpretative differences have resulted. Since 1927, when T. S. Eliot described Othello as a self-dramatizer 'cheering himself up' in his last speech, critics have debated whether or not the Moor is truly noble. Earlier commentators (Dr. Johnson, Bradley) took Othello at his own estimate. Others, like Leavis, have charged him with 'an obtuse and brutal egotism', to which Holloway, Marsh, and many others have replied. Among Christian interpreters a comparable polarity developed between those who regarded Othello as damned or as saved (surveyed by West). Fortunately, Jane Adamson has moved the discussion beyond this adversarial debate to discern in Othello a complex personality, with both strengths and weaknesses.

About Iago there has been much wider agreement. Interpreters worry Coleridge's phrase concerning his 'motiveless malignity'

(Raysor, Shaffer), arguing about how much his malignity is due to the tradition of the Vice (Spivack), the devil (Scragg, Bethell), or the Calumniator Credited (Stoll). Taking Iago's motives as a 'pluralist test-case', Hyman studies him as a stage villain, Satan, an artist, a latent homosexual, and a Machiavel; but he leaves it to his reader to interrelate these identities. Interpreters also differ about the degree of Iago's success, G. R. Elliott treating him as a bungler, Evans as a 'masterful but, after all, a flawed practiser', Auden as so masterful that he accomplishes everything he wishes, including his own destruction. Yet about Iago's essential nature there is remarkable consensus: his is a spirit of negation—of doubt, hatred, destruction, death.

In contrast, Desdemona has been seen as embodying trust and faith, charity and life. Hawkes (1964) finds in her a wise and intuitive kind of reason as distinguished from Iago's lower rationality. Such contrasts are frequent; often Othello has been regarded as a morality hero, torn between his bad angel and his good. Angelic purity is perhaps better rendered in music—as in Verdi's opera *Otello* (Hartnoll, Kerman)—than on the stage, where it can seem dull. Until recently, Rosenberg was one of the few interpreters who recognized Desdemona as a complex and developing character, a recognition that has been much enhanced lately by the insights of female scholars (Garner, Cook, W. D. Adamson, Jardine), some of whom have commented as well on Emilia and Bianca (Neely, Greene, Jane Adamson, Grennan).

When considering the three main characters and their relation-ships, most critics since Leavis have played down Iago's role in the tragedy (even though he has more lines than Othello). They have been more inclined to locate the cause of the tragedy within Othello's personality and within his relationship with Desdemona. The sex lives of the two lovers, especially Othello's sexual anxiet-ies, have been much scrutinized. In particular there has been an excessive amount of gossip concerning the physical consummation of their marriage. Is the strawberry-worked handkerchief em-blematic of the blood-stained sheet, traditionally displayed to confirm the deflowering of the bride (Boose)? There is nothing in the text to clinch the connection. Does the bloody on-stage brawl at Cyprus reflect what is going on off-stage in the bedroom of the newly-weds (Novy)? Does the murder of Desdemona in her wedding-sheets represent Othello's attempt to undo his act of defloration (Snow)? Was the marriage consummated at all (Pryse,

Nelson, Whallon)? The evidence is too slim to be sure of anything but that Shakespeare chose to leave the couple's honeymoon door closed and without a peephole. The tendency to locate the tragedy primarily within Othello's sexual makeup reaches an ultimate in Snow (who treats Othello's sexual aberrations in the latter part of the play not as Iago-inspired derangements but as expressions of attitudes latent in his psyche from the first) and in Stockholder (who reads the entire play as if it were Othello's dream, involving in addition to the heterosexual triangle a homosexual triangle of Othello/Iago/Cassio). As analyses of Othello's character, these two studies are obvious distortions; at best their free associations may bring to the surface subliminal attitudes in the creating author or a responding audience.

Preoccupation with Othello's sexual anxiety is especially to be regretted in the influential and otherwise estimable work of Cavell and of Greenblatt. In each, *Othello* emerges unexpectedly yet climactically within broad philosophical and historical contexts. Cavell uses the play as his best example of the deep connections between tragedy and scepticism, both of which are fuelled, he maintains, by a fierce denial of belief. Othello wishes to deny that Desdemona is less than perfect; he cannot forgive her for being *other* than himself, 'separate from him, outside, beyond command, commanding, her captain's captain' (p. 491). Such denial of belief in an unwelcome reality is highly resonant; it may be seen in Desdemona, Iago, and other characters as well. But to Cavell it is Othello's appalled discovery of Desdemona's sexuality, not her presumed infidelity, that causes his change of heart. Far from resisting Iago's slander, Cavell's Othello wishes to believe it, as a way of denying that the Desdemona he had idealized is—in bed—flesh and blood. Yet Othello says nothing about such a 'discovery'; on the contrary, when in his soliloquy he laments 'O curse of marriage, | That we can call these delicate creatures ours | And not their appetites' (iii. iii 272–3), his regret is not that his wife has appetites but rather that they are not subject to his complete possession. Greenblatt valuably deepens and makes more sympathetic what Leavis scorned as Othello's self-dramatization by putting it in the context of the 'self-fashioning' of More and Wyatt, Marlowe and Spenser. But he, too, is distracted by Othello's sexual anxieties, seeing him as vulnerable because he is appalled by the realization of his own sexuality, a view that depends on the slim thread of an ambiguous

pronoun reference in Iago's plan 'to abuse Othello's ear, / That he
is too familiar with his wife' (I. iii. 387–8). Greenblatt understands this to mean that it is Othello himself who is 'too familiar',
not Cassio as is usually thought, and cites theological warnings
against adulterous lust in marriage. Yet we never hear Iago
abusing Othello's ear in Greenblatt's sense, whereas he of course
often does so in the usual sense.

There is a need for more studies which strike a balance among
the inter-connections of Othello, Iago, and Desdemona. The best
such is Jane Adamson's. She discerns at the heart of their inner
lives a fear of deep and complex feelings, feelings which they
seek to evade by construing their lives into self-justifying patterns
that are simpler and less threatening to live with than reality. For
Othello, for instance, it is less painful to regard his wife as a
whore than to face even the possibility that Desdemona might
not love him or that he might not be worthy of her love. Until too
late, Desdemona cannot accept Othello's distrust of her because
of what it implies about the man she married. Iago's 'whole
mind's endeavour is rigidly and permanently geared to prevent
him from having to see his own vulnerability'. The defensiveness
of the three characters is a fresh insight; unfortunately, Adamson
overemphasizes it to the neglect of the dynamic power of the
actively destructive forces in the play—such as Iago's hatred and
Othello's jealousy. Her work may well be read in tandem with
Grudin, who is less sympathetic with the two lovers than she,
and more sympathetic with Iago.

However the individual characters may be interpreted, certain
of the relationships that recur among them firmly delineate the
unique 'world' Shakespeare envisaged for this tragedy. One of
its features is *displacement*, signalized when Shakespeare chose
his subtitle: 'The Moor of Venice'. His hero is a black man among
whites, a soldier in society (Jorgensen, 1956; Proser, Ide); his
heroine is a very domestic girl (Knight) who elopes with a very
exotic stranger (Van Doren). Locales are important. Resemblances
to the setting of *The Merchant of Venice* have been explored by
Fiedler and Nuttall. Commentators disagree about the function
of Venice: to Heilman it represents a sound and supportive
society; to Fergusson it seems so sterile that even Desdemona
could find nothing in it to command her love and loyalty. But
they agree that the outpost on Cyprus is a place in which the
characters seem lost. Here the harsh military hierarchy is the

nearest thing to a social order, and all the soldiers are sooner or later estranged even from that—as they are passed over, cashiered, or transferred. There is nothing like the sense of great national and cosmic involvement that one customarily finds in Shakespearian tragedy (Hibbard) and what scope there is narrows progressively (Brown, 1976). Thrown on themselves as they are, these displaced persons at the outset also seem remote from one another. As Hazlitt puts it: 'These characters and the images they stamp upon the mind are the farthest asunder possible, the distance between them is immense.' They cluster around the magnetic and expansive Othello (Fergusson). He stands at the centre of a network of bonds (Everett) that soon become bondages, a strange net of relationships that finally enmeshes them all.

One focus of their very intense relationships involves questions of *control*. All the leading characters are strong-willed. None of them knows when to stop. When at the beginning Othello and Desdemona dominate, they feel 'free' and sure of themselves, wonderfully poised and self-controlled. Their self-possession will be lost, utterly (Mack), as their inner and domestic lives are thrown into chaos. As Iago more and more takes control, he more and more defines the world of the play. It is one of torment and cruelty (Spurgeon), in which impulses toward destruction and self-destruction have been released, in which sexual passion turns perverse to the point of madness, in which the controlled violence of justice becomes a mask for revenge. This has become a world in which consequences enormously exceed their causes (McElroy). The consequent sufferings also release overwhelming surges of grief, pity, and—ironically—love. Eventually, the chaos extends so far that Iago himself loses control, and chance and circumstance increasingly take charge (Bradley).

It is concerning overall meanings or themes that Shakespeare's intentions are least clear. Levin has made this point in general (1979), and in particular he has convincingly attacked (1988) those who read *Othello* and other Shakespearian tragedies as anti-patriarchal statements. The play itself seems engaged in a search for meaning. Interpreters differ about the degree to which the search is successful. Skulsky finds an initial period of 'moral suspense' for the play's spectators before its ultimate affirmation of 'intrinsic value'. To Bradshaw Shakespeare in *Othello* as elsewhere is 'both more sceptical than his idealistic characters and more tentatively—sceptically—affirmative than his nihilists and dogmatic sceptics' (p. 37). Felperin follows the processes by which the action is first allegorized in terms of Christian morality, then de-allegorized by Emilia's plain-speaking, then re-allegorized at the end, ultimately producing an 'acknowledged indeterminacy' (p. 85). To Granville-Barker, *Othello* seems 'a tragedy without meaning, and that is the ultimate horror of it'. The truth is, I believe, that the play is not a 'statement' of any kind. At most, one can identify in it areas of interest. Here questions of *fidelity*, of truth to self and others, are dominant. Like the characters, commentators have rightly dwelt on such matters as trust and mistrust, faith and cynicism, integrity and hypocrisy—to the point of prostitution, of honesty in all its senses, of deception and self-deception, of seeming and being, of reputation and honour. Many of these matters, of course, also figure in other plays by Shakespeare; it is their particular combination in *Othello* that makes it unique. Through them the play engages our minds but without reducing itself to a single message or moral. At most its upshot, as Jane Adamson argues, should make us resist our need for moral simplicities, whether of condemnation or simple pity, and run the risks entailed by complex feelings and judgements.

In addition to outlining the imagined characters and actions of the story, each of Shakespeare's texts provides guidelines for its enactment by actors and its reception by audiences, implying the kind of theatre-event best suited to the imagined story. *Othello*'s power in performance has long been recognized. It is one of the few plays by Shakespeare to have had a continuously successful life in the theatre. Yet until recent decades commentaries with a theatrical orientation have been disappointing. Granville-Barker's *Preface* is less inspired than usual. Stanislavsky's production notes are fragmentary and much given to speculation about political intrigues in Venice before the play began. Stoll occupies a special place in *Othello* commentary, having written more of it than anyone else, and occasioned innumerable replies. Yet the attention thus given to his views far exceeds their value; and for all his talk about 'stage convention', his theories—as Rosenberg has shown—are not really based upon theatrical experience.

Subsequent studies have been much more rewarding. In running notes to his edition Brown (1976) visualizes the play in performance, aided by photographs and details from actual productions. Hankey's edition emphasizes stage history, surveyed in a full introduction and itemized in pages facing the text (as if in a promptbook). The role of Othello as a part to be played has been analyzed by Goldman and Hapgood (1988); Brown (1981) has commented on the play's text as dialogue to be spoken. Particular performances have been celebrated by Sprague on Edmund Kean's Othello and Edwin Booth's Iago; Spector on Margaret Webster's *Othello*, starring Paul Robeson; Tynan on Olivier's Othello; Wine on performers of Othello, Iago, and Desdemona, 1943–82; Jorgens on filmed versions. Comments by actors themselves have been collected by Rosenberg, Carlisle, Meryman, and Jackson. Such accounts can help one to define the spectrum of options for interpretation that Shakespeare has provided for performers.

The text can also be read as a scenario for audience responses, guiding not only the vicarious experiences that come through identifying with characters but also the direct experiences that members of an audience must undergo in coming to terms with what happens. In many ways spectators are placed in a position analogous to Othello's. They are obliged to determine the trust-worthiness of Iago—critics still argue about whether certain statements of Iago are to be credited or not. They are made to feel Iago's all-compelling powers; if Sedgewick is right, Iago masters the audience (along with Brabanzio, Roderigo, and Cassio) before he masters Othello. Unless the spectators walk out, they must then suffer helplessly Iago's horrible imaginings, and by Act IV may well feel as compelled as does Othello to find release from these oppressions (Nowottny).

Often spectators have been as inclined as the characters to go to extremes. Under the influence of the contrasting verbal styles of Othello and Iago, some have tended to regard the play in an idiom of general glorification, as does Swinburne, or of general vilification, as does Leavis. A good many have judged the charac-ters as self-righteously as does Othello (surveyed by Hapgood, 1966) or as compassionately as does Desdemona (Wilson). Like Emilia, spectators may resist the lovers' commitments to absolutes (Neely, Grudin) and yet feel with Burke that such resistance is 'placed' through her expression of it. The playwright himself seems to enter into the dynamics of the theatre event he has imagined for the performers and spectators of *Othello*. He out-does Iago in the subtle craft and daring of his plotting. And like all his characters in this play, he drives relentlessly beyond his source (Spencer) to devastating extremes. So all concerned, it seems, are caught up in the same distinctive act of imagination.

To conclude: In the 1973 edition of this survey, I predicted that 'The time seems near for some fundamental advances in *Othello* criticism and commentary' (p. 160). I believe that, in the varied ways specified in the present survey, this prediction has come true. As new approaches and attitudes have developed that are more congenial to the play than before, scholars and critics have addressed difficult, delicate, neglected aspects of *Othello* that have indeed advanced our understanding of it. The 1973 survey concluded, however, by observing that 'the most important studies of *Othello* remain to be made', and this continues to be true. Large scale, richly inclusive projects are what is needed. Adamson's book, Hankey's edition, Martin Elliott's monograph are steps in the right direction. We need edited and annotated versions of the Quarto and Folio texts, for example, and a synthesis of specialized findings about the diverse features of the dialogue. Surveys would be welcome which place the play in broad cultural contexts and which relate it to literary traditions other than tragedy. It is tempting simply to call for more books devoted solely to *Othello*. Almost all of the commentary surveyed here has been in the form of sharply focused articles or single chapters in books where *Othello* was only one item on a larger agenda. But the true issue is more one of breadth of perspective than of length. After all, the best appreciations of the play to date are chapters in books by Bradley and Knight. And it is their achievement that best exemplifies the Arnoldian perspective I would recommend: as different as they are, they each help us to see *Othello* whole.

REFERENCES

For guidance to *Othello* commentary until 1915, see Stoll; until 1956, see Heilman; until 1972, see Quinn. My references below emphasize subsequent studies. For a fuller guide until 1984, see Martin Elliott. An annotated bibliography from 1940 is promised by Garland Publications in 1990.

TEXTS AND TEXTUAL STUDIES

Brown, John Russell (ed.), *Shakespeare in Performance: An Introduction through Six Major Plays* (New York, 1976).

Coghill, Nevill, *Shakespeare's Professional Skills* (Cambridge, 1964).

Hankey, Julie (ed.), *Othello: Plays in Performance* (Bristol, 1987).

Hinman, Charlton (ed.), *Othello 1622* (Shakespeare Quarto Facsimiles, Oxford, 1975).

—— *The Norton Facsimile: The First Folio of Shakespeare* (New York, 1968).

Honigmann, E. A. J., 'Shakespeare's Revised Plays: *King Lear* and *Othello'*, *The Library*, 6th ser., 4 (1982), 142–73.

—— *The Stability of Shakespeare's Text* (London, 1965).

Muir, Kenneth (ed.), *Othello* (New Penguin Shakespeare, Harmondsworth, 1968).

Ridley, M. R. (ed.), *Othello* (Arden Shakespeare, London, 1958.

Sanders, Norman (ed.), *Othello* (New Cambridge Shakespeare, Cambridge, 1984).

Schröer, M. (ed.), *Othello: Paralleldruck der ersten Quarto und der ersten Folio* (Heidelberg, 1949).

Wells, Stanley, and Gary Taylor (gen. eds.), *William Shakespeare: The Complete Works* (Oxford, 1986; compact edn., 1988).

CRITICISM AND COMMENTARY

Adamson, Jane, *'Othello' as Tragedy* (London, 1980).

Adamson, W. D., 'Unpinned or Undone?: Desdemona's Critics and the Problems of Sexual Innocence', *Shakespeare Studies*, 13 (1980), 169–86.

Altman, Joel B., ' "Preposterous Conclusions": Eros, *Enargeia*, and the Composition of *Othello'*, *Representations*, 18 (1987), 129–57.

Auden, W. H., *The Dyer's Hand* (New York, 1962).

Bamber, Linda, *Comic Women, Tragic Men: A Study of Gender and Genre in Shakespeare* (Stanford, Calif., 1982).

Barthelemy, Anthony Gerard, *Black Face Maligned Race: The Representation of Blacks in English Drama from Shakespeare to Southerne* (Baton Rouge, La., 1987).

Bayley, John, *The Characters of Love* (London, 1960).

—— *Shakespeare and Tragedy* (London, 1981).

Bethell, S. L., 'The Diabolic Images in *Othello'*, *Shakespeare Survey* 5 (1952), 62–80.

Boose, Lynda E., 'Othello's Handkerchief: "The Recognizance and Pledge of Love" ', *English Literary Renaissance*, 5 (1975), 360–74.

Bradley, A. C., *Shakespearean Tragedy* (London, 1904; reprinted 1978).

Bradshaw, Graham, *Shakespeare's Scepticism* (New York, 1987).

Brown, John Russell, *Discovering Shakespeare* (London, 1981).

Bulman, James C., *The Heroic Idiom of Shakespearean Tragedy* (Newark, Del., 1985).

Burke, Kenneth, '*Othello*: An Essay to Illustrate a Method', *Hudson*

Review, 4 (1951–2, 165–203); reprinted in *Perspectives by Incongruity*, ed. S. E. Hyman (Bloomington, Ind., 1964).

Calderwood, James, 'Speech and Self in *Othello*', *Shakespeare Quarterly*, 38 (1987), 293–303.

Carlisle, Carol Jones, *Shakespeare from the Greenroom* (Chapel Hill, NC, 1969).

Cavell, Stanley, *The Claim of Reason: Wittgenstein, Scepticism, Morality, and Tragedy* (Oxford, 1980).

Clemen, Wolfgang H., *The Development of Shakespeare's Imagery* (London, 1951; 2nd edn., with new preface, 1977).

Colie, Rosalie, *Shakespeare's Living Art* (Princeton, NJ, 1974).

Cook, Ann Jennalie, 'The Design of Desdemona: Doubt Raised and Resolved', *Shakespeare Studies*, 13 (1980), 187–96.

Danson, Lawrence, *Tragic Alphabet: Shakespeare's Drama of Language* (New Haven, Conn., 1974).

Dash, Irene, *Wooing, Wedding, and Power: Women in Shakespeare's Plays* (New York, 1981).

de Mendonça, B. H., '*Othello*: A Tragedy Built on a Comic Structure', *Shakespeare Survey 21* (1968), 31–8.

Doran, Madeleine, 'Iago's "if": Conditional and Subjunctive in *Othello*', in her *Shakespeare's Dramatic Language* (Madison, Wis., 1976), 63–91.

Eliot, T. S., 'Shakespeare and the Stoicism of Seneca', in his *Selected Essays 1917–1932* (London, 1932), 126–40.

Elliott, G. R., *Flaming Minister* (Durham, NC, 1953).

Elliott, Martin, *Shakespeare's Invention of Othello* (London, 1988).

Empson, William, *The Structure of Complex Words* (London, 1951; reprinted 1985).

Erickson, Peter, *Patriarchal Structures in Shakespeare's Drama* (Berkeley, Calif., 1985).

Evans, Bertrand, *Shakespeare's Tragic Practice* (Oxford, 1979).

Everett, Barbara, 'Reflections on the Sentimentalist's *Othello*', *Critical Quarterly*, 3 (1961), 127–39.

Felperin, Howard, *Shakespearean Representation* (Princeton, NJ, 1977).

Fergusson, Francis, *Shakespeare: The Pattern in His Carpet* (New York, 1970).

Fiedler, Leslie, *The Stranger in Shakespeare* (New York, 1972).

Foreman, Walter, *The Music of the Close: The Final Scenes of Shakespeare's Tragedies* (Lexington, Ky., 1978).

French, Marilyn, *Shakespeare's Division of Experience* (New York, 1981).

Gardner, Helen, '*Othello*: A Retrospect, 1900–67', *Shakespeare Survey 21* (1968), 1–11.

Garner, S. N., 'Shakespeare's Desdemona', *Shakespeare Studies*, 9 (1976), 233–52.

Gohlke, Madelon, ' "All that is spoke is marred": Language and Consciousness in *Othello*', *Women's Studies*, 9 (1982), 157–76.

Goldman, Michael, 'Othello's Cause', in his *Acting and Action in Shakespearean Tragedy* (Princeton, NJ, 1985, 46–70).

Granville-Barker, Harley, *Prefaces to Shakespeare*, Fourth Series (London, 1945).

Greenblatt, Stephen, *Renaissance Self-Fashioning* (Chicago, Ill., 1980).

Greene, Gayle, ' "This That You Call Love": Sexual and Social Tragedy in *Othello*', *Journal of Women's Studies in Literature*, 1 (1979), 16–32.

Greg, W. W., *The Shakespeare First Folio* (Oxford, 1955).

Grennan, Eamon, 'The Women's Voice in *Othello*: Speech, Song, Silence', *Shakespeare Quarterly*, 38 (1987), 275–92.

Grudin, Robert, *Mighty Opposites: Shakespeare and Renaissance Contrariety* (Berkeley, Calif., 1979).

Hapgood, Robert, *Shakespeare the Theatre-Poet* (Oxford, 1988).

—— 'The Trials of Othello', in *Pacific Coast Studies in Shakespeare*, ed. W. F. McNeir and T. N. Greenfield (Eugene, Oreg., 1966), 134–47.

Hartnoll, Phyllis (ed.), *Shakespeare in Music* (London, 1964).

Hawkes, Terence, *Shakespeare and the Reason* (London, 1964).

—— *Shakespeare's Talking Animals* (London, 1973).

Hazlitt, William, *Characters of Shakespear's Plays* (London, 1817; World's Classics, London, 1917).

Heilman, Robert B., *Magic in the Web* (Lexington, Ky., 1956).

Hibbard, G. R., '*Othello* and the Pattern of Shakespearian Tragedy', *Shakespeare Survey 21* (1968), 39–46.

Hill, Erroll, *Shakespeare in Sable* (Amherst, Mass., 1984).

Holland, Norman, *Psychoanalysis and Shakespeare* (New York, 1964).

Holloway, John, *The Story of the Night* (London, 1961).

Hunter, G. K., *Othello and Colour Prejudice*, British Academy Lecture, 1968; reprinted in his *Dramatic Identities and Cultural Tradition* (Liverpool, 1978), 31–59.

Hyman, Stanley Edgar, *Iago. Some Approaches to the Illusion of His Motivation* (New York, 1970).

Ide, Richard S., *Possessed with Greatness: The Heroic Tragedies of Chapman and Shakespeare* (Chapel Hill, NC, 1980).

Jackson, R., and R. Smallwood (eds.), *Players of Shakespeare 2* (Cambridge, 1988).

Jardine, Lisa, *Still Harping on Daughters: Women and Drama in the Age of Shakespeare* (Brighton, 1983).

Jones, Eldred, *Othello's Countrymen* (London, 1965).

Jones, Emrys, *Scenic Form in Shakespeare* (Oxford, 1971).

Jorgens, Jack, *Shakespeare on Film* (Bloomington, Ind., 1977).

Jorgensen, Paul, ' "Perplex'd in the Extreme": The Role of Thought in *Othello*', *Shakespeare Quarterly*, 15 (1964), 265–75.

—— *Redeeming Shakespeare's Words* (Berkeley, Calif., 1962).

—— *Shakespeare's Military World* (Berkeley, Calif., 1956).

Kahn, Coppélia, *Man's Estate: Masculine Identity in Shakespeare* (Berkeley and Los Angeles, Calif., 1981).

Kerman, Joseph, *Opera as Drama* (New York, 1956).

Kirsch, Arthur, *Shakespeare and the Experience of Love* (Cambridge, 1981).

Knight, G. Wilson, *The Wheel of Fire: Interpretations of Shakespearian Tragedy* (London, 1930; rev. edn., 1949).

Leavis, F. R., 'Diabolic Intellect and the Noble Hero', *Scrutiny*, 6 (1937), 259–83; reprinted in his *The Common Pursuit* (London, 1952), 136–59.

Levin, Richard, 'Feminist Thematics and Shakespearean Tragedy', *PMLA* 103 (1988), 125–38.

—— *New Readings vs. Old Plays: Recent Trends in the Reinterpretation of English Renaissance Drama* (Chicago, Ill., 1979).

McDonald, Russ, 'Othello, Thorello, and the Foolish Hero', *Shakespeare Quarterly*, 30 (1979), 51–67.

McElroy, Bernard, *Shakespeare's Mature Tragedies* (Princeton, NJ, 1973).

Mack, Maynard, 'The Jacobean Shakespeare', in *Jacobean Theatre*, ed. J. R. Brown and B. Harris (Stratford-upon-Avon Studies, 1; London, 1960), 11–42.

Marsh, D. R. C., *Passion Lends Them Power* (Manchester, 1976).

Melchiori, Giorgio, 'The Rhetoric of Character Construction: "Othello" ', *Shakespeare Survey 34* (1981), 61–72.

Meryman, Richard, 'The Great Sir Laurence', *Life* 56 (1 May 1964), 80–98.

Morozov, Mikhail, M., 'The Individualization of Shakespeare's Characters through Imagery', *Shakespeare Survey* 2 (1949), 83–106.

Neely, Carol Thomas, *Broken Nuptials in Shakespeare's Plays* (New Haven, Conn., 1985).

Nelson, T. G. A., and Charles Haines, 'Othello's Unconsummated Marriage', *Essays in Criticism*, 33 (1983), 1–18.

Nevo, Ruth, *Tragic Form in Shakespeare* (Princeton, NJ, 1972).

Newman, Karen, ' "And wash the Ethiop white": Femininity and the Monstrous in *Othello*', in *Shakespeare Reproduced*, ed. J. Howard and M. O'Connor (London, 1987), 143–62.

Novy, Marianne, L., *Love's Argument: Gender Relations in Shakespeare* (Chapel Hill, NC, 1984).

Nowottny, Winifred M. T., 'Justice and Love in *Othello*', *University of Toronto Quarterly*, 21 (1952), 330–44; reprinted in *A Casebook on 'Othello'*, ed. L. F. Dean (New York, 1961).

Nuttall, A. D., *A New Mimesis: Shakespeare and the Representation of Reality* (London, 1983).

Orkin, Martin, 'Othello and the "Plain Face" of Racism', *Shakespeare Quarterly*, 38 (1987); reprinted in his *Shakespeare Against Apartheid* (Craighall, 1987), 59–129.

Parker, Patricia, 'Shakespeare and Rhetoric: "Dilation" and "Delation" in *Othello'*, in *Shakespeare and the Question of Theory*, ed. P. Parker and G. Hartmann (London, 1985), 54–74.

Proser, Matthew N., *The Heroic Image in Five Shakespearean Tragedies* (Princeton, NJ, 1965).

Pryse, M., 'Lust for Audience: An Interpretation of *Othello'*, *ELH* 46 (1976), 461–78.

Quinn, E., J. Ruoff and J. Grennen (eds.), *The Major Shakespearean Tragedies: A Critical Bibliography* (Riverside, NJ, 1973).

Raysor, T. M., *Coleridge's Shakespearean Criticism*, 2 vols. (Cambridge, Mass., 1930); reprinted Everyman's Library (London, 1960).

Rosenberg, Marvin, *The Masks of Othello* (Berkeley, Calif., 1961).

Rymer, Thomas, *The Critical Works of Thomas Rymer*, ed. C. Zimansky (New Haven, Conn., 1956).

Scragg, Leah, 'Iago—Vice or Devil?' *Shakespeare Survey 21* (1968), 53–65.

Sedgewick, G. G., *Of Irony, Especially in Drama* (Toronto, 1948).

Shaffer, Elinor S., 'Iago's Malignity Motivated: Coleridge's Unpublished "Opus Magnum"', *Shakespeare Quarterly*, 19 (1968), 195–203.

Shaw, G. B., 'A Word More about Verdi', *Anglo-Saxon Review*, 8 (1901), 221–29.

Shirley, Frances A., *Swearing and Perjury in Shakespeare's Plays* (London, 1979).

Skulsky, Harold, *Spirits Finely Touched* (Athens, Ga., 1976).

Snow, Edward, 'Sexual Anxiety and the Male Order of Things in *Othello'*, *English Literary Renaissance*, 10 (1980), 384–412.

Snyder, Susan, *The Comic Matrix of Shakespeare's Tragedies* (Princeton, NJ, 1979).

Spector, Susan, 'Margaret Webster's *Othello'*, *Theatre History Studies*, 6 (1986), 93–108.

Spencer, T. J. B. (ed.), *Elizabethan Love Stories* (Harmondsworth, 1968).

Spivack, Bernard, *Shakespeare and the Allegory of Evil* (New York, 1958).

Sprague, Arthur Colby, *Shakespearean Players and Performances* (Cambridge, Mass., 1953).

Spurgeon, Caroline F. E., *Shakespeare's Imagery and What It Tells Us* (Cambridge, 1935).

Stanislavski, Konstantin, *Stanislavsky Produces 'Othello'*, trans. H. Nowak (London, 1948).

Stewart, J. I. M., *Character and Motive in Shakespeare* (London, 1965).

Stockholder, Karen, *Dream Works: Love and Families in Shakespeare's Plays* (Toronto, 1988).

Stoll, E. E., *Othello: An Historical and Comparative Study* (Minneapolis, Minn., 1915).

Swinburne, Algernon Charles, *A Study of Shakespeare* (London, 1909).

Tynan, Kenneth, *Othello: The National Theatre Production* (New York, 1966).

Van Doren, Mark, *Shakespeare* (New York, 1939).

West, Robert, 'The Christianness of *Othello*', *Shakespeare Quarterly*, 15 (1964), 333–43.

Whallon, William, *Inconsistencies* (Cambridge, 1983).

Wheeler, Richard P., ' ". . . And my loud crying still": The *Sonnets*, *The Merchant of Venice*, and *Othello*', in *Shakespeare's Rough Magic*, eds. P. Erickson and C. Kahn (Newark, Del., 1985), 193–209.

Wilson, H. S., *On the Design of Shakespearian Tragedy* (Toronto, 1958).

Wimsatt, W. K. (ed), *Samuel Johnson on Shakespeare* (New York, 1960); reprinted as *Dr. Johnson on Shakespeare* (Penguin Shakespeare Library, Harmondsworth, 1969).

Wine, Martin L., *Othello: Text and Performance* (London, 1984).

12 | King Lear

KENNETH MUIR

It has been suggested by several critics that *King Lear* has replaced *Hamlet* as the tragedy which finds the most direct response from the modern reader. As L. C. Knights puts it, *King Lear* 'is the great central masterpiece, the great exploratory allegory'. This suggestion is certainly borne out by the large number of books and articles which have been published in recent years.

TEXTS

Until recently, all editions of *King Lear* were based on the two original texts—the First Quarto published in 1608, and the First Folio published in 1623—in varying proportions. It was generally agreed that the Folio text was the better, but, even so, editors felt bound to accept a number of readings, extended passages, and even whole scenes from the quarto.

The play appeared, of course, in all editions of Shakespeare's works from 1623 to the present day, but the first separate edition that need be mentioned is H. H. Furness's New Variorum (1880) which gives all the readings of previous editions and a summary of previous commentary and criticism. Although the edition has been superseded textually and critically, it still contains information not easily obtainable elsewhere.

The most valuable conflated edition from the textual point of view is G. I. Duthie's old-spelling edition. This contains a detailed examination of all the variants: but it is so austerely textual, without anything other than textual annotation, that only the specialist will find it useful. Some years later, Duthie collaborated with J. Dover Wilson in the New (Cambridge) edition. This has a good introduction, succinct notes, a stage history, and a glossary. Fuller annotation is provided in Kenneth Muir's new Arden edition. This, which has been revised many times, also includes a selection from the main sources of the play—Sidney's *Arcadia*, *King Leir*, Holinshed's *Chronicles*, Spenser's *Faerie Queene*, *A Mirror for Magistrates*, and Harsnett's *Declaration of Egregious Popish Impostures*. Russell Fraser's Signet

edition contains a shorter selection of sources and some representative criticism. Like Alfred Harbage's Pelican edition, this
has brief glosses at the foot of the page. Another American
edition by G. L. Kittredge has a good introduction, a conservative
text, and useful notes. G. K. Hunter's New Penguin edition has a
freshly considered text and ample annotation. Among other
editions Philip Edwards's may be mentioned.

In recent years, however, it has been argued that all these
editions fell into the mistake of conflating the Quarto and Folio
texts, since these represent two separate versions of the play.
This idea was propounded by Michael J. Warren and Steven
Urkowitz and developed by Gary Taylor and others, most persuasively in *The Division of the Kingdoms*. The new Oxford
Shakespeare, therefore, prints two separate texts of *King Lear*. It
is established that many Folio readings were substitutions for
those of the Quarto; and it is probable that Shakespeare was
ultimately responsible for both versions. Yet the cuts in the Folio
text may have been forced upon the poet by theatrical expediency
(e.g. a tour) and we cannot be certain that he intended them to be
permanent.

CRITICISM AND COMMENTARY

So much has been written about *King Lear*—many books, hundreds of articles, scores of chapters in books concerned with
wider aspects of Shakespeare's work—that in a survey of this
kind it will be necessary to make a representative selection.
There are useful bibliographies by S. A. Tannenbaum and in *The
'King Lear' Perplex* by H. Bonheim, and a superb annotated
bibliography by Larry S. Champion. The criticism written between
1604 and 1904 (when Bradley's *Shakespearean Tragedy* was published) will be considered in roughly chronological order. But
during the present century the proliferation has been such that it
will be necessary to consider the criticism under various headings.

1604–1904

The first substantial criticism of the play appeared in Nahum
Tate's preface to his adaptation, in which he complacently defended his alterations by enumerating Shakespeare's 'faults',
such as the introduction of the Fool and the insufficient motive
for Cordelia's conduct in the first scene, faults which made the
play 'a Heap of Jewels, unstrung and unpolished'. The adaptation,

in which Cordelia is in love with Edgar, and Lear is restored to the throne, held the stage throughout the eighteenth century. It was condemned by Joseph Addison in *The Spectator* and defended by Samuel Johnson in his edition because he found the death of Cordelia unbearably painful and a violation of poetic justice. Charles Lamb, who had seen only modifications of Tate's version in the theatre, argued that *King Lear*, and all Shakespeare's tragedies, could not be adequately performed. William Hazlitt quoted Lamb's essay with approval. (Kean restored the tragic ending, though retaining the love story. It was not until 1838 that the Fool was restored by Macready.)

Meanwhile, the eighteenth-century habit of weighing Shakespeare's beauties against his faults (for example in Joseph Warton's essays on the play) had given place to the enthusiasm of Romantics. Schlegel, unlike Warton, realized the function of the Gloucester underplot. Coleridge in his courses of lectures had perceptive comments on several scenes and in his *Table Talk* (29 December 1822) he called the play 'the most tremendous effort of Shakespeare as a poet'. Shelley in his 'Defence of Poetry' described the play as 'the most perfect specimen of dramatic poetry existing in the world'. But the poet who made the most profound remarks about *King Lear* was Keats. He speaks of the play in his letters and stresses the way in which the disagreeables are evaporated by the intensity of the poetry (21 December 1817). He also has some marginalia in his copy of Hazlitt's *Characters*—on the relation between the play and Shakespeare's experience and on the Fool. D. G. James discusses Keats's views on *King Lear* in *Shakespeare Survey 13*.

A. C. Swinburne set the tone for much later criticism by proclaiming that Gloucester's words after his blinding—

> As flies to wanton boys are we to the gods
> They kill us for their sport—

were the keynote of the play. He spoke of Shakespeare's 'tragic fatalism' and declares that 'Requital, redemption, amends, equity, explanation, pity, mercy, are words without a meaning here'. Edward Dowden more soberly stressed the stoical attitude revealed in the play, and, in asserting that 'all that is tragically sublime is also grotesque', he anticipated Wilson Knight. The first full analysis of the structure of the play, of the parallelism of the two plots, and of the trio of madness (Lear, Poor Tom, the Fool) in the storm scenes was made by Richard G. Moulton in *Shakespeare as a Dramatic Artist*.

A. C. Bradley's *Shakespearean Tragedy* contains two chapters on *King Lear*, which raise all the main questions concerning the play: whether it is a good stage play, whether it is well constructed, whether it can be acted, whether it is pessimistic, to what extent it reflects Shakespeare's personal feelings, whether the opening scene is credible, whether the death of Cordelia is dramatically justifiable, whether Lear is redeemed, and what is the function of the animal imagery. Later critics do not always agree with Bradley's answers, but they agree that most of these questions should be asked.

Bradley, though a keen playgoer, never had the chance of seeing *King Lear* in the theatre without drastic alterations, and some of his views—on the structural weakness of the play, that the blinding of Gloucester was too horrible for the stage, that the ending was not inevitable—might well have been modified. He thought the play might be entitled 'The Redemption of King Lear', but Helen Gardner is one of several critics who argue that Lear does not acquire wisdom.

Bradley's second chapter is concerned mainly with the characters of the play, and this side of his work has not worn so well. It was attacked by those who believed that it diverted attention from the poetry (to which, in fact, Bradley was fully responsive) and it was criticized by those, such as Elmer Edgar Stoll, who felt that Bradley failed to appreciate the conventions of poetic drama, and by Lily B. Campbell who showed that Bradley's character analysis failed to use Elizabethan terminology and was 'made on a foundation of morality without morals, as well as a psychology untrue to psychological thinking of any period'. Bradley's terminology may be dated, and sometimes confused, but neither his morality nor his knowledge of human nature deserves this blanket condemnation.

Sources

The sources of the play are discussed briefly in most editions and they are printed and discussed in Geoffrey Bullough's *Narrative and Dramatic Sources of Shakespeare*, Vol. VII. Earlier, in *The Story of King Lear*, W. Perrett had made an exhaustive study of all versions previous to Shakespeare's; and W. W. Greg had discussed Shakespeare's indebtedness to Holinshed's *Chronicles*, Spenser's

Faerie Queene, A Mirror for Magistrates, and the old tragi-comedy, *King Leir.* The use of Sidney's *Arcadia* in the Gloucester underplot has been discussed by Fitzroy Pyle, D. M. McKeithan and John Danby, and Kenneth Muir. R. A. Law analysed Shakespeare's use of Holinshed and *King Leir* and Muir discussed Shakespeare's use of Samuel Harsnett's *Declaration of Egregious Popish Impostures.* (Muriel C. Bradbrook has some good comments on the tone of Harsnett and of Shakespeare's reaction to it.) Arthur F. Kinney suggested that Shakespeare was indebted to Lipsius; but Leo Salingar did not find the parallels convincing. The influence of Florio's translation of Montaigne is discussed by G. C. Taylor and W. B. Drayton Henderson. Gary Taylor suggested that Shakespeare was influenced by *Eastward Ho!* and G. M. Young argued that the true story of Brian Annesley and his three daughters was known to Shakespeare. The youngest daughter who succoured him in his dotage was named Cordell. Bullough discusses this theory with some scepticism.

Critics differ as to the skill with which Shakespeare constructed his play from these materials. Some have deplored his haste and exhaustion (Nicoll), his failure to write a good stage play (Tucker Brooke), its loose episodic structure (Perkinson), its being too huge for the stage (Bradley), its absurdity, contrivance, and falsity (Gide, after seeing Olivier in the title-role), and its radical incoherence (Mason). John Middleton Murry, while allowing that Shakespeare took immense pains in the composition of the play, complained that the result was an artefact, its failure being due to Shakespeare's 'terrible primitive revulsion against sex'.

Tolstoy used *King Lear* as his main exhibit in his attack on Shakespeare for his triviality, irreligion, immorality, vulgarity, and insincerity, *King Leir* being superior to Shakespeare's tragedy. As Y. Levin pointed out, Tolstoy was one of a number of Russians who attacked what they regarded as Shakespeare's inflated reputation. But, as G. Wilson Knight showed, Tolstoy made the mistake of treating Shakespeare as a would-be naturalistic writer, and George Orwell argued that Tolstoy was more like Lear than he could admit and his attitude to the play was due to the way Shakespeare had treated the theme of renunciation. Both Lear and Tolstoy clung to the power from which they had abdicated.

Harley Granville-Barker's preface to *King Lear* is the best answer to those critics—now few in number—who think that the play cannot be acted. Not merely does he give admirable advice on how the various parts should be played, he also replies directly to Lamb and Bradley by showing how the storm scenes, long regarded as unactable, should be staged. He allows that they cannot be performed on a stage with elaborate scenery and stage effects, but if played as Shakespeare intended, with Lear personifying the storm, they can be supremely effective. Bradley had assumed that the Elizabethan stage with its limited resources was even less able to provide an adequate representation of those scenes; but, as Granville-Barker points out, Shakespeare obtains his effects largely by means of the poetry. Sir John Gielgud, in a production for which Barker was unofficially responsible, was able to validate these arguments; and Gielgud's *Stage Directions* includes the hints offered him by Barker. It may be added that Shakespeare did not expect his actor to shout above the noise of the thunder; in the First Folio the stage directions show that the thunder is heard only between speeches and in natural pauses.

Marvin Rosenberg has given a detailed account of the way *King Lear* has fared on the stage, and shown the interaction of criticism and performance, and Gregori Kozintsev has shown both in his great film and in his book that the play can succeed in a different medium. Emrys Jones has given a detailed defence of the scenic structure of the play, though he admits that some of the final scene is on a lower level. Goldberg and others even claim that the final scene—before the entrance of Lear—is badly written.

Christian or Agnostic

One of the questions that have aroused most controversy during the present century is whether *King Lear* is the expression of scepticism or nihilism; or is it, as J. C. Maxwell once said, 'a Christian play about a pagan world'? The danger is, of course, that critics tend to find in the play a reflection of their own views; and the decline of faith during the last seventy years has had its effect on the interpretation of the play. The older generation of critics were anxious to find vestiges of Christian belief or sentiment. More recently critics have sought in the play a reflection of their own scepticism. To R. W. Chambers, the play presents the world as, in Keats's phrase, 'a vale of soul-making'. G. L. Bickersteth comes to a similar conclusion. John F. Danby maintains that the play is essentially Christian, with Cordelia as an allegorical Christlike figure. The conflict in the play is between two conceptions of nature: one benignant, rational, and divinely ordered, the other based on the assumption that man is governed merely by appetite and self-interest. Danby's view of Cordelia is shared by S. L. Bethell and Paul N. Siegel. Terence Hawkes (writing in 1964) gave a directly Christian interpretation. Paul A. Jorgensen argued that the King, through suffering, is brought to an understanding of himself and of mankind. Kenneth Myrick in 'Christian Pessimism in *King Lear*' declared that the play conformed to the orthodox views of Shakespeare's day. Virgil K. Whitaker regarded the play as 'profoundly Christian in thought', containing the Christian answer to the problem of suffering. H. S. Wilson claimed that the play affirmed the value of human love; and L. C. Knights declared that the mind 'is directed towards affirmation in spite of everything'.

Finally, on this side of the question, D. G. James suggested that although Shakespeare deliberately denied himself any expression of Christian belief, he exhibited 'the limits merely of our human experience as they are reached by souls of surpassing excellence and beauty.' Although there is no escape from evil, the good is 'altogether proof against all that is brought against it'.

On the other side of the debate are ranged a large number of recent critics. Clifford Leech argues that a Christian tragedy is impossible. Sylvan Barnet warns against Christian interpretations. Barbara Everett attacks all those critics who have attempted to turn the tragedy into an allegory or miracle play. Nicholas Brooke in his scene-by-scene commentary and in an article argues that the ending is 'without any support from systems of moral or artistic belief at all'. Edgar's 'morality play is exposed by Lear's experience'. Robert G. Hunter thinks that Shakespeare dramatizes the possibility that there is no God. To Sears Jayne the play is harshly pagan. To John Holloway, Lear, like other tragic heroes, is a scapegoat, and he stresses the continued sequence of disasters and the meagreness of consolation at the end. Jan Kott regards *King Lear* as part of the Theatre of the Absurd, comparing it to Beckett's *Endgame*. John D. Rosenberg, repudiating this, complains that 'modern' criticism has made the terror and the tragedy peripheral to the play. Both L. L. Schücking and Helen Gardner deny that Lear learns anything from experience. J. K. Walton and J. Stampfer agree that it is wrong to interpret Lear's last speech to

mean that he imagines Cordelia is alive; and John Shaw, showing
that Albany's penultimate (in the Quarto) speech resembles the
final speeches of other tragedies, argues that its effect is 'to throw
a fresh and shocking emphasis on the last confused words of the
play'. Derek Peat maintains that *King Lear* 'forces every spectator
to choose between the contrary possibilities it holds in unresolved
suspension'. (Much, however, will depend on the director's own
interpretation.) James Black suggests that the pattern of *King Lear*
is not that of a wheel, but one 'which overturning all conventions,
justice, expectations and hopes, takes us down and down and
down'.

   The fullest and most learned treatment of the subject is William
R. Elton's *King Lear and the Gods*. After a detailed consideration of
the evidence, he concludes that the play is not 'a drama of
meaningful suffering and redemption, within a just universe
ruled by providential higher powers'. Lear is not regenerated;
providence is not operative; and the last act 'shatters the foundations of faith itself'. Elton shows that the characters in the play
exhibit four attitudes to the gods: Edgar and Cordelia are virtuous
pagans; the evil characters are all atheists; Gloucester is super-
stitious; and Lear himself represents the view that God is mysterious and unintelligible to mortal eyes. Elton's strongest arguments
are that the ironical structure of the play is nicely calculated to
destroy one's faith not merely in poetic justice but in divine
justice, and a dusty answer is given to Albany's prayer for
Cordelia's safety. All this is true, but it does not inevitably lead to
Elton's conclusion. As Muir points out in *King Lear: A Critical
Study*, a Christian need not believe that God intervenes to protect
the good, nor suppose that the virtuous triumph in this life.
Shakespeare had to start from the dramatic hypotheses available
to a pagan. He shows that the sins of the comparatively good
characters (Lear and Gloucester) open the door to the worse sins
of the evil characters and to the murder of the innocent. It may be
said that the Christian ethic—the ethic of any of the great
religions—is vindicated without any support from the Christian
hope. As Oscar J. Campbell implies in 'The Salvation of Lear' and
as Enid Welsford says 'The metaphysical comfort of the Scriptures
is deliberately omitted, though not therefore necessarily denied'.
A chapter in Walter Stein's *Criticism as Dialogue* replies convincingly to Kott and, perhaps, to Nicholas Brooke. Mary Lascelles
has written on the Last Judgement in connection with the play

and Joseph Wittreich on the prevailing influence of the Apoca-
lypse. Maynard Mack and Rosalie L. Colie have both analysed
the biblical influence on the play; but since he had reverted to the
pre-Christian era for his setting, Shakespeare's biblical allusions
are more discreet than those of the author of *King Leir*.

Imagery and Symbol

The imagery of *King Lear* has attracted a great deal of attention.
Bradley commented on the significance of the animal imagery,
making use of an article by J. Kirkman entitled 'Animal Nature
versus Human Nature in *King Lear*', written years before. Caroline
Spurgeon calculated, however, that the dominant 'iterative'
image of the play is that of a body racked and tortured. Her article
was published in 1930 and incorporated in her big book on
Shakespeare's Imagery. W. H. Clemen soon afterwards demonstrated in *Shakespeares Bilder* (later revised and translated as *The
Development of Shakespeare's Imagery*) how the imagery is fully
integrated with the structure of the play. By the time the translation
appeared, Clemen had had the advantage of reading R. B. Heilman's *This Great Stage*, the most elaborate analysis of the imagery
of a single play then attempted. Heilman showed that Spurgeon's
method of concentrating on the largest group of images was
bound to give a one-sided view of the play. He realized, as
Clemen had done, that it was necessary to show 'the inter-
dependence of style, diction, imagery, plot, technique of charac-
terisation, and all the other constituent elements of drama.' The
various groups of images discussed by Heilman included those
relating to sight and blindness, to clothes, to madness in reason
and reason in madness, and to the gods. Blindness has also been
treated by J. I. M. Stewart in *Character and Motive in Shakespeare*
and later by Thelma Greenfield and Maurice Charney (see Colie
and Flahiff). Nature was treated at length by Danby, as we have
seen, and by Robert Speaight in a chapter in *Nature in Shakespearian Tragedy*. Elton discussed the gods; and Muir and Josephine W. Bennett discussed the theme of madness in the play.
Heilman makes use of the iteration of words as well as metaphors
and similes. In this respect he was forestalled by F. C. Kolbe's
brief study, *Shakespeare's Way*, based on articles written years
before its publication in 1930. Sometimes Heilman carries his
analysis too far. Alpers complained of the way sight imagery was
misinterpreted and W. R. Keast attacked Heilman's method for

the ponderous way in which it reached platitudinous conclusions; but no one before Heilman had brought out so clearly the basic paradoxes of the play.

One such paradox is to be found in the wisdom of the Fool. All those critics who have written of this character have been led into broader questions of interpretation. Enid Welsford, for example, suggests that 'Lear's tragedy is the investing of the King with motley: it is also the crowning and apotheosis of the Fool'. She, like William Empson, brings out the importance of an idea which goes back to Erasmus's *Praise of Folly*. There is a sensible treatment of the subject in Robert H. Goldsmith's book on wise fools and a short article by Carolyn S. French. Leslie Hotson discusses the Fool's costume in *Shakespeare's Motley*.

Russell A. Fraser's misleadingly entitled book, *Shakespeare's Poetics in Relation to 'King Lear'*, is a finely illustrated discussion of Elizabethan ideas on providence, fortune, anarchy, order, and reason, as represented in emblem books, and as used in the play. Martha Andresen writes on sententiae and commonplaces in *King Lear* (see under Colie and Flahiff) and also makes use of emblem writers. Winifred Nowottny has two valuable essays which may be mentioned here—'Lear's Questions' and 'Some Aspects of the Style of *King Lear*'.

Characterization

This subject, of major concern to Bradley, is now less central to criticism of the play. Characters are now discussed in relation to the thematic structure of the play and to their theatrical roles. Freud's idea of Lear derives from his interpretation of the symbolic significance of the three daughters (Cordelia representing death) and Lear having reached the age when he ought 'to renounce love, choose death, and make friends with the necessity of dying'. Stanley Cavell, to take another example, writes on 'The Avoidance of Love' and interprets not merely Lear but other characters in the light of this theme.

John Holloway, writing on Shakespearian heroes as scapegoats, can easily accommodate Lear to this role; and Reuben A. Brower finds the greatness of Lear in the fact that he is able to 'Love and hope with full tragic knowledge of the injustice, cruelty and confusion of life'. D. A. Traversi shows that Lear was himself responsible for the breaking up of reciprocal loyalties, but that he acquires understanding through suffering. Ivor Morris writes on

Lear and Cordelia, Paul Siegel on the way adversity leads to the miracle of love, Robert P. Adams on 'Lear's Revenges', and Robert H. West on 'Sex and Pessimism' as exemplified by Lear's speeches in Act IV.

There is not much disagreement about Cordelia, except that Elliott, Battenhouse, and Sewell accuse her of sinful pride and, at the other extreme, Bethell and Danby allegorize her almost out of existence. On Edgar, however, there are sharp disagreements. Goldberg thought that Shakespeare must have been slightly irritated by 'his fundamentally self-protective moralism'. Kirschbaum declared that Edgar was not a consistent character, but merely a dramatic function. Mooney illuminatingly argues that we should distinguish Edgar's role as an active participant in the illusionistic action from his function as the symbolic figure of Poor Tom, and from the choric figure 'who stands, as it were, outside the play'. Russell A. Peck argues that Edgar's search for identity parallels Lear's. Flahiff (see Colie and Flahiff) shows that he is anachronistically fused with the historical figure of King Edgar, who restored order after a period of anarchy. Kenneth Muir sought to show that Edgar was a developing character as a result of his experiences as well as by his role-playing—as Bedlam beggar, demoniac, peasant, his father's guide and protector, heroic challenger, future king.

Albany has aroused less interest and his importance is minimized by the Folio revision; but there are interesting articles by Leo Kirschbaum and Peter Mortensen.

Many critics use single scenes as means of suggesting wider interpretations of the play. William Frost, for example, starts from the ritual element in the first scene and goes on to show the importance of ritual in the remainder of the play; Harry Levin has a famous article that, though concentrating on Gloucester's attempted suicide, broadens the discussion to include not merely the relationship of Gloucester with his two sons but also the significance of the parallel plots; and John Bayley, starting also from Dover Cliff, proceeds to a general discussion of *King Lear* and, indeed, of Shakespearian tragedy.

Shakespearian tragedy was the subject of G. Wilson Knight's early books. In *The Wheel of Fire* he had two influential chapters on *King Lear*. In the first he discusses 'the comedy of the grotesque' which Dowden had found in the play, in the other what he calls 'the *Lear* universe'. He stresses the element of absurdity in Lear's madness, underlined by the Fool's commentary, and the ludicrous nature of Gloucester's suicide attempt. He speaks of the 'demonic laughter that echoes in the *Lear* universe'. The basis of the play, in his view, is that 'a tremendous soul is . . . incongruously geared to a puerile intellect'. (Lear's intellect, it should be said, is defended by Frances G. Schoff and G. R. Elliott). When Knight played the part in 1951 the grotesque element was confined to the action and was excluded from his own performance. Some modern directors have combined Knight's view with that of Kott, not always with happy results.

His other chapter touches on several themes that have been elaborated by later critics: the importance of 'nature' in various senses in the course of the play, the animal imagery, our ambivalent attitude to Edmund, Cordelia as the principle of ideal love, the resemblance of the play to the book of *Job*, and the action considered as a kind of *Purgatorio*.

Maynard Mack in his essay on Jacobean Tragedy declared that Lear 'is one of the most profoundly human figures ever created in a play; but he is not, certainly, the Platonic ideal laid up in heaven, or in critical schemes, of regenerate man'. A few years later, in *King Lear in Our Time*, he stressed the archetypal nature of the play, and in the final chapter he rejects two opposite forms of sentimentality—the views that Cordelia at the end of the play is transported to a better world, and that the play leads us to believe that 'we inhabit an imbecile universe'. We are rather driven, as Mack says, 'to seek the meaning of our human fate not in what becomes of us, but in what we become'.

The seminal importance of Mack's book can be seen from the collection of essays it inspired, edited by Rosalie L. Colie and F. T. Flahiff. Nearly every chapter starts from one or other of Mack's insights. Bridget Gellert Lyons writes on the sub-plot as simplification of the main plot; F. D. Hoeniger on 'the artist exploring the primitive'; Colie on biblical echoes; Nancy R. Lindheim on *King Lear* as pastoral tragedy; all these are indebted to Mack. The book also contains Colie's essay developing Laurence Stone's views that there was a crisis of the aristocracy in Shakespeare's day, and that this crisis is reflected in *King Lear*. (Edwin Muir had earlier argued that the play reflected a conflict in society, and this was the view of Danby and Arnold Kettle from their very different ideological standpoints.) John Reibetanz, another contributor, discusses in his own book the play in its dramatic context. Susan Snyder's chapter on *King Lear* in *The Comic Matrix of Shakespeare's Tragedies* follows up Mack's suggestions on the pastoral and romance elements in the play as well as Knight's on the grotesque.

It has been impossible in this short survey to mention the valuable points on *King Lear* to be found in books on wider subjects by Raleigh, Masefield, P. Alexander, Theodore Spencer, Stauffer, and dozens of others; but we may conclude with Robert Ornstein's remarks that

Shakespeare alone penetrates beneath . . . the outworn cosmology and archaic systems, to bring to light the indestructible certainties of the human spirit: its capacity for love, devotion and joy: its resources of courage and compassion in the face of unimaginable terror. . . . Like all great tragedy *Lear* actually celebrates the vulnerability of man.

REFERENCES

TEXTS

Duthie, G. I. (ed.), *King Lear* (Oxford, 1949).
—— and Wilson, J. Dover (eds.), *King Lear* (Cambridge, 1960).
Fraser, Russell (ed.), *King Lear* (Signet Shakespeare, New York, 1963).
Furness, H. H. (ed.), *King Lear* (New Variorum Shakespeare, Philadelphia, 1880).
Harbage, Alfred (ed.), *King Lear* (Pelican Shakespeare, Baltimore, 1958).
Hunter, G. K. (ed.), *King Lear* (New Penguin Shakespeare, Harmondsworth, 1972).
Kittredge, G. L. (ed.), *King Lear* (New York, 1940).
Muir, Kenneth (ed.), *King Lear* (Arden Shakespeare, London, 1952, 1985).
Wells, Stanley, and Gary Taylor (eds.), *William Shakespeare: The Complete Works* (Oxford, 1986).

CRITICISM AND COMMENTARY

Adams, Robert P., 'King Lear's Revenges', *Modern Language Quarterly*, 21 (1960), 223–7.
Addison, Joseph, *The Spectator* (16 April 1711).
Alexander, Peter, *Shakespeare's Life and Art* (London, 1939).
Alpers, Paul, 'King Lear and the Theory of the Sight Pattern', in *In Defense of Reading*, ed. R. Brower and R. Poirier (New York, 1963), 133–152.
Andresen, Martha, ' "Ripeness is All": Sententiae and Commonplaces in *King Lear*', in *Some Facets of 'King Lear'*, ed. R. L. Colie and F. T. Flahiff (Toronto, 1974), 145–68.

Barnet, Sylvan, 'Some Limitations of a Christian Approach to Shakespeare', *ELH* 22 (1955), 81–92.

Battenhouse, R. W., *Shakespearean Tragedy: Its Art and Its Christian Premises* (Bloomington, Ind., and London, 1969).

Bayley, John, *Shakespeare and Tragedy* (London, 1981).

Bennett, Josephine W., 'The Storm within: The Madness of Lear', *Shakespeare Quarterly*, 13 (1963), 137–55.

Bethell, S. L., *Shakespeare and the Popular Dramatic Tradition* (London, 1944).

Bickersteth, G. L., *The Golden World of 'King Lear'* (London, 1946).

Black, James, 'King Lear: Art Upside Down', *Shakespeare Survey 33*, (1980), 35–42.

Bonheim, H., *The King Lear Perplex* (San Francisco, Calif., 1960).

Bradbrook, Muriel C., *Shakespeare: The Poet in His World* (London, 1978).

Bradley, A. C., *Shakespearean Tragedy* (London, 1904; reprinted 1978).

Brooke, Nicholas, 'The Ending of *King Lear*', in *Shakespeare 1564–1964*, ed. E. A. Bloom (Providence, RI, 1964), 71–87.

—— *Shakespeare: King Lear* (London, 1963).

Brower, Reuben A., *Hero and Saint: Shakespeare and the Graeco-Roman Tradition* (New York, 1971).

Bullough, Geoffrey, 'King Lear and the Annesley Case', in *Festschrift Rudolf Stamm*, ed. E. Kolb and J. Hasler (Bern and Munich, 1969), 43–50.

—— *Narrative and Dramatic Sources of Shakespeare*, vol. vii (London, 1973).

Campbell, Lily B., *Shakespeare's Tragic Heroes* (Cambridge, 1930).

Campbell, Oscar J., 'The Salvation of Lear', *ELH* 15 (1948), 93–109.

Cavell, Stanley, 'The Avoidance of Love', in *Must We Mean What We Say?* (New York, 1969; reprinted Cambridge 1976), 267–353, reprinted in *Disowning Knowledge in Six Plays of Shakespeare* (Cambridge, 1987), 39–123.

Chambers, R. W., *King Lear* (Glasgow, 1940).

Champion, Larry S., *King Lear: An Annotated Bibliography* (New York, 1980).

Charney, Maurice, ' "We Put Fresh Garments on Him": Nakedness and Clothes in *King Lear*', in *Some Facets of 'King Lear'*, ed. R. L. Colie and F. T. Flahiff (Toronto, 1974), 77–88.

Clemen, W. H., *The Development of Shakespeare's Imagery* (London, 1951).

Coleridge, S. T., *Coleridge's Shakespearean Criticism*, ed. T. M. Raysor, 2 vols., (Cambridge, Mass., 1930).

Colie, Rosalie, L., and F. T. Flahiff (eds.), *Some Facets of 'King Lear'* (Toronto, 1974).

Danby, John F., *Elizabethan and Jacobean Poets* (London, 1964).

—— *Shakespeare's Doctrine of Nature* (London, 1949).

Dowden, Edward, *Shakspere: A Critical Study of His Mind and Art* (London, 1875).

Elliott, G. R., *Dramatic Providence in 'Macbeth'* (Princeton, NJ, 1960).

Elton, William R., *King Lear and the Gods* (San Marino, Calif., 1966).

Empson, William, *The Structure of Complex Words* (London, 1951).

Everett, Barbara, 'The New King Lear', *Critical Quarterly*, 2 (1960), 325–39.

Flahiff, F. T., 'Edgar: Once and Future King', in *Some Facets of 'King Lear'*, ed. R. L. Colie and F. T. Flahiff (Toronto, 1974), 221–37.

Fraser, Russell, *Shakespeare's Poetics in Relation to 'King Lear'* (London, 1962).

French, Carolyn S., 'Shakespeare's "Folly": *King Lear'*, *Shakespeare Quarterly*, 10 (1959), 523–9.

Freud, S., *Collected Papers*, vol. iv (London, 1934).

Frost, William, 'Shakespeare's Rituals and the Opening of *King Lear'*, *Hudson Review*, 10 (1958), 577–85.

Gardner, Helen, *King Lear* (London, 1967).

Gide, André, *Journals*, trans. J. O'Brien (New York, 1956).

Gielgud, John, *Stage Directions* (London, 1963).

Goldberg, S. L., *An Essay on King Lear* (Cambridge, 1974).

Goldsmith, Robert H., *Wise Fools in Shakespeare* (East Lansing, Mich., and Liverpool, 1955).

Granville-Barker, Harley, *Prefaces to Shakespeare*, First Series (London, 1927).

Greenfield, Thelma, 'The Clothing Motif in *King Lear'*, *Shakespeare Quarterly*, 5 (1954), 281–6.

Greg, W. W., 'The Date of *King Lear* and Shakespeare's Use of Earlier Versions of the Story', *The Library*, 20 (1940), 377–400.

Hawkes, Terence, *Shakespeare and the Reason* (London, 1964).

Hazlitt, William, *Characters of Shakespear's Plays* (London, 1817).

Heilman, R. B., *This Great Stage* (Baton Rouge, La., 1948).

Henderson, W. B. Drayton, 'Montaigne's *Apologie of Raymond Sebond*, and *King Lear'*, *Shakespeare Association Bulletin*, 14 (1939), 209–15, and 15 (1940), 40–54.

Holloway, John, *The Story of the Night* (London, 1961).

Hotson, Leslie, *Shakespeare's Motley* (London, 1952).

Hunter, Robert G., *Shakespeare and the Mystery of God's Judgements* (Athens, Ga., 1976).

James, D. G., *The Dream of Learning* (Oxford, 1951).

—— 'Keats and *King Lear'*, *Shakespeare Survey* 13 (1960), 58–68.

Jayne, Sears, 'Charity in *King Lear'*, in *Shakespeare Quarterly*, 15 (1964), 277–88.

Jones, Emrys, *Scenic Form in Shakespeare* (Oxford, 1971).

Jorgensen, Paul A., *Lear's Self-Discovery* (Berkeley, Calif., 1967).

Keast, W. R., 'Imagery and Meaning in the Interpretation of *King Lear*', *Modern Philology*, (1949–50), 45–64.

Keats, John, *The Letters of John Keats, 1814–21*, ed. H. E. Rollins. 2 vols. (Cambridge, Mass., 1958).

Kettle, Arnold (ed.), *Shakespeare in a Changing World* (London, 1964).

Kinney, Arthur F., 'Some Conjectures on the Composition of *King Lear*', *Shakespeare Survey 33* (1980), 13–25.

Kirkman, J., 'Animal Nature *versus* Human Nature in *King Lear*', *New Shakespeare Society Transactions*, 6 (1877–9), 385–408.

Kirschbaum, Leo, 'Albany', *Shakespeare Survey 13* (1960), 20–9.

——— *Character and Characterization in Shakespeare* (Detroit, Mich., 1962).

Knight, G. Wilson, *The Wheel of Fire: Interpretations of Shakespearian Tragedy* (London, 1930; rev. edn., 1949).

Knights, L. C., *Some Shakespearean Themes* (London, 1959).

Kolbe, F. C., *Shakespeare's Way* (London, 1930).

Kott, Jan, *Shakespeare Our Contemporary* (London, 1967).

Kozintsev, Grigori, *King Lear: The Space of Tragedy* (London, 1977).

Lamb, Charles, 'On the Tragedies of Shakespeare' (1811); reprinted in *Shakespeare Criticism*, ed. D. Nichol Smith (London, 1916).

Lascelles, Mary, '*King Lear* and Doomsday', *Shakespeare Survey 26* (1973), 69–79.

Law, R. A., 'Holinshed's Leir Story and Shakespeare's', *Studies in Philology*, 48 (1950), 42–50.

——— '*King Leir* and *King Lear*', in *Studies in Honor of T. W. Baldwin*, ed. D. C. Allen (Urbana, Ill., 1958), 112–24.

Leech, Clifford, *Shakespeare's Tragedies* (London, 1950).

Levin, Harry, 'The Heights and the Depths', in *More Talking of Shakespeare*, ed. J. Garrett (London, 1959), 87–103; reprinted in his *Shakespeare and the Revolutions of the Time* (Oxford, 1976), 162–86.

Levin, Y., 'Tolstoy, Shakespeare and the Russian Writers of the 1860's', *Oxford Slavonic Papers*, NS 1 (1968), 85–104.

Mack, Maynard, 'The Jacobean Shakespeare', in *Jacobean Theatre*, ed. J. R. Brown and B. Harris (London, 1960), 11–42.

——— *King Lear in Our Time* (Berkeley, Calif., 1965).

McKeithan, D. M., '*King Lear* and Sidney's *Arcadia*', *University of Texas Studies in English*, 14 (1934), 45–9.

Masefield, John, *Shakespeare* (London, 1911).

Mason, H. A., *Shakespeare's Tragedies of Love* (London, 1970).

Maxwell, J. C., 'The Technique of Invocation in *King Lear*', *MLR* 45 (1950), 142–7.

Mooney, Michael F., ' "Edgar I nothing am": *Figurenposition* in *King Lear*', *Shakespeare Survey 38* (1985), 153–66.

Morris, Ivor, 'Cordelia and Lear', *Shakespeare Quarterly*, 8 (1957), 141–58.

Mortensen, Peter, 'The Role of Albany', *Shakespeare Quarterly*, 16 (1965), 215–25.

Moulton, Richard G., *Shakespeare as a Dramatic Artist* (Oxford, 1885; rev. 1906).

Muir, Edwin, *Essays on Literature and Society* (London, 1949).

Muir, Kenneth, *King Lear: A Critical Study* (Harmondsworth, 1986).

—— 'Madness in *King Lear*', *Shakespeare Survey* 13 (1960), 30–40.

—— 'Samuel Harsnett and *King Lear*', *RES* NS 2 (1951), 11–21.

Murry, John Middleton, *Shakespeare* (London, 1936).

Myrick, Kenneth, 'Christian Pessimism in *King Lear*' in *Shakespeare 1564–1964*, ed. E. A. Bloom (Providence RI, 1964), 56–70.

Nicoll, Allardyce, *Studies in Shakespeare* (London, 1927).

Nowottny, Winifred, 'Lear's Questions', *Shakespeare Survey* 10 (1957), 90–7.

—— 'Some Aspects of the Style of *King Lear*', *Shakespeare Survey* 13 (1960), 47–57.

Ornstein, R., *The Moral Vision of Jacobean Tragedy* (Madison, Wis., 1960).

Orwell, George, 'Lear, Tolstoy and the Fool', in *Shooting an Elephant and Other Essays* (New York, 1945), 32–52.

Peat, Derek, '"And that's true too": *King Lear* and the Tension of Uncertainty', *Shakespeare Survey* 33 (1980), 43–53.

Peck, Russell A., 'Edgar's Pilgrimage', *SEL* 7 (1967), 219–37.

Perkinson, Richard H., 'Shakespeare's Revision of the Lear Story and the Structure of *King Lear*', *Philological Quarterly*, 22 (1943), 315–29.

Perrett, W., *The Story of King Lear* (Berlin, 1964).

Pyle, Fitzroy, '*Twelfth Night, King Lear*, and *Arcadia*', *MLR* 43 (1948), 449–55.

Raleigh, W., *Shakespeare* (London, 1907).

Reibetanz, John, *The Lear World* (Toronto and London, 1977).

Rosenberg, John D., 'King Lear and His Comforters', *Essays in Criticism*, 16 (1966), 135–46.

Rosenberg, Marvin, *The Masks of King Lear* (Berkeley, Calif., 1972).

Salingar, Leo, *Dramatic Form in Shakespeare and the Jacobeans* (Cambridge, 1986).

Schlegel, A. W., *A Course of Lectures on Dramatic Art and Literature* (London, 1846).

Schoff, Frances G., '*King Lear*: Moral Example or Tragic Protagonist?' *Shakespeare Quarterly*, 13 (1962), 157–72.

Schücking, L. L., *Character Problems in Shakespeare's Plays* (London, 1922).

Sewell, A., *Character and Society in Shakespeare* (Oxford, 1951).

Shaw, John, 'King Lear: The Final Lines', *Essays in Criticism*, 16 (1966), 261–7.

Shelley, P. B., 'A Defence of Poetry', in e.g. *Peacock's 'Four Ages of Poetry . . .'*, ed. H. F. B. Brett-Smith (2nd edn., Oxford, 1923).

Siegel, Paul N., 'Adversity and the Miracle of Love in *King Lear*', *Shakespeare Quarterly*, 6 (1955), 325–36.
—— *Shakespearean Tragedy and the Elizabethan Compromise* (New York, 1957).
Snyder, Susan, *The Comic Matrix of Shakespeare's Tragedies* (Princeton, NJ, 1979).
Speaight, Robert, *Nature in Shakespearean Tragedy* (London, 1955).
Spencer, Theodore, *Shakespeare and the Nature of Man* (Cambridge, Mass., 1942).
Spurgeon, Caroline F. E., Shakespeare's Imagery (Cambridge, 1935).
Stampfer, J., 'The Catharsis of *King Lear*', *Shakespeare Survey* 13 (1960).
Stauffer, D. A., *Shakespeare's World of Images* (New York, 1949).
Stein, Walter, *Criticism as Dialogue* (Cambridge, 1969).
Stroup, T. B., 'Cordelia and the Fool', *Shakespeare Quarterly* (1961).
Steward, J. I. M., *Character and Motive in Shakespeare* (London, 1949).
Stoll, E. E., *Art and Artifice in Shakespeare* (New York, 1933)
Swinburne, A. C., *A Study of Shakespeare* (London, 1880).
Tannenbaum, S. A., *Shakespeare's 'King Lear': A Concise Bibliography* (New York, 1940).
Tate, Nahum, *The History of King Lear* (London, 1681).
Taylor, G. C., *Shakespeare's Debt to Montaigne* (Cambridge, Mass., 1925).
Taylor, Gary, 'A New Source and an old Date for *King Lear*' *RES*32 (1982).
—— and Warren, Michael (eds.), *The Divison of the Kingdoms* (Oxford, 1986).
Tolstoy, L., *Tolstoy on Art* (Boston, Mass., 1924).
Traversi, D. A., *An Approach to Shakespeare*, 2 vols. (London, 1968–9).
Walton, J. K., 'Lear's Last Speech', *Shakespeare Survey* 13 (1960).
Warton, Joseph, 'King Lear' in *The Adventurer* 1733–4 (Reprinted in *Shakespeare Criticism* ed. D. Nichol Smith (London, 1916)).
Welsford, Enid, *The Fool* (London, 1935).
West, Robert H., 'Sexual Pessimism in *King Lear*' (SQ 1960).
Whitaker, Virgil K., *The Mirror up to Nature* (San Marino, 1965).
Wilson, Harold S., *On the Design of Shakespearian Tragedy* (Toronto, 1957).
Young, G. M., *Today and Yesterday* (London, 1948).

13 | Macbeth

R. A. FOAKES

TEXTS AND TEXTUAL STUDIES

The Arden edition by Kenneth Muir (1951, with later revisions) remains for the time being the fullest; it has an ample commentary, and the critical introduction is notable for its comments on the language of the play, and its defence of the Porter scene. Dover Wilson's New (Cambridge) edition presents in its Introduction a very heroic image of Macbeth, and has a useful brief stage-history; this editor thought the text to be a reworked version of an abridgement by Shakespeare of his original play. If his edition is used, it should be in conjunction with William Empson's defence of the integrity of the text. Both of these editions are old enough to have been troubled by the last flurry of what had been a major debate about the text. When it was discovered in the late eighteenth century that the full text of the songs in III. v and IV. i might be found in Thomas Middleton's play, *The Witch*, Shakespeare's authorship of these and a variety of other scenes began to be disputed, so that by the early twentieth century a tradition of regarding parts of the play as suspect came to be taken for granted. Some sense of this dispute may be recovered from the New Variorum edition, which provides in appendices a record of early criticisms, and also excerpts from Middleton's play. The whole matter is considered in J. M. Nosworthy's defence of the integrity of the text, in which he discusses possible revision and augmentation. The New Variorum edition contains extracts from the revision of *Macbeth* staged by William Davenant in 1673–4, which may preserve some readings from an original version of the play, and which has a Witch's song not included in the First Folio: the evidence is set out in Christopher Spencer's edition of Davenant's text.

The revised Yale edition by Eugene Waith concentrates on presenting the text attractively, and pares down additional material to a minimum. The Bobbs-Merrill edition by R. A. Foakes offers an ample range of aids to reading the play, but no critical introduction. The Pelican edition by Alfred Harbage has a brief critical introduction, which rather overdoes the notion of 'stark simplicity', and provides minimal annotation. Much better is the New Penguin edition by G. K. Hunter, which has an excellent introduction that is alert to the dangers of simplification. Hunter is especially concerned to show how Macbeth brings 'his world into conformity with the man he has become'. The main feature of the Signet edition is the inclusion of seventy-five pages of extracts from critical accounts of the play, and it seems designed for students who prefer reading commentaries to reading the play itself. New full-scale editions are in preparation for the Oxford and New Cambridge editions of single plays; meanwhile, the textual commentary by Gary Taylor and Stanley Wells, issued as the third volume of the Oxford Shakespeare, provides textual notes and the latest account of the textual problems of the play.

CRITICISM AND COMMENTARY

Character and Action

'Lady Macbeth is merely detested, and though the courage of Macbeth preserves some esteem, every reader rejoices at his fall.' Dr Johnson's comment reflects a tendency in the early criticism of *Macbeth* to see the play rather simply in terms of evil or villainy, and to regard the protagonists as 'great criminal characters', in the phrase of Charles Lamb, who linked Macbeth with Iago. Johnson thought the play had 'no nice discriminations of character', and an understanding of the character of Macbeth began to be developed by later eighteenth-century critics, especially in their comparisons of Macbeth with Richard III. The most notable are those by Thomas Whately, who saw Macbeth as soft and vain in contrast to the hard and proud Richard, and by J. P. Kemble, who, not quite grasping the subtlety of Whately's argument, defended Macbeth as equal in courage to Richard, and wrought upon by insecurity rather than by fear in his murderous progress.

The powerful interpretation of Lady Macbeth by Mrs Siddons helped to foster from 1777 onwards a new esteem for this character. She wrote an interesting commentary on her engagement with the role, and her concept of Lady Macbeth as having a 'frailer frame, and keener feelings' than Macbeth needs to be set against William Hazlitt's account of her performance as full of power and grandeur: 'she was tragedy personified', he wrote. This sense of grandeur, and what Hazlitt called its 'lofty imagination', provided the groundwork for much later criticism, which culminated in two very different readings of the play at the end of the nineteenth century. R. G. Moulton stressed the heroic, rugged aspects of Macbeth as 'essentially the practical man, the man of action', finding his antithesis in Lady Macbeth as representing the inner life. By contrast, A. C. Bradley stressed the degree to which Macbeth is possessed by his imagination, 'the best of him, something usually deeper and higher than his conscious thoughts; and if he had obeyed it he would have been safe'. For him the greatness of Lady Macbeth lay 'almost wholly in courage and force of will'. Although differing in their readings, both critics stressed the relationship of Macbeth and Lady Macbeth, and both agreed on the stature of the play ('the most tremendous of the tragedies', according to Bradley).

In the twentieth century the pre-eminence of *King Lear* among Shakespeare's tragedies has come to be an article of faith with many critics, and some, like William Rosen, have sought to demonstrate its superiority over *Macbeth*, though his argument turns on the rather simplistic view that 'Macbeth loses his humanity and descends to the bestial'. The growing influence of the disintegrators, who disputed Shakespeare's authorship of many parts of the play (see the section on 'Texts' above), contributed to a diminishing regard for it, shown in a number of studies that schematize it. So Lily B. Campbell described it as 'A Study in Fear'; E. E. Stoll discovered an implausible psychological gap between the nature of Macbeth and his deed; Willard Farnham called it a 'morality play'; and Larry S. Champion found in it a 'fearful drivelling nihilism'. The discussion of the play by these critics is often more subtle than these labels suggest, but they represent a tendency that found its cleverest exponent in R. B. Heilman: in his essay 'The Criminal as Tragic Hero', he argued that too little is demanded of the reader because Shakespeare was too sympathetic towards his hero, so that 'we see the world judging Macbeth, but not Macbeth judging himself', and he concluded that 'This is not the best that tragedy can offer'.

If some critics have been content with such formulations as that of H. B. Charlton, 'Macbeth destroys human nature in himself. It is all as simple as that', the later twentieth century has brought a strong reaction against simplistic readings. Matthew Proser defended Macbeth in *The Heroic Image*, arguing that his manliness is shown in the dignity with which he faces his end. J. C. Bulman takes a more complex view of Macbeth as 'affirming a heroic role to which he is never fully committed'. The idea of 'manliness' in *Macbeth* has, indeed, come under increasing scrutiny since E. M. Waith showed the limitations of Lady Macbeth's insistence on it ('When you durst do it, then you were a man'), and claimed that she drove Macbeth into 'brutishness' rather than heroism. Terence Hawkes has been followed by others in arguing that Macbeth's attempt to achieve manliness in fact unmans him. A number of critics have explored the relation of 'manliness' to sexual potency or impotence, femininity, motherhood, and the nursing infant, and have revealed new psychological dimensions; the most notable essays are those by Dennis Biggins, Carolyn Asp, David Willbern, and Harry Berger Jr., who sees 'Man's fear of being unmanned' as 'the basic theme of the text'. Berger's long essay is especially interesting on the difference between the 'Shakespearean intention constituted by the reader', and that 'constituted by the spectator and the performed script'.

In his judicious 1966 survey of commentary on *Macbeth*, G. K. Hunter concluded that most recent critics had been reductive in their anxiety 'to de-sentimentalize Macbeth'; but in the last twenty years the emphasis has been on the richness and complexity of the play, and critics have sought to give due weight to the contradictory qualities of Macbeth, rather than stressing his failure or his heroism. Rebutting Stoll on the question of psychological probability, J. I. M. Stewart emphasized a sense of something inexplicable in the play's exploration of evil. Later critics have stressed equivocation, double vision, illusion, or paradox as central; so William O. Scott comments on the proliferation of conflicting messages in the play, while Barbara L. Parker and Lucy Gent see illusion as the key to the play's complexity, the latter observing how 'Nothing is but what is not' relates both to evil and to 'harmless aesthetic illusion'. Others have explored the ambivalence of sexuality, childishness, and concepts of manhood, from a psychological viewpoint, and if terms like 'matricide' (David Willbern) or 'rape' (Dennis Biggins) in relation to the murder of Duncan seem overpitched, these critics have suggested new depths in the play. The most subtle reading of this kind is Janet Adelman's exploration of what she sees as 'the play's central fantasy of escape from woman', as exemplified in Macbeth, Malcolm, and Macduff, leading to a final 'consolidation of male power.' She incidentally provides a comprehensive range of references to other psychological approaches to the play. Another notable essay is that by Bert O. States, who takes off from the way Macbeth's mind works as if it were processing dream images.

Some have explored what John Lawlor called Macbeth's 'realized incapacity to sustain the role' he has chosen, while Howard Felperin has stressed the gap between the roles of tyrant and hero adopted respectively by Macbeth and Malcolm and their 'precarious selves'. In a brilliant essay Stephen Booth considers a more profound gap between the sense of limitlessness, or the unmanageable truths the play conveys, and the 'irrationally comforting framework' of its artistic pattern. His post-structuralist emphasis on indefinition links with the clever but too consciously playful book by James L. Calderwood, which reassesses *Macbeth* in relation to current critical theorizing, finding in the play only the 'postponement of a beginning', and no ending, only the start of a 'new cycle of violence'. In his essay, 'An Unknown Fear', Wilbur Sanders seeks to bridge the gap between 'the act of judgment', which sees through Macbeth, and the 'act of imagination', which sees the world with him, and finds a 'tremulous equilibrium between affirmation and despair'. In relation to these accounts, Maynard Mack Jr.'s argument that there are two plays in *Macbeth*, one the 'familiar morality of crime and punishment', the other 'a more familiar tragedy of self-destruction', begins to look old-fashioned.

The most sensitive accounts of character and action in *Macbeth* seek to explain not merely Macbeth's crime, ambition, or deterioration, but what glows through in spite of these, an enormous vitality and attractiveness, those 'sympathetic qualities' noted by John Russell Brown, which help to provide the 'sources of Macbeth's life'. Such readings of the play may be seen as expanding the brief but incisive comments of S. T. Coleridge and Lascelles Abercrombie, who strikingly formulated a complex response in 1925: 'For we see not only what he feels, but the personality that feels it; and in the very act of proclaiming that life is "a tale told by an idiot, *signifying nothing*", personal life announces its virtue, and superbly *signifies itself*.' In a notable full-length study of the play, Paul A. Jorgensen enriches our sense of its complexity by setting it in the context of the thought of Shakespeare's age, and by analysing a number of key terms, like 'strange', 'labour', and 'fear'.

Poetic Imagery and Thematic Interpretations

Jorgensen was making good use of the analysis of imagery popularized in 1935 by Caroline Spurgeon, who first studied in detail patterns of related images, noticing, for instance, how Macbeth is seen metaphorically as a small man in clothes too large for him. In the reaction of the 'new critics' of the 1930s against A. C. Bradley's emphasis on character, *Macbeth* became a test case for an approach to Shakespeare's plays as 'dramatic poems', with the stress on language and imagery. L. C. Knights tilted at Bradley in the title of his essay, 'How many children had Lady Macbeth?', but effectively reduced the play to a 'statement of evil'; his later essay in *Some Shakespearean Themes* is much more incisive. In another influential essay Cleanth Brooks brought out the importance of the image of the 'naked babe' as a symbol of the future Macbeth cannot control.

The concentrated power of the poetry of the play has stimulated a number of critics to write well on various aspects of its language. The best essays include those by Molly Mahood in her study of *Shakespeare's Wordplay*; by Donald Stauffer, on blood, clothing, and the stars; and a notable piece by William Blissett on sterility and fruitfulness, and the 'contrast between blood as stain and blood as life'. Since Kenneth Muir's 1966 survey of commentary on the imagery and symbolism of Macbeth, interest in poetic imagery as such has declined, even as much more attention has been given to spectacle and the play in performance. This shift has proved fruitful, for a preoccupation with imagery and themes too often led to schematic readings of the play as, for example, a 'vision of evil' (Wilson Knight in *The Wheel of Fire*) or 'a tragedy about damnation in Christian terms' (Irving Ribner). D. J. Enright's lively essay, 'Macbeth and the Henpecked Hero', offers a useful corrective to such schematizations, and a fuller response has come from those who, like Muriel Bradbrook, have seen 'new possibilities for joining poetry and spectacle' in the play. Stage images of jewels, the cauldron, the dagger, decapitated heads, and more, have been analysed by John Doebler; David Palmer has considered the importance of the play's sensational sights, and of what is not staged to our view; and N. S. Brooke has written incisively on the disjunction between the speaker and the image, between the reality of the character and the fantastic quality of the language in the speeches of Macbeth and Lady Macbeth.

Is Macbeth a Christian Tragedy?

In some sense the answer must be yes, in relation to a play in which Macbeth gives his soul ('mine eternal jewel') to the devil ('the common enemy of man'), and in which Duncan and Edward are 'sainted' or 'holy' kings. Specifically Christian readings of the play, however, like those by G. R. Elliott and Ivor Morris, rarely seem to do justice to its complexity. In Roy Walker's *The Time Is Free*, his close analysis of the text is more persuasive than his sense that the murder of Duncan is 'profoundly impregnated with the central tragedy of the Christian myth'; and J. A. Bryant's incidental insights are more interesting than his attempt to impose a Christian framework on the play. Robert G. Hunter is more illuminating in arguing that Macbeth both exemplifies and calls in question a providential pattern. Brian Morris goes further in astutely observing Macbeth's 'inability to register the religious dimension' in life. Few would now claim with Harold S. Wilson that 'Christian assumptions control' the play, or with Lawrence Danson that 'the form of the play triumphantly asserts its thematic moral resolution'. Indeed, some of the more notable recent essays on Macbeth have sought to present him not as a villain, but rather as a victim; so E. A. J. Honigmann sees him as a 'sufferer who demands the audience's sympathetic response', and John Bayley even goes so far as to claim that the 'intensely private' Macbeth has a 'moral superiority' over the other public characters in the play. Wilbur Sanders and Howard Jacobson also explore Macbeth's inner growth, arguing that he had to murder Duncan 'in order to become moral'. If this argument strains too far, the idea may be better formulated in secular terms by Bernard McElroy, who sees Macbeth's act as one of self-definition: 'The primary purpose of his act has been to define his manhood'.

Some critics have treated the play in ritualistic or quasi-religious terms while avoiding a specifically Christian reading. So Terence Hawkes contrasts the lower world of 'fact' with the 'miraculous' world of 'reality' represented in the 'King's dispersal of evil'; and Frederick Turner sees Macbeth as trapped in time, and so 'fatally vulnerable to the forces of timelessness' represented by Malcolm. Such readings again tend to become schematic, and

John Holloway's vision of the play as concerned with a retributive justice operating under 'Fate or Fortune', a justice that makes Macbeth in the end a ritual victim, has come under attack by Harry Berger, Jr., who finds the oppositions in the play much less clear, and sees Duncan as a weak monarch, whose régime is shaken by contention and distrust; for him the justice at the end works for the audience, but not for the characters.

Background, Sources, and Special Studies

W. C. Curry's learned seminal study of the background of witchcraft and demonology now seems too categorical in claiming that the Weird Sisters 'are in reality demons opposed to good', and that the whole play is 'saturated with the malignant presences of demons'. Robert H. West sensibly rejected the need for 'any one demonological explanation' while emphasizing the importance of the supernatural. Arthur McGee widened the context of the Weird Sisters by showing how they relate to the Furies, biblical demons, and to the fairies of folklore. Robin Grove has tried to bring out the conventional aspects of the Weird Sisters as both comic and sinister dramatic figures; and Peter Stallybrass has sought to show that witchcraft in the play is 'associated with female rule and the overthrowing of patriarchal authority'. Terry Eagleton goes further in his challenging Marxist interpretation, claiming that the 'witches are the heroines of the piece', who expose the 'pious self-deception of a society based on routine oppression'.

Shakespeare may have found some of his lore concerning witches in Reginald Scot's *Discovery of Witchcraft* (1584), and in King James I's treatise on *Demonology* (1597). H. N. Paul pressed the connection with James into arguing that *The Royal Play of Macbeth*, Shakespeare's only play on a Scottish theme, was written for performance before the King, and that the dramatist made use of the King's book of advice to his son, *Basilikon Doron*, in which he sets out the qualities of a tyrant and those of a good monarch. Paul's passion for finding topical references rather unbalances his book, which is put into perspective in the excellent analysis of the historical context of the play by Michael Hawkins. Alan Sinfield castigates all those who see the play as reflecting the ideology of the state under James, and attempts a subversive reading designed 'to expose, rather than to promote, State ideologies'. In 1604 the King's Men performed a play about the conspiracy by the Earl of Gowrie to murder James near Perth, and Shakespeare must have known of this; it is not so clear as Arthur Melville Clark claims, and Stanley J. Kozikowski also argues, that many details in the text of *Macbeth* are based on the account of the conspiracy published in London in 1600, though Shakespeare may have found there the character name 'Lennox'. It is more helpful to see the Gowrie conspiracy as having a kind of metaphorical relationship to the play; so Steven Mullaney uses it to interpret ambiguities and equivocations in *Macbeth* as marking an aspect of language that authority cannot control.

The play's sources are comprehensively presented and discussed in the standard work on this subject, Geoffrey Bullough's *Narrative and Dramatic Sources of Shakespeare*. A judicious survey of the sources may also be found in M. C. Bradbrook's essay, in which she attends not only to the sources in the chronicles, but, following Muir, points to the play's connections with *The Rape of Lucrece*. Paul and others have observed that *Macbeth* is the most Senecan of Shakespeare's tragedies, and Inga-Stina Ewbank has noted links especially with Seneca's *Medea*. Kenneth Muir's helpful essay in *Shakespeare's Sources* contains a critique of Paul's book, a detailed treatment of the chronicles, and also notes links with Seneca, especially the *Agamemnon*. Marion Lomax finds somewhat tenuous connections between the play and Thomas Campion's *Lord Hay's Masque*. Following a different line of investigation, Ruth L. Anderson has traced the background of conventional ideas about ambition and tyranny, and claims that Shakespeare relied on these ideas in creating Richard III and Macbeth. The topic of Macbeth's ambition has been further explored in different ways by R. A. Foakes, who finds in the play Shakespeare's 'most searching analysis of the effects of ambition'; by Arthur Kirsch, who sees Macbeth's ambition as a suicidal 'fantasy grotesquely beyond the reach of reality'; and by Robert N. Watson, who argues that Macbeth's ambition is a common human instinct, and that 'the hazards of ambition are an essential component of human experience.' Watson thus finds another way of explaining why Macbeth retains our sympathy.

The Porter scene (II. iii), which Coleridge dismissed as an interpolation by the actors, has stimulated much commentary in attempts to explain its function. John B. Harcourt's analysis of its language and its thematic content did much to demonstrate its relevance to the rest of the play. Frederic B. Tromly stresses the links between the Porter and Macbeth himself, and Michael J. B. Allen more interestingly argues that the Porter represents the evil genius of Macbeth himself. Glynne Wickham has thrown further light on the scene as a theatrical image by relating it to the 'Harrowing of Hell' in medieval cycle plays. Starting from the Porter scene, Joan Hartwig finds analogy, or what she calls parody, extending as a principle of dramaturgy through the whole play. Wolfgang Clemen has written a commentary on the play's soliloquies, and Horst Breuer argues that Macbeth's 'Tomorrow, and tomorrow, and tomorrow . . .' speech is pivotal in his reading of *Macbeth* as a 'document of historical progress'. Michael Goldman's essay on the play is notable for a good analysis of Macbeth's 'Is this a dagger . . .' soliloquy.

Macbeth in performance has received increasing attention. Dennis Bartholomeusz has provided a detailed account of the play on the stage between 1606 and 1964, arguing that actors and directors have insights denied to critics, though it seems these are not easily demonstrable in relation to the elusive art of the stage. Marvin Rosenberg's huge book, *The Masks of Macbeth*, offers a scene-by-scene commentary, noting what various actors and directors have done; the book is full of matter, if it almost overwhelms by the mass of detail. An appendix on images of children in the play deserves notice. The particular studies by R. W. David of Laurence Olivier and Paul Rogers in the title-role, and by Gareth Lloyd Evans of productions at Stratford between 1946 and 1980, also show what great actors can contribute to interpreting the play. The importance of *Macbeth* for the Romantic period is brought out by Joseph Donohue, and developed notably in terms of political action in an age of revolution by Mary Jacobus.

Conclusion

In all this commentary curiously little attention has been given directly to the structure of the play. If it is in some sense classical, as the Senecan analogies suggest, then perhaps it ought to be amenable to an Aristotelian analysis. So Francis Fergusson argues, in '*Macbeth* as the Imitation of an Action'—the key to it being the phrase, 'to outrun the pauser reason'. In a reply to Fergusson, Julian Markels claimed that the structure of the play is not consonant with the *Poetics* since *Macbeth* depends so much on what to Aristotle was peripheral, namely, 'the choice of episodes and the visual machinery'. T. B. Tomlinson has also argued that the play is a failure in Aristotelian terms, because it makes the 'subtle introspection' of the chief character primary, and tries, unsuccessfully in his view, to raise this to the status of tragedy. Taking a very different view of the structure, R. A. Foakes sees it as falling into three parts, divided by the choric scenes of the Old Man (II. iv) and Lennox (III. vi). Emrys Jones also stresses this three-part division into sections that he labels 'Duncan', 'Banquo', and 'Macduff'; he finds a 'satisfying simplicity' and 'formal coherence' in the play's scenic design. Deconstructionist, feminist, Marxist, and new historicist critics have often simply ignored this coherence in emphasizing transgression, disorder, violence, and subversion in the action; but criticism surely needs to bring the action and the meanings of the play into relation with its formal 'elegance', to use Jones's term, and of all the critics, Stephen Booth (in *King Lear, Macbeth, Indefinition and Tragedy*) has best shown the way to do this.

REFERENCES

TEXTS AND TEXTUAL STUDIES

Barnet, Sylvan (ed.), *Macbeth* (Signet Shakespeare, New York, 1963).

Empson, William, 'Dover Wilson on *Macbeth*', *Kenyon Review*, 14 (1952), 84–102.

Foakes, R. A. (ed.), *Macbeth* (Bobbs-Merrill Shakespeare Series, Indianapolis, Ind., 1968).

Furness, H. H. (ed.), *Macbeth* (New Variorum Shakespeare, Philadelphia, Pa., 1873).

Harbage, Alfred (ed.), *Macbeth* (Pelican Shakespeare, Baltimore, Md., 1956).

Hunter, G. K. (ed.), *Macbeth* (New Penguin Shakespeare, Harmondsworth, 1967).

Muir, Kenneth (ed.), *Macbeth* (Arden Shakespeare, London, 1951).

Nosworthy, J. M., *Shakespeare's Occasional Plays* (London, 1965).

Spencer, Christopher (ed.), *Davenant's 'Macbeth' from the Yale Manuscript* (New Haven, Conn., 1961).

——Davenant's *Macbeth* in *Five Restoration Adaptations of Shakespeare* (Urbana, Ill., 1965).

Waith, E. M. (ed.), *Macbeth* (Yale Shakespeare, New Haven, Conn., 1954).

Wells, Stanley, and Gary Taylor, with John Jowett and William Montgomery, *William Shakespeare: A Textual Companion* (Oxford, 1987).

Wilson, John Dover (ed.), *Macbeth* (New Shakespeare, Cambridge, 1947).

CRITICISM AND COMMENTARY

Abercrombie, Lascelles, *The Idea of Great Poetry* (London, 1925); reprinted with *The Theory of Poetry* (New York, 1968).

Adelman, Janet, ' "Born of Woman": Fantasies of Maternal Power in *Macbeth*', in *Cannibals, Witches, and Divorce: Estranging the Renaissance*, ed. Marjorie Garber (Selected Papers from the English Institute, 1985, NS 11; Baltimore Md., 1987), 90–121.

Allen, Michael J. B., 'Macbeth's Genial Porter', *English Literary Renaissance*, 4 (1974), 326–36.

Anderson, Ruth L., 'The Pattern of Behavior Culminating in *Macbeth*', *SEL* 3 (1963), 151–73.

Asp, Carolyn, ' "Be bloody, bold and resolute": Tragic Action and Sexual Stereotyping in *Macbeth*', *Studies in Philology*, 78 (1981), 153–69.

Bartholomeusz, Dennis, *Macbeth and the Players* (Cambridge, 1969).

Bayley, John, *Shakespeare and Tragedy* (London, 1981).

Berger, Harry, Jr., 'The Early Scenes of *Macbeth*: Preface to a New Interpretation', *ELH* 47 (1980), 1–31.

—— 'Text against Performance in Shakespeare: The Example of *Macbeth*', in *The Power of Forms in the English Renaissance*, ed. Stephen Greenblatt (Norman, Okla., 1982), 49–79.

Biggins, Dennis, 'Sexuality, Witchcraft, and Violence in *Macbeth*', *Shakespeare Studies*, 8 (1975), 255–77.

Blissett, William, ' "The Secret'st Man of Blood". A Study of Dramatic Irony in *Macbeth*', *Shakespeare Quarterly*, 10 (1959), 397–408.

Booth, Stephen, *'King Lear', 'Macbeth', Indefinition and Tragedy* (New Haven, Conn., 1983).

Bradbrook, Muriel C., *The Living Monument: Shakespeare and the Theatre of His Time* (Cambridge, 1976).

—— 'The Sources of *Macbeth*', *Shakespeare Survey* 4 (1951), 35–48.

Bradley, A. C., *Shakespearean Tragedy* (London; 1904; reprinted 1978).

Breuer, Horst, 'Disintegration of Time in Macbeth's Soliloquy "Tomorrow, and Tomorrow, and Tomorrow" ', *Modern Language Review*, 71 (1976), 256–71.

Brooke, N. S., ' "Language most shows a man . . .?" Language and Speaker in *Macbeth*', in *Shakespeare's Styles*, ed. Philip Edwards, Inga-Stina Ewbank, and G. K. Hunter (Cambridge, 1980), 67–77.

Brooks, Cleanth, ' "The Naked Babe" and the Cloak of Manliness', in his *The Well-Wrought Urn* (New York, 1947), 22–49.

Brown, John Russell, *Shakespeare's Dramatic Style* (London, 1970).

Bryant, J. A., *Hippolyta's View: Some Christian Aspects of Shakespeare's Plays* (Lexington, Ky., 1961).

Bullough, Geoffrey, *Narrative and Dramatic Sources of Shakespeare*, vol. vii (London, 1973).

Bulman, J. C., *The Heroic Idiom of Shakespearean Tragedy* (Newark, Del., 1985).

Calderwood, J. L., *If It Were Done: Macbeth and Tragic Action* (Amherst, Mass., 1986).

Campbell, Lily B., *Shakespeare's Tragic Heroes* (Cambridge, 1930).

Campbell, T., *The Life of Mrs Siddons* (London, 1834).

Champion, Larry S., *Shakespeare's Tragic Perspective* (Athens, Ga., 1976).

Charlton, H. B., *Shakespearean Tragedy* (Cambridge, 1948).

Clark, Arthur Melville, *Murder under Trust or The Topical Macbeth* (Edinburgh, 1981).

Clemen, Wolfgang, *Shakespeare's Soliloquies*, trans. Charity Scott Stokes (London, 1987), 141–63.

Coleridge, S. T., *Coleridge's Criticism of Shakespeare*, ed. R. A. Foakes (London, 1989).

Curry, W. C., *Shakespeare's Philosophical Patterns* (Baton Rouge, La., 1937).

Danson, Lawrence, *Tragic Alphabet: Shakespeare's Drama of Language* (New Haven, Conn., 1974).

David, Richard W., 'The Tragic Curve', *Shakespeare Survey* 9 (1956), 122–31.

Doebler, John, *Shakespeare's Speaking Pictures: Studies in Iconic Imagery* (Albuquerque, N. Mex., 1974).

Donohue, Joseph, *Dramatic Character in the English Romantic Age* (Princeton, NJ, 1970).

Eagleton, Terry, *William Shakespeare* (Rereading Literature Series, Oxford, 1986).

Elliott, G. R., *Dramatic Providence in 'Macbeth'* (Princeton, NJ, 1958).

Enright, D. J., *Shakespeare and the Students* (London, 1970).

Evans, Gareth Lloyd, 'Macbeth: 1946–80 at Stratford-upon-Avon', in *Focus on Macbeth*, ed. John Russell Brown (London, 1982), 87–110.

Ewbank, Inga-Stina, 'The Fiend-Like Queen: A Note on Macbeth and Seneca's *Medea*', *Shakespeare Survey*, 19 (1966), 82–94; reprinted in *Aspects of 'Macbeth'*, ed. Kenneth Muir and Philip Edwards (Cambridge, 1977), 53–65.

Farnham, Willard, *Shakespeare's Tragic Frontier* (Berkeley, Calif., 1950).

Felperin, Howard, *Shakespearean Representation* (Princeton, NJ, 1977).

Fergusson, Francis, 'Macbeth as the Imitation of an Action', *English Institute Essays* (New York, 1952); reprinted in *Shakespeare: The Tragedies*, ed. A. Harbage (Englewood Cliffs, NJ), 1964.

Foakes, R. A., 'Images of Death: Ambition in Macbeth', in *Focus on Macbeth*, ed. John Russell Brown (London, 1982), 7–29.

—— 'Macbeth', in *Stratford Papers on Shakespeare 1962*, ed. B. W. Jackson (Toronto, 1963), 150–74.

Gent, Lucy, 'The Self-Cozening Eye', *RES* NS 34 (1983), 419–28.

Goldman, Michael, *Acting and Action in Shakespearean Tragedy* (Princeton, 1985), pp. 94–111.

Grove, Robin, 'Multiplying Villainies of Nature', in *Focus on Macbeth*, ed. John Russell Brown (London, 1982), 113–39.

Harcourt, John B., ' "I Pray You, Remember the Porter" ', *Shakespeare Quarterly*, 12 (1961), 393–402.

Hartwig, Joan, *Shakespeare's Analogical Scene* (Lincoln, Nebr., 1983).

Hawkes, Terence, *Shakespeare and the Reason* (London, 1964).

—— *Shakespeare's Talking Animals* (London, 1973).

Hawkins, Michael, 'History, Politics and *Macbeth*', in *Focus on Macbeth*, ed. John Russell Brown (London, 1982), 155–88.

Hazlitt, William, *Characters of Shakespear's Plays* (London, 1817); reprinted in *Works*, ed. P. P. Howe (1930), vol. iv.

Heilman, R. B., 'The Criminal as Tragic Hero: Dramatic Methods', *Shakespeare Survey 19* (1966), 12–24.

Holloway, John, *The Story of the Night* (London, 1961).

Honigmann, E. A. J., *Shakespeare, Seven Tragedies: the Dramatist's Manipulation of Response* (London, 1976).

Hunter, G. K., '*Macbeth* in the Twentieth Century', *Shakespeare Survey 19* (1966), 1–11.

Hunter, Robert G., *Shakespeare and the Mystery of God's Judgments* (Athens, Ga., 1976).

Jacobus, Mary, ' "That Great Stage Where Senators Perform": *Macbeth* and the Politics of Romantic Theatre', *Studies in Romanticism,* 22 (1983), 353–87.

Jones, Emrys, *Scenic Form in Shakespeare* (Oxford, 1971).

Jorgensen, Paul A., *Our Naked Frailties* (Berkeley and Los Angeles, Calif., 1971).

Kemble, J. P., *Macbeth and King Richard the Third* (London, 1817).

Kirsch, Arthur, 'Macbeth's Suicide', *ELH* 51 (1984), 269–96.

Knight, G. Wilson, *The Imperial Theme: Further Interpretations of Shakespeare's Tragedies Including the Roman Plays* (London, 1931).

—— *The Wheel of Fire: Interpretations of Shakespearian Tragedy* (London, 1930; rev. edn., 1949).

Knights, L. C., 'How Many Children Had Lady Macbeth? An Essay in the Theory and Practice of Shakespeare Criticism' (Cambridge, 1933); reprinted in his *Explorations* (London, 1946), 13–50.

—— '*Macbeth*', in his *Some Shakespearean Themes* (London, 1959), 120–42.

Kozikowski, Stanley J., 'The Gowrie Conspiracy against James VI: A New Source for Shakespeare's *Macbeth*', *Shakespeare Studies,* 13 (1980), 197–212.

Lawlor, John, *The Tragic Sense in Shakespeare* (London, 1960).

Lomax, Marion, *Stage Images and Traditions: Shakespeare to Ford* (Cambridge, 1987).

Mack, Maynard, Jr., *Killing the King* (New Haven, Conn., 1973).

Mahood, M. M., *Shakespeare's Wordplay* (London, 1957).

Markels, Julian, 'The Spectacle of Deterioration: *Macbeth* and the "Manner" of Tragic Imitation', *Shakespeare Quarterly*, 12 (1961), 293–303.

McElroy, Bernard, *Shakespeare's Mature Tragedies* (Princeton, NJ, 1973).

McGee, Arthur R., '*Macbeth* and the Furies', *Shakespeare Survey* 19 (1966), 55–67.

Morris, Brian, 'The Kingdom, the Power and the Glory in *Macbeth*', in *Focus on Macbeth*, ed. John Russell Brown (London, 1982), 30–53.

Morris, Ivor, *Shakespeare's God: The Role of Religion in the Tragedies* (London, 1972).

Moulton, R. G., *Shakespeare as a Dramatic Artist* (Oxford, 1885; rev. 1906).

Muir, Kenneth, 'Image and Symbol in *Macbeth*', *Shakespeare Survey* 19 (1966), 45–54.

—— *Shakespeare's Sources*, vol. i (London, 1957); rev. as *The Sources of Shakespeare's Plays* (London, 1977).

Mullaney, Steven, 'Lying Like Truth: Riddle, Representation and Treason in Renaissance England', *ELH* 47 (1980), 32–47.

Palmer, D. J.,' "A New Gorgon": On Visual Aspects of *Macbeth*', in *Focus on Macbeth*, ed. John Russell Brown (London, 1982), 54–69.

Parker, Barbara L., 'Macbeth: The Great Illusion', *Sewanee Review*, 78 (1970), 476–87.

Paul, H. N., *The Royal Play of Macbeth* (New York, 1950).

Proser, Matthew N., *The Heroic Image in Five Shakespearean Tragedies* (Princeton, NJ, 1965).

Ribner, Irving, *Patterns in Shakespearian Tragedy* (London, 1960).

Rosen, William, *Shakespeare and the Craft of Tragedy* (Cambridge, Mass., 1960).

Rosenberg, Marvin, *The Masks of Macbeth* (Berkeley and Los Angeles, Calif., 1978).

Sanders, Wilbur, *The Dramatist and the Received Idea* (Cambridge, 1968).

—— and Howard Jacobson, *Shakespeare's Magnanimity* (London, 1978).

Scott, William O., 'Macbeth's—and Our—Self-Equivocations', *Shakespeare Quarterly*, 37 (1986), 160–74.

Sinfield, Alan, '*Macbeth*: History, Ideology and Intellectuals', *Critical Quarterly*, 28 (1986), 63–77.

Spurgeon, Caroline F. E., 'Leading Motives in the Imagery of Shakespeare's Tragedies' (Shakespeare Association Lecture, 1930); incorporated into *Shakespeare's Imagery* (Cambridge, 1935).

Stallybrass, Peter, '*Macbeth* and Witchcraft', in *Focus on Macbeth*, ed. John Russell Brown (London, 1982), 189–209.

States, Bert O., 'The Horses of Macbeth', *Kenyon Review*, 7 (1985), 52–66.

Stauffer, Donald A., *Shakespeare's World of Images: The Development of His Moral Ideas* (New York, 1949).

Stewart, J. I. M., *Character and Motive in Shakespeare* (London, 1949).

Stoll, E. E., *Art and Artifice in Shakespeare* (New York, 1934).

Tomlinson, T. B., 'Action and Soliloquy in *Macbeth*', *Essays in Criticism*, 8 (1958), 147–55.

Tromly, Frederic B., 'Macbeth and His Porter', *Shakespeare Quarterly*, 26 (1975), 151–6.

Turner, Frederick, *Shakespeare and the Nature of Time* (Oxford, 1971).

Waith, E. M., 'Manhood and Valor in Two Shakespearean Tragedies', *ELH* 17 (1950), 262–73.

Walker, Roy, *The Time Is Free* (London, 1949).

Watson, Robert, N., *Shakespeare and the Hazards of Ambition* (Cambridge, Mass., 1984).

West, Robert H., *Shakespeare and the Outer Mystery* (Lexington, Ky., 1968).

Whately, Thomas, *Remarks on Some Characters of Shakespeare* (London, 1785); reprinted in *Shakespeare Criticism*, ed. D. Nichol Smith (London, 1916).

Wickham, Glynne, 'Hell-Castle and Its Door-Keeper', *Shakespeare Survey* 19 (1966), 68–74.

Willbern, David, 'Phantasmagoric Macbeth', *English Literary Renaissance*, 16 (1986), 520–49.

Wilson, Harold S., *On the Design of Shakespearian Tragedy* (Toronto, 1957).

Wimsatt, W. K., Jr. (ed.), *Samuel Johnson on Shakespeare* (New York, 1960); reprinted as *Dr. Johnson on Shakespeare* (Harmondsworth, 1969).

14

Julius Caesar
and
Antony and
Cleopatra

R. J. A. WEIS

SHAKESPEARE AND ROMAN HISTORY

In the *Annals of English Drama* Harbage and Schoenbaum note that approximately one classical drama appeared for every year of Shakespeare's life and that some forty-three Roman plays for the period from 1588 to 1651 are recorded. Like everyone who went through the Elizabethan grammar school syllabus, Shakespeare was early on exposed to a rich diet of classical authors, including particularly Ovid, Virgil, and Terence. His lasting interest in, and indebtedness to, the classics span his writing career, from *Titus Andronicus* and *The Rape of Lucrece* at the beginning to *Coriolanus* and *Cymbeline* towards the end. In between he wrote *Julius Caesar* (1599) and *Antony and Cleopatra* (1607), which flank the period of the great tragedies. Both works are inspired primarily by Sir Thomas North's rendering in English of Amyot's brilliant French translation of Plutarch's *The Lives of the Noble Grecians and Romanes, Compared*. T. S. Eliot's claim in his essay 'Tradition and the Individual Talent' that Shakespeare 'acquired more essential history from Plutarch than most men could from the whole British Museum' articulates the measure of Shakespeare's debt to the first-century Chaeronean historical biographer. In the so-called Plutarchan plays Shakespeare follows his source-texts to a degree unprecedented even in his English histories. Plutarch did more than just provide an anecdotal window on the worlds of ancient Greece and Rome. History for him formed the canvas on which to sketch the actions and reflections of men and women who transformed the events in which they participated. In the 'Life of Alexander', the parallel life to 'Julius Caesar', he explains:

My intent is not to write histories, but only liues. For, the noblest deedes not alwayes shew mens vertues and vices, but oftentimes a light occasion, a word, or some sporte makes mens naturall dispositions and manners appeare more plaine, then the famous battells wonne, wherein are slaine tenne thowsande men, or the great armies, or cities wonne by siege or assault.

In North's lively and rhetorically inventive Elizabethan translation Shakespeare and his contemporaries encountered a world peopled with imaginatively credible characters. The Roman *Lives* are informed by a strain of temperate republicanism and a strong moral awareness, whether Plutarch deals with Caesar and Brutus or Antony and Cleopatra. Underlying Plutarch's histories is a belief that men and women are the shapers of their destinies, hence the emphasis in them on moral choice and responsibility. Shakespeare, more ambiguously, followed suit, and Plutarch's *Lives* became his favoured source, although some credit for this must be given to North's prose. That Shakespeare, and before him Spenser in the *Faerie Queene*, also drew repeatedly on Plutarch's *Moralia*, available in Latin throughout the 1590s and in Philemon Holland's English translation after 1603, is likely, as the essays in it are concerned with ethics, politics, and history, as well as providing a treasure house of information on classical and esoteric cults, such as the oracles and Isis and Osiris.

Like Jonson in *Sejanus* and *Catiline*, Shakespeare would have been familiar with Tacitus' *Annals of Imperial Rome* and Suetonius' *The Historie of Twelve Caesars*, both works which nostalgically look back at the republican period of a frugal Rome in its heyday. Suetonius in particular provides a hostile view of a cynical and calculating Octavius Caesar. It is likely that Shakespeare also read *The Civil Wars* by Appian of Alexandria, translated by W. B. in 1578, even if he did not necessarily share W. B.'s contention that the history of Rome provides a punitive providential pattern, which culminates in the birth of Christ under the Empire.

Although Sir M. W. MacCallum published *Shakespeare's Roman Plays and Their Background* nearly eighty years ago, his detailed and methodical study of the Plutarchan plays and their sources remains a model of scholarly investigation. A substantial part of the book is taken up by a thorough survey of plays on Roman themes before Shakespeare's, particularly those of the French Senecans and their English followers; and MacCallum's lucid pages on the merits and demerits of Plutarch's histories and the prose styles of Amyot and North retain their freshness and speak to the contemporary reader with unrivalled authority. The discussions of the individual plays have proved seminal in their critical fortunes since. Equally indispensable is Geoffrey Bullough's collection of sources and analogues for the Plutarchan tragedies, *Narrative and Dramatic Sources of Shakespeare's Plays*, vol. V (1964). Bullough conveniently reproduces large chunks of Plutarch, entire plays such as Garnier's *Marc Antoine* (in the English version by the Countess of Pembroke), and Samuel Daniel's *Cleopatra*. He also reproduces excerpts and summaries of relevant historical texts by Appian, Sallust, and Suetonius, as well as several 'analogues' for Shakespeare's plays. The material for each tragedy is prefaced by a valuable introductory essay on the relationship between text and context.

Bullough's volume complements T. J. B. Spencer's modest but useful *Shakespeare's Plutarch*, published the same year, which annotates the relevant 'Lives' with entire passages from Shakespeare to show the intimacy of the text-source relationship and the process of literary transformation. A few years earlier Spencer published a masterly and much needed study of the imaginative reception of Rome in Elizabethan England, 'Shakespeare and the Elizabethan Romans' (*Shakespeare Survey 10*). In it he remarked that 'in spite of literary admiration for Cicero, the Romans in the imagination of the sixteenth century were Suetonian and Tacitan rather than Plutarchan', thereby firmly casting his lot with the republicans. The implications of this critique of Rome and Shakespeare's contemporaries for reading *Julius Caesar* and *Antony and Cleopatra* are momentous, and further the view that Shakespeare found his Roman material profoundly enabling: it allowed him to explore relationships of power and hierarchy in a structured but non-monarchical and pre-Christian setting, emancipated from the shackles of Tudor orthodoxy which he had had to acknowledge in the two English tetralogies. For this reason the argument propounded by J. A. K. Thomson in *Shakespeare and the Classics*, that Plutarch provided an imaginative trigger for Shakespearian tragedy as a whole—through the intermediary of *Julius Caesar*—commands a measure of assent.

The most ambitious recent study of the meanings and uses of 'Romanitas' in Shakespeare is Robert S. Miola's *Shakespeare's Rome*. Unlike his predecessors, Miola does not treat the Plutarchan plays apart, but integrates them in the wider spectrum of all the Roman works, including *The Rape of Lucrece* and *Cymbeline*. His approach is 'organic' and 'sequential', and he notes: 'Just as the examination of a cell reveals the biology of an entire organism, examination of the sources behind these speeches reveals Shakespeare's creative method in his Roman works'. Miola's strategy is to proceed not only chronologically, but act by act, and he discusses the plays in a manner reminiscent of D. A. Traversi's close readings of the Plutarchan tragedies in *The Roman Plays*. Miola eschews merely annotating the works, however, and his considerable erudition throws interesting new light on dark places, such as the imagery of Cassius' recollection of saving Caesar from drowning and the extent to which *Julius Caesar* 'marks Shakespeare's ongoing dialogue with Vergil'. While valuable, Miola's preferred formula precludes the kind of study that would reassess Shakespeare's Rome against the background of political philosophy and poetic endeavours. Two particularly useful surveys of criticism of Shakespeare's Roman works are provided by J. C. Maxwell, 'Shakespeare's Roman Plays: 1900–1956', published in *Shakespeare Survey 10*; and John W. Velz, *Shakespeare and the Classical. Tradition: A Critical Guide to Commentary, 1660–1960*, which lists and briefly summarizes the most important books and articles in the period on Shakespeare's use of the classics.

Julius Caesar

TEXTS

Julius Caesar was first printed in the First Folio of 1623. The text of the play is exceptionally clean and may have been set up from a scribal transcript of the playhouse prompt-book rather than from 'foul' papers, because of the absence from the Folio text of characteristic Shakespearian spellings. There is possible evidence of revision, notably in IV. iii, when Brutus denies to Messala that he has had news of Portia, a mere forty lines after telling Cassius of her death. Furthermore, the canonical line 'Know, Caesar doth not wrong, nor without cause / Will he be satisfied' (III. i. 47) was recorded by Ben Jonson, in a famous gibe at Shakespeare, as 'Caesar did never wrong, but with just cause' (*Timber: or, Discoveries*). Jonson had a practising playwright's and actor's memory so that it is likely that the editors of the First Folio—or even

Shakespeare himself—changed the text in the event to dispose of
the charge of meaninglessness.

The New Variorum edition of the play by H. H. Furness is of
limited usefulness and is now mostly of historic interest. Its
appendix reproduces parts of Plutarch's *Lives* and anthologies of
Victorian and earlier critical opinion on the main characters. It
also conveniently gives the entire text of the Senecan play *The
Tragedy of Julius Caesar* by William Alexander. Its brief, republican
introduction calls Caesar 'a braggart, inflated with the idea of his
own importance', and its text is extensively annotated. If the
notes contain much redundant information, they can at times be
genuinely informative, as in the case of the interpretation of the
crucial 'he' in Cassius' famous aside 'If I were Brutus now, and he
were Cassius, / He should not humour me' (1. ii. 313–14).

John Dover Wilson's New Shakespeare edition retains its
appeal by virtue of its passionate and engaging introduction, as
well as its idiosyncratic notes, which conflate exegesis and
textual commentary. For Dover Wilson *Julius Caesar* is 'the greatest
of political plays' because it makes 'its public men convincingly
private persons' and through exposing, in the nobility of Brutus,
the lesson that 'Caesarism is a secular threat to the human spirit'.

In stark contrast to Dover Wilson, T. S. Dorsch's Arden edition
champions Caesar and attacks the conspirators, particularly Brutus
whom Dorsch execrates as the deliverer of self-righteous homilies
on the virtues of conspiracy and the sacredness of a Roman
promise: 'Caesar grows in stature as the play proceeds: Brutus
deteriorates', Dorsch notes, while granting that Brutus is at his
most attractive in intimate, personal relationships. The textual
and critical notes in this edition are clear and helpful, and the
appendix reproduces excerpts from Plutarch.

The New Penguin edition of *Julius Caesar* by Norman Sanders
offers excellent notes and includes a useful survey of 'Further
Reading' in addition to a short but level-headed introduction.

The outstanding edition to date is A. R. Humphreys's in The
Oxford Shakespeare. Humphreys's ninety pages on the critical
fortunes of the play and its history in performance are compelling
reading. He eschews polarizing the ideological movement of the
play into Caesarism and republicanism, and instead views it as a
'Hegelian' tragedy, 'balancing conflicting goods rather than contrasting good and evil'. Humphreys writes with authority on the
play's reshaping of its sources, and considers the extent to which

Shakespeare's understanding of 'Romanitas' keeps the characters at a distance. He finds the style of the play lucid and vigorous and reappraises its austere blend of concrete images with an absence of figurative qualities. His notes on the text are invariably illuminating and economical.

The most recent edition to date is Marvin Spevack's in the New Cambridge Shakespeare series. It has a sound introduction, which reassesses the textual and historical evidence in the light of recent scholarship. Spevack remarks that one of Shakespeare's most arresting achievements in Julius Caesar is the degree of individuality conferred on the characters. The notes are attractively laid out on the page, and are clear and helpful; and the appendix reproduces excerpts from Plutarch. The section on the play's stage history is particularly good, as are the accompanying illustrations.

CRITICISM

Dr Johnson thought Julius Caesar was 'somewhat cold and un-affecting compared with some other of Shakespeare's plays', and Coleridge professed his dismay at Brutus' famous soliloquy ('It must be by his death . . .' II. i. 1 ff.), because 'nothing can seem more discordant with our historical preconceptions of Brutus, or more lowering to the intellect of this Stoico-Platonic tyrannicide, than the tenets here attributed to him, to him, the stern Roman republican'. Less troubled by the work's marmoreal coldness and its alleged failure to champion Brutus as a committed re-publican, Shaw describes it as 'the most splendidly written political melodrama we possess'. Some, like J. E. Phillips in The State in Shakespeare's Greek and Roman Plays, have followed Shaw in reading Julius Caesar as a primarily political play, against the background of Tudor doctrine, thereby downgrading the psycho-logical and moral dilemmas experienced by Brutus and justifying the association between 'regicide and social chaos' made by Antony in his soliloquy over Caesar's dead body. R. A. Foakes chooses a similar, if more flexible, approach, when he argues in 'An Approach to Julius Caesar' that the play primarily dramatizes the story of a rebellion in which the main actors are participants in, rather than makers of, their destinies; and in Shakespearian Tragedy H. B. Charlton aligns Julius Caesar with Shakespeare's English History Plays, but concedes that the political setting of Rome proved liberating to Shakespeare's imagination, because 'patriotic sentiments' do not come into play. Brutus, according to Charlton, is not developed enough as a character to mould 'the whole play to a tragic pattern'.

Most critical enquiry, however, has taken the shape of moral essays on the conjunction in the play of characters' motivation and the Roman political scene, agreeing with Philip Edwards (*Shakespeare: A Writer's Progress*) that the play projects a world in which 'the fulfilment is social and political as well as personal'. Among the best Victorian readings is Edward Dowden's *Shakspere: A Critical Study of His Mind and Art*, in which he identifies in *Julius Caesar* studies of the corrupting effects of power and idealism. Caesar epitomizes the man who, by losing touch with his humanity, becomes to himself a legend and a myth, while in Brutus Shakespeare proposes to show the grounds upon which idealists act. As Dowden notes, 'It is idealists who create a political terror; they are free from all desire for blood . . . to them the lives of men and women are accidents; the lives of ideas are the true realities; and, armed with an abstract principle and a suspicion, they perform deeds which are at once beautiful and hideous'. A similar view of Brutus, as 'an intellectual hideously corrupted by high-mindedness', is advanced a century later by E. A. J. Honigmann in *Shakespeare: Seven Tragedies*, where he charts a tripartite 'serial' arrangement, which generates an unfavourable view of Brutus. In *Shakespearean Iconoclasm* James R. Siemon further develops the enquiry into what Honigmann terms the 'mistakes', 'muddled thinking', and 'conceitedness' of Brutus. Using a semiotic framework of 'essence' and 'perception' —as pioneered by Bertrand Evans in *Shakespeare's Tragic Practice* which identified four significant 'gaps' in the play that undermine Brutus—Siemon studies the myth-making processes in *Julius Caesar* and their deconstruction. He writes shrewdly on Caesar's futile attempt to transcend his frail humanity—as evidenced by his aborted swim across the Tiber and his deafness —through his use of the third person singular, and notes that the play endorses one's awareness of the fact that 'the personal name "Caesar" is a homonym for the name given to the class of Roman rulers'. But Brutus is seen to participate in similar self-fashioning and ultimately bad faith, both in his adopting the name 'Brutus' instead of the 'I', and in his Roman suicide, a way of escape which he had earlier dismissed as 'cowardly and vile'. Brutus and Caesar have much in common, Siemon notes, and the noblest of all the Romans appears as 'a figure carved upon the human material that constitutes the others.'

In *Shakespeare and the Common Understanding* Norman Rabkin concedes that Brutus and Caesar are equally generous men who 'are alike predictably unable to relax a self-destructive moral rigidity'. He construes both men's weaknesses as an essential part of their common humanity and views Brutus' predicament after the assassination as that of a victim caught in the maelstrom of a revenge tragedy. In this context the high principles which motivate the leader of the conspiracy become a mockery, and Brutus, the self-professed rationalist, finds that he is 'governed by irrational forces in himself'. Matthew N. Proser argues in *The Heroic Image in Five Shakespearean Tragedies* that the central issue of *Julius Caesar* is that of freedom in both the political and philosophical senses, and that Brutus is 'Rome's acknowledged artist of the good.' But Brutus, despite himself, becomes like Caesar as he achieves some of Caesar's power, and subscribes to his own self-created role as a sacrificial priest. In an article, 'Or Else This Were a Savage Spectacle', Brents Stirling, who had earlier written on Shakespeare's empathy with the 'people' in *The Populace in Shakespeare*, suggests that Brutus' idealism provides the means to the wrong end; and in *Shakespeare's Use of Learning* Virgil K. Whitaker agrees, when he compares Brutus' soliloquy on the assassination with that of Marlowe's Dr Faustus, concluding that 'Brutus is the first of Shakespeare's superb tragic figures who fail through false moral choice'.

Disagreeing with Ernest Schanzer's view of *Julius Caesar* as a problem play (*The Problem Plays of Shakespeare*), Kenneth Muir casts Brutus as the hero of *Julius Caesar* in *Shakespeare's Tragic Sequence*, while being severe on the character for desiring 'to enjoy the spiritual satisfaction of a good conscience . . . and a moral superiority in comparison with those others'. John Palmer anticipated Muir's championing of Brutus to the extent that he made 'Marcus Brutus' the first of his character studies in *Political Characters of Shakespeare*. For Palmer Brutus exhibits 'precisely the qualities which in every age have rendered the conscientious liberal ineffectual in public life', while Caesar's greatness is unchallenged, as the elemental disturbances before his death symbolically indicate. Caesar's human failings keep him anchored in the world of ordinary beings and underline his vulnerability. Palmer views Caesar's possibly apocryphal claim of never doing

wrong without just cause—reported by Jonson—as the 'characteristic assumption of the man who lives for power that the
wrong he does is right'.

In a short but important study, *The Structure of 'Julius Caesar'*,
Adrien Bonjour comments on the duality of the play and its
oscillatory character, already noted by W. Warde Fowler in
Roman Essays and Interpretations. For Bonjour *Julius Caesar* is
primarily 'the story of a political murder and a posthumous
revenge', and its multiple antitheses form its very texture. Bonjour
highlights the parallel conjugal relationships of Brutus and Caesar
and the importance of the tributes paid to both by Antony. In
Patterns in Shakespearian Tragedy Irving Ribner studies the 'unique
manipulation of two tragic situations' in *Julius Caesar* and argues
that the play's main imaginative source derives not from Plutarch
but from the 'long tradition of Senecan Caesar plays which
preceded' it. Reuben A. Brower disagrees, and in *Hero and Saint*
Brower, like Willard Farnham in *Shakespeare's Tragic Frontier*,
champions *Julius Caesar* as a seminal work in Shakespeare's
career as a tragic dramatist. Shakespeare, Brower argues, discovered in North's Plutarch the 'Graeco-Roman hero in a relatively
pure form.' He writes convincingly on the oratorical style of
Julius Caesar and suggests that, compared to the later tragedies,
soliloquies in *Julius Caesar* are public and impersonal in tone. In
an essay entitled 'Style in the Roman Plays' (in *Discussions of
Shakespeare's Roman Plays*), Maurice Charney notes that with the
exception of *The Comedy of Errors* and *The Two Gentlemen of
Verona*, *Julius Caesar* uses the smallest lexicon of any Shakespeare
play and that its stock of imagery is equally limited: *Julius Caesar*
comes twenty-sixth in the canon on an image count, while
Antony and Cleopatra comes third. Two close, perceptive readings
of the play by D. A. Traversi and David Daiches should be noted.
In *Shakespeare: The Roman Plays* Traversi studies the Plutarchan
tragedies and demonstrates how *Julius Caesar* resists a simple
polarizing of empire/tyranny with republicanism/freedom by
endowing its characters with complex and conflicting emotions.
In *Julius Caesar* Daiches locates the central theme of the tragedy in
the uneasy relationship between Brutus, the abstract idealist,
and Cassius, the plotting but loyal and ultimately limited friend.

One of the most searching enquiries into the characters
and ethical issues of the play comes from Dieter Mehl in *Shakespeare's Tragedies: An Introduction*. Mehl views Caesar's deafness

as paradoxically enhancing the force of his presence and draws a
thought-provoking comparison between Othello and Brutus.
Both men, he argues, delude themselves into believing that
murder can be 'stylized into a ritual act of higher justice or even a
necessary sacrifice.' He writes sympathetically on the private toll
exacted from Brutus in his marriage by the conspiracy and the
extent to which his isolation from Portia brings us closer to him.
Of value and interest is John Ripley's *'Julius Caesar' on Stage in
England and America 1599–1973*, which offers detailed accounts of
performances of the play from Elizabethan times to the present.

Two collections of essays, *Twentieth Century Interpretations of
'Julius Caesar'*, edited by Leonard F. Dean, and *Shakespeare: Julius
Caesar. A Casebook*, edited by Peter Ure, between them gather
excerpts from some of the seminal writings on the play. Essential
background material is provided by Friedrich Gundolf's *The
Mantle of Caesar*, which proposes an anti-republican reading of
the play on the basis that Shakespeare's view of the characters
would have coincided with Dante's and the pro-Caesar popular
opinion of his contemporaries, and by Ernle Bradford's informative study of Caesar, *Julius Caesar: The Pursuit of Power*, which
outlines the political and historical background to the conspiracy.

Antony and Cleopatra

TEXTS

Our only early text for *Antony and Cleopatra* exists in the First
Folio of 1623 and was probably set from some form of Shakespeare's own manuscript, possibly from 'fair copy', as the Folio
shows a number of Shakespearian spellings. On the whole the
play has not been as well served by editors as the other two
Plutarchan tragedies.

The New Variorum edition by H. H. Furness produces a good
text which is often sounder than those of his successors, as for
example in the placement of the important stage-direction *'Enter
Cleopatra'* at I. i. 80, or in the retaining of the Folio's *'Antony'* at v. ii.
86, where others have substituted 'autumn'. Furness's notes are
overly elaborate, but useful. His introduction attempts to rehabilitate Octavius, 'the Power, representing Justice', and the
massive appendices reprint selections from Plutarch, Dryden's
All For Love, several excerpted pre-Shakespearian dramas on

Antony and Cleopatra, and a collection of English and European critical appraisals of the play.

The New Shakespeare edition by John Dover Wilson carries a characteristically mercurial introduction which exalts the play's eponymous lovers for their vitality and mutuality. Dover Wilson shrewdly notes that Act V of the play, which is Cleopatra's, shows that the tragedy is also hers and that 'she too must find her true greatness and be touched to finest issues'. His notes incorporate passages from Plutarch where relevant.

M. R. Ridley's Arden edition of the play retains much of R. H. Case's original edition and reprints his valuable introduction. Ridley's notes on the text and his interpretative glosses are often idiosyncratic and of limited usefulness. Maynard Mack's Pelican edition and Barbara Everett's Signet contain brief introductions; the Signet reproduces a selection of important essays on the play. The best edition of *Antony and Cleopatra* to date is by Emrys Jones in the New Penguin. Its text is generally sound, and the notes, of varying length, are informative and judicious. Jones's introductory essay provides a cogent and fluid account of the play's relationship to Plutarch's *Lives*, its contested structure and multiple scenic breaks, and the lovers themselves in a world of power politics. Jones approvingly quotes Hazlitt on *Antony and Cleopatra*, that Shakespeare

brings living men and women on the scene, who speak and act from real feelings, according to the ebbs and flows of passion, without the least tincture of pedantry of logic or rhetoric.

Jones's five pages of 'Further Reading' are thorough and highly informative.

The New Swan Shakespeare: Advanced Series edition of *Antony and Cleopatra* by John Ingledew has a sound introduction and reproduces brief passages from influential critics of the play. It is attractively illustrated and, in its notes and glossings, takes nothing for granted.

CRITICISM

Lecturing on *Antony and Cleopatra* Coleridge wondered whether the play 'in all exhibitions of a giant power in its strength and vigor of maturity' did not rival the great tragedies. He described its motto as '*feliciter audax*' and noted that 'this happy valiancy of style is but the representative and result of all the material excellencies so exprest'. Critical attention to *Antony and Cleopatra* has traditionally concentrated on its grand rhetoric, its titular characters' love-affair against the background of political reality, and its structure. Dr Johnson remarked that the play's events follow history and 'are produced without any art of connection or care of disposition', but then chose *Antony and Cleopatra* as his example to defend Shakespeare's art against the charge of ignoring the neo-classical unities. The multiple dramatic shifts in *Antony and Cleopatra*, which number forty-two editorially derived scenes, are addressed and theatrically justified by Harley Granville-Barker in his *Prefaces to Shakespeare*, with particular reference to Elizabethan playhouse conditions and the argument that *Antony and Cleopatra* is 'a play of action . . . not of spiritual insight'. In a brilliant essay on the play in *Oxford Lectures on Poetry*, A. C. Bradley calls it 'the most faultily constructed of all the tragedies', but then astutely reflects on its unique blending of comedy and tragedy, poetry and passion, and the privilege accorded Cleopatra by granting her the entire last act. The problematic structure of *Antony and Cleopatra* is the subject of a searching essay by Anne Barton, 'Nature's Piece 'Gainst Fancy: The Divided Catastrophe in *Antony and Cleopatra*', in which she views the split between Act IV and Act V as an integral part of a Shakespearian audience-response strategy.

Some of the lovers' detractors have used the play's straining towards sublimity as evidence of artistic failing. In *Character Problems in Shakespeare's Plays* L. L. Schücking maintains that the reclaimed Cleopatra of the last two acts is simply a different and unconnected character from the wayward queen of the first half of the play. But E. E. Stoll, by arguing that Cleopatra's 'very Cleopatraness' is the basis of her tragedy, dissents, as does J. I. M. Stewart in *Character and Motive in Shakespeare*. The politico-moralist school of thought has developed the view first propounded about the historical Antony by Bacon in the essay 'Of Love', where Bacon suggests that Antony epitomized the folly of love for giving up an empire for a whore. Shaw's gibe in *Three Plays for Puritans* that in *Antony and Cleopatra* Shakespeare strains his huge command of rhetoric to vindicate a 'soldier broken down by debauchery, and the typical wanton in whose arms such men perish', receives a more elaborate and less ironic treatment in *Not Wisely But Too Well* by F. M. Dickey. Dickey maintains, with reference to literary and historical tradition, that

'Antony and Cleopatra are examples of rulers who threw away a kingdom for lust, and this is how, despite the pity and terror which Shakespeare makes us feel, they appear in his play'. Lord David Cecil denies Cleopatra the prominence granted her by the play's title in 'Antony and Cleopatra: The Fourth Ker Memorial Lecture', and takes the Renaissance moralist's stance by suggesting that the play ought rightly to be known as a de casibus tragedy about the decline and fall of Antony. Leeds Barroll pursues a similarly moralist reading in an erudite but unduly narrow essay, 'Antony and Pleasure'. In Shakespeare and the Craft of Tragedy William Rosen takes a hostile view of the lovers and suggests that the absence of a chorus or choric figure such as Enobarbus in the last two acts allows them to mediate an unqualified but mistaken view of each other and themselves.

L. C. Knights admires the pathos of Cleopatra's imaginative and transcendent aspirations which create an 'unbearable pathos', but notes in Some Shakespearean Themes that death seals up her fate and Antony's alike, and that it is this stark fact which makes the play 'so little comforting to the romantic imagination'. F. R. Leavis in 'Antony and Cleopatra and All For Love: A Critical Exercise' praises Cleopatra for her vitality and compares the characters of Shakespeare's 'poem as drama' favourably to Dryden's statuesque tragic personae. The most responsive and effusive champion of Antony and Cleopatra is G. Wilson Knight, who in The Imperial Theme devotes four chapters to the play and charts its movement towards apotheosis. That Antony and Cleopatra reaches out to, and obtains, a 'victorious vision, a fulfilment of immortal longings', is argued by D. A. Stauffer in Shakespeare's World of Images. His chapter on the play is significantly called 'Roads to Freedom', to indicate that the lovers' deaths constitute a defeat of the political and temporal order of Rome. The distinctive rhetorical features of Antony and Cleopatra are hyperbole and paradox, the latter of which is the subject of a distinguished study by Benjamin T. Spencer, 'Antony and Cleopatra and the Paradoxical Metaphor'. That Antony and Cleopatra differs from other tragedies in its definition of identity and internal struggle was noted by A. C. Bradley; and J. F. Danby in Poets on Fortune's Hill develops the idea of the lovers' symbiosis against the background of what he sees as Shakespeare's most dialectical and deliquescent play. According to Danby, the characters merge into each other, and the play pulls towards androgynous mysticism as in 'The Phoenix and the Turtle', not least through the pressure of its mythopoeic imagery. In *The Problem Plays of Shakespeare* Ernest Schanzer similarly studies the 'near-identity of Antony and Cleopatra' and traces its genesis through a series of verbal and thematic echoes in the play. David Daiches concurs, and in *More Literary Essays* he notes that the identities of the two protagonists together constitute the heart and mystery of the play. In an important article, 'Shakespeare's Boy Cleopatra, the Decorum of Nature, and the Golden World of Poetry', Phyllis Rackin relates the play's concerns with androgynous identity to the bisexual conditions of the Elizabethan theatre and extrapolates from the alleged limitations of the prevailing stage icon Cleopatra's strategies of recreating for Antony and herself a redeemed world of poetry.

Three valuable studies of *Antony and Cleopatra* which appeared at almost the same time are Robin Lee, *Shakespeare: Antony and Cleopatra*, A. P. Riemer, *A Reading of Shakespeare's 'Antony and Cleopatra'*, and P. J. Traci, *The Love Play of Antony and Cleopatra*. Traci's is of particular interest, not least for its use of Florentine Neoplatonism to provide a wider context for the gender ambiguities contemplated in Shakespeare's play.

That the opposition between Rome and Egypt can be interpreted as an integral part of a wider courtly, and therefore romantic, metaphor is argued in *The Pillar of the World* by J. Markels, who suggests that in *Antony and Cleopatra* 'the political order of the histories may in the end become an artistic one'. In 'The Comic Pattern and Vision in *Antony and Cleopatra*' and later in *Shakespeare's Pagan World*, J. L. Simmons undertakes to read *Antony and Cleopatra* as a 'tragedy of heroic love' cast generically in the mould of a divine comedy. The lovers' exalted status in the political world of history confers imaginative credibility on their *contemptus mundi*, and 'the glory of empire is . . . necessary as the setting of their love'. In *Shakespeare's Rome: Republic and Empire*, Paul Cantor offers a similarly partisan reading of the lovers by subordinating the political and moral issues in the play to a love-affair which soars above domestic comedy and exacts as its validation the Roman Empire.

The liberating and uplifting pressure of the play's mythopoeia, its interweaving uses of Hercules, Mars, and Isis, have attracted considerable critical attention. The Hercules-analogy with Antony invariably entails a casting of Cleopatra as an Omphale figure, who emasculates the ensnared warrior through inflicting domestic chores on him. But as Eugene Waith remarks in *The Herculean Hero*, in *Antony and Cleopatra* the function of the myth is more ambiguous, as the collapsing of the heroic ideal precedes the creation of a richer and perhaps preferable identity. 'The Choice of Hercules in *Antony and Cleopatra*' by J. Coates develops and reassesses the role of the myth in the play, and in '*Antony and Cleopatra*: What Venus Did with Mars', R. B. Waddington links Hercules' leaving Antony in Act IV to the further absorption of Antony in his role of a Mars in conjunction with a Venus, a union which mythographically constellates harmony. That the Isis-myth—as derived from Plutarch's *Moralia*, Apuleius' *The Golden Ass*, and Spenser's *The Faerie Queene*—feeds into Shakespeare's conception of Antony and Cleopatra is argued by Michael Lloyd, 'Cleopatra as Isis', and by Harold Fisch, '*Antony and Cleopatra*: The Limits of Mythology', both of whom relate it to the play's concern with fertility and immortality. A more specifically Christian and Eucharistic imagery is traced in the texture of the play's rhetoric by John Middleton Murry in *Shakespeare*. Antony's lines in IV. ii to his faithful, 'Tend me to-night; / Maybe it is the period of your duty', remind Murry of Christ in Gethsemane, and Enobarbus' claim to be 'a master-leaver' casts him as a Judas. In *Shakespeare and the Popular Dramatic Tradition*, S. L. Bethell argues further that the sensuality of *Antony and Cleopatra* translates into the apocalyptic 'new heaven, new earth' of Antony's definition of love, following the patristic model of reading the *Canticles* as the *hieros gamos*. In '*Antony and Cleopatra* and the *Book of Revelation*' Ethel Seaton studies Cleopatra's dream vision of Antony in the context of the famous Dürer drawing of St John's vision of the angel from which the relevant illustration in the 1568 *Bishops' Bible* derived. One of the seminal recent works on *Antony and Cleopatra* is Janet Adelman's distinguished book *The Common Liar: An Essay on 'Antony and Cleopatra'*. Adelman offers a comprehensive reassessment of the conflicting myths and images in the play and writes with authority on its dynamic and fluctuating concepts of selfhood in an imaginative world 'in which nothing stays to scale'. Identity in *Antony and Cleopatra* is, Adelman notes, not in being but in becoming, and the limits to human metamorphosis recede into infinity. In *Possessed with Greatness: The Heroic Tragedies of Chapman and Shakespeare*, Richard S. Ide considers the range of the lovers' lyric imagination and suggests that the grandeur of their love 'is predicated on the acceptance of human frailty in themselves and in others'. Russell Jackson sensitively studies the paradoxes inherent in Antony's and Cleopatra's 'intimate' and 'private triumphs' in 'The Triumphs of *Antony and Cleopatra'*, while in *'Antony and Cleopatra*: The Challenge of Fiction' René Weis reconsiders the implications of Cleopatra's vision of 'an Antony' who is the product of a transcending imagination.

Barbara J. Bono's *Literary Transvaluation: From Vergilian Epic to Shakespearean Tragicomedy* is a brilliant and wide-ranging study of Shakespeare's play and its transvaluing—that is, creatively appropriating—of a complex and dialectical literary tradition. Bono astutely surveys the fields of myth as well as the classical and medieval receptions of the Antony and Cleopatra story, and relates them to a sympathetic reading of the lovers' ideals.

Two collections of criticism, *Shakespeare: Antony and Cleopatra. A Casebook*, edited by J. R. Brown, and *Twentieth Century Interpretations of Antony and Cleopatra*, edited by M. Rose, offer useful excerpts from important work on the play.

REFERENCES

SHAKESPEARE AND ROMAN HISTORY

Appian, of Alexandria, *An Auncient Historie and exquisite Chronicle of the Romanes warres, both Ciuile and Foren . . . from the death of Sextus Pompeius . . . till the overthrow of Antonie and Cleopatra*, trans. W. B. (London, 1578); *Shakespeare's Appian*, ed. E. Schanzer (Liverpool, 1956).

Bullough, Geoffrey (ed.), *Narrative and Dramatic Sources of Shakespeare*, vol. v (London, 1964).

MacCallum, (Sir) M. W., *Shakespeare's Roman Plays and Their Background* (London, 1910); new edn. with introduction by T. J. B. Spencer (London, 1967).

Maxwell, J. C., 'Shakespeare's Roman Plays: 1900–1956', *Shakespeare Survey 10* (1957), 27–38.

Miola, Robert S., *Shakespeare's Rome* (Cambridge, 1983).

Plutarch, *The Lives of the Nobel Grecians and Romanes, Compared . . . Translated out of Greeke into French by Iames Amyot . . . and out of French into English by Thomas North* (London, 1579, etc.)

——— *The Philosophie, commonlie called The Morals. Written by . . . Plutarch . . . Translated out of Greeke into English, and conferred with the Latine translations and the French by Philemon Holland* (London, 1603).

Spencer, T. J. B., 'Shakespeare and the Elizabethan Romans', *Shakespeare Survey 10* (1957).

——(ed.), *Shakespeare's Plutarch* (London, 1964).

Suetonius, C. Tranquillus, *The Historie of Twelve Caesars Emperours of Rome . . . newly translated into English by Philemon Holland* (London, 1606).

Tacitus, Publius Cornelius, *The Annals of Imperial Rome*, trans. with an introduction by Michael Grant (London, 1956, etc.).

Thomson, J. A. K., *Shakespeare and the Classics* (London, 1952).

Traversi, Derek A., *Shakespeare: The Roman Plays* (London, 1963).

Velz, J. W., *Shakespeare and the Classical Tradition: A Critical Guide to Commentary, 1660–1960* (Minneapolis, Minn., 1968).

Julius Caesar

TEXTS

Dorsch, T. S. (ed.), *Julius Caesar* (Arden Shakespeare, London, 1955, etc.)

Furness, H. H. (ed.), *Julius Caesar* (New Variorum Shakespeare, Philadelphia, Pa., 1913).

Humphreys, Arthur, *Julius Caesar* (Oxford Shakespeare, Oxford, 1984).

Sanders, Norman (ed.), *Julius Caesar* (New Penguin Shakespeare, London, 1967, etc.).

Spevack, Marvin (ed.), *Julius Caesar* (New Cambridge Shakespeare, Cambridge, 1988).

Wilson, J. Dover (ed.), *Julius Caesar* (New Shakespeare, Cambridge, 1949).

CRITICISM

Bonjour, Adrien, *The Structure of 'Julius Caesar'* (Liverpool, 1958).

Bradford, Ernle, *Julius Caesar: The Pursuit of Power* (London, 1984).

Brower, Reuben A., *Hero and Saint: Shakespeare and the Graeco-Roman Heroic Tradition* (Oxford, 1971).

Charlton, H. B., *Shakespearian Tragedy* (Cambridge, 1948).

Charney, Maurice (ed.), *Discussions of Shakespeare's Roman Plays* (Boston, Mass., 1964).

Coleridge, S. T., *Shakespearean Criticism*, ed. T. M. Raysor, 2 vols. (London, 1960, etc.).

Daiches, David, *Julius Caesar* (London, 1976).

Dean, Leonard F. (ed.), *Twentieth Century Interpretations of 'Julius Caesar'* (Englewood Cliffs, NJ, 1968).

Dowden, Edward, *Shakspere: A Critical Study of His Mind and Art* (London, 1875).

Edwards, Philip, *Shakespeare: A Writer's Progress* (Cambridge, 1986).

Evans, Bertrand, *Shakespeare's Tragic Practice* (Oxford, 1979).

Farnham, Willard, *Shakespeare's Tragic Frontier: The World of his Final Tragedies* (Berkeley, Calif., 1950).

Foakes, R. A., 'An Approach to *Julius Caesar*', *Shakespeare Quarterly*, 5 (1954), 259–70.

Fowler, W. Warde, *Roman Essays and Interpretations* (Oxford, 1920).

Gundolf, Friedrich, *The Mantle of Caesar* (London, 1929).

Honigmann, E. A. J., *Shakespeare, Seven Tragedies: The Dramatist's Manipulation of Response* (London, 1976).

Mehl, Dieter, *Shakespeare's Tragedies: An Introduction* (Cambridge, 1983).

Muir, Kenneth, *Shakespeare's Tragic Sequence* (Liverpool, 1972, etc.).

Palmer, John, *Political Characters of Shakespeare* (London, 1945).

Phillips, J. E., *The State in Shakespeare's Greek and Roman Plays* (New York, 1940).

Proser, Matthew N., *The Heroic Image in Five Shakespearean Tragedies* (Princeton, NJ, 1965).

Rabkin, Norman, *Shakespeare and the Common Understanding* (New York, 1967).

Ribner, Irving, *Patterns in Shakespearian Tragedy* (London, 1960, etc.).

Ripley, John, *'Julius Caesar' on Stage in England and America, 1599–1973* (Cambridge, 1980).

Schanzer, Ernest, *The Problem Plays of Shakespeare* (London, 1963).

Siemon, James R., *Shakespearan Iconoclasm* (London, 1985).

Stirling, Brents, 'Or Else This Were a Savage Spectacle', *PMLA* 66 (1951), 765–74.

—— *The Populace in Shakespeare* (New York, 1949).

Ure, Peter (ed.), *Shakespeare: Julius Caesar* (Casebook Series, London, 1969).

Whitaker, Virgil K., *Shakespeare's Use of Learning* (San Marino, Calif., 1953).

Antony and Cleopatra

TEXTS

Case, R. H. (ed.), *Antony and Cleopatra* (Arden Shakespeare, London, 1906, rev. edn., 1930).

Everett, Barbara (ed.), *Antony and Cleopatra* (Signet Shakespeare, New York, 1964, etc.).

Furness, H. H. (ed.), *Antony and Cleopatra* (New Variorum Shakespeare, Philadelphia, Pa., 1907).

Ingledew, John (ed.), *Antony and Cleopatra* (New Swan Shakespeare, London, 1971, etc.).

Jones, Emrys (ed.), *Antony and Cleopatra* (New Penguin Shakespeare, London, 1977, etc.).

Ridley, M. R. (ed.), *Antony and Cleopatra* (Arden Shakespeare, London, 1954, etc.).

Wilson, J. Dover (ed.), *Antony and Cleopatra* (New Shakespeare, Cambridge, 1950).

CRITICISM

Adelman, Janet, *The Common Liar: An Essay on 'Antony and Cleopatra'* (London, 1973).
Barroll, Leeds J., 'Antony and Pleasure', *JEGP* 57 (1958), 708–20.
Barton, Anne, 'Nature's Piece 'Gainst Fancy: The Divided Catastrophe in *Antony and Cleopatra'*. An Inaugural Lecture (London, 1973).
Bethell, S. L., *Shakespeare and The Popular Dramatic Tradition* (London, 1944).
Bono, Barbara J., *Literary Transvaluation: From Vergilian Epic to Shakespearean Tragicomedy* (Berkeley, Calif., 1984).
Bradley, A. C., *Oxford Lectures on Poetry* (London, 1909).
Brown, John Russell (ed.), *Shakespeare: Antony and Cleopatra* (Casebook Series, London, 1968).
Cantor, Paul, *Shakespeare's Rome: Republic and Empire* (London, 1976).
Cecil, Lord David, '*Antony and Cleopatra*', The Fourth Ker Memorial Lecture, 1944; reprinted in *Poets and Storytellers* (London, 1949).
Coates, J., 'The Choice of Hercules in *Antony and Cleopatra*', *Shakespeare Survey 31* (1978), 45–52.
Coleridge, S. T., *Shakespearean Criticism*, ed. T. M. Raysor, 2 vols. (London, 1960, etc.).
Daiches, David, *More Literary Essays* (London, 1968).
Danby, John F., *Poets on Fortune's Hill* (London, 1952, etc.).
Dickey, F. M., *Not Wisely But Too Well* (San Marino, Calif., 1966).
Fisch, Harold, '*Antony and Cleopatra*: The Limits of Mythology', *Shakespeare Survey 23* (1970), 59–67.
Granville-Barker, Harley, *Prefaces to Shakespeare*, 2nd ser. (London, 1930).
Ide, Richard S., *Possessed with Greatness: The Heroic Tragedies of Chapman and Shakespeare* (London, 1980).
Jackson, Russell, 'The Triumphs of *Antony and Cleopatra*', *Shakespeare Jahrbuch* (West) (1984), 128–48.
Johnson, S., *Johnson on Shakespeare*, ed. Arthur Sherbo, vols. vii and viii in *The Yale Edition of the Works of Samuel Johnson* (London, 1968).
Knight, G. Wilson, *The Imperial Theme: Further Interpretations of Shakespeare's Tragedies Including the Roman Plays* (London, 1954).
Knights, L. C., *Some Shakespearean Themes* (London, 1959).
Leavis, F. R., '*Antony and Cleopatra* and *All for Love*: A Critical Exercise', *Scrutiny*, 5 (1936), 158–69.
Lee, Robin, *Shakespeare: Antony and Cleopatra* (London, 1971).
Lloyd, Michael, 'Cleopatra as Isis', *Shakespeare Survey 12* (1959), 88–94.
Markels, J., *The Pillar of the World: 'Antony and Cleopatra' in Shakespeare's Development* (Columbus, Ohio, 1968).

Murry, John Middleton, *Shakespeare* (London, 1936, etc.).

Rackin, Phyllis, 'Shakespeare's Boy Cleopatra, the Decorum of Nature, and the Golden World of Poetry', *PMLA* 87 (1972), 201–12.

Riemer, A. P., *A Reading of Shakespeare's 'Antony and Cleopatra'* (Sidney, 1971).

Rosen, William, *Shakespeare and the Craft of Tragedy* (Cambridge, Mass., 1960).

Rose, M. (ed.), *Twentieth Century Interpretations of 'Antony and Cleopatra'* (Englewood Cliffs, NJ, 1968).

Schanzer, Ernest, *The Problem Plays of Shakespeare* (London, 1963).

Schücking, L. L., *Character Problems in Shakespeare's Plays* (London, 1922).

Seaton, Ethel, '*Antony and Cleopatra* and the *Book of Revelation*', *RES* 22 (1946), 219–24.

Shaw, G. B., *Three Plays for Puritans* (London, 1901).

Simmons, J. L., 'The Comic Pattern and Vision in *Antony and Cleopatra*', *ELH* 36 (1969), 493–510.

—— *Shakespeare's Pagan World: The Roman Tragedies* (Hassocks, Sussex, 1974).

Spencer, B. T., '*Antony and Cleopatra* and the Paradoxical Metaphor', *Shakespeare Quarterly*, 9 (1958), 373–8.

Stauffer, D. A., *Shakespeare's World of Images. The Development of His Moral Ideas* (New York, 1949).

Stewart, J. I. M., *Character and Motive in Shakespeare* (London, 1949).

Stoll, E. E., *Poets and Playwrights* (Minneapolis, Minn., 1930, etc.).

Traci, P. J., *The Love Play of 'Antony and Cleopatra'* (The Hague, 1970).

Waddington, R. B., '*Antony and Cleopatra*: What Venus Did with Mars', *Shakespeare Studies*, 2 (1966), 210–27.

Waith, Eugene, *The Herculean Hero in Marlowe, Chapman, Shakespeare, and Dryden* (London, 1962).

Weis, R. J. A., '*Antony and Cleopatra*: The Challenge of Fiction', *English*, 32 (1983), 1–14.

15

Coriolanus and Timon of Athens

MAURICE CHARNEY

Coriolanus

TEXTS AND TEXTUAL STUDIES

Coriolanus first appeared in print in the Folio of 1623, seven years after Shakespeare's death. The printer seems to have used a carefully prepared manuscript, perhaps in the author's own hand. The stage directions are unusually elaborate, and the text is longer than would be normal for an acting version. The chief difficulty is with mislineation, or lines that do not scan properly as blank verse. Most editors rearrange the lines to improve the scansion, but G. B. Harrison argues strongly for following the Folio pattern in most cases.

For students' purposes, the most useful editions of the play are the New Penguin (edited by G. R. Hibbard) and the Signet (edited by Reuben Brower). The New Penguin has a long and comprehensive introduction, with extensive notes that appear, unfortunately, after the text of the play; the remarks on the dramatic function of each scene are particularly illuminating. Although the Signet edition has many brief notes (chiefly explaining what the words mean), its emphasis is different. Brower's introduction is one of the most original essays on the play, and the volume reprints a generous sampling from North's translation of Plutarch, as well as selections from Bradley, Wyndham Lewis, and Traversi.

The best modern edition is by Philip Brockbank in the new Arden series. This has very full notes and puts a valuable emphasis on history and politics. The Cambridge edition by John Dover Wilson, the last volume for which he was solely responsible, has notes that are remarkable for their wide learning and keen insight, especially into problems of lexicography. Furness's New Variorum edition is also very learned, although a good part of its 762 pages culled from critics of the eighteenth and nineteenth centuries now seems merely of antiquarian interest. Among other editions, the Pelican by Harry Levin is modest in scope, with a brief and searching introduction.

CRITICAL STUDIES AND COMMENTARY

When T. S. Eliot in 1919 praised *Coriolanus* for being, 'with *Antony and Cleopatra*, Shakespeare's most assured artistic success', he was paradoxically revaluing the tragedies from Bradley's traditional 'great four': *King Lear, Othello, Macbeth*, and *Hamlet*. It is no longer necessary to defend *Coriolanus* from its imagined detractors. To recent critics it has seemed one of Shakespeare's most original accomplishments, and commentary has been intent on discovering what makes it unique as a tragedy.

In his British Academy lecture of 1912, Bradley was keenly aware that *Coriolanus* stands apart from other tragedies of Shakespeare. 'That peculiar *imaginative* effect or atmosphere is hardly felt', because the play is intensely secular and public and has no natural or supernatural support. As usual, Bradley's descriptive powers are impressive even when we may disagree with his conclusions. The same holds true for O. J. Campbell's argument that *Coriolanus* is a 'tragical satire', full of the spirit of mockery and derision. Although Campbell is too energetic in the pursuit of his thesis, he has an acute sense of what is special in tone and mood. D. J. Enright's essay, '*Coriolanus*: Tragedy or Debate?', is more moderate and subtle than Campbell, but he too is trying to discover why the play cannot be understood within the conventional criteria of tragedy. The range of tone and feeling in the verse 'is unusually narrow for Shakespeare', and the play in general 'has certain qualities of an intellectual debate'. I. R. Browning's answer to Enright, 'Coriolanus: Boy of Tears', seems to misunderstand the scope of the discussion, because Enright chooses to deal with style and tone, whereas Browning concentrates on a psychological approach to character.

In *Shakespeare's Tragic Frontier*, Farnham creates a separate paradoxical world for Shakespeare's final tragedies: *Timon of Athens, Macbeth, Antony and Cleopatra*, and *Coriolanus*. This world of taints and honours waging equally, of deeply flawed yet

noble characters, has its most characteristic expression in Coriolanus, whose pride produces 'not only everything bad but also
everything good by which he comes to be a subject for Shakespearean tragedy'. Even if we disagree with aspects of Farnham's
presentation, we are still indebted to him for trying to discern the
place of *Coriolanus* in Shakespeare's development.

One of the most original suggestions about the genre of
Coriolanus is that of Kenneth Burke, who sees it as a 'grotesque'
tragedy resembling a Greek satyr-play. His essay, '*Coriolanus*
and the Delights of Faction', is one of the best accounts of the
play's tragic structure, derived deductively from Aristotelian
principles. Virtues and vices work together to fit Coriolanus for
his sacrificial function: his vices make him vulnerable, but his
virtues establish his stature as a victim worth the killing. There is
a comparable balancing of opposites in Jan Kott's chapter, '*Coriolanus*, or Shakespearian Contradictions' (in *Shakespeare Our Contemporary*), in which political and moral ambiguity lies at the
heart of the tragedy. Kott makes it clear why this play appealed so
strongly to Brecht and his followers. H. J. Oliver's essay, 'Coriolanus as Tragic Hero', is a perceptive evaluation of modern
thinking on the subject. Samuel Johnson does not deem *Coriolanus*
tragic at all—it is 'one of the most amusing of our author's
performances', and Shaw goes so far as to call it 'the greatest of
Shakespear's comedies'.

Our interpretation of *Coriolanus* depends, of course, on our
own moral values. Critics associated with *Scrutiny* expressed
their indignation at the growth of an impersonal, violent, mass
society through their comments on Coriolanus, especially in his
guise as heroic warrior—heroic values are vigorously reprehended
for their harshness and inhumanity. D. A. Traversi is constantly
reproaching Coriolanus for being an 'iron, mechanical warrior',
a 'human war-machine'. For him, the crucial problem in the play
is 'a failure in sensitivity, a failure in living; and it represents a
failure on the part of a whole society.' Although L. C. Knights
couches his argument (in *Further Explorations*) in terms of 'political
wisdom', this too is essentially a moral concept. Tragedy arises
from the 'defective humanity' of the central figure, his 'failure to
achieve integration', his scorn for 'mutuality' in the state, his lack
of 'maturity'. G. Wilson Knight pursues a comparable moral
theme in his essay, where War and Love oppose each other as
life-denying and life-giving forces.

Whatever one's sympathies for humane values, in the play itself military honour and personal heroism do not merely represent 'a failure in sensitivity, a failure in living'. Brower renders a notable service to students of *Coriolanus* by pursuing his discussion in the heroic, epic mode, and by making cogent comparisons between Shakespeare's protagonist and Homer's Achilles (but a completely Romanized Achilles). Coriolanus 'comes nearest to the essence of Homer's hero in his absoluteness, in his determination to imitate "the graces of the gods", in his will to push the heroic to the limit. . . .' This approach insists on complex moral assumptions, because abstract values are set against a necessary historical background of *virtus* and military honour. Eugene Waith enlightens us on the moral force of the classical tradition by interpreting Coriolanus as a Herculean hero. In *Possessed with Greatness*, Richard S. Ide has an original account of the heroic tragedies of Chapman and Shakespeare. He sees *Coriolanus* as an attempt to out-Chapman Chapman, especially in *The Conspiracy and Tragedy of Byron*. As a titanic hero, Coriolanus is superior to Byron.

Knight's questioning of the 'maturity' of Coriolanus raises one of the most often debated (but not necessarily most significant) issues about the play. Is the hero merely a 'boy of tears' (I. R. Browning), a 'huge boy' (Bradley), an 'incorrigible boy' (Granville-Barker), 'one that never became anything but a schoolboy (razed with notions of privilege and social distinction' (Wyndham Lewis), and can the play properly be called 'a tragedy of youth' (F. H. Rouda)? Psychoanalytic criticism has strongly emphasized Coriolanus's infantile relation to his castrating mother, and Charles Hofling sees the threatened attack on Rome as a sadistic but futile gesture against the mother. Emmett Wilson also interprets the play as the story of a son who is destroyed for his rebellion against his mother. In this schematic representation, both Menenius and Aufidius serve as surrogate fathers for the orphaned hero. To Rufus Putney, the problems of Coriolanus arise from the bleak and loveless atmosphere in which he was raised, so that his overpowering rage against his mother must be displaced on to other objects. Also relevant are D. W. Harding's incisive comments on Volumnia as 'Shakespeare's most blood-chilling study of the destructive consequences of a woman's living out at someone else's expense her fantasy of what manhood should be'.

Of the newer psychoanalytic criticism, some of the best is both psychoanalytic and feminist. Janet Adelman's essay, ' "Anger's My Meat": Feeding, Dependency, and Aggression in *Coriolanus*', uses the imagery of eating as a central metaphor for the play. The mob transforms hunger into phallic aggression, while Volumnia is the non-nurturant mother who has not fed her children enough. Basically, the taking in of food is a sign of one's dependence and also of one's vulnerability, which Coriolanus, in his self-suffi-ciency, refuses to acknowledge. His male identity is discussed in conjunction with Macbeth in Coppélia Kahn's *Man's Estate*. Both warrior-heroes are unfinished men who are convinced that only through violence will they achieve manhood. Their manhood is infused into them by women who are themselves half men. Madelon Sprengnether develops the theoretical implications of this position for Shakespeare's tragedies in 'Annihilating Intimacy in *Coriolanus*': 'Shakespeare's tragedies demonstrate, with a terrible consistency, the ways in which love kills.' *Coriolanus* reveals a deep fantasy of maternal destructiveness, since the hero both desires and fears the annihilation of his identity that intimacy with a woman either threatens or requires. The feminist-psychoanalytic arguments are summed up in Lisa Lowe's essay, ' "Say I play the man I am": Gender and Politics in *Coriolanus*'.

An older style of character analysis fills the pages of the New Variorum edition: small details are assiduously garnered in order to build a vivid, 'rounded' characterization. The elaborate account of the characters in M. W. MacCallum's *Shakespeare's Roman Plays* is the most highly wrought study of this kind. What remains impressive in MacCallum is his careful reasoning and critical insight, which shine through the ponderousness of his approach. Another general book, half of which is devoted to *Coriolanus*, is Paul A. Cantor's *Shakespeare's Rome*. He sums up what is happening in the play, especially in relation to character, with particular skill.

Modern critics have been more interested in character functions than in characterization as an autonomous entity. Dean Frye has investigated the commentary on Coriolanus by other characters, and he reaches conclusions that rehabilitate the protagonist in the eyes of the audience. In a similar line, Una Ellis-Fermor sees the character of Coriolanus revealed by 'secret impressions', especially in his relation to Virgilia. E. A. M. Colman interprets Coriolanus from the perspective of his final speech, which, like

Othello's, is exultantly self-assertive. Jay L. Halio shows an excellent sense of Coriolanus as a character and his need to come to terms with the humanity he rejects in '*Coriolanus*: Shakespeare's "Drama of Reconciliation" '. One of the best character studies, especially from a theatrical point of view, is Michael Goldman's 'Characterizing Coriolanus', in which Goldman tries to understand the performance aspects of the dramatic role.

On the broad question of politics in *Coriolanus*, Hazlitt's observation that 'Shakespeare himself seems to have had a leaning to the arbitrary side of the question' has not found much support. Modern commentators are more likely to begin with Coleridge's remark about the 'wonderful philosophic impartiality in Shakespeare's politics'. A study of what Shakespeare did with Plutarch supports this notion of a deliberate balancing of the conflict between patricians and plebeians. As Knights insists in 'Shakespeare and Political Wisdom', the politics of the play are not separable from questions of character and morality. John Palmer's pragmatic, commonsensical account of Coriolanus as a 'political character' best illustrates this approach. Coriolanus fares rather poorly in Palmer's scale of values, whereas the Tribunes are seen to be 'Shakespeare's counterfeit presentment of two labour leaders', who work for their party without claiming to be 'working disinterestedly for the nation'. Only Kenneth Muir seconds Palmer 'In Defence of the Tribunes', because they are 'much less unscrupulous than their opponents'. There may be some confusion between 'politic' and 'political', although *Coriolanus* lends itself to amoral speculations about the true source of power in the state. 'Politics' in a more general sense is the theme of Norman Rabkin's '*Coriolanus*: The Tragedy of Politics' and of Rossiter in *Angel with Horns*. Rossiter calls *Coriolanus* Shakespeare's 'only great political play'. R. B. Parker presents a searching political account of the play in '*Coriolanus* and "th' interpretation of the time" ', and Gail Kern Paster has a full analysis of the idea of Rome in 'To Starve with Feeding: The City in *Coriolanus*'.

For a more historical approach, Phillips's considerable book on *The State in Shakespeare's Greek and Roman Plays* has a long chapter on the 'Violation of Order and Degree in *Coriolanus*'. Menenius' fable establishes a norm for the political ideology of the play, against which we may measure the excesses of Coriolanus and the Tribunes. David Hale, however, objects to the normative use of the fable of the belly; ultimately, the political analogy cannot be made relevant to the complex issues of the play. In 'Tragic Superfluity in *Coriolanus*', James Holstun makes us aware of the complexity of the body politic analogy in the belly and members fable. The play dramatizes 'a monarchical threat to mixed republican stability'. Further complexities are explored in Andrew Gurr's essay, '*Coriolanus* and the Body Politic', and in Chapter 2 of Leonard Barkan's book, *Nature's Work of Art*.

The most thorough examination of the contemporary political background is in Clifford Chalmers Huffman's book, '*Coriolanus*' *in Context*, which interprets 'context' with excessive literalness. Jorgensen's book, *Shakespeare's Military World*, has important political implications for understanding the role of Coriolanus; his tragedy arises from his inability to move 'from the casque to the cushion', from military to civic life. There is a useful account of Jacobean politics in the article by Gordon Zeeveld; Clifford Davidson's essay, '*Coriolanus*: A Study in Political Dislocation', is also relevant. Patricia K. Meszaros's article, ' "There is a world elsewhere": Tragedy and History in *Coriolanus*', is impressive in its scope.

The mob as a political force is the subject of Stirling's book, *The Populace in Shakespeare*, and it is quite clear that the Roman mob is conceived in contemporary terms. Stirling notes the topical significance of the enclosure riots in the Midlands in 1607, a point which is developed by E. C. Pettet and Sidney Shanker. As a substantial landowner in Warwickshire, Shakespeare must have been disturbed by the news of this popular insurrection at the very time he was writing *Coriolanus*. There is an intriguing account of the mob in Chapter VIII of Michael Goldman's *Shakespeare and the Energies of Drama*.

Our best guide to the classical background of *Coriolanus* is T. J. B. Spencer, who establishes a contemporary context for 'Shakespeare and the Elizabethan Romans'. Spencer's brief treatment of the play in his 'Writers and Their Work' pamphlet also emphasizes Shakespeare's concern 'to get things historically correct, to preserve Roman manners and customs and allusions'. In Spencer's view, 'to write *Coriolanus* was one of the great feats of the historical imagination in Renaissance Europe'. Brower's introduction to the Signet edition draws a significant parallel between *Coriolanus* and the heroic, epic tradition, as seen especially in the figure of Achilles. To Brower, Coriolanus is 'the most Roman, the least Christian, of Shakespeare's major heroes'.

On the sources, our chief authority is Geoffrey Bullough, *Narrative and Dramatic Sources of Shakespeare*, Volume V, which reprints selections from Livy and Florus as well as from Plutarch, and includes historical documents to illustrate the Jacobean context. In his introduction Bullough makes a strong case for Shakespeare's knowledge of Livy. MacCallum's book has a very detailed account of Shakespeare's use of Plutarch, a subject that is also profitably explored by Hermann Heuer and Ernst Honigmann. Kenneth Muir has written extensively about the literary traditions that lie behind *Coriolanus*, and Shakespeare's view of *Romanitas* is examined by Robert S. Miola. If Shakespeare was not actually erudite, he must have read widely and unpredictably in the books and pamphlets of his own time, or at least have been well informed about them. Farnham's book also has a good deal to say about contemporary sources. Plutarch's Life of Coriolanus in North's translation is conveniently available in *Shakespeare's Plutarch* (edited by Spencer), which prints the relevant passages from the play at the bottom of the page. Recently, John W. Velz has argued for Shakespeare's debt to Vergil's *Aeneid* and Anne Barton has made a strong case for Shakespeare's use of Livy, *Ab Urbe Condita*, which best represents republican Rome. Barton also discusses Machiavelli's commentary on Livy in his *Discourses*.

Our understanding of the poetic quality of *Coriolanus* has been much influenced by G. Wilson Knight, who stresses the imagery of hardness, constriction, and violence: 'We are limited by city walls. And cities are here metallic, our world constricted, bound in by hard walls: and this constriction, this suggestion of hardness, is rooted deep in our theme.' Traversi pursues a similar line of imagery, but with greater sensitivity to the sinuous, muscular movement of the verse. L. C. Knights, in *Further Explorations*, has valuable comments on Shakespeare's poetic achievement in this play. An interesting study by R. F. Hill tries to show how contrarieties in the play are expressed by a pervasively antithetical style. James L. Calderwood has a significant essay on the breakdown of language in *Coriolanus*: 'Wordless Meanings and Meaningless Words', a theme that is pursued further in Carol M. Sicherman's essay, '*Coriolanus*: The Failure of Words'.

Spurgeon's standard work on Shakespeare's imagery has little to point out in *Coriolanus* except the fairly obvious theme of the body and sickness. In *The Development of Shakespeare's Imagery*, Clemen stresses the patrician-plebeian conflict as the source of symbolic contrasts. The most extensive discussion of imagery is in Charney's book on the Roman plays, in which the images are related to their dramatic function. Food, disease, and animals dominate, but the tragedy of Coriolanus is also presented by an imagery of acting and isolation. Maxwell's brief account of the animal imagery is one of the best studies of how a detail of Shakespeare's symbolism can illuminate his poetic method. The animal imagery reveals that '*Coriolanus* is characteristically a play in which the most momentous and vehement statements are made in the most literal form.' In the penetrating article by F. N. Lees, '*Coriolanus*, Aristotle, and Bacon', the animal and god imageries show the hero poised between the alternatives proposed by Aristotle: 'He that is incapable of living in a society is a god or a beast.' Leonard Dean's essay on 'Voice and Deed in *Coriolanus*' adds to our awareness of the acting imagery, while D. J. Gordon's handling of a similar topic, 'Name and Fame', relates Shakespeare to the *topoi* of classical tradition. In 'Sexual Imagery in *Coriolanus*', Ralph Berry takes up the relations of war and sexuality, especially the homoerotic theme in the attachment of Coriolanus to Aufidius. An excellent general study of the style of the play is Madeleine Doran's chapter on the language of contention in *Shakespeare's Dramatic Language*. In an ingenious essay, Lawrence N. Danson devotes his attention specifically to 'Metonymy and *Coriolanus*', in which he argues that metonymy and synecdoche rather than metaphor are the most prominent rhetorical figures in the play.

Critics pay lip-service to the dramatic power of *Coriolanus*, yet there has been little serious consideration of its dramaturgy, or even of practical problems of staging. Glynne Wickham's comments on the play grow out of his experience in producing it at Bath in 1952, and there is a rewarding sense here of how staging may clarify the text. The fullest discussion of dramaturgy is in Granville-Barker's *Prefaces*. Unfortunately, *Coriolanus* was the last Preface Granville-Barker wrote, and it shows a certain laboriousness in its points about characters, but its final sections on the dramatic verse and on the use of silence represent the author at his best. He tries to deal with the presented play in its own medium, and this concern gives his work a special freshness and relevance. Charney's book also pays close attention to dramaturgic problems and necessities, especially in the use of a non-verbal 'presentational' imagery.

Brockbank's Arden edition has a good deal to say about the stage history of *Coriolanus*, which is also summarized briefly by C. B. Young in the New Cambridge edition. An article by Ralph Berry, 'The Metamorphoses of *Coriolanus*', concentrates on the interesting relation of stage history and politics. Further details about later versions of the play, often radically rewritten, may be found in Hazelton Spencer's *Shakespeare Improved* and Odell's *Shakespeare—from Betterton to Irving*. Trewin discusses English productions of the twentieth century. The New Variorum edition has useful material in its appendix on dramatic versions, stage history, and actors' interpretations.

For further discussion of the many books and articles on *Coriolanus* and its background, the reader should consult John W. Velz's bibliography, *Shakespeare and the Classical Tradition*, which goes as far as 1960. There is also valuable commentary on the critical literature in Hibbard's New Penguin edition; in Spencer's 'Writers and Their Work' pamphlet; and in his foreword to the reprint of MacCallum in 1967. Maxwell assesses the main lines of investigation in *Shakespeare Survey 10*, a volume devoted to the Roman plays. There is a collection of essays, edited by Charney, on Shakespeare's Roman plays.

Timon of Athens

TEXTS AND TEXTUAL STUDIES

There is an air of mystery surrounding the first publication of *Timon* in the Shakespeare Folio of 1623. We know from bibliographical evidence that three pages of *Troilus and Cressida* were already set up and printed when it was suddenly withdrawn, presumably because of difficulties over rights. As a stopgap, *Timon* was inserted in the space left blank between *Romeo and Juliet* and *Julius Caesar*. Whether *Timon* ever would have been published had this contretemps not arisen is an open question, but it seems clear that the manuscript the printer used must have been a rough draft rather than a final version, because it is full of inconsistencies in plot, irregularities in verse, and odd ineptitudes in writing.

It is apparent, for example, from Terence Spencer's fascinating note about money, that Shakespeare either did not know or had forgotten how much a talent was worth, but in the course of writing he found out and then rectified some of his figures. The conclusion from the evidence of the talents seems to be that the play was never 'reasonably completed, polished, or corrected for performance or perusal'. Maxwell has some additional comments on this matter in his edition. The curious history and status of the text of *Timon* are discussed in J. Q. Adams's article, '*Timon of Athens* and the Irregularities in the First Folio'; in Greg's book, *The Shakespeare First Folio*; and in the editions of Maxwell and Oliver. Hinman's brief note in the Pelican edition should also be consulted.

We are fortunate in having excellent scholarly editions of the play: the Arden by H. J. Oliver and the New Cambridge by J. C. Maxwell. Oliver keeps closely to the Folio text on the principle that 'there are many things in *Timon* about which Shakespeare had presumably not made up his mind at all . . . and I do not myself think it is an editor's business to make Shakespeare's mind up for him.' The notes in this edition are particularly rewarding for their explication of difficult passages, and Oliver's introduction offers a judicious review of the main lines of thinking about the play. Maxwell's introduction and style of editing are more adventurous than Oliver's, so that the two editions complement each other. The New Penguin edition by G. R. Hibbard has full notes and an eclectic and well-balanced introduction.

The notes in the Signet edition by Maurice Charney are much concerned with word-play, and this edition reprints commentary by David Cook, William Richardson, and Roy Walker. Charlton Hinman's Pelican edition has brief notes, but it has the special merit of being edited by one of the leading authorities on the First Folio.

CRITICAL STUDIES AND COMMENTARY

Questions about the text of *Timon* impinge closely on interpretation. Theories of divided authorship persist, and the play is ascribed to Shakespeare and Thomas Middleton in the *Complete Oxford Shakespeare*. Arguments are summarized in Wells and Taylor: *William Shakespeare: A Textual Companion*. In any case it is generally agreed that the play as we have it is unfinished. But unfinished in what sense? Chambers, in his chapter in *Shakespeare: A Survey*, thinks that parts of *Timon* 'might be rough notes, first drafts of scenes, jotted down in half prose of gnomic couplets, just as they came to the surface in the early stages of composition, to be taken up and worked over again during the process of revision'. The notion that *Timon* is unfinished both in conception and execution has been persuasively developed by Una Ellis-Fermor in her essay, '*Timon of Athens*: An Unfinished Play'. It is 'a play such as a great artist might leave behind him, roughed out, worked over in part and then abandoned; full of inconsistencies in form and presentation, with fragments (some of them considerable) bearing the unmistakable stamp of his workmanship scattered throughout'. This is the heart of the matter, and Miss Ellis-Fermor's later argument about our not really 'knowing' Timon as a character seems to me weak.

Miss Ellis-Fermor's article, in its wide and enthusiastic acceptance, has had a most pernicious effect on the appreciation of *Timon*. If the play is indeed so chaotic and so fragmentary as it is represented to be, then it is not worth bothering about, and *Timon* has been neglected not only in the classroom, but also in general studies of Shakespeare's tragedies. Even if one admits that it is an unfinished play, the caution Honigmann has proposed is still relevant: 'Stylistic and textual peculiarities have been overstressed while the vital fact that *Timon* appears to be an almost finished play has escaped the attention it deserves.' For all its faults, the poetic interpretation of G. Wilson Knight in *The Wheel of Fire* assumes that the play is a coherent work of art. H. S. Wilson strongly supports Knight: 'as an imaginative conception, as a symbolic poem, *Timon* is splendidly complete in its effect.' It is interesting that in Miss Bradbrook's eloquent inaugural lecture at the University of Cambridge (1966) there is no mention at all of *Timon* as an unfinished play.

The problem of disappointed expectations also arises in the position usually accorded *Timon* in Shakespeare's development. Older critics tended strongly to think of the play in Coleridge's terms as an 'after vibration' of *King Lear*: 'It is a *Lear* of the satirical drama, a *Lear* of domestic or ordinary life . . . a *Lear*, therefore, without its soul-scorching flashes, its ear-cleaving thunder-claps, its meteoric splendours. . . .' In Bradley's *Shakespearean Tragedy*, *Timon* is confidently placed after *King Lear*, and Bradley devotes Note S and many passing references to exploring their similarities. This pairing is one of the commonplaces of *Timon* criticism, although there is no external evidence at all, or even a specific allusion, by which to date the play. No one would deny similarities of theme and handling between *Timon* and *King Lear*, but, as Honigmann points out, the forms of the two plays are 'so utterly unlike that their collocation can only be misleading'.

Approaching *Timon* with different assumptions, Chambers locates it after *Coriolanus* and before *Pericles*. In this perspective, *Timon* is the last of Shakespeare's tragedies, and it looks ahead to the romances. It is not a failed version of *King Lear*, but something quite different. As Northrop Frye observes, 'It seems to me that this extraordinary play, half morality and half folk tale, the fourth and last of the Plutarchan plays, is the logical transition from *Coriolanus* to the romances, and that it has many features making for an *idiotes* comedy rather than a tragedy.' Clifford Leech develops a similar point of view in *Shakespeare's Tragedies*, where he compares Timon and Leontes. In a wide-ranging essay, 'The Last Tragic Heroes', G. K. Hunter explores the special status of *Timon* (and *Coriolanus*) between *King Lear* and the romances.

The best (and only) general book on the play is Rolf Soellner's *Timon of Athens: Shakespeare's Pessimistic Tragedy*. Soellner places *Timon* in a contemporary intellectual tradition of misanthropy and pessimism and argues strongly that it is a fully conceived tragedy. This is a very solid and full study, which sees *Timon* in relation to general ideas of its age such as Fortune, the conflict of Nature and Art, and the ills of society (especially economic ills). Soellner also discusses the characters in detail. In 'The Ending of "Timon of Athens": A Reconsideration', Richard D. Fly emphasizes the complexity of the play, its double perspective especially in the disjunction between Timon and Alcibiades. The complexity of *Timon* is also the theme of Lesley W. Brill in 'Truth and *Timon of Athens*', in which the 'efflorescence of internal commentary' in the play is given special prominence.

If *Timon* cannot be considered a tragedy like *King Lear*, then the question of its genre is once more open to discussion. O. J. Campbell makes a case for 'tragical satire' in the mode of Jonson's *Sejanus* and *Volpone*, but it is difficult to see how satire can be the end rather than the means of the tragedy. Campbell weakens his excellent points about *Timon* by pursuing so narrow a thesis. Farnham's notion of 'paradoxical tragedy' also suffers from the need to prove a thesis about the deeply flawed heroes of Shakespeare's 'tragic frontier'. Unlike Coriolanus, Timon is so thoroughly alienated that there is no norm against which we may understand his tragedy. The 'schematism' of the play is noted by

Van Doren, and Charney, in his introduction to the Signet edition, calls the structure a dramatic fable: the 'action separates itself into a series of well-defined episodes related to each other analogically rather than causally.' In an incisive article, William W. E. Slights proposes that *Timon* draws on a variety of dramatic genres, especially masque and anti-masque. The masque idea is well pursued by Robert C. Fulton, III, in 'Timon, Cupid, and the Amazons', which uses an iconographic approach. In another excellent iconographic study, Clifford Davidson illustrates the theme of false friendship in the play.

In an important article, Collins uses the tradition of the medieval morality play in order to explain the special features of *Timon*. The characters are 'subtilized Virtues and Vices', and their conflict illustrates moral principles. A good deal of squeezing is necessary to fit everything into the allegorical mode, but Collins has a keen sense of what the play is trying to do. To Anne Lancashire, *Timon* is Shakespeare's *Dr. Faustus*, because it so consciously reverses the morality-play expectations of *Everyman*. Traversi also draws on the morality-play aspect of *Timon* to argue the theme of excess. The morality-play context is much invoked by Bradbrook in her wide-ranging lecture, *The Tragic Pageant of 'Timon of Athens'*, but she is also intent on demonstrating that the play is a show, or masque, or pageant, as Jacobean audiences would understand these terms. Bradbrook is strongly conscious of paradox and parody in *Timon*, which she considers not so much a play in the ordinary sense as 'an experimental scenario for an indoor dramatic pageant'—presented, presumably, before the sophisticated audience of the private theatres. Lewis Walker very specifically relates *Timon* to the morality tradition, especially as this may be seen in the *Castle of Perseverance*.

Timon as a character has not fared well at the hands of the critics, who have endowed both his philanthropy and his mis-anthropy with a complexity far beyond the scope of Timon's own limited awareness. As Samuel Johnson reads the play, 'The catastrophe affords a very powerful warning against that ostenta-tious liberality, which scatters bounty, but confers no benefits, and buys flattery, but not friendship.' From somewhat later in the eighteenth century, William Richardson offers a perceptive psychological analysis of Timon in *Essays on Shakespeare's Dramatic Characters*. The 'love of distinction' is Timon's ruling passion, and 'through an undue relish for adulation' he comes to solicit distinction, 'not so much for the pleasure it yields him as to remove a disagreeable craving'. Dowden puts a similar emphasis on the dream-like compulsion of Timon in *Shakspere: A Critical Study of His Mind and Art.*

G. Wilson Knight's portrait of Timon, in an essay called 'The Pilgrimage of Hate', is an extravagant idealization. 'Timon himself is the flower of human aspiration.... Timon's world is poetry made real, lived rather than imagined. He would break down with conviviality, music, art, the barriers that sever consciousness from consciousness. He would build a paradise of love on earth.' Andor Gomme takes just exception to this sentimentalizing of Timon in defiance of the dramatic context. There is much that is brilliant in Knight's reading of the play as an extended metaphor, but the conclusions seem to be superimposed on the evidence. A study by Jarold W. Ramsey extends Knight's heroic portrait of Timon into a literal imitation of Christ. In an essay that opens the G. Wilson Knight festschrift, L. C. Knights quietly demolishes any favourable view of the protagonist. He is particularly interesting on Timon's self-hatred. Harry Levin has a very harmonious essay on 'Shakespeare's Misanthrope', in which he compares Timon to Melville's *The Confidence Man*—judging from his heavy annotations, Melville was strongly interested in Shakespeare's play.

Among general discussions, one of the best is by David Cook, who is helpful on the role of Apemantus as 'relentless mentor'. Maxwell has an inventive essay in *Scrutiny* that tries to understand why *Timon* is not more successful, even though it gives promise of being a more profound play than *Coriolanus*. Of all critics who have written on the play, the most enthusiastic still remains William Hazlitt, who found that *Timon* is 'written with as intense a feeling of his subject as any one play of Shakespeare. It is one of the few in which he seems to be in earnest throughout, never to trifle nor go out of his way. He does not relax in his efforts, nor lose sight of the unity of his design.'

There is general agreement that the world of *Timon* is corrupt and that Athens is a materialistic, money-grubbing city in which virtue is doomed to cynical betrayal. Pettet sees the play narrowly as a 'straightforward tract for the times' on the disruption of feudal morality. Timon in Act I is the ideal feudal lord, a dispenser of bounty, but the new forces of commercialism, money, and economic self-interest shatter his traditional beliefs. Karl Marx was particularly drawn to *Timon*, as Kenneth Muir informs us in an important article, '*Timon of Athens* and the Cash Nexus.' Everything in Athens has its market value, and the 'sex nausea of *Timon* is an appropriate criticism of a society which is dominated by the acquisitive principle, a society which is bound together by what Marx calls the cash-nexus'. James Emerson Phillips also comments on the social corruption of Athens, chiefly in the light of Renaissance political thinking. Jorgensen adds to this discussion by examining the notion of a 'peace-rotten' society—war is manly and character-building, whereas peace promotes idleness and vice. Alcibiades figures significantly in this argument. Another aspect of the corruption of Athens is the contemporary reputation of Greeks as a 'licentious, luxurious, frivolous, bibulous, venereal, insinuating, perfidious, and unscrupulous' people, as Terence Spencer sums up their national qualities in his essay, ' "Greeks" and "Merrygreeks" '. The subject is also explored by Clifford Leech in *Stratford Papers on Shakespeare, 1963*.

There is no extensive study of the imagery of *Timon*. Spurgeon calls attention to dogs, especially in the sequence of dogs licking sweets to express fawning. 'Timon's Dog' is the subject of a subtle expatiation by Empson in *The Structure of Complex Words* that ranges far beyond its avowed subject. Farnham's chapter on *Timon* puts special emphasis on the beast theme. Knight's essay has many fine perceptions about imagery, but the best brief discussion is in Clemen's book, *The Development of Shakespeare's Imagery*. Hilda Hulme makes some controversial points about the language of *Timon*, especially in defence of a number of Folio readings that are usually emended. '*Timon* and the Conceit of Art' is the topic of a very original study by W. M. Merchant, which he develops further in his book, *Shakespeare and the Artist*.

Timon has been closely related to Shakespeare's life by older critics, who saw in the subject of the play a disturbing expression of Shakespeare's personal troubles. Even so sober and factual a commentator as E. K. Chambers cannot resist the temptations of romantic biography: 'Both *King Lear* and *Timon of Athens* seem to show symptoms of mental disturbance. But mental disturbance may come in waves. It may very likely only be a whimsy of my own that during the attempt at *Timon of Athens* a wave broke, that an illness followed, and that when it passed, the breach between the tragic and the romantic period was complete.' The historical context of this topic is wittily developed in Sisson's British Academy lecture, *The Mythical Sorrows of Shakespeare*. The subject, however, has a medical aspect that equates Shakespeare's physical symptoms with those of Timon, who is not only suffering from megalomania, but also from brain damage brought about by syphilis. This is Somerville's thesis in *Madness in Shakespearian Tragedy*. Andrew H. Woods corroborates the paretic dementia in a learned professional article, and W. I. D. Scott, in *Shakespeare's Melancholics*, treats the same malady under the heading 'Timon: The General Paralytic'. The best of the psychoanalytic studies is Susan Handelman's '*Timon of Athens*: The Rage of Disillusion', which is also strongly feminist. The play is 'a demonstration of the rage which refuses to accept loss'. It is significant that the play presents a world without women, since accepting women means accepting loss. This essay is reprinted in part in the new Signet edition of *Timon*.

The problem of sources is complicated by the fact that, although most critics claim Lucian's dialogue as the main source, there is no contemporary edition of Lucian that Shakespeare can confidently be shown to have used. The first English translation of Lucian was by Thomas Heywood in 1637. These matters are discussed at some length in Bullough's introduction to the *Narrative and Dramatic Sources of Shakespeare*, Volume VI, but the reader should also consult the provocative and original article by Honigmann. John M. Wallace makes a strong claim for Shakespeare's indebtedness to Seneca's *De beneficiis*. Farnham has a valuable section in *Shakespeare's Tragic Frontier* on the Renaissance tradition of Timonism.

The best account of the relation of *Timon of Athens* to the 'old' *Timon* play, a comedy based closely on Lucian's *Misanthropos*, is by James C. Bulman, Jr., in two articles. Bulman argues convincingly that this is an Inns of Court play from which Shakespeare derived his Lucian and that it was presented no later than 1602. Shakespeare's *Timon* may thus be quite early—earlier than the Roman plays and perhaps even than *King Lear*. Bulman agrees with Muriel Bradbrook's lively and speculative account of *The Comedy of Timon* as a revelling play of the law students of the Inner Temple, but he disagrees strongly that this play is later than Shakespeare's *Timon*. For other views, see Bonnard, Honigmann, Bullough, and Farnham. A date for the *Timon* comedy before 1600 is argued by G. C. Moore Smith and J. Q. Adams.

When Shadwell undertook to rewrite *Timon of Athens* as *The Man-Hater* (1678), he admitted that Shakespeare 'never made more Masterly strokes', yet, he insisted, 'I can truly say I have made it into a Play.' The stage history of *Timon of Athens* is part of literary criticism, because the alterations and omissions of playwrights clearly express their opinion of the original. The best account of the theatrical history of *Timon* is by Gary Jay Williams in a long appendix to Soellner's book. There is also a shorter stage history in the new edition of the Signet Shakespeare by Maurice Charney.

In 'Wormwood in the Wood outside Athens: *Timon* and the Problem for the Audience', Ninian Mellamphy pays particular attention to the Robin Phillips production in Stratford, Ontario, in 1976. Some of the earlier stage history is traced in Hazelton Spencer's *Shakespeare Improved*, and in Odell's *Shakespeare—from Betterton to Irving*. Stanley Williams has a useful article on 'Some Versions of *Timon of Athens* on the Stage'. There are brief accounts by C. B. Young in the New Cambridge edition and by Oliver in the new Arden. For more modern productions see Trewin's *Shakespeare on the English Stage 1900–1964*, and an informative presentation in the *Times Educational Supplement* for 30 May 1952 ('*Timon of Athens:* Some Earlier Appearances').

There is a full bibliography of the play by John J. Ruszkiewicz, but it is not scrupulously accurate. In *Shakespeare and the Classical Tradition*, John W. Velz lists and briefly describes what has been written on *Timon* up to 1960. Francelia Butler devotes a whole book, full of miscellaneous information, to *The Strange Critical Fortunes of Shakespeare's 'Timon of Athens'*, but its judgements are often ill considered.

REFERENCES

Coriolanus

TEXTS AND TEXTUAL STUDIES

Brockbank, Philip (ed.), *Coriolanus* (Arden Shakespeare, London, 1976).
Brower, Reuben (ed.), *The Tragedy of Coriolanus* (Signet Shakespeare, New York, 1966); introduction reprinted in revised form in his *Hero and Saint: Shakespeare and the Graeco-Roman Heroic Tradition* (New York, 1971), 354–81.

Furness, H. H., Jr. (ed.), *The Tragedie of Coriolanus* (New Variorum edition, Philadelphia, Pa., 1928).

Harrison, G. B., 'A Note on *Coriolanus*', in *Joseph Quincy Adams Memorial Studies*, ed. James G. McManaway *et al.* (Washington, DC, 1948), 239–52.

Hibbard, G. R. (ed.), *Coriolanus* (New Penguin Shakespeare, Harmondsworth, 1967).

Levin, Harry (ed.), *The Tragedy of Coriolanus* (Pelican Shakespeare, Baltimore, Md., 1956).

Wilson, John Dover (ed.), *The Tragedy of Coriolanus* (New Shakespeare, Cambridge, 1960).

CRITICAL STUDIES AND COMMENTARY

Adelman, Janet, ' "Anger's My Meat": Feeding, Dependency, and Aggression in *Coriolanus*', in *Shakespeare: Pattern of Excelling Nature*, ed. David Bevington and Jay L. Halio (Cranbury, NJ, 1978), 108–24; reprinted in *Representing Shakespeare*, ed. Murray M. Schwartz and Coppélia Kahn (Baltimore, Md., 1980), 129–49.

Barkan, Leonard, *Nature's Work of Art: The Human Body as Image of the World* (New Haven, Conn., 1975).

Barton, Anne, 'Livy, Machiavelli, and Shakespeare's *Coriolanus*', *Shakespeare Survey 38* (1985), 115–29.

Berry, Ralph, 'The Metamorphoses of *Coriolanus*', *Shakespeare Quarterly*, 26 (1975), 172–83.

—— 'Sexual Imagery in *Coriolanus*', *SEL* 13 (1973), 301–16.

Bradley, A. C., '*Coriolanus*', British Academy Lecture 1912, reprinted in *Studies in Shakespeare*, ed. Peter Alexander (London, 1964), 219–37.

—— *Shakespearean Tragedy* (London, 1904).

Browning, I. R., '*Coriolanus*: Boy of Tears', *Essays in Criticism*, 5 (1955), 18–31.

Bullough, Geoffrey (ed.), *Narrative and Dramatic Sources of Shakespeare*, vol. v (London, 1964).

Burke, Kenneth, '*Coriolanus* and the Delights of Faction', *Hudson Review*, 19 (1966), 185–202.

Calderwood, James L., '*Coriolanus*: Wordless Meanings and Meaningless Words', *SEL* 6 (1966), 211–24.

Campbell, Oscar James, *Shakespeare's Satire* (New York, 1943).

Cantor, Paul A., *Shakespeare's Rome* (Ithaca, NY, 1976).

Charney, Maurice, *Shakespeare's Roman Plays: The Function of Imagery in the Drama* (Cambridge, Mass., 1961).

—— (ed.), *Discussions of Shakespeare's Roman Plays* (Boston, Mass., 1964).

Clemen, Wolfgang H., *The Development of Shakespeare's Imagery* (London, 1951; 2nd edn., with new preface, 1977).

Coleridge, Samuel Taylor, *Shakespearean Criticism*, ed. T. M. Raysor, 2 vols. (Cambridge, Mass., 1930; Everyman's Library, London, 1960).

Colman, E. A. M., 'The End of Coriolanus', *ELH* 34 (1967), 1–20.

Danson, Lawrence N., 'Metonymy and *Coriolanus*', *Philological Quarterly*, 52 (1973), 30–42.

Davidson, Clifford, 'Coriolanus: A Study in Political Dislocation', *Shakespeare Studies*, 4 (1968), 263–74.

Dean, Leonard F., 'Voice and Deed in *Coriolanus*', *University of Kansas City Review* 21 (1955), 177–82.

Doran, Madeleine, ' "All's in anger": The Language of Contention in *Coriolanus*', in her *Shakespeare's Dramatic Language* (Madison, Wis., 1976), 182–217.

Eliot, T. S., 'Hamlet' (1919), in *Selected Essays 1917–1932* (London, 1932), 141–6.

Ellis-Fermor, Una, 'Coriolanus', in *Shakespeare the Dramatist*, ed. Kenneth Muir (London, 1961), 60–77.

Enright, D. J., '*Coriolanus*: Tragedy or Debate?', in his *The Apothecary's Shop* (London, 1957), 32–53; reprinted in *Discussions*, ed. Charney (Boston, Mass.), 156–70.

Farnham, Willard, *Shakespeare's Tragic Frontier* (Berkeley, Calif., 1950).

Frye, Dean, 'Commentary in Shakespeare: The Case of Coriolanus', *Shakespeare Studies*, 1 (1965), 105–17.

Goldman, Michael, 'Characterizing Coriolanus', *Shakespeare Survey 34* (1981), 73–84.

—— 'Coriolanus and the Crowd', in his *Shakespeare and the Energies of Drama* (Princeton, NJ, 1972), 109–23.

Gordon, D. J., 'Name and Fame: Shakespeare's Coriolanus', in *Papers Mainly Shakespearian*, ed. G. I. Duthie (Edinburgh, 1964), 40–57.

Granville-Barker, Harley, *Prefaces to Shakespeare*, Fifth Series (London, 1947).

Gurr, Andrew, '*Coriolanus* and the Body Politic', *Shakespeare Survey 28* (1975), 63–9.

Hale, David G., '*Coriolanus*: The Death of a Political Metaphor', *Shakespeare Quarterly*, 22 (1971), 197–202.

—— 'Intestine Sedition: The Fable of the Belly', *Comparative Literature Studies*, 5 (1968), 377–88.

Halio, Jay L., '*Coriolanus*: Shakespeare's "Drama of Reconciliation" ', *Shakespeare Studies*, 6 (1972), 289–303.

Harding, D. W., 'Women's Fantasy of Manhood: A Shakespearian Theme', *Shakespeare Quarterly*, 20 (1969), 245–53.

Hazlitt, William, *Characters of Shakespear's Plays* (London, 1817; World's Classics, London, 1917).

Heuer, Hermann, 'From Plutarch to Shakespeare: A Study of Coriolanus', *Shakespeare Survey 10* (1957), 50–9.

Hill, R. F., '*Coriolanus*: Violentest Contrariety', *Essays and Studies*, 17 (1964), 12–23.

Hofling, Charles K., 'An Interpretation of Shakespeare's Coriolanus', *American Imago*, 14 (1957), 407–35.

Holstun, James, 'Tragic Superfluity in *Coriolanus*', *ELH* 50 (1983), 485–507.

Honigmann, E. A. J., 'Shakespeare's Plutarch', *Shakespeare Quarterly*, 10 (1959), 25–33.

Huffman, Clifford Chalmers, '*Coriolanus' in Context* (Lewisburg, Pa., 1971).

Ide, Richard S., *Possessed with Greatness: The Heroic Tragedies of Chapman and Shakespeare* (Chapel Hill, NC, 1980).

Johnson, Samuel, *Johnson on Shakespeare*, ed. Arthur Sherbo (New Haven, Conn., 1968), vol. viii of the Yale Johnson.

Jorgensen, Paul A., *Shakespeare's Military World* (Berkeley, Calif., 1956).

Kahn, Coppélia, *Man's Estate: Masculine Identity in Shakespeare* (Berkeley and Los Angeles, Calif., 1981).

Knight, G. Wilson, *The Imperial Theme: Further Interpretations of Shakespeare's Tragedies Including the Roman Plays* (London, 1931).

Knights, L. C., *Further Explorations* (London, 1965).

—— 'Shakespeare and Political Wisdom: A Note on the Personalism of *Julius Caesar* and *Coriolanus*', *Sewanee Review*, 61 (1953), 43–55.

—— *Some Shakespearean Themes* (London, 1959).

Kott, Jan, *Shakespeare Our Contemporary* (London, 1964).

Lees, F. N., '*Coriolanus*, Aristotle, and Bacon', *RES* NS 1 (1950), 114–25.

Lewis, Wyndham, *The Lion and the Fox* (London, 1927).

Lowe, Lisa, ' "Say I play the man I am": Gender and Politics in *Coriolanus*', *Kenyon Review*, 8 (1986), 86–95.

MacCallum, M. W., *Shakespeare's Roman Plays and Their Background* (London, 1910; reprinted with a new foreword, 1967).

Maxwell, J. C., 'Animal Imagery in *Coriolanus*', *MLR* 42 (1947), 417–21.

—— 'Shakespeare's Roman Plays: 1900–1956', *Shakespeare Survey* 10 (1957), 1–11.

Meszaros, Patricia K., ' "There is a world elsewhere": Tragedy and History in *Coriolanus*', *SEL* 16 (1976), 273–85.

Miola, Robert S., *Shakespeare's Rome* (Cambridge, 1983).

Muir, Kenneth, 'The Background of *Coriolanus*', *Shakespeare Quarterly*, 10 (1959), 137–45.

—— 'In Defence of the Tribunes', *Essays in Criticism*, 4 (1954), 331–3.

—— 'Menenius's Fable', *N & Q* 198 (1953), 240–2.

—— 'Shakespeare and Politics', in *Shakespeare in a Changing World*, ed. Arnold Kettle (London, 1964), 65–83.

—— *Shakespeare's Sources*, vol. i (London, 1961).

Odell, G. C. D., *Shakespeare—from Betterton to Irving*, 2 vols. (New York, 1920).

Oliver, H. J., 'Coriolanus As Tragic Hero', *Shakespeare Quarterly*, 10 (1959), 53–60.

Palmer, John, *Political Characters of Shakespeare* (London, 1945).

Parker, R. B., '*Coriolanus* and "th' interpretation of the time"', in *Mirror up to Shakespeare: Essays in Honour of G. R. Hibbard*, ed. J. C. Gray (Toronto, 1984), 261–76.

Paster, Gail Kern, 'To Starve with Feeding: The City in *Coriolanus*', *Shakespeare Studies*, 11 (1978), 123–44.

Pettet, E. C., '*Coriolanus* and the Midlands Insurrection of 1607', *Shakespeare Survey 3* (1950), 34–42.

Phillips, James Emerson, Jr., *The State in Shakespeare's Greek and Roman Plays* (New York, 1940).

Putney, Rufus, '*Coriolanus* and His Mother', *Psychoanalytic Quarterly*, 31 (1962), 364–81.

Rabkin, Norman, '*Coriolanus*: The Tragedy of Politics', *Shakespeare Quarterly*, 17 (1966), 195–212.

Rossiter, A. P., *Angel with Horns* (London, 1961).

Rouda, F. H., '*Coriolanus*—A Tragedy of Youth', *Shakespeare Quarterly*, 12 (1961), 103–6.

Shanker, Sidney, 'Some Clues for *Coriolanus*', *Shakespeare Association Bulletin*, 24 (1949), 209–13.

Shaw, G. Bernard, *Shaw on Shakespeare*, ed. Edwin Wilson (London, 1962; Penguin Shakespeare Library, Harmondsworth, 1969).

Sicherman, Carol M., '*Coriolanus*: The Failure of Words', *ELH* 39 (1972), 198–207.

Spencer, Hazelton, *Shakespeare Improved* (London, 1927).

Spencer, T. J. B., foreword to reprint of MacCallum, *Shakespeare's Roman Plays* (London, 1967).

—— 'Shakespeare and the Elizabethan Romans', *Shakespeare Survey 10* (1957), 27–38; reprinted in *Discussions*, ed. Charney.

—— *Shakespeare: The Roman Plays* (Writers and Their Work, 157; London, 1963).

—— (ed.), *Shakespeare's Plutarch* (Harmondsworth, 1964).

Sprengnether, Madelon, 'Annihilating Intimacy in *Coriolanus*', in *Women in the Middle Ages and the Renaissance*, ed. Mary Beth Rose (Syracuse, NY, 1986), 89–111.

Spurgeon, Caroline F. E., *Shakespeare's Imagery and What It Tells Us* (Cambridge, 1935).

Stirling, Brents, *The Populace in Shakespeare* (New York, 1949).

Traversi, D. A., *An Approach to Shakespeare*, 3rd edn., 2 vols. (London, 1968–9).

—— '*Coriolanus*', *Scrutiny*, 6 (1937), 43–58.

—— *Shakespeare: The Roman Plays* (London, 1963).

Trewin, J. C., *Shakespeare on the English Stage 1900–1964* (London, 1964).

Velz, John W., 'Cracking Strong Curbs Asunder: Roman Destiny and the Roman Hero in *Coriolanus*', *English Literary Renaissance*, 13 (1983), 58–69.

—— *Shakespeare and the Classical Tradition: A Critical Guide to Commentary*, *1660–1960* (Minneapolis, Minn., 1968).

Waith, Eugene M., *The Herculean Hero* (New York, 1962).

Wickham, Glynne, '*Coriolanus*: Shakespeare's Tragedy in Rehearsal and Performance', in *Later Shakespeare*, ed. J. R. Brown and B. Harris (Stratford-upon-Avon Studies, 8; London, 1966), 167–81; reprinted in his *Shakespeare's Dramatic Heritage* (London, 1969), 232–48.

Wilson, Emmett, Jr., '*Coriolanus*: The Anxious Bridegroom', *American Imago*, 25 (1968), 224–41.

Zeeveld, W. Gordon, '*Coriolanus* and Jacobean Politics', *MLR* 57 (1962), 321–34.

Timon of Athens

TEXTS AND TEXTUAL STUDIES

Adams, Joseph Quincy, '*Timon of Athens* and the Irregularities in the First Folio', *JEGP* 7 (1908), 53–63.

Charney, Maurice (ed.), *The Life of Timon of Athens* (Signet Shakespeare, New York, 1965).

Greg, W. W., *The Shakespeare First Folio* (Oxford, 1955).

Hibbard, G. R. (ed.), *Timon of Athens* (New Penguin Shakespeare, Harmondsworth, 1970).

Hinman, Charlton (ed.), *The Life of Timon of Athens* (Pelican Shakespeare, Baltimore, Md., 1964).

Maxwell, J. C., (ed.), *The Life of Timon of Athens* (New Shakespeare, Cambridge, 1957).

Oliver, H. J. (ed.), *Timon of Athens* (Arden edition, London, 1963).

Spencer, T. J. B., 'Shakespeare Learns the Value of Money: The Dramatist at Work on *Timon of Athens*', *Shakespeare Survey 6* (1953), 75–8.

Wells, Stanley, and Gary Taylor, with John Jowett and William Montgomery, *William Shakespeare: A Textual Companion* (Oxford, 1987).

CRITICAL STUDIES AND COMMENTARY

Adams, Joseph Quincy, 'The Timon Plays', *JEGP* 9 (1910), 506–24.

Bonnard, Georges, 'Note sur les sources de *Timon of Athens*', *Études anglaises*, 7 (1954), 59–69.

Bradbrook, Muriel C., '*The Comedy of Timon*: A Reveling Play of the Inner Temple', *Renaissance Drama*, 9 (1966), 83–103.

—— *The Tragic Pageant of 'Timon of Athens'* (Cambridge, 1966); reprinted in her *Shakespeare the Craftsman* (London, 1969), 144–67.

Bradley, A. C., *Shakespearean Tragedy* (London, 1904; reprinted 1978).

Brill, Lesley W., 'Truth and *Timon of Athens*', *Modern Language Quarterly*, 40 (1979), 17–36.

Bullough, Geoffrey (ed.), *Narrative and Dramatic Sources of Shakespeare*, vol. vi (London, 1966).

Bulman, James C., Jr., 'The Date and Production of "Timon" Reconsidered', *Shakespeare Survey* 27 (1974), 111–27.

—— 'Shakespeare's Use of the "Timon" Comedy', *Shakespeare Survey* 29 (1976), 103–16.

Butler, Francelia, *The Strange Critical Fortunes of Shakespeare's 'Timon of Athens'* (Ames, Ia., 1966).

Campbell, Oscar James, *Shakespeare's Satire* (New York, 1943).

Chambers, E. K., *Shakespeare: A Survey* (London, 1925).

—— *William Shakespeare: A Study of Facts and Problems*, 2 vols. (Oxford, 1930; reprinted 1989); abridged by Charles Williams, *A Short Life of Shakespeare with the Sources* (Oxford, 1933).

Clemen, Wolfgang H., *The Development of Shakespeare's Imagery* (London, 1951; 2nd edn., with new preface, 1977).

Coleridge, Samuel Taylor, *Shakespearean Criticism*, ed. T. M. Raysor, 2 vols. (Cambridge, Mass., 1930; Everyman's Library, London, 1960).

Collins, A. S., '*Timon of Athens*: A Reconsideration', *RES* 22 (1946), 96–108.

Cook, David, '*Timon of Athens*', *Shakespeare Survey* 16 (1963), 83–94; reprinted in the Signet edition.

Davidson, Clifford, '*Timon of Athens*: The Iconography of False Friendship', *Huntington Library Quarterly*, 43 (1980), 181–200.

Dowden, Edward, *Shakspere: A Critical Study of His Mind and Art* (London, 1875).

Ellis-Fermor, Una, '*Timon of Athens*: An Unfinished Play', *RES* 18 (1942), 270–83; reprinted in her *Shakespeare the Dramatist*, ed. Kenneth Muir (London, 1961), 158–76.

Empson, William, *The Structure of Complex Words* (London, 1951).

Farnham, Willard, *Shakespeare's Tragic Frontier* (Berkeley, Calif., 1950).

Fly, Richard D., 'The Ending of *Timon of Athens*: A Reconsideration', *Criticism*, 15 (1973), 242–52.

Frye, Northrop, *A Natural Perspective: The Development of Shakespearean Comedy and Romance* (New York, 1965).

Fulton, Robert C., III, 'Timon, Cupid, and the Amazons', *Shakespeare Studies*, 9 (1976), 283–99.

Gomme, Andor, '*Timon of Athens*', *Essays in Criticism*, 9 (1959), 107–25.

Handelman, Susan, '*Timon of Athens*: The Rage of Disillusion', *American Imago*, 36 (1979), 45–68; reprinted in part in the new Signet edition.

Hazlitt, William, *Characters of Shakespear's Plays* (London, 1817; World's Classics, London, 1917).

Honigmann, E. A. J., '*Timon of Athens*', *Shakespeare Quarterly*, 12 (1961), 3–20.

Hulme, Hilda M., *Explorations in Shakespeare's Language* (London, 1962).

Hunter, G. K., 'The Last Tragic Heroes', in *Later Shakespeare*, ed. J. R. Brown and B. Harris (Stratford-upon-Avon Studies, 8; London, 1966), 11–28.

Johnson, Samuel, *Johnson on Shakespeare*, ed. Arthur Sherbo (New Haven, Conn., 1968), vol. viii of the Yale Johnson.

Jorgensen, Paul A., *Shakespeare's Military World* (Berkeley, Calif., 1956).

Knight, G. Wilson, *The Wheel of Fire: Interpretations of Shakespearian Tragedy* (London, 1930; rev. edn., 1949).

Knights, L. C., 'Timon of Athens', in his *The Morality of Art: Essays Presented to G. Wilson Knight*, ed. D. W. Jefferson (London, 1969), 1–17.

Lancashire, Anne, 'Timon of Athens: Shakespeare's *Dr. Faustus*', *Shakespeare Quarterly*, 21 (1970), 35–44.

Leech, Clifford, 'Shakespeare's Greeks', in *Stratford Papers on Shakespeare, 1963*, ed. B. W. Jackson (Toronto, 1964), 1–20.

—— *Shakespeare's Tragedies* (London, 1950).

Levin, Harry, 'Shakespeare's Misanthrope', *Shakespeare Survey* 26 (1973), 89–94.

Maxwell, J. C., 'Timon of Athens', *Scrutiny*, 15 (1948), 195–208.

Mellamphy, Ninian, 'Wormwood in the Wood outside Athens: *Timon* and the Problem for the Audience', in *'Bad' Shakespeare*, ed. Maurice Charney (Rutherford, NJ, 1988), 166–75.

Merchant, W. M., *Shakespeare and the Artist* (London, 1959).

—— '*Timon* and the Conceit of Art', *Shakespeare Quarterly*, 6 (1955), 249–57.

Muir, Kenneth, 'Timon of Athens and the Cash Nexus', *Modern Quarterly Miscellany*, 1 (1947), 57–76; reprinted in his *The Singularity of Shakespeare and Other Essays* (Liverpool, 1977), 56–75.

Odell, G. C. D., *Shakespeare—from Betterton to Irving*, 2 vols. (New York, 1920).

Pettet, E..C., 'Timon of Athens: The Disruption of Feudal Morality', *RES* 23 (1947), 321–36.

Phillips, James Emerson, Jr., *The State in Shakespeare's Greek and Roman Plays* (New York, 1940).

Ramsey, Jarold W., 'Timon's Imitation of Christ', *Shakespeare Studies*, 2 (1966), 162–73.

Richardson, William, *Essays on Shakespeare's Dramatic Characters*, 2nd edn. (London, 1785; section on *Timon* reprinted in the Signet edition).

Ruszkiewicz, John J., *Timon of Athens: An Annotated Bibliography* (New York, 1986).

Scott, W. I. D., *Shakespeare's Melancholics* (London, 1962).

Sisson, C. J., *The Mythical Sorrows of Shakespeare*, British Academy Lecture, 1934.

Slights, William W. E., '*Genera mixta* and *Timon of Athens*', *Studies in Philology*, 74 (1977), 39–62.

Smith, G. C. Moore, 'Notes on Some English University Plays', *MLR* 3 (1907–8), 141–56.

Soellner, Rolf, *Timon of Athens: Shakespeare's Pessimistic Tragedy* (Columbus, Ohio, 1979). With a stage history by Gary Jay Williams.

Somerville, H., *Madness in Shakespearian Tragedy* (London, 1929).

Spencer, Hazelton, *Shakespeare Improved* (London, 1927).

Spencer, T. J. B., ' "Greeks" and "Merrygreeks": A Background to *Timon of Athens* and *Troilus and Cressida*', in *Essays on Shakespeare and Elizabethan Drama in Honor of Hardin Craig*, ed. Richard Hosley (Columbia, Mo., 1962), 223–33.

Spurgeon, Caroline F. E., *Shakespeare's Imagery and What It Tells Us* (Cambridge, 1935).

'*Timon of Athens*: Some Earlier Appearances', *Times Educational Supplement* (30 May 1952).

Traversi, Derek A., *An Approach to Shakespeare*, 3rd edn., 2 vols. (London, 1968–9), vol. ii.

Trewin, J. C., *Shakespeare on the English Stage 1900–1964* (London, 1964).

Van Doren, Mark, *Shakespeare* (London, 1939).

Velz, John W., *Shakespeare and the Classical Tradition: A Critical Guide to Commentary, 1660–1960* (Minneapolis, Minn., 1968).

Walker, Lewis, '*Timon of Athens* and the Morality Tradition', *Shakespeare Studies*, 12 (1979), 159–77.

Wallace, John M., '*Timon of Athens* and the Three Graces: Shakespeare's Senecan Study', *Modern Philology*, 83 (1986), 349–63.

Williams, Stanley T., 'Some Versions of *Timon of Athens* on the Stage', *Modern Philology*, 18 (1920), 269–85.

Wilson, Harold S., *On the Design of Shakespearian Tragedy* (Toronto, 1957).

Woods, Andrew H., 'Syphilis in Shakespeare's Tragedy of Timon of Athens', *American Journal of Psychiatry*, 91 (1934), 95–107.

16 | The First Tetralogy and King John

MICHAEL HATTAWAY

TEXTS AND TEXTUAL STUDIES

Presenting the Henry VI plays and *King John* to modern readers has been seen, until recently, primarily as a massive task in textual criticism and theatrical history (Alexander, 1929; Honigmann, 1982, 1985; Carroll, 1985). Solving the problems of text and provenance left editors and scholars little time to describe the particular forms of these early Elizabethan history plays, and to attend, without condescension, to their ceremonious theatrical forms and overtly rhetorical verbal styles.

Only one text of *1 Henry VI* survives, that printed in the Folio of 1623. *2* and *3 Henry VI*, on the other hand, are related respectively to a series of quarto texts, entitled *The First Part of the Contention betwixt the Two Famous Houses of York and Lancaster* and an octavo text *The True Tragedy of Richard Duke of York*, which was reprinted in quarto. The best scholarly opinion (see Wells and Taylor, 1987) now believes that these are 'bad quartos', that is texts reconstructed from memory generally by actors, rather than first drafts or early versions of the story by other writers (Wilson, Cambridge edition, 1952). However they contain stage directions which may well record certain details of early performances and which may also offer evidence of revision after the first performances, by the author or by the company, for touring productions. Editors who believe that these texts are bad quartos are likely to include in their texts some of Q's stage directions, unlike editors who still believe that they are early drafts.

Doubts about the plays' authorship (particularly of *1 Henry VI*) began in the eighteenth century with Edmond Malone, who

Michael Hattaway

posed questions which are still the matter for debate (Wells and Taylor, 1987). Editors found the styles of the Henry VI plays unfamiliar and, assuming that Q's title *The First Part* ... indicated the beginning of a series of plays rather than describing the content of the action within that series, argued that *1 Henry VI* was written after Parts 2 and 3, probably in collaboration with the so-called University Wits.

The editions of the Henry VI plays by John Dover Wilson for Cambridge's New Shakespeare (1952) represent the culmination of a long line of historical criticism which, because it was sceptical of Shakespeare's sole authorship, found little merit in the texts. In his edition of *1 Henry VI*, Wilson offers many verbal parallels to passages in the writings of Greene, Peele, and Nashe whom he believed to have collaborated on the play. There is little critical analysis although there is some useful material on theatrical history. The new Arden editions by Andrew Cairncross (1962–1964) are the most substantial modern editions (the plays did not appear in the New Variorum series). Cairncross displayed a sturdy belief that the plays were by Shakespeare and written in the order of the events that they dramatize—offering a clear account of contrary arguments. His (briefer) critical accounts of the plays follow the orthodoxy that obtained when he wrote his introductions: that the plays portray 'the retribution on Henry VI for the original sin of his grandfather' (i, p. xlii). There is little theatrical analysis but some useful source material in appendices. His textual hypotheses and editorial interventions are often highly contentious. The Signet editions of the plays (*1 Henry VI* by Lawrence V. Ryan (1967), *2 Henry VI* by Arthur Freeman (1967), and *3 Henry VI* by Milton Crane (1968)), have brief lively introductions but little annotation, and each usefully reprints some source material and a relevant part of the essay by Philip Brockbank (see below), which established modern critical interest in the play, as well as essays by Samuel Johnson and Sir Barry Jackson (1953) among others. Norman Sanders, who edited the plays for the New Penguin series (1981), offers straightforward introductions to the politics of each play and, within the limited compass of the series, helpful notes that deal particularly fully with Shakespeare's use of his sources; he also gives biographies of the characters, as well as useful genealogical tables. Other editions for the Pelican Shakespeare (Part I edited by David Bevington, Parts 2 and 3 by R. K. Turner and G. W. Williams

(1967)), offer brief introductions and less full annotation. The BBC Television Shakespeare texts with introductions by John Wilders (1983) offer useful material by the director Jane Howell of productions which were particularly successful (see below).

A new wave of disintegrationism was signalled by the appearance of the edition of *The Complete Works* by Stanley Wells and Gary Taylor and the accompanying *Textual Companion*. The editors conclude from stylistic analysis and rare word tests that 1 *Henry VI* was written after Parts 2 and 3. It is, accordingly, printed after the two other parts which carry the titles of their Quarto forms (see above). The findings of these editors, however, have to be weighed against the experience of those theatre audiences who find 1 *Henry VI* a necessary synopsis of parts of the Hundred Years' War before parts 2 and 3 focus in on the Wars of the Roses, and of those critics who, by investigating themes and structures as well as textual matters, see no reason to insist too loudly on the possibility of multiple authorship or on composition in an order different from that offered by the Folio. Readers will find in the Oxford Shakespeare a contentiously high degree of editorial interventionism in the text which derives from the results of these statistical analyses, as well as a commendable attempt to make explicit in stage directions what is latent in the text.

The Arden edition of *Richard III*, edited by Antony Hammond, did not appear until 1981. Hammond offers an extremely full analysis of the complex relationship between the Folio text and the eight quartos that appeared from 1597 to 1634 (a testimony to the play's popularity), of the play's sources (see also Brooks, 1979, 1980), and its performance history. Kristian Smidt published a very useful parallel text version of the first quarto and first Folio (Oslo, 1969), and Julie Hankey (1981), in the Plays in Performance Series, offers a text the annotations of which record details of theatrical business in notable past productions as well as a full history of the play in performance. The Pelican text, edited by G. Blakemore Evans (1959), the Signet edited by Mark Eccles (1964), and the New Penguin edited by E. A. J. Honigmann (1968), all have useful but brief introductions. The New Variorum edition, by H. H. Furness, appeared in 1908. Clemen's book length study of the play (1968) works through it scene by scene.

E. A. J. Honigmann's introduction to his Arden Edition (1954) offers a defence of the unity of *King John* based on an examination of its themes. Honigmann makes the case that *King John* came first and that *The Troublesome Raigne of King John*, an anonymous two-part play printed in 1591, is a bad quarto. He was followed by William H. Matchett in his Signet Edition. The essays reprinted by Matchett also concentrate on image and theme. R. L. Smallwood, however, in his New Penguin edition (1974), reverses these priorities and strongly argues that *The Troublesome Raigne* is a source of *King John*, as did John Dover Wilson in his New (Cambridge) Shakespeare of 1936, and as does A. R. Braunmuller in the Oxford Shakespeare edition of 1989. The New Variorum edition, by H. H. Furness, appeared in 1919.

CRITICISM AND COMMENTARY

For many years the Henry VI plays and *King John* did not get a good critical press (Jenkins, 1953; Burden, 1985; Berry, 1986; Hinchcliffe, 1986). Because, on the other hand, *Richard III* has always been popular in the theatre because of the histrionic possibilities of its central part (Shaw, 1961; Sher, 1985; Hassell, 1985), it has received its share of critical attention, although usually as a tragedy rather than a historical drama (Brownlow, 1977; Brooke, 1984). Now that the Henry VI plays too have been demonstrated to possess striking theatrical virtues of their own (Hodgdon, 1980), directors and critics have explored *Richard III* anew, seeing it possessed of links as significant with the history plays that precede as with the 'great tragedies' which succeed (French, 1968). Notable modern productions have placed it as the last movement in the 'first tetralogy'—a notion, however, which is as contentious in this context as in that of the *Richard II–Henry V* 'cycle'.

King John, more verbally sophisticated, has continued to puzzle because of its form, even though it has been performed regularly since the Restoration—unlike the Henry VI plays. It has been seen to be dominated by tragedy (Price, 1970) but important modern productions (Smallwood, 1976; David, 1978) have confirmed those critics who have seen it possessed of a sardonic comic texture (Grennan, 1978), and as an innovative and experimental play of debate, one that fits but awkwardly with the dominant genres of tragedy and comedy, but which may well look forward to the 'problem' plays with their 'politician-actors' written in the first decade of the seventeenth century (Schanzer,

1963; Elliott, 1965; Burckhardt, 1968; Wixson, 1981; Vaughan, 1984).

A series of modern revivals of the *Henry VI* plays has surprised and delighted modern audiences (Jackson, 1953; Sprague, 1964; Brown, 1966; Barton, 1970) and placed in perspective the negative opinions of those critics who, paying more attention to problems of theatrical history and textual criticism, felt bound to critically abuse the corpses they were cutting up. Instead of attempting to dress the plays up in historical costumes and place them in illusionistic sets, directors have set them in empty spaces with as much emphasis on theatrical rhythm as on poetry, on ensemble work as on individual performance (Hattaway, 1982). They have been treated as epics, but epics in the Brechtian sense, concerned with the origins, nature, and transfer of power, rather than as epics in the nineteenth-century sense, texts illustrating the manifest destiny of England. They have thereby been revealed, perhaps, as political rather than 'history' plays, demonstrations of *how* history is made with an emphasis on the relationships between political groups and contesting ideologies. Knights (1957), however, offers a useful reminder that critical accounts of the texts which divorce 'politics' from moral experience are bound to be reductive. It is noteworthy that the productions of the 'tetralogy' for the BBC television series in 1983 were generally held to be some of the most successful (Bulman and Coursen, 1988)—because of the refusal to go for any kind of historical realism. The players did wear 'Plantagenet' costumes, but the action was filmed in a kind of modern adventure playground, knocked together out of old doors and pieces of wood, suggesting the fragility of the institutions Shakespeare was anatomizing.

Perhaps as a consequence of these theatrical analyses, it can be demonstrated that the plays have their own, functional styles (Turner, 1974; Watkins, 1975; Clemen, 1980; Knights, 1980; Hibbard, 1981; Bulman, 1985), and need not be written off as failures to achieve the more musical qualities of the great tragedies. John W. Blanpied (1983) examines style in the context of meta-drama (compare Bergeron, 1977), writing about the evolving relationship of subject to medium, history to drama. Shakespeare's mind at once imposes and reveals forms; his style is perpetually self-reflexive.

The fundamental change in modern accounts of the plays is that few critics are now able to see them simply aligning

themselves with one great schematic view of history or 'order'
(Tillyard, 1944). This challenge to orthodoxy has come from
several directions. First, there has been closer attention to what
is actually in the texts and the way in which references to
a transcendental power controlling the action might serve to
illustrate character rather than derive from the author (French,
1968, 1969, 1974). Shakespeare, rather than being an ideological
time-server to the Tudor régime, may offer an ironic and comprehensive analysis which encouraged a historian to call him
'the greatest of all Tudor thinkers' (Morris, 1953). Man might be
seen to be making his own history—and contriving his own
destruction (Brockbank, 1961; Brooke, 1968). Characters concentrate on the claims of family at the expense of claims of state
(Berry, 1975; Berman, 1962) and, even in these early plays, an
analysis of motive as complex as that we bring to the bond
between Prince Hal and Falstaff in the Henry IV plays might be
applied to the relationship between Henry VI and his protector
Gloucester (Robinson, 1977). Robert Ornstein (1972), on the
other hand, argued that the plays are shaped more by dramatic
than dogmatic considerations, and Burckhardt (1968; compare
Riddell, 1977) showed the degree of artfulness that enables
complex meaning to be found in episodes, the significance of
which tended to be obliterated by the imposition of schematic
readings.

We might also note developments in the writing of history of
the period, in the analysis of Elizabethan political ideas (Morris,
1953; Kelly, 1970), and in modern critical theory. An earlier
generation of critics, led by Lily B. Campbell, with her *Shakespeare's
'Histories': Mirrors of Elizabethan Policy* (1947), cleared the way by
indicating that these plays were not to be regarded as flawed
chronicles of what had actually happened in Plantagenet times
but as 'mirrors' of political matters pertinent to the age in which
they were written (Bevington, 1968). As political plays their
concern is with power, with the relationship between what is
and what ought to be (Leggatt, 1988), with encounters between
different kinds of historiography (Goy-Blanquet, 1986); they
deal with groups, factions, political themes (Prior, 1973), with the
construction of the feminine and an analysis of the roles of
women (Williamson, 1987; Jackson, 1988), and with changes in
notions of honour and heroism (Riggs, 1971). They are not just
narratives peopled with psychologically consistent 'characters',

but look at the mutually determining relationships between personality and circumstance (Wilders, 1978), at institutions as well as events (Boris, 1978). There are no heroes in the Henry VI plays or *King John*: Dover Wilson's assumption that Talbot was the only candidate to be 'hero' of *1 Henry VI* and his observation that the 'hero' of the first play was not mentioned in the later ones led him to a distorted view of the history of the play's composition.

The history of the reign of Elizabeth has been revised, particularly in the light of what has been discovered by social historians (Williams, 1979; Palliser, 1983; Slack, 1984; Sharpe, 1987), so that now it has become customary to see the period as one of crisis rather than settlement, of political and religious debate and scepticism rather than certainty. Shakespeare may have appeared more of a radical and oppositional writer to his contemporaries (Hattaway, 1988) than, as Tillyard (1944) presented him, as an apologist for 'the Tudor Myth' as that myth seemed to Tillyard to be expounded in the chronicles of Edward Hall. It can now be demonstrated that it was Holinshed's chronicle in the edition of 1587 rather than Hall which lay to hand during the composition of the Henry VI plays (Boswell-Stone, 1896; Bullough, 1960; Hosley, 1968; Saccio, 1977). Shakespeare did turn to Hall for the 'essays'—pen portraits of individuals, reflections on the shapes of events—which stud the chronicle, but, like Hall himself, shows signs of as much scepticism as endorsement of the idea of history as providentially ordered (Kelly, 1970; Kastan, 1983–4).

Certainly history plays made the authorities uncomfortable: on 12 November, 1589 the Privy Council wrote to the Archbishop of Canterbury, the Lord Mayor of London, and the Master of the Revels asking them each to appoint someone to scrutinize all plays performed in and about the City of London because the players had taken 'upon themselves certain matters of divinity and state unfit to be suffered' (Chambers, 1923, iv. 306). This suggests not only that playhouses were seen as centres of disorder and riot but that the drama played in them could appear subversive. (If Shakespeare had started to write some of these plays as early as 1587 (Honigmann, 1982, 1985) it could even be that the Privy Council sought to censor the writings of England's 'national poet'). Alternative 'oppositional' readings have also been encouraged by developments in critical theory (Holderness, 1985; Tennenhouse, 1986; Kastan, 1986), developments which 'decentre' the author as the origin of a play's meaning, analyse how readings and critical accounts of the plays can be a function of the ideological assumptions of readers or audiences, and show how, in the text and the study, scenes which an earlier generation had taken as positives, can be viewed from other perspectives (Braunmuller, 1988). Readings of the texts which can accept openness in endings rather than closure (Kastan, 1982), inconsistency rather than consistency (Smidt, 1982), have been characteristic of recent criticism. In particular, a coherent reading of this first cycle can be generated which is materialist and pragmatic—men make their own history (Siegel, 1986)—to complement if not displace readings which show history as made by God.

When Shakespeare wrote *Richard III* there is little doubt that he intended the play to sound at its ending a note of celebration for the birth of the new Tudor dynasty (Ornstein, 1972). The play is often grimly comic and matches political virtuosity against political naïveté (Rossiter, 1961). These emphases in the play may be weighed against those critics who have seen it dominated by a grim providential scheme of retributive justice. Shakespeare's main source was Sir Thomas More's *The History of King Richard the Third* as it appeared filtered through Hall and Holinshed, and More was a servant of the Tudors. There is no doubt, either, that he was aware of the old form of the morality play, a form that cast Richard into the role of the vice, a witty villain, and which worked generally by justifying the ways of God to man (Spivack, 1958)—although Evans (1982) argues that More fails to provide Shakespeare with antagonists forceful and sharply observed enough to make Richard's evil credible. But Shakespeare was also interested in the relationships between an individual and his role (Reese, 1961; Prior, 1973; Manheim, 1978), and between the King and the institution of monarchy (Braunmuller, 1984), and, in the case of Richard of Gloucester, his ability to create a fictional self and impose his fictions upon the world, a manifestation of his power. Instead therefore of seeing the play as a document which deploys an archaic form and a residual ideology to construct a simplified moral perspective on the action, it is possible to see it as a text that explores emergent ideas of self (Ure, 1974; Van Laan, 1978) and of varying relationships between power and authority (Sanders, 1968), and that questions the legitimacy of rebelling against an evil but legitimate ruler—Richard himself—a topic dramatized by Stanley's decision to change sides to Richmond (Gurr, 1974).

Henry A. Kelly (1970) even argues that the play burlesques the providential myth.

The play is dominated by the character of the hero. He is obviously witty, and, despite his appearance, not unattractive (Ornstein, 1972, p. 67; Berry, 1984). He does have a conscience—at the end of the play—but chooses to die bravely without exposing his vulnerabilities to the world (Armstrong, 1946). Perhaps he was brought into being by the world he inhabited (Prior, 1973) or putting this more subtly, his deformity was a presupposition of those about him which he was able to manipulate, in the words of a Freudian, 'by projecting and displacing its characteristics onto others' (Garber, 1987).

The form of *King John* has not ceased to puzzle, particularly those 'providentialist' critics who have to confront the play's obvious secularism. It seems a transitional piece with the Bastard both traditional bogey Machiavel and an acceptable and typical social figure, attractive in his 'outward accoutrement' (Danby, 1961). The play stands alone, unsupported by other texts in a tetralogy (Vaughan, 1984). Again the search for a hero can distort, although Adrien Bonjour (1951) sees a moral turning point for John when he commands the murder of Arthur. Reese (1961) and Ornstein (1972) brand it an artistic failure. Others have found unity through an analysis of themes as did James Calderwood (1959–60) who saw it dramatizing a clash between honour and commodity. William H. Matchett (1962) sees the play examining a range of candidates for kingship, and Bevington (1968) stresses the clash, topical in Tudor times, between the Bastard and the papacy. A collection of essays on various aspects of the play edited by Deborah T. Curren-Aquino was due to appear as this volume went to press.

Critical debate over the ideological content of these plays has predominated over their formal qualities. F. P. Wilson (1953) saw Shakespeare as the 'inventor' of the Elizabethan history play although Ribner (1957) saw Shakespeare's works related to earlier plays, moral and academic, and, like Tillyard, argued that the genre tended to inculcate patriotism and a Christian scheme of history. Dean (1982; compare Bulman, 1985) took further the analysis of romance elements described by Ribner, and Brooks (1979, 1980) studied the indebtedness of *Richard III* to the non-Christian Senecan tradition. Descriptions of the plays' theatrical forms were pioneered by Hereward T. Price (1951), who isolated the significance of interrupted ceremonies, and were developed, notably, in Emrys Jones's *Scenic Form in Shakespeare* (1971). Long analysed the use of music (1972), Clemen (1951) wrote on the set speech, Laroque (1988) analysed carnival elements. Theatrical images can be studied in Fleischer (1974). Emrys Jones, *The Origins of Shakespeare* (1977), revealed how rather than being primitive 'drum and trumpet things' as an eighteenth-century writer dismissed *Henry VI*, Shakespeare's early plays consciously and artfully draw upon the achievements and insights of Christian humanism and a rich heritage of earlier dramatic forms.

REFERENCES

TEXTS

Bevington, David (ed.), *The First Part of King Henry the Sixth* (Pelican Shakespeare, Baltimore, Md., 1966).

Cairncross, Andrew S. (ed.), *The First Part of King Henry VI* (Arden Shakespeare, London, 1962).

—— *The Second Part of King Henry VI* (Arden Shakespeare, London, 1957).

—— *The Third Part of King Henry VI* (Arden Shakespeare, London, 1964).

Crane, Milton (ed.), *Henry VI, Part Three* (The Signet Shakespeare, New York, 1968).

Freeman, Arthur (ed.), *Henry VI, Part Two* (The Signet Shakespeare, New York, 1967).

Hattaway, Michael (ed.), *Henry VI, Part One* (The New Cambridge Shakespeare, Cambridge, 1990).

Ryan, Lawrence V. (ed.), *Henry VI, Part One* (The Signet Shakespeare, New York, 1967).

Sanders, Norman (ed.), *Henry VI, Part One* (New Penguin Shakespeare, Harmondsworth, 1981).

—— *Henry VI, Part Two* (New Penguin Shakespeare, Harmondsworth, 1981).

—— *Henry VI, Part Three* (New Penguin Shakespeare, Harmondsworth, 1981).

Turner, R. K., and G. W. Williams, *The Second and Third Parts of King Henry the Sixth* (Pelican Shakespeare, Baltimore, Md., 1967).

Wilders, John (ed.), *Henry VI, Part 1* (BBC TV Shakespeare, London, 1983).

—— *Henry VI, Part 2* (BBC TV Shakespeare, London, 1983).

—— *Henry VI, Part 3* (BBC TV Shakespeare, London, 1983).

Wilson, John Dover (ed.), *The First Part of King Henry VI* (New Shakespeare, Cambridge, 1952).

—— *The Second Part of King Henry VI* (New Shakespeare, Cambridge, 1952).

—— *The Third Part of King Henry VI* (New Shakespeare, Cambridge, 1952).

Braunmuller, A. R. (ed.), *King John* (Oxford Shakespeare, Oxford, 1989).
Honigmann, E. A. J. (ed.), *King John* (Arden Shakespeare, London, 1954).
Matchett, William H. (ed.), *King John* (Signet Shakespeare, New York, 1966).
Smallwood, R. L. (ed.), *King John* (New Penguin Shakespeare, Harmondsworth, 1974).
Wilson, John Dover (ed.), *King John* (New Shakespeare, Cambridge, 1931).

Eccles, Mark (ed.), *The Tragedy of Richard III* (Signet Shakespeare, New York, 1964).
Evans, G. Blakemore (ed.), *King Richard III* (Pelican Shakespeare, Baltimore, Md., 1959).
Hammond, Antony (ed.), *King Richard III* (Arden Shakespeare, London, 1981).
Hankey, Julie (ed.), *Richard III* (Plays in Performance, London, 1981).
Honigmann, E. A. J. (ed.), *King Richard III* (New Penguin Shakespeare, Harmondsworth, 1968).
Smidt, Kristian (ed.), *The Tragedy of King Richard the Third: Parallel Texts of the First Quarto and the First Folio with Variants of the Early Quartos* (Oslo, 1969).

CRITICISM AND COMMENTARY

Alexander, Peter, *Shakespeare's Henry VI and Richard III* (Cambridge, 1929).
Armstrong, William A. (ed.), *Shakespeare's Histories: An Anthology of Modern Criticism* (Harmondsworth, 1972).
Berry, Edward I., *Patterns of Decay: Shakespeare's Early Histories* (Charlottesville, Va., 1975).
—— 'Twentieth-Century Shakespeare Criticism: The Histories', in *The Cambridge Companion to Shakespeare Studies*, ed. Stanley Wells (Cambridge, 1986), 249–56.
Bevington, David, *Tudor Drama and Politics: A Critical Approach to Topical Meaning* (Cambridge, Mass., 1968).
Blanpied, John W., *Time and the Artist in Shakespeare's History Plays* (Newark, Del., 1983).
Boris, Edna Zwick, *Shakespeare's English Kings, the People and the Law* (Rutherford, NJ, 1978).
Boswell-Stone, W. G., *Shakespeare's Holinshed, the Chronicle and the Historical Plays Compared* (London, 1896).
Brown, John Russell, *Shakespeare's Plays in Performance* (London, 1966; Penguin Shakespeare Library, Harmondsworth, 1969).
Brownlow, F. W., *Two Shakespearean Sequences* (London, 1977).

Bullough, Geoffrey, *Narrative and Dramatic Sources of Shakespeare*, vols. iii and iv (London, 1960–2).

Bulman, James C., *The Heroic Idiom of Shakespearean Tragedy* (Newark, Del., 1985).

—— and H. R. Coursen (eds.), *Shakespeare on Television* (Hanover, NH, 1988).

Burden, Dennis H., 'Shakespeare's History Plays: 1952–1983; *Shakespeare Survey 38* (1985), 1–18.

Campbell, Lily B., *Shakespeare's 'Histories': Mirrors of Elizabethan Policy* (San Marino, Calif., 1947).

Chambers, E. K., *The Elizabethan Stage*, 4 vols. (Oxford, 1923).

Fleischer, Martha Hester, *The Iconography of the English History Play* (Salzburg, 1974).

French, A. L., 'The Mills of God and Shakespeare's Early History Plays', *English Studies*, 55 (1974), 313–24.

Hattaway, Michael, *Elizabethan Popular Theatre, Plays in Performance* (London, 1982).

Hibbard, G. R., *The Making of Shakespeare's Dramatic Poetry* (Toronto, 1981).

Holderness, Graham, *Shakespeare's History* (Dublin and New York, 1985).

Honigmann, E. A. J., *Shakespeare: The 'Lost Years'* (Manchester, 1985).

—— *Shakespeare's Impact on His Contemporaries* (London, 1982).

Hosley, Richard, *Shakespeare's Holinshed* (New York, 1968).

Jenkins, Harold, 'English History Plays: 1900–1950', *Shakespeare Survey* 6 (1953), 1–15.

Johnson, Samuel, *Johnson on Shakespeare*, ed. Arthur Sherbo, 2 vols. (New Haven, Conn., and London, 1968).

Jones, Emrys, *The Origins of Shakespeare* (Oxford, 1977).

—— *Scenic Form in Shakespeare* (Oxford, 1971).

Kastan, David Scott, 'Proud Majesty Made a Subject: Shakespeare and the Spectacle of Rule', *Shakespeare Quarterly*, 37 (1986), 459–75.

—— *Shakespeare and the Shapes of Time* (Hanover, NH, 1982).

Kelly, Henry A., *Divine Providence in the England of Shakespeare's Histories* (Cambridge, Mass., 1970).

Knights, L. C., 'Shakespeare's Politics: With Some Reflections on the Nature of Tradition' (1957), in *Interpretations of Shakespeare*, ed. Kenneth Muir (Oxford, 1985), 85–104.

Leggatt, Alexander, *Shakespeare's Political Drama* (London, 1988).

Long, J. H., *Shakespeare's Use of Music: The Histories and the Tragedies* (Gainesville, Fa., 1971).

Manheim, M., *The Weak King Dilemma in the Shakespearean History Play* (Syracuse, NY, 1973).

Morris, Christopher, *Political Thought in England: Tyndale to Hooker* (London, 1953).

Ornstein, Robert, *A Kingdom for a Stage* (Cambridge, Mass., 1972).

Palliser, D. M., *The Age of Elizabeth* (London, 1983).

Prior, Moody E., *The Dream of Power* (Evanston, Ill., 1973).

Reese, M. M., *The Cease of Majesty* (London, 1961).

Ribner, Irving, *The English History Play in the Age of Shakespeare* (Princeton, NJ, 1957; rev. edn., 1965).

Saccio, Peter, *Shakespeare's English Kings: History, Chronicle, and Drama* (Oxford, 1977).

Sharpe, J. A., *Early Modern England: A Social History 1550–1760* (London, 1987).

Siegel, Paul N., *Shakespeare's English and Roman History Plays: A Marxist Approach* (Madison, NJ, 1986).

Slack, Paul (ed.), *Rebellion, Popular Protest and the Social Order in Early Modern England* (Cambridge, 1984).

Smidt, K., *Unconformities in Shakespeare's History Plays* (London, 1982).

Sprague, Arthur Colby, *Shakespeare's Histories: Plays for the Stage* (London, 1964).

Tennenhouse, Leonard, *Power on Display: The Politics of Shakespeare's Genres* (London, 1986).

Tillyard, E. M. W., *Shakespeare's History Plays* (London, 1944).

Turner, Robert Y., *Shakespeare's Apprenticeship* (Chicago, Ill., 1974).

Wells, Stanley, and Gary Taylor, with John Jowett and William Montgomery, *William Shakespeare: A Textual Companion* (Oxford, 1987).

Wilders, John, *The Lost Garden: A View of Shakespeare's English and Roman History Plays* (London, 1978).

Williams, Penry, *The Tudor Regime* (Oxford, 1979).

Williamson, Marilyn L., ' "When Men are Rul'd by Women": Shakespeare's First Tetralogy', *Shakespeare Studies*, 19 (1987), 41–60.

Wilson, F. P., *Marlowe and the Early Shakespeare* (Oxford, 1953).

The Henry VI Plays

Barton, John, *The Wars of the Roses* (London, 1970).

Bergeron, David M., 'The Play-within-the-Play in *3 Henry VI*', *Tennessee Studies in Literature*, 22 (1977), 37–45.

Berman, Ronald S., 'Fathers and Sons in the *Henry VI* Plays', *Shakespeare Quarterly*, 13 (1962), 487–97.

Brockbank, J. P., 'The Frame of Disorder—*Henry VI*', in J. R. Brown and B. Harris (eds.), *Early Shakespeare* (Stratford-upon-Avon Studies, 3; London, 1961, pp. 73–99); reprinted in Armstrong (1972), 92–122.

Bulman, James C., 'Shakespeare's Georgic Histories', *Shakespeare Survey* 38 (1985), 37–47.

Burckhardt, Sigurd, *Shakespeare's Meanings* (Princeton, NJ, 1968).

Carroll, D. Allen, 'Greene's "Vpstart Crow" Passage: A Survey of

Commentary', *Research Opportunities in Renaissance Drama*, 28 (1985), 111–27.

Clemen, Wolfgang H., 'Some Aspects of Style in the *Henry VI* Plays', in *Shakespeare's Styles: Essays in Honour of Kenneth Muir*, ed. P. Edwards, I.-S. Ewbank, and G. K. Hunter (Cambridge, 1980), 9–24.

Dean, P., 'Shakespeare's Henry VI Trilogy and Elizabethan "Romance" Histories: The Origins of a Genre', *Shakespeare Quarterly*, 33 (1982), 34–48.

French, A. L., '*Henry VI* and The Ghost of Richard II', *English Studies*, 50 (1969), xxxvii–l.

—— 'Joan of Arc and *Henry VI*', *English Studies*, 49 (1968), 425–29.

Goy-Blanquet, D., *Le roi mis à nu: l'histoire d'Henri VI de Hall à Shakespeare* (Paris, 1986).

Hattaway, Michael, 'Rebellion, Class Consciousness, and Shakespeare's 2 *Henry VI*', *Cahiers Élisabéthains*, 33 (1988), 13–22.

Hinchcliffe, Judith, *King Henry VI, Parts 1, 2, and 3* (Garland Shakespeare Bibliographies, New York and London, 1984).

Hodgdon, B., 'Shakespeare's Directorial Eye: A Look at the Early History Plays', in *Shakespeare's 'More than Words can Witness'*, ed. S. Homan (Lewisburg, Pa., 1980), 115–29.

Jackson, Sir Barry, 'On Producing *Henry VI*', *Shakespeare Survey 6* (1953), 49–52.

Jackson, Gabriele Bernhard, 'Topical Ideology: Witches, Amazons, and Shakespeare's Joan of Arc', *English Literary Renaissance*, 18 (1988), 40–65.

Knights, L. C., 'Rhetoric and Insincerity', in *Shakespeare's Styles: Essays in Honour of Kenneth Muir*, ed. P. Edwards, I.-S. Ewbank, and G. K. Hunter (Cambridge, 1980), 1–8.

Laroque, François, *Shakespeare et la fête* (Paris, 1988), 264–9.

Price, Hereward T., *Construction in Shakespeare*, University of Michigan Contributions in Modern Philology, 17 (Ann Arbor, 1951).

Riddell, J. A., 'Talbot and the Countess of Auvergne', *Shakespeare Quarterly*, 28 (1977), 51–7.

Riggs, D., *Shakespeare's Heroical Histories: Henry VI and Its Literary Tradition* (Cambridge, Mass., 1971).

Robinson, Marilynne, S., 'A New Look at Shakespeare's *Henry VI, Part II*: Sources, Structure, and Meaning' (Univ. of Washington Ph.D. diss., 1977).

Warren, Roger, ' "Contrarieties Agree": An Aspect of Dramatic Technique in *Henry VI*', *Shakespeare Survey 37* (1984), 75–83.

Watkins, Ronald, 'The Only Shake-Scene', *Philological Quarterly*, 54 (1975), 47–67.

Richard III

Armstrong, W. A., 'The Elizabethan Conception of the Tyrant', *RES* 22 (1946), 161–81.

Berry, Ralph, 'Richard III: Bonding the Audience', in *Mirror up to Shakespeare*, ed. J. C. Gray (Toronto, 1984).

Braunmuller, A. R., 'Early Shakespearean Tragedy and Its Contemporary Context: Cause and Emotion in *Titus Andronicus, Richard III*, and *Lucrece*', in *Shakespearean Tragedy*, ed. Malcolm Bradbury and David Palmer (Stratford-upon-Avon Studies, 20; London, 1984), 97–128.

Brooke, Nicholas, 'Reflecting Gems and Dead Bones: Tragedy versus History in *Richard III*', in *Shakespeare's Wide and Universal Stage*, ed. C. B. Cox and D. J. Palmer (Manchester, 1984), 104–16.

—— *Shakespeare's Early Tragedies* (London, 1968).

Brooks, Harold F., '*Richard III*: Antecedents of Clarence's Dream', *Shakespeare Studies*, 32 (1979), 145–50.

—— *Richard III*: Unhistorical Amplifications: the Women's Scenes and Seneca', *MLR* 75 (1980), 721–37.

Clemen, Wolfgang H., *A Commentary upon Shakespeare's 'Richard III'*, trans. J. Bonheim (London, 1968).

—— *The Development of Shakespeare's Imagery* (London, 1951).

Evans, Gareth Lloyd, *The Upstart Crow* (London, 1982).

French, A. L., 'The World of Richard III', *Shakespeare Studies*, 4 (1968), 25–39.

Garber, Marjorie, 'Descanting on Deformity: Richard III and the Shape of History', in her *Shakespeare's Ghost Writers* (London, 1987), 28–51.

Gurr, Andrew, '*Richard III* and the Democratic Process', *Essays in Criticism*, 24 (1974), 39–47.

Hassell, R. Chris, Jr., 'Context and Charisma: The Sher-Alexander *Richard III* and Its Reviewers', *Shakespeare Quarterly*, 36 (1985), 630–43.

Rossiter, A. P., 'Angel with Horns: The Unity of *Richard III*', in his *Angel with Horns* (London, 1961), 1–22; reprinted in Armstrong (1972), 123–44.

Sanders, Wilbur, *The Dramatist and the Received Idea* (Cambridge, 1968).

Shaw, George Bernard, *Shaw on Shakespeare*, ed. Edwin Wilson (London, 1961).

Sher, Antony, *Year of the King* (London, 1985).

Spivack, Bernard, *Shakespeare and the Allegory of Evil* (New York, 1958).

Ure, Peter, 'Character and Role from *Richard III* to *Hamlet*', in his *Elizabethan and Jacobean Drama* (Liverpool, 1974).

Van Laan, Thomas F., *Role Playing in Shakespeare* (Toronto, 1978).

King John

Bonjour, Adrien, 'The Road to Swinstead Abbey: a Study of the Sense and Structure of *King John*', *ELH* 18 (1951), 253–74.

Braunmuller, A. R., '*King John* and Historiography', *ELH* 55 (1988), 309–32.

Calderwood, James, 'Commodity and Honour in *King John*', *University of Toronto Quarterly*, 29 (1959–60), 341–56.

Curren-Aquino, Deborah T. (ed.), '*King John': New Perspectives* (Delaware, NJ, 1989).

Danby, John F., *Shakespeare's Doctrine of Nature* (London, 1961).

David, Richard, *Shakespeare in the Theatre* (Cambridge, 1978).

Elliott, John R., 'Shakespeare and the Double Image of King John', *Shakespeare Studies*, 1 (1965), 21–38.

Grennan, Eamon, 'Satirical History: A Reading of *King John*', *Shakespeare Studies*, 11 (1978), 21–38.

Kastan, David Scott, ' "To Set a Form upon that Indigest": Shakespeare's Fictions of History', *Comparative Drama*, 17 (1983–4), 1–16.

Matchett, William H., 'Richard's Divided Heritage in *King John*', *Essays in Criticism*, 12 (1962), 231–53; reprinted in Armstrong (1972), 145–169.

Price, Jonathan R., '*King John* and Problematic Art', *Shakespeare Quarterly*, 21 (1970), 25–8.

Schanzer, Ernest, *The Problem Plays of Shakespeare* (London, 1963).

Smallwood, R. L., 'Shakespeare Unbalanced: The Royal Shakespeare Company's *King John*, 1974–5', *Deutsche Shakespeare-Gessellschaft West Jahrbuch 1976*, 79–99.

Vaughan, Virginia Mason, 'Between Tetralogies: *King John* as Transition', *Shakespeare Quarterly*, 35 (1984), 407–20.

Wixson, Douglas C., ' "Calm Words Folded up in Smoke": Propaganda and Spectator Response in Shakespeare's *King John*', *Shakespeare Studies*, 14 (1981), 111–27.

17 | The Second Tetralogy

RICHARD DUTTON

The first part of this essay looks at general approaches to the second tetralogy, criticism primarily interested in all four plays as a sequence. The second deals with the plays individually, listing recommended editions and giving prominence to discussions of them as separate pieces or as lesser sequences (the Henry IV plays or the three containing Hal/Henry V). The third looks at accounts of productions of the plays, on both stage and screen, and at discussions of their theatrical potential. For brevity's sake, there are few cross-references between the three parts. Anyone looking for the fullest record of a particular play should read all three accordingly. 'Tetralogy' here means a 'series of four related dramatic . . . compositions' (*OED*) and is a term to be treated with caution. The plays do deal with a continuous passage of history, from 1398 to 1420, and several characters naturally recur in them, but this need not mean that Shakespeare planned them as a sequence or with a consistent political/philosophical framework in mind.

This essay owes a debt to previous review studies of Shakespeare's histories by Harold Jenkins (1953), Arthur Humphreys (1973), and Dennis H. Burden (1985). It supplements but does not supplant them.

GENERAL

Intensive study of Shakespeare's English histories begins, not entirely accidentally, with the Second World War. Before that, although anything associated with Shakespeare provoked interest, the stock of the histories never stood very high: they did not enjoy the sustained critical attention or theatrical acclaim accorded to the tragedies and comedies. As a broad picture of medieval England they were part of the national heritage, sometimes claimed as a national epic. A few critical issues still current —notably how far the history plays (particularly those relating to

Hal/Henry V) were to be considered a deliberate sequence, and the nature of our response to Falstaff—indeed go back to Dr Johnson's time. But 'the history play' did not fall into the traditional formal categories of drama, and Shakespeare's artistry in this genre (was it, indeed, a genre?) was only fitfully appreciated. The supposed deficiences of the first tetralogy might be written off on the presumption that they were not wholly his own creations; the plays of the second were at least recognized as his own work, but still generated relatively little enthusiasm. Indeed, had it not been for 'unimitated, unimitable Falstaff' (Johnson's phrase), and to an extent the patriotic potential of *Henry V*, the attention accorded to the second tetralogy would have been lukewarm at best. The kind of attention Falstaff himself received partly explains this. Maurice Morgann's striking early *Essay* (1777), dedicated to proving him no coward, was not widely known but typical in its tendency to treat Falstaff as a real person. Here, and more broadly in his English histories (so constrained, it seemed, by the factual record), Shakespeare was credited with recreating nature rather than creating art, a two-edged commendation since it acknowledged the vitality of characters like Hal, Hotspur, and Falstaff, whose virtues and vices could be debated, but largely ignored the formal, theatrical, and intellectual qualities of the plays in which they were located.

Three books in the space of four years transformed the standing of these plays: Dover Wilson's *The Fortunes of Falstaff* (1943), E. M. W. Tillyard's *Shakespeare's History Plays* (1944), and Lily B. Campbell's *Shakespeare's 'Histories': Mirrors of Elizabethan Policy* (1947). These did not, of course, emerge from a critical vacuum. Dover Wilson, well into his own Cambridge edition of Shakespeare, built on the scholarship of the 'New Variorum' editors of the *Henry IV* plays (respectively S. B. Hemingway, 1936; and M. A. Schaaber, 1940) in formulating his influential view of them as a Morality play, structured around Hal as Everyman, with Hotspur as Chivalry, Falstaff as the Vice, Vanity, and so on; his sympathetic, rather indulgent view of Falstaff was essentially the traditional one (memorably advanced by A. C. Bradley, 1909, talking of 'the bliss of freedom gained in humour'), but related to the growing scholarly appreciation of Morality plays and interludes, and quasi-anthropological interest in the Vice and the clown/fool (see Enid Welsford's *The Fool*, 1935). Campbell's book gives more prominence to the first tetralogy than the second, but was stimu-

lating for its view of the histories as attuned to Elizabethan
political issues and historiography—moral/political mirrors for
those in power. Earlier attempts to relate the histories to the
1590s when they were written, rather than to the fifteenth century
they depicted, either fell on deaf ears, like Richard Simpson's
prescient 'The Politics of Shakespeare's Historical Plays' (1874),
or squandered their case by making rash 'identifications' and
assumptions about Shakespeare's sympathies, as in Evelyn M.
Albright's essays of the 1920s and 1930s. Campbell's strength lay
in relating her claims both to Renaissance notions of history-as-
instruction and to more sophisticated views of Shakespeare's
creative adaptation (rather than simple translation) of his source
materials. Hitherto, scholarly investigation of the sources had
run rather ahead of the critical appreciation of what the dramatist
made of them. W. G. Boswell-Stone rather mechanically edited
the principal source, Holinshed's *Chronicles* (though he did
helpfully cross-reference with other sources) in 1896; Allardyce
and Josephine Nicoll produced a handy Everyman edition in
1927. C. L. Kingsford usefully surveyed all the relevant fifteenth-
century chronicles (1913), in a way that clearly influenced Tillyard.
Alfred Hart (1934) suggested the influence of the Anglican church
homilies on Shakespeare's rendering of his sources, while
Campbell herself (1938) edited a key source, *A Mirror for
Magistrates.*

Dover Wilson and Campbell were, in different ways, spurred
on by the war-time context in which they wrote—the former to a
view of '*Henry IV* as Shakespeare's vision of the "happy breed of
men" that was his England', the latter to a sense of these plays of
civil and international warfare speaking to the tensions of the
time in which they were written, and so to the times in which
they were read. But Tillyard seems in retrospect the writer most
complexly responding to his own time: not just the war, but the
decades of mass-destruction and totalitarianism before it. His
approach was based on an essentialist view of human nature and
an idealized 'freezing' of Elizabethan political values into a late-
medieval framework of divinely ordained hierarchic order and
stability. The framework of ideas derived from such studies as
Hardin Craig's *The Enchanted Glass* and A. O. Lovejoy's *The Great
Chain of Being* (both 1936), which were specifically applied to
Shakespeare in Theodore Spencer's *Shakespeare and the Nature of
Man* (1942). The emphasis in all these works on supposed corres-

pondences between the political state and the God-given harmony of the cosmos was made the central theme of Tillyard's *Elizabethan World Picture* (1943), a conscious prelude to his work on the histories. In the latter, he finds that behind 'all the confusion of civil war in Shakespeare's histories is the belief that the world is a part of eternal law'. The 'total sequence' of the plays 'expressed successfully a universally held and still comprehensible scheme of history: a scheme fundamentally religious, by which events evolve under a law of justice and under the ruling of God's Providence, and of which Elizabeth's England was the acknowledged outcome'—the so-called Tudor myth of history. Tillyard's views have been widely challenged, and arguably superseded, but his remains the most influential single work on the history plays, setting much of the critical agenda described below.

With the impetus of these three works, scholarly activity gathered pace, the sources continuing to provide fruitful approaches. Denys Hay (1950) edited Polydore Vergil's *Anglia Historia*, a key text in the 'Tudor myth', particularly as echoed in Edward Hall's 1548 chronicles (available in modern reprint, 1970)—though most scholars are more persuaded of the influence of Vergil/Hall on the first tetralogy than on the second. The second tetralogy is, however, acknowledged to have adopted something of its emotional tone and imaginative outlook from Samuel Daniel's *Civil Wars* (1595), while borrowing much of its factual material from the second (1587) edition of Holinshed (edited in a readable, modernized form by Richard Hosley, 1968). Shakespeare is also thought to have borrowed details from John Stow's *Chronicles* and *Annals* (1580, 1592) and from Thomas Elyot's *The Governour* (1531), evidence for the latter being advanced by Harold Brooks (1963). The great culmination of Shakespeare source-study, providing an indispensable quarry of material and judicious (if not ideologically neutral) comment is Geoffrey Bullough's *Narrative and Dramatic Sources of Shakespeare*. Vol. IV, *Later English History Plays* (1962) is the relevant volume here. This was complemented by Kenneth Muir's overview, *The Sources of Shakespeare's Plays* (1977). Discussions of the sources, extracts from which they reprint, are a feature of the Arden editions, especially those of the *Henry IV* plays by A. R. Humphreys (1960, 1966). The indeterminate relationship of Shakespeare to his (usually conservative) chronicle sources has been argued by Michael Tomlinson (1984).

Broader thematic studies of the plays, and of the tetralogy-as-sequence, also followed, in many ways testing the Tillyard thesis to breaking point. R. A. Law (1954) challenged the inclusive sweep of Tillyard's approach, suggesting that Shakespeare moved more tentatively from play to play. Virgil Whitaker, in *Shakespeare's Use of Learning* (1953), made a more substantial case of this, seeing a maturing in Shakespeare's grasp of dramatic possibilities coupled with a more sophisticated reading of source materials, but driven by artistic and theatrical motives rather than philosophical ones. Tillyard himself (1954) conceded that there was room for local artistic initiatives within his overall pattern. However, Christopher Morris's *Political Thought in England: Tyndale to Hooker* (1953) significantly questioned the orthodoxy of the Tillyard picture and its absolutist emphases, suggesting that the reality—even in such matters as what the homilies actually said—was more complex than often assumed. A. P. Rossiter, in 'Ambivalence: the Dialectic of the Histories' (1961, though written earlier), examined the ironic and indeterminate interactions of tragic and comic elements, which he saw as subverting 'the Tudor myth'. L. C. Knights (1957) also argued against reading predetermined political theses into Shakespeare, stressing the scope for his own experience and imagination in 'recreating' his materials. Derek Traversi (*Shakespeare: From 'Richard II' to 'Henry V'*, 1957: the first book-length study devoted solely to the tetralogy) applied *Scrutiny*-type close reading to the plays, looking in the verbal texture for the immediate tensions and human complications of the political themes, overlooked in historiographical generalizations, and finding in them an evolving critique of political behaviour. Robert Hapgood (1963) argued that the plays deliberately cultivate unresolved moral and political oppositions, playing off tensions between actions that we may know on one level to be right (the deposition of Richard II, the rejection of Falstaff) but feel on another to be wrong. Norman Rabkin in *Shakespeare and the Common Understanding* (1957) sees the plays deliberately dealing in problems and 'areas of turbulence' rather than offering answers or following prescribed patterns of thought, while C. G. Thayer (1967) resists ideological interpretations of the tetralogy, advancing Bolingbroke as a compelling character study rather than an element in a metaphysical political pattern. Henry A. Kelly's *Divine Providence in the England of Shakespeare's Histories* (1970) goes back to the chronicles to demonstrate that there was more than one 'Tudor myth' about the sequence of events stemming from the deposition of Richard II—not only the Yorkist view, foregrounded by Tillyard, of a sequence of retribution on the House of Lancaster, but also the Lancastrian argument justifying the removal of a corrupt government heedless of the kingdom's welfare. (The second tetralogy is sometimes dubbed the 'House of Lancaster' plays, to distinguish them from the Yorkist protagonists of the first tetralogy). Edna Zwick Boris's *Shakespeare's English Kings, the People, and the Law* (1978) further explores the context of Elizabethan understanding of the plays by examining their contemporary constitutional and legal implications. Robert Ornstein's *A Kingdom for a Stage* (1972) commonsensically proposes that the histories are about rebellion and reconciliation, not providence or protracted retribution; Shakespeare was more constrained by the disciplines of drama than by political orthodoxies. Ornstein constantly draws parallels between what he sees as the strengths and weaknesses of the plays (for example suggesting that the last act of *Richard II* is an anti-climax) and the fortunes of their protagonists. H. R. Coursen looks to other indicators in *The Leasing Out of England: Shakespeare's Second Henriad* (1982)—war as commercial enterprise, social and economic disruptions—as leading indicators of the growth of the series. Kristian Smidt's *Unconformities in Shakespeare's History Plays* (1982) insists that the plays' many anomalies and inconsistencies refute any suggestion of their being written to a pre-formed plan

Cutting somewhat across the debate over Tillyard's thesis is a continuing interest in the play's depiction of kingship as an institution, posing dilemmas for those invested with it. Una Ellis-Fermor (1945) concentrated on the four plays as 'the Elizabethan phase of Shakespeare's portrait of the statesman-king', also an issue in Traversi though not located by him in the development of Shakespeare's career. M. M. Reese in *The Cease of Majesty* (1961) broadly accepts Tillyard's contextualization, but goes beyond it to see the plays as centrally concerned with issues of social partnership, pointing up the human qualities required of kings in a crisis and the qualities of justice, charity, and compassion that must underpin kingship if a healthy community is to be preserved. Jan Kott's influential *Shakespeare Our Contemporary* (1964) turned all the kings into faceless existential beings confronting a grim, arbitrary, but unrelenting historical process, light years removed in tone and ideology from S. C. Sen Gupta's *Shakespeare's Historical Plays* (1964), which reads the plays as character studies, subordinating issues of politics and history to the human dilemmas of those caught up in them. H. M. Richmond, by contrast, builds *Shakespeare's Political Plays* (1967) around the thesis that the histories demonstrate the evolution of man as a political animal, while James Winny in *The Player King* (1968)—confined to the second tetralogy—traces the *idea* of the king from play to play, where successive monarchs strive to fulfil what is less a political office than an imaginative identity. John Bromley's *The Shakespearean Kings* (1971) seeks to show how the kings are destroyed by the weight of kingship itself and the unpleasant realities of power. Robert B. Pierce in *Shakespeare's History Plays: The Family and the State* (1971) approaches the issue from a different perspective, seeing in the family a recurrent dramatic motif which mediates between grand affairs of state and the personal experience of the audience, though the king as father of the nation is never far from the centre of attention. Moody E. Prior's *The Dream of Power* (1973) suggests that each of the plays explores a different problem about kingship, related to Renaissance categories of political thought, while Michael Man-heim's *The Weak King Dilemma in the Shakespearean Henriad* (1973) acknowledges more frankly than most of its predecessors (excepting Kott) that its thesis—the plays show weak, traditional monarchy proving inadequate and being superseded by un-scrupulous Machiavellism—owes as much to twentieth-century preoccupations as it does to Renaissance thinking. C. G. Thayer's *Shakespeare's Politics* (1983) is more traditional in historical method, arguing that the second tetralogy as a coherent group analyses alternative governors and forms of government, a topic of special urgency at the end of the Tudor era; Henry V emerges as an ideal of 'man-centred kingship', an antithesis to Richard II, with 'none of Richard's illusions and none of Richard's problems'. More radical views of the power politics in these plays and of their ideological 'appropriation' by modern critics have been advanced by Graham Holderness in *Shakespeare's History* (1985) and by the New Historicists (see under *Henry V*).

History is inevitably concerned with time, permanence, and mutability, the seeing of then from now, themes that have been much discussed. L. C. Knights (1959) linked *Richard II* and *2 Henry IV* with the Sonnets in these thematic preoccupations.

Tom F. Driver's *The Sense of History in Greek and Shakespearean Drama* (1960) sharpens our perception of Shakespeare's essentially Christian sense of time by comparing this aspect of his plays with what we find in classical Greek drama. Northrop Frye (1965) found within the plays cosmic patterns of retribution, disintegration, and re-growth, while A. R. Humphreys (1968) in a more down-to-earth way emphasized how firmly their perspectives are located in temporal and geographical co-ordinates. Wolfgang Clemen (1966) examined the ways in which the plays present events as pressured both from the past and from the future, while David Scott Kastan in *Shakespeare and the Shapes of Time* (1982) emphasizes large areas of dramatic irony, in which discrepancies between what we know of what was to happen and what the characters hoped or expected reverberate open-endedly. Ricardo J. Quinones' *The Renaissance Discovery of Time* (1972) influentially demonstrated how different ways of registering the passing of time changed conceptions of the phenomenon itself, ushering in a number of substantial studies on related themes: Soji Iwasaki's *The Sword and the Word* (1973), Gary F. Waller's *The Strong Necessity of Time* (1976), and F. Wylie Sypher's *The Ethic of Time* (1976). John Wilders in *The Lost Garden* (1978) most fully articulates the strain of elegy, melancholy, and nostalgia that many have found in the second tetralogy, extending its clear representation in *2 Henry IV* to a tragic reading of the sequence as a whole. Complementing these studies of historical sense *within* the plays, a number of useful studies of Tudor historiography have helped us to place Shakespeare's drama in the context of the (non-dramatic) practice of his contemporaries. These include F. J. Levy's *Tudor Historical Thought* (1967) and May McKisack's *Medieval History in the Tudor Age* (1971). Herschel Baker's *The Race of Time* (1967) notes the growing insistence on factual accuracy demanded by historians like Camden and Bacon, but largely ignored by creative writers. Rather differently, Peter Saccio's *Shakespeare's English Kings* (1977) is an account of the reigns covered by Shakespeare's plays, but from both Elizabethan and modern perspectives, indirectly emphasizing the elements on which Shakespeare chose to concentrate. Others (following on from Campbell) have suggested that Shakespeare's focus was often dictated by the specific concerns of the 1590s. S. L. Bethell (1953) makes something of deliberate anachronisms in this connection, while Paul Jorgensen's *Shakespeare's Military World*

(1956) concentrates on the topical dimensions of the depiction of warfare—always a central issue in these plays. The most balanced and considered study of contemporary political references in Shakespeare's Elizabethan plays is David Bevington's *Tudor Drama and Politics* (1968), which is traditional (pre-New Historicist) about what constitutes a topical allusion and properly sceptical, for example, about Shakespeare's supposed affiliations with Essex. W. Gordon Zeeveld's *The Temper of Shakespeare's Thought* (1974) is concerned less with the persons and events of the 1590s than with the climate of thought at the time, for example linking the histories' emphasis on ceremony with the Puritan controversies. E. W. Ives (1985) helpfully considers what Shakespearians may find enlightening in historians' current thinking about Tudor/Stuart England (especially in the fields of factional politics, highly relevant to these plays, and family and social history).

The generic qualities of the plays have also generated debate, here often reacting against both Dover Wilson and Tillyard, who in different ways argued for the Morality play as the model for Shakespeare's histories. Irving Ribner's *The English History Play* (1957, rev. ed. 1965) is the most systematic study of the chronicle history play, tracing it as a form from the middle ages to the Commonwealth, defined by its concern with the nation's political and religious evolution, where links between the past and present are stressed; both of Shakespeare's tetralogies are firmly located in this tradition and discussed at length. David Riggs in *Shakespeare's Heroical Histories* (1971) attempts to construct a narrower popular tradition of heroical history, in which *Tamburlaine* is central; the heroic ideal is lost in the first tetralogy, partly recovered in the second. Herbert Lindberger's *Historical Drama: The Relation of Literature and Reality* (1978) links the plays with a wide range of English and continental historical fictions (for example Walter Scott, Brecht) in ways that may help narrow Renaissance specialists to re-think their premises. Others are less convinced that the histories belong to a stable, identifiable genre, finding it helpful to relate them to tragedy, comedy, romance, or a mixture of these forms. S. L. Bethell (1953) surveyed the various forms of comedy in the histories, R. J. Dorius (1960) contrasted the virtues of historical heroes (prudence, economy) with those of tragic ones (daring, risk-taking), while Charles R. Forker (1965) pointed to recurrent pastoral elements. But this is one area where differences between the plays often seem to outweigh the similarities, *Richard II* frequently being linked with tragedy, the *Henry IV* plays with comedy, *Henry V* more problematically with comedy and romance (see below). Leonard F. Dean (1967) proposed a view of Shakespeare moving progressively into his material in the second tetralogy, discovering new possibilities in it as he worked, mixing dramatic modes and consciously going beyond the naïve formulae of earlier chronicle and history plays; this chimes well with Harold E. Toliver's analysis (1965) of Shakespeare grappling with the generic indeterminacies of the plays, and giving the form a whole new stature. Both of these are more sophisticated in approach than F. P. Wilson's essay (1969), which advances Shakespeare as possible inventor of the history play and certainly its first significant proponent. Leonard Tennenhouse has argued for the ideological implications of dramatic genres in *Power on Display: The Politics of Shakespeare's Genres* (1986), though dealing only intermittently with these plays.

Discussions of structural features of the histories have been less contentious but generally useful. Madeleine Doran's *Endeavors of Art* (1954), with its discussions of the literary and rhetorical traditions behind the drama, is the starting point for this line of study. Richard Levin's *The Multiple Plot in Renaissance Drama* (1971) expands upon William Empson's exhilarating essay, 'Double Plots' (in *Some Versions of Pastoral*, 1935), in ways that particularly illuminate the structures of the *Henry IV* plays and *Henry V*, though not everyone will agree with his suggestion that the low-life scenes serve to *enhance* the dignity of the principal actions. Emrys Jones's *Scenic Form in Shakespeare* (1971), Mark Rose's *Shakespearean Design* (1972), and James E. Hirsch's *The Structure of Shakespearian Scenes* (1981) all in their different ways point to the individual scene (or binary combinations of scenes) as the essential building block of Shakespearian structure, rather than to the five-act design (which perhaps owes more to printing than to theatrical practice). Larry S. Champion's *Perspective in Shakespeare's English Histories* (1980) shows how scenic alternations create a multiplicity of angles of vision from which to consider the implications of the action; the first tetralogy is marked by deliberate fragmentation of vision, replaced by a concentration on a single character in the two *Richard* plays, in turn superseded by the mature multiple perspectives of the Hal plays.

Questions of language and style have provided a variety of

points of entry to these plays. R. A. Foakes (1952) usefully warned against the book-centred, anti-theatrical bias of early studies of the imagery (Spurgeon *et al.*). Several studies have looked to stylistic developments in the histories as a measure of Shakespeare's maturing artistry. Kenneth Muir's *Image and Symbol in Shakespeare's Histories* (1967) found a gradual progression in the iterative imagery—sparse in the first tetralogy, much more marked in the second. Robert Y. Turner's *Shakespeare's Apprenticeship* (1974) shows how the oratorical mode of the earlier histories, analysed in a variety of scenes and speeches, develops into a much more theatrically flexible and responsive medium in the later plays. G. R. Hibbard's *The Making of Shakespeare's Dramatic Poetry* (1981) suggests that Shakespeare became dissatisfied with the extravagant style of his early historical plays and worked on developing a more varied and comprehensive style in the later ones, where he perfected the dramatic instrument to be deployed in the mature tragedies. Others have focused on the relationship (perceived to be more problematic in successive studies) between language, other representational forms (symbol, ceremony, ritual), and the 'reality' they embody. Joan Webber (1963) observes that the sequence is 'an analysis of the nature of kingship and royal rhetoric which directly concerns the relationship between language and reality'. Eric La Guardia (1966) focuses on the evolution of cultural symbolism, seeing in the sequence 'the movement from medieval figural reality . . . toward a more secular view of reality'. Alvin Kernan (1969) describes it as 'in the most summary terms . . . a movement from ceremony and ritual to history'; he sees the 'Henriad' (his own coinage for the tetralogy, the wide adoption of which is a mark of the influence of this essay) as an epic tracing the transition from medieval England, politically and culturally secure in its ritualistic feudalism, to its modern counterpart, marked by uncertain individualism and role-playing. Anne Barton (1971) explores the conflict of imagination and fact in the second tetralogy, a conflict in which language is pushed to its limits and beyond; Richard II and Falstaff emerge as interestingly parallel characters, attempting but failing to dominate reality through language. Barbara D. Palmer (1985) examines the use of civic pageantry in the four plays, stressing that it does not disappear after *Richard II* but takes different forms, all related to the political realities being explored. Richard Lanham devotes a chapter of *The Motives of Eloquence* (1976) to the second tetralogy,

which he sees as a structure of styles and attitudes so complex
that it is impossible to impose a rigid scheme on the material
they comprehend; language dissolves and re-shapes history,
resisting its schematization. Virginia Carr (1978) is once more
concerned with lost ritual and ceremony. Sigurd Burckhardt's
Shakespeare's Meanings (1968) is often bafflingly indirect in its
argument but sometimes brilliantly illuminating, especially
where it has been most influential, in treating language not as a
means but as an object of representation, self-referentially aware
of itself, contributing to the plays' self-conscious explorations of
themselves and their own artistry; his chapter, ' "Swoll'n with
Some Other Grief': Shakespeare's Prince Hal Trilogy' has left its
mark on subsequent metadramatic criticism of the histories,
notably the work of James L. Calderwood: *Shakespeare's Metadrama* (1971) has a chapter on *Richard II*, while *Metadrama in
Shakespeare's Henriad* (1979) subjects the whole sequence to a
self-referential methodology in which speech and drama become
the protagonists of the plays, art monitoring its own and its
author's artistry. Ronald R. Macdonald (1984) also acknowledges
a debt to Burckhardt in his reading of language-as-history.
Joseph A. Porter's *The Drama of Speech Acts* (1979) similarly sees
in these plays a decisive shift in Shakespeare's conception and
use of language, tracing a progress towards *Henry V*, where the
triumphs of language, drama, and Henry complement and sanction
each other. John W. Blanpied's *Time and the Artist in Shakespeare's
Histories* (1983) again sees the plays as a process of self-education
for the dramatist, partly realized in production, but most consistently apparent in the linguistic self-consciousness.

Richard II

TEXTS

Black, Matthew W. (ed.), *Richard II* (New Variorum Shakespeare,
Philadelphia, Pa., 1955).

The most comprehensive edition of the play, with exhaustive
collations of earlier editions, extensive textual commentary, and
detailed examination of the sources.

Gurr, Andrew (ed.), *Richard II* (New Cambridge Shakespeare,
Cambridge, 1984).

Replaces the previous Cambridge series volume (ed. J. Dover

Wilson, 1939); full introduction, especially strong on the staging and stage history; detailed explanatory notes on the page, but textual analysis at the end of the text; appendices deal with Shakespeare's use of Holinshed, and include extensive extracts from Daniel and 'An Homilie against Disobedience'; reading list.

Muir, Kenneth (ed.), *Richard II* (Signet Shakespeare, New York, 1963). Useful student edition, with helpful glosses at foot of page, selections from the sources, and from Pater, Altick, and Traversi, cited below.

Ure, Peter (ed.), *Richard II* (Arden Shakespeare, London, 1956; rev. edn., 1966).

Full introduction, most useful on the sources and textual matters; very detailed and reasoned textual and explanatory notes on the page, often tracing the editorial history of *cruces*; extracts from the sources. One of this formerly near-definitive series beginning to show its age.

Wells, Stanley (ed.), *Richard II* (New Penguin Shakespeare, Harmondsworth, 1969).

Useful general introduction, especially strong on style and language, suggestions for further reading; text presented plain (ideal for acting and uncluttered reading), full commentary and account of the text at the end.

Richard II is the most distinctively lyrical of Shakespeare's histories, written entirely in verse, with a high proportion of rhyme. These qualities have been central to its critical reputation this century, from the aestheticism of Pater (1889) and Yeats (1903), which saw in the soliloquizing Richard an artist-poet (a tradition epitomized in the theatre by a number of productions with John Gielgud in the role), through the New Critical enthusiasm for the play's rich and sustained threads of imagery, to an identification of the mannered style with a conscious 'medievalism'. Conversely, the play also has a special status as Shakespeare's only work demonstrably subjected to political censorship during his lifetime (the excision of the deposition scene from the Elizabethan quartos; though see D. M. Bergeron, 1974), the topical sensitivity underlined by its (apparent) choice for a performance on the eve of the Essex rebellion: 'I am Richard II, know ye not that?' Elizabeth herself is recorded as saying. The style of the play and its special history have ensured critical interest outside the general attention paid to the tetralogy, the full range of which is reflected in Josephine Roberts's two-volume annotated bibliography (1988), awesomely comprehensive in its coverage of post-1940 material.

Much has been made of the complex array of literary sources Shakespeare used for this play: Holinshed, Hall, the anonymous play of *Woodstock* (see A. P. Rossiter's edition, 1946), Daniel's *The Civil Wars* and Berners's translation of Froissart's *Chronicle* (sometimes given credit for the play's medieval flavour). These have been widely discussed by Matthew W. Black (in both his New Variorum edition and essay), Bullough (1962), Muir (1977), and by Ure and Gurr in their editions. George M. Logan's (1976) close examination of Shakespeare's use of Daniel has implications for dating. Discussions of the topical context of the play, and its famous early productions, include Campbell (1947), S. Schoenbaum (1975), and David M. Bergeron (1975).

The view of Richard as artist-poet gave him the potential dignity of a tragic hero, and the play has often been approached from this angle. Travis Bogard (1955) and Peter Phialas (1961) both see the play as an important step in Shakespeare's development of a tragic mode, though R. F. Hill (1958; 1961) sees it as a dead end, the last refinement of rhetorical tragedy rather than a tragedy of character. Michael Quinn (1959) saw the play as a perfect blend of history and tragedy—a political narrative set in an ethical perspective—though John R. Elliott, Jr. (1968) argued that Richard's personal tragedy was circumscribed by the need to do justice to the wider historical themes, notably the rise of Bolingbroke: the play forges its own genre. See also R. J. Dorius (1960). Richard himself, like Charles I, is sometimes seen as a martyr (see Karl F. Thompson, 1957; Donald H. Reiman, 1964; Sidney Homan, 1972; Moody E. Prior, 1973) and sometimes as a clever, or devious, politician (see Nicholas Brooke, in *Shakespeare's Early Tragedies*, 1968; Harold F. Folland, 1973; Lois Potter, 1974; S. Schoenbaum, 1975; Larry S. Champion, 1975). Richard's tragedy is often posed in terms of his being a player-king, an actor unsuited to his role, as for example in Leonard F. Dean (1952), who examines parallels between the state and the theatre, James Winny (1968) who emphasizes the loss of Richard's name and identity, and Thomas F. Van Laan in *Role-Playing in Shake-*

speare (1978). A. D. Nuttall (1988) reflects on the self-regarding nature of his character, and the depiction of its interiority, by over-reading his role with Ovid's Narcissus myth. Even Paul Gaudet's study of the 'parasitical counsellors' (1982) concludes that the ultimate responsibility for the tragedy lies in Richard's own character. Complementing the emphasis on the play as quasi-tragedy have been attempts to find comedy in the bumbling character of York (see Arthur Humphreys, 1967, and Roy Battenhouse, 1974) and the burlesque elements of the Aumerle conspiracy (which earlier generations had difficulty in reconciling with the play's overall solemnity, sometimes doubting their authenticity); see Sheldon P. Zitner (1974), though also James Black (1985). Comic or not, York is often seen as a key commentator; see Norman Rabkin in *Shakespeare and the Common Understanding* (1967), Michael F. Kelly (1972), and James A. Riddell (1979).

Ernst H. Kantorowicz's influential *The King's Two Bodies* (1957) drew on medieval and Renaissance discussions of the difference between the natural body of the king and the spiritual body of continuing government to examine the constitutional relationship between the king and kingship, the man and the office. Not everyone would accept that Shakespeare saw matters in precisely these terms, though Marie Axton in *The Queen's Two Bodies* (1977) acutely reassesses the issue in the light of Henry VIII's will and as it surfaced in pressing form in the 1590s succession debate. Philip Edwards (1972) stressed that identity between a person and the office he held was an ideal to be aspired to, not necessarily always a reality. Kantorowicz fuelled the debate about the play's 'medievalism'. Tillyard had seen the play as a deliberate, elegiac re-creation of a medieval world secure in its values. A. P. Rossiter ('*Richard II*', 1961) was typically sceptical about this. Peter Phialas ('The Medieval in *Richard II*', 1961) pointed out that the play itself was nostalgic about an even earlier era (that of Edward III) and that the balance was not simply between an outmoded, medieval Richard and a pragmatic, modern Bolingbroke, a point developed and expanded by Robert D. Hapgood (1963). These should be borne in mind in relation to Alvin Kernan's otherwise cogent view of the 'Henriad' (1969, see above), which sees Richard as undermining by his own inadequacies a world he believes immutable, a tragic precursor who creates a road all his successors will have to travel. John R. Elliott, Jr. (1966) emphasized that the political terms of reference in the play were Elizabethan and not medieval. Arthur Humphreys (1964) even-handedly summarized the main conflicts in Elizabethan political thought which the play encapsulates; his 1967 monograph points out how in III. iii Richard's assertion of divine right is countered by Northumberland's insistence on the rights of subjects. E. W. Talbert, in *The Problem of Order* (1962), suggested that the play advanced the Yorkist (Richardian, divine right) and Lancastrian (legalistic, rights of subjects) positions with almost schematic scrupulousness. Peter Ure (1968), however, saw much more of the Yorkist position in the play, while A. L. French, answering him (1968), narrowed things very much to the Lancastrian perspective. *Modern* views of the play's politics have shifted away from the scarcely concealed royalist sympathies of Tillyard and Bullough, through more even-handed assessments such as that by Robert P. Merrix (1979), to Graham Holderness's impatience (1981; expanded in his 1985 book) with earlier critics' attempts to contain the play's radical indeterminacies within conservative ideologies: the emblematic scene of the Gardeners is about good husbandry, not divine right. Perhaps Allan Bloom (1981) represents the most usual current view: the play raises a number of political issues without resolving any of them.

R. D. Altick (1947) was the first to identify a systematic pattern in the play's imagery, an insight reinforced in subsequent studies by Arthur Suzman (1956) and Kathryn M. Harris (1970); M. M. Mahood's chapter on the play in *Shakespeare's Wordplay* (1967) is perhaps the most generally admired close study of its language and imagery. Stanley R. Maveety offers a very detailed interpretation of the Christian imagery in the play. Richard's personal 'poetic' mode has been characterized by Stanley Wells (1982), while his obsession with time has been examined by L. C. Knights (1959), Robert L. Montgomery (1969), and Michel Grivelet (1970). Gaunt's famous deathbed speech has been examined from many angles, perhaps most persuasively by Donald M. Friedman (1976). The distinctive style and manner of the play have also provoked much comment. J. A. Bryant, Jr. (1957) proposes a wry perspective from which we can see the material of the chronicles being turned into poetic symbols and analogues. Dorothy C. Hockey (1964) applies the criteria of Renaissance rhetoric to the language of the play, as does T. McAlindon, who examines the play's fascination with ceremony in *Shakespeare and Decorum* (1973), seeing Richard's stylistic inconsistencies as markers of his political perversities. Ernest B. Gilman, in *The Curious Perspective* (1978), has a chapter in which he links the play's shifts of perspective to sixteenth-century artistic modes, which require the viewer simultaneously to entertain contradictory impressions. John Baxter's *Shakespeare's Poetic Styles* (1980) is very largely concerned with *Richard II*, analysing it in the light of Yvor Winters's distinction between Petrarchan and plain styles. The play's self-conscious concern with language almost invites post-structuralist analyses, focused on the gap between words and what they represent; Terence Hawkes's *Shakespeare's Talking Animals* (1973) is in this mode, as are James L. Calderwood's two metadramatic essays on the play (1971, 1979).

1 and 2 Henry IV

TEXTS

Bevington, David (ed.), *Henry IV, Part 1* (Oxford Shakespeare, Oxford, 1987).

Exhaustive and scrupulous (127-page) introduction, impressive in its grasp of critical, textual, and stage history; thorough and helpful annotation, with index; appendix considers, but does not reprint, the sources.

Davison, P. H. (ed.), *Henry IV, Part 1* (New Penguin Shakespeare, Harmondsworth, 1968).

Useful general introduction, surveying the issues from Hal standing over the fallen Hotspur and Falstaff, ending with Falstaff's zest for life as a key to the play's popularity; suggestions for further reading; text presented plain (ideal for acting and uncluttered reading), full commentary and account of the text at the end.

Hemingway, S. B. (ed.), *Henry IV, Part 1* (New Variorum Shakespeare, Philadelphia, Pa., 1936).

Most comprehensive edition of the play, with exhaustive collations of earlier editions, extensive textual commentary, and detailed examination of the sources; supplementary material by G. Blakemore Evans in *Shakespeare Quarterly*, 7 (1956).

Humphreys, A. R. (ed.), *Henry IV, Part 1* (Arden Shakespeare, London, 1960).

Extensive introduction, notable for its treatment of the sources and examination of the early history (including its relation to *Part 2* and *The Merry Wives of Windsor*); detailed and reasoned textual and explanatory notes on the page, often tracing the editorial history of *cruces*; extracts from the sources.

Mack, Maynard (ed.), *Henry IV, Part 1* (Signet Shakespeare, New York, 1965, 1987).

Useful student edition, with helpful annotations at foot of page; selections from the sources and Dover Wilson, Traversi, Ornstein, Goldman, and Sylvan Barnet's review of the play's theatrical history up to the mid 1980s.

Holland, Norman L. (ed.), *Henry IV, Part 2* (Signet Shakespeare, New York, 1965).

Useful student edition, with helpful annotations at foot of the page; selections from the sources and older criticism.

Humphreys, A. R. (ed.), *Henry IV, Part 2* (Arden Shakespeare, London, 1966).

Complements and completes his excellent edition of *Part 1* in the same series, reviewing again relations between the two parts; detailed and reasoned textual and explanatory notes on the page, often tracing the editorial history of *cruces*; extracts from the sources.

Shaaber, Matthias A. (ed.), *Henry IV, Part 2* (New Variorum Shakespeare, Philadelphia, Pa., 1940).

The most comprehensive edition of the play, by an editor convinced that it is a completely distinct play from *Part 1*; with exhaustive collations of earlier editions, extensive textual commentary, and detailed examination of the sources.

Davison, P. H. (ed.), *Henry IV, Part 2* (New Penguin Shakespeare, Harmondsworth, 1977).

Useful general introduction, mainly concerned to define the play by differentiating it from others in the tetralogy; suggestions for further reading; text presented plain (ideal for acting and uncluttered reading), full commentary and account of the text at the end.

So much criticism deals with the two *Henry IV* plays together that it would be artificial to try to separate them, though failure to do so blurs the very real differences between them, and can leave *Part 2* overshadowed by the generally more popular *Part 1*. Dr Johnson judged them 'to be two [plays] only because they are too long to be one', a view which—with elaborations—has found modern support; see, for example, G. R. Hibbard (1977). G. K. Hunter (1954) relates them to other Elizabethan examples of two-part plays, independent works, but offering a diptych-like parallelism in which common features stand out with repetition, an argument supported by Sherman Hawkins (1982). Hawkins earlier (1975) suggested that Shakespeare always had in mind a two-part play dealing with Hal's advances in the virtues crucial to good kingship, though he may have changed his mind about the structure and certain features of *Part 2*. Against the notion that Shakespeare always had two plays in mind, Harold Jenkins developed a long and technical argument in *The Structural Problem in Shakespeare's Henry IV* (1956) to demonstrate that Shakespeare set out to write a single play, but midway opted to defer the rejection of Falstaff to a sequel, a decision requiring the infusion of some new material but also a recapitulation of the reformation of Hal. More radically, M. A. Shaaber (1948) argued that *Part 2* is an after-thought, a vehicle to exploit the popularity of Falstaff. H. E. Cain (1952) similarly sees the plays as totally independent of each other (*Part 2* effectively requiring us to forget *Part 1*). Both plays are commonly thought to be essentially comic, the generic case for this being furthered by C. L. Barber's influential *Shakespeare's Festive Comedy* (1959), with its quasi-anthropological perspective, and by Jonas Barish (1965), though the tragic dimensions have been spelled out by Catherine M. Shaw (1985) and Derek Cohen (1985). There is virtual unanimity that *Part 2* is a more sombre, brooding piece than *Part 1*, a point elaborated from different angles by Clifford Leech (1953), L. C. Knights (1959), and Harry Levin (1981), and given stylistic support in Brian Vickers's extensive analysis of the prose in the two plays in *The Artistry of Shakespeare's Prose* (1968). Even where *Part 2* may share heroic themes with its predecessor, these are ironized and turned to mock-heroic (James Black, 1973); it lacks the dramatic action of both *1 Henry IV* and *Henry V*, a deliberate shift of tempo in the tetralogy as a whole and an effective prelude to the latter play (B. T. Spencer, 1961). J. A. B. Somerset (1977) also sees it as a unique play, similar to the estate plays of the 1580s and 1590s in the questions it raises about social and moral issues. R. A. Law

(1961) examined the use of sources in the *Henry IV* plays as a way of underlining the differences between them, suggesting that *Part 1* is itself the primary source for *Part 2*, a reinforcement of Shaaber's case.

The principal sources for both plays—Holinshed, Hall, Daniel, Stow, *The Famous Victories of Henry V*—have been assembled by Bullough and their use further analysed by Muir (1977). Humphreys dealt thoroughly with the sources in his Arden editions of the plays, as David Bevington has with Part 1 in his Oxford edition. Studies of Shakespeare's handling of his material based on comparisons with the sources include Seymour V. Connor on the role of Douglas (1948), Charles Fish on character motivation and audience response (1964), Mary Olive Thomas on Hal (1972), and Margaret B. Bryan on Sir Walter Blunt (1975). But the sources and analogues to provoke most recent interest have been those bearing on the character of Falstaff. Dover Wilson (1943) linked him most particularly with the Vice of the Morality plays, a line developed and expanded in Bernard Spivack's 'Falstaff and the Psychomachia' (1957) and his *Shakespeare and the Allegory of Evil* (1958), which examines changing audience reactions as the role was secularized, and Alan C. Dessen (1974). Falstaff has also been linked with the Braggart Soldier (D. C. Boughner, 1944 and 1954), with the tradition of the picaro (Herbert B. Rothschild, Jr., 1973), and with the centaur who educated the Greek hero in his cave (Douglas J. Stewart, 1977); his characteristics have been traced in emblem literature, from his associations with the moon and the hare, against Hal's sun and lion (James Hoyle, 1971), and his parodic gestures of wrath (Lawrence L. Levin, 1977). C. L. Barber (1959) cast the fat knight as a Lord of Misrule, a holiday king, a role which perhaps, in its parodic nature, encompasses the ambivalent biblical role of remorseful tempter ascribed him by D. J. Palmer (1970) and that of the Holy Fool assigned by Roy Battenhouse (1975). Walter Kaiser's *Praisers of Folly* (1963) saw him as a wise fool in the tradition of Erasmus's *Praise of Folly* and Rabelais, though Sukanta Chaudhuri's *Infirm Glory* (1981) carefully distinguishes his scepticism from that of Rabelais and Montaigne. Among theatrical precedents D. B. Landt (1966) pointed out how much of the character could have been constructed from a variety of roles in *The Famous Victories*, while Leo Salingar (1980) stressed the folk elements, including his St George-like 'resurrection';

J. A. Bryant, Jr. (1954) saw his unruly wit as built on the example of professional clowns like Dick Tarleton and Will Kempe, bringing their licentiousness within the authorial script. David Wiles, taking Kempe's professionalism more seriously than many have been prepared to do, has argued in *Shakespeare's Clown* (1987) that the role was written around his clown persona; Kempe's leaving of the Chamberlain's Men c.1599 may explain why Shakespeare did not revive Falstaff in *Henry V*, as he seemingly promises to do in 2 *Henry IV* (Epilogue).

Most of these critics insist that Shakespeare's handling of the character is superior to anything he found in the precedents, and wonderfully comic. But the emphasis on 'placing' Falstaff, or tracing his ancestry, or indeed exploring the implications of his name—see T. W. Herbert (1954), R. F. Willson, Jr. (1976), Norman Davis (1977), G. Walton Williams (1979)—parallels a decline in the earlier, often sentimental, celebration of the old rogue, strains of which were still apparent in Dover Wilson and hover, perhaps surprisingly, over two otherwise engagingly idiosyncratic essays: W. H. Auden (1948) sees him as an irresistibly endearing Unworldly Man, while William Empson (1953) makes of him a live-wire of amoral dramatic energy, an apt subject for his own critical wit, assaulting the complacent and the virtuous. Since then a growing concern with the grimmer social and political aspects of the plays may have tempered responses to Falstaff. He has been seen to represent an opportunistic social philosophy in the post-feudal world (Axel B. Clark, William B. Stone, both 1972), as the type of impoverished gentry in that period (Paul N. Siegel, 1974), and the antithesis of the Protestant ethic (Robert G. Hunter, 1978)—roles with uncomfortably immediate Elizabethan resonances. Robert N. Watson in *Shakespeare and the Hazards of Ambition* (1984) sees the Freudian and mythic elements of his relationship with Hal in much less indulgent terms than Auden did. Much has also been made latterly of the long-established fact that Shakespeare originally called his character Oldcastle (after the soldier and Lollard martyr, Lord Cobham), and that he changed it to Falstaff, presumably following protests from the Elizabethan Cobhams—again emphasizing local rather than universal aspects of the character. R. Fiehler (1955) extensively lists links between Oldcastle and Falstaff, while in *Shakespeare's Typological Satire* (1979) Alice-Lyle Scoufos pushes matters further than most people would in seeing the Elizabethan Cobhams as butts of the plays'

satire. Yet a growing school of thought does centre the Oldcastle/
Falstaff controversy in some way on William, Lord Cobham's
term as Lord Chamberlain (see R. J. Fehrenbach, 1986). Coupling
this with the theory that the third Falstaff play, *The Merry Wives
of Windsor*, was written/revised in connection with the younger
Lord Hunsdon's assumption of that office after him, there is an
argument for dating *Part 1* 1596 and *Part 2* 1597 (as Humphreys
tentatively does in the Arden editions), about a year earlier in
each case than many authorities suggest. Gary Taylor (1987), one
of the editors of *The Complete Oxford Shakespeare* has reviewed
all this (1985) in connection with his decision to restore 'Oldcastle'
to the text of *Part 1* as the truest reflection of Shakespeare's
intention in that play (though not to *Part 2*, since he concludes
that Shakespeare's mind had been changed before that was
staged); he has also (1987) strengthened the evidence for the
Cobhams insisting on the change being made. John Jowett (1987)
has argued, on the same principle, that Peto and Bardolph should
also be replaced by their originals, Harvey and Sir John Russell
(both of which may have had unfortunate contemporary connotations)—this in connection with a wider review of the names
and disposition of some of the lesser low-life characters, one of
the few major textual problems posed by these plays (also addressed by Fredson Bowers, 1981). David Bevington has not
followed either of these radical suggestions, nor been completely
convinced about the earlier dating, in his Oxford Shakespeare
1 Henry IV.

There have been some surprisingly sympathetic accounts of
the king in these plays, Charles Fish (1964) placing the responsibility for rebellion in *Part 1* upon the rebels, David Evett (1981)
seeing him as a suffering King David to his Absalom/Hal of a
son, while James Black (1983) sees the death in the Jerusalem
Chamber as a blessed, and not ironic, alternative to the crusade/
pilgrimage Henry had promised. But most people agree that
Hal—rather than Henry, or even Falstaff—is the focal point of
the plays. Many accounts examine the prince in the light of the
king he becomes, but I defer those to the next section. Opinions
divide as to whether Hal is a more-or-less temperate machiavel
(A. D. Nuttall coins the term 'White Machiavel' in an interesting
discussion, 1983), observing and manipulating other people to
his own ultimate advantage (in which case it may be inappropriate
to talk of him growing or being educated in the course of the

action), or whether he admirably matures towards some princely ideal. The first camp includes J. F. Danby (1949), Derek Traversi (1957), Jonas Barish (1965) who associates Hal's killjoy spirit and rejection of Falstaff with the likes of Shylock and Malvolio, and Stephen Greenblatt (1981; see below). Against this, following Tillyard and Dover Wilson, Hal has been seen as redeeming himself to become a model of Christian action (J. A. Bryant, Jr., 1959; Paul A. Jorgensen, 1960; Franklin B. Newman, 1966; D. J. Palmer, 1970) or of the Renaissance courtier/prince (William B. Hunter, Jr., 1950; W. Gordon Zeeveld, 1952; Charles Mitchell, 1967; Sherman Hawkins, 1975; J. P. Sisk, 1977; G. M. Pinciss, 1978; Gerard H. Cox, 1985), or simply an English paragon (Maynard Mack in his Signet edition of *Part 1*, 1965). These latter readings have somewhat to gloss over Hal's having no more legitimate claim to the throne than his father, an issue considered by Hugh Dickinson (1961) and Alan Gerald Cross (1968). Whatever view is held of Hal, there is a general consensus that the key scenes in determining his politics and personality are those, particularly in *Part 1*, in the Eastcheap taverns and involving his parodic play-acting with Falstaff, which have come in for close scrutiny (see Fredson Bowers, 1966; Waldo F. McNeir, 1966; Richard L. McGuire, 1967; J. D. Shuchter, 1968; Sheldon P. Zitner, 1968; Paul A. Gottschalk, 1974; and J. McLaverty, 1981). Steven Mullaney (1988) parallels Hal's 'learning experience' in the taverns and brothels with the marginalized place of the Elizabethan popular theatre, situated in the anomalous Liberties outside the City of London, a New Historicist perspective consonant with those discussed in the next section.

Henry V

TEXTS

Brown, J. R. (ed.), *Henry V* (Signet Shakespeare, New York, 1965).
    Useful student edition; helpful glosses at foot of page; with extracts from sources and Hazlitt, Yeats, Tillyard.

Humphreys, A. R. (ed.), *Henry V* (New Penguin Shakespeare, Harmondsworth, 1968).
    Useful introduction, aware of the darker sides of the play but seeing Henry rising above these at Agincourt; suggestions for further reading; text presented plain (ideal for acting and un-

cluttered reading), full commentary and account of the text at the end.

Taylor, Gary (ed.), *Henry V* (Oxford Shakespeare, 1982).
   Very full introduction, especially notable for its coverage of the play's stage history; text notable for its re-valuation of the 1600 quarto, largely ignored by earlier editors; appendices focus on specific textual details, *cruces*, direct borrowings from Holinshed (though there is no general reprinting of the sources), profanities, and early allusions to the play.

Walter, J. H. (ed.), *Henry V* (Arden Shakespeare, London, 1954).
   Full introduction (argues for Henry as a Christian hero), most useful on the sources and textual matters; detailed and reasoned textual and explanatory notes on the page, often tracing the editorial history of *cruces*; extracts from the sources. One of this formerly near-definitive series beginning to show its age.

   Joseph Candido and Charles R. Forker have compiled a thorough, dispassionately annotated bibliography (1983). Bullough, as usual, is the starting-point for a consideration of the sources, mainly Holinshed, Hall, and *The Famous Victories*, though doubts have been cast on Bullough's acceptance of Tacitus's *Annals* as a source for Henry's going disguised among his troops. Anne Barton (1975) posits a variety of historical romance plays of the 1590s as more likely analogues, if not exactly sources. Her general thesis, that Shakespeare is ironizing and rejecting the romantic mode, is part of an on-going debate about the play's generic bearings. Rose Zimbardo (1969) argued that it was a formal work of celebration, perfectly balanced and unironic. Roy W. Battenhouse (1963), however, sees a strain of warm, Chaucerian satire aimed at reprobate heroism and false glory in what he construes as the play's heroic comedy, while Robert Egan (1968) sees Henry's potentially tragic dilemma—outwardly conquering monarch, inwardly Christian conscience—resolved in comic fashion by his final discovery of his true identity. But Paul Dean and Joanne Altieri (both 1981) both find something disturbing in the play's mixture of history and romance.
   Worries about the generic identity of the histories are commonplace, but with *Henry V* they seem to go to the heart of the play's reception. Is it a celebration of national glory, with Henry a truly heroic warrior prince? Or is it a dark satire on warfare and the

abuses of power, a prelude to the tragedies soon to follow? Is it symptomatic of the lack of unanimity on this point that Tillyard (1944), for whom the play might logically have been the climax of a providential sequence, found it a disappointment, suggesting that Shakespeare jettisoned the subtle ironist Hal he had created to build an unsatisfactory play around the Henry of the chronicles and popular tradition? Our view of Henry is perhaps the crucial issue. At one extreme Keiji Aoki argues in *Shakespeare's 'Henry IV' and 'Henry V': Hal's Heroic Character and the Sun-Cloud Theme* (1973) that Henry's is always an ideal nature, though skilfully hidden successively from the English and French courts: the drama is one of repeated, stage-managed revelations of his true self—his defeat of Hotspur carefully revealed only to Falstaff (who has his own reasons for not making it public) so as to allow for a subsequent, more overwhelming revelation. Western critics who have found Henry on balance admirable tend to have seen it as a matter of growth or development. J. H. Walter in his Arden edition argued for Henry as a Christian epic hero. Arthur Humphreys in his New Penguin edition recognizes the darker elements in the play, but sees a confidence emerging in the Agincourt speech, Henry matured by trial and not finally a tragic figure. Norman Sanders (1977) sees him overcoming a dissociation of identity in the earlier plays to find a true resolution of self in the public political role given him in *Henry V*. W. Babula (1977) similarly sees Henry achieving real success as a national leader, but only at the end of *Henry V*—his progress to that point, including even Agincourt, being subjected to harsh criticism. Karl P. Wentersdorf (1976) points out that Shakespeare says nothing in the play about Cambridge's claim to the throne, a silence which absolves Henry from having publicly to argue his own claim and subtly weighs in our sympathies. Joseph Candido (1984) considers the variety of titles by which Hal is known in the plays, as a key to the forms of linguistic and political integrity he achieves. Kent T. van den Berg in *Playhouse and Cosmos: Shakespearean Theater as Metaphor* (1985) confronts the play's self-conscious theatricality (the 'wooden O') in arguing that Henry is presented as an ideal king, but that the audience have to concur in declining ironic perspectives, which the play acknowledges are possible. The other side of the coin—Henry as cold-blooded hypocrite—was most forcefully argued for by Gerald Gould (1919) in the wake of the First World War, and picked up in the wake of the Second by H. C. Goddard in *The Meaning of Shake-speare* (1951). The most jaundiced recent reading is that by Andrew Gurr (1977), who sees it as a play dominated by the self-interest of the king and others, sceptical in the extreme about what can be achieved in the political world. Between the antithetic views of the play as national epic, with a heroic king, or as anti-war satire, dominated by a self-interested hypocrite, several readings have tried to reconcile the possibilities in terms of tension or ambiguity: Traversi (1957) sees Henry reconciling his humanity with the superhumanity of his office by a process of consciously accepted mortification. But his most telling perception is one of Henry constantly endeavouring to place the responsibility for his actions on other people—a point echoed by Honor Matthews in *Character and Symbol in Shakespeare's Plays* (1962), who sees him at best as an ambiguous hero. Norman Rabkin (1977) sees two plays in one, a heroic sequel to 1 *Henry IV* and a darker, more interesting sequel to 2 *Henry IV*, with the audience left to mediate between the two. Brownell Salomon (1980) detects a similar ambivalence deliberately built into the play's scenic alternations. Jonathan Bate (1985) ingeniously traces how various facets of the ambivalent Hal/Henry character were applied to the Prince of Wales during the Regency period.

Gordon Ross Smith (1976) offers corroboration of a kind for the notion of a two-faced play by demonstrating that Elizabethan opinions of Henry were distinctly more mixed than proponents of a simple patriotism often assume. Another aspect of the play's contemporary derivations, its relations to England's imperial aspirations, is interestingly dealt with in Philip Edwards's *Threshold of a Nation* (1979). The apparent reference to Essex's 1599 Irish expedition in the Chorus to Act 5 has led to much speculation about the play's political affinities and dating. W. D. Smith (1954), noting the absence of the reference in the 1600 quarto, argued that it was a later reference to Mountjoy, not Essex; he was reasonably answered by R. A. Law (1956). G. P. Jones (1978) has argued for an earlier date of composition, with the possibility of a court performance. All of this, together with a re-think of the status of the 1600 quarto, was thoroughly re-examined by Gary Taylor in 'The Text of *Henry V*: Three Studies' (1979), the findings of which were the basis for the editorial procedures he used in his Oxford edition of the play (1982).

The *Henry IV* plays and *Henry V* have been central texts in the critical movement known variously as New Historicism and Cultural Materialism, translating the humanist concern with the character of Hal/Henry into a concern for the ideological implications of the style of power he represents. Stephen Greenblatt offers 'a poetics of Elizabethan power', in what is already an influential, much reprinted essay, 'Invisible Bullets' (1981, expanded 1985), based on a Foucauldian model of authority sustaining itself by encouraging its own opposition, a cyclic process of subversion and containment. Leonard Tennenhouse (1985) relates these plays in a cross-generic manner to *A Midsummer Night's Dream*, Petrarchan lyrics, and *Henry VIII*, all advanced as forms of literature employing 'radically discontinuous political strategies for idealizing political authority'. Jonathan Dollimore and Alan Sinfield (1985) consider *Henry V* as a test case of modern 'appropriations' of Shakespeare; Günther Walch (1988) also approaches it as a 'working-house of ideology'. See also Graham Holderness (1984) on the Olivier film of *Henry V*.

STAGE AND FILM PRODUCTION

The second tetralogy was staged as a sequence at Stratford in 1951 (directed by Antony Quayle and markedly influenced by Tillyard). It is a measure of the subsequent rise in esteem of these plays that Richard David (1953) began his review of that Stratford season with the words: 'Shakespeare's Histories are not popular. They are generally regarded as inferior works . . .'; by 1968, following complete cycles of both tetralogies at Stratford in 1964 (directed by John Barton with Peter Hall), Kenneth Tynan was of the opinion that 'the two parts of *Henry IV* are the twin summits of Shakespeare's achievement . . . great public plays in which a whole nation is under scrutiny and on trial. . . . To conceive the state of mind in which the Henries were written is to feel dizzied by the air of Olympus' (quoted by A. R. Humphreys, 1973). The 1951 season was also considered by Dover Wilson and T. C. Worsley in *Shakespeare's Histories at Stratford, 1951* (1952), while the 1964 productions were the subject of J. R. Brown in *Shakespeare's Plays in Performance* (1966), though see Humphreys's 1973 caveats. John Barton directed *Richard II* at Stratford in 1973, with Richard Pasco and Ian Richardson alternating Richard and Bolingbroke in one of the most discussed productions of recent times. There are accounts by James Stredder (1976), Stanley Wells— fittingly, since the production owed more than a little to the introduction of his New Penguin edition of the play—in *Royal Shakespeare* (1977), Richard David (1978), Malcolm Page in *Richard II: Text and Performance* (1987), and in Andrew Gurr's New Cambridge edition. Michael L. Greenwald's *Directions by Indirections* (1986) considers John Barton's role as director in both the 1964 sequence and the *Richard II*. Three Royal Shakespeare Company productions of *Richard II*—John Barton's, Terry Hands's (1980–81), and Barry Kyle's (1986–7) are assessed in an extended comparative study, *In One Person Many People* (1988), by Liisa Hakola. The Henry plays of the second tetralogy, with *The Merry Wives of Windsor*, were staged at Stratford (director, Terry Hands) in 1975 and analysed in Richard David's *Shakespeare in the Theatre* (1978), with special consideration going to the *Henry V* in Sally Beauman's *The Royal Shakespeare Company's Production of 'Henry V' for the Centenary Season at the Royal Shakespeare Theatre* (1976) and an essay by Gary Taylor on the audience's response to that production (1985). Trevor Nunn directed the Royal Shakespeare Company in the *Henry IV* plays at the Barbican in 1982. T. F. Wharton usefully compared and contrasted these with their 1964 and 1975 productions, and the BBC TV 1979 productions, in *Henry IV, Parts 1 and 2. Text and Performance* (1983). The Royal Shakespeare Company inevitably if unfortunately receives the lion's share of attention, but the general production history of the plays throughout the world can be traced in the annual reviews in *Shakespeare Quarterly* (Washington, DC) and *Shakespeare Survey* (Cambridge). The earlier stage history of the second tetralogy is covered in A. C. Sprague's *Shakespeare's Histories: Plays for the Stage* (1964) and J. C. Trewin's *Shakespeare on the English Stage* (1964), while the Oxford editions of the plays make the stage history an important element of their introductions. Michael Goldman's *Shakespeare and the Energies of Drama* (1972) is particularly perceptive about the theatrical potential of these plays and the ways in which production can resolve what in the study may seem to be problems. Anthony B. Dawson's *Watching Shakespeare: A Playgoer's Guide* (1988) helpfully surveys the plays as pieces for the theatre. Harry Berger, Jr. (1987) uses the *Henriad* to explore what he calls textual dramaturgy—'the indications of staging given by the Shakespeare text'.

The second tetralogy has given rise to two feature films. Laurence Olivier's film of *Henry V* (1944 and dedicated to Britain's war-time commandos and airborne troops; script published

1971 by Garrett *et al.*, and see Olivier, 1984) was imaginative, visually splendid, and clearly demonstrates the patriotic potential of the play—though it is useful to consider the amendments made to achieve that. In 1966 Orson Welles adapted the *Henry IV* plays into *Chimes at Midnight* (*Falstaff* in the US) revolving around himself in the role of Falstaff, in elegiac rather than comic mood. The BBC has twice broadcast the tetralogy as a sequence, in 1960 as part of *An Age of Kings* and in 1978/79 as part of the BBC/Time–Life Television Shakespeare. A filmography by Holderness and McCullough (1987) gives production details of all the significant film and TV versions of these plays. The two feature films are discussed by Roger Manvell (1971) and Jack J. Jorgens (1977). Harry M. Geduld incisively analysed Olivier's *Henry V* (1973), while Graham Holderness (1984) has considered the ideological implications of the film and responses to it; *Chimes at Midnight* is discussed by Samuel Crowl (1980) and Robert Hapgood (1987). There is a round-table discussion with David Giles, director of the second tetralogy plays in the BBC Television Shakespeare, and an analysis of both tetralogies in that series by Michèle Willems, in a collection of pieces edited by Willems herself (1987).

REFERENCES

GENERAL

Albright, Evelyn, M., 'Shakespeare's *Richard II* and the Essex Conspiracy', *PMLA* 42 (1927), 686–720.
—— 'Shakespeare's *Richard II*, Hayward's History of Henry IV, and the Essex Conspiracy', *PMLA* 46 (1931), 694–719.
Baker, Herschel, *The Race of Time* (Toronto, 1967).
Barton, Anne, 'Shakespeare and the Limits of Language', *Shakespeare Survey 24* (1971), 19–30.
Bergeron, David M. (ed.), *Pageantry in the Shakespearean Theater* (Athens, Ga., 1985).
Bethell, S. L., 'The Comic Element in Shakespeare's Histories', *Anglia*, 71 (1952–3), 82–101.
Bevington, David, *Tudor Drama and Politics: A Critical Approach to Topical Meaning* (Cambridge, Mass., 1968).
—— (ed.), *Henry IV, Parts 1 & 2: Critical Essays* (details under *1 & 2 Henry IV*, below).
Blanpied, John W., *Time and the Artist in Shakespeare's English Histories* (Newark, Del., 1983).

Boris, Edna Zwick, *Shakespeare's English Kings, the People, and the Law* (Rutherford, NJ, 1978).

Boswell-Stone, W. G. (ed.), *Shakespeare's Holinshed: The Chronicle and the Historical Plays Compared* (London, 1896).

Bradley, A. C., 'The Rejection of Falstaff', in *Oxford Lectures on Poetry* (London, 1909), 247–73; reprinted in *Henry IV, Parts 1 & 2: Critical Essays*, ed. D. Bevington (1986), 77–98.

Bromley, John C., *The Shakespearean Kings* (Boulder, Colo., 1971).

Brooks, Harold, 'Shakespeare and *The Governour*', *Shakespeare Quarterly*, 14 (1963), 195–9.

Bullough, Geoffrey (ed.), *Narrative and Dramatic Sources of Shakespeare*, vol. iv, *Later English History Plays* (London, 1962).

Burckhardt, Sigurd, ' "Swoll'n with Some Other Grief": Shakespeare's Prince Hal Trilogy', in his *Shakespearean Meanings* (Princeton, NJ, 1968), 144–205.

Burden, Dennis H., 'Shakespeare's History Plays: 1952–1983', *Shakespeare Survey 38* (1985), 1–18.

Calderwood, James L., *Metadrama in Shakespeare's Henriad: 'Richard II' to 'Henry V'* (Berkeley, Calif., 1979).

—— *Shakespearean Metadrama* (Minneapolis, Minn., 1971).

Campbell, Lily B., *Shakespeare's 'Histories': Mirrors of Elizabethan Policy* (San Marino, Calif., 1947).

Carr, Virginia, 'Once More into the Henriad: A Two-Eyed View', *JEGP* 77 (1978), 530–45.

Champion, Larry S., *Perspective in Shakespeare's English Histories* (Athens, Ga., 1980).

Clemen, Wolfgang H., *Past and Future in Shakespeare's Drama*, British Academy Lecture 1966.

Coursen, H. R., *The Leasing Out of England: Shakespeare's Second Henriad* (Washington, DC, 1982).

Craig, Hardin, *The Enchanted Glass: The Elizabethan Mind in Literature* (New York, 1936; reprinted Westport, Conn., 1975).

Daniel, Samuel, *The First Fowre Bookes of the Civile Warrs between the Two Houses of Lancaster and Yorke* (London, 1595, 1609).

Dean, Leonard F., 'From *Richard II* to *Henry V*: A Closer View', in *Studies in Honour of DeWitt T. Starnes*, ed. Thomas P. Harrison and James H. Sledd (Austin, Tex., 1967), 37–52.

Doran, Madeleine, *Endeavors of Art: A Study of Form in Elizabethan Drama* (Madison, Wis., 1954).

Dorius, R. J., 'A Little More Than a Little', *Shakespeare Quarterly*, 11 (1960), 13–26; reprinted in *Henry IV, Parts 1 & 2: Critical Essays*, ed. D. Bevington (1986), 263–76.

Driver, Tom F., *The Sense of History in Greek and Shakespearean Drama* (New York, 1960).

Ellis-Fermor, Una, 'Shakespeare's Political Plays', in her *The Frontiers of Drama* (London, 1945; reprinted 1964 (University Paperbacks)), 34–55.

Elyot, Thomas, *The Boke Named The Governour* (London, 1531); ed. S. E. Lehmberg (Everyman's Library, London, 1962).

Empson, William, 'The Double Plot', in *Some Versions of Pastoral* (London, 1935).

Foakes, R. A., 'Suggestions for a New Approach to Shakespeare's Imagery', *Shakespeare Survey* 5 (1952), 81–92.

Forker, Charles R., 'Shakespeare's Chronicle Plays as Historical-Pastoral', *Shakespeare Studies*, 1 (1965), 84–104.

Frye, Northrop, 'Nature and Nothing', in *Essays on Shakespeare*, ed. Gerald W. Chapman (Princeton, NJ, 1965), 35–58.

Hall, Edward, *The Union of the Two Noble and Illustre Famelies of Lancastre and Yorke* (London, 1548; ed. Henry Ellis (London, 1809, and Scolar Press, Menston, 1970).

Hapgood, Robert, 'Shakespeare's Delayed Reactions', *Essays in Criticism*, 13 (1963), 9–16.

Hart, Alfred, *Shakespeare and the Homilies* (Melbourne, 1934).

Hibbard, G. R., *The Making of Shakespeare's Dramatic Poetry* (Toronto, 1981).

Hirsch, James E., *The Structure of Shakespearian Scenes* (New Haven, Conn., 1981).

Holderness, Graham, *Shakespeare's History* (Dublin and New York, 1985).

Hosley, Richard (ed.), *Shakespeare's Holinshed: An Edition of Holinshed's Chronicles (1587)* (New York, 1968).

Humphreys, Arthur R., 'Shakespeare and the Tudor Perception of History', in *Stratford Papers on Shakespeare, 1964*, ed. B. W. Jackson (Toronto, 1965), 51–70, reprinted in *Shakespeare Celebrated*, ed. L. B. Wright (Ithaca, NY, 1966), 89–112.

—— *Shakespeare's Histories and the 'Emotion of Multitude'*, British Academy Lecture 1968 (London, 1970).

Ives, E. W., 'Shakespeare and History: Divergencies and Agreements', *Shakespeare Survey* 38 (1985), 19–35.

Iwasaki, Soji, *The Sword and the Word* (Tokyo, 1973).

Jenkins, Harold, 'Shakespeare's History Plays: 1900–1951', *Shakespeare Survey* 6 (1953), 1–15.

Jones, Emrys, *Scenic Form in Shakespeare* (Oxford, 1971).

Jorgensen, Paul, *Shakespeare's Military World* (Berkeley, Calif., 1956).

Kastan, David Scott, *Shakespeare and the Shapes of Time* (Hanover, NH, 1982).

Kelly, Henry Ansgar, *Divine Providence in the England of Shakespeare's Histories* (Cambridge, Mass., 1970).

Kernan, Alvin B., '*The Henriad*: Shakespeare's Major History Plays', *Yale*

Review, 59 (1969), 3–32; reprinted in *Modern Shakespearean Criticism*, ed. Alvin B. Kernan (New York, 1970), 245–75.

Kingsford, C. L., *English Historical Literature in the Fifteenth Century* (Oxford, 1913).

Knights, L. C., 'The Public World: First Observations', in his *Some Shakespearean Themes* (London, 1959), 26–44.

—— *Shakespeare's Politics*, Annual Lecture of the British Academy 1957 (London, 1958); reprinted in his *Further Explorations* (London, 1965), 11–32.

Kott, Jan, *Shakespeare Our Contemporary* (London, 1964).

La Guardia, Eric, 'Ceremony and History: The Problem of Symbol from *Richard II* to *Henry V*', in *Pacific Coast Studies in Shakespeare*, ed. W. F. McNeir and T. N. Greenfield (Eugene, Oreg., 1966), 68–88.

Lanham, Richard, *The Motives of Eloquence* (New Haven, Conn., 1976).

Law, R. A., 'Shakespeare's Historical Cycle: Organism or Compilation?', *Studies in Philology*, 51 (1954), 34–9.

Levin, Richard, *The Multiple Plot in Renaissance Drama* (Chicago, Ill., 1971).

Levy, F. J., *Tudor Historical Thought* (San Marino, Calif., 1967).

Lindberger, Herbert, *Historical Drama: The Relation of Literature and Reality* (Chicago, Ill., 1978).

Lovejoy, Arthur O., *The Great Chain of Being: A Study of the History of an Idea* (Cambridge, Mass., 1936).

Macdonald, Ronald R., 'Uneasy Lies: Language and History in Shakespeare's Lancastrian Tetralogy', *Shakespeare Quarterly*, 35 (1984), 22–39; reprinted in *Henry IV, Parts 1 & 2: Critical Essays*, ed. D. Bevington (1986), 359–85.

Manheim, Michael, *The Weak King Dilemma in the Shakespearean History Play* (Syracuse, NY, 1973).

McKisack, May, *Medieval History in the Tudor Age* (Oxford, 1971).

Morgann, Maurice, *An Essay on the Dramatic Character of Sir John Falstaff* (London, published for T. Davies, 1777); in *Maurice Morgann: Shakespearian Criticism*, ed. Daniel A. Fineman (Oxford, 1972), and reprinted in *Henry IV, Parts 1 and 2: Critical Essays*, ed. D. Bevington (1986), 15–40.

Morris, Christopher, *Political Thought in England: Tyndale to Hooker* (London, 1953).

Muir, Kenneth, *Image and Symbol in Shakespeare's Histories* (Manchester, 1967).

—— *The Sources of Shakespeare's Plays* (London, 1977).

A Myrroure for Magistrates (London, 1559); ed. Lily B. Campbell (Cambridge, 1938).

Nicoll, Allardyce and Josephine (eds.), *Holinshed's Chronicle, As Used in Shakespeare's Plays* (Everyman's Library: London, 1927).

Nuttall, A. D., 'Ovid's Narcissus and Shakespeare's Richard II: The Reflected Self', in *Ovid Renewed: Ovidian Influences on Literature and Art from the Middle Ages to the Twentieth Century*, ed. Charles Martindale (Cambridge, 1988).

Ornstein, Robert, *A Kingdom for a Stage* (Cambridge, Mass., 1972).

Palmer, Barbara D., ' Ciphers to This Great Accompt": Civic Pageantry in the Second Tetralogy', in *Pageantry in the Shakespearean Theater*, ed. David M. Bergeron (Athens, Ga., 1985), 114–29.

Pierce, Robert B., *Shakespeare's History Plays: The Family and the State* (Columbus, Ohio, 1971).

Porter, Joseph A., *The Drama of Speech Acts* (Berkeley, Calif., 1979).

Prior, Moody E., *The Drama of Power: Studies in Shakespeare's History Plays* (Evanston, Ill., 1973).

Quinones, Ricardo J., *The Renaissance Discovery of Time* (Cambridge, Mass., 1972).

Rabkin, Norman, *Shakespeare and the Common Understanding* (New York, 1967).

Reese, M. M., *The Cease of Majesty* (London, 1961).

Ribner, Irving, *The English History Play in the Age of Shakespeare* (Princeton, NJ, 1957; rev. edn., 1965).

Richmond, H. M., *Shakespeare's Political Plays* (New York, 1967).

Riggs, David, *Shakespeare's Heroical Histories* (Cambridge, Mass., 1971).

Rose, Mark, *Shakespearean Design* (Cambridge, Mass., 1972).

Rossiter, A. P., 'Ambivalence: The Dialectic of the Histories', in his *Angel with Horns* (London, 1961).

Saccio, Peter, *Shakespeare's English Kings* (Oxford, 1977).

Sen Gupta, S. C., *Shakespeare's Historical Plays* (London, 1964).

Simpson, Richard, 'The Politics of Shakspere's Historical Plays', *Transactions of the New Shakspere Society*, 1 (1874), 396–441.

Smidt, Kristian, *Unconformities in Shakespeare's History Plays* (London, 1982).

Spencer, Theodore, *Shakespeare and the Nature of Man* (New York, 1942; 2nd edn., 1949).

Spurgeon, Caroline, *Shakespeare's Imagery and What It Tells Us* (Cambridge, 1935; reprinted Boston, 1958).

Stow, John, *The Annales of England* (London, 1592).

—— *The Chronicles of England* (London, 1580).

Sypher, F. Wylie, *The Ethic of Time* (New York, 1976).

Tennenhouse, Leonard, *Power on Display: The Politics of Shakespeare's Genres* (London, 1986).

Thayer, C. G., *Shakespeare's Politics* (Athens, Ohio, and London, 1983).

—— 'Shakespeare's Second Tetralogy: An Underground Report', *Ohio University Review*, 9 (1967), 5–15.

Tillyard, E. M. W., *The Elizabethan World Picture* (London, 1943).

Tillyard, E. M. W.; Links between Shakespeare's History Plays', *Studies in Philology*, 50 (1953), 168–87.
—— *Shakespeare's History Plays* (London, 1944).
Toliver, Harold E., 'Falstaff, the Prince, and the History Play', *Shakespeare Quarterly*, 16 (1965), 63–80.
Tomlinson, Michael, 'Shakespeare and the Chronicles Reassessed', *Literature and History*, 10 (1984), 46–88.
Traversi, Derek A., *Shakespeare: From 'Richard II' to 'Henry V'* (Stanford, Calif., 1957).
Turner, Robert Y., *Shakespeare's Apprenticeship* (Chicago, Ill., 1974).
Vergil, Polydore, *The Anglia Historia of Polydore Vergil, A.D. 1486–1537*, ed. Denys Hay (Camden Society, 3rd Ser. 74, London, 1950).
Waller, Gary F., *The Strong Necessity of Time* (The Hague, 1976).
Webber, Joan, 'The Renewal of the King's Symbolic Role: From *Richard II* to *Henry V*', *Texas Studies in Literature and Language*, 4 (1963), 530–8.
Welsford, Enid, *The Fool: His Social and Literary History* (London, 1935).
Whitaker, Virgil, *Shakespeare's Use of Learning* (San Marino, Calif., 1935).
Wilders, John, *The Lost Garden: A View of Shakespeare's English and Roman History Plays* (London, 1978).
Wilson, F. P., 'The English History Play', in his *Shakespearian and Other Studies*, ed. Helen Gardner (Oxford, 1969), 1–53.
Wilson, John Dover, *The Fortunes of Falstaff* (Cambridge, 1943).
Winny, James, *The Player King* (London, 1968).
Zeeveld, W. Gordon, *The Temper of Shakespeare's Thought* (New Haven, Conn., 1974).

Richard II

Altick, R. D., 'Symphonic Imagery in *Richard II*', *PMLA* 62 (1947), 339–65; reprinted in the Signet edition, *'Richard II': A Casebook*, ed. N. Brooke (1973), and *'Richard II': Critical Essays*, ed. J. T. Newlin (1984).
Axton, Marie, *The Queen's Two Bodies: Drama and the Elizabethan Succession* (London, 1977).
Battenhouse, Roy, 'Tudor Doctrine and the Tragedy of *Richard II*', *Rice University Studies*, 60 (1974), 31–53.
Baxter, John, *Shakespeare's Poetic Styles* (London, 1980).
Bergeron, David M., 'The Deposition Scene in *Richard II*', *Renaissance Papers* (1974), 31–7.
—— 'The Hoby Letter and *Richard II*: a Parable of Criticism', *Shakespeare Quarterly*, 26 (1975), 477–80.
Black, James, 'The Interlude of the Beggar and the King', in *Pageantry in the Shakespearean Theater*, ed. David M. Bergeron (Athens, Ga., 1985), 104–113.

Black, Matthew W., 'The Sources of Shakespeare's *Richard II*', in *Joseph Quincy Adams Memorial Studies*, ed. J. G. McManaway, G. E. Dawson, and E. E. Willoughby (Washington, DC, 1948), 199–216.

Bloom, Allan, '*Richard II*', in *Shakespeare as a Political Thinker*, ed. J. Alvis and T. G. West (Durham, NC, 1981), 51–61.

Bogard, Travis, 'Shakespeare's Second Richard', *PMLA* 70 (1955), 192–209.

Brooke, Nicholas, *Shakespeare's Early Tragedies* (London, 1968), 110–33.

—— (ed.), '*Richard II*': *A Casebook* (London and Basingstoke, 1973): contains extracts from Altick, J. R. Brown, Brooke, Bryant, Gielgud, Kantorowicz, Mahood, Rossiter, Tillyard.

Bryant, J. A., Jr., 'Linked Analogies of *Richard II*', *Sewanee Review*, 65 (1957), 420–33.

Champion, Larry S., 'The Function of Mowbray: Shakespeare's Maturing Artistry in *Richard II*', *Shakespeare Quarterly*, 26 (1975), 3–7.

Dean, Leonard F., '*Richard II*: The State and the Image of the Theater', *PMLA* 67 (1952), 211–18; reprinted in *Shakespeare: Modern Essays in Criticism*, ed. Leonard F. Dean (New York, 1957), 188–205.

Edwards, Philip, 'Person and Office in Shakespeare's Plays', British Academy Lecture 1970; reprinted in *Proceedings of the British Academy*, 56 (1972), 93–109.

Elliott, John R., Jr., 'History and Tragedy in *Richard II*', *SEL* 8 (1968), 253–71.

—— '*Richard II* and the Medieval', in *Renaissance Papers, 1965*, ed. G. W. Williams and Peter Phialas (1966), 25–34.

Folland, Harold F., 'King Richard's Pallid Victory', *Shakespeare Quarterly*, 24 (1973), 390–9.

French, A. L., '*Richard II*: A Rejoinder', *Essays in Criticism*, 18 (1968), 229–33.

Friedman, Donald M., 'John of Gaunt and the Rhetoric of Frustration', *ELH* 43 (1976), 274–99.

Gaudet, Paul, 'The "Parasitical" Counselors in Shakespeare's *Richard II*: A Problem of Dramatic Interpretation', *Shakespeare Quarterly*, 33 (1982), 142–54.

Gielgud, John, 'Introduction, *King Richard II*' (London, 1958), revised in his *Stage Directions* (London, 1963); reprinted in *Shakespeare's Histories: An Anthology of Modern Criticism*, ed. W. A. Armstrong (Penguin Shakespeare Library, Harmondsworth, 1972), 196–201, and '*Richard II*': *A Casebook*, ed. N. Brooke (London, 1973), 77–81.

Gilman, Ernest B., *The Curious Perspective: Literary and Pictorial Wit in the Seventeenth Century* (New Haven, Conn., 1978).

Grivelet, Michel, 'Shakespeare's "War with Time": The Sonnets and *Richard II*', *Shakespeare Survey 23* (1970), 69–73.

Hapgood, Robert, 'Three Eras in *Richard II*', *Shakespeare Quarterly*, 14 (1963), 281–3.

Harris, Kathryn M., 'Sun and Water Imagery in *Richard II*', *Shakespeare Quarterly*, 21 (1970), 157–65.

Hawkes, Terence, *Shakespeare's Talking Animals* (London, 1973).

Hill, R. F., 'Dramatic Technique and Interpretation in *Richard II*', in *Early Shakespeare*, ed. J. R. Brown and B. Harris (Stratford-upon-Avon Studies, 3; London, 1961), 100–21.

—— 'Shakespeare's Early Tragic Mode', *Shakespeare Quarterly*, 9 (1958), 455–69.

Hockey, Dorothy C., 'A World of Rhetoric in *Richard II*', *Shakespeare Quarterly*, 15 (1964), 179–91.

Holderness, Graham, 'Shakespeare's History: *Richard II*', *Literature and History*, 7 (1981), 2–24; expanded in his *Shakespeare's History* (1985), 40–144.

Homan, Sidney, '*Richard II*: The Aesthetics of Judgement', *Studies in the Literary Imagination*, 5 (1972), 65–71.

Humphreys, Arthur R., *Shakespeare: 'Richard II'* (Arnold's Studies in English Literature, 31; London, 1967).

—— 'Shakespeare's Political Justice in *Richard II* and *Henry IV*', in *Stratford Papers on Shakespeare, 1964*, ed. B. W. Jackson (Toronto, 1965), 30–50.

Kantorowicz, Ernst H., *The King's Two Bodies: A Study in Medieval Political Theology* (Princeton, NJ, 1957).

Kelly, Michael F., 'The Function of York in *Richard II*', *Southern Humanities Review*, 6 (1972), 257–67.

Logan, George M., 'Lucan-Daniel-Shakespeare: New Light on the Relation between *The Civil Wars* and *Richard II*', *Shakespeare Studies*, 9 (1976), 121–40.

Mahood, Molly M., *Shakespeare's Wordplay* (London, 1957).

Maveety, Stanley R., 'A Second Fall of Cursed Man: The Bold Metaphor in *Richard II*', *JEGP* 72 (1973), 175–93.

McAlindon, T., *Shakespeare and Decorum* (London, 1973).

Merrix, Robert P., 'Shakespeare's Histories and the New Bardolators', *SEL* 19 (1979), 179–96.

Montgomery, Robert L., 'The Dimension of Time in *Richard II*', *Shakespeare Studies*, 4 (1969), 73–85.

Newlin, Jeanne T. (ed.), *'Richard II': Critical Essays* (New York and London, 1984).

Pater, Walter, 'Shakespeare's English Kings', in his *Appreciations* (London, 1889), 192–212; reprinted in the Signet edition and *'Richard II': Critical Essays*, ed. J. T. Newlin (1984).

Phialas, Peter, 'The Medieval in *Richard II*', *Shakespeare Quarterly*, 12 (1961), 305–10.

—— '*Richard II* and Shakespeare's Tragic Mode', *Texas Studies in Literature and Language*, 3 (1961), 344–55.

Potter, Lois, 'The Antic Disposition of Richard II', *Shakespeare Survey 27* (1974), 33–41.

Quinn, Michael, ' "The King Is Not Himself: The Personal Tragedy of *Richard II'*, *Studies in Philology*, 56 (1959), 169–86.

Reiman, Donald H., 'Appearance, Reality and Moral Order in *Richard II'*, *Modern Language Quarterly*, 25 (1964), 34–45.

Riddell, James A., 'The Admirable Character of York', *Texas Studies in Literature and Language*, 21 (1979), 492–502.

Roberts, Josephine A., *'Richard II': An Annotated Bibliography*, 2 vols., (Garland Shakespeare Bibliographies, 14; New York, 1988).

Rossiter, A. P., *'Richard II'*, in his *Angel with Horns* (London, 1961), 23–29.

——(ed.), *Woodstock: A Moral History* (London, 1946).

Schoenbaum, S., *'Richard II* and the Realities of Power', *Shakespeare Survey 28* (1975), 1–13; reprinted in his *Shakespeare and Others* (Washington, DC and London, 1985), 80–96.

Suzman, Arthur, 'Imagery and Symbolism in *Richard II'*, *Shakespeare Quarterly*, 7 (1956), 350–70.

Talbert, E. W., *The Problem of Order: Elizabethan Political Commonplaces and an Example of Shakespeare's Art* (Chapel Hill, NC, 1962).

Thompson, Karl F., 'Richard II, Martyr', *Shakespeare Quarterly*, 8 (1957), 159–66.

Ure, Peter, *'Richard II*: or "To Find Out Right With Wrong" ', *Essays in Criticism*, 18 (1968), 225–9.

Van Laan, Thomas F., *Role-Playing in Shakespeare* (1978).

Wells, Stanley, 'The Lamentable Tale of Richard II', *Shakespeare Studies*, 17 (Tokyo, 1982), 1–23.

Yeats, W. B., 'At Stratford-upon-Avon', in his *Ideas of Good and Evil* (London, 1903); reprinted in *'Richard II': Critical Essays*, ed. J. T. Newlin (1984).

Zitner, Sheldon P., 'Aumerle's Conspiracy', *SEL* 14 (1974), 239–57.

1 and 2 Henry IV

Auden, W. H., 'The Prince's Dog', in *'The Dyer's Hand' and Other Essays* (New York, 1948), 182–208; reprinted in *'Henry IV, Parts 1 and 2': A Casebook*, ed. G. K. Hunter (1970), 187–211, and *Henry IV, Parts 1 and 2: Critical Essays*, ed. D. Bevington (1986).

Barber, C. L., 'Rule and Misrule in *Henry IV'*, in his *Shakespeare's Festive Comedy* (Princeton, NJ, 1959); reprinted in *'Henry IV, Parts 1 and 2': A Casebook*, ed. G. K. Hunter (1970), 212–30, and *Henry IV, Parts 1 and 2: Critical Essays*, ed. D. Bevington (1986).

Barish, Jonas A., 'The Turning Away of Prince Hal', *Shakespeare Studies*,

1 (1965), 9–17; reprinted in *Henry IV, Parts 1 and 2: Critical Essays*, ed. D. Bevington (1986), 277–88.

Battenhouse, Roy, 'Falstaff as Parodist and Perhaps Holy Fool', *PMLA* 90 (1975), 32–52.

Bevington, David (ed.), *Henry IV, Parts 1 and 2: Critical Essays* (New York and London, 1986): contains extracts from Auden, Bradley, Barber, Barish, Burckhardt, Dorius, Gottschalk, R. G. Hunter, Macdonald, Palmer, Spivack, Tillyard, Watson, Dover Wilson, Wharton.

Black, James, 'Counterfeits of Soldiership in *Henry IV*', *Shakespeare Quarterly*, 24 (1973), 372–82.

—— 'Henry IV's Pilgrimage', *Shakespeare Quarterly*, 34 (1983), 18–26.

Boughner, Daniel C., 'Traditional Elements in Falstaff', *JEGP* 43 (1944), 417–28.

—— 'Vice, Braggart, and Falstaff', *Anglia*, 72 (1954), 35–61.

Bowers, Fredson, 'Establishing Shakespeare's Text: Poins and Peto in 1 *Henry IV*', *Studies in Bibliography*, 34 (1981), 189–98.

—— 'Hal and Francis in *King Henry IV, Part 1*, *Renaissance Papers 1965* (1966), 15–20.

Bryan, Margaret B., ' "Sir Walter Blunt. There's Honor For You" ', *Shakespeare Quarterly*, 26 (1975), 292–8.

Bryant, J. A. Jr., 'Prince Hal and the Ephesians', *Sewanee Review*, 67 (1959), 204–19.

—— 'Shakespeare's Falstaff and the Mantle of Dick Tarleton', *Studies in Philology*, 51 (1954), 149–62.

Cain, H. E., 'Further Light on the Relation of 1 and 2 *Henry IV*', *Shakespeare Quarterly*, 3 (1952), 21–38.

Chaudhuri, Sukanta, *Infirm Glory: Shakespeare and the Renaissance Image of Man* (Oxford, 1981).

Clark, Axel B., 'The Battle of Shrewsbury', *Critical Review*, 15 (1972), 29–45.

Cohen, Derek, 'The Rite of Violence in 1 *Henry IV*', *Shakespeare Quarterly Survey 38* (1985), 77–84.

Connor, Seymour V., 'The Role of Douglas in *Henry IV, Part One*', *University of Texas Studies in English*, 27 (1948), 215–21.

Cox, Gerard H., ' "Like a Prince Indeed": Hal's Triumph of Honor in 1 *Henry IV*', in *Pageantry in the Shakespearean Theater*, ed. David M. Bergeron (Athens, Ga., 1985), 130–49.

Cross, Alan Gerald, 'The Justification of Prince Hal', *Texas Studies in Literature and Language*, 10 (1968), 27–35.

Danby, J. F., *Shakespeare's Doctrine of Nature* (London, 1949).

Davis, Norman, 'Falstaff's Name', *Shakespeare Quarterly*, 28 (1977), 513–15.

Dessen, Alan C., 'The Intemperate Knight and the Politic Prince: Late Morality Structure in 1 *Henry IV*', *Shakespeare Studies*, 7 (1974), 147–71.

Dickinson, Hugh, 'The Reformation of Prince Hal', *Shakespeare Quarterly*, 12 (1961), 33–46.

Empson, William, 'Falstaff and Mr. Dover Wilson', *Kenyon Review*, 15 (1953), 213–62; reprinted in *'Henry IV, Parts 1 and 2': A Casebook*, ed. G. K. Hunter (1970), 135–54.

Evett, David, 'Types of King David in Shakespeare's Lancastrian Tetralogy', *Shakespeare Studies*, 14 (1981), 139–61.

Fehrenbach, Robert J., 'When Lord Cobham and Edmund Tilney "were att odds"', *Shakespeare Studies*, 18 (1986), 87–101.

Fiehler, R., 'How Oldcastle Became Falstaff', *Modern Language Quarterly*, 16 (1955), 16–28.

Fish, Charles, 'Henry IV: Shakespeare and Holinshed', *Studies in Philology*, 61 (1964), 205–18.

Gottschalk, Paul A., 'Hal and the "Play Extempore" in *1 Henry IV*', *Texas Studies in Literature and Language*, 15 (1974), 605–14; reprinted in *Henry IV, Parts 1 and 2: Critical Essays*, ed. D. Bevington (1986).

Hawkins, Sherman, '*Henry IV*: The Structural Problem Revisited', *Shakespeare Quarterly*, 33 (1982), 278–301.

—— 'Virtue and Kingship in Shakespeare's *Henry IV*', *English Literary Renaissance*, 5 (1975), 313–43.

Herbert, T. Walter, 'The Naming of Falstaff', *Emory University Quarterly*, 19 (1954), 1–11.

Hibbard, G. R., '*Henry IV* and *Hamlet*', *Shakespeare Survey 30* (1977), 1–12.

Hoyle, James, 'Some Emblems in Shakespeare's Henry IV Plays', *ELH* 38 (1971), 512–27.

Hunter, G. K., '*Henry IV* and the Elizabethan Two-Part Play', *RES* NS 5 (1954), 236–48.

—— (ed.), *'Henry IV, Parts 1 and 2': A Casebook* (London, 1970); contains extracts from Auden, Barber, Bradley, Empson, Knights, Jenkins, Jorgensen, Morgann, Tillyard, Dover Wilson.

Hunter, Robert G., 'Shakespeare's Comic Sense As It Strikes Us Today: Falstaff and the Protestant Ethic', in *Shakespeare: Pattern of Excelling Nature*, ed. David Bevington and Jay L. Halio (Newark, NJ, 1978), 125–32; reprinted in *Henry IV, Parts 1 and 2: Critical Essays*, ed. D. Bevington (1986).

Hunter, William B., Jr., 'Prince Hal, His Struggle Toward Moral Perfection', *South Atlantic Quarterly*, 50 (1950), 86–95.

Jenkins, Harold, *The Structural Problem in Shakespeare's 'Henry IV'* (London, 1956); extract reprinted in *'Henry IV, Parts 1 and 2': A Casebook*, ed. G. K. Hunter (1970), 155–73.

Jorgensen, Paul A., '"Redeeming Time" in Shakespeare's *Henry IV*', *Tennessee Studies in Literature*, 5 (1960), 101–9; reprinted in *'Henry IV, Parts 1 and 2': A Casebook*, ed. G. K. Hunter (1970), 231–42.

Jowett, John, 'The Thieves in *1 Henry IV*', *RES*, NS 38 (1987), 325–33.

Kaiser, Walter, *Praisers of Folly: Erasmus, Rabelais, Shakespeare* (Cambridge, Mass., 1963; London, 1964).

Knights, L. C., 'Time's Subjects: The Sonnets and *King Henry IV, Part II*', in his *Some Shakespearean Themes* (London, 1959), 45–64.

Landt, D. B., 'The Ancestry of Sir John Falstaff', *Shakespeare Quarterly*, 17 (1966), 69–76.

Law, R. A., 'The Composition of Shakespeare's Lancastrian Trilogy', *Texas Studies in Literature and Language*, 3 (1961), 321–7.

Leech, Clifford, 'The Unity of *2 Henry IV*', *Shakespeare Survey 6* (1953), 16–24.

Levin, Harry, 'Falstaff's Encore', *Shakespeare Quarterly*, 32 (1981), 5–17.

Levin, Lawrence L., 'Hotspur, Falstaff, and the Emblem of Wrath in *1 Henry IV*', *Shakespeare Studies*, 10 (1977), 42–66.

McGuire, Richard L., 'The Play-within-the-play in *1 Henry IV*', *Shakespeare Quarterly*, 18 (1967), 47–52.

McLaverty, J., 'No Abuse: The Prince and Falstaff in the Tavern Scenes', *Shakespeare Survey 34* (1981), 105–10.

McNeir, Waldo F., 'Structure and Theme in the First Tavern Scene (II. iv.) of *1 Henry IV*', in *Pacific Coast Studies in Shakespeare*, ed. W. McNeir and T. Greenfield (Eugene, Oreg., 1966), 89–105.

Mitchell, Charles, 'The Education of the True Prince', *Tennessee Studies in Literature*, 12 (1967), 13–21.

Mullaney, Steven, *The Place of the Stage: Licence, Play, and Power in Renaissance England* (Chicago, Ill., and London, 1988).

Newman, Franklin B., 'The Rejection of Falstaff and the Rigorous Charity of the King', *Shakespeare Studies*, 2 (1966), 153–61.

Nuttall, A. D., *A New Mimesis* (London, 1983), 143–61.

Palmer, D. J., 'Casting Off the Old Man: History and St. Paul in *Henry IV*', *Critical Quarterly*, 12 (1970), 267–83; reprinted in *Henry IV, Parts 1 and 2: Critical Essays*, ed. D. Bevington (1986).

Pinciss, G. M., 'The Old Honour and the New Courtesy', *Shakespeare Survey 31* (1978), 85–91.

Rothschild, Herbert B., Jr., 'Falstaff and the Picaresque Tradition', *MLR* 68 (1973), 14–21.

Salingar, Leo, 'Falstaff and the Life of Shadows', in *Shakespearean Comedy*, ed. Maurice Charney (New York, 1980), 185–205.

Scoufos, Alice-Lyle, *Shakespeare's Typological Satire* (Athens, Ohio, 1979).

Shaaber, M. A., 'The Unity of *Henry IV*', in *Jospeh Quincy Adams Memorial Studies*, ed. J. G. McManaway, G. E. Dawson, and E. E. Willoughby (Washington, DC, 1948), 217–27.

Shaw, Catherine M., 'The Tragic Substructure of the *Henry IV* Plays', *Shakespeare Survey 38* (1985), 61–8.

Shuchter, J. D., 'Prince Hal and Francis: The Imitation of an Action', *Shakespeare Studies*, 3 (1968), 129–37.

Siegel, Paul N., 'Falstaff and His Social Milieu', *Shakespeare Jahrbuch West*, 110 (1974), 139–45.

Sisk, J. P., 'Prince Hal and the Specialists', *Shakespeare Quarterly*, 28 (1977), 520–4.

Somerset, J. A. B., 'Falstaff, the Prince, and the Pattern of 2 *Henry IV*', *Shakespeare Survey 30* (1977), 35–45.

Spenser, B. T., 'The Stasis of *Henry IV, Part 2*', *Tennessee Studies in Literature*, 6 (1961), 61–9.

Spivack, Bernard, 'Falstaff and the Psychomachia', *Shakespeare Quarterly*, 8 (1957), 449–50.

—— *Shakespeare and the Allegory of Evil* (New York, 1958); extract reprinted in *Henry IV, Parts 1 & 2: Critical Essays*, ed. D. Bevington (1986).

Stewart, Douglas J., 'Falstaff the Centaur', *Shakespeare Quarterly*, 28 (1977), 5–21.

Stone, William B., 'Literature and Class Ideology: *Henry IV, Part 1*', *College English*, 33 (1972), 891–900.

Tayor, Gary, 'The Fortunes of Oldcastle', *Shakespeare Survey 38* (1985), 85–100.

—— 'William Shakespeare, Richard James and the House of Cobham', *RES* NS 38 (1987), 334–54.

Thomas, Mary Olive, 'The Elevation of Hal in *1 Henry IV*', *Studies in the Literary Imagination*, 5 (1972), 73–89.

Vickers, Brian, *The Artistry of Shakespeare's Prose* (London, 1968).

Watson, Robert N., 'The *Henry IV* Plays', in his *Shakespeare and the Hazards of Ambition* (Cambridge, Mass., 1984), 47–75; reprinted in *Henry IV, Parts 1 and 2: Critical Essays*, ed. D. Bevington (1986).

Wiles, David, 'Falstaff', in his *Shakespeare's Clown: Actor and Text in the Elizabethan Playhouse* (Cambridge, 1987), 116–35.

Williams, George Walton, 'Some Thoughts on Falstaff's Name', *Shakespeare Quarterly*, 39 (1979), 82–4.

Willson, Robert F., Jr., 'Falstaff in *1 Henry IV*: What's in a Name?', *Shakespeare Quarterly*, 27 (1976), 199–200.

Zeeveld, W. Gordon, ' "Food for Powder"—"Food for Worms" ', *Shakespeare Quarterly*, 3 (1952), 249–53.

Zitner, Sheldon P., 'Anon, Anon: or, a Mirror for a Magistrate', *Shakespeare Quarterly*, 19 (1968), 63–70.

Henry V

Altieri, Joanne, 'Romance in *Henry V*', *SEL* 21 (1981), 223–40.

Aoki, Keiji, *Shakespeare's 'Henry IV' and 'Henry V': Hal's Heroic Character and the Sun-Cloud Theme* (Kyoto, 1973).

Babula, W., 'Whatever Happened to Prince Hal?', *Shakespeare Survey 30* (1977), 47–59.

Barton, Anne, 'The King Disguised: Shakespeare's *Henry V* and the Comical History', in *The Triple Bond*, ed. Joseph G. Price (University Park, Pa., 1975), 92–117.

Bate, Jonathan, 'Hal and the Regent', *Shakespeare Survey 38* (1985), 69–76.

Battenhouse, Roy W., '*Henry V* as Heroic Comedy', in *Essays on Shakespeare and Elizabethan Drama in Honor of Hardin Craig*, ed. Richard Hosley (Columbia, Mo., 1963), 163–82.

Berman, Ronald (ed.), '*Henry V': Twentieth Century Interpretations* (Englewood Cliffs, NJ, 1968): contains extracts from Bradley, Jorgensen (1956), Reese, Rossiter, Tillyard, Traversi, Yeats.

Candido, Joseph, 'The Name of King: Hal's "Titles" in the "Henriad" ', *Texas Studies in Literature and Language*, 26 (1984), 61–73.

—— and Charles R. Forker, *Henry V: An Annotated Bibliography* (Garland Shakespeare Bibliographies, 4; New York, 1983).

Dean, Paul, 'Chronicle and Romance Mode in *Henry V*', *Shakespeare Quarterly*, 32 (1981), 18–27.

Dollimore, Jonathan, and Alan Sinfield, 'History and Ideology: The Instance of *Henry V*', in *Alternative Shakespeares*, ed. John Drakakis (London, 1985), 206–27.

Edwards, Philip, *Threshold of a Nation* (Cambridge, 1979).

Egan, Robert, 'A Muse of Fire: *Henry V* in the Light of *Tamburlaine*', *Modern Language Quarterly*, 29 (1968), 15–28.

Goddard, H. C., *The Meaning of Shakespeare* (Chicago, Ill., 1951).

Gould, Gerald, 'A New Reading of *Henry V*', *The English Review*, 29 (1919), 42–55; reprinted in *Shakespeare: 'Henry V', a Casebook*, ed. M. Quinn (1969), 81–94.

Greenblatt, Stephen, 'Invisible Bullets', *Glyph*, 8 (1981), 40–61; revised and expanded in *Political Shakespeare*, ed. Jonathan Dollimore and Alan Sinfield (Manchester, 1985), 18–47; reprinted in his own *Shakespearean Negotiations* (Berkeley, Calif., 1988), 21–65.

Gurr, Andrew, '*Henry V* and the Bees' Commonwealth', *Shakespeare Survey 30* (1977), 61–72.

Jones, G. P., '*Henry V*: The Chorus and the Audience', *Shakespeare Survey 31* (1978), 93–104.

Law, R. A., 'The Choruses in Henry the Fifth', *University of Texas Studies in English*, 35 (1956), 11–21.

Matthews, Honor, *Character and Symbol in Shakespeare's Plays* (London, 1962); reprinted in *Shakespeare: 'Henry V', a Casebook*, ed. M. Quinn (1969), 202–27.

Quinn, Michael (ed.), *Shakespeare: 'Henry V', a Casebook*, (London, 1969): contains extracts from Gould, Ellis-Fermor, Walter (Arden Introduction), Traversi, Zimbardo, Sprague, Matthews, Knights (1957).

Rabkin, Norman, 'Rabbits, Ducks and *Henry V*', *Shakespeare Quarterly*, 28 (1977), 279–96.

Salomon, Brownell, 'Thematic Contraries and the Dramaturgy of *Henry V*', *Shakespeare Quarterly*, 31 (1980), 343–56.

Sanders, Norman, 'The True Prince and the False Thief: Prince Hal and the Shift of Identity', *Shakespeare Survey* 30 (1977), 29–34.

Smith, Gordon Ross, 'Shakespeare's *Henry V*: Another Part of the Critical Forest', *Journal of the History of Ideas*, 37 (1976), 3–26.

Smith, Warren D., 'The *Henry V* Choruses in the First Folio', *JEGP* 53 (1954), 38–57.

Taylor, Gary, 'The Text of *Henry V*: Three Studies', in Wells and Taylor, *Modernizing Shakespeare's Spelling, with Three Studies in the Text of 'Henry V'* (Oxford, 1979).

Tennenhouse, Leonard, 'Strategies of State and Political Plays: *A Midsummer Night's Dream, Henry IV, Henry V* and *Henry VIII*', in *Political Shakespeare*, ed. Jonathan Dollimore and Alan Sinfield (Manchester, 1985), 109–28.

Van den Berg, Kent T., *Playhouse and Cosmos: Shakespearean Theater as Metaphor* (Newark, Del., 1985).

Walch, Günther, '*Henry V* as Working-House of Ideology', *Shakespeare Survey* 40 (1988), 63–8.

Wentersdorf, Karl P., 'The Conspiracy of Silence in *Henry V*', *Shakespeare Quarterly*, 18 (1976), 264–87.

Zimbardo, Rose, 'The Formalism of *Henry V*', in *Shakespeare: 'Henry V', a Casebook*, ed. Michael Quinn (London, 1969), 163–70.

STAGE AND FILM PRODUCTION

Beauman, Sally, *The Royal Shakespeare Company's Production of 'Henry V' for the Centenary Season at the Royal Shakespeare Theatre* (Oxford, 1976).

Berger, Harry, Jr., 'Textual Dramaturgy: Representing the Limits of Theatre in *Richard II*', *Theatre Journal*, 39 (1987), 135–55.

Brown, John Russell, *Shakespeare's Plays in Performance* (London, 1966; Penguin Shakespeare Library, Harmondsworth, 1969).

Crowl, Samuel, 'The Long Goodbye: Welles and Falstaff', *Shakespeare Quarterly*, 31 (1980), 369–80.

David, Richard, *Shakespeare in the Theatre* (Cambridge, 1978).

—— 'Shakespeare's History Plays: Epic or Drama?', *Shakespeare Survey* 6 (1953), 129–39.

Dawson, Anthony B., *Watching Shakespeare: A Playgoer's Guide* (London and Basingstoke, 1988).

Garrett, George P., O. B. Hardison, Jr., and Jane Gelfman (eds.), *Film Scripts One* (New York, 1971).

Geduld, Harry M., *Filmguide to 'Henry V'* (Bloomington, Ind., 1973).

Goldman, Michael, *Shakespeare and the Energies of Drama* (Princeton, NJ, 1972).

Greenwald, Michael L., *Directions by Indirections: John Barton of the Royal Shakespeare Company* (Newark, Del., 1986).

Hakola, Liisa, *In One Person Many People: The Image of the King in Three RSC Productions of William Shakespeare's 'King Richard II'* (Helsinki, 1988).

Hapgood, Robert, '*Chimes at Midnight* from Stage to Screen: The Art of Adaptation', *Shakespeare Survey* 39 (1987), 39–52.

Holderness, Graham, 'Agincourt 1944: Readings in the Shakespeare Myth', *Literature and History*, 10 (1984), 24–45; reprinted in his *Shakespeare's History* (1985), 164–200.

—— and Christopher McCullough, 'Shakespeare on the Screen: A Selective Filmography', *Shakespeare Survey* 39 (1987), 13–38.

Jorgens, Jack J., *Shakespeare on Film* (Bloomington, Ind., 1977).

Manvell, Roger, *Shakespeare and the Film* (London, 1971).

Olivier, Laurence, *Filmscript of 'Henry V' (1944)* (Classic Film Scripts, London, 1984).

Page, Malcolm, '*Richard II': Text and Performance* (London and Basingstoke, 1987).

Sprague, Arthur Colby, *Shakespeare's Histories: Plays for the Stage* (London, 1964).

Stredder, James, 'John Barton's Production of *Richard II* at Stratford-on-Avon 1973', in *Deutsche Shakespeare-Gesellschaft West Jahrbuch 1976* (1976), 23–42.

Taylor, Gary, *Moment by Moment by Shakespeare* (London and Basingstoke, 1985).

Trewin, J. C., *Shakespeare on the English Stage* (London, 1964).

Wells, Stanley, *Royal Shakespeare: Four Major Productions at Stratford-upon-Avon* (Manchester, 1977).

Wharton, T. F., '*Henry IV, Parts 1 and 2': Text and Performance* (London and Basingstoke, 1983); extracts reprinted in *Henry IV, Parts 1 and 2: Critical Essays*, ed. D. Bevington (1986).

Willems, Michèle, *Shakespeare à la télévision* (Publications de l'Université de Rouen; Rouen, 1987).

Wilson, John Dover, and T. C. Worsley, *Shakespeare's Histories at Stratford, 1951* (London, 1952).

18

Henry VIII (All is True), The Two Noble Kinsmen, and the Apocryphal Plays

G. R. PROUDFOOT

Henry VIII (All is True)

TEXT AND AUTHORSHIP

The Life of King Henry VIII was first printed in the First Folio of 1623, where it appears in chronological sequence of subject as the last of the histories, in a good text with unusually full and elaborate stage directions. Its date is established by the fact that the Globe playhouse was destroyed on 29 June 1613 by a fire which started when wadding from a cannon (required by the stage direction at I. iv. 49) ignited the thatched roof during the performance. One eye-witness, Sir Henry Wotton, called the play a new one and described it, under the title *All Is True*, as containing 'some principal pieces of the reign of Henry VIII'. Further evidence that *All Is True* was its original title has been found by H. R. Woudhuysen. It seems likely that it was written with performance at the Blackfriars playhouse also in mind, whether or not, as G. Wickham supposes, it was first performed there—as that playhouse occupied the very room in which the trial of Queen Katherine (II. iv) had taken place in 1527. Though never one of Shakespeare's most read plays, it has had a consistent history of success in the theatre, and more recently on television (topping a poll of members of the Shakespeare Association of America about the BBC Shakespeare Series, as M. Willems reports).

Criticism has been bedevilled by controversy about the authorship: equally, the history of controversy about the authorship of *Henry VIII* cannot be considered without critical judgement being involved. Doubts about its integrity were expressed in the late eighteenth century, and since 1850 many critics and scholars have argued that, in spite of its inclusion in the First Folio, the play is not wholly by Shakespeare but a product of his collaboration with John Fletcher. This view appears to have originated with Tennyson, but was first aired in public in 1850 by James Spedding in an article entitled 'Who wrote Shakespeare's *Henry VIII*?'. His dissatisfaction with the play's attitude to its subject, especially with its morally equivocal handling of the King and its evasive treatment of the Reformation, goes hand in hand with stylistic and metrical arguments tending to shift the onus for its alleged failure onto John Fletcher. There followed a period in which various metrical statistics were presented, generally in support of a modified version of Spedding's scene-by-scene division of the play between Shakespeare and Fletcher. Reassertion of Shakespeare's sole authorship by Swinburne in *A Study of Shakespeare* was the first powerful challenge to Spedding's hypothesis. His objection was simply that many speeches assigned to Fletcher, such as Buckingham's farewell (II. i. 55–136), had 'a comparative severity and elevation which will be missed when we turn back . . . to the text of Fletcher', but he also regarded the play as one of Shakespeare's earliest works.

The two opinions of the play are still current. The theory of collaborative authorship was reinforced by closer stylistic and linguistic analysis, notably by Marco Mincoff in '*Henry VIII* and Fletcher' and by A. C. Partridge in *The Problem of 'Henry VIII' Reopened*. Mincoff's stylistic analysis takes full account of the observed effects of collaboration on Fletcher's style in the plays he wrote with Francis Beaumont. He finds in *Henry VIII* both the characteristic sentence structure and imagery of Fletcher and his typical humour, while agreeing with Swinburne that Fletcher here achieved an untypical success, which Mincoff attributes to the influence of 'another mind behind Fletcher's'. Partridge's aim was to supplement the metrical tests, which had come in for deserved criticism, with evidence of two patterns of linguistic usage in the play.

Defending Shakespeare's sole authorship, Peter Alexander, in 'Conjectural History, or Shakespeare's *Henry VIII*', drew attention to the play's participation in the 'compassionate outlook' of Shakespeare's latest period and argued that stylistic variation could be seen as the deliberate device of Shakespeare for his own artistic ends and claimed that variation as extreme was to be found in many of his plays. These positions were elaborated by G. Wilson Knight, whose estimate of the play as 'the only fitting culmination of Shakespeare's work' remains a minority view, despite the fertility of his essay in ideas about the play's themes and leading characters. The consistency of the play's use of its historical source materials has been seen as arguing for unity of authorship by, among others, Geoffrey Bullough in his introduction to a reprint of those sources.

R. A. Foakes, in his Arden edition, gives the fullest commentary and the most comprehensive critical account of the play, stressing its unity of design and deducing from this a unity of conception hard to reconcile with the orthodox theory of absolute division of authorship between Shakespeare and Fletcher. J. C. Maxwell in his Cambridge edition and A. R. Humphreys in his New Penguin edition (which includes a full and impartial survey of the controversy) accept the theory of divided authorship and allow the play only a qualified artistic success, a position which R. Ornstein develops in an able hostile analysis of *Henry VIII* as 'an extended *double entendre*', a play merely pretending to seriousness and more akin to Beaumont and Fletcher's *Philaster* than to *The Tempest*. F. D. Hoeniger recommends 'scholarly caution' in the matter of authorship and sees the play as truly Shakespeare's final work, both in its experimental use in a historical play of 'some of the themes and devices and even the symbolism of the Romances' and in its completion of the pattern of English history 'begun in the early histories by extending the view to the birth of Queen Elizabeth, in a sense even to 1613'. Necessarily all the evidence for Fletcher's hand in *Henry VIII* is internal, so that the question to be asked must remain 'Did Fletcher write any of the play and if so, how much?'

CRITICISM AND COMMENTARY

Dispute about the authorship of *Henry VIII* has been in part responsible for critical neglect of the play, as well as itself stemming from doubts about its achievement. Dissatisfaction with *Henry VIII* has been variously explained as resulting from its episodic structure, from its lack of a strong central character, from its ambiguous attitude to its historical material, even from its failure to tackle those aspects of the reign of Henry VIII which its critics themselves regard as most significant. Attempts to relate it to Shakespeare's earlier histories are hampered by its peaceful action and unheroic mode, as well as by the gap of thirteen years of dramatic experience that separates it from *Henry V*, while its relation to the late romances is equally complicated by its historical subject and its offer of 'truth'. Of the earlier histories, that to which *Henry VIII* has most often been related is *King John*. Cumberland Clark anticipated Tillyard's description of the two plays by calling *King John* the prologue and *Henry VIII* the 'epilogue to the historical dramas', having in common a concern with 'the victory of Protestantism'. Though England and kingship and penitence and rebirth may be among its themes, it is neither simply a political play nor a romance.

The play has never lacked admirers. Dr Johnson laid his finger on two perennial sources of its appeal in his comment that it 'still keeps possession of the stage, by the splendour of its pageantry. . . . Yet pomp is not the only merit of this play. The meek sorrows and virtuous distress of Catherine have furnished some scenes which may be justly numbered among the greatest efforts of tragedy'. Its pomp has motivated revivals on the occasion of several coronations from 1727 to 1953, while its leading roles, especially Katherine, Wolsey, and Henry himself, have attracted the leading Shakespearian players of every period, from Thomas Betterton (who is said to have learned his part from John Lowin, the original Henry) and Sarah Siddons to John Gielgud and Peggy Ashcroft. In the nineteenth century the play was lavishly presented, with huge processions and meticulously historical settings and costumes. Such productions as those of Charles Kean in 1855 and Henry Irving in 1892 are described by G. C. D. Odell, who also reveals the cost in textual cuts (often including the whole of Act V) imposed by lavish scenic elaboration. The twentieth century has seen notable revivals and the restoration of the full text. Tyrone Guthrie's 1953 production at Stratford-upon-Avon, fully described by Muriel St Clare Byrne, did much to revive critical curiosity about the play. Trevor Nunn's Stratford production in 1969 was a straightforward account of the play, distinguished by the forceful though deeply puzzled King of Donald Sinden and a Katherine of exemplary quiet dignity from Peggy Ashcroft. The religious bearing of the action (tentatively traced by Gervinus in 1863), in which the English Reformation, though never directly treated, is implied by the falling fortunes of Wolsey and Queen Katherine and the rise of Anne Bullen and Cranmer, was clearly projected and did much (despite the eccentric and fussy playing of Cranmer as a near-simpleton) to answer the familiar charge that Act V is irrelevant and uninteresting. The subtle interrelation between the stage history of *Henry VIII* and the course of criticism is one of many aspects of the play discussed by A. C. Sprague in *Shakespeare's Histories: Plays for the Stage*. Sprague's praise of the play achieves a happy balance between the uncritical adulation and the impatient dismissal which it has too often provoked.

Critics have been drawn to the interrelated questions of the play's historical and political ideas, its structural and thematic unity, and its relation to the other late plays. The central position of the King affords a clear link with the earlier histories, but in no other play is the disparity between the King's private actions and his public significance so marked. R. A. Foakes in his edition proposes that Henry's central position resembles that of Prospero, both rulers 'being central in as much as they are permanent, influencing others, and uniting a complex plot'. His emphasis on Henry's 'growth in spiritual stature during the play' stems from a consideration of the King's emergence from Wolsey's domination into full self-awareness and beneficent exercise of his royal power, as this is reflected in Henry's role in the four trials of Buckingham, Queen Katherine, Wolsey, and Cranmer which are the major crises of the action. He here develops Frank Kermode's view of the play as 'a new "Mirror for Magistrates" ', a morality in which Henry presides over three tragic falls before intervening in the role of Mercy to save Cranmer. Foakes regards Shakespeare's choice of a historical subject as an intelligible step in his gradual renunciation of supernatural intervention in the plays from *Cymbeline* to *The Tempest*: 'Perhaps after abjuring magic as a means to his end, the dramatist turned to real life again, to fact in the form of history'. Developing this point in a later book, Foakes relates it to Shakespeare's emphasis on the 'truth' of his action, which comprises 'human activities within a framework of government or rule'. Simple judgement is forbidden by 'the variety of perspectives' on men and their motives, and 'the generosity of providence' in the birth of Elizabeth shines the brighter among the 'fumbling inadequacies of men and their laws in a given

historical situation'. Compassing at once the historical particu-
larity of the action and its constant suggestion of spiritual significance, this view of the play serves to differentiate it from the
earlier histories, whose concern with political dogma and dyn-
astic struggles it does not share, and provides an answer both to
the complaint of Irving Ribner that *Henry VIII* 'does not give us a
coherent and meaningful philosophy of history' and to E. M. W.
Tillyard's disappointment at its lack of dramatic 'event'. Madeleine
Doran, reviewing Foakes's edition, urged some caution in relating
it to the late romances. To his claim that 'a contrast between
private suffering and public good, or private sorrow and public
joy' serves to unify the play, she replied with a reminder of its
uneven quality—'One difficulty is that the private sorrow is so
much more moving than the public joy'.

'*All Is True*', quoth Shakespeare (and Fletcher), whether jesting
or not. What may constitute the 'truth' of *Henry VIII* has become
the focus of many different lines of enquiry. 'Truth Topical' has
been explored, or alleged, by those who see Shakespeare's late
works as direct reflectors of the politics and predilections of King
James I. While all the best critics are sensitive to the topicalities of
1612–13, only a few have wished to locate the play's centre in
covert allusion to contemporary politics. For Frances Yates, it
forms part of an 'archaising revival' of the cult of Queen Elizabeth;
for W. M. Baillie, it comments on the scandalous Essex divorce
case (concurrent with its performances in 1613); while Glynne
Wickham sees it as a propagandist rehabilitation of Katherine of
Aragon timed to soften up public opinion in preparation for the
possibility of a Catholic marriage for one of the children of James I.
Can they all be right? 'Truth Metaphysical' remains the objective
of others, like A. Leggatt, who find transcendental values in the
play, although the pacific two-way vision of Cranmer's prophecy
has lost an earlier gloss of innocence in the political world of the
1970s and 1980s, and T. McBride, detecting the coexistence of a
'truth' of *realpolitik*, labels the play 'Machiavellian Romance'.

'Truth Multiple' and 'Truth Biographical' have been the subjects
of two of the best and most substantial contributions to understanding of *Henry VIII*. Lee Bliss, in an essay whose argument is
pursued in the later work of E. I. Berry, F. W. Brownlow, and F. V.
Cespedes, contends that the 'truth' of *Henry VIII* reveals 'an
essential ambiguity' as 'prior certainty repeatedly dissolves in
the face of later revelations'. She rejects the reading of the play as

'the education of a model king' as perversely blind to 'Henry's shifting (and shifty) character' and his 'acceptance and exploitation of fallen men's vices and passions'. Cranmer's prophecy is thus 'endowed with an effect of prayer rather than statement', leading 'the hopes of the fictional world of 1533' to 'face the realities of 1613' and offering no more than 'a glimpse of what transformed England, under an inspired monarch, might be'. Judith H. Anderson approaches the play from the early Tudor angle and finds in it a central concern with that 'changing relation between fiction and truth, poetic feigning and history' which is her own broader subject in a book on the representation of historical persons in Tudor–Stuart writing. *Henry VIII* is 'not . . . more historical but . . . less fictional' than Shakespeare's 'more universally admired' histories, revealing a keen awareness of the discrepancy between 'the aspects of reality'. She traces aesthetic dissatisfaction with the characters of Henry and Wolsey to their lack of artistic idealization or tidying: 'They are too true'. The ambiguity of Wolsey rather than his corruption is what the play emphasizes— an ambiguity which culminates in the contrasting epitaphs spoken by Katherine and Griffith—and this ambiguity, or disjunction between inner and outer, makes him 'thematically focal' as the embodiment of 'discord and divorce'. Shakespeare, sharing Thomas More's awareness of the 'fiction in biographical truth', conducts in *Henry VIII* a self-conscious exploration of 'the nature and varieties of truth in the portrayal of historical persons in art and in chronicle'.

The Two Noble Kinsmen and the Apocryphal Plays

TEXTS, AUTHORSHIP, AND CRITICISM

The canon of Shakespeare's dramatic work was established in 1623 by John Heminges and Henry Condell in their epistle 'To the great Variety of Readers' prefaced to the First Folio, where they add to their claim to offer the best texts of the plays previously published the statement that their book also includes 'all the rest, absolute in their numbers, as he conceived them'. Despite this specific claim, substantial reasons exist for attributing to Shakespeare at least a share in some plays excluded from the Folio and for questioning his sole authorship of a few of the plays in it, notably *Henry VIII*, *1 Henry VI*, and *Timon of Athens* (which the Oxford edition of *The Complete Works* boldly presents as *All Is*

True (Henry VIII) by Shakespeare and Fletcher, *The First Part of Henry VI* by Shakespeare and others, and *Timon of Athens* by Shakespeare and Thomas Middleton).

The possibility of Shakespeare's hand in plays outside the Folio won support from the discovery that problems encountered during printing nearly led to the exclusion of *Troilus and Cressida* and that only its near exclusion left room for *Timon of Athens*. Although in either eventuality the great variety of readers might have been notified, they might equally well not have. Even before 1623 plays had been published as Shakespeare's which Heminges and Condell omitted. *The London Prodigal*, 'By *William Shakespeare*', was published in 1605 and *A Yorkshire Tragedy*, '*Written by* W. Shakespeare', in 1608. They were followed, in 1609, by *Pericles, Prince of Tyre*, 'By William Shakespeare'. During these years, the reluctance of the King's Men to release Shakespeare's plays for publication gave printers an incentive to misattribute plays to him. This is probably what happened with the first two, although *Pericles* presents a different problem and is generally held to be substantially Shakespeare's work.

A second issue of the Third Folio of 1663, published in 1664, added these three plays in a supplement, together with four more, alleged on even flimsier grounds to be Shakespeare's because of claims made on the title-pages of earlier quarto editions. One, *The First Part of Sir John Oldcastle*, was written in 1599 by Antony Munday, Michael Drayton, Robert Wilson, and Richard Hathaway as a retort to Shakespeare's Falstaff plays, but was fraudulently attributed to Shakespeare in its second edition (falsely dated '1600', though printed in 1619 as part of Thomas Pavier's attempt to bring out an unauthorized collected edition of 'Shakespeare'). The others were attributed on the strength of the mere initials 'W. S.', as sole author of *The Life and Death of Thomas Lord Cromwell* (1602) and *The Puritan, or the Widow of Watling Street* (1607, perhaps the work of Thomas Middleton), but only as overseer and corrector of *The Lamentable Tragedy of Locrine* (1595). None of these plays affords internal evidence for the identification of 'W. S.' with William Shakespeare.

Stronger claims have been made for Shakespeare's hand in other plays not attributed to him in his lifetime. *The Tragedy of Master Arden of Faversham* (1592) and *The Reign of King Edward III* (1596) were both written about 1591–2, when Shakespeare was beginning to make a name as a playwright. Neither was attributed to him, except haphazardly in unreliable booksellers' catalogues, until Edward Capell edited *Edward III* in 1760 with a tentative but enthusiastic suggestion of his authorship and Edward Jacob did likewise for *Arden of Faversham* in 1770. As both cases depend exclusively on the internal evidence of style and linguistic usage and as both plays date from a time before Shakespeare's style had fully diverged from that of his immediate forerunners, conviction has not been reached about either attribution, though the case for *Edward III* is immeasurably the stronger of the two. The documentary mode and 'naked' style in which *Arden of Faversham* dramatizes a notorious murder committed in 1552 contrast with Shakespeare's early addiction to classical allusion and elaborate rhetoric, whereas *Edward III* is linked by vocabulary, imagery, structure, and thematic concerns not only with his early histories and sonnets but with other plays of much later date, notably *Henry V* and *Measure for Measure*. Kenneth Muir, in *Shakespeare as Collaborator*, gives a clear account of the main arguments for Shakespeare's participation in the latter play together with discussion of its use of historical material, while G. R. Proudfoot offers a survey of the play's main textual, historical, and theatrical issues and places *Edward III* on the frontier of the Shakespeare canon.

Shakespeare's hand as collaborator or reviser has also been suggested elsewhere, for instance in the additions to *Mucedorus* (1598) printed in 1610. Fuller and more convincing arguments have built up around *The Book of Sir Thomas More*, a play which survives in a single manuscript that has undergone extensive revision (first printed in an edition by Alexander Dyce in 1844). Dates proposed for the composition and revision of this play have ranged from about 1591 to about 1603, with some weight in favour of the earlier dating. Two additions to the manuscript, one a three-page scene in its author's hand, the other a scribal copy of a single speech, have come to be regarded as very probably the work of Shakespeare. The suggestion was launched in 1871 by Richard Simpson, who proposed that much more of the manuscript was in Shakespeare's hand. It has continued to generate lively controversy and endless modification ever since. Two landmarks in the history of this question were W. W. Greg's edition of 1911, which not only provided the best text to date but laid the basis for identification of the hands in the manuscript, and the collection of essays edited by A. W. Pollard in 1923 as

Shakespeare's Hand in the Play of 'Sir Thomas More'. The essays by
Sir E. Maunde Thompson comparing the handwriting of the
scene in question (known as 'Hand D') with that of Shakespeare's
signatures and by R. W. Chambers on the political ideas in the
additions and in Shakespeare's English and Roman histories
remain among the strongest links in the chain of evidence
connecting Shakespeare with the play. The case for the shorter
speech was greatly reinforced by J. M. Nosworthy's analysis of it
in relation to passages within the Shakespeare canon, a process
which K. P. Wentersdorf has extended to both of the passages in
question.

   Controversy persists about two issues: whether or not the
'Hand D' addition is by Shakespeare, and whether the major
revision to the play took place soon after initial composition or
some six to eight years later. Scepticism about the identification
of 'Hand D' as Shakespeare's is expressed by M. L. Hays and C.
Chillington, while P. Ramsey surveys the full range of evidence
and concludes that it falls short of a compelling case for the
identification, while not precluding it. Chillington's proposal of
John Webster as an alternative candidate for 'Hand D' is weakly
argued and has won little support. The other issue depends on
close scrutiny and interpretation of the manuscript and its additions as well as of the theatrical history of the 1590s. The work of
S. McMillin and G. Melchiori has brought new life to the question.
Assuming (contrary to previous opinion) that it may well have
been performed, McMillin seeks to identify the companies likely
to have been associated with *Sir Thomas More* in both its original
and revised states. He accepts Shakespeare's participation, which
he locates in the period of initial composition, probably for Lord
Strange's Men in the early 1590s, rather than that of the revision,
which he dates late and associates with the Admiral's Men in the
early years of the seventeenth century. The main motive for the
revision is revealed as the need to adapt the play for a reduced
cast. Melchiori's articles are in effect prolegomena for a projected
English edition of the play, to follow that already published in
Italy, in which he collaborated with V. Gabrieli. He argues for
dates in the mid-1950s for both composition and revision. Mc-
Millin and Melchiori vindicate the stageworthiness of *Sir Thomas
More*: its recurring 'verbal and ideological patterns' are the
subject of C. R. Forker and J. Candido. The incongruity of
Shakespeare's evocation of pity for the oppressive foreigners

who are the *casus belli* in the famous speech with which More quells the 'Ill May Day' riots is subtly explored by M. M. Lascelles.

The remaining important attributions to Shakespeare are of plays belonging to the latest years of his career and are thus related to the question of collaboration already raised by *Henry VIII*. In each case it is claimed that Shakespeare collaborated with his younger colleague John Fletcher, soon to succeed him as principal playwright for the King's Men. *The Two Noble Kinsmen*, written in 1613 and based on Chaucer's *Knight's Tale*, was printed in 1634 as a play 'Presented at the Blackfriars by the King's Majesty's servants, with great applause' and attributed to Fletcher and Shakespeare. The printers used a good manuscript bearing traces of performance about 1625–6. Most attentive readers have found clear indications of two styles, not always in distinct scenes, which can reasonably be identified as those of Fletcher and of Shakespeare in his latest period. Internal evidence of the kinds found in *Henry VIII* has also accumulated in the attempt to discern the separate contributions of the two playwrights. Some measure of consensus has been reached and the question 'Did Shakespeare write any of it?' is increasingly answered in the affirmative by the inclusion of the play in series and in such collected editions of his plays as *The Riverside Shakespeare*, edited by G. Blakemore Evans and in the Oxford *Complete Works*, where it was edited by W. Montgomery.

Controversy about *The Two Noble Kinsmen* antedates that about *Henry VIII*. One early contributor was Charles Lamb, whose description of the two styles remains classic. Systematic division of the play began with W. Spalding's *Letter on Shakespeare's Authorship of the Drama Entitled 'The Two Noble Kinsmen'* (1833) and followed a course parallel with *Henry VIII*. H. Littledale's collection of parallels of thought and expression between the parts attributed to Shakespeare (mainly in the first and last acts) and the canonical plays greatly strengthened the case for his participation. The play's move from the Beaumont and Fletcher canon towards inclusion in editions of Shakespeare began in the 1840s with Charles Knight's *Pictorial Shakespeare*. Denial of Shakespeare's participation has been frequent, but divided authorship has usually been accepted and Paul Bertram stands alone in claiming the whole play for Shakespeare. This position is the major weakness of a book that does much to illuminate the history of the play and is forceful in its criticism of the lack of rigour in the tests used by many nineteenth-century investigators of the authorship. Among such cogent evidence against single authorship, Alfred Hart's analysis of the play's vocabulary stands out. Work on disputed authorship in relation to Shakespeare (including the controversies about *Titus Andronicus* and *1 Henry VI*) is usefully summarized by D. Erdman and E. Fogel in *Evidence for Authorship* (1966), while S. Schoenbaum gives a cautionary account of the whole history of disputed authorship in *Internal Evidence and Elizabethan Dramatic Authorship*.

A play called *Cardenno* or *Cardenna* was acted at court by the King's Men in the winter of 1612–13 and on 8 June 1613. 'The History of Cardennio, by Mr. Fletcher & Shakespeare' was registered by Humphrey Moseley in the Stationers' Register on 9 September 1653. This lost play would seem to have dramatized the episode of Cardenio and Lucinda from Cervantes's *Don Quixote*, translated into English by Thomas Shelton and published in 1612. Over a century later Lewis Theobald claimed to have rescued a lost play by Shakespeare, which he had performed, in a text adapted by himself, at Drury Lane in 1727. It was published in 1728 as *Double Falsehood, or the Distress'd Lovers*. Though the characters' names have been changed, this play shows signs of being based on Shelton's 1612 version of the Cardenio episode from *Don Quixote*. Theobald's silence after 1728 about his claim that the play was Shakespeare's lent weight to the general view that it was a forgery, but modern investigators have reopened the case and some argue for a Jacobean original underlying Theobald's avowedly thorough adaptation. E. H. C. Oliphant presents the scanty evidence for two styles in that original play, which he holds to be a collaborative work of Fletcher and Shakespeare. J. Freehafer traces a strong train of external links back from Theobald to the early seventeenth century and at least discourages too impatient a dismissal of Theobald's story of owning several manuscripts of the play. Harriet C. Frazier attempts to reassert the case against Theobald in a book that casts light on the history of *Double Falsehood* in the eighteenth century and establishes Theobald's skill in imitation and propensity for plagiarism. However, the weight of circumstantial evidence is vitiated by partial and illogical pleading, so that her conclusions, though appealing, must remain wholly conjectural: they are that *Double Falsehood* 'is not *Cardenio*. Rather it is Theobald's misguided attempt to establish a vital relationship between the author of *Hamlet* and the author of *Don Quixote* . . . Theobald wrote the play which we all wish Shakespeare might have written'.

Apart from *Double Falsehood* (edited by Walter Graham in 1920), all these plays are included in *The Shakespeare Apocrypha*, edited by C. F. Tucker Brooke (1908, revised 1929: reprinted 1968 from 1908 edition), together with a handful of other plays even more tenuously associated with Shakespeare's name. The texts, except for *Sir Thomas More*, are generally reliable, but commentary is scanty and the introduction long out of date. Littledale's major edition of *The Two Noble Kinsmen* remains an indispensable source for commentary and gives a full account of early criticism. Useful students' editions include those of *Sir Thomas More* by Harold Jenkins; *Arden of Faversham* and *A Yorkshire Tragedy* by K. M. Sturgess; *Arden of Faversham* by T. W. Craik, M. Wine (the most comprehensive), and M. White; *A Yorkshire Tragedy* by A. C. Cawley and B. Gaines (a full and balanced account of the play and its problems); *Edward III* by W. A. Armstrong, F. Lapides, and G. Parfitt (though the last is unduly prone to textual error); and *The Two Noble Kinsmen* by Clifford Leech, G. R. Proudfoot, N. W. Bawcutt (the most readable critical introduction) and E. M. Waith. The more recent of these editions reflect a growing interest in the staging of the plays, all five of which have had professional productions in the 1970s and 1980s. Among other plays in the *Apocrypha*, editions of *Sir John Oldcastle* by J. Rittenhouse and *Fair Em, the Miller's Daughter of Manchester: With the Loves of William the Conqueror* by S. Henning may be recommended. Not so the 'editions' of *The Birth of Merlin* by M. Dominik (which merely reprints a nineteenth-century text and claims to validate the implausible 1662 attribution to William Rowley and William Shakespeare) and *Edmond Ironside* by Eric Sams (which attempts to present that play, probably written about 1593–6, as an example of Shakespeare's 'lost' *juvenilia*) both of which are more remarkable for their return to the Victorian values of forensic energy and special pleading than for any light they cast on the plays. Such is the current interest in Shakespearian attributions that these plays too have been professionally staged, *Edmond Ironside* in London and *The Birth of Merlin* at Theatr Clwyd, Mold, North Wales.

A balanced and fully documented account of the ascription to Shakespeare of plays omitted from the First Folio constitutes

G. R. Proudfoot

chapter X of E. K. Chambers's *William Shakespeare: A Study of Facts and Problems.* Further useful surveys of scholarship are G. Harold Metz's annotated bibliography of *Four Plays Ascribed to Shakespeare (Edward III, Sir Thomas More, Cardenio,* and *The Two Noble Kinsmen);* T. P. Logan and D. S. Smith's *The Predecessors of Shakespeare* (which surveys scholarship and criticism of *Edward III, Fair Em, Mucedorus, Arden of Feversham* and *Locrine);* and the *Textual Companion* to the Oxford Shakespeare, in which Gary Taylor surveys 'The Canon and Chronology of Shakespeare's Plays', including attributed works omitted from the edition.

Though much writing about the apocryphal plays has concentrated on the question of their authorship, critical commentary, sometimes extended, will be found in many of the editions cited, in Kenneth Muir's *Shakespeare as Collaborator* and in Baldwin Maxwell's studies of *Locrine, Thomas Lord Cromwell, The London Prodigal, A Yorkshire Tragedy,* and *The Puritan,* which also explore thoroughly the issues of sources, historical context, and authorship. Of many general studies which pay attention to the apocryphal plays, mention can be made of Irving Ribner's *The English History Play in the Age of Shakespeare* for the historical plays in the group and of Wolfgang Clemen's *English Tragedy before Shakespeare* for its account of the rhetoric of *Locrine.*

Various critics have tried to define and account for the divided nature of *The Two Noble Kinsmen,* notably Theodore Spencer in a bravura piece which presents the play as emanating from the imagination of an ageing and exhausted Shakespeare. More moderately, Philip Edwards discerns a thematic pattern in the opening and closing acts which collaboration has blurred and left incomplete: this pattern both brings the play into relation with *The Winter's Tale* and points to a new departure in Shakespeare's art and in his view of love as radical and as disturbing as that which leads from *Twelfth Night* to *Troilus and Cressida.* Una Ellis-Fermor finds that the style of the scenes usually attributed to Shakespeare is 'not strictly dramatic' and concludes that he cannot have written them. Authorship is again deeply implicated in discussions of the play's imagery by M. Mincoff, E. A. Armstrong, and P. Bertram.

Criticism of *The Two Noble Kinsmen* has moved imperceptibly towards acceptance of dual authorship and away from dismay at that fact. Source study has advanced, with the work of Ann

Thompson, whose full discussion of the dramatists' handling of Chaucer is refreshingly complemented from a medievalist's view-point by E. Talbot Donaldson. M. C. Bradbrook and G. Wickham extend their discussions of Jacobean topicality in late Shakespeare to include *The Two Noble Kinsmen*, both finding links with the royal funeral and wedding of the winter of 1612–13 (which is reasonable), whether or not their further allegations—that the play was written expressly to exploit the popularity of the anti-masque from Beaumont's wedding masque, or that it expresses the personal predicaments of Princess Elizabeth and her father, King James I, at the time of her wedding—seem congruous with the usual standards and behaviour of professional playwrights. The stage history of the play is outlined by G. H. Metz, whose list of twentieth-century productions, though not complete, is sub-stantial, while comments on some of those productions (notably by P. Holland and L. Potter on the production by the Royal Shakespeare Company which opened the Swan Theatre at Strat-ford in April 1986) reveal that the much-scorned subplot is indeed, as C. Leech and others had supposed, the centre of human interest and audience involvement in the play, with the Jailor's Daughter as its star role. Analogies and contrasts with *A Midsummer Night's Dream* are differently developed by F. W. Brownlow and G. Wickham, but both use the comparison to sharpen awareness of *The Two Noble Kinsmen* as (in Brownlow's words) 'a stern, rather dark play' in which the prevailing sense is of disenchantment and loss, while 'the destructive elements flow through men and cities, and have the name of gods' and 'Athens, modest, reasonable and self-limiting, is the name of our humane city'. Wilder shores have now been sighted and await further exploration, perhaps along the lines of R. H. Abrams, who opens a pathway towards the play's pervasive homosexual motifs and deals sensitively with the predicament of Emilia and the centrality of her opposition to Theseus.

Earlier, simpler estimates of *Arden of Faversham* are yielding to revelation of a play whose surface naiveté belies its author's art. Alexander Leggatt discusses it as a play whose design is to keep us guessing, whose world we enter without a guide: its tension between tragedy and sordid fact, between reporting and inter-preting, reflects engagement with metaphysical problems, forcing us to confront the question whether life is random or meaningful, man a free agent or mere slave of passion and accident. G. R.

Proudfoot, reviewing the Royal Shakespeare Company's 1982 production, found a fine balance between the comic and the horrific, the near-absurd and the providential. The play's uses and critique of rhetoric are the subject of I. and H. D. Ousby, who conclude that 'the playwright is warning us that rather than functioning as graceful adornment, "filed points" can be as deadly as dagger points'. C. Belsey finds a reason for the notoriety of the murder of Arden by his wife in its 'challenge to the institution of marriage, itself publicly in crisis in the period' and delineates the dilemma of Alice, caught between the 'chain of bondage' of the traditional view of marriage and the newer and more insidious 'net of power' awaiting her should she remarry with Mosby. L. C. Orlin discerns a political dimension, seeing Mosby not only as the seducer of Arden's wife but the usurper of his house, while for W. Tydeman the play is 'alive with the tensions of the late Elizabethan era' and portrays London in a more 'anarchic and sinister aspect' than any other play of the sixteenth century.

M. Hattaway offers a lively introduction to one of the best-known plays of its time by relating *Mucedorus* to popular dramatic conventions of the Elizabethan theatre, but is unreliable in matters of fact and confuses issues by failing to separate the original text printed in 1598 from its Jacobean additions, printed in 1610. R. Thornberry argues persuasively for an early Jacobean revival of the play between 1604 and 1606. *Mucedorus* is placed in an anthropological and structuralist perspective by R. Marienstras, who finds it full of pointed oppositions between the civilized and the savage, the cooked and the raw, while M. D. Bristol co-opts both *Locrine* and *The Merry Devil of Edmonton* into a discussion of 'plebeian culture and the structure of authority in Renaissance England'. *Locrine* is treated in more conventional terms by P. Berek, who sees it as a professional revamping in the mode of *Tamburlaine* of an amateur Senecan tragedy written by Charles Tilney.

REFERENCES

Henry VIII (*All is True*)

TEXT

Alexander, Peter, 'Conjectural History, or Shakespeare's *Henry VIII*', *Essays and Studies*, 16 (1931), 85–120.

Bullough, Geoffrey (ed.), *Narrative and Dramatic Sources of Shakespeare*, vol. iv (London, 1962).

Foakes, R. A. (ed.), *Henry VIII* (Arden Shakespeare, London, 1957).

Hoeniger, F. D. (ed.), *Henry VIII* (Pelican Shakespeare, Baltimore, Md., 1966).

Humphreys, A. R. (ed.), *Henry VIII* (New Penguin Shakespeare, Harmondsworth, 1971).

Knight, G. Wilson, '*Henry VIII* and the Poetry of Conversion', in *The Crown of Life* (London, 1947; 2nd edn., London, 1948), 256–336.

—— *Shakespearean Production* (London, 1964).

Maxwell, J. C. (ed.), *Henry VIII* (The New Shakespeare, Cambridge, 1962).

Mincoff, M., '*Henry VIII* and Fletcher', *Shakespeare Quarterly*, 12 (1961), 239–60.

Partridge, A. C., *The Problem of 'Henry VIII' Reopened* (Cambridge, 1949); reprinted in his *Orthography in Shakespeare and Elizabethan Drama* (London, 1964).

Spedding, J., 'Who Wrote Shakespere's *Henry VIII*?', *Gentleman's Magazine* (Aug. 1850), NS 34, 115–23.

Swinburne, A. C., *A Study of Shakespeare* (London, 1880).

Willems, M., 'Verbal-Visual, Verbal-Pictorial or Textual-Televisual? Reflections on the BBC Shakespeare Series', *Shakespeare Survey 39* (1987), 91–102.

Woudhuysen, H. R., '*King Henry VIII* and *All Is True*', *N & Q* 229 (1984), 217–18.

CRITICISM AND COMMENTARY

Anderson, Judith H., *Biographical Truth: The Representation of Historical Persons in Tudor-Stuart Writing* (New Haven, Conn., and London, 1984).

Baillie, W. M., '*Henry VIII*: A Jacobean History', *Shakespeare Studies*, 12 (1979), 247–66.

Berry, E. I., '*Henry VIII* and the Dynamics of Spectacle', *Shakespeare Studies*, 12 (1979), 229–46.

Bliss, Lee, 'The Wheel of Fortune and the Maiden Phoenix in Shakespeare's *King Henry the Eighth*', *ELH* 42 (1975), 1–25.

Byrne, M. St C., 'A Stratford Production: *Henry VIII*', *Shakespeare Survey* 3 (1950), 120–9.

Cespedes, F. V., ' "We are one in fortunes": The Sense of History in *Henry VIII*', *ELH* 45 (1978), 413–38.

Clark, Cumberland, *A Study of Shakespeare's 'Henry VIII'*, (London, [1931]).

Doran, Madeleine, review of *Henry VIII*, ed. R. A. Foakes (London, 1957), in *JEGP* 59 (1960), 287–91.

Foakes, R. A., *Shakespeare: The Dark Comedies to the Last Plays* (London, 1971).

Gervinus, G. G., *Shakespeare Commentaries*, trans. F. E. Bennett, 2 vols. (London, 1863).

Kermode, Frank, 'What Is Shakespeare's *Henry VIII* About?', *Durham University Journal*, NS 9 (1948), 48–55; reprinted in *Shakespeare's Histories*, ed. W. A. Armstrong (Penguin Shakespeare Library, Harmondsworth, 1972).

Knight, G. Wilson, '*Henry VIII* and the Poetry of Conversion', in *The Crown of Life* (London, 1947; 2nd edn., London, 1948).

Leggatt, Alexander, '*Henry VIII* and the Ideal England', *Shakespeare Survey 38* (1985), 131–43.

McBride, T., '*Henry VIII* as Machiavellian Romance', *JEGP* 76 (1977), 26–39.

Odell, G. C. D., *Shakespeare—from Betterton to Irving* (New York, 1920).

Ornstein, R., *A Kingdom for a Stage* (Cambridge, Mass., 1972).

Ribner, Irving, *The English History Play in the Age of Shakespeare* (Princeton, NJ, 1957; rev. edn., London, 1965).

Sprague, Arthur Colby, *Shakespeare's Histories: Plays for the Stage* (London, 1964).

Tillyard, E. M. W., *Shakespeare's History Plays* (London, 1944).

—— 'Why did Shakespeare write *Henry VIII*?', *Critical Quarterly*, 3 (1961), 22–7.

Wickham, Glynne, 'The Dramatic Structure of Shakespeare's *King Henry VIII*: An Essay in Rehabilitation', *Proceedings of the British Academy*, 70 (1985), 149–66.

Wimsatt, W. K. (ed.), *Samuel Johnson on Shakespeare* (New York, 1960; reprinted as *Dr Johnson on Shakespeare*, Harmondsworth, 1969).

Yates, Frances A., *Shakespeare's Last Plays: A New Approach* (London, 1975).

The Two Noble Kinsmen, and the Apocryphal Plays

TEXTS, AUTHORSHIP, AND CRITICISM

Editions

Armstrong, W. A. (ed.), *Edward III*, in *Elizabethan History Plays* (World's Classics, London, 1965).

Bawcutt, N. W. (ed.), *The Two Noble Kinsmen* (The New Penguin Shakespeare, Harmondsworth, 1977).

Brooke, C. F. Tucker (ed.), *The Shakespeare Apocrypha* (Oxford, 1908, rev. 1929; reprinted from 1908 edn., Oxford, 1968).

Capell, E. (ed.), *King Edward III*, in *Prolusions, or Select Pieces of Ancient Poetry* (London, 1760).

Cawley, A. C., and B. Gaines (eds.), *A Yorkshire Tragedy* (The Revels Plays, Manchester, 1986).

Craik, T. W. (ed.), *Arden of Faversham*, in *Minor Elizabethan Tragedies* (London, 1974).

Evans, G. Blackmore (ed.), *The Two Noble Kinsmen* in The Riverside Shakespeare (Boston, Mass., 1974).

Dyce, A. (ed.), *Sir Thomas More* (Shakespeare Society, London, 1844).

Gabrieli, V., and G. Melchiori (eds.), *The Book of Sir Thomas More* (Biblioteca Italiana di Testi Inglesi, 25; Bari, 1981).

Graham, Walter (ed.), *Double Falsehood* (Cleveland, Ohio, 1920).

Greg, W. W. (ed.), *The Book of Sir Thomas More* (Malone Society Reprints, Oxford, 1911); reprinted with *Supplement* by H. Jenkins (Oxford, 1961).

Henning, S. (ed.), *Fair Em* (New York and London, 1980).

Jacob, E. (ed.), *Arden of Feversham* (Faversham, 1770).

Jenkins, Harold (ed.), *Sir Thomas More*, in *William Shakespeare: The Complete Works*, ed. C. J. Sisson (London, 1953).

Knight, Charles (ed.), *The Pictorial Shakespeare*, 8 vols. (London, 1838–43).

Lapides, F. (ed.), *The Raigne of King Edward the Third* (New York and London, 1980).

Leech, Clifford (ed.), *The Two Noble Kinsmen* (Signet Shakespeare, New York, 1966).

Littledale, H. (ed.), *The Two Noble Kinsmen* (New Shakspere Society, London, 1874–85).

Montgomery, W. (ed.), *The Two Noble Kinsmen* (The Oxford Shakespeare, Oxford, 1986).

Parfitt, G. (ed.), *Edward III* (Nottingham Drama Texts, Nottingham, 1985).

Proudfoot, G. R. (ed.), *The Two Noble Kinsmen* (Regents Renaissance Drama Series, Lincoln, Nebr., and London, 1970).

Rittenhouse, J. (ed.), *Sir John Oldcastle* (New York and London, 1984).

Sams, Eric (ed.), *Shakespeare's Lost Play: 'Edmund Ironside'* (London, 1985).

Sturgess, K. M. (ed.), *Arden of Faversham* and *A Yorkshire Tragedy*, in *Three Elizabethan Domestic Tragedies* (Harmondsworth, 1969).

Waith, E. M. (ed.), *The Two Noble Kinsmen* (The Oxford Shakespeare, Oxford, 1989).

Wine, M. L. (ed.), *Arden of Faversham* (The Revels Plays, London 1973).

White, M. (ed.), *Arden of Faversham* (New Mermaids, London, 1982).

Other Studies

Abrams, R. H., 'Gender Confusion and Sexual Politics in *The Two Noble Kinsmen*', *Themes in Drama*, vol. vii, *Drama, Sex and Politics* (Cambridge, 1985), 69–76.

Armstrong, E. A., *Shakespeare's Imagination* (London, 1946; 2nd edn., Lincoln, Nebr., 1963).

Belsey, C., 'Alice Arden's Crime', *Renaissance Drama*, 13 (1982), 83–102.
—— *The Subject of Tragedy* (London, 1985).

Berek, P., '*Locrine* Revised, *Selimus*, and Early Responses to *Tamburlaine*', *Research Opportunities in Renaissance Drama*, 23 (1980), 33–54.
—— '*Tamburlaine*'s Weak Sons: Imitation as Interpretation before 1593', *Renaissance Drama*, 13 (1982), 55–82.

Bertram, Paul, *Shakespeare and the 'Two Noble Kinsmen'* (New Brunswick, NJ, 1965).

Bradbrook, Muriel C., *The Living Monument: Shakespeare and the Theatre of his Time* (Cambridge, 1976).

Bristol, M. D., *Carnival and Theater: Plebeian Culture and the Structure of Authority in Renaissance England* (New York and London, 1985).

Brownlow, F. W., *Two Shakespearean Sequences* (London, 1977).

Chambers, E. K., *William Shakespeare: A Study of Facts and Problems*, 2 vols. (Oxford, 1930; reprinted 1989); abridged by Charles Williams, *A Short Life of Shakespeare with the Sources* (Oxford, 1933).

Chambers, R. W., 'The Expression of Ideas—Particularly Political Ideas—in the Three Pages, and in Shakespeare', in *Shakespeare's Hand in the Play of 'Sir Thomas More'*, ed. A. W. Pollard (Cambridge, 1923; reprinted 1967).

Chillington, C. A., 'Playwrights at Work: Henslowe's, Not Shakespeare's *Book of Sir Thomas More*', *English Literary Renaissance*, 10 (1980), 439–79.

Clemen, Wolfgang H., *English Tragedy before Shakespeare*, trans. T. S. Dorsch (London, 1961).

Dominik, M., *William Shakespeare and 'The Birth of Merlin'* (New York, 1985).

Donaldson, E. Talbot, *The Swan at the Well: Shakespeare Reading Chaucer* (New Haven, Conn., and London, 1985).

Edwards, Philip, 'On the Design of *The Two Noble Kinsmen*', *Review of English Literature*, 5 (1964), 89–105; reprinted in *The Two Noble Kinsmen*, ed. C. Leech (Signet Shakespeare, New York, 1966).

Ellis-Fermor, Una, '*The Two Noble Kinsmen*', in her *Shakespeare the Dramatist*, ed. K. Muir (London, 1961).

Erdman, D. V., and E. G. Fogel (eds.), *Evidence for Authorship* (Ithaca, NY, 1966).

Forker, C. and J. Candido, 'Wit, Wisdom, and Theatricality in *The Book of Sir Thomas More*', *Shakespeare Studies*, 13 (1980), 85–104.

Frazier, Harriet C., *A Babble of Ancestral Voices: Shakespeare, Cervantes, and Theobald* (The Hague and Paris, 1974).

Freehafer, J., '*Cardenio*, by Shakespeare and Fletcher', *PMLA* 84 (1969), 501–13.

Hart, Alfred, 'Shakespeare and the Vocabulary of *The Two Noble Kinsmen*', *RES* 10 (1934), 274–87; reprinted in his *Shakespeare and the Homilies* (Melbourne, 1934), 242–56.

Hattaway, Michael, *Elizabethan Popular Theatre, Plays in Performance*, (London, 1982).

Hays, M. L., 'Watermarks in the Manuscript of *Sir Thomas More*', *Shakespeare Quarterly*, 26 (1975), 66–9.

——'Shakespeare's Hand in *Sir Thomas More*: Some Aspects of the Palaeographic Argument', *Shakespeare Studies*, 8 (1975), 241–53.

Holland, P., 'Style at the Swan', *Essays in Criticism*, 36 (1986), 193–209.

Jackson, MacD. P., *Studies in Attribution: Middleton and Shakespeare* (Salzburg Studies in English, Jacobean Drama Studies, 79; Salzburg, 1979).

Lamb, Charles, *Specimens of English Dramatic Poets* (London, 1808).

Lascelles, M. M., *The Story-Teller Retrieves the Past: Historical Fiction and Fictitious History in the Art of Scott, Stevenson, Kipling and Some Others* (Oxford, 1980).

Leggatt, Alexander, '*Arden of Faversham*', *Shakespeare Survey 36* (1983), 121–33.

Logan, Terence P., and Denzell S. Smith (eds.), *The Predecessors of Shakespeare: A Survey and Bibliography of Recent Studies in English Renaissance Drama* (Lincoln, Nebr., 1973).

Marienstras, R., *New Perspectives on the Shakespearean World*, trans. J. Lloyd (Cambridge, 1985).

Maxwell, Baldwin, 'Conjectures on *The London Prodigal*', in *Studies in Honor of T. W. Baldwin*, ed. D. C. Allen (Urbana, Ill., 1958).

——*Studies in the Shakespeare Apocrypha* (New York, 1956).

McMillin, S., *The Elizabethan Theatre and 'The Book of Sir Thomas More'*, (Ithaca, NY, 1987).

Melchiori, G., '*The Book of Sir Thomas More*: A Chronology of Revision', *Shakespeare Quarterly*, 37 (1986), 291–308.

——'The Contextualisation of Source Material: The Play within the Play in *Sir Thomas More*', *Le Forme del Teatro*, 3 (Rome, 1984), 59–94.

——'Hand D in *Sir Thomas More*: An Essay in Misinterpretation', *Shakespeare Survey 38* (1985), 101–14.

Metz, G. Harold, *Four Plays Ascribed to Shakespeare . . . : An Annotated Bibliography* (Garland Shakespeare Bibliographies, 2; New York, 1982).

Mincoff, M., 'The Authorship of *The Two Noble Kinsmen*', *English Studies* 33 (1952), 97–115.

Muir, Kenneth, *Shakespeare as Collaborator* (London, 1960).

Nosworthy, J. M., 'Shakespeare and *Sir Thomas More*', *RES* NS 6 (1955), 12–25.

Oliphant, E. H. C., *The Plays of Beaumont and Fletcher* (New Haven, Conn., 1927).

Orlin, L. C., 'Man's House as His Castle in *Arden of Faversham*', *Medieval and Renaissance Drama in English*, 2 (1985), 57–89.

Ousby, I., and H. D. Ousby, 'Art and Language in *Arden of Faversham*', *Durham University Journal*, 68 (1975–6), 47–54.

Pollard, A. W. (ed.), *Shakespeare's Hand in the Play of 'Sir Thomas More'* (Cambridge, 1923; reprinted 1967).

Potter, L., 'Two *Noble Kinsmen*', *En Torno a Shakespeare*, 3 (Valencia, 1987), 137–49.

Proudfoot, G. R., '*Arden of Faversham*', review of 1982 Royal Shakespeare Company production, *Cahiers Elisabéthains*, 22 (1982), 121–2.

—— 'The *Reign of King Edward the Third* (1596) and Shakespeare', *Proceedings of the British Academy*, 71 (1986), 159–85.

Ramsey, P., 'Shakespeare and *Sir Thomas More* Revisited: Or a Mounty on the Trail', *Papers of the Bibliographical Society of America*, 70 (1976), 333–46.

Ribner, Irving, *The English History Play in the Age of Shakespeare* (Princeton, NJ, 1957; rev. edn., London, 1965).

Schoenbaum, S., *Internal Evidence and Elizabethan Dramatic Authorship* (Evanston, Ill., 1966).

Simpson, Richard, 'Are There Any Extant MSS. in Shakespeare's Handwriting?', *N & Q* 4th Ser. 8 (1871).

Spalding, W., *A Letter on Shakespeare's Authorship of the Drama Entitled 'The Two Noble Kinsmen'* (Edinburgh, 1833); reprinted in *Transactions of the New Shakspere Society* (London, 1876).

Spencer, Theodore, 'The *Two Noble Kinsmen*', *Modern Philology*, 36 (1939), 255–76; reprinted in *The Two Noble Kinsmen*, ed. C. Leech (Signet Shakespeare, New York, 1966).

Thompson, Ann, 'Jailers' Daughters in *The Arcadia* and *The Two Noble Kinsmen*', *N & Q* 224 (1979), 400–1.

—— *Shakespeare's Chaucer: A Study in Literary Origins* (Liverpool, 1978).

Thompson, E. Maunde, 'The Handwriting of the Three Pages Attributed to Shakespeare Compared with His Signatures', in *Shakespeare's Hand in the Play of 'Sir Thomas More'*, ed. A. W. Pollard (Cambridge, 1923; reprinted 1967), 57–112.

Thornberry, R., 'A Seventeenth-Century Revival of *Mucedorus* in London before 1610', *Shakespeare Quarterly*, 28 (1977), 362–4.

Tydeman, W., 'The Image of the City in English Renaissance Drama', *Essays and Studies*, NS 38 (1985), 29–44.

Wells, Stanley and Gary Taylor, with John Jowett and William Montgomery, *William Shakespeare: A Textual Companion* (Oxford, 1987).

Wentersdorf, K. P., 'Linkages of Thought and Imagery in Shakespeare and *More*', *Modern Language Quarterly*, 34 (1973), 384–405.

Wickham, G., '*The Two Noble Kinsmen* or *A Midsummer Night's Dream, Part II*?', in *Elizabethan Theatre 7* ed. G. R. Hibbard (Port Credit, Ont., 1980).

19 | Critical Developments

Cultural
Materialism,
Feminism and
Gender
Critique, and
New Historicism

JONATHAN DOLLIMORE

Sometimes fairly, sometimes not, the new defines itself against the established. To that extent it might be said to depend upon what it seeks to displace. For its part, the established, though it does not want to be displaced, needs innovation if it is to survive in the long run; and because it has the greater power it tends to respond to this tension by allowing the new in a 'policed' form. At the same time it may seek to pretend that it is not changing at all, especially by misrepresenting or misunderstanding those challenging developments which it cannot or will not accommodate. Generally speaking, the resistance, misunderstanding, and misrepresentation are greater the more established the institution. Nothing is more established than 'Shakespeare', and nowhere in the humanities are vested interests more apparent. The situation is further complicated by the fact that time passes and what were once thought to be sharp differences may dissolve into obscure similarities, while new differences emerge (one need only think of the complicated relationship of modernism to romanticism).

What I've just described is a process of cultural struggle and change in which real power is at stake. There is a good reason for beginning this essay by invoking power struggles in the academy: the foregounding of such issues, and of the cultural contest they imply, is central to many of the new approaches in English studies, both in their consideration of the historical contexts of literature, and in their account of critical practice (theirs and others'). For the perspectives I shall be outlining there is no question of simply describing some new interpretations of Shakespeare's plays, or indeed of restricting this chapter to Shakespeare in the narrow sense typical of conventional literary criticism. Here are four reasons why not.

First, some of the most challenging work has originated in a wider context and often has not even been by those primarily identified as 'Shakespearians'. Second, this work is often inter-disciplinary, and rather than focussing primarily on Shakespeare, it seeks to interrelate him with other aspects of culture. Third, materialist studies of the reproduction of 'Shakespeare' have shown him/it to be a powerful cultural institution. More is at stake in the cultural struggle over what he represents and embodies than for any other figure in the literary canon, and maybe within the humanities more generally. There was a time when it was thought bad form for critics to write on other critics rather than the authors themselves. Now, however, traditions of criticism are seen as significant aspects of cultural history, and worth attending to for that reason; they not only reflect but help to make that history. Fourth, the student has too often been presented with review/survey essays which describe alternative interpretations as if they simply reflect either the rich tapestry of literary criticism, or of Shakespeare's 'vision' of life, or both, the first reflecting the second. And when specific earlier interpretations do become so embarrassing that they must be stamped 'obsolete', it is often in a way which suggests that they have become so in the course of a natural progression towards critical enlightenment, with the happy consequence that the current orthodoxy is always the closest to the truth of the matter. In contrast, materialist criticism relates changing interpretations to the cultural formations which produce them, and which those interpretations in turn reproduce, or help to change. It is probably true to say that behind every substantial literary-critical disagreement can be found a substantial cultural and political difference rooted in the society of its time. It is this which makes the new self-reflexive aspect of literary studies a contribution to cultural history.

The recent and controversial changes in literary criticism are due mainly to the influence of a range of intellectual perspectives in post-war Europe, including anthropology, post-structuralism,

Marxism, deconstruction, psychoanalysis, feminism, and cultural studies. To make this essay manageable, but also because I consider tham to be the most interesting and important in this context, I shall be concerned mainly with three critical movements influenced by these perspectives: feminism and gender critique, new historicism, and cultural materialism. Even within this self-imposed limitation (and bias) this introduction is not exhaustive. If, further, it fails in some areas to be adequately representative, I have nevertheless tried to cite work which constitutes significant points of access or departure—pláces to begin, to return to, to contest.

The three critical movements which make up the subject of this essay draw selectively on the perspectives just mentioned while also developing their own forms of cultural theory and critical practice, and, in significant cases, doing this in studies of the Renaissance period and of Shakespeare. This is especially true of *Renaissance Self-Fashioning* by Stephen Greenblatt, a pioneering work in hew historicism and still one of the most important contributions in the field, and one of the most rewarding for students to read. Greenblatt's later *Shakespearean Negotiations* continues and develops his earlier work. Although only a couple of its contributors write specifically on Shakespeare, a number of essays which first appeared in an important journal *Representations* and which are now reprinted under the title *Representing the English Renaissance* (ed. Greenblatt), indicate the scope and influence of new historicism in this field. This collection continues to reflect, but also broadens, the initial new historicist concern with the relations between the aesthetic and the political, especially the connections between art and state power.

Cultural materialism has a different history. Originating in the UK it grows from an eclectic body of work which can be broadly defined as cultural studies; major influences include Raymond Williams and Stuart Hall. Perhaps the best introduction to cultural materialism is the collection of interviews with Raymond Williams published under the title *Politics and Letters*. In the UK Renaissance Studies were among the first areas to benefit from a growing feeling in literary and cultural theory that theory itself had reached a level of sophistication which required historical engagement as its next stage, meaning by this not *just* a re-reading of past literature through theoretical lenses, but an historical testing of theory, using history to 'read' theory as well as vice versa. This is another reason why the three approaches I'm concerned with here are more than just new ways of interpreting old texts; they also involve different and contested conceptions of (for instance) human identity, cultural, social, and historical process, as well as the activity of criticism itself. The introductions to *Political Shakespeare* (ed. Jonathan Dollimore and Alan Sinfield) and the 1987 reprint of J. W. Lever's *The Tragedy of State* try to indicate some of these differences in a way accessible to students. With a similar intention now, and to counter the necessary generality of much of this essay, I want to proceed through a specific example and contrast.

Kenneth Muir, discussing the supernatural elements in *Macbeth* (he is speaking specifically of Lady Macbeth's sleepwalking scene), remarks:

The fact that we no longer believe in demons, and that Shakespeare's audience mostly did, does not diminish the dramatic effect for us; for with the fading of belief in the objective existence of devils, they and their operations can yet symbolize the workings of evil in the hearts of men. . . . The changes in custom and belief do not seriously detract from the universality of the tragedy. (p. lxx)

Contrast this with Terry Eagleton in *William Shakespeare*, speaking of the witches in *Macbeth*:

The witches are the heroines of the piece . . . they . . . by releasing ambitious thoughts in Macbeth, expose [the] hierarchical social order for what it is . . . the pious self-deception of a society based on routine oppression and incessant warfare. . . . Their riddling, ambiguous speech . . . promises to subvert this structure: their teasing word-play infiltrates and undermines Macbeth from within, revealing in him a lack which hollows his being into desire. The witches signify a realm of non-meaning and poetic play which hovers at the work's margins. . . . [They] catalyse this region of otherness and desire within [Macbeth] so that by the end of the play it has flooded up from within him to shatter and engulf his previously assured identity. . . . The witches figure as the 'unconscious' of the drama, that which must be exiled and repressed as dangerous but which is always likely to return with a vengeance. . . . The witches inhabit an anarchic, richly ambiguous zone both in and out of official society. . . . But official society can only ever imagine its radical 'other' as chaos rather than creativity. . . . Foulness—a political order which thrives on bloodshed—believes itself fair, whereas the witches do not so much invert this opposition as deconstruct it. (pp. 2–3)

I've chosen these two critics because each is deservedly respected, representative of his respective critical context, and, to a large extent, his generation.

For Muir the demons constitute an awkward aspect of Shakespeare; we don't believe in them, and if it turns out that Shakespeare did, then his universal appeal might be diminished. He will become too much of his time with the embarrassing consequence that a fundamental aspect of his reputation as the greatest playwright, namely that he transcends his time, is put in question. Muir's solution to the problem is to reconstitute demons as symbols of evil. This way Shakespeare is saved. Note that Muir does not say Shakespeare believed in demons, only that his audience mostly did. But the implication is that even if he did, he and/or we could also see a deeper truth behind the surface superstition. I say 'and/or we' because, to be fair to Muir, he is quite scrupulous in this passage, and doesn't actually attribute the symbolic view to Shakespeare either; that 'can yet' includes what it does not actually specify. But the effect is to dissolve an awkward piece of history via an appeal to symbolism; history is dissolved into transhistorical truth.

What Muir seeks to remove, Eagleton seizes upon and stresses. I have quoted him at length because the passage represents something rather important in the new work, which Eagleton is here voicing though not directly specifying: a concern with the subordinate, the marginal, and the displaced. In the new work these individuals, groups, or sub-cultures are seen as being (i) of importance in their own right, aspects of our past which literary criticism and official history have ignored or repressed; (ii) of further importance for understanding the society which has rendered them marginal (for example, the dominant is understood in terms of its deviants; those whom it defines itself over and against; (iii) sources of a potential or actual instability and disruption in that society. So, for Eagleton, the witches are fascinatingly deviant, but they also reveal much about, and subvert, the social order which demonizes them.

Here then is the process which has so fascinated cultural anthropologists—in the words of Barbara Babcock, the culturally peripheral turn out to be symbolically central. Though in quite different ways, this is so both in the society of early modern England that demonized them, and in the contemporary criticism that foregrounds and appropriates them. But this is a very different kind of symbolism to Muir's symbolic dissolution of the witches into 'the hearts of men'.

A similar concern with the paradoxically central significance of marginality is taken up by contributors to *Political Shakespeare*, with the difference that here an attempt is made to give the subordinate more of a history: two essays analyze English colonialism in the New World and Ireland in relation to Shakespeare's history plays and *The Tempest*: other essays consider the prostitutes in *Measure for Measure*, the representation of women's subordination in this same play, in *King Lear*, and in early modern England. A concern with the subordinate and the marginal is likewise apparent in *Rewriting the Renaissance: The Discourses of Sexual Difference in Early Modern Europe* (ed. Margaret Ferguson *et al.*), one of the best recent collections on the period: I have in mind especially Peter Stallybrass's 'Patriarchal Territories: The Body Enclosed', which includes a discussion of *Othello*, Coppélia Kahn's 'The Absent Mother in *King Lear*', Stephen Orgel's 'Prospero's Wife', Louis Montrose's study of gender, power, and form *vis-à-vis A Midsummer Night's Dream*, and Ann Rosalind Jones's study of sixteenth-century women poets and their audiences. This collection is a persuasive reminder that some of the most rewarding recent work has been interdisciplinary and concerned with the period as a whole rather than a single author. Likewise with Walter Cohen's *Drama of a Nation*, another recent cross-cultural study which integrates diligent historical research into an ambitious theoretical and political perspective. Cohen describes his project thus:

The entire study pursues a single and simple hypothesis: that the absolutist state, by its inherent dynamism and contradictions, first fostered and then undermined the public theatre. More precisely, the similarities between Spanish and English absolutism help account for the parallels between the two dramatic traditions, while the divergent courses of economic and religious development in England and Spain begin to explain the differences.

Of other recent collections of essays which concentrate on Shakespeare, three should be mentioned: *Alternative Shakespeares*, edited by John Drakakis; *Shakespeare and the Question of Theory*, edited by Patricia Parker and Geoffrey Hartman; and *Shakespeare Reproduced*, edited by Jean E. Howard and Marion F. O'Connor. The first two exemplify the variety of the alternative perspectives now available; the accessible style of most of the essays in the Drakakis volume also makes it especially useful for students. *Shakespeare Reproduced* addresses important differences as well as similarities between the three perspectives discussed here.

As enjoyably different as it is from Muir's account, Eagleton's celebration of the witches shares something in common with it: both fail to supply an adequately historical dimension to witchcraft. Moreover Eagleton, like Muir, appropriates the witches as symbols, except that instead of the tired cliché about evil in the hearts of men, they become symbols of an anarchic, decentred desire, occupying a radically ambiguous zone. Additionally—and this is another reason for quoting him at length—Eagleton engagingly 'rereads' the witches as prototype literary theorists, remarkable not least for the breadth of their theoretical sophistication: they are at once Marxist, Lacanian, and Deconstructionist. In fact, they are not a little Eagletonian.

But—and how can this be said without sounding gauche?—to become eclectic literary theorists was not the fate of most 'witches' in Renaissance Europe. All three of our perspectives, feminist, historicist, materialist, would insist on the importance of addressing the history of witchcraft, and doing so via a cultural analysis which is more inclusive and interdisciplinary than some conventional history and most literary criticism.

Recently critics have learned much from historians exploring similar areas. Stuart Clark's dense but informative 'Inversion, Misrule and the Meaning of Witchcraft' indicates how witchcraft was conceived in the context of a 'vocabulary of misrule', an inversion of right order, an antithetical component in a world view which was also a legitimation of 'ordered' relations. Examining *Macbeth* from this perspective, Peter Stallybrass shows the way the play associates witchcraft with a whole range of inversions and disorders—rebellion, the world upside-down, female rule, and the overthrowing of patriarchal authority. Again the marginal becomes symbolically central, thoroughly implicated in both the structure and the instabilities of rule. Addressing similar issues but now from a psychoanalytic perspective, Janet Adelman has argued that *Macbeth* fantasizes a destructive maternal power and then displaces this with another fantasy: an escape by men from this power. By the end of the play 'the problem of masculinity' is solved by eliminating the female: 'in *Macbeth*, maternal power is given its most virulent sway and then abolished; at the end of the play we are in a purely male realm'. Belief in witchcraft facilitates the creation of these fantasies and the displacement of the one by the other. Adelman reminds us that the evil attributed to witches in England was not as virulent as that attributed to their Continental counterparts. Generally the things the latter were supposed to do—the ritual murder and eating of infants, attacking male genitals, engaging in sexual perversity with demons—the former were not. But, argues Adelman, the extreme evil associated with Continental witches does figure in the play and is identified with Lady Macbeth.

Reading such work, we begin to see that witchcraft beliefs were inseparable from gender beliefs, and that the important connections are not always the obvious ones. Catherine Belsey, in *The Subject of Tragedy*, sees the witchcraft craze as coterminous with a crisis in 'the definition of women and the meaning of the family'. Reminding us that 'Of the witches executed in England, 93% were women', she explores the relation between witchcraft and women speaking out of turn: 'These women, at the extreme edges of the social body, old, poor and often beggars . . . broke silence and found an unauthorized voice, but the social body required that they paid a high price for the privilege of being heard.' Moreover: 'The supreme opportunity to speak was the moment of execution.' On this same issue of women's subordinate speech, D. E. Underdown sees witchcraft as part of the crisis in gender relations. He remarks that the period of public anxiety about scolding women and witches is roughly similar, and paralleled by the chronology of a third category of rebellious women, the 'woman on top'.

Such then would be the beginnings of a materialist approach to *Macbeth*: attending to, rather than suppressing the problematic presence of the witches, the inquiry opens out into an historical study which is necessarily also theoretical, and vice versa; which asks questions about gender, language, and social order from an interdisciplinary perspective, and does so because it wants to do much more than simply provide a persuasive modern interpretation of *Macbeth*.

The example of witchcraft is important for two further reasons. First, by exploring its history we are led to reject the view that the marginal are usually or easily the source of subversion. Second, witchhunting has been extremely difficult to explain adequately; no single, and certainly no simple, explanation is adequate to the historical reality. Like other forms of discrimination and demonizing—misogyny, racism, homophobia, for example—witchcraft seems to work at different though interrelated levels. If a psychological explanation ignoring the material conditions which foster the demonizing of minorities is inadequate, so too would be a sociological argument which presented witchcraft as simply functional for the prevailing social order. What is required is an interdisciplinary analysis, by which I mean not just a loose combination of perspectives, but a conjunction which provokes each into transgressing disciplinary boundaries, the tension between incompatible methodologies itself becoming a source of insight rather than confusion.

Christopher Hill (even more mischievously than Eagleton's transvaluation of the witches?) began a recent review by remarking that for many years now the best history of seventeenth-century England has been written by literary critics (*TLS* 1–8 Jan. 1988, p. 17). If there is any truth at all in that, it is largely because of what critics have learned from historians who have themselves crossed interdisciplinary boundaries. Hill is an eminent example; in his review he has in mind especially Margot Heinemann's pioneering study *Puritanism and Theatre: Thomas Middleton and Opposition Drama under the Early Stuarts.*

> contradiction and struggle: *the materialist senses of these words are important for recovering the complexity of both the historical processes which Renaissance drama represents, and the complexity of these plays' actual dramatic structure. By contradiction I mean a development which is at once necessary to something yet destructive of it, and by struggle I mean a conflict between (for example) classes, or within a class (between contending fractions), or between dominant and emergent groups of other kinds.*

The theatre of early modern England shows a sophisticated knowledge of conflict, be it within human subjectivity, within society and the state, or within large-scale historical change. However such issues are often difficult to grasp and students are sometimes at a loss as to how to approach them in actual critical practice. 'History and Ideology: The Instance of Henry V' by Dollimore and Sinfield (in Drakakis) tries to show how theoretical, historical, and textual analysis might be integrated in critical practice.

It is partly because of the complexity in the representation of historical and social process *within* Shakespearian drama itself that there is a thriving debate as to whether these plays are more conservative than challenging or vice versa; in particular—and the point is recorded here somewhat simply for the sake of brevity—did his plays reinforce the dominant order, or do they interrogate it to the point of subversion? According to a rough-and-ready division, new historicists have inclined to the first view, cultural materialists to the second, while feminism and gender critique have operated in both categories. Actually the materialist perspective also crosses between categories; it might, for example, contrast the challenge offered by Shakespeare's plays on the Jacobean stage with the often highly conservative appropriation of those plays in subsequent criticism and theatre productions. At this point it is useful to mention several recent essays comparing the three perspectives in this and other respects; three of the best are Jean Howard's 'The New Historicism in Renaissance Studies', Walter Cohen's 'Political Criticism of Shakespeare', and Don E. Wayne's 'Power, Politics, and the Shakespearean Text: recent criticism in England and the United States'; the second and third of these are in *Shakespeare Reproduced*; the first is separately listed in the bibliography section below. Alan Sinfield's 'Power and Ideology: An Outline Theory and Sidney's *Arcadia*' develops, through a criticism of early new historicist work, a way of approaching texts which shows them not so much as conservative *or* radical, but as sites of struggle. Another essay by Sinfield exemplifies this perspective in a reading of *Macbeth* ('*Macbeth*: History, Ideology and Intellectuals').

If new historicists see a conservative dimension in Shakespeare, they do so in terms very different from earlier criticism. Those like Greenblatt in *Renaissance Self-Fashioning*, Jonathan Goldberg in *James I and the Politics of Literature*, and Stephen Mullaney in *The Place of the Stage*, make use of concepts like 'rehearsal' and 'containment' whereby the theatre is seen to explore subversive elements in contemporary culture in ways which may harness or neutralize their challenge, but which also show their ability to disrupt. Leonard Tennenhouse in *Power on Display* begins from the proposition that Shakespeare's plays were not enclosed within an aesthetic framework of the kind subscribed to by modern critics. He develops from this an argument for the collaboration between statecraft and stagecraft in producing spectacles of power, and explores the ways gender and class, misogyny and patriarchy figure in such spectacles.

It is around the representation of gender that historicist critics with a materialist bias have become increasingly aware of the way authority's attempt to control divergent and dissident cultures is often marked by instability. In '*A Midsummer Night's Dream* and the Shaping Fantasies of Elizabethan Culture: Gender, Power, Form', Louis Montrose explores the problems created for a patriarchal culture by Queen Elizabeth, as focused for example in male fantasies of dependence and domination. In Shakespeare's play he finds 'a fantasy of male dependency upon woman . . . expressed and contained within a fantasy of male control over woman'. Alert to the dialectical, political, and often unstable aspects of cultural representations, Montrose also shows how the Elizabethan regime generated tensions which threatened its fragile stability, and how strategies of containment in *A Midsummer Night's Dream* intermittently undermine themselves. In another essay, 'Professing the Renaissance: The Poetics and Politics of Culture', Montrose has written an informative article on the history and development of new historicism, its connections with materialist criticism, and the controversies which surround both.

To contain a threat by rehearsing it one must first give it a voice, a part, a presence—in the theatre, as in the culture. Through this contradiction the very condition of something's containment may constitute the terms of its challenge: opportunities for resistance become apparent, especially on the stage, even as they are denied. This would be one of several things materialists would stress in elucidating the challenge of this theatre, a challenge which, according to critics like Dollimore in *Radical Tragedy* and Moretti in *Signs Taken for Wonders*, helped undermine the legitimacy of established authority.

Similar questions arise when we consider further the representation of gender in the plays, especially the comedies. Of all the differences, analysis of gender is one of the most important.*

---

* My formulation 'feminism and gender critique' is a shorthand way of indicating not so much two separate perspectives as several overlapping ones. The analysis of gender from feminist, lesbian, gay, and materialist perspectives —to name but four—will typically interrelate. At the same time there may be

There are two contrasts to be noted here. The first is between the traditional and the new work, the second between different emphases within the latter. Nothing has dated conventional Shakespearian criticism so much as its attitude to, or its ignoring of, gender. It has been ready to reproduce the most tired and oppressive clichés about female 'virtue' and more than ready to reprove female 'vice', and either deny the existence of the sexually unconventional (especially where it is an embarrassment to canonical dignity) or to endorse punitive attitudes towards it (for example sexual deviance as a metaphor for evil). Conservative literary critics have often felt superior to and in advance of the prevailing social order, contrasting their own cultivated values with those of the vulgar. I doubt if this has ever been justified; as regards their attitudes to gender and sexuality I am sure it is not: they are attitudes which often reveal critics to be up-market moral hacks, giving a certain academic respectability to conventional wisdom, that is, bigotry. Linda Woodbridge's critique of male critics writing about *Antony and Cleopatra* is especially telling in this respect.

The distance from traditional approaches is equally apparent in that recent work which would see Shakespeare as conservative in his treatment of gender, as well as that which sees him as relatively (historically speaking) progressive. This is the second contrast, and one worth further attention. Again let me put the question directly if somewhat crudely: do these plays endorse the conservative and, to us, oppressive views of gender which prevailed in their society, or do they challenge them?

In 1975 Juliet Dusinberre published *Shakespeare and the Nature of Women*, a pioneering and still inspiring study which argues that 'the drama from 1590 to 1625 is feminist in sympathy', and

important areas of dispute or, at the very least, different histories and diverse objectives which it is important to recognise. Also, the very concept of gender itself may be the subject of critique since it is sometimes used in a way which takes no account of sexual orientation, or of class and race with which it is inevitably connected. I believe that some of the most crucial issues in gender are around the points of connection (though not necessarily agreement) between these perspectives. Some have questioned this. Carol Thomas Neely in 'Constructing the Subject: Feminist Practice and the New Renaissance Discourses' and Lynda E. Boose in 'The Family in Shakespeare Studies; or—Studies in the Family of Shakespeareans; or—the Politics of Politics' argue that some gender analysis, and even some feminist analysis, of Shakespeare is in fact inimical to feminist objectives.

relates this to the development of more positive views of marriage within protestantism and puritanism. Another important book, *The Woman's Part: Feminist Criticism of Shakespeare*, a collection of essays edited by Lenz, Greene, and Neely, appeared in 1980. These two books have been points of departure for much subsequent feminist criticism. A further significant influence in the development of a feminist perspective on Shakespeare in America has been the psychoanalytic work of (for example) Janet Adelman, especially her essay on masculinity in *Coriolanus*, and of Coppélia Kahn in her book *Man's Estate: Masculine Identity in Shakespeare*.

Often, though not invariably, these writers read Shakespeare for positive identifications of women. Subsequent work has tended to be more critical, examining the ways in which Shakespeare's plays represent the patriarchal values of his period, and in particular how women are represented in relation to social crisis and change. Thus Lisa Jardine argues that the strong interest in women shown by Elizabethan and Jacobean drama does not reflect an increasing liberty for women at that time, but 'is related to the patriarchy's unexpressed worry about the great social changes which characterise the period'. This is brought out especially well in chapters on dress codes, sumptuary law and 'natural' order, and the disorderly woman.

Likewise Kathleen McLuskie in 'The Patriarchal Bard' (in *Political Shakespeare*) dissents from what she calls the 'liberal feminism' which would co-opt Shakespeare: 'Feminist criticism need not restrict itself to privileging the woman's part or to special pleading on behalf of female characters. It can be equally well served by making a text reveal the conditions in which a particular ideology of femininity functions and by both revealing and subverting the hold which such an ideology has for readers both female and male.' Her study of *King Lear* is exemplary of an important trend in feminist criticism, one which connects with other kinds of gender analysis:

The misogyny of King Lear, both the play and its hero, is constructed out of an ascetic tradition which presents women as the source of the primal sin of lust, combining with concerns about the threat to the family posed by female insubordination. However the text also dramatises the material conditions which lie behind assertions of power within the family, even as it expresses deep anxieties about the chaos which can ensue when the balance of power is altered.

Ann Thompson in ' "The Warrant of Womanhood": Shakespeare and Feminist Criticism' provides a survey which I commend to readers of this one; one of the works she discusses is Elaine Showalter's 'Representing Ophelia: Woman, Madness and the Responsibilities of Feminist Criticism'. This is a fascinating essay which exemplifies an important connection between the materialist and feminist perspectives. Showalter explores the cultural refiguring of Ophelia not only in the arts but in 'reality' also; she shows among other things how 'illustrations of Ophelia have played a major role in the theoretical construction of female insanity.'

Jacqueline Rose in 'Sexuality in the Reading of Shakespeare: *Hamlet* and *Measure for Measure*' (in *Alternative Shakespeares*, ed. Drakakis) looks at the representation of two other heroines, Gertrude from the first play in the title, and Isabella from the second, showing how 'the question of aesthetic form and the question of sexuality are implicated in each other'. Drawing on a psychoanalytic perspective she shows how in these plays and in criticism of them the woman is made a focus 'for a set of ills which the drama shows as exceeding the woman *at the same time* as it makes of her their cause'. Dollimore in 'Transgression and Surveillance in *Measure for Measure*' (in *Political Shakespeare*), though from a different perspective, offers a comparable approach to *Measure*, showing how social crisis is displaced onto the prostitutes of the play. They are indeed made 'symbolically central' even while remaining utterly marginal: everything in the play presupposes them, yet they have no voice or presence. Those who speak on their behalf do so as exploitatively as those who want to destroy them. The prostitutes are precisely 'spoken for'.

Even those who have felt that, when all is said and done, these plays relocate desire and gender within the conservative confines of patriarchy and family as ordained by the metaphysic of nature and divine law would probably agree that, somewhere on the way, the conservative view is questioned, perhaps even sub-verted. Through the very attributes of theatre itself—artifice, cross-dressing, disguise, role-playing—the cultural construction of gender can be explored and its contradictions and discriminations revealed. The artifice of the theatre becomes the grounds for deconstructing the idea that gender is the result of divine or natural law; for exploring the artifice of gender (that it is a social construction and not a natural or biological fact) and the creative and the potentially creative perversity of desire itself: this theatre revelled in what Ray Davies rediscovered in *Lola*—in the sphere of the social, boys will be girls and girls will be boys. Catherine Belsey in 'Disrupting Sexual Difference' (in *Alternative Shakespeares*) and Dollimore in 'Subjectivity, Sexuality, and Transgression' explore how artifice, in keeping with its nature, takes on a double aspect: if it is the precondition for the safe taking apart of gender (it's not true really) it can also be the basis for its critique. The controversy around cross-dressing in the Renaissance involves real anxieties about real challenges to class and gender hierarchies. In the most radical texts of the period, gender and sexual difference are demystified, shown to be the effect not of divine law but of social custom. Jean Howard in 'Crossdressing, the Theatre and Gender Struggle in Early Modern England' very usefully explores some of the differences in the manifestations of cross-dressing in the period, and with reference to several plays, including Shakespeare's *Twelfth Night* and *As You Like It*, shows how the theatre played a contradictory role in the controversies over dress. One implication of this and other recent work—for example Mary Beth Rose's 'Women in Men's Clothing: Apparel and Social Stability in *The Roaring Girl*'—is that Shakespeare's treatment of gender may be more conservative than that of some of his contemporaries.

For a modern audience one of Shakespeare's most problematic treatments of gender is *The Taming of the Shrew*. Ann Thompson observes in the introduction to her New Cambridge edition of the play: 'Since the late nineteenth century the movement for the liberation of women has done for [this play] what reaction to the antisemitism of our time has done for *The Merchant of Venice*: turned it into a problem play'. Karen Newman in 'Renaissance Family Politics and Shakespeare's *The Taming of the Shrew*' brings to the play the more recent perspective described above: the play's 'patriarchal master narrative' is subverted when it is exposed 'as neither natural nor divinely ordained, but culturally constructed'.

Problematic in a different way are Shakespeare's *Sonnets*. Joseph Pequigney's *Such Is My Love* is the most sustained argument ever for the homosexual basis of these Sonnets: the sequence is seen as not only 'extraordinary amatory verse, but the great masterpiece of homoerotic poetry'. This book makes

explicit aspects of gender and sexuality which have traditionally been suppressed in Shakespeare criticism, including some
feminist criticism. But in certain respects this book remains
quite traditional, especially in the way it uses Freud, and its
understanding of homosexuality. In the same year as Pequigney's
book appeared (1985), Eve Kosofsky Sedgwick published *Between
Men*, which contains a chapter on the Sonnets. She sees them not
so much homosexual as 'homosocial'. In an article called 'A Poem
Is Being Written', highly recommended to all Shakespearians,
she defines 'the male–homosocial structure' as that 'whereby
men's "heterosexual desire" for women serves as a more or less
perfunctory detour on the way to a closer, but homophobically
proscribed, bonding with another man'. Sedgwick's category of
the homosocial is subtly if incompletely developed, encouraging
us to rethink the history of sexuality in Shakespeare and the
Renaissance by taking apart our own reductive psychosexual
categories, and developing new ones. Discussing Sonnets 136
and 137, she says

> My point is . . . again not that we are here in the presence of homosexuality
> (which would be anachronistic) but rather (risking anachronism) that
> we are in the presence of male heterosexual desire, in the form of a desire
> to consolidate partnership with authoritative males in and through the
> bodies of females. (*Between Men*, 38)

Another respect in which Pequigney's analysis is traditional is
in his critical practice, which works through close textual analysis
of an ahistorical kind. Contrary to conventional wisdom, materialist criticism does not object to close textual analysis, nor to
analysis of form and genre. In fact, its project often requires it. It
objects rather to the ahistorical and indeed antihistorical tendency
of this analysis as it has sometimes been practised. For example,
Pequigney's reading of the Sonnets is intelligent and sensitive
yet largely ignores the seventeenth-century constructions of
gender and sexual differences, and invokes instead, ahistorically
and arguably anachronistically, the work of Freud to 'explain'
homosexuality. Alan Bray's *Homosexuality in Renaissance England*
is considered by many to be an indispensable study, even when
its conclusions are questioned; not so for Pequigney.

In certain respects the more illuminating discussions of homosexuality begin by analysing its representations in modern literary
criticism. Simon Shepherd in his book on Marlowe and an essay

on Shakespeare's *Sonnets* shows how such an approach can reveal much about the culturally specific, often confused, not so say hypocritical, assumptions of that criticism.

What a materialist analysis can achieve through a close analysis of language which is at once historically aware and textually sensitive is exemplified in John Barrell's fine chapter on Sonnet 29 in his *Poetry, Language and Politics*. Patronage, whether possessed or lacked, was a crucial factor in the production (or not) of Renaissance poetry; Barrell explores its relation to, and its representation in, Sonnet 29, right down to crucial issues of punctuation. In the process he shows how the pathos of this poem is 'inextricably a function of how it represents the specificity of the historical moment it produces and which produced it: a pathos which arises from the narrator's attempt to claim a transcendence he cannot achieve.'

Whatever the critical position taken on gender in Shakespeare, recent work has proved beyond doubt that the representations of it in his plays are as fascinating and important as they are complex and unstable. It has also established beyond doubt that gender was a controversial topic outside the theatre. Society at that time was obsessed with sexual difference and gender, especially the real and supposed violations of it. A book which gives a wide-ranging, scholarly, and readable introduction to some of the controversies around gender as they figured in literature is Linda Woodbridge's *Women and the English Renaissance: Literature and the Nature of Womankind, 1540–1620*.

---

dialectic: *the concept refers in part to the inevitability and pervasiveness of struggle and conflict, but also to the idea that what is ideologically represented as absolutely separate and distinct, is often deeply interrelated with that which it is supposed to be distinct from. Especially with subjectivity: existing conditions, be they economic, linguistic, cultural, ideological—or a complex formation of all these—pre-exist and shape the consciousness of individuals more thoroughly than most of us ever subjectively realise, and nowhere more so than in formation of gender identity. Psychic disorder always signifies more than subjective breakdown, and cultural conflict more than social breakdown.*

Gender is inseparable from questions of subjectivity and identity. Muir, in the passage quoted above, (p. 408) is representative of a criticism which has seen truly great literature as affirming

trans-historical truths, be they about human nature or the universe
of existence more generally. Typically, and especially in criticism of
tragedy, these truths are seen to be embodied or perceived by the
unique individual. Both individuality and truth, being and
knowledge, are conceived as a profound ultimate unity; dislocation
and discord are overcome, be it in the individual psyche, the
social body or the universe itself. The belief in or desire for this
profound unity, psychic and metaphysical (the first being an
instantiation of the second), a unity beyond the actual strife and
disunity of existence, and beneath the experience of psychic
confusion, is fundamental to western culture and so has a history
far beyond literary criticism. It is just this belief that is attacked
by virtually all those post-war intellectual developments mentioned at the outset of this essay, which are loosely and sometimes misleadingly collected under the general heading of 'theory'.

Materialist and feminist critics draw on such theory, especially
its critique of humanist individualism. Dollimore in *Radical
Tragedy*, Barker in *The Tremulous Private Body*, and Belsey in *The
Subject of Tragedy* assess the implications of this for the view of
the Renaissance as the supposed origin of modern 'man'. There
are important differences here: Barker offers a critique of the
subjectivity produced in and by bourgeois culture, Belsey of an
equally large historical development which she categorizes as
'liberal humanism'; Dollimore speaks more specifically of 'essentialist humanism'. But all three challenge some central assumptions
of the traditional reading of character, human nature, and individual identity as they are found in studies of Shakespeare, of
Renaissance literature, and more generally still, in the practice of
English Studies.

All three proceed via a twofold analysis—a critique of the way
literary critics have reproduced Renaissance drama in terms of a
modern depoliticized subjectivity, and an attempt to recover a
more adequate history of subjectivity, especially in the Renaissance period. Belsey begins with the proposition that 'Man is the
subject of liberal humanism. Woman has meaning in relation to
man. And yet the instability which is the result of this asymmetry is
the ground of protest, resistance, feminism.' Barker points out
how successive generations of critics, especially Romantics and
those since, have attempted to discover the essence of Hamlet,
finding in him (for example) the 'alienated modern individual
dejected in the market place of inauthentic values'. But for Barker

'At the centre of Hamlet, in the interior of his mystery, there is, in short, nothing'; at this time the modern forms of bourgeois subjectivity are only—could only be—gestured towards; they were incipient, not yet formed. Dollimore explores the way that, in Elizabethan and Jacobean tragedy, subjectivity is conceived not as the antithesis of the social and political, but as their focus. Psychic discord is seen in terms of the struggle and conflict which inevitably characterize social existence.

Much has already been written on subjectivity and gender. Nevertheless they will probably remain at issue in Renaissance studies, as well as in literary theory and cultural analysis more generally. This is surely justified: the constructions of gender and subjectivity are central to the literature and history of western culture, and those constructions are being foregrounded at a time when they are in process of change.

It has been a commonplace of literary criticism that every age interprets Shakespeare for itself. The implication of this is that Shakespeare is only what we make of him. Or it might be, were this commonplace not generally harnessed within another: in each age we discover new (locally appropriate) ways of perceiving the transhistorical truths perceived by the genius who was Shakespeare and embodied in his plays. So an interpretation or production for our time isn't changing the meaning of the play so much as making it more accessible to a modern audience.

Materialist work on the reproduction of Shakespeare contests this. It argues that the way a particular culture reads Shakespeare reveals the 'nature' of that same culture, especially its dominant formations, and in so doing materialism also dismantles the myth of genius. The title of Part II of *Political Shakespeare*— 'Reproductions, Interventions'—suggests that to uncover the political basis of supposedly non-political or apolitical criticism is also to show that other kinds of political criticism (interventions) are not only possible but to be encouraged. But this concern with reproduction is not primarily concerned with the readings of this or that literary critic. Much more important is the institutional reproduction of Shakespeare: separate chapters discuss the re-production of Shakespeare in education, the RSC, film, and television, as well as the interpretation and appropriation of Shakespeare in the theatre of Bertolt Brecht. *The Shakespeare Myth* (ed. Graham Holderness) continues this kind of analysis showing how, for example, Shakespeare can be used to sustain delusions of unity and harmony in what is in fact a divided and strife-ridden culture. Representative of this analysis are the essays of Alan Sinfield; two in *Political Shakespeare* (one on education and another on the RSC), a third in *The Shakespeare Myth* on the 'appropriation and confrontation' of Shakespeare in recent British plays (Stoppard's *Rosencrantz and Guildenstern*, Marowitz's *Collage Hamlet* and *Measure for Measure*, Wesker's *The Merchant*, and Bond's *King Lear*.)

The Shakespeare Myth also has sections on education, popular culture, ideology, the theatre, sexual politics, and broadcasting. An interesting feature of this collection is the juxtaposition of critical essays alongside interviews with prominent cultural practitioners of Shakespeare in education, the theatre, and television.

Other important studies of the reproduction of Shakespeare have recently appeared. Terence Hawkes's *That Shakespeherian Rag* explores some intriguing points of connection between politics—for example colonialism and nationalism—and the processes of literary criticism. This is a challenging and witty analysis of major figures in Shakespearian literary criticism, including A. C. Bradley, Sir Walter Raleigh, T. S. Eliot, and John Dover Wilson. By exploring the influence on these critics of large-scale ideological formations as well as specific historical events, Hawkes shows how thoroughly, often alarmingly so, criticism is of its time.

In another enlightening piece, 'The Authentic Shakespeare', Stephen Orgel shows how the traditions of textual and editorial scholarship, for all their aura of judicious scholarship and impartial scrutiny of the evidence, can be as time-bound as criticism, reproducing Shakespeare just as evaluatively. Orgel begins with a consideration of the controversy over whether or not the poem 'Shall I Die?' was written by Shakespeare. Little written on the in/authenticity of the poem is as informative as this discussion by Orgel, largely because he addresses not the question of the actual poem's authenticity but the assumptions behind the dispute itself, especially the assumption that a bad poem cannot be by Shakespeare. Orgel shows how the question of authenticity involves doctrinal and political elements; authenticity itself is shown to be something bestowed, not inherent.

Marjorie Garber in *Shakespeare's Ghost Writers* considers

reproduction from a very different but equally fascinating and illuminating perspective. Via Freud's notion of the uncanny, she explores the way Shakespeare has come to haunt our culture, his plays having mined themselves into it.

The perspectives considered in this chapter try to understand not just the theatre but the wider culture of early modern England. They are helping to generate not only new readings, but substantial historical and cultural debates with an importance beyond Shakespeare and even beyond English Studies. In this connection I mention finally Martin Orkin's *Shakespeare against Apartheid*, which unashamedly appropriates the dramatist for an anti-racist criticism, and Ania Loomba's *Gender, Race, Renaissance Drama*, which analyses race as it affects diverse recent discussions. Loomba shows the way women and black people are similarly constructed as the 'others' of white patriarchal society and the connections between this and other kinds of exclusion such as that based on class. Yet the consideration of race also problematizes efforts to make easy analogies between different aspects of women's subordination; for Loomba the *specificity* of each emerges more clearly. She also discusses the uses of Shakespeare in a colonialist and post-colonialist context. In these respects and others this is a truly challenging book, not only for traditionalists, but for us all.

REFERENCES

Adelman, Janet, ' "Anger's My Meat": Feeding, Dependency and Aggression in *Coriolanus'*, in *Shakespeare: Pattern of Excelling Nature*, ed. David Bevington and Jay L. Halio (Cranbury, NJ, 1978), 108–24; reprinted in *Representing Shakespeare*, ed. Murray M. Schwartz and Coppélia Kahn (Baltimore, Md., 1980), 129–49.

——' "Born of Woman": Fantasies of Maternal Power in *Macbeth'*, in *Cannibals, Witches, and Divorce: Estranging the Renaissance*, ed. Marjorie Garber (Baltimore, Md., and London, 1987), 90–121.

Babcock, Barbara A. (ed.), *The Reversible World: Symbolic Inversion in Art and Society* (Ithaca, NY, and London, 1978).

Barker, Francis, *The Tremulous Private Body: Essays on Subjection* (London and New York, 1984).

Barrell, John, *Poetry, Language and Politics* (Manchester, 1988).

Belsey, Catherine, *The Subject of Tragedy: Identity and Difference in Renaissance Drama* (London and New York, 1985).

Boose, Lynda E., 'The Family in Shakespeare Studies: or—Studies in the

Family of Shakespeareans; or—the Politics of Politics', *Renaissance Quarterly*, 40 (1987), 707–42.

Bray, Alan, *Homosexuality in Renaissance England* (London, 1982).

Clark, Stuart, 'Inversion, Misrule and the Meaning of Witchcraft', *Past and Present*, 87 (1980), 98–127.

Cohen, Walter, *Drama of a Nation: Public Theater in Renaissance England and Spain* (Ithaca, NY, and London, 1985).

Dollimore, Jonathan, *Radical Tragedy: Religion, Ideology and Power in the Drama of Shakespeare and his Contemporaries* (Brighton, 1984; 2nd edn., 1989).

—— 'Subjectivity, Sexuality and Transgression: The Jacobean Connection', in *Renaissance Drama*, NS 17 (1986), 53–81.

—— and Alan Sinfield (eds.), *Political Shakespeare: New Essays in Cultural Materialism* (Manchester and Ithaca, NY, 1985).

Drakakis, John (ed.), *Alternative Shakespeares* (London and New York, 1985).

Dusinberre, Juliet, *Shakespeare and the Nature of Women* (London, 1975).

Eagleton, Terry, *William Shakespeare* (Rereading Literature Series, Oxford, 1986).

Ferguson, Margaret W., Maureen Quilligan, and Nancy J. Vickers, (eds.), *Rewriting the Renaissance: The Discourses of Sexual Difference in Early Modern Europe* (Chicago, Ill., and London, 1986).

Garber, Marjorie, *Shakespeare's Ghost Writers: Literature as Uncanny Causality* (London, 1987).

Goldberg, Jonathan, *James I and the Politics of Literature* (Baltimore, Md., and London, 1983).

Greenblatt, Stephen, *Renaissance Self-Fashioning: From More to Shakespeare* (Chicago, Ill., and London, 1980).

—— *Shakespearean Negotiations: The Circulation of Social Energy in Renaissance England* (Oxford, 1988).

—— (ed.), *Representing the Renaissance* (Berkeley and Los Angeles, Calif., and London, 1988).

Hawkes, Terence, *That Shakespeherian Rag: Essays on a Critical Process* (London and New York, 1986).

Heinemann, Margot, *Puritanism and Theatre: Thomas Middleton and Oppositional Drama under the Early Stuarts* (Cambridge, 1980).

Holderness, Graham (ed.), *The Shakespeare Myth* (Manchester, 1988).

Howard, Jean E., 'Crossdressing, the Theatre and Gender Struggle in Early Modern England', *Shakespeare Quarterly*, 39 (1988), 418–40.

—— 'The New Historicism in Renaissance Studies', *English Literary Renaissance*, 16 (1986), 13–43.

—— and Marion F. O'Connor, (eds.), *Shakespeare Reproduced: The Text in History and Ideology* (New York and London, 1987).

Jardine, Lisa, *Still Harping on Daughters: Women and Drama in the Age of Shakespeare* (Brighton, 1983).

Kahn, Coppélia, *Man's Estate: Masculine Identity in Shakespeare* (Berkeley, 1981).

Lenz, Carolyn, Gayle Greene, and Carol Neely (eds.), *The Woman's Part: Feminist Criticism of Shakespeare* (Urbana, Ill., 1980).

Lever, J. W., *The Tragedy of State: A Study of Jacobean Drama*, with a new introduction by J. Dollimore (1971; reprinted London, 1987).

Loomba, Ania, *Gender, Race, Renaissance Drama* (Manchester, 1989).

Montrose, Louis A., '*A Midsummer Night's Dream* and the Shaping Fantasies of Elizabethan Culture: Gender, Power, Form', in *Rewriting the Renaissance*, see Ferguson, above. A longer version of this piece is reprinted in *Representing the English Renaissance*, ed. Greenblatt.

—— 'Professing the Renaissance: The Poetics and Politics of Culture', in *The New Historicism*, ed. H. A. Veeser (New York and London, 1989), 15–36.

Moretti, Franco, *Signs Taken for Wonders: Essays in the Sociology of Literary Forms* (London, 1983).

Muir, Kenneth (ed.), *Macbeth* (The Arden Shakespeare, London, 1951).

Mullaney, Steven, *The Place of the Stage: Licence, Play, and Power in Renaissance England* (Chicago, Ill., and London, 1988).

Neely, Carol Thomas, 'Constructing the Subject: Feminist Practice and the New Renaissance Discourses', *English Literary Renaissance*, 18 (1988), 5–18.

Newman, Karen, 'Renaissance Family Politics and Shakespeare's *The Taming of the Shrew*', *English Literary Renaissance*, 16 (1986), 86–100.

Orgel, Stephen, 'The Authentic Shakespeare', *Representations*, 21 (1988), 1–26.

Orkin, Martin, *Shakespeare against Apartheid* (Craighall, South Africa, 1987).

Parker, Patricia, and Geoffrey Hartman (eds.), *Shakespeare and the Question of Theory* (New York and London, 1985).

Pequigney, Joseph, *Such Is My Love: A Study of Shakespeare's Sonnets* (Chicago, Ill., and London, 1985).

Rose, Mary Beth, 'Women in Men's Clothing: Apparel and Social Stability in *The Roaring Girl*', *English Literary Renaissance*, 14 (1984), 367–91.

Sedgwick, Eve Kosofsky, *Between Men: English Literature and Male Homosocial Desire* (Gender and Culture Series, New York, 1985).

—— 'A Poem Is Being Written', *Representations*, 17 (1987), 110–43.

Shepherd, Simon, *Marlowe and the Politics of Elizabethan Theatre* (Brighton, 1986).

—— 'Shakespeare's Private Drawer: Shakespeare and Homosexuality', in *The Shakespeare Myth*, ed. Graham Holderness (Manchester, 1988), 96–109.

Showalter, Elaine, 'Representing Ophelia: Women, Madness, and the Responsibilities of Feminist Criticism', in *Shakespeare and the Question* of Theory, ed. Patricia Parker and Geoffrey Hartman (New York and London, 1985), 77–94.

Sinfield, Alan, '*Macbeth*: History, Ideology and Intellectuals', in *Futures for English*, ed. Colin MacCabe (Manchester, 1988), 63–77.

—— 'Power and Ideology: An Outline Theory and Sidney's *Arcadia*', *ELH*, 52 (1985), 259–77.

Stallybrass, Peter, 'Macbeth and Witchcraft', *Focus on 'Macbeth'*, ed. John Russell Brown (London, 1982), 189–209.

Tennenhouse, Leonard, *Power on Display: The Politics of Shakespeare's Genres* (New York and London, 1986).

Thompson, Ann, ' "The Warrant of Womanhood": Shakespeare and Feminist Criticism', in *The Shakespeare Myth*, ed. Graham Holderness (Manchester, 1988), 74–88.

—— (ed.), *The Taming of the Shrew* (The New Cambridge Shakespeare, Cambridge, 1984).

Underdown, D. E., 'The Taming of the Scold: The Enforcement of Patriarchal Authority in Early Modern England', in *Order and Disorder in Early Modern England*, ed. Anthony Fletcher and John Stevenson (Cambridge, 1985), 116–36.

Williams, Raymond, *Politics and Letters* (London, 1979).

Woodbridge, Linda, *Women and the English Renaissance: Literature and the Nature of Womankind 1540–1620* (Brighton, 1984).

—— [L. T. Fitz], 'Egyptian Queens and Male Reviewers: Sexist Attitudes in *Antony and Cleopatra* Criticism', *Shakespeare Quarterly*, 28 (1977), 297–316.

Notes on the Contributors

MAURICE CHARNEY is Distinguished Professor of English at Rutgers University. He is the author of *Shakespeare's Roman Plays, Style in 'Hamlet',* and *Hamlet's Fictions.* Most recently, he has written a critical introduction to *Titus Andronicus* in the Harvester–Wheatsheaf series. He is past President of the Shakespeare Association of America and is on the editorial boards of *Shakespeare Quarterly, Shakespeare Bulletin, Assaph,* and *Psychoanalytic Books.*

DAVID DANIELL is Senior Lecturer in the Department of English at University College London. His publications on Shakespeare include books on *Coriolanus* and *The Tempest* as well as many articles. For some years he wrote the Shakespeare chapter for *The Year's Work in English Studies,* which he helped to edit. He also writes on the Bible in English (he has edited Tyndale's 1534 New Testament) and on John Buchan.

JONATHAN DOLLIMORE is author of *Radical Tragedy: Religion, Ideology and Power in the Drama of Shakespeare and his Contemporaries* (Chicago and Brighton, 1984; second edition Brighton, 1989), and co-editor of *Political Shakespeare: New Essays in Cultural Materialism* (Manchester and Cornell, 1985). His next book will be *Perverse Dynamics: Sexuality, Transgression and Sub-cultures.*

KATHERINE DUNCAN-JONES is a Tutorial Fellow in English Literature at Somerville College, Oxford; she has edited a selection of the writings of Sir Philip Sidney for Oxford University Press.

RICHARD DUTTON is Reader in English Literature at Lancaster University. His publications include *Ben Jonson: To the First Folio* (Cambridge, 1983); *Modern Tragicomedy and the British Tradition* (Brighton, 1983); and *William Shakespeare: A Literary Life* (London, 1989) in the Macmillan *Literary Lives* of which he is General Editor. He is currently completing a study of the censorship of English Renaissance drama.

R. A. FOAKES is Professor of English at the University of California, Los Angeles. Among the more recent of his many publications on Shakespeare and the drama are an edition of *A Midsummer Night's Dream* (Cambridge, 1984) and *Illustrations of the English Stage* (London and Stanford, 1985).

ROBERT HAPGOOD is Professor of English at the University of New Hampshire. His publications include *Shakespeare the Theatre-Poet* (Oxford,

1988) and numerous articles, mostly concerned with Shakespeare's plays in performance.

MICHAEL HATTAWAY is Professor of English Literature at the University of Sheffield. He is author of *Elizabethan Popular Theatre* (1982) among other books. His editions of *1–3 Henry VI* for the New Cambridge Shakespeare are in process of publication, and with A. R. Braunmuller he has edited *The Cambridge Companion to English Renaissance Drama* (forthcoming).

MICHAEL JAMIESON is a Lecturer in English at the University of Sussex. He has edited *Three Comedies* by Ben Jonson and published a study of *As You Like It* as well as articles on the boy actor, on Shakespeare's problem plays, and on the American actress Elizabeth Robins.

KENNETH MUIR is Emeritus Professor and Honorary Senior Fellow of Liverpool University. Among his many publications on Shakespeare are editions of five of the plays (including the Arden *King Lear* and *Macbeth*) and a critical study of *King Lear*.

D. J. PALMER is Professor of English at the University of Manchester. He is the author of *The Rise of English Studies*, was formerly a general Editor of Stratford-upon-Avon Studies, and has edited Macmillan casebooks on *The Tempest* and *Twelfth Night*.

G. R. PROUDFOOT is Professor of English Literature at King's College London. He was General Editor of the Malone Society from 1971 to 1985 and is currently General Editor of the Arden Shakespeare, as well as continuing to work on his Oxford edition of the *Shakespeare Apocrypha*.

NORMAN SANDERS is Lindsay Young Professor of English at the University of Tennessee. Among his publications are editions of the three parts of *Henry VI* for the New Penguin Shakespeare and of Othello for the New Cambridge Shakespeare, and Volume 2, Part 2 of *The Revels History of the Drama in English*. He is working on a New Variorum edition of the *Two Noble Kinsmen*.

R. L. SMALLWOOD is Deputy Director of the Shakespeare Birthplace Trust in Stratford-upon-Avon and Honorary Fellow of the Shakespeare Institute of the University of Birmingham. He is editor of *King John* for the New Penguin Shakespeare and of *Players of Shakespeare* (Cambridge).

MICHAEL TAYLOR is Professor of English at the University of New Brunswick and has published critical essays on Shakespeare and his contemporaries.

R. J. A. WEIS, Lecturer in English Literature at University College London, has edited the plays of John Webster (Oxford, forthcoming), and *King Lear* (Longman).

STANLEY WELLS is Professor of Shakespeare Studies and Director of the Shakespeare Institute, University of Birmingham. He is General Editor of the Oxford Shakespeare, editor of *Shakespeare Survey*, and has published extensively on Shakespeare and his contemporaries.

R. S. WHITE, Professor of English at the University of Western Australia, was formerly Senior Lecturer at the University of Newcastle upon Tyne. His publications on Shakespeare include many articles and several books, among them *Keats as a Reader of Shakespeare* (1987).

JOHN WILDERS is John Hamilton Fulton Professor of the Humanities at Middlebury College, Vermont and Emeritus Fellow of Worcester College, Oxford. His publications include *The Lost Garden: A View of Shakespeare's English and Roman History Plays* (1978) and *New Prefaces to Shakespeare* (1988), written initially for the BBC television series, to which he was literary adviser.